Second
Edition

INTERVIEWING

Speaking, Listening, and Learning
for Professional Life

Rob Anderson

Saint Louis University

G. Michael Killenberg

University of South Florida St. Petersburg

New York   Oxford

OXFORD UNIVERSITY PRESS

2009

Oxford University Press, Inc., publishes works that further Oxford University's
objective of excellence in research, scholarship, and education.

Oxford   New York
Auckland   Cape Town   Dar es Salaam   Hong Kong   Karachi
Kuala Lumpur   Madrid   Melbourne   Mexico City   Nairobi
New Delhi   Shanghai   Taipei   Toronto

With offices in
Argentina   Austria   Brazil   Chile   Czech Republic   France   Greece
Guatemala   Hungary   Italy   Japan   Poland   Portugal   Singapore
South Korea   Switzerland   Thailand   Turkey   Ukraine   Vietnam

Published by Oxford University Press, Inc.
198 Madison Avenue, New York, New York 10016
http://www.oup.com

Oxford is a registered trademark of Oxford University Press

Library of Congress Cataloging-in-Publication Data
Anderson, Rob, 1945–
   Interviewing : speaking, listening, and learning for professional
life / Rob Anderson, George M. Killenberg. — 2nd ed.
       p. cm.
   Includes index.
   ISBN 978-0-19-536771-3 (alk. paper)
   1. Interviewing.   I. Killenberg, George M.   II. Title.
   BF637.I5A53   2009
   158'.39—dc22
                                              2007043226

Printed in the United States of America
on acid-free paper

Contents

One of the many things we've learned from our students is that they can react to interviewing assignments in dramatically different ways. Some are almost pathologically nervous about asking and answering questions, especially if they're videotaped. They find an interviewing class similar to a public speaking class in that it asks them—they think—to perform. They overestimate the difficulties of interviewing because they interpret it as a tense performance challenge. Other students, however, underestimate its difficulties, figuring an interviewing class should be a breeze. After all—they think—talking is easy, and talkative people should have no trouble exchanging information in conversational, informal settings.

More than 35 years of teaching interviewing and interpersonal communication to students, managers, and career journalists have convinced us that this is one of the most practical skills a professional can develop. And it isn't as intimidating as some people fear, or as automatic as others assume.

Interviews as Opportunities

Interviewing is not a simple behavioral skill or procedure that can be practiced over and over until it's done "right." As authors and teachers, we cannot prescribe exactly what students should do or say, because we can't anticipate the specific people or situations they'll encounter. Experienced interviewers and interviewees discover that each interview is brand new, with a fresh set of invitations and challenges. A class, and a textbook, shortchanges students if it doesn't encourage flexibility and creativity in a variety of interviewing concepts. An effective interview isn't a collection of techniques, carefully practiced and skillfully orchestrated. It is a mutual improvisation between two or more people who probably have different ways of seeing the world. It is an opportunity for learning through dialogue.

Although interview talk can be unpredictable, it isn't random. Learning baseline communication tendencies along with new behavioral skills will put interviewing tasks in context, freeing participants' creativity. So, in reading this book, we suggest that students:

- Think about current professional goals and future career possibilities.

- Relate interviewing tasks to previously learned concepts from other communication, social science, and humanities courses.

- Understand how this class is connected to "real-life" situations (assignments in such a course are not likely to involve throwaway practice interviews, but real ones with family, acquaintances, and professional decision makers).
- Don't just read about skills but try them out at every opportunity.
- Understand that the basic motivation for interviewing is learning something new.

Boiled down: People are unlikely to become effective interviewers if they're not curious about learning new things; people are unlikely to become effective interviewees if they're not knowledgeable. Curiosity and knowledge support each other, as do theory and practice.

Features of This Book

Interviewing is for students who want to build practical skills, and who expect a course to be interesting, thoughtful, and engaging beyond the skill-building. A practical course does not simply ask students to mimic how-to-do-it performance skills; it also starts them thinking about the process and demonstrates the relevance of interviewing for daily life. Here, then, are the key features of this book:

- *"Skills-plus" orientation:* Throughout, we describe essential skills and place them in conceptual context. With an effective blend of skills, tips, and knowledge, interviewing easily can be linked to other courses in the major, such as communication theory, research methods, interpersonal communication, mass communication, journalism, organizational communication, and intercultural communication. Students fresh from their other communication courses will recognize many of those ideas in this new setting, but *Interviewing* is not a theoretical book. We want to help students understand the ideas supporting behavioral advice, but we've tried to be selective in the research we cite. Long footnotes about scholarly studies aren't essential for beginning students, although instructors may choose to supplement assignments with additional resources found in the online *Instructor's Resource Guide.* Our bottom line: We are just as interested in motivating students to become more interested in interviewing as we are in teaching the details of how to interview. Both goals are important, but some texts, we believe, emphasize the latter at the expense of the former.

- *Helpful and flexible organization within chapters:* Each chapter includes two sections, "The Basics" and "Beyond the Basics"—allowing instructors more choice in making assignments and adapting the text to their courses. For example, some instructors may choose to assign only "The Basics" in each chapter, supplementing this material with their own content and emphases.

- *Clear division of basic interviewing skills into three interrelated types—listening, questioning, and framing. Listening* enables interview-based learning in the first place; *questioning* focuses learning through inquiry; and *framing* interprets and places learning in appropriate context. As you'll notice, the goals of different chapters will demand that we vary how this troika is presented. Listening will at times appear to be the dominant skill, whereas at other times questioning or framing will take center stage. All interviewing books overtly teach the importance of questioning. Few if any, we believe, stress the importance of listening more than this one. Perhaps none make more of a case for why students must understand how framing determines their success as communicators.

- *Helpful and flexible overall organization of chapters:* Part One develops basic skills and appreciations, and Part Two describes specific interview contexts and strategies. Part Three places interviewing in a wider analytical context, and includes a chapter we believe is unique to interviewing texts, "Understanding and Analyzing Interviews in Popular Media Culture." Here at the end of the book we depart from the listening–questioning–framing pattern so that students can see how contemporary culture's most visible celebrity interviewers do not necessarily offer viable models for other interviewing situations students and professionals are likely to encounter.

- *Student-friendly writing:* The chapters feature an informal narrative style with many stories and anecdotes, often about everyday college life. We keep the "laundry lists" to a minimum and try to describe interviewing styles through example more than with abstract theory. We suggest exercises to involve students directly in their learning. We offer some interview excerpts for analysis, but we have usually attempted to encourage learners to focus on their own life experiences. In this way, students can become more introspective as they learn also about their campuses, their families and friends, and, of course, professional responsibilities.

- *Emphasis on how interviewing contributes to the quality of public dialogue:* The fact that 21st-century social and technological trends have created an "interview society" (Gubrium & Holstein, 2001), in which interviewing is woven throughout our personal lives, careers, and media systems, presents new challenges for an interviewing class. No longer is this an individual skill largely compartmentalized from broader social interraction; it has become how we handle our information publicly. Effective interviewing skills and values support democratic action. Perhaps more than other textbooks, this one stresses that ethical interviewing creates better citizens, whose rhetoric will become more civil, sensitive, and attuned to other voices in the political process.

- *Integrated approach to both interviewer and interviewee roles:* This book prepares students to be more responsive and effective interviewees, in addition to becoming more successful interviewers. Unless they understand the interdependence of these roles, students may learn to approach professional tasks in selfish or fragmented ways. In particular, *Interviewing* offers a blended one-chapter treatment of employment interviewing, stressing the synergy of roles, rather than separating them in different chapters.

- *Integrated ethics approach:* Ethics, we stress, is not a separate concern for interview communicators; it is involved in all message choices. Incidents with ethical implications illustrate concepts in each chapter and challenge students to articulate their own responses to ethical choices inherent in the interview.

- *Integrated cultural approach:* As with ethics, cultural sensitivity is a topic that's relevant to all contexts of interviewing, and we explore its implications as they arise in those contexts. We include straightforward discussions, examples, and analyses of multicultural issues, such as "political correctness," within each chapter.

- *Innovative boxed supplements:* A series of highlighted examples helps students enrich their learning. We have streamlined this feature a bit in the second edition, while retaining the basic ideas. "Interviewer/Interviewees in Action" boxes offer first-person accounts of professional successes and failures. "Reminders" boxes develop important ideas and help students summarize and remember key skills. "Trying Out Your Skills" boxes encourage practical examinations of the depth of learning, often by analyzing brief interview excerpts. End-of-chapter "Making Your Decision" boxes present hypothetical situations, often oriented toward ethics, that lead students to apply insights creatively in ambiguous contexts sure to stimulate class discussion. In addition, each chapter includes "The Interview Bookshelf," an annotated section recommending books students will find helpful for further reading or future interviewing-related assignments in other classes.

• *Thorough* Instructor's Resource Guide *for the teacher:* The online *Guide* supplements the text with additional suggestions for class activities, resources, and assignments. It also explores the many practical decisions involved in teaching with a skills-plus approach.

Opportunities of a New Edition

When given a fresh opportunity to assess this book's contributions, we jumped at the chance. We liked some of what we saw when revisiting the chapters, and still felt committed to the basic premise of skills-plus learning and to the specific features already outlined. Other things, however, called out for a makeover. First, we reorganized the context-based chapters of Part Two, giving them more flow, and making the book more accessible to students and more "teachable" for instructors. It's clearer to move the journalistic interviewing chapter closer to the basic informational interviewing styles discussed in Part One, and to follow the kind of research reporters do with a fuller discussion of research interviewing in academic and organizational life. Employee selection interviewing, still the longest chapter, introduces the following chapter dealing with other forms of organizational assessment through interviews. The final two contexts of Part Two, interviews in persuasive and helping situations, clarify problems of one-on-one communication skill that are still relevant in many ways, of course, to journalists, job applicants, organizational professionals, and researchers.

Second, we took the opportunity to update sources extensively and put research trends in a fresher context. The years since the first edition have seen substantial advances in such areas as qualitative research interviewing, patient care in medical contexts, employment selection, and forensic interviewing. The book reflects those trends with dozens of new sources, while retaining important classic references that give students a sense of the history behind their learning.

Finally, we've attempted to stress even more often and more deeply how cultural assumptions frame virtually any interviewing encounter, sometimes making dialogue far more difficult while it makes it potentially far more productive. Cultural difference can be frustrating, but it is less a roadblock to communication than a rich resource of productive new understanding that can come when communicators pay attention to the process. New examples and many new cultural sources ground the book, we hope, in just this point.

Where a Book Comes From

Textbook authors do a lot of thanking, because they, more than anyone else, understand their debt to others.

Without our families, especially our wives Dona and Penny, we wouldn't have had the spark or the support that encouraged us to write. Somebody who cares about you needs to say something like, "Sure, that's important, too—spend a lot of time cooped up in a cluttered office without me and get it done." Although we think they know how much we love them, we want to say it again here.

Without our students, we wouldn't have been able to test-drive many of the ideas that made it into the book, and some that didn't. They have been delightfully willing to share what works for them and what broke down.

Without our friends and colleagues, we would have missed conversations that stimulated what we hope are some of the book's special strengths. Nobody gets many good ideas sitting around alone, but in conversations we come alive: "Oh, yeah! I'd never thought of it that way before. Tell me more. I wonder if I can use that in Chapter 6. . . ." Specifically, for this revision, we appreciate the library, Web, and manuscript assistance of graduate students extraordinaire Joselyn Howell, Matt Zerrip, and Kathryn Bradshaw. Patreece Boone-Broadus and her interviewing students at Saint Louis University shared their impressions of the book, and we appreciate their helpful feedback.

Without each other, we would have had far fewer resources for writing such a book. As we have been since 1972, your authors were indispensable friendly critics for each other's writing—nitpicking, admiring, arguing, and, most often, agreeing.

Without editors and staff both at Roxbury Press and Oxford University Press, and reviewers at various colleges and universities across the country, we would have missed a variety of excellent teaching and learning options we'd never have considered on our own. Claude Teweles of Roxbury first offered us the opportunity to revise the text, and with Scott Carter, helped us make necessary early decisions. Later, after Oxford University Press acquired Roxbury, executive editor Peter Labella served admirably to shepherd the book to completion. Others on the OUP book team, including Josh Hawkins, Chelsea Gilmore, and Mary Araneo, helped make our words into an attractive, readable book. Reviewers, all experienced teachers, helped us fine-tune our message. We incorporated some of their suggestions and didn't use others, but we took them all seriously. We appreciate the range of options and ideas they provided. There are many ways to teach this course, and many (occasionally, mutually exclusive) ways to organize its content. Ultimately, of course, we're responsible for the choices you see reflected here. The following reviewers provided excellent feedback, and the book is vastly improved because of their careful attention: Amy Aldridge Sanford, Northeastern State University; Jerry Allen, University of New Haven; Sandra Chesborough, St. Cloud State University; Phillip Clampitt, University of Wisconsin-Green Bay; Timothy Cline, Notre Dame College of Maryland; Robert Cocetti, University of Nebraska, Kearney; Stacey L. Connaughton, Rutgers University; David Droppa, Seton Hall University; Charles Figley, Florida State University; Peggy Fisher, Ball State University; Connie Fletcher, Loyola University; Sheryl Friedley, George Mason University;

Maurice Hall, Villanova University; Cara W. Jacocks, Texas Christian University; Rosalind W. Kennerson-Baty, Baylor University; Sue Lockett John, University of Washington; Vern Miller, Michigan State University; Kathleen I. Powell, Marietta College; Meera Rastogi, University of Wisconsin, Madison; Richard Rieke, University of Utah; Veronica Ross, Greenville College; Ralph Webb, Purdue University; David Weber, University of North Carolina, Wilmington; Cory Young, University of Wisconsin, Oshkosh; and thank you also to those reviewers who wished to remain anonymous.

About the Authors

Rob Anderson has enjoyed university teaching and learning for almost 35 years. He has applied his research in the theory of dialogue to practical problems of interviewing, conflict management, listening, and everyday communication ethics, and has facilitated numerous workshops in interpersonal communication for student and professional audiences. Now professor of communication at Saint Louis University (SLU), he has received major teaching awards at two universities, and has published 11 books and many articles in journals in communication, journalism, education, English, and psychology. When not at SLU, he enjoys sitting on the screened-in porch with Dona and two super-Labs, Sophie and Ben; savoring crisp northeast Wisconsin and southern Illinois mornings; reading the poetry of William Stafford and Wendell Berry; dabbling in Taoism, soccer, and Frisbee; listening to acoustic folk and bluegrass music; and yearning for the best audio system he can almost afford.

G. Michael (Mike) Killenberg has extensive professional interviewing experience as a reporter and editor for daily newspapers, in addition to teaching journalism and mass communication at several colleges and universities. His current research focuses on newspaper–community relations, the public journalism controversy, and encouraging diversity within professional journalism. He is professor of journalism at the University of South Florida St. Petersburg, where he was that program's founding director. He received the USF Professorial Excellence award for 1999. His previous publications include numerous articles in academic and professional periodicals and four books, including a new edition of his public affairs reporting textbook for Focal Press. Off-campus, his passions include magnificent dinners with Penny; reading biographies, military history, and *The New York Times*; puttering around his garage; and playing some pretty respectable golf.

Together, Anderson and Killenberg have coauthored *Interviewing* (Mayfield, 1998), *The Conversation of Journalism* (Praeger, 1994, 1996; with Robert Dardenne; Korean edition 2007), and *Before the Story* (St. Martin's, 1989; Chinese edition 1992). They've also honed their skills as washer-tossing teammates at the Al Theis Memorial Washer Pit in Jacksonport, WI.

INTERVIEWING

Chapter One

Beyond the Q&A Presumption

Interviewing with a Listening/Learning Perspective

LEARNING GOALS

After reading this chapter, you should be able to

- Understand the implications of an "inter-view" perspective

- Discuss the three complementary facets of interviewing: listening, speaking, and framing

- Recognize the major qualities of effective interviews

- Know the various ways interview types are used in professional and personal lives

- Approach interviewing with an ethical orientation

A young married couple, Kristen and Jason, spend an afternoon driving around town to visit three different day-care centers. They want to talk to the directors and get a feel for the atmosphere of each place. They are appropriately careful about researching the centers, as they know how important this decision can be for the education of their daughter. They have prepared a list of questions to ask and concerns to check out; in other words, they have become interviewers whether they have had formal training in interviewing or not.

After visiting the three centers, Kristen and Jason stop at the mall to grab a bite to eat. Just outside the food court, a nicely dressed man with a clipboard asks for their cooperation in responding to a brief marketing survey. Which stores do they usually visit? How often do they eat at the mall? What draws them to the mall? Advertised sales? Special events? A wide selection of products? Ease of parking? Down the aisle, a volunteer for a local politician wants their opinions about the school district. The couple takes three or four minutes to talk over their shopping habits and their attitudes about education; they have become interviewees.

Interviews can be like a warm bath or a cold shower, verbal massage or medieval torture. Interviews can motivate or they can alienate, push, or pull, join or separate you from those you interview.

—Frank MacHovec,
Interview and Interrogation

Returning home, they thank and pay their babysitter and ask a series of questions about their daughter's day: Did she like the sitter's games? Was she fussy? Did she eat well? Although this conversation feels informal and spontaneous, it serves many of the same functions as a formal interview. Persons who don't have the information they need use a focused conversation to obtain it.

Conversation and interviews are alike in that both, if done right, lead to knowledge and understanding. Not all conversations are interviews and not all interviews have the tone of conversations, but they share a common goal of helping people learn. Researchers Rubin and Rubin (2005) refer to the "conversational partnership" that develops in effective interviews (p. 79). In his classic book on interviewing, Gorden (1969) writes that interviewing cannot be separated "from the basic skills of ordinary conversation. Any two-way conversation involves many of the same skills and insights needed for successful interviewing. The main difference is in the central purpose of interviewing as opposed to other forms of conversation" (p. 30).

Interviewing's central purpose is assisted learning, to satisfy the need for information and insight. Gorden warns about the dual dangers that confront beginning interviewers and interviewees: first, the notion that interviewing is "just talking to people in a spontaneous social way" and, second, the belief that interviewing is "a magical and mysterious formula" that is directed by known techniques. It is neither. Interviewing is conversational, to be sure, but it is a specialized form of creative conversation that can't be learned by memorizing a repertoire of handy techniques, gimmicks, or formulas. The rest of this book is an elaboration of this basic but complex theme of speaking, listening, and, especially, learning.

The Basics

The Interview as "Inter-View"

In a basic sense, an **interview** is an interpersonal or public communication event in which someone seeks information and insight from someone else. Most interviews therefore must rely on questions and responses, but it's limiting and misleading to think of interviews only as occasions for asking and answering questions.

Although interviews often appear to be conducted to benefit one or the other party, effective interviews usually lead to mutual understanding, helping participants as they make decisions affecting their own lives and the lives of others. Consider the outcome the word suggests—"inter-view," a sharing of views (Killenberg & Anderson, 1989; Kvale, 1996). In this sense, an interview becomes a partnership in which interviewer and interviewee realize that more can be gained for both by a genuine attempt to collaborate. Success comes from thorough and reciprocal exchanges, not from a competition of winning and losing. An interview conducted as a partnership isn't a tea party with phony polite talk; although civility is usually expected, professionals often use words such as *challenging, confrontational, intense, exhausting,* or *irritating* to describe interviews.

Interviews are indispensable for many types of routine data collection. Beyond the routine, however, interviews can be turning points for us individually and collectively. Although some interviews seem far more important than others, everything is relative. To a supermarket manager hiring a minimum-wage clerk, the employment interview is no big deal; to the young mother who has spent weeks looking for work, it's a crucial moment. Interviews often involve high personal stakes—hiring decisions, medical diagnoses, marriage counseling, highway crash investigations—in which the potential for error and misunderstanding is great, even when the communicators see each other as partners.

Some people consider interviews only as a means of data accumulation, not as opportunities to go beyond the data to achieve understanding or shared learning. Social scientist Steiner Kvale (1996) uses the metaphors of the miner and the traveler to illustrate the difference between mere collection of facts and the search for understanding. The miner acquires information by extracting previously hidden nuggets of fact or meaning, digging and scraping and treating the interviewee's experience like so much debris to sift through. Mining has its place in interviews, but it also has its limitations. The interviewer-as-traveler understands that interviewing is not something one person does to another. Travelers explore with others rather than take from them. A partnership model stresses attitudes over final products, and can offer no guarantee of success, but it is far more promising than its alternatives because it takes relationships into account.

Anyone can imagine legitimate exceptions to partnership styles of interviewing. Police questioning witnesses to an abduction may need to "mine" accurate facts quickly; a social worker investigating child abuse may not have time for a leisurely negotiation with an uncooperative relative. Exceptions aside, though, the gap between the norm and the ideal remains sizable. Interviewers and interviewees often work at cross-purposes unnecessarily, playing roles that encourage selfish objectives over mutual ones. Interviewers then assume a superior, controlling position; interviewees react accordingly. The interviewer questions and the interviewee answers, rarely developing anything like the spirit of an "inter-view."

Common Stereotypes of Interviews

The interview as partnership? Most readers are more likely to picture someone in a suit sizing up a job prospect with a gruff opening question ("Tell me why my company should hire you") or Diane Sawyer or Tim Russert boring in with questions that leave politicians and policymakers squirming before a TV audience of millions. The word *interview* suggests for some a formal, structured, controlled inquiry at the hands of a stranger who asks penetrating questions while we sit consumed with anxiety. Or perhaps we're the stranger, trying to be tough and tender at the same time. For most people, interviews are associated with the *Q&A presumption*—the belief that questions and answers are the only important outcomes. In this case, the prospect of an interview is about as appealing as visiting a dentist for a root canal. No wonder a popular book on the subject was titled *Sweaty Palms* (Medley, 1992).

An education in interviewing based on studying communication research and applied practice isn't part of the average person's schooling. Even specialists perceived as skillful interviewers, such as police or journalists, seldom receive more than a cursory exposure to the literature and research of interviewing. Most of us go through life experiencing interviews here and there, perhaps knowing less about the subject than we do about microbrewing or Tom Cruise's personal life. We've learned through snippets of experience or the anecdotal advice of self-help books. The average interviewee's sparse repertoire probably consists of basic survival skills: what to be nervous about, what not to say, how to behave, how to protect yourself. A so-called trained interviewer may have a slight advantage—perhaps a three-hour company workshop on the subject. Few people, however, are adequately prepared to make the most out of interview opportunities.

Don't assume, either, that those exposed to a formal, textbook-driven communication curriculum possess a broad perspective on the potential of interviewing. Some books are written primarily from the interviewer's perspective, an approach that overlooks several important considerations. When teachers and students focus so intently on the interviewer, they're likely to underestimate the potential value of an interview as a collaboration. They are also likely reinforce the misconception that interviewers must always be dominant, which encourages energy-sapping countertactics from interviewees, as the employment interviewing research shows.

Even in such helping professions as medicine and counseling, the interviewer is emphasized. Despite a recent emphasis on "patient-centered communication" in medical education (Thompson & Parrott, 2002), many doctors and other health-care specialists aren't likely to see the patient interview as a cooperative venture. The interviewee may benefit from the attention, but the approach might be perceived as paternalistic even when the specialist is sincerely trying to help. The patient or client is treated as someone to be probed, inspected, analyzed, assessed, and—ultimately—helped.

Although some people wind up as formal interviewers, almost everyone is interviewed at one time or another. All of us could benefit from studying key components of interviewing, such as listening, choosing appropriate language, interpreting others' behavior, and assessing information. This book defines the topic broadly enough to consider a wide range of situations and activities, presenting the interview as a fundamental form of human communication that cannot be taken for granted (see Box 1.1).

Characteristics of an Interview

No definition of an interview can be universal or comprehensive. However, most interviews share certain key characteristics, functions, and qualities. Let's extend our earlier definition a bit. At its most basic level, an interview is a form of communication, usually between two people, talking face-to-face, in a more or less organized way. The participants in an interview assume complementary roles, usually with the interviewer initiating and sustaining the talk. The interview has a purpose, usually understood by all parties: to learn something useful in making a decision or planning a course of action. Occasionally, the interview is a step in the further communication of ideas to audiences who would not have had access to them otherwise. No two interviews are alike, however. At times, for example, the interview has no immediately discernible plan; other times it has an exceptionally clear (and possibly conflicting) plan or purpose. Our

Box 1.1

Interviewers in Action *James G. Goodale*

Management consultant and author James Goodale warns against the assumption that effective interviewing is intuitive:

> Many of us have known people who appear to conduct effective interviews almost by intuition and seem to have the knack to say the right thing at the right time. We are inclined to attribute their success to personality and intuitive feel and therefore conclude that a good interviewer is born not made.

> This conclusion, however, is simply not true.

> . . . Just as the ballet dancer, the professional athlete, and the professional comedian have planned and practiced each individual action we observe in their seemingly effortless performance, successful interviewers have worked very hard to perfect their art.

Source: Goodale (1982, pp. 1–2)

description is also deceptively simple. In practice, there's nothing simple about most interviews. See Box 1.2 for a summary of our definition.

As researchers confirm, the term *communication,* which seems so straightforward at first glance, is remarkably complex and dense. Although **communication** usually refers generally to the development of shared meaning between persons in a relationship, that shared meaning can never be completely or exactly understood the same way by all participants. Although much of the meaning is shared symbolically through language (verbal messages), significant aspects of human life also are influenced directly by the nonverbal messages we interpret in each other's behavior and in the contexts for our talk.

As a form of human communication, the interview consists of three fundamental but interdependent processes: listening, speaking, and framing. *Listening* involves the essentially internal, but still active, means of focusing on the messages of interviewing. *Speaking* involves the active questioning and responding that constitute the "out loud" experience of interviewing. *Framing* indicates a different kind of activity—the complex inner processes of interpreting and evaluating messages in context. Although we'll discuss them in sequence, try to imagine their overlaps. Listening and speaking are not separate processes but are interwoven at every level. Listening and framing are both interpretive processes that create meanings; speaking is possible because of our abilities to frame meanings. The more each participant knows about the subtleties of communication, the more likely the interview will contribute to genuine learning.

We address communication problems in more detail later, but for now, think about the basic processes of listening, speaking, and framing in nontechnical ways.

Listening

Listening is basic because it enables purposeful communication. Meaningful talk tends to occur only when speakers assume that the potential for attentive listening is already

Box 1.2

Reminders *Defining the Interview*

An interview can be understood as

- A form of interpersonal communication (emphasizing questions and answers at times).
- Usually between two complementary roles.
- Usually involving face-to-face presence.
- With mutually agreed-on focus or purpose.

- Resulting in better or more information or insight.
- Leading to a decision, a course of action, or further communication with additional audiences.

present. We'll examine interesting implications of this for interview partners in Chapter 3, but for now, just note the defining characteristics of effective listening.

Merely hearing something is not the same thing as listening. **Hearing** is a physiological process through which the human ear and auditory apparatus perceive sounds. **Listening,** on the other hand, is a much more important concept for communicators. It's the holistic process of attending to, comprehending, and interpreting oral messages and their contexts. It is holistic because people listen with their eyes, bodies, minds, emotions, and cultural assumptions. Listening involves effort, commitment, and concentration.

The ability to listen is tested at times by occupational, personal, and psychological distractions. Ringing phones, nagging headaches, problems at home, or personal biases, for example, can impede listening. People must occasionally work in conditions where they have little control, but whenever possible, interview participants should position themselves physically and attitudinally to listen at their best. A willingness to listen, and the skill to do it well, is under your control even in the most trying circumstances.

Listening is important as a means of enhancing the relationship between interview partners. An attentive, responsive interviewer says nonverbally, "I'm with you." In fact, listening becomes a message in itself, confirming the identities of the speakers and the importance of the occasion. It can inspire more revealing and more complete talk because people tend to speak more earnestly and more often to careful listeners. Those who mishear us or are easily distracted receive less of our attention.

Listening is important, too, for creating an accurate record of the interview. It requires questions and probes to double-check what we hear, or what we think we hear—such as saying, "Could I rephrase what you just said to be sure I've got it right?" Interviewers, in particular, must guard against becoming so absorbed with recording the results of an interview that they listen narrowly only to what's obvious, and not for the meanings that are often shaded in nuance or in subtle behaviors. Skillful interviewees will probe to ensure they are in fact addressing the issues the interviewer raises. Careful listening also helps interviewees, such as medical patients, keep their own record of the interview.

Finally, listening is not only receptive; it is also interpretive. What people say, even when expressed in simple terms, can be far more complex than it first sounds.

Interviewers' discriminating, interpretive listening can detect inconsistencies, improbabilities, evasions, doubts, ambiguities, half-truths, metaphors, and other intricacies of speech, enabling the interview to reach its potential.

Speaking

The language of interviewing is crucial because questions and responses can energize further talk or stifle it; they can inspire eloquence or prompt monosyllabic grunts; they can build trust or raise suspicions. Participants must respect the power of language to enhance or damage communication. This text asks that you sensitize yourself to what your language might suggest to others in addition to what you intend.

Knowing what to say depends on how you anticipate the context of the interview, the personalities involved, and the subjects to be addressed. Before each interview, participants should commit themselves to assessing the situation and to seeking background information and insights necessary to facilitate understanding.

Although most speakers would like their speech to be clear, interesting, and provocative enough to generate further speech, speech problems (using a wrong word, mispronunciation, stuttering) occur fairly often in otherwise-effective interviews just because we're human. However, the best interview partners become reasonably mindful of how their speaking is shaped by the conversation and vice versa; they monitor and regulate their speech to accomplish flexible objectives. Communicators can be guided by speech in addition to "using" it. For that step to occur, the next component of the interview plays a central role—the ability to frame information well.

Framing

Speaking and listening are ultimately linked to our ability to **frame;** that is, to interpret what we think is really going on in social situations (Goffman, 1974). Three brief connotations might clarify the concept. First, think of framing as it relates to a picture frame—something that defines the boundaries of something else and creates its context. (That photo of Mom, you might think, would look better in a wood frame or a gold one, rather than in silver. The frame tells a perceiver how to "take" or interpret the picture.) Second, you might also want to consider how a framework is a pattern made of parts fitted together for mutual support, as in the wood frame that supports a house as it is built or a car's frame that gives it strength and stability. (Carpenters know that a subpar frame causes huge construction problems later.) Finally, think of concocting a story to frame someone else for a crime—that's a kind of patterned portrayal designed to be interpreted in a certain way. ("He framed me" means that he created a coherent story that falsely implicates me in something.) Some sort of supportive pattern is fundamental to all of these connotations.

For example, what one person intends as a friendly series of questions showing sincere curiosity might be framed by a respondent as a personal attack or cross-examination. Some communication scholars call this kind of framing **punctuation** (Watzlawick, Beavin, & Jackson, 1967). It is the mental act of taking complex processes and mentally labeling causes and effects, or starts and stops, within them, much like punctuation marks (periods, question marks, commas, etc.) indicate similar intentions in writing.

Punctuation helps us to understand how the same words can be heard by one person as a new topic but by another as a response to a previous comment (you think your questions were "caused" by your interest in me; I, punctuating the speech differently, think the questions come from your desire to criticize).

Different people punctuate differently, and this can create framing problems. When a politician, for example, answers a reporter's question curtly, it may be because the question is perceived as an extension of last month's contentious give-and-take in a press conference. The reporter, on the other hand, punctuates differently by seeing this interview as a new event, thinking, "This is my first question and I'm being nice. Why is this guy so mad already? That's not fair." The tone of the interchange sours from there, becoming more strained, as neither interviewer nor interviewee considers that there may be different frames for the "same" sequence of interaction. Yet they both think they know what's going on. The interview opportunity, used effectively, allows us to confirm what we know and identify what we don't know; to separate, as best we can, truth from untruths and facts from fiction; to confront the ambiguity of conflicting frames; and to obtain clarification, elaboration, or amplification (see Box 1.3).

Framing is also a basic human style of handling similarities and differences: "A frame, as the name suggests, sets a boundary around the details and highlights how those details are related to each other" (Agar, 1994, p. 130). To Agar, an anthropologist, frames are holistic (they disclose whole interrelationships and patterns); comparative (they tell us how to move knowledge and insight from old situations to new, from known to unknown); and based on fieldwork (they're understood and changed through direct experience in the "field" of everyday communication). Agar provides a good model for everyday learning: (1) be alert for patterns, (2) compare situations in which you find those patterns, (3) try out what you think you know to see if it works.

Qualities of Interviewing

Every interview has an emotional climate, and its participants will be affected by its conversational weather. An inhospitable climate is marked by tension, suspicion, anxiety, and other draining, counterproductive qualities. A supportive climate enhances the

---

Box 1.3

Reminders *Connotations of the Framing Metaphor*

- The *picture frame* (reminds us that framing is a way of establishing the limits, definitions, or boundaries of an idea).

- The *frame for structural support* (reminds us that a good frame—such as in a house or a car—bolsters and strengthens interpretations).

- The *frame-up* in which someone is implicated in another person's story (reminds us that frames are narratives that structure experience, and that persons are all woven into each others' stories).

ability to communicate, reducing or eliminating concerns that characterize many encounters between strangers. The common qualities of emotionally satisfying interviewing—whatever the context—are empathy, honesty, respect, and validation.

Empathy

In the behavioral sciences, **empathy** means the attempt to sense someone else's world, more or less as she or he senses it, without leaving your own experience. In part, it's the ability to detect and appreciate another's feelings, emotions, and concerns. Empathy is not *sympathy,* which involves two people in agreement or harmony in feelings or beliefs. It's not a full identification with the other, in which someone loses a separate sense of self. Empathy doesn't necessarily signal approval or disapproval, either, but it does say, "I'm trying to see things from your perspective." Interestingly, according to a popularized summary of recent research into babies' brains, "One of the earliest emotions that even tiny babies display is, admirably enough, empathy. In fact, concern for others may be hard-wired into babies' brains" (Wingert & Brant, 2005, p. 35).

Honesty

Nothing derails an interview more quickly than the perception of dishonesty. Various shades of dishonesty—hidden agendas, deception, half-truths, lies, and even "BS" (Frankfurt, 2005)—might go undetected and even produce results in the short run. More often than not, however, listeners will sense when someone is not forthright or honest. Even when full disclosure by interview partners is unrealistic—because, for example, of prior commitments, ethical restraints, or time limits—an attitude of honesty should guide interviewer and interviewee. In some settings, withholding information perhaps can be justified. A doctor, for example, interviewing a patient with symptoms of a potentially serious illness, might hide some of her suspicions until tests confirm a tentative diagnosis. In negotiating a real estate sale, both sides might hedge as they assess each other's relative interest in buying or selling. Yet occasional compromises of total honesty or full disclosure, perhaps even in the service of etiquette or politeness, should not undermine the fundamental expectation that interview partners will be direct and honest. Interview partners' fullest appropriate disclosure allows the interview to move into substantive talk and past a suspicion-laden contest of thrust and parry. Empathy can support honesty in interviews, and an honest, empathic approach helps demonstrate respect.

Respect

Respect in an interview goes beyond pleasantries and politeness to an authentic concern for differences in status, gender, age, and culture. It means honoring essential human qualities, such as dignity, self-esteem, courage, humor, and determination. Without respect, we are likely to see what we expect to see. A job interviewer, for example, meets an applicant who is young, shy, socially awkward, and nervous. With an attitude of respect, the interviewer discovers a fresh side of the applicant's personality—a previously unexpressed maturity. Interviews are occasions for respectful listening and speech. In many instances, the interviewer holds the power cards, such as choosing where to talk, when to change topics, or how to terminate the conversation. Still, cutting an interview short, showing impatience with another's halting speech, and glancing often at a clock are readily experienced as signals of disrespect. When empathy, honesty, and respect blend in an interview, communicators can be said to be validating each other's basic worth as persons.

Validation

Validation occurs when communicators acknowledge that they recognize the other's presence and that they have attempted to cooperate in a sincere exchange of views. Perhaps the outcome remains unsatisfactory—you didn't get the job, or that friendly couple didn't buy your car—but the interviewer or interviewee acknowledges your position; you've been given a fair opportunity to be heard. An interview, even when conducted as a partnership, still has elements of yours, mine, and ours. Participants cannot will or guarantee the outcome they desire. Without validation, however, the interview probably will feel incomplete and unsatisfactory. Validation is a somewhat more general term for what we call confirmation in Chapter 3.

Traditional Types of Interviews

Identifying interview categories helps explain how one interview differs from another. The categories, although not entirely arbitrary, vary, depending on how broadly *interview* is defined. Parents and children practice interviewing, especially when talking through problems. A popular guide from the past, *Parent Effectiveness Training* (T. Gordon, 1975), stressed active listening through nonjudgmental inquiries—conversational family interviews in a sense—about a child's anger, poor grades, or withdrawal, for example. Police and social workers regularly use interviews as investigative tools (Yeschke, 2003). Despite these examples, we don't label one category "family interviews" and another "institutional investigation interviews." Objectives and participants differ, of course, but all interview types overlap considerably. Notice, for example, how almost all kinds of interviews involve the four qualities just discussed, and how they all involve some kinds of information gathering, persuasion, and decision making. Here, we've chosen the most common contexts for these activities as our categories; they suggest nearly every possible type of interview. We address each in detail in the chapters of Part Two.

Journalistic Interviews

Probably the most common informational interview in modern society is the news interview, and the skills it requires are broadly applicable to the interviewing process whether or not you'll ever become a reporter. The interview is the basic vehicle of journalists as they gather information, verify facts, elicit quotes, clarify conflicting accounts, and reconstruct events. Because the public relies on journalists for its perspectives on the world, news accuracy is crucial. Mistakes, amplified and spread through mass media accounts, can do tremendous economic, political, social, or personal damage. Thus, news interviews require not only careful listening, but confirmation of information. Moreover, the quality and reliability of our news system depend largely on the joint conversational efforts of reporters and the people they sometimes call their "sources."

Research Interviews

Journalists obviously do research, but experts in interviewing usually use the term *research interview* to refer to collecting data that is essential for a larger task of advancing knowledge. Social scientists gather quantitative and qualitative data in their work, such as geographers studying population shifts or sociologists investigating perceptions of crime in an inner city. Marketing firms working for corporations use surveys and focus group interviews to determine consumer preferences and needs. Political consultants interview citizens to measure voter attitudes and the salience of social issues; this research helps generate policies and campaign strategies. Research interviews are usually more important to interviewers than to interviewees, although there are clear exceptions to this rule. For example, interviewers doing oral history research may help a group become more familiar with its own cultural narratives; thus, the "researched" may be enriched immeasurably by the shared research experience.

Selection Interviews

The selection interview often involves hiring decisions. Personnel experts or managers in corporations rely on job interviews for screening and selecting employees, from office clerks to CEOs. In most job interviews the outcome boils down to a "yes" or a "no," and therefore these interviews exhibit an obvious power structure. Interviewees can feel vulnerable: Most interviews are face-to-face, occur on the interviewer's turf, and are played by the interviewer's ground rules. Other types of selection interviews exhibit the same power dynamics, including screening for membership in groups, determining who among a group of bidders gets a contract, and deciding among plans or courses of action by asking their advocates to present and defend them.

Organizational Interviews

Selection interviews usually occur in organizations, of course, but other interview forms also support and advance organizational goals. Today's organizational environment demands great emphasis on teamwork and decentralized decision making. Instead of bosses dictating from on high, employees increasingly have a say in plotting the course and implementing procedures. Interviews help uncover problems and find solutions, and they generate ideas and cost-saving innovations. On another level, appraisal interviews assess the performance of individuals or groups within the organization. Still other interviews might occur at a point of crisis or intervention to discipline, correct, or even fire an employee. The methods might range from a narrative evaluation of an employee's work record to a discussion with a quality-control focus group.

Persuasive Interviews

Clearly, all professional communication involves some aspect of persuasion. Yet traditionally, what interviewers term the *persuasive interview* involves such attitude-change tasks as closing business deals, selling products, or negotiating contracts. At the center of such decisions are obvious issues of financial gain or loss, basic fairness, convenience, safe working conditions, and many other factors. The persuasive dimension of interviews also arises outside business settings. Candidates for political office, for example, may appear before the editorial staff of a newspaper or meet with the officers of a labor union to seek endorsements.

Helping Interviews

Doctors, teachers, counselors, therapists, and religious leaders, among others, conduct helping interviews that typically involve such tasks as diagnosis, therapy, and problem solving. Candor is important in all interviews, but it becomes especially crucial when helping is the objective. In these interviews, talk may focus on personal feelings and issues that are painful or embarrassing to disclose. The path toward helping may require a series of interviews, each progressing from building rapport to defining the problem, exploring answers, and diagnosing possible solutions. Clearly, issues of trust, relationship duration, credibility, and openness can be even more important in helping situations than in most other forms of interviewing.

For a summary of the six major types of interviews, see Box 1.4.

Getting Started on a Basic Informational Interview

At the heart of most interviews is a straightforward and broadly practical task—the need to learn something specific that another person knows well. Almost all specialized interviewing tasks are variations on this theme. Sometimes called the **information-gathering interview,** this is the prototypical form for most interviewers and interviewees. It most closely resembles the journalist's task, although the metaphor of gathering is somewhat misleading; skillful journalistic interviewers know that information (or news) is never

---

Box 1.4

Reminders   *Major Types of Interviews*

- Journalistic (to develop information and insight necessary for providing news to public audiences).

- Research (to develop information and insight necessary for developing better theories and practices of human behavior).

- Selection (to develop information and insight necessary for making a decision, usually about matching a person or group to a position or task).

- Organizational (to develop information and insight necessary for coordinating or appraising people and policies within complex organizations).

- Persuasive (to develop information and insight within situations of direct interpersonal influence).

- Helping (to develop information and insight necessary for assisting people in meeting their own psychological and health goals).

simply lying around ready to be gathered. Information that matters is rarely prepackaged and ready for consumption.

Often the people who are most able to inform you aren't even fully aware of what they know, such as the laboratory scientist who has deep knowledge about a new drug but has given scant thought to the social or political changes its legalized use might bring. You engage information experts, talk with them, let them know why you're curious, and convince them you will listen carefully. Then—if you're skilled or lucky—you begin to find they will open up to you. They'll even surprise themselves with what they are able to articulate. This is the true excitement of interviewing: coming up with what neither person expected. The scientist who knows about the chemical nature of a drug that counteracts male impotence, or one who fully understands the science of cloning, discovers that she or he wants to share an opinion about the social consequences of the innovation. Many otherwise competent communicators overlook this dialogic potential of talk.

Before moving further into the finer points of interviewing, let's bypass jargon and reduce informational interviewing, defined as one person's, or group's, attempt to learn specific information from another person or group, to its basic elements: the stimulus, the participants, the relationship, the content, the process, and the outcome.

• The *stimulus* (why does an interview happen?): In informational interviewing, someone has an itch to learn that needs to be scratched. There is a knowledge gap, a crisis, or a problem that someone wants solved.

• The *participants* (who participates in an interview?): The interviewer wants to obtain information or insight not already possessed, and identifies a resource person who's ideally knowledgeable or qualified enough to provide guidance—a responding interviewee.

• The *relationship* (how are participants connected?): Interviewers who need information or insight must rely on the goodwill and responsiveness of respondents. Informational interviews are usually requested by interviewers and arranged at the convenience of interviewees. Yet the benefits are mutual; interviewers help interviewees talk about things they might not have articulated before and help them to reach new audiences. Ideally, each party serves the needs of the other.

• The *content* (what do participants say and do?): As focused conversations, interviews generally are propelled by questions and answers. However, don't assume that all the questions will belong to interviewers and that all answers come from interviewees. Each will probably ask, answer, and need to clarify at various times.

• The *process* (how do speech and action develop in interviews?): Generally, the primary responsibility for "maintenance" in interview situations lies with the interviewer, and the question—or in some cases, an inquiry implied by a comment or observation—is the prime way to move things forward. Interviewing is a conversation that is managed and pointed in certain directions, to make certain outcomes more likely than others. Interviews that aren't limited by external commitments (e.g., "I have to leave by 5:30 to pick up my daughter") usually last as long as the parties perceive progress toward meeting their goals, which probably include getting the interviewer's question(s) answered.

The informational interviewing process is often relatively directive. In other words, an interviewer may lead with a brief statement of task, then introduce a fairly general and open-ended question. He or she would quickly move to requests for specific details, phrased in relatively closed ways. Interviewers must signal clearly what is needed for respondents to reply efficiently. Then, each topic change thereafter could be noted with a general question. For example:

LUCAS (interviewer): To project a budget for student government this coming year, I need the final figures on the Spring Fling promotion. You and Monique handled that, right? [SIGNALS TASK AND GENERAL PURPOSE]

SERENA (interviewee): Well, yes and no. I did most of the planning, but then after I got sick, Monique took it over. We both handled PR and ads, but she was much more responsible for the legwork.

LUCAS: I just need the final figures. Should I ask her, or do you have that information, too? [VERIFIES THAT SERENA IS AN APPROPRIATE SOURCE FOR THE INFORMATION HE NEEDS]

SERENA: I've got them right here, but they're just copied down in pencil in my notebook—I don't have the official report. Is that OK?

LUCAS: Right. No problem. All I need is ballpark estimates for the different parts of the Fling. How much for equipment rental? [ASKS FIRST CONTENT QUESTION]

SERENA: Looks like about $250. Much less than we'd thought, by the way.

LUCAS: How about ads—print and radio both? [ASKS SECOND QUESTION]

SERENA: We did only print this year, but we did both the *College News* and the *Herald-Investigator* in town. Quite a chunk. Total came to just over $500.

LUCAS: Do you think that the lack of radio ads hurt the attendance? Maybe we should go back to them next year. [ASKS FOLLOW-UP TO SECOND QUESTION]

SERENA: Not a problem, I'd say. Attendance was actually up. Monique and her group did a great job on banners and fliers.

LUCAS: They cost next to nothing, right? Well, that's about all I need. Thanks. See you at Monday's meeting; take care. [CAPS THE CONVERSATION BY ACKNOWLEDGING THE INFORMATION AND SERENA'S HELPFULNESS]

Lucas's approach is informal, yet straightforward and appropriate to the task. He was clear in asking for the information he needed from Serena and helpful in clarifying why she could help. Compare his systematic approach with a second, and less effective, way he could have approached his task:

LUCAS: Hi, Serena. You were involved in the Spring Fling, right? What could you tell me about it? [ASKS GENERAL QUESTION WITHOUT CONTEXT]

SERENA: Yeah, I was—it was so much fun. What do you want to know?

LUCAS: I've got to get some figures together. I wish someone else could get this done, but they asked me to do it. [RESPONDS TANGENTIALLY TO SERENA'S REQUEST FOR CLARIFICATION]

SERENA: For what?

LUCAS: Why'd they ask me? [RESPONDS WITH SIDE QUESTION, AS IF IT'S SERE-
NA'S JOB TO GUESS WHAT HE WANTS TO KNOW]

SERENA: No, silly. What are the figures for?

Six turns into this second conversation, Serena still wouldn't know exactly why they're talking together. She likes Lucas, perhaps, but is wondering, "What is he talking about? Are we just passing the time here, or does he need something more specific from me?" In this example, Lucas is not efficiently matching his need to know something with Serena's ability to share information. There's nothing wrong with this conversation as conversation, but at times its elliptical tendency to waste time will not be appreciated. Note that in the first example, Lucas and Serena are also talking informally; being focused and systematic doesn't mean being stuffy or excessively formal. You can be sure that in most professional contexts, efficient informational interviewing is a skill much appreciated by coworkers.

• The *outcome* (what is learned?): In many interviews, both parties will learn something new; the process can be seen usefully from both perspectives. However, it's probably fair to say that most people think about such interviews from the vantage point of the original inquirer, and they assume an effective interview is one that helps the interviewer learn what is necessary.

Therefore, in seeking basic information, think of your inquiry strategy as variations on just a few steps. Although these five steps look like a textbook presciption, they develop quite naturally in most interview situations: (1) State what you need; (2) phrase a general question about the respondent's ability or willingness to share information; (3) listen to the response well enough to follow up with specific questions that clarify, extend, and test the information; (4) revisit steps 2 and 3 when probing subtopics or further issues; and (5) cap the interview by ensuring you've understood the information accurately and showing appreciation for the help you've received.

Now reverse the roles; you're being interviewed. Imagine a situation in which you have information you suspect an interviewer needs, but you don't know quite how to provide or package it. From an interviewee's perspective, simply mirror the steps: (1) Make sure you clarify what the interviewer needs, and what it's needed for; this will suggest how you might phrase your responses or, in some cases, whether you might even want to avoid discussing the matter (e.g., "You want to discover who did what in the Tompkins incident?"); (2) Clarify the general question (e.g., "You want to know whether I was responsible for hiring Tompkins?"); (3) Ask if your specific responses are providing the information the interviewer needs ("I recommended Tompkins, but you may know that two other people did, too. And The Big Boss was really pushing for her. So I was in on it, sure, but I wouldn't say I was primarily responsible. Does that make sense?"); (4) Continue to check on the other person's listening as the conversation progresses. You have at least as much concern for accurate messages as the interviewer does; (5) Conclude the interview with a summary of what you think you've told your partner.

Trying Out Your Skills

- Pair up with a partner from your interviewing class, or let your teacher match you on the basis of dissimilar interests.

- Talk for five minutes, each of you disclosing some basic, not-too-personal facts about hobbies, politics, school activities, and family life.

- Decide on one specific aspect of your partner's life that you'd like to know more about ("You're a concert pianist? What kind of practice schedule do you have to keep?"; "I've heard a lot of students try to get into the physical therapy major, but I've never understood what jobs you might be aiming for. What are the most common career goals?"). Each of you should have time to play the interviewer role.

- Each should interview the other for five to ten minutes. When you are the interviewer, start by phrasing a general question that indicates your interest in that aspect (see earlier examples). Use the reply to that question to suggest other, perhaps more specific, directions. Be sure to help your partner talk by phrasing your curiosity as clearly as you can and by following up as specifically as possible on the details. (Your general question we will later call a "primary question," and the follow-ups we'll later term "probes"; for now, though, don't worry about the distinctions.

- Your teacher may ask you to use the information obtained in these mini-interviews as material to help you introduce your partner to the class. This is often a good way to let class members sense, early in the semester, what they have in common and what is unique about each person.

Beyond the Basics

Ethical Implications and Dimensions

Organizational leaders are increasingly emphasizing the importance of ethical communication, stressing ethics through advertising, diversity and other human relations training, in-house workshops on labor–management relations, written rules and policies, ethical "audits," and lofty mission statements. Most professional organizations, such as the Society of Professional Journalists and the American Psychological Association, have formal codes of ethics, some with recommended sanctions for violations. However, the ethics of interviewing is an issue still too often found at the periphery of study, discussion, and practice, if it's considered at all.

Ethical Orientations

Understanding ethics in an interviewing context begins with understanding ethical orientations. First, we consider the two major types of orientation, teleology and deontology, although we'll discuss other approaches later. **Teleology** comes from the Greek *telos*, meaning "end" or "goal." It looks at ethical behavior from the perspective of outcomes or consequences. Teleology is often referred to as *consequentialist* ethics. An example of consequentialist ethics is **utilitarianism,** which itself takes several forms. For example, one of those forms promotes a noble ethical objective: Do what is most likely to produce the greatest good for the greatest number of people. Another consequentialist approach puts individual interests first: ethical **egoism.** An egoism-based ethic, although consequentialist in orientation, would result in doing what is most likely to produce the greatest good for the deciding individual, and does not necessarily ask deciders to factor in others' welfare.

Applied to an interview, a utilitarian approach taken by one participant and egoism by another could result in an acceptable outcome for both—but probably won't. The manager of a security firm, for example (putting the overall good of the company first), decides it's too risky to hire an ex-convict and so simply goes through the motions of an interview, never revealing or discussing her knowledge of the applicant's criminal record. The applicant, guided by egoism, withholds this part of the record, figuring he'll never get hired and have a shot at straightening out his life if he comes clean. In a narrow sense, both are adhering to their separate ethical codes, based on a weighing of possible consequences. Is a middle ground possible? Perhaps, but consequentialist ethical positions are often held individually and privately. Although the idea of partnership perhaps should guide interviews, overt cooperation about what's ethical in problem situations is often difficult.

Deontology, the second major ethical orientation, comes from the Greek *deon,* meaning "duty." Deontology stresses that communicators should adhere to rules or duties, often regardless of the consequences. A strict deontologist could argue that anticipated consequences should have no bearing in determining what is ethically right or wrong. For example, if we have an obligation to tell the truth, there should be little justification for lying, even if people might be spared harm as a consequence. Attempting to practice an unbending form of deontology can tie you in ethical knots, but generally, ethical behavior based on moderate forms of deontology will not completely reject how consequences might be relevant; rather, it simply emphasizes the consistency of duties and principles. Sometimes, though, general duties, such as the doctor's dictum "do no harm" and other guidelines such as "tell the truth" will clash. Journalists often find that publishing truthful stories about interviewees—one "duty"—can hurt innocent people, which can violate another expectation of their profession. Balancing duties and responsibilities might be necessary, based on assessing possible consequences. That teleological–deontological balancing might result in telling the truth in ways that minimize harm.

Whether schooled in philosophical frameworks of ethics or operating from an intuitive sense of right and wrong, ethical interviewers typically consider both principles and consequences in their deliberations.

Ethical Deliberations

Most interview partners would like to think we're sensitized to ethical ways of thinking and communicating before they ever meet us. So we'd do well to develop an ethical standard operating procedure (SOP) to provide a touchstone of acceptable behavior in the ever-changing contexts of professional life. This touchstone could be a personal guide; it could be based on professional or organizational norms; it could be a combination of both. Ethics isn't mathematics, with set formulas and axioms, so we must expect the unexpected.

In the professional world, setting the ethical tone is a responsibility that usually falls primarily to the interviewer. From an ethically sensitive grounding, he or she can work from an implicit checklist of sorts, asking at each stage of the interaction about whether behaviors are right or wrong, not just effective or ineffective. Here is a sample of such a checklist:

• What is the purpose of the interview? Is there a shared understanding of the purpose? If not, is there a justifiable reason to withhold or disguise the real purpose of the interview? Full disclosure should be the rule, with rare exceptions.

• What preparation has been done? Have I done enough reading, study, and deliberation to conduct a fruitful interview? Has the interviewee been given comparable opportunity to prepare?

• Who will be interviewed? Can the selection of the interviewees be justified as fair and appropriate? Are any of the interviewees emotionally vulnerable or in need of special care or consideration?

• What will be the substance and impact of the questions asked? Are the questions well intentioned? Honest? Will they upset, disturb, or cause harm in any way? Is the information sought essential to the purpose of the interview? How will the acquired information be used? Is there any reason to believe that information might be misused? What safeguards might be necessary?

• Am I listening well? What distractions or listening difficulties might arise? Have I tried to create a listening environment conducive to appropriately open communication? Have I listened with the interviewee's interests in mind in addition to my own?

• What is the outcome? Has the interviewee been given ample time and opportunity to be heard and understood? Could others be harmed by interview outcomes? Is my behavior at every stage ethical and justifiable if subjected to public scrutiny? Have I been true to whatever duties find my conduct, and have I weighed the consequences for all who might have a stake in the outcome? What has been accomplished in this interview? Has mutual learning and understanding occurred? If roles were reversed, would I feel I'd been treated fairly, honestly, and respectfully?

Although this isn't a one-size-fits-all checklist, it can be valuable for beginning conversations about interview ethics. The ultimate ethical act is a commitment to ethical decision making itself, even if that means saying no when under pressure to compromise beliefs. People have quit jobs rather than submit to pressures to act unethically. This kind of sacrifice may not be necessary; ethical people often prevail by the strength of their convictions. An experienced organizational consultant once told one of the authors that the most radically powerful member of an organization is usually the person who is both effective and nonmanipulative.

Some ethical concerns include a legal dimension. Federal and state statutes, for example, legally restrict interview inquiries about sexual orientation, age, race, and some personal matters. There is some ethical foundation to why many laws exist, but law and ethics are not the same thing. Law generally sets a minimal standard—a lowest common denominator guide to behavior. Privacy laws, for example, limit disclosures of confidential student academic records; a teacher's personal ethical code regarding students' rights to confidentiality may encompass far more than the law protects.

Public Dialogue

Studying interviewing brings rewards that extend far beyond participating in interviews. It emphasizes a research sensibility, an openness to listening, a respect for diverse voices, an ability to be introspective, and a willingness to be thorough. These characteristics that some critics believe are too rare in public discourse. Have we lost track of civil ways to talk with each other? Does a preoccupation with advocacy and a habit for dismissing arguments of others deplete our public life? In this book you'll find an essentially dialogic model for interview communication, one that can be translated readily into larger spheres of family and public life. As you listen, question, and frame messages responsibly in one-on-one interviews, you're practicing the same basic skills that will help you manage relationships and meanings in other life contexts. Interviewing skills are directly applicable in many other work, home, and public interactions.

Interviewing Skills in the Workplace

Look around an office, school, factory, or any place where people work together, and you'll find too many communication glitches. These misunderstandings and misperceptions lead to costly mistakes, morale problems, lost business, reduced productivity, or disruptive behavior. (Of course, even effective communication can lead to morale problems and lost business, but that is another story.) In the long run, bet that poor communication will create mistrust, detachment, lack of purpose, and dissatisfaction. Those conditions are far less common in workplaces where people generally listen and talk things out, even when they're working with others who are quite different in terms of cultural and personal background. Workplaces are challenging because the very differences that make communication difficult are what energize organizational productivity and teach us new ways of relating. Increasingly, companies and institutions are encouraging new forms of communication, sometimes from the bottom up, through groups and teams that readily acknowledge difference. Such groups discuss, listen, and seek mutual solutions. Effective interviewers direct these programs.

Interviewing Skills at Home

If organizations have gotten more complex, so too have family lives. Recent decades have seen the rise of two, three, or more incomes in a complex family dance of schedule conflicts, misperceived motives, and transportation snafus. Many families are strained to the breaking point. If there has been a breakdown of the family, it's been partly a radical shift in expectations about communication. Relations tend to improve when parents and children commit themselves to ask thoughtful and nonjudgmental questions, phrase reasonable answers, understand one another's dilemmas, and work toward

Making Your Decision

Unplanned, informal interviews happen frequently in the course of our lives, and we usually participate in those interviews without giving them a second thought. We help friends talk out personal problems. We ask questions about issues affecting us. We share aspirations and job advice with family members. As you become more aware of the practices of interviewing, you'll see these occurrences as opportunities to apply what you've learned. At the end of each chapter, we'll put "Making Your Decision" boxes like this one. As a warm-up exercise, consider several fairly typical interviews from everyday life, and determine how you'd address each one.

- *Helping a friend:* Over coffee, a friend says "I'm having trouble at work. I can never seem to please my boss. Frankly, I'm worried about losing my job. What do you think I'm doing wrong?" You're not a trained counselor, but friends often play a similar informal role. What would you say? You could change the subject and reply, "Hey, I don't know what to say." But assume you want to help. How would you go about it? Would you mostly listen and clarify rather than inquire and advise? Would you ask questions, asking information about your friend's behavior and attitudes at work? What types of questions? Would you go immediately to the step of offering advice? Would you be frank? Indirect? Noncommittal? What about consequences of your talk? For you? For your friend? For your relationship?

- *Questioning the candidate:* A flyer stuck in your car door handle announces a neighborhood forum with a candidate for city council. You decide to attend; it's a small gathering of fewer than a dozen people. The candidate introduces herself, states her plans in general terms, then asks for questions. Here's your opportunity to become informed as a voter—an opportunity for face-to-face dialogue. What would you want to learn? Why? Qualifications? Issues? Character? Family and personal life? What questions would elicit information that helps you assess whether the candidate warrants your vote? What would you do if you believe the candidate is being evasive? How persistent or aggressive should you be in your questions and reactions?

- *Making a sale:* It's time to sell your 1997 Toyota, a dependable car that is past its prime. A nervous young man answers your classified ad. He's looking for his first car, and he has a list of questions to ask you. To some extent, this is a moment of truth. You're not going to lie about the car's condition, because it does have some problems. But it's safe and runs. Do you volunteer information? Would you sidestep some questions? What might they be? Could you justify withholding information? Would you try to maneuver the conversation away from the negatives about the car? How far would you go in using your powers of persuasion to make a sale?

Try to imagine these episodes playing themselves out. Raise questions of your own and try answering them, as well. The objective is not to test whether you have the "right" answers, because there aren't any. The exercise is meant to reinforce the notion that interviews are both common and uncommon. They're common because so many of our communication encounters involve elements of interviewing. They're uncommon because the unique dynamics of a particular interview can be incredibly complicated. No prior knowledge guarantees how an interview will turn out.

solving problems together. Of course, we see no shortage of pop culture gurus willing to tell us all exactly how to live. That isn't our goal. We simply suggest that good interviewing skills might be applied at home to raise the quality of family life, too. Practicing interviewing is practicing ways to enhance your quality of life.

Interviewing Skills in Public Life

The United States was founded as a republic, which means supreme power rests in the citizenry. Without an informed, involved public, the ideal and practice of republican government will die a slow death. What grows in its place may not be a totalitarian system, but it may well be one that is far less of, by, and for the people. Passive citizens surrender their authority and power by default. Special-interest groups and political operatives quickly fill the void. Public life prospers through our ability and willingness to communicate; public life withers when communication does. Through civic talk at all levels of public life, people settle problems, set priorities, and establish policy. At least that is how it should work. Stay alert, too, to how diatribes, sloganeering, harassment, threats and, when all else fails, bombs take the place of civic discourse.

The interview is a useful model for communication throughout society. It stresses abilities of language, listening, and analyzing. It's based on principles of collaboration and honesty under conditions of not knowing something. It recognizes the complexity and layers of human life. Its goal is mutual understanding. We hope *Interviewing* proves to be valuable well beyond its obvious applications in interviewing situations. A broadly based education in interviewing will mean that, for example, more citizens may feel comfortable questioning mayoral candidates at public forums and assessing their performance; parents may be more likely to attend conferences with their children's teachers; officers in neighborhood organizations may be better prepared to research the preferences of other residents. Surely everyone can benefit from being better interviewers and interviewees.

Summary

This chapter introduced the basic themes that will recur throughout the book. We view interviews as conversations focused on information and, ideally, guided by a sense of mutual involvement. Although popular stereotypes often make the process sound like unpleasant competition, the best interviews are more likely to resemble partnerships.

Interviews can be analyzed by emphasizing their characteristics, qualities, and types. We defined the three characteristic subprocesses of interviewing as listening, speaking, and framing. Effective interview partners find qualities such as empathy, honesty, respect, and validation extraordinarily practical in a variety of communication settings. In this book we focus on six such settings for interviews: journalistic, research, personnel selection, organizational, persuasive, and helping.

In "Beyond the Basics" we placed the interviewing process in larger context by discussing ethical implications of interviewing at work, home, and in civic life. Interviewers and interviewees can contribute significantly to democratic discourse, but only if they remain sensitive to questions of interpersonal ethics.

Chapter Two

Before Skills

Appreciations and Habits of Dialogue

After reading this chapter, you should be able to

- Describe the difference between a *skills* approach to interviewing and this book's *skills-plus* approach

- Discuss the characteristics of a dialogic appreciation of interviewing and be able to point to examples from everyday life

- Begin to analyze your personal interviewing style in terms of such skills-plus concepts as credibility, content and process knowledge, multiculturalism, communication reticence or apprehension, and empathic ways of being

- Build on your basic knowledge of interviewing to understand how the more theoretical notions of conversation—such as communication rules, the cooperative principle, and conversational maxims of quantity, quality, relevance, and manner—can enhance interviewing decisions

Cassaundra, a recent college graduate, encounters trouble landing the job to launch her career in public relations. Her solid work in classes, along with excellent experience doing volunteer service for several local nonprofits, helped her construct an impressive résumé and earned her several interviews with good companies. With no job offers to date, however, she fears she'll have to give up her apartment and ask Mom and Dad if she can live at home until she gets full-time work. Now she's after a position she really wants, for an organization she has admired for years—a breakthrough job, she thinks. As she approaches the door of the interviewer's office, she thinks, "Everything rides on this interview."

Loren, a freelance writer, has tried for several years to break into the major magazine market with articles on important social issues. He's sold a few pieces to industry publications and smaller magazines, and although they supplemented the family income, none established his reputation or opened new doors for him. He recently learned that an attorney from his hometown, a woman he knew slightly in high school, helped defend a high-profile celebrity who was charged with murder in an eastern state. While on a visit to Baileyville to see family, the attorney agrees to talk with

We can . . . take courage from the fact that many people are longing to be in conversation again. We are hungry for a chance to talk. People want to tell their story, and are willing to listen to yours. People want to talk about their concerns and struggles. Too many of us feel isolated, strange, or invisible. Conversation helps end that.

—**Margaret J. Wheatley,**
Turning to One Another

Loren about the trial, which just ended in a controversial acquital. This is the kind of article that could be a career-maker. As he drives to his parents' home, Loren dwells on his big opportunity and how "Everything rides on this interview."

Kathryn, a community organizer, has worked tirelessly for the past two years to provide services to teenagers from troubled families in tense, sometimes violent, neighborhoods. Most of her work, and most of its benefit, has occurred behind the scenes. Yet several days ago, a news story broke that threatens the entire project: Two youth counselors were arrested on charges of selling cocaine to minors. Public suspicion about her program is mounting, and its very existence is threatened. Somehow she must explain, without defensiveness, that the two counselors—even if guilty—should not taint an otherwise successful and necessary program. "Everything," she says to herself as the newspaper's most cynical investigative reporter knocks on her door, "rides on this interview."

These sincere but ego-involved interview participants are all probably wrong on one count—rarely does "everything" hinge on a single interview. Yet they can be forgiven for their emotional involvement, because interviews so often seem like pivotal incidents in life. People feel nervous, and naturally so, because in interviews they know something important is likely to happen. Someone is on the spot; something is being listened to especially carefully. The interview, as a focused occasion for direct talk, can put interaction under the magnifying glass and occasionally expose its imperfections. The potential for miscommunication is high. The personal and professional stakes are typically just as significant. Interviews can, indeed, lead to life-changing decisions: Who gets the job? Who gets the story? Whose impressive work might be dismissed unfairly because of a single misstatement?

It's easy to think of interviews as tests for individuals. In fact, it is easiest, perhaps, for many people to think of interviews as occasions either for personal crisis or for personal crisis management, and often they are. In this chapter, however, we want to remind you of the extent to which successful interviews are not merely the result of individual successes. Likewise, disappointing interviews are not simply caused by individual failures. Rather, the quality of interview experience is based more fundamentally on collaborative efforts—the appreciations and habits of dialogue that participants enact in the interview.

The Basics

A Skills-Plus Approach

Most of this book concentrates on describing the skills necessary for effective interviewing. **Skills,** often defined as the behaviors necessary to adapt to the demands of different contexts, create much of the foundation for competent communication. Most college classes and organizational workshops in interviewing are conceived as skill-building exercises. Participants learn new ways of acting and speaking, as they should. Yet, as

R. B. Rubin (1990) suggests, the competent communicator goes beyond mere skills to consider a wider context. Rubin defines **communication competence** in these terms:

> [It is] knowledge about appropriate and effective communication behaviors, development of a repertoire of skills that encompass both appropriate and effective means of communicating, and motivation to behave in ways that are viewed as both appropriate and effective by interactants. This definition implies that communication competence can be taught through enhancing this knowledge, these skills, and this motivation. (p. 96)

Rubin's definition stressed three components of competence we, in turn, should stress in this book: Interviewers and interviewees should be knowledgeable, skillful, and motivated. *Knowledge* means concepts, vocabulary, ideas, facts, research findings—the issues communicators need to understand. *Skills* depend on putting that knowledge into practice. The ability to behave differently will not be very valuable unless we know when and where to do so, but complete knowledge of situations will not increase competence unless we have a wide range of behavioral alternatives—skills—available. Neither knowledge nor skill will be sufficient without the motivation to use them. *Motivations* are those inner impulses, goals, or choices that lead us in certain directions but not in others. They are influenced by what we value and what we expect from the interview.

As you build skills by reading this book, you'll also be building a framework of knowledge that supports your efforts, and developing new motivation for improvement. We call this kind of competence a **skills-plus approach** to interviewing. It emphasizes skills, but in the context of values and motivations of the people who use them. In skills-plus interviewing, the "plus" part must involve a consistent, informed motivation toward dialogue and an appreciation of its power. In the rest of this section, we describe several attitudes of dialogic interviewing that will help fuel your interest in high-quality interviews (see Box 2.1 for an example of skills-plus thinking).

Appreciations of Dialogic Interviewing

People sometimes associate the word *dialogue* with faddish feelings of warm, cuddly friendships and mystical communion (see Truss, 2004). Such a view misrepresents dialogue, which, as a research subject, is large and complex. Far from presuming a full union or merging of souls, most references to dialogue in contemporary philosophy and social science actually acknowledge the inadequacy of our knowledge about other people. We therefore attempt dialogue not because we already love others or already know who they are but because, most assuredly, we do not know what we are getting into. Dialogue partners, however, are convinced that the sustained attempt at connection is worth the effort.

Let's start with a fundamental question: What is dialogue? We can begin to answer the question by examining what Grudin (1996) believes are dialogue's key ingredients—*reciprocity* and *strangeness*:

> By reciprocity I mean a give-and-take between two or more minds or two or more aspects of the same mind. This give-and-take is open-ended and is not controlled or limited by any single participant. By strangeness I mean the shock of new information—divergent opinion, unpredictable data, sudden emotion, etc.—on those to whom it is expressed. Reciprocity and strangeness carry dialogue far beyond a mere conversation between two

Box 2.1

Interviewers in Action   *Richard Farson*

Richard Farson, a psychologist and management consultant, used interview research to discover how people improve as parents and business managers. Interestingly, he decided to study effectiveness from the standpoint of what children and employees remembered and were influenced by, rather than from the perspective of what parents and supervisors actually did. He asked children and employees what they remembered about significant moments in these relationships with their supposed leaders and role models. Perhaps surprisingly, he found that it was almost never techniques that mattered, but people's responsiveness to concrete and immediate situations. Farson concludes from his interviews and a variety of other evidence that mere techniques and skills are not central to effective communication; instead, the core requirement is the personal presence of a perceptive "other" who wants to keep the relationship going. Farson values communication deeply, even as he expresses equally deep suspicion of a skills- or technique-centered assumption about communication:

> In both parenthood and management, it's not so much what we do as what we are that counts. . . . Each new human relations technique promises to make the leader more effective. Managers who are taught to listen nonjudgmentally or to reward certain behaviors in others may initially feel that they have found the answer. At last, something that works! But the feeling seldom lasts. Over time, they usually discover that their newfound techniques are actually working to prevent closer human relationships— just the opposite of their intended effect. The most obvious reason is that any technique loses its power when it becomes evident that it is a technique. "Don't listen to me that way." "Don't treat me as if you were my therapist." "I see what you're doing." "Are you rewarding me now?"

Source: Farson (1996, pp. 34–35)

monolithic information sources. Through reciprocity and strangeness, dialogue becomes an evolutionary process in which the parties are changed as they proceed. (p. 12)

Philosopher Martin Buber (1965a) thought dialogue was a complex process, but it relied on an easily understood principle: Genuine dialogue is "where each of the participants really has in mind the other or others in their present and particular being and turns to them with the intention of establishing a living mutual relation" (p. 19). Considering Grudin and Buber in the context of our skills-plus approach, we define **dialogue** as a mutually interactive relationship, not based in technique or deception, that is open to continual change. The attitude of dialogue, in turn, creates the opportunity for a series of moments of insight through which communicators are changed in new and surprising ways (Anderson, Baxter, & Cissna, 2004).

Another way to examine the meaning of dialogue is to compare it to *monologue*, in which one person tries to establish a single voice as the dominant one and treats another communicator as an object rather than a person. Monologic speakers hog the spotlight, transforming other persons into mere sources of reward ("admire me"), or into mere means to another end ("you are useful to me"). As one psychologist (Sampson, 1993) explains, "When I construct a *you* designed to meet my needs and desires, a *you* that is serviceable for me, I am clearly engaging in a monologue as distinct from a dialogue. Although you and I may converse and interact together, in most respects the you with whom I am interacting has been constructed with me in mind. Your sole function has been to serve and service me" (p. 4).

Can such monologue happen in everyday interviewing? You bet. Think of the journalist who interviews the grieving parents of a child killed in a plane crash and leaves immediately after eliciting the most harrowing emotional disclosures, filing her story before the other media catch up to the parents. Think of the retired mayor who appears on a local television show only to plug his book, while ignoring inquiries about the performance of the current mayor, his handpicked successor. Think of the university researcher who schedules interviews with students to investigate their study habits but gets angry with one who leaves early with an upset stomach. Think of the magazine writer who, while interviewing a celebrity just recovering from the depths of alcohol addiction, seems interested only in the lurid and sensational aspects of "drunkenness" rather than the star's newfound calm satisfaction with his life. Or imagine the perfunctory way a press secretary or corporate spokesperson answers questions at a press conference; are the questions likely to be interesting after the questioners have become cynical about hearing anything new?

All these situations feature interviewers and interviewees who are interested in others but only to the extent that they can supply immediate rewards. If Farson (1996) is right that skills aren't as important as who we are, such behavior is ironically counterproductive; the attitude of objectifying others to get more information results in less information sharing.

Scholars (e.g., Cissna & Anderson, 1994; Johannesen, 2002, pp. 55–75) have compiled long lists of dialogue's characteristics, but for our purposes here, consider five basic appreciations and habits of effective dialogue, described in everyday words: curiosity, knowledge, diversity, flexibility, and empathy. Any professional who interviews would profit by paying careful attention to them.

Curiosity

Effective interviews are characterized by *embodied curiosity*. Although it is tempting to think of interviewing as a systematic search for certainty, actually it's recognizing ambiguity that more commonly fuels the interview. Those who are absolutely sure about what they must "get" from the other person will never be consistently good interviewers or interviewees. Every interview, in other words, should begin with some assessment of what is *not* understood, *not* known, and *not* certain. Curious interviewers have a healthy respect for what they don't know and a focused desire to fill that gap (see Box 2.2). No amount of technical skill will offset an absence of curiosity. Respondents notice "I don't care" attitudes, even if they accompany slick techniques. How would you respond to an interviewer who asks a series of appropriate questions but sounds bored and not especially interested in your answers? Truly effective questions are not just effective because of a linguistic formula; they have to be genuine and sincere. We suspect you'd respond more expansively to the interviewer who seems most curious about who you are as a person. An interviewer's healthy curiosity might include such interests as these: What motivates the other person? What does he or she know? What

Box 2.2

Interviewers in Action   *Lawrence Grobel*

Putting together an interview involves many skills: One must be able to converse like a talk-show host, think like a writer, understand subtext like a psychiatrist, have an ear like a musician, be able to select the best parts like a book editor, and know how to piece it together dramatically like a playwright.

Source: Grobel (2004, p. 18)

can I discover that helps explain the world, solve problems, educate audiences, improve social institutions, or meet our goals?

Interviewees, too, are rewarded by demonstrating curiosity. Curiosity is formed in questions and is demonstrated in them as well. What is the perspective of the interviewer, and how can I find out more about it? What is the basis for these questions and their underlying assumptions? What motivates the interviewer's curiosity? Who needs this information, and how will it ultimately benefit them? The moment people become convinced that they know "exactly where the other person is coming from," they quit listening carefully. Complacency clearly leads to missed opportunities and diminished dialogue.

Knowledge

Successful interviewers and interviewees prepare well, time after time. Although preparation often involves behavioral rehearsal—as job applicants surely understand—the most crucial aspects of preparation involve how participants acquire relevant knowledge about what they're about to do. Because interviews are occasions for focused communication about information that often can be anticipated, prior research is almost always essential.

Lack of preparation undermines the ability of an interviewee to be perceived as credible and, in turn, persuasive. As we describe more fully in a later chapter, all communication contexts involve some kind of persuasion; people, intentionally or not, constantly influence each other. This is true not only when a salesperson from Don's Ford Country inquires about your driving habits while standing in the middle of the lot on a Friday evening but also when the boss asks you after two weeks on the job how you like it. Even in the simplest interviews, participants are rarely, if ever, completely unconcerned with how they're seen or what effects they'll have on the other person. One of the most important factors of persuasive success, **credibility**, depends primarily on listeners' estimates of speakers' *expertise* (how much they think the speaker knows) and their *trustworthiness* (how much they can rely on the speaker). In the interview, both basic aspects of credibility, but especially expertise, depend on knowledgeable preparation.

Interviewers, who are usually responsible for initiating the action, should begin interviews with curiosity and a willingness to tolerate ambiguity. However, this is far from saying they should underestimate the importance of knowledge, particularly knowledge based on experience as interviewers. Indeed, successful interviewers in any field find that while they are still willing to be surprised, the more they interview, the less they are blindsided by completely unexpected responses. Their knowledge base has familiarized them with the likely language, background, values, and motivating interests of their conversation partners. Such a knowledge base is equally important for interviewees, although for different reasons. Wise interviewees try to anticipate the interviewer's specific focus on content, which is not an easy task, and also anticipate the kind of interview structure the interviewer might use.

Two types of knowledge assist interviewers and interviewees alike: *content knowledge* (what-is-known understandings) and *process knowledge* (how-to understandings). For example, Fish (1990) analyzed crisis-line telephone communication between callers and counselors. She found that callers retain control over content, and over initiation and termination choices. The counselors, however, had power largely over the process or structure of the call—"length, timing, and duration of probing questions, the degree to which the caller needs to be supported" (p. 161). Both the content and process of interviews are affected by the quality of participants' knowledge.

Diversity

Appreciating diversity means that interview participants can use cultural and social differences to energize their talk and make it meaningful, often in unexpected ways. Some interviews involve persons who know each other quite well, or come from similar social, cultural, and economic backgrounds, and can interact well because of an easygoing familiarity with each other. A reporter, for example, might be assigned to interview a famous journalist at a competing paper because the two have known each other for many years. More commonly, interview partners are largely unfamiliar with each other's lives before they begin researching how they want to handle the content and process. Their knowledge gaps give the interview a special character of discovery that has implications far beyond basic curiosity and the will to know more.

A particularly challenging characteristic of many interviews is that they depend on people's willingness to talk across a variety of differences—of culture, ethnicity, gender, power, age, status, sexual preference, and other ways people invest their identities (see, e.g., Dunbar, Rodriguez, & Parker, 2001; Prewett-Livingstone & Field, 2000; Ryen, 2001; Shah, 2004). Later we will make many more specific suggestions for improving your communication skills in cross-cultural interview settings; here, simply consider how certain relatively narrow cultural or social habits can hinder your interviews.

We cannot tell you what kind of personality or what kind of person is "best." Nor will we try to manipulate you into a cultural or political position with which you are uncomfortable. Yet the research into communication competence is clear, and it suggests that a certain style of culturally sensitive interviewing tends to lead to better information and increased satisfaction. Although the word *multicultural* has become politically charged lately, we intend to use it benignly and straightforwardly. No other term better describes what's necessary for interviewers and interviewees who must talk with others who might not look or talk like themselves.

Stated simply for the interview context, **multiculturalism** is an appreciation for the fact that others' cultural habits and expectations appear as normal and reasonable to them as yours do to you. "Multi-" suggests that there are many such cultural systems; "-ism" suggests that you will profit from developing a generalized reminder for yourself that these other systems are not necessarily wrong, dysfunctional, evil, or inefficient from the standpoint of your interview partners. In other words, the more you interview, the more you'll tend to develop a pluralistic worldview in which a wide range of behavior is possible and functional (see Box 2.3). As you appreciate multiculturalism, you acknowledge and value diversity instead of being intimidated, frustrated, or frightened by it.

Most interviews, excepting, of course, mental health contexts and certain types of ethnographic research, aren't concerned with deep relationships involving personality analysis or intense emotional involvement. Generally, interview partners are not going to change each others' lives radically. Your goals will usually involve understanding other persons much more than attempting to change them (see Box 2.4). Acknowledging and respecting diversity is not the same as agreeing artificially with the specific people who are different from yourself or adopting a banal tolerance in which you think you must always love everybody. You can still be effective in interviews if you disagree with some differences you encounter, but you will have problems if you don't appreciate how other communicators have built worlds of meaning that are just as important to them as your values and beliefs are to you.

Box 2.3

Reminders   *Problems of Avoiding or Ignoring a Pluralistic Worldview*

You will be frustrated with the results of your interviews if:

- You believe you already know what someone thinks or should think.

- You think you should use the interview to persuade others not to be who they are.

- You can justify avoiding certain interviewers or interviewees because they are too different from you—assuming you'll never understand each other.

- You are convinced that only your religion, your view on social controversies, or your own ethnic culture holds a patent on essential truth. (This does not mean that you must abandon your own beliefs in interviews, only that you

should check constantly to ensure you're not using them unfairly to dismiss the value of others' beliefs.)

- You believe it is your duty to moralize publicly about others' behavior, even if morality isn't the subject of the interview.

- You hold grudges, not only against persons but against the groups they supposedly represent.

- You depend on relatively static or frozen evaluations of groups and people to carry you from situation to situation.

- You believe you represent a substandard or inadequate culture or group whose voice does not need to be heard.

Box 2.4

Interviewers in Action   *Hugo Slim and Paul Thompson*

Slim, senior research officer for Save the Children Fund in Great Britain, and Thompson, professor and director of Britain's National Life Story Collection, have practiced their craft of narrative, oral history, and life
stories interviewing in a variety of world cultures. Their book is a rich resource in cross-cultural interviewing
that describes problems they and similar researchers have faced and, often, surmounted.

While the interview is now a common form of enquiry and communication in the West—where the job
interview is a prerequisite for most employment, the media feature endless interviews, both informative
and entertaining, and few people escape having to take part in polls and questionnaires—this is by no
means a universal experience. . . . In some societies the interview is not an established type of speech
event, and there can often be an incompatibility between standard interview techniques and indigenous
systems of communication. This incompatibility can create problems for people who, as interviewees, are
forced to express themselves in an unfamiliar speech format. In particular, the interview form has
a tendency to put unnatural pressure on people to find ready answers, to be concise and to summarise
a variety of complex experiences and intricate knowledge. It may also mean that researchers and interviewers unwittingly violate local communication norms relating to turn-taking, the order of topics for
discussion or various rituals attached to story-telling. In some societies, individual interviews are considered dangerously intimate encounters. In others, the recounting of group history can be a sacred
ritual and certain people must be consulted before others. Sometimes, a number of clearly prescribed
topics should be used to start proceedings, while other topics may be taboo, or should not be introduced
until a particular level of intimacy and trust has been achieved.

Source: Slim & Thompson (1995, p. 62)

Flexibility

Communicators usually develop everyday habits they comfortably rely on from relationship to relationship. For example, some speak up readily in a group of strangers;
others try to stay in the background. Some share their emotions openly and don't care
who knows what they feel; others protect their privacy and rarely disclose personal
experience. Some tell jokes loudly and laugh easily; others reveal their senses of humor
more subtly.

Many students inexperienced at interviewing find it takes courage on the interviewer's part to make the social requests necessary to question others and, perhaps, equivalent courage from interviewees to agree to be listened to carefully and taken seriously.
An interview presents social risks of embarrassment, vulnerability, and the possibility of
mistakes made and witnessed in public. It is not always a comfortable experience, and
some reticence is normal. However, for many people, more intense experiences such
as interaction apprehension and shyness create deeper difficulties (Daly & McCroskey,
1984; Phillips, 1981, 1984, 1991; Zimbardo, 1977). For many people, appreciating
flexibility is more a mental goal than a behaviorally realistic option. Phillips's (1984) research shows that most people are not reticent in all interchanges. Virtually everyone, in

fact, feels confident in particular communication contexts in their lives. However, he reports, people who identify themselves as reticent commonly avoid situations (e.g., asking questions in classes, starting small talk with a stranger, participating in groups, asserting oneself to get even deserved attention, talking with authority figures) to avoid the discomfort associated with them (p. 60).

Extremely reticent, shy, or apprehensive people who avoid such situations are unlikely to be as flexible as the situation demands, even if they try to exhibit "correct" behavior. This obviously applies to interviewing, which involves questions and answers coordinated in specific ways that often depend on small talk and developing rapport. Interviews typically involve persons of different genders and gender orientations, and often occur in public or semipublic settings in which communicators must draw attention to themselves. Interviews often cross lines of prestige, as those who have comfortable jobs talk with unemployed applicants, a rookie reporter interviews a governor, or a world-renowned brain surgeon is asked a series of possibly naïve questions by a patient about to have an operation. Perhaps almost as much as in public speaking contexts, nervousness affects interview partners. Most people deal with it, and a sense of coping or even mastery develops. Others may need additional assistance, such as specific training

Trying Out Your Skills

Read the following interview excerpt. Using the concepts of this chapter, can you make the case that this is an example of dialogic interviewing? Or is there more evidence here that these communicators do not appreciate dialogue?

Delores Wilson, an African American student with a history of campus activism, is talking with her 60-ish white male political science professor, Michael Van Allen. This is one of a series of interviews conducted by a small group of students to determine whether faculty and administration would support the establishment of an African American Studies interdisciplinary major. Many students, black and white, support such a program, but others on campus, including some faculty, believe there are already too many majors and interdisciplinary programs. Some faculty also wonder if diversity-oriented programs might not "water down" traditional education. The two meet in Van Allen's office late one afternoon.

DW: Thanks, Dr. Van Allen, for meeting with me. I know you're busy.

MVA: This isn't a problem, Delores, I'm happy to help. What can I do for you?

DW: Well, there are a lot of us who feel . . .

MVA: A lot of you? Who do you mean?

DW: A lot of students, and a lot of black students especially, who feel that the campus just kind of, well, doesn't give us many options.

MVA: At last count, there were over 25 different majors in Arts & Science alone. Now that I think about it, there was a faculty council meeting last Wednesday, and that number may be in the hundreds by now.

DW: (smiles) I know. There are a lot. Well, I didn't know there were that many, but I knew there were quite a few. That counts sciences, doesn't it? But what I mean—we mean—by "not many options" is that so many of the humanities and social science majors seem like just different ways to look at the same traditional things like elections, politics, great books, and so on.

programs in coping strategies or desensitization that are available at many universities and other institutions.

Although most so-called inflexible behaviors appear to relate to personality characteristics or traits, other comfortable–uncomfortable behaviors could have cultural roots. For example, some people are comfortable maintaining consistent eye gaze at close quarters, whereas others are not. This is not necessarily a personality habit but a culturally ingrained expectation. Some cultures train young people to avert direct eye contact from those of perceived higher status, no matter who is speaking. Similarly, some people regard a high incidence of touching as perfectly normal during conversation, whereas others find touch invasive. Different cultural groups appear to mandate such behaviors in ways that are clearer to social researchers than to individual communicators, for whom they are simply enacted—or avoided—habitually.

Empathy

Psychologist Carl Rogers (1959), one of the most famous of counseling interviewers, defined *empathy* as the ability "to perceive the internal frame of reference of another with accuracy and with the emotional components and meanings which pertain thereto as if

But you think that the 25 majors give enough choices to all students?

MVA: Doesn't sound so bad to me. Those things you mentioned are the core issues of society—things all citizens need to come to grips with. No matter what color they are. The article in the paper made it seem like black students want to do their own thing, read only minority authors. I very much liked your performance in my class last semester, Delores, but I have to admit I'm not in favor of an African Americans–only major. Why not stick with doing well in traditional majors like English, political science, or even business?

DW: Thanks for the compliment, Dr. Van Allen. I do work hard in school. The article in the paper was misleading, though. Rasheed got misquoted, and it did sound like the new proposal might be for African Americans and minorities exclusively. It's not designed that way at all. Has anyone shown you the proposal itself?

MVA: No. I've heard people refer to it, but haven't seen it.

DW: I can get you a copy tomorrow morning. OK? I could be wrong, but to me it seems like it would attract a lot of students from all cultural groups. It's not just a club kind of atmosphere. One of the things that's different about it is that it would be a second major for any student who declared it; it'd be a substitute for a minor, not a major.

MVA: I didn't know that. How many hours would be included? What departments and faculty have expressed interest? How are the courses going to be coordinated? Cross-listed? There are lots of questions.

DW: That's true. Would you still like to see the proposal? It answers some of those things, but, I have to admit, maybe not all of them. Teachers have different ways of looking at classes than students do, I know.

MVA: Sure. I'd like to read it. Drop it by during my ten o'clock office hours, if you can.

one were the person, but without ever losing the 'as if' condition" (p. 210). Interestingly, empathy has often been taught and learned as if it were a simple skill of peering into another's experience and understanding it almost as if it were mind reading. Rogers saw it less as a skill and more as a "way of being." His attempts to understand clients often took the form of tentative restatements of their speech, to ensure he was understanding them, as well as offering out loud his tentative verbal explorations of their experience. His partner could correct the interpretations if necessary. Rogers became frustrated late in his life that his genuine curiosity about the distinctive "otherness" of the client came to be taught as a simplistic technique of "reflective listening" in which the listener only tries to mirror exactly what the speaker just said.

To Rogers, however, being empathic was a far more inclusive way of being a person. Empathy could be obvious in conversation as a kind of active listening we explore in other chapters, but Rogers believed the essence of empathy can be found in an attitude of respect, an attitude that links several of the other appreciations in this chapter. Rogers (1959) reminded interviewers that empathy could "dissolve alienation" (p. 151), help persons feel "accepted" (p. 152), and communicate a "nonjudgmental" stance (pp. 153–154). Empathy is not only a phenomenon of therapeutic communication. Rogers thought that it characterized all effective relationships as a way to free effective and honest talk. Few insights could be more functional for beginning interviewers and interviewees. However, this is because empathy suggests a basic respect for persons, not because it is a handy technique for unlocking someone's thoughts or for keeping them talking.

Beyond the Basics

A skills-plus approach to interviewing must depend on more than "how-to" formulas of asking and answering questions. Success comes beyond tactics, when participants fully recognize the complexity of what they are cooperating to accomplish. Over the past few decades, many researchers have explained subtle ways conversants appreciate this complexity, or how they fail to appreciate it. In this section, we are especially concerned with baseline concepts of *communication rules* and the *cooperative principle*.

Communication Rules

Discussions about communication "rules" refer to the complex set of guidelines that help communicators adjust their behavioral choices with others' behaviors in different contexts. A **communication rule**, writes Shimanoff (1980), is a "followable prescription that indicates what behavior is obligated, preferred, or prohibited in certain contexts" (p. 57). Many times in conversations we adjust ourselves to each other in predictable ways—but these are ways that no one specifically dictated to us or necessarily taught us. In fact, most of our interactions are governed in these kinds of subtle ways, by implicit "rules" that are never codified but are constantly affirmed in our mutual understanding of what is right to do in a given situation.

Of course, not everyone will agree with or enact the rules in exactly the same ways. Rules are broken all the time. Your conversation partner is edging toward the door as you talk and has looked at her watch twice in the past few minutes, but you continue to press new questions, not acknowledging that she needs to leave. Your ignorance of the implications of her behavior are, in effect, rule violations; if you share the same culture, you "should" have noticed. These everyday rules governing how talk is regulated are broken less often by people who make themselves aware of the cultural contexts of communication and the kinds of diversity required in them (see the discussion of diversity earlier in this chapter). The rules are broken less often, too, by communicators who have developed a high degree of behavioral flexibility.

Interviewing demands what we call **high-flex communicators**—those who are aware of not only the content stream (what's being discussed) but also the process stream of conversational rules and can coordinate their behaviors accordingly. They aren't chameleons, changing their behavior constantly to fool others; ideally they are highly ethical speaker-listeners who know how to adapt in a variety of situations to help others communicate as well as possible. High-flex communicators can infer the linguistic and nonlinguistic rules that seem to guide their partners and, when necessary, adapt their own talk to those rules. This is more than a skill; it is an inherent appreciation for the constant changes in human sense making.

The Cooperative Principle and Its Maxims

H. P. Grice (1975), a researcher specializing in analyzing conversational talk, suggested that speakers and listeners, especially in the Western world, are bound by what he calls an overall cooperative principle and, further, by four "maxims" that help speakers decide when and how they need to be flexible. These insights (pp. 45–47), paraphrased here, will help explain the importance of a skills-plus approach:

The Cooperative Principle

Each speaker should contribute in ways that are appropriate to the seemingly mutually accepted stage, purpose, and direction of their conversation. We begin to talk when we assume that others will cooperate rather than try to undercut us, interfere with our talk, or otherwise work against understanding. (For example, politicians start to turn down interviews if they think a reporter will not write a fair story, or they will speak only in generalities about a tax reform plan if they think a reporter hasn't taken the time to research the plan's basic economics.)

The Conversational Maxims

Quantity—Speakers should not provide more or less information than is required by the type of conversation being conducted.

Quality—Speakers share only those observations and statements they believe to be true and supportable by external evidence.

Relevancy—Speakers concentrate on providing information and commentary that fits the situation.

Manner—Speakers avoid expressions likely to confuse the other person, cause misunderstanding, or lead to unnecessary ambiguity.

It's hard to overestimate the importance of Grice's insights for interviewers and interviewees. Several examples from the standpoint of interviewees illustrate the point, although we could just as easily provide interviewers' examples. An interviewee who filibusters in answering a question violates the maxim of quantity (See Sunday morning news interview programs for intentional examples of this, although most instances are probably unintentional.) The interviewer should consider polite but direct ways to nudge the speaker back toward pointed, streamlined, and more efficient discussion. An interviewee who misleads listeners on purpose, who lies, or who tells a half-truth violates the maxim of quality and, depending on the context, shouldn't be surprised if an alert interviewer calls attention to the violation in immediate interaction or later, perhaps in a story written about the interview. A political science professor who, when asked pointedly by a reporter for an opinion on the outcome of a mayoral election, responds with a long discussion of how qualified he is to assess the charisma of the

Making Your Decision

As an active member of your campus's Student Activities Board, you're asked by the student government president to investigate why international students and their organizations are less active in campus governance and in planning activities. To supply this kind of information, you decide to interview the most important and active members of each international student group (e.g., the Korean Student Association, the African Student Alliance, etc.).

- How would you decide whom to interview from each group?

- What would you do if a significant population of students on campus was not represented by a formal organization? Would you attempt to interview someone anyway? If so, how would you decide whom to interview?

- It's possible that interviewees could feel they are being singled out or blamed for not participating. You want to avoid this impression, because you're genuinely interested in facilitating increased learning between cultures. (In other words, although you may be a skillful interviewer, you want the appropriate attitude to be apparent to interviewees.) How would you try to convince students from different cultures that you are sincere in your curiosity and desire to help? Would you have a specific plan for how to establish this kind of rapport early in each interview?

- Would you want to do research to discover any special communication rules that characterize cultural assumptions? Where would you go to discover some basic rules that would help you avoid potential situations in which you unintentionally insult or offend interviewees, or just avoid significant misunderstandings? Hint: You might want to think about coursework in cross-cultural communication and Internet research capabilities. See the current edition of *Communication Research: Strategies and Sources* (Rubin, Rubin, & Piele, 2005) or one of the many guides for interviewers on information collection, such as *The Reporter's Handbook: An Investigator's Guide to Documents and Techniques* (Ullmann & Colbert, 1991).

candidates, has violated the maxim of relevancy. Finally, a scientist trying to explain the greenhouse effect in a broadcast interview launches into a long discussion of reactivity and stability in fluorocarbon chemistry; she has certainly violated the maxim of manner, even though the information's relevance, quality, and quantity may be appropriate.

Summary

When interviewing is effective, it involves the most practical communication skills in professional life. In the following chapters, we divide various skills into three major categories—listening, questioning, and framing—before we survey basic contexts for interviewing in your career and personal life.

We've found it unhelpful to study interviewing as a collection of skills, as if they can be used like tools at the disposal of communicators. This chapter has placed interviewing skills in a broader context of competence in which habits of dialogic communication can guide your choice of skills. This skills-plus approach emphasizes five basic appreciations that can guide effective interviews: persistent curiosity, thorough knowledge, sensitivity to diversity, behavioral and attitudinal flexibility, and a willingness to be empathic.

The Interview Bookshelf

On the appreciation of dialogue and conversation in professional interviewing:

Schumacher, M. (1990). *Creative conversations: The writer's complete guide to conducting interviews.* Cincinnati, OH: Writer's Digest Books.

This practical book is by an interviewer experienced in writing human interest profiles. Schumacher avoids the trap of trying to make a formula of interviewing, and urges that interviewers should rely on curiosity, habits of dialogue, and the creative experience of conversational approaches.

On multicultural interviewing:

Fetterman, D. M. (1989). *Ethnography: Step by step.* Newbury Park, CA: Sage.

Ethnography is a qualitative research method in which researchers attempt to "get inside" a culture or cultural group to experience and describe its inner patterns. In addition to various styles of interviewing, it usually involves participant observation methods and a series of assumptions on the part of investigators that the culture studied will be "strange," different, and new in yet-to-be-discovered ways.

On a coherent way to think about interviewing, beyond a skills approach:

Gubrium, J. F., & Holstein, J. A. (Eds.). (2001). *Handbook of interview research: Context and method.* Thousand Oaks, CA: Sage.

The editors portray interviewing research not as the study of individual interviews, but as a story of how ours has become an "interview society." Interviewing contexts influence almost every aspect of social life. We find this view compatible with our skills-plus approach.

On the philosophical foundations of the interview relationship:

Rubin, H. J., & Rubin, I. S. (2005). *Qualitative interviewing: The art of hearing data* (2nd ed.). Thousand Oaks, CA: Sage.

Rubin and Rubin underscore the importance of imagining most interviews as dialogue; they use the term "conversational partnership" throughout the book to stress the uniqueness of each interview and how each participant can affect the outcomes.

Chapter Three

Skillful Listening

(LEARNING GOALS)

*After reading this chapter,
you should be able to*

- Describe the psychological and communicative process of listening and distinguish it from the more physiological process of hearing

- Develop effective strategies that will prepare you to listen with more focus and sensitivity

- Identify five major types of listening skills and discuss how different interviewing contexts depend on these types

- Practice the verbal and nonverbal skills of *active listening,* a style that confirms communicators and allows listeners and speakers to verify the extent of their mutual understanding

April Robinson, a senior at a nearby university, has talked with a campus counselor twice now to try to resolve a scary personal problem: Just one semester away from graduating, she now finds herself oversleeping, avoiding classes, and just not turning in assignments. This, she has said, is "not like me." In fact, her first three years were almost too easy, and she was able to glide to a 3.5 grade-point average. After firm and persistent questioning by her counselor, though, April feels more stuck than ever. She left the counseling center last week determined never to go back. After a week of skipping almost every class, however, she got nervous and made another appointment. This time, the assigned counselor was ill and a last-minute substitute, Marty Smith, sat and talked briefly with April about campus pressures. They sat silent for a time. Ms. Smith didn't press, but it was clear to April that she was paying close attention. Then, for some reason, April found herself telling the new counselor important details about family expectations and fears of workplace insecurities—facts and emotions she'd never told the other counselor. After about 45 minutes, the two had drafted a three-part agreement that laid out motivational options for April to experiment with.

No one would deny that talking
necessarily implies listening, and yet no
one bothers to point out, for example,
that in our culture there has always been a
vast profusion of scholarly works focusing
on expressive activity and very few, almost
none in comparison, devoted to the study
of listening.

—Gemma Corradi Fiumara,
The Other Side of Language

No one can know exactly why we open up to some listeners and not to others. Perhaps April and the first counselor had already prepared the way for a more productive third visit. Or perhaps April just found the kind of listener for whom her words resonated more deeply and, buoyed by this small success, she explored other conversational directions more freely. While imagining April's situation, ask yourself several questions about your own experience of being listened to: When faced with a decision that's important to talk through, whom do I call? Are there certain topics I won't bring up with certain people? Do I have some friends who are nice enough, but after a conversation with them I never seem to feel understood? When giving directions to some people, do I have to repeat things two or three times, and they still don't get it? Do I look forward to talking with people who show little interest in what I have to say?

Your answers should provide clues about why we think it's important to study listening in the interviewing context. If you are like most people, you can appreciate poor listeners for their other qualities (they may be generous, wise, or witty), but you aren't likely to trust them with sensitive information, with personal dilemmas you're trying to sort out, or with decisions to be made carefully, on the basis of nuanced information. Simply put, some people you want to talk to, and others you avoid because you're sure they'll misunderstand you somehow.

Now consider the chilling possibility that friends or coworkers might sometimes find *you* the kind of listener they will want to avoid. Maybe you're the one who mixes up messages; you're the interrupter; you're the one who selfishly turns the topic back to yourself when your friends talk about their problems; you're the one whose own opinions engulf the other person's; you're the one whose judgments stifle different opinions.

If you're a poor listener, it's probably not because you have some sort of generalized condition or trait that keeps you from listening well. According to recent research (Bommelje, Houston, & Smither, 2003), it's more likely that you're simply not flexible enough to adapt your listening skills to "situation-specific social interactions" (p. 42). Chances are, people in your life have not told you about the problem, not wanting to hurt your feelings by lecturing you about your limitations. Instead, they just end conversations prematurely or they don't call you as often as you'd hope. Remember, these are friends and acquaintances; what could strangers be expected to do? Similarly, if you are interviewing others in professional settings, or being interviewed by them, and you display poor listening habits, they aren't likely to explain the real reason when a discussion suddenly ends with a "I have a meeting, I have to go to now" or "I can't think of anything more that needs to be covered."

This chapter will help you inventory your habits and skills to diagnose how your own listening style can make or break your interviews. The first part of the chapter surveys the basics of what experienced interviewers know about listening, and touches lightly on research. You'll see how this knowledge can be translated into observable skills. You'll learn how listening is not a process that's separate from speaking, and how it's not the same thing as merely hearing, either. You'll get hints for preparing to listen before you ever encounter an interview partner. Knowing the functions of different listening goals will further help you adjust your style to the demands of each interviewing challenge. Finally, you'll understand how listening is an intensely active process, far from the passive kind of reception most people associate with it. Then, in "Beyond the Basics," you'll move past fundamental skills to a wider philosophical appreciation of how listening can improve the communication between interviewer and interviewee.

The Basics

Defining Listening

After you learn that a customer in your store is a German tourist with little skill in English, you change your speech patterns and word choices. After you learn that your roommate's brother is hearing impaired, it's natural to avoid speaking to him when he can't also see you. In a less obvious but equally real example, you don't ask friends for favors unless you believe they are able to understand the basis for the request. This doesn't mean that you know beforehand whether a friend will comply, or even if the request will be understood in the way you intend. It only means that you have some reason to assume that people you talk with will not tune you out. In short, you act on the assumption we're highlighting here: Talk is based on the presumption of listening.

Speaking to Others' Listening

The best mediators, therapists, diplomats, and parents know that people don't just decide to "say something"; speakers decide to say something to somebody and to say it in a certain way. Their assessment of the other's listening skill, or lack of it, influences that speech. A listener, in other words, is not just hearing "speech," but the *kind* of speech a speaker believes is appropriate for the listener to process, or the kind of speech that the listener has invited.

If this sounds obvious, you'd be surprised at the thousands of interviewers who forget this fact, perhaps believing that the "interviewee was a nervous guy" or "the governor doesn't want to talk about the budget." In reality, the interviewee may have been a usually calm person who was agitated only when talking with you (because of your poor eye contact and constant interruptions). Or maybe the governor wanted to avoid fiscal topics with you because of previous interviews in which you showed your inability to follow the ins and outs of statistical reasoning. It's true that we constantly listen to other people's speech; it's equally true that we constantly speak to other people's listening.

We define **listening**, therefore, as the active process through which communicators process aural (sound) stimuli, intepret them as messages, and use them to construct meanings. This definition should explain why we chose to present the topic of listening before the topic of questioning. Listening is not the effect caused by speaking. It is the very condition within which speaking becomes relevant at all. As Box 3.1 shows, understanding and being understood is a doorway to personal growth and everyday sanity. While listening, we create the conditions within which others feel more human. Beyond that, listening creates a space in which speakers find they have more and better things to say. What could be more practical?

Box 3.1

Interviewers in Action　　*Earl Koile*

Years ago, a college senior in one of my classes came for a conference. She was working part time as a dorm advisor to freshmen, and, after talking about the class, she stayed to talk about how weighted down she felt listening to so many girls with seemingly insoluble problems. For an hour she described their problems and her worries about them. The next day she stopped by to announce that she had discovered something quite wonderful. "When you listened to me without taking over my worries," she said, "I found out that I could listen better to them." Then she asked, "I wonder if I might come by once in a while to let off a little steam when hearing their problems gets me down?" As she was walking out she looked back over her shoulder and then stopped. I was struck by her appreciation for what it is like to be heard, when she asked, "But is there someone who will then listen to you?"

Source: Koile (1977, pp. 122–123)

Listening Is Not Hearing

Recall that in our definition, listening involves the active processing of aural stimuli. The word *processing* is important because some students believe listening is primarily a matter of accurately receiving or remembering the details of what someone else has said. "Yes, I was listening," you might say. "You just asked if you could borrow my car." Or, "Yes, I listened in ethics class; the lecture yesterday was about Rawls's theory of justice." However, does either of these comments tell us much about how well you listened?

Listening and hearing are different. *Hearing* is primarily a physiological process by which various stimuli are perceived as present or absent. Most of the time it occurs relatively automatically, and at least some of what we hear will stick. Hearing is what happens when you turn suddenly toward that loud noise downstairs, or recognize as soon as you pick up the phone that this is Anita calling you and not Marquita. Hearing is noticing that Mark is talking louder now than he did a while ago. Listening, though, involves processing the information gained through hearing sounds, to make more and more sense out of it. If hearing is physiological, listening is better understood as a psychological process that uses what is heard in the person's attempt to make sense of experience.

Another implication of our definition is that the listening process doesn't involve simply getting another person's message "right." Accurate understanding of auditory stimuli is important, of course. For example, interviewees who consistently misunderstand interviewers' questions and intentions are unlikely to be sought for subsequent interviews and may pay other prices, too, such as a damaged public reputation. Interviewers who consistently misunderstand or misquote interviewees will relay poor information, and may lose their jobs. Yet effective listeners go beyond simply registering the basic messages to imagine the deeper or wider meanings that accompany speech. The effective listener is a verbal detective, using the words and acts of the partner as clues to other meanings that might not be spoken or demonstrated overtly. Effective listeners can get things wrong, and they might not have a full enough context to understand people and their motives completely, but like other detectives, they follow their leads doggedly.

Preparing to Listen

Effective listening is not something you make yourself do by force of will. If you've just been fired from your part-time job, the meeting you've scheduled for the Student Government Association will probably not receive your full attention. Despite wanting to listen carefully to your friends, your state of mind will tend to interfere. This extra set of stimuli will create what communication theorists call *noise*—a condition in which messages you don't need or want to attend to will distract you from what's more important. **Noise** is any message or other factor that interferes with messages to which you want to listen. Noise can be psychological, such as fear about losing a job, or physiological, such as the jackhammer outside your window that interferes with all but the most superficial and trivial conversations. Noise is a problem because it is composed of competing stimuli that limit not just hearing but listening, too. In other words, the conditions for listening can be all wrong. How can you prepare more effectively for them, whatever the professional context in which you find yourself?

Roach and Wyatt (1988) discuss the problem of a listener who was severely distracted. An interviewer found herself asking questions from a couch with no back, which compelled a hunched-over posture. "The interview lasted half an hour," she reported, "and when I tried to stand up I practically fell down. I had a cramp in my leg and my neck was getting stiff. I can't remember anything that was said" (p. 24). The physical discomfort was an example of communication noise, and controlling it depends in part on preparation. When possible, effective listeners choose conditions and occasions in which interference is minimal, and they look for ways to minimize the noise of daily life. Although you obviously can't anticipate all conditions, here are some practical ways to plan your listening:

• Do a listening self-assessment. Everyone has unique listening strengths and particular problem areas. Some listen well in assessing personalities and emotional climates, whereas others specialize in accurate recall of facts or critical thinking. Be introspective and open to feedback from friends and coworkers, and try to glimpse the style you've developed to this point.

• Review and acknowledge immediate sources of noise—such as nervousness or a toothache—and, if necessary, clear your mind. Some professionals set aside a half-hour or more before important interviews to review notes and immerse themselves in the topics important to the other person.

• Imagine how psychological noise might affect how you interpret questions, answers, and intentions. For example, if you're interviewing a school board candidate whose positions you personally dislike, prepare yourself to give every benefit of the doubt to your interviewee. Otherwise, your own feelings could function as unwanted noise. On the other hand, if you're being interviewed and your experience tells you that this reporter has written unflattering stories before, remind yourself that this interview is a fresh opportunity to present your views.

• Anticipate possible sources of physiological noise, and if necessary, try to alter those conditions or change the interview site. For example, if you know a professor is busy with student questions in a noisy hallway right after class, you might want to wait until her more leisurely and quiet office hours to ask about her new assignment as advisor to the school newspaper.

• Predict the specialized kinds of language or jargon the other person is likely to use and be ready to "enter" the new vocabulary readily or explain your own vocabulary succinctly. For example, if a popular professor has been denied tenure (a status of faculty no longer on probation and who can't be terminated without extraordinary cause), you wouldn't want to interview the dean about the case without first reviewing the definition and guidelines concerning tenure itself; similarly, the dean would want to anticipate the possible misunderstandings of tenure outside academic life.

• Clarify the major goals for the interview. If both partners know a series of interviews is planned, they may find a somewhat meandering first conversation to be satisfying in setting the stage and breaking the ice. That same relatively unfocused conversation could be seen as a waste of time in a briefer, one-shot interview or when partners haven't thought carefully beforehand about listening goals.

Preparation also helps to counteract what behavioral researchers call the **self-fulfilling prophecy**. In it, people encounter a new situation with old perceptual habits, ultimately finding what they expect to find or creating conditions that wouldn't have occurred if not for the expectations. In fact, what they "find" exists largely as a product of their prophecies and expectations. In one famous experiment (Snyder, Tanke, & Berscheid, 1977), people in separate rooms connected by an intercom who thought they were speaking with "attractive" people were found to speak in more social, more humorous, more interesting, and more enjoyable conversational styles. However, researchers noticed something even more interesting when the recordings were analyzed further. The partners who were presumed to be "attractive" *also* changed their speech styles. When they were spoken to as someone attractive, their speech began to match that assumption, and they started to act more "attractive": Their talk was more animated, interesting, enthusiastic, and confident. In other words, speakers' presumptions about their listeners influenced (in this case, positively) the others' behaviors, even when those presumptions were never verbalized. It was a self-fulfilling prophecy. Our expectations may create the very conditions under which people say more, or less, or different things, or say them with more or less enthusiasm, or have different feelings about the interaction.

Types of Listening

Clearly, listening at some level occurs almost constantly when people interact. Humans are meaning-making creatures who try to use others' speech to interpret what's going on, what others might mean, and what they might want to say but are unable to say. Yet this meaning-making occurs differently in different contexts. Effective interview partners know they must vary their approaches according to the context, not only to accomplish their own goals, but also to allow their partners to develop their own meanings.

Wolvin and Coakley (1996) identify five basic forms of listening, which are helpful for diagnosing your interview behavior. Whether you find yourself primarily asking questions or answering them, you should think of your different listening tasks. At times a listener's goal is to pay careful attention to distinguish one type of message from another, or, perhaps, distinguish sincerity from deceit. Wolvin and Coakley call this **discriminative listening** because the listener discriminates among different types and subtleties of messages. When engaged in **comprehensive listening,** a listener wants to ensure that he or she "gets it"—understands and processes as many messages as possible according to a speaker's intention. On other occasions, listeners must use their relational skills to help the speaker accomplish his or her own goals by supportive listening styles; this is **therapeutic listening.** Listeners also find themselves responsible for judging the worth of communication and evaluating—perhaps for a distant audience—the quality of messages through a process known as **critical listening.** Finally, in **appreciative listening,** we listen simply to appreciate the particularly interesting, creative, or aesthetic features of messages. We consider each type of listening from the standpoint of interview participants.

Discriminative Listening

This is probably the most basic type of listening because nearly all human listening involves some degree of discrimination—that is, some need to be able to understand, judge, and react to what's being said. The good discriminative listener, then, can become effective in the other modes. Interviewers who are ineffective at distinguishing messages carefully, however, will be unsure about what they are hearing, about what notes to take, and about what to remember; further, they won't have the raw materials to accomplish more sophisticated listening tasks. Interviewees deficient at discriminative listening will also find it difficult to perceive subtle vocal cues by which interviewers often signal their intentions.

Any interaction involves a variety of skills. In discussing each listening type, it is useful to identify two basic skills by which listeners can monitor their own effectiveness. Although we use Wolvin and Coakley's overall typology, the labels we apply here are not necessarily theirs.

The key skills of discriminative listening are **recognition skills** (attentiveness to verbal, vocal, and behavioral cues of meaning) and **regulation skills** (sensitivity to cues that guide the process). Examples of recognition skills include your familiarity with the language used by your partner; recognizing how your partner signals irony, sarcasm, or kidding by tone of voice; understanding how verbal context can affect which meaning of a word is actually intended; and so forth. It's important to recognize basic meanings, even if it's impossible to get everything right. Regulation skills let you use cues to manage conversational turn-taking (e.g., how do you know it's your turn to speak? How do you know when you've spoken too long? How do you know when it's OK to overlap another's speech and not have that interpreted as an interruption?).

Comprehensive Listening

Listening comprehensively is a prime goal of information-gathering interviewers, such as detectives or investigative reporters. They must emphasize the accurate reception of messages and the accurate recall of responses given by interviewees. Of course, it's also the responsibility of interviewees to comprehend the full implications of questions and issues that arise, because they must decide how to address each question. Although the ability to remember and reconsider the results of the interview usually is more crucial for interviewers, interviewees will also profit by an accurate memory and comprehensive understanding of the content of the interview—when quotations are remembered differently by each party, for example.

The key skills of comprehensive listening are **full mental focus**, which means the ability to capitalize on "listening spare time" (taking advantage of the difference between the rate of speech and the [much faster] rate of thought), and **paraphrasing** (repeating the speaker's ideas and facts in your own words to verify that you've heard them accurately). Many technically capable communicators who know how to ask and answer questions glibly find themselves curiously bogged down in details, awkward at making transitions between points, or unable to recognize internal contradictions in the speaker's

Trying Out Your Skills

Read the following diagnostic interview between doctor and patient, and identify the times when recognition skills and regulation skills are used effectively or not so effectively as the doctor listens discriminatively.

PATIENT: Hello (fidgeting, looking away).

DOCTOR: How are you? It's been a long time since I've seen you. I guess that's a good thing, huh? You must have been healthy. What brings you in today? What a great day!

P: Hi, Doctor Payne. I'm here because of my leg. It's a rash or something, but I can't figure out why it begins to get sensitive in the afternoons. By evening it hurts so much that I have to sit down.

D: Hmmm. How long have you had it?

P: (fidgeting) I don't remember. Long time. I thought it would go away, but it never did.

D: You said it was a rash "or something." You think it's not like the rash you had on your arm last year? Let's have a look (rolling up leg of jeans).

P: The arm rash went away in a week or so. Besides, it didn't swell up like this.

D: Ah . . . swelling, too? How much?

P: Some. It's not swollen now, much. There are times when it is and times when it isn't. Gets redder, then less red, then real red again, then . . .

D: (Interrupting) How much swelling is "some"? Enough to keep you from your evening jog? I used to see you chugging down Elm. Have you changed your route?

P: Actually, no. Haven't been running since mid-March. Maybe that was when the swelling started. Really, Doctor Payne, I don't know what to think. This isn't just a rash, is it? I'm scared.

D: I know you are. I'll bet it swells quite a bit. How much? . . .

assertions. With practice, your listening spare time will allow you to comprehend others while simultaneously engaged in a focused and active inner dialogue about the implications of the conversation. The most rapid speaker you know, for example, probably speaks no faster than 180 words a minute in everyday speech, and most of us speak 125 to 150 words per minute. Yet studies of compressed speech, in which talk is electronically squished by reducing silences without changing vocal pitch, show that most people can understand speech at twice the normal rate without sacrificing comprehension. Most texts on listening describe how much this spare time allows listeners to compare, analyze, add examples, paraphrase, and in a variety of other ways supplement the speaker's content. Of course, paraphrasing is not only an inner skill but also an interpersonal method of checking on the accuracy of perception. Listeners should develop the habit of reflecting or paraphrasing significant aspects of the message back smoothly: "Your office will cut back workers by 50 percent, you say?" Or, "You said you have no plans to run for Congress; should I take this to mean you will not campaign under any circumstances?"

Therapeutic Listening

Far from being the exclusive province of mental health professionals, therapeutic listening can occur in any context where the listener tries to help the speaker meet personal goals, disclose difficult or personally involving situations, solve interpersonal problems, or establish emotional equilibrium. Therapeutic listening can also occur when a speaker needs to be understood fully on several rational or emotional levels at the same time; in other words, it is a style that fits many complex interview situations. Many listeners who are especially effective at discriminative or comprehensive listening are not particularly good at therapeutic listening because, unlike those tasks, therapeutic listening must be to some extent demonstrable externally. The person being listened to must recognize the support and see that the partner's listening is, in fact, sensitive (Burleson & MacGeorge, 2002). The speaker must not only *be* understood, but also must *feel* understood.

The key skills of therapeutic listening are emotional sensitivity and nonjudgmental response. **Emotional sensitivity** is the ability to infer, from words and behaviors, the emotional state of mind that lies behind the overt messages (see Metts & Planalp, 2002). No listener will always accomplish this task, but some culture-specific guidelines can help. For example, consider past experiences with your own nervousness and with nervous people. The outward signs of the inner feelings, although not inevitable, are at least common enough to allow generalizations. In North American culture, nervous people tend to speak faster, make more verbal slips, fidget, perspire, suffer from dry mouth, and find it hard to maintain eye contact with conversation partners. You can use such information directly to diagnose how to help an interviewee who is going through personal turmoil. Knowledge about others and what they are feeling will always be a matter of educated guesswork. Still, the observant and sensitive listener will be better able to infer what life is like from the other person's perspective. Professionals in helping professions call this kind of insight *empathy*, a concept we discussed in Chapter 2.

Similarly, a listener using **nonjudgmental response** avoids attacking or judging the essential humanity of the other person, even when disagreeing with the other person's actions. The nonjudgmental listener not only listens more supportively but also responds by speaking for self instead of putting words or ideas into the other's mouth. For example, instead of the **you-messages** typical of blaming responses ("You should have taken more control over your life years ago"; "You made your wife unhappy"), the nonjudgmental response opens the door for more speech, and more expansive explanation, by supplying **I-messages**: "I'm unsure of your point about your home situation" or even, "I don't know why, but I'm feeling sad hearing this." Although judgment tends to increase defensiveness and shut down disclosure (Gibb, 1961), I-messages tend to encourage more talk. It may seem surprising that a brief message about the *listener's* personal response can focus attention on a speaker's meaning, but it appears that speakers feel safe when encountering personalized, yet nonjudgmental, listening. Therefore, it's no accident that this style is so often used by anthropological researchers or trainers who facilitate cross-cultural communication in groups and organizations (see Box 3.2).

Critical Listening

Interviews often serve the specific purpose of selecting which persons or messages provide the most important or valuable information. In buying a car, for example, shoppers typically ask a series of questions to determine the willingness of the dealership to service

---

Box 3.2

Interviewers in Action   *Elizabeth Bird*

Some professional interviewers may overlook therapeutic listening just because they don't consider themselves to be therapists. Here, an anthropologist and journalist explores how empathic listening can be extremely practical in everyday journalism:

> The empathetic approach may in the end be more effective than the confrontational approach in reading a deeper understanding, and professional journalists may be guilty of fostering the idea that only adversarial, "60 Minutes" style reporting is really effective in discovering the "truth." I have certainly been struck by the pervasiveness of this attitude among my journalism students, eager as they are to rush out into the "real world" and expose evil. . . .
>
> In discussing this point in class, I use my own experience, including one instance in which I had the opportunity to interview a local Ku Klux Klan leader. I found the use of a wide-ranging, non-confrontational approach to be extremely effective in encouraging the source to expand his ideas, and even to seek me out for further interviews when he recalled other topics he wished to develop. The final picture that emerged was more complete and informative than would have been painted using an adversarial approach. It was certainly more useful than a quick round-up of phone calls to local official sources asking standard questions on Klan activity.
>
> The problem of over-identification with sources is shared by journalists and anthropologists. Nevertheless, while it is not an easily resolved problem, its existence is not enough for journalists to reject the deeper understanding that [such anthropological approaches as empathy] may offer.

Source: Bird (1987, p. 9)

and stand behind its product. Salespersons rarely express reservations about their company's ability to service cars or treat customers fairly, but experience shows that not all dealerships are alike. Critical listening provides answers to such questions as: How can I use interview information to make the right decisions? How can I keep from being misled or deceived by others, or simply victimized by my own temptations?

The key skills of critical listening are testing and clarification. **Testing** skills involve a persistent willingness to make comparisons (using your listening spare time) between, first, what you're hearing and what you've known before to be true; second, what you're hearing and fallacies of reasoning; and third, what you're hearing and previously formulated criteria for making decisions (e.g., which applicant to hire, which candidate to vote for, or which lawnmower to buy).

In certain cases, interviewers and interviewees must be willing to discuss openly the problems exposed by tests of critical listening. Some journalistic interviews, for example, are purposely confrontational; the reporter might confront the school board president about the *ad hominem* attack on her opponent or the inconsistency between her recent reference to budget cuts and the budget flexibility she touted just last spring. Often, however, as in selection interviews, both parties are expected to leave the encounter politely pretending that they had not been engaged in intense critical listening designed to assess the suitability of the applicant for the job, or, conversely, the company's culture and reward system for the applicant.

The second major skill of critical listening, clarification, comes in handy when you suspect you may disagree with the other person, but you aren't sure. **Clarification** is similar to the skill of paraphrasing, described earlier in the chapter, but clarifying is more proactive. Listeners cannot evaluate the worth of a course of action, a candidate, or a product without ensuring that the speaker's definitions of claims and benefits match the listener's definitions. An interviewer who listens critically will ask a job applicant, for example, to define what a previous job title of "office assignments coordinator" means. The applicant in the same situation will want to get a clear definition of what the personnel manager calls a "state-of-the-art benefits package." Clarification can come from direct questions ("What do you mean by 'assignments coordinator'? Were you responsible for assigning duties, or did a supervisor ask you to check up on other people's projects?"), or the strategy might be less direct ("I assume from your description that your benefits package is at least equivalent to Gomez & Martino's benefits on the health insurance side"). What you want as a critical listener is not only to get raw information, but also to build a picture or pattern of information on which to base a decision.

Appreciative Listening

Most people don't participate in interviews to exercise their skills in appreciative listening; interviewing is usually considered to be more instrumental and goal-driven. Appreciative listening, though, emphasizes a relatively goal-free enjoyment of the beauty of a message, such as when a listener draws enjoyment and inspiration from a jazz musician's intricate sax solo. Comparable appreciations might enhance the experience of everyday communication, but they hardly seem to be at the core of interpersonal listening. You might, however, consider the ability to be transported by the beauty of improvisation to be helpful in interviewing: What else is effective interviewing but verbal jazz, a collaborative improvisational performance that has essentially artistic elements as well as technical or instrumental goals?

The key skills here are clearing and concentration. By **clearing**, we refer to the process of eliminating extraneous objects of attention, so you can participate without distraction. Sir Yehudi Menuhin (1992), the renowned violinist and conductor, once wrote, "Until we can create a still centre within ourselves we will be unable to attune the 'third ear' to the messages that are broadcast to us, loud and clear for the most part, but rendered futile due to our incapacity to listen" (p. 7). Some people clear themselves by clearing their environments and situations of stimuli that act as communication noise. Some audiophiles will never put on a CD or record of a symphony, a jazz group, or a singer as background music, but instead will listen only when they can sit quietly, giving all their attention to the music. Many interviewers, too, prefer a nearly isolated environment for the occasion, where interruptions will not detract from the miniature world of meaning created by the participants. Other communicators clear their minds before an interview by physiological techniques such as breathing or centering exercises, guided imagery, or creative visualization. They counter nervousness and at the same time create a receptive psychological space.

By **concentration**, we refer to a listener's ongoing ability to focus on the messages or ideas most important to the communication after diminishing the effects of distractions by the skill of *clearing*. For most of us, the process of concentrating is not an automatic state of interest that maintains itself in some stable or predictable way; rather, it's an ongoing process of perceptual adjustment in which we constantly remind ourselves of the reasons for listening and the centrality of the message(s) for us. In a sense, appreciative listening comes from concentration that is persistently achieved and reachieved from moment to moment. This is why you may feel tired after following closely a long speech or lecture on one of your favorite subjects. You may also be energized and excited, but your involvement and appreciation have been deep enough that you've participated in the talk, not just received it passively.

Responsive and Active Listening

Clearly, listening can be helpful to those in interviewing situations, but is one habit of listening especially important? The answer, we believe, is yes. If, in a workshop that brought together interviewees and interviewers from all walks of life, we only had 30 minutes to practice an activity, that activity would be what Rogers and Farson (1957) called **active listening**: the willingness of a listener to test emerging interpretations by verbalizing them, reflecting essential elements back to the speaker, and when necessary, going beyond what the speaker said to verbalize inferences about other possible meanings.

Active listening can take different forms in different contexts, but the general pattern usually resembles one or more of the following example forms:

• "Your brother let you all down" (a response after your partner complains about her brother not doing his part in supporting the family). Or, "You really want the new highway as a top priority" (a reporter's response after the mayor in a press conference stresses the need for a new major thoroughfare through the city). These are *paraphrases* or **mirror responses**. With them, you hope to verify for speakers that you've heard their basic ideas accurately.

• "Let me see. What seems to be bothering you is . . ." or, "Although you haven't said so directly, you seem to emphasize the values of a public school education over a private school experience. Is that true?" (responses to a school superintendent's public statements about building a new elementary school). These are **content inference responses**. They attempt to show speakers that listeners are trying to understand the implications beyond the overt or obvious message.

• "When you speak about your family, I hear a lot of anger and your body tightens up" (response to a client in a counseling session). This is a perception that offers a behavioral or nonverbal interpretation rather than focusing directly on content. Such responses can be termed **affective/behavioral inference responses**.

Active listening responses are not necessarily questions. Nor is it necessary that the interviewer's paraphrasing or inferring be correct. They are only educated guesses. Good listeners must be willing to be wrong if high-quality communication is their goal. It's still valuable if the active listener is corrected by the speaker (e.g., "No, that wasn't my point at all"); both parties then know what kind of conversational work must be done to repair the misunderstanding. This is a positive outcome, not a failure. You're not trying to read the speaker's mind, but showing the speaker that you're at least trying hard to communicate well.

Nor is active listening the province only of interviewers. Savvy interviewees know that they often must say things like, "I want to be sure to talk about what you're most interested in. I think you're most interested in how I'd handle difficult employees. Right?" Or: "When you ask about 'health-care providers,' I think you're referring to hospital and clinic doctors and nurses. But you may mean administrators, too. Do you include them all?" Although the simplest level of active listening is direct mirroring of the other's actual words, most active listening involves more subtle guesswork and displays the state of the listener's interpretation. It's a difficult task with no guarantees, one that sets the stage for subsequent trust.

Beyond the Basics

Deeper Issues of Listening

The study of listening and how to improve it is a growing area within communication research, and the private sector is realizing the importance of such research and applying its results (Purdy & Borisoff, 1997). Like any research area, the complexity and sophistication of specialists' knowledge cannot be summarized in a brief chapter. To supplement the basic topics, however, we've chosen two deeper issues of listening for more attention: research that shows effective listening within any culture carries certain

Trying Out Your Skills

An activity teachers call "listening triads" is helpful for practicing active listening skills. You can do the experiment outside class, with two partners—or your teacher might want the class to try it during a class session.

- Think of an emotionally involving experience that you're willing to tell as a story to an acquaintance or stranger—not one that's too private or would embarrass someone else in your life (examples: your anger when you were treated badly at the bookstore; your disappointment and sadness when your best friend moved away; your joy when you found out you received a scholarship).

- Divide your available time into three equal parts. The minimum time for the exercise to work well is 30 minutes; 45 minutes or so would be better.

- For each segment of time, decide on three different roles: speaker, listener, and monitor. The speaker tells the story, the listener practices active listening, and the monitor is the observer who discusses the effects of active listening on the story, after the conversation. The monitor should take notes to highlight especially striking instances of understanding or misunderstanding.

- The basic rule of the exercise is that the listener cannot comment on, add to, or shift the content of the story until the conversation is over. During the conversation, he or she can only use paraphrasing, content inference, or affective/behavioral inference statements—not contribute personal evaluations or ideas.

- After the conversation (which could last five minutes or so), the monitor should discuss the listener's strengths and how the story was affected.

Note: Don't expect an active listening interchange to sound like entirely "natural" conversation. One problem of interviewing, and everyday conversations, is that listeners often don't care enough to ensure that they understand fully, so this exercise might seem artificial or strained at first. Unfortunately, too, communicators often experience attempts to listen carefully as abnormal. However, the proof is in the results: Did the story emerge with more detail, more vivid detail, and more comprehension? Observe famous interviewers, such as Oprah Winfrey, to see how they subtly build active listening into an informal and friendly conversational style without calling attention to it.

behavioral expectations, and research that demonstrates how practical some philosophical approaches to listening can be.

Listening seems to be a fundamentally psychological process. However, as you will see consistently in Part Two—where we explore the skills relevant to various professional contexts—the *behavior* of listeners is crucial. It does not happen only inside someone's head, but also involves observable behaviors. Speakers observe listeners, believe they know when they're being listened to, and adjust their speech accordingly. To understand listening in this way, consider two communication research traditions—nonverbal immediacy and interpersonal confirmation and disconfirmation.

Immediacy

Mehrabian's (1981) **immediacy theory** research investigated how face-to-face communication tends to be experienced as successful and satisfying when people behave in ways that bolster both perceived *directness* and perceived *intensity*. To grasp the concept, think of immediacy as a kind of direct contact that removes unnecessary barriers or distance from between communicators. It is related to how people perceive "presence."

Immediacy can be studied in verbal or nonverbal contexts. When someone says "the death of a parent is upsetting to anyone," it's perceived as more distant and impersonal than, say, "Your father's death has naturally upset you, LaVerne." The "your" and using the name increases immediacy. Many relationship-defining moments also occur when someone nonverbally reduces the distance between self and other. You might increase eye contact, come around from behind a desk, lean toward the speaker to indicate interest in the topic, reach out to touch another person appropriately (as when consoling someone after the passing of a family member), or in many other ways make it clear that the speaker is the unique person with whom the listener wants to establish direct connection.

Researchers of communication rules (Pearce & Cronen, 1980; Shimanoff, 1980; M. J. Smith, 1984) have provided good clues about how we can demonstrate listening nonverbally. Rules, you will recall, are those implicit social agreements that tell communicators what behaviors are expected socially to "fit" various occasions. We usually don't articulate the rules that guide how we talk in our own cultures and cultural situations in everyday life because the rules are rarely taught explicitly. More often, they are learned informally in routine interaction with others. For example, you've probably never had a class in how to know when someone is interested in your stories, but you would typically be irritated when, during an emotional account of an argument with your supervisor, a listener starts to watch TV. Although it's technically possible for a listener to track much of your story without looking interested, most listeners (at least in general North American culture) are expected to display the attention overtly.

Unfortunately, because interviewing doesn't happen for most of us every day, because many beginners are naturally nervous, and because many interviews involve touchy topics or high-prestige partners, people may forget what they do naturally in other situations. Because rules might be broken or ignored inadvertently under such circumstances, effective interview participants remind themselves to build immediacy messages into their listening behavior (see Box 3.3).

Confirmation

Awareness of immediacy rules is important in interviewing because of people's desire to be confirmed. In communication studies, confirmation theory (Cissna & Keating, 1979; Cissna & Sieberg, 1981) explains how we experience acknowledgment and recognition by others, both verbally and nonverbally, and how our messages encourage or discourage such reactions in others. To think about confirmation concretely, consider what it's like to walk into a small party and have your host and a couple of other people approach you to start conversations. Whether they like you or not, whether you agree with them or not, the fact remains that you are noticed and you make a difference.

Box 3.3

Reminders   *Immediacy Behaviors Associated with Listening: Generalizations from North American Culture*

• *Eye contact*: Speakers expect that listeners will look at them—not all the time, as in staring, but at especially important or emotional moments.

• *Appropriate distance*: Speakers expect that listeners will neither be too distant nor too close, considering the topic and context at hand. Hall's (1966) research into *proxemics* (how people send messages by their decisions about physical distance) shows that most conversations about nonintimate social topics occur in a zone from about 4 to 12 feet.

• *Forward lean*: Speakers tend to associate listeners' inclined posture, especially when seated, with interest and involvement. This doesn't mean listeners should get sore backs from constant leaning, but it does mean that leaning corresponds with moments when speakers emphasize especially important meanings.

• *Nodding and other interest indicators*: Speakers tend to assume that "connected" listeners will be nodding up and down (as opposed to nodding off), signaling that they're tracking the speaker's ideas. This is often coupled with vocal encouragements such as "uh-huh" or "hmmmm," which indicate "I'm still with you" to speakers. Although we also nod when agreeing with a speaker, most conversational head nods are experienced as simple recognition rather than agreement.

• *Removal of barriers*: Speakers expect that serious listeners won't rely on unnecessary barriers. Listeners, then, should ask themselves what behaviors or artifacts could be interpreted as a barrier. Dark glasses, large notebooks, baseball caps with low brims, expansive desktops, and intrusive recording devices or laptop computers placed directly between interviewer and interviewee could all impede communication through introducing artificial barriers. Notice that we do not mean to judge whether someone has the right to wear sunglasses, for example. You may have the right to do a lot of things, and it might be unfair for the other person to judge you for them; still, that doesn't change the fact that when immediacy rules are violated, efficiency and satisfaction are likely to suffer.

To try out your skills further, watch a video recording of yourself as an interviewer or interviewee. Using the immediacy behaviors just described, rate yourself from one to ten on each behavioral area. Decide on one thing in each area that you will either be sure to do again or be sure to do differently next time you're in an interview.

Helping professionals believe that confirmation of this sort helps people establish self-esteem and identity.

On the other hand, imagine that people at the party make no eye contact to acknowledge or welcome your presence. Everyone remains busily engaged in conversations that don't include you. This unfortunate but fairly common experience (at least for some) is disconfirming. However, interpersonal disconfirmation extends beyond being ignored and applies to a variety of other messages we use to diminish each other. Researchers analyze three general categories of disconfirmations: indifferent responses, impervious

Box 3.4

Reminders   *Confirmation in Interviews*

Professionals should not just avoid indifference, imperviousness, and disqualification. Stated more positively, they should stress *recognition, acknowledgment*, and *endorsement* in their messages. In effect, these approaches say to your partner, "I'm fully present with you," "I'm trying to see and hear you accurately," and "I'm accepting you as you are," respectively (Cissna & Sieberg, 1981). These behaviors occur in clusters that work together to reinforce confirmation.

- **Recognition cluster**: "I'm with you." Direct engagement in a clearly defined space and time; nonverbal behaviors suggesting focused attention and increased immediacy.

- **Acknowledgment cluster**: "I see you and hear you." Willingness to follow the train of thought and remain engaged; direct response to the other's topics and roles, whether that response is agreement or disagreement.

- **Endorsement cluster**: "I accept you." Statements and behaviors that suggest acceptance of the other person's messages as important or OK ("I see what you mean," "That's a point I hadn't considered," various kinds of vocal and visual "encouragers."

responses, and disqualifying responses (Cissna & Sieberg, 1981). For purposes of illustration, first examine the major forms of disconfirmation from an interviewer's standpoint; then we will specify positive suggestions for how any interview participant can increase confirmation (see Box 3.4).

• **Indifferent responses:** When interviewers are indifferent, they are suggesting that the interviewee for all practical purposes either isn't fully present or isn't worth communicating with. Common examples of indifferent responses are lack of eye contact, rapid cutting off of the interview without explanation, not calling back to verify information after promising to do so, and monotonic vocal style indicating the interviewer is bored.

• **Impervious responses:** When interviewers are impervious, they may acknowledge presence and communication but fail to perceive interviewees accurately or carefully. This can take the form of implying the speaker doesn't know his or her own mind as well as the interviewer does. Common examples of impervious responses include "You don't really mean that," or "I know you're going to come out of this a better person" when the interviewee has suggested otherwise. Some listeners make a habit of creating a false front for others and then speaking only to that role or front, or they constantly reinterpret the other's stated experience. Understanding this potential problem should also remind us of some potential dangers of active listening—it is effective only when listeners don't intrude on others' speech or seem to be putting words in their mouths.

• **Disqualifying responses:** When interviewers are disqualifying, they adopt an attitude of dismissing, blaming, or disparaging the other person, or reacting as if the interviewee's topics are trivial, irrelevant, too obvious to pay close attention to, or not as important as the contributions the interviewer could make on the same subject. Common examples of disqualifying responses are derisive sighing as the partner explains a point, inappropriate or unexplained interruptions or rapid topic shifts, attempts to place the interviewer's own stories center stage to deflect attention from an interviewee, and judgmental comments like, "Don't you think that's a naïve thing to say?"

Being asked to be an interviewee is itself a confirming message for most people. The request itself suggests that you're important, or what you have to say is worth listening to. Yet within the interview itself, the listening styles of both interviewer and interviewee might undercut confirmation. Certainly, not all disconfirmations are intentional or evil. Similarly, not all confirming messages are certain evidence of genuine warmth or sincerity, as many people (sales clerks, customer relations personnel, and others) have trained themselves to display a false front without necessarily experiencing interest or warm positive feelings. Both sides of this coin—the potential for unintentional disconfirmation even when someone is sincere, and the potential for phony or tactical confirmation when someone is trying to be deceptive—underscore the importance of videotaped analysis of your own interviewing behavior. Many students are surprised at what they see ("I didn't know I did that!").

A Brief Philosophy of Listening for Interviewers

We realize that students in interviewing courses are usually more concerned with being effective than with pondering deep philosophical issues. They want and need extensive practical experience and ways to speak, listen, and frame ideas more skillfully. However, we also think it's not responsible for us to ignore deeper contexts. Don't forget how practical your other humanities, liberal arts, or general education courses might be to your education in interviewing. For example, consider how the insights of important philosophical traditions provide practical reminders for how to listen in interviews (see Box 3.5).

For philosopher Martin Heidegger, listening was a key for understanding what it is to be human. In one essay (1982), he wrote:

> Speaking is known as the articulated vocalization of thought by means of the organs of speech. But speaking is at the same time also listening. It is the custom to put speaking and listening in opposition. . . . But listening accompanies and surrounds not only speaking such as takes place in conversation. The simultaneousness of speaking and listening has a larger meaning. Speaking is of itself a listening. Speaking is listening to the language as we speak. Thus, it is a listening not *while* but *before* we are speaking. (pp. 123–124)

The first point toward an informal philosophy of listening is that without listening, we don't know what to say or how language can create new futures for us. Humans

---

Box 3.5

Reminders *Practical Advice from Philosophers of Listening*

- Listening well is the basis for creative communication. You are not listening just for the purpose of gauging another's intentions accurately. He or she may not even have a well-formed idea that you are supposed to "get," so let listening be a creative experience you share.

- Listening and speaking are interdependent; if you are bored by someone's talking, consider the possibility that your listening style might have contributed to that boredom too. Consider that more *interested* listening from you can stimulate more *interesting* speech from others.

- Listening and questioning are intimately related. Good interviewers try to discover what led an interviewee to be the kind of listener she or he

has become, or, if you are the interviewee, you try to figure out what kinds of listening your interviewer believes is important.

- Use your listening style and even your silence to create a space for dialogue, in which something unexpected and surprising is likely to be said.

- Listen not *to* words, but *through* the words to the larger issues your interview partner must be motivated by, or to his or her existence as a person. Try not to concentrate so hard on getting the words right that you miss the real message of the other person's talk (or life). In other words, philosophers support our earlier insight that listening is much more than just hearing the words correctly.

---

speak from the standpoint of a *listening* consciousness; no one who fails to listen well can expect, therefore, to have much to say. What lesson in communication could ultimately be more practical than this?

Another philosopher, Mikhail Bakhtin, also examined the relationship of listening and speaking in communication. He stressed that human life, being dialogic, depends on a "double-voicedness" and a "surplus of seeing" in which humans together become partners in completing each other. To Bakhtin (1986), the idea of **surplus of seeing** means that each person sees or hears—and thus contributes—something the other partner(s) cannot. His analogy is simple: At any moment, I can look at you and see what is in my field of vision even if it is behind you and outside your field of vision as you look toward me. The same goes for your own vision. Neither of us individually can see what's behind us, the full scope of our own context, without turning away from the other person. Yet together—and only together—we can take each other into account and, with each other's help, see (understand) our full context. In a similar way, whenever speech occurs, both parties are listening, and both are, in a sense, engaged in speaking. Bakhtin (1986) observes that

when the listener perceives and understands the meaning (the language meaning) of speech, he simultaneously takes an active, responsive attitude toward it. He either agrees or disagrees with it (completely or partially), augments it, applies it, prepares for its execution, and so on. And the listener adopts this responsive attitude for the entire duration of the process of listening and understanding, from the very beginning. . . . Any understanding of live speech, a live utterance, is inherently responsive. (p. 68)

Several other recent philosophers have contributed to a practical understanding of listening. Hans-Georg Gadamer (1982) believed that listening was closely tied to the questions persons are able to ask. Every genuine question arises in listening, and each statement made in response to some question or other can be thought of as an answer. Any topic we want to study, Gadamer thought, could be considered as a group of answers to questions that previous thinkers have asked. To understand their "texts"—their books, speeches, poems, or interviews, for example—we have to understand how they listened well enough to question the world in new ways. Therefore, if you are unsure of what Picasso's paintings mean, one way to approach them is to assume they are ways for the artist to answer questions he had about art, the world, loving relationships, and so on. An interviewer who wants to know how Barack Obama got interested in social action and political life should assume that his life hasn't been a random series of acts and events, but instead a series of answers to questions he had. What are those questions, and how did he listen to them? If you get a chance, ask him! Interviewers should remember this practical insight: When perplexed about what to ask next, think of ways to ask about your interviewee's listening habits. Whom does he ask for advice? To whom does she turn for inspiration? How did an author's last book try to answer new questions raised by other authors? Try to relate such choices and habits to the essential questions in their lives.

Gadamer and philosopher Martin Buber (1965) were both interested (although in different ways) in how listening and questioning enhanced dialogue—that experience of creative communication is only possible when two or more people interact with the full expectation that they will be changed and surprised by the encounter. In dialogue the meanings emerge not from psyches but from meetings.

Two other philosophers, Gemma Corradi Fiumara (1990) and Don Ihde (1976, 1983), have shown how listening creates a "space" in which dialogue can develop. Listening is an immediate experience, one that potentially immerses the listener in what is happening here and what is happening now. As such, it demands the kind of total attention that makes others feel safe investing their own creative thoughts. To Fiumara (1990), "The highest function of silence is revealed in the creation of a coexistential space which permits dialogue to come along (p. 99). In everyday language, effective listeners not only hear more but also enable their conversation partners to think of newer, better, and more creative things to say. Ihde relates dialogue to a curious experience you may have had, in which you were listening so hard to something that you understood the words but couldn't connect with the meaning or the sense behind them. (You may have a similar experience reading this, about philosophical approaches to listening!) If he were to give practical interviewing advice, he might say: Instead of hard concentration on each other's words, listen "soft" and holistically for the larger senses that are available in any conversation. Listen through

Making Your Decision

- You are writing a personality profile of your college president for the student newspaper, and she has been extremely generous with her time. Not only has she granted an interview of over an hour, but she's invited you to follow her around as she moves from meeting to meeting throughout the afternoon. This is a rare opportunity.

  Around mid afternoon, however, you overhear her in a phone call telling a board of trustees member that there is nothing to worry about in the school's transition from Division I sports programs to Division II, that alumni are clearly supportive of this move. But you've also heard from her best friend, the academic vice president, that the president is quite concerned that annual giving from alumni might in fact diminish if there are no major conference football and basketball programs to energize the campus image for the public. Although these two perceptions aren't exactly contradictory, your critical listening skills have exposed what may be at least a slight inconsistency. However, the matter must be handled delicately to avoid the appearance of accusing her of lying or deception. At the end of the day, President McLish gives you a chance to ask a few final questions.

  Would you use what you've overheard to phrase a new question? If not, why not? If so, phrase a diplomatic but clear "active listening" and empathic response that would give her a chance to explain her position.

- Reread Elizabeth Bird's account of how she interviewed a Ku Klux Klan member by using an empathic style of listening. She chose to get a fuller story by letting the Klan member talk out his feelings and perceptions, and she expressed no judgment, argument, or disapproval. She decided that a confrontational approach would have been counterproductive, even though her account implies she felt negative about the interviewee.

  Consider the implications of Bird's choice. What if she had advertised her disapproval. Would that have been fair? Should she have assumed she already knew enough to disagree with the interviewee, or is that part of what the interview is for? We've suggested that empathy is not the same thing as agreement, but could it deceptively imply that the interviewer is on the side of the interviewee? Are ethical dilemmas, perhaps of misrepresentation, involved here? On another front, would you be able to put aside your personal prejudices when interviewing someone you disagree with and proceed to listen in this way—perhaps having therapeutic effects on the other person? Remember that Bird not only got a story, but also, if we are to believe her account, helped the Klan member develop his ideas with more thoroughness and detail. The interview may have helped him just as much as it helped her. Did he deserve that help? How would you handle such a situation?

the words to the person, not just to the words for their separate meanings. Sound familiar?

Summary

In this chapter, we've defined listening as the active process through which communicators process aural stimuli, interpret them as messages, and use them to construct meanings of speech, speakers, and contexts. Listening is a vastly more complex process than most interviewers and interviewees conceive it to be and one that, if understood fully, can enhance every other aspect of interviewing.

Listening and speaking regulate each other. We listen when someone else speaks to address us, but the process isn't just a matter of receiving their meaning as if listeners were tape recorders. Your manner as a listener often regulates how others will speak with you and what they will decide to say. Perhaps no other single insight is more valuable for, but more often overlooked by, beginning interviewing students.

In this chapter, too, you read how listening transcends the physiological process of hearing, and how you can eliminate some unwanted effects of noise and distraction by preparing to listen systematically. You've learned about the five basic types of listening—discriminative, comprehensive, therapeutic, critical, and appreciative—and how each of them indicates slightly different skills to interview communicators. You've also read about how all interviewing tasks inherently involve an active, responsive style of listening. Active listening is a basic attitude of inquiry much more than it is a bag of behavioral or verbal skills.

Finally, in "Beyond the Basics," we introduce two topics often treated in interpersonal communication courses—rules theory and the philosophy of communication. In each topic, we concentrate on pragmatic challenges faced by people in real situations rather than on introducing the ideas in theoretically sophisticated ways. Still, we believe students should know that theory and practice, the abstract and the concrete, the philosophical and the everyday, are not that far apart.

The Interview Bookshelf

On a general appreciation of listening:

Berendt, J.-E. (1992). *The third ear: On listening to the world* (T. Nevill, Trans.). New York: Henry Holt Owl Books.

An entertaining and literate appreciation of how listening contributes to the quality of human life. Berendt, an internationally recognized jazz critic, has integrated amazingly diverse research and stories, covering the full range of listening concerns from physiology to literature, philosophy to music, personal growth to social science.

On a style of engaged listening:

Gross, T. (2004). *All I did was ask: Conversations with writers, actors, musicians, and artists.* New York: Hyperion.

Terry Gross hosts a daily interview show on National Public Radio on which her interviewees have the benefit of a whole human being to react to. In these interviews with artists in popular culture, Gross manages to be an active listener while still being herself.

On applying listening to professional interview settings:

Purdy, M., & Borisoff, D. (Eds.). (1997). *Listening in everyday life: A personal and professional approach* (2nd ed.). Lanham, MD: University Press of America.

A collection of essays that show how high-quality listening is a practical requirement for a variety of professions. After several essays about the concept of listening, you will read how listening contributes to careers in education, training, service industries, helping professions, law, health-care professions, and journalism.

On placing listening and interviewing in a philosophical context:

Fiumara, G. C. (1990). *The other side of language: A philosophy of listening.* London: Routledge.

One of the best syntheses of philosophical approaches to listening. Probably most readable for those with some philosophical background, this book is nevertheless surprisingly accessible. Interviewers and interviewees will develop useful perspectives from the author's ability to place listening in the context of a "tradition of questioning."

Skillful Questioning

Edna Buchanan (1987/2004), now a successful mystery novelist, received a Pulitzer Prize in journalism for her coverage of mayhem and murder in Miami. She quickly learned the importance of asking the right questions after missing an unusual detail in a homicide investigation. "The case seemed routine—if one can ever call murder routine. But I later learned that at the time the victim was shot he was wearing a black taffeta cocktail dress and red high heels" (p. 265). She tracked down the detectives and asked why they hadn't told her about the dead man's wardrobe. Their response? *You didn't ask*.

"Now I always do," she said.

Questions are versatile, powerful tools of communication for anyone seeking answers. They are versatile because they enable us to learn everything from the mundane ("What time is it?") to the complex ("Why do you say you hate your mother?"). They are powerful because they can uncover buried truths and even alter lives. (Q: "Will you marry me?" A: "Hmmm . . . let me think about that.") Used wisely and properly in interviews, questions help us acquire vital information by which to assess relationships, identify problems, find solutions, make decisions, and gain insights. Beyond simply requesting answers, questions kindle candid, comfortable talk by their ability to challenge, amuse, flatter, and entice us.

Almost everything of moment reaches us through one [person] asking questions of another. Because of this, the interviewer holds a position of unprecedented power and influence.

—Denis Brian,
Murderers and Other Friendly People

An interview, although not exclusively an exercise in questioning, often succeeds or fails on the ability to ask and answer questions. Used carelessly or thoughtlessly, questions can easily extinguish thoughtful communication. Skilled professional interviewers know this, and they consider not only the wording, but also such important aspects as tone, timing, and sequence of their questions.

Although asking questions is more art than science, even interviewers with seemingly inborn talent can profit from a fuller knowledge of how questions function to stimulate further communication. Too much is at stake in most interviews to take the question-and-answer exchange for granted. Edna Buchanan learned a fundamental lesson of questioning early in her career, but her success as a journalist and as a novelist suggests she continued her education in the craft of asking questions.

The first section of this chapter opens by asking why we ask questions. From there, the common uses of questions are discussed, followed by a catalogue of question types, including the advantages and limitations of each. In "Beyond the Basics" we discuss the complex motives behind questioning and the ethical and emotional complications of questions and answers. We don't address every facet of skillful questioning in this chapter because the type of interview must define the goals and methods of questioning. Each chapter in Part Two considers questions in particular contexts and circumstances. Here, we focus on spoken questions; Chapter 7 describes criteria for wording questions precisely in standardized surveys and written questionnaires.

A caveat before moving on: Questioning cannot be divorced in real life from the complementary skills of listening and framing. As you read this chapter, remember that questioning itself is not an independent process. It is part of the intricate, dynamic enterprise of human communication. Even an interviewer's "best" questions will fail if they are not accompanied by the ability and commitment to listen and understand.

The Basics

Asking Questions: Why?

Before determining *what* to ask and *how* to ask, interviewers first need to ask themselves: Why do I ask? Answering that question isn't simple or easy. At least it shouldn't be.

Interviewing is a purposeful communication activity, with explicit and implicit objectives or goals. The questions at the core of most interviews should be carefully crafted and designed to serve those objectives or goals. Despite how obvious this sounds, many professionals overlook such a simple insight. A personnel manager who has conducted thousands of interviews over a 20-year career might operate with only the vaguest purpose to guide her: "I want to hire a good person." Although that could be called a goal, does it provide the foundation for a series of focused, effective questions? Interviewers ideally want to stimulate accurate, helpful answers, so one answer to the question, Why do I ask?, is that interviewers ask to learn. But learn what?

An interview with a vague or generalized purpose might succeed, but is more likely to flounder.

A Starting Point

Where do you begin in establishing a purpose—the "why" behind interview questions? J. T. Dillon (1990), an expert on questioning, suggests beginning at the *end*. "A smart way to proceed is to plan right away in terms of answers rather than questions," he advises (p. 167). Dillon is not suggesting that you ask questions that lead to desired or expected answers—artificially predetermined destinations. By "answers" he means: What do you want to learn? What is your specific, well-thought-out goal? What do you hope to accomplish? In a sense, you start with self-questioning. A news reporter, for example, assigned to do a story about the local school district's teacher of the year, consults with editors to determine a focus. The conclusion: Readers will want to know how the teacher explains the secret of her own success, and perhaps what she thinks of the qualities that brought her special recognition. It is a starting point. Next, the reporter needs to devise questions to elicit the fullest answers possible. Asking about a favorite recipe probably wouldn't help achieve this goal, but questions like these probably would: "Do you remember your first teacher?" or "What inspired you to become a teacher?" Of course, dozens of other questions might follow to add detail and dimension to the story.

Deciding on questions in advance and sticking to them rigidly negates the power of spontaneity. Questions explore the unknown or the unexpected. Flexibility allows for discovery of fresh but rewarding alternatives. These observations also apply to interviewees, whose questions will be partly preconsidered and partly spontaneous, depending on the ebb and flow of an interview.

Using a typical example, let's follow through on Dillon's advice of first considering potential answers you seek, and building on that to determine what questions to ask. Metro State University advertises for a new English professor with an announcement in the *Chronicle of Higher Education*: "Metro State University seeks an assistant professor of English to teach American literature and advise the campus literary magazine, *The Muse*. PhD required. Candidates should expect to teach four classes a semester and be active in research and publication."

The advertisement (streamlined here for purposes of illustration) outlines the bare-bones expectations and requirements and suggests a few generic questions about a candidate's credentials and professional experience. The goal, obviously, is finding a well-qualified person to hire. But what moves interviewers toward that goal? Faculty, administrators, and students conducting interviews can't expect much progress without a set of standards, expectations, or criteria to guide their questions. (To streamline our example further, we focus only on questions likely to be put to the candidate, and dispense with sample questions the candidate might want to ask.)

Imagine you're on the selection committee, and it's time to interview the first prospect, Dr. Mary Stinson. As a student representing the interests of other students in the department, your perspective, and the answers you seek, may differ from those of the professors or dean. Your focus is on Dr. Stinson, the teacher. So how do you go about finding answers? What questions would help?

Trying Out Your Skills

"Analyze the following interview between a newspaper reporter and a cancer researcher; decide what the interviewee might assume about the purpose of the interview. Could she develop a clear perspective on why she's being interviewed? What could the reporter—and the doctor—have done differently to help the interview progress with more clarity?"

REPORTER: I'd like to talk to you today about your work. OK?

DOCTOR: That's fine. About how much time do you think we'll need? I have a meeting in 30 minutes.

R: Oh, it's not going to take anywhere near that long.

D: All right. Let's sit down here, in the conference room . . . Now, how can I help you?

R: I just wanted to ask a few questions.

D: I see. What do you want to know?

R: I was told by my editor that you were in the forefront of a new cancer initiative. Is that right?

D: Well, I've been involved in basic research since 1978, and our team has come up with some remarkable findings. There have been two breakthroughs in the past three years. I'm wondering which one you might have in mind.

R: Uh . . . Could you tell me about them?

D: I don't know where to begin. One of them concerns the physical exercise habits of women who discover breast lumps in early middle age. The other is a new approach to chemotherapy. But maybe I'm not the best person to discuss these things. Do you know why your editor asked you to interview me in particular?

R: Well, it probably has something to do with the *USA Today* article last Friday. Did you read it?

D: Yes. But that article was only about breast cancer generally and about some faith-centered treatments. You don't want me to comment on those, do you?

R: Are we going to run out of time? Do you want me to call back when we have more time to talk? . . .

You'd probably want Dr. Stinson's answers to disclose tangible information about her classroom experience, such as the courses she's taught, the student evaluation scores she's earned, and the instructional workshops she's attended. You'd also want her to talk about her demeanor, relationship with students, and reasons for becoming a teacher; you'd then have access to important intangibles of values and attitudes. You'd hope she would share insights into her teaching, classroom management, and grading methods, moving into the area of behavior. In other words, your questions originate from who she is, relative to who you are and whom you represent. Given your focus, you'd probably be interested in answers to questions like these:

- How much experience do you have in teaching freshman composition?
- What are your grading criteria on essays or other written papers?
- How do you involve students in class discussions?
- Why did you become a teacher?
- What do you like best about teaching?

- Have you ever caught a student plagiarizing? What did you do?
- If you could describe the ideal student, what would be his or her characteristics?
- If your superior asked you to change the grade of a student-athlete to avoid academic suspension, what would you do?
- What are some of your own special interests as a learner and writer?

Answers to these questions would form the basis for additional questions, by you and others participating in the interview. Pursuit of the ultimate decision—whom to hire—could generate hundreds of questions as various interviewers attempted to determine which candidate would best fit within the educational milieu of students, colleagues, campus, and community. The process, according to Dillon (1990, p. 168), resembles a *pas de deux*—a dance with answers and questions in constant motion.

Sound a bit daunting? Interviews can be, especially if you haven't prepared with a clear purpose and a plan for seeking answers and asking questions.

Clear Purpose

Ideally, the questions asked and answered serve a shared, clearly understood purpose. Realistically, we cannot expect a common purpose—a partnership—in every interview. People sometimes act in selfish, deceitful, or misguided ways. It won't necessarily occur to them to state their purposes or to seek common ground. Even the most self-serving interviewers, however, should be concerned about the dangers of clashing purposes or hidden agendas. Even though full teamwork may be impossible, clarity of purpose is quite attainable. A car salesperson interviews a potential buyer about driving habits and price range; they are both focused on a cobalt blue sport utility vehicle, but for different reasons. The salesperson's questions might serve one prime purpose: get a signed contract. The buyer's response serves another purpose: don't get ripped off. They may find cooperation difficult for understandable reasons. The salesperson may ask aggressive questions in an exasperated manner, bordering on insulting: "What do I have to *do* to earn your business?" The buyer, wary of high-pressure tactics, responds in kind, "Do you think I just fell off a turnip truck?" The goals of interviewer and interviewee in such a persuasive interview will likely never be exactly the same. Still, it might be worthwhile to clarify a mutual purpose toward which both could work: a satisfying purchase of a good product at a fair price.

Uses of Questions

Questions help accomplish particular information-seeking goals, such as encouraging disclosure or acquiring accurate information. Teachers, for example, use questions at times to determine what their students know and how well they can recall what they are supposed to know: "What American president developed the U.S. space program?" On a higher cognitive plane, teachers use questions to encourage learning by challenging students to integrate and build on the facts they know: "What do you think President Kennedy considered as he decided to invest American resources in space exploration?" On still another level, teachers will probe attitudes or assess values: "Do you think President Kennedy was right or wrong to lead us into space in an era of social turmoil?"

Questioning ranges from basic fact gathering to far more complex incursions into the mind and emotions. Interview participants often draw on a variety of question types, a subject covered later in this chapter. First, though, consider an inventory of common uses that fall under three broad categories: preparatory, primary, and supportive.

Preparatory Uses

Naturally, many people are nervous or tense when beginning an interview. As a result, interviews often begin with questions designed to establish a comfort level before embarking on substantive matters. **Preparatory questions**, then, prepare communicators to accomplish other tasks later by establishing rapport or screening information in a nonthreatening atmosphere. The most common preparatory questions include ones of hospitality or housekeeping:

"How was your trip here?" (Interviewer)

"Would you like a cup of coffee or soft drink?" (Interviewer)

"Are you comfortable talking in my office, or would you like to go down to the coffee shop?" (Interviewer)

"Did you get my message that I won't be needing a ride to the airport? My aunt will be picking me up." (Interviewee)

In another stage of preparatory use, questions build goodwill; they also help everyone ease into the interview gradually. These questions can pop up spontaneously, usually prompted by surroundings or situations:

"That's a really handsome briefcase. Did you buy it locally?" (Interviewer)

"I saw the Orioles memorabilia outside your office. Is Baltimore your hometown?" (Interviewee)

Simple research can provide material for questions, such as looking over a list of references attached to a resume and finding a familiar name:

"We know someone in common—Virginia Matthews of Samuels Construction. How's she doing?" (Interviewer)

To use their time together efficiently, interviewers and interviewees both should study background information in advance. A portfolio, job application, or company report can provide answers, but they also suggest questions about missing details. Common background questions include:

"I see you graduated from Illinois College with a bachelor's degree in English. Did you specialize in any particular field?" (Interviewer)

"Who actually founded the company? There wasn't a history in the material I looked at." (Interviewee)

Other preparatory questions accomplish screening tasks, such as determining whether an applicant meets minimum requirements for the job. These questions might be asked as part of a separate process, such as a telephone interview, test, or questionnaire:

"Because you applied for our training slot, I'm assuming that you probably conducted orientation training while you were at Electronic Systems. Am I right?"

Preparatory questions and the answers they elicit can be crucial. They enable deeper understanding later in the exchange, or they block it. Although they can seem deceptively casual and even unplanned, these inquiries are more important than they appear.

Primary Uses

With the stage set, interviews can progress to **primary questions**, the purpose of which is to uncover basic information or problems, search for solutions, or test or confirm attitudes. They also move the interview into more challenging terrain that calls for even greater care and alertness. Questions used for preparatory purposes usually skirt sensitive subjects; primary questions frequently must address them. Moreover, the consequences of primary questions loom larger. The following sample questions illustrate the functions of primary questions associated with job interviews.

No company wants unhappy employees, so one line of questions might serve to explore the working environment or identify potential problems:

"How do you feel about working for a company that's known for its civic involvement? Many employees take on extensive volunteer duties." (Interviewer)

"What is the company's policy on a father taking days off to care for a sick child?" (Interviewee)

A question that explores a problem might ultimately lead to follow-up questions that, in turn, find a solution or compromise:

"My family supports a move to another city if necessary. But we hope to see this as a long-term commitment, too. Is there a possibility of being transferred in a couple of years or less?" (Interviewee)

"What if I could more or less guarantee that you'll be assigned here for at least five years? Would that work for you?" (Interviewer)

Behaviorally based questions have become common in job interviews because interviewers find them valuable for assessing future performance under trying conditions. Behavioral questions often ask the respondent to relate a story or anecdote about previous experiences: "Tell me about . . ." or, "Describe a situation where . . ." are typical openings for this type of question.

"Tell me about a time when you showed creativity in resolving a customer's complaint." (Interviewer)

Interviewees could ask behavioral questions in return:

"Could you tell me about an occasion when the company dealt with a factory worker who reported a safety hazard? I'm especially interested in what happened next, after the first report." (Interviewee)

Certain qualities of a good employee aren't evident on résumés or in portfolios. That is why primary questions cover such areas as attitudes about communication with co-workers, consensus building, loyalty, or work ethic:

"Have you had the experience of delegating authority?" (Interviewer)

"How often do managers sit down with staff to discuss how things are going?" (Interviewee)

Some of the toughest primary questions address issues of integrity:

"Your résumé doesn't reveal this, but we learned you were dismissed from your previous job. Would you explain why that position isn't mentioned anywhere in your application material?" (Interviewer)

"Last year, your company was investigated by the Securities and Exchange Commission for alleged price fixing. How has the company answered those allegations?" (Interviewee)

Primary uses of questions move both participants forward. They define the central topics motivating the communicators and in many ways determine the ultimate success of the interview.

Supportive Uses

Supportive questions bolster, set up, or follow up primary questions. They can be as simple as "Tell me more," "What happened next?" or "I'm going to switch gears now, with some questions about your first job. OK?"

Supportive communication shows respect and attentive involvement. In a supportive approach, an interviewer or interviewee sometimes summarizes the other participant's statements, thereby ensuring what has been said by one participant is understood by the other. The interviewer would ask, for example, "Let me see if I fully understand what you mean by the term 'educationally challenged,'" and proceed to offer a tentative definition. The interviewee, then, could either confirm, correct, or modify with a response.

Often, supportive questions seek amplification or provide encouragement. In this role, they nurture primary questions through expanded responses, a point developed later in the chapter when probes are discussed. Supportive questions also act as barometers of the interview's climate:

"Are these questions meaningful for you?" (Interviewer)

"Am I fully answering your questions?" (Interviewee)

When you're concerned about how primary questions are heard, you guard against unnecessary misinterpretations and can head off hurt feelings that might arise.

Finally, some questions help you make transitions from one subject to another. Maintaining a smooth pace of questioning helps keep everyone in focus, whereas a sharp change of direction can be disruptive. A simple question can serve as both a turn signal and a sign of consideration for your interview partner.

"I don't want to cut short our discussion on this point, but if you're ready, would you mind if we move on to another subject?" (Interviewer)

Although these examples have been tailored to job interviews, the general framework applies to question functions in many other interview contexts (see Box 4.1). With this overall structure in mind, we can examine particular types of questions and learn how they work.

Box 4.1

Reminders   *Common Uses of Questions*

Preparatory

- Establish rapport or break the ice
- Screen information
- Acquire background

Primary

- Collect data or factual information
- Confirm the truthfulness or accuracy of information
- Explore attitudes, values, and beliefs

- Identify a problem
- Arrive at an outcome—a solution or decision, for example
- Predict behavior
- Persuade

Supportive

- Control, direct, or regulate communication
- Clarify ambiguous or uncertain information
- Provide transitions

Types of Questions

Choosing appropriate questions is like picking the best tool for a job, and you wouldn't use a pipe wrench for carburetor adjustments. On the other hand, questioning is not auto repair; sometimes a question that seems perfect for the situation won't work, and one that seems ill suited will succeed. Although no question comes with a warranty or a foolproof set of instructions, we can expect certain results from particular types. In the family of questions, the two general forms of *open* and *closed* illustrate opposite ends of a continuum.

Open Questions

By letting respondents choose their own directions and context as much as possible, **open questions** (sometimes called open-ended) invite talk. "Could you talk about the South as a place to live?" opens up a wide array of response choices and thus is relatively open. Open questions reduce the interviewer's role as questioner and intensify the interviewer's roles of listener and observer. With open-ended questions, respondents are freer to roam; interviewers lose some control over the conversation's direction and structure. Interviewees might produce meandering answers that lead, at one extreme, to panoramic vistas or, at the other, to fruitless dead ends.

Open questions have important advantages:

- They encourage people to rely on their own words as they determine the content and depth of answers.
- They help respondents reveal the importance of a topic, its *salience*, to their lives.
- They can provide excellent clues to a respondent's priorities.

- They create conversational space for disclosing unexpected feelings, attitudes, or behaviors.
- They gauge the depth of a respondent's knowledge, insight, eloquence—or the absence of such qualities.
- They can encourage a conversational flow to interviews, which helps diminish a feeling of being interrogated.
- They can help someone talk through a problem.

Open questions can backfire, though, if people aren't clear about the interview context or goals. Among their disadvantages:

- They can encourage rambling, disorganized answers.
- They take time—and can even waste time.
- They pressure people who aren't comfortable marshaling thoughts or experiences spontaneously.
- They complicate recording and analysis of interviews by producing more "data" than might be needed for a given purpose.

These observations about open-ended questions should not suggest absolutes. The success of an open question depends on a willingness and ability to answer. In some respects, they afford perhaps too much freedom—freedom to filibuster, freedom to obscure, freedom to evade.

An open question needn't be long or complex. A simple question can prompt a well-developed response (see Box 4.2). Open questions, however, should be specific enough to elicit a significant answer, not merely a bulky one. "Tell me about yourself" could touch off an avalanche of personal details, or it could stump a respondent ("I don't know where to begin").

Closed Questions

At the other end of the continuum, closed questions come from the desire for specific and limited information. They discourage unwanted answers by marking the boundaries of an interview. They are particularly useful and effective for gathering, confirming, or screening factual information, which is why market researchers often rely on closed questions. Among their advantages:

- They allow accurate comparisons and analysis among answers from a large number of respondents, a result usually most useful in social science surveys.
- They give interviewers greater control, especially with inexperienced or uncooperative interviewees.
- They are efficient.
- They help provide focus for people who find it difficult to express themselves.
- They reduce the effort of answering.
- They confirm an agreement or understanding.
- They discourage unnecessary equivocation.

Box 4.2

Interviewers in Action   *David Fetterman*

David Fetterman, a cross-cultural researcher, discusses the importance of open questions in his projects:

> An open-ended question allows participants to interpret it. For example, in studying an emergency room, I asked a regular emergency room nurse, "How do you like working with the helicopter nurses?" This question elicited a long and detailed explanation about how aloof she thought they were and how unfair it was that the helicopter nurses did not pitch in during the busy periods. She said she could list five or six activities that emergency room and helicopter nurses did together during the week, but said these activities were all superficial.
>
> This response opened new doors to my study. I followed up with questions to helicopter nurses, who indicated that they did wait around a great deal of the time waiting for a call to rush to the helicopter. They explained that they could not pitch in during regular emergency room busy periods because they might be called away at any time, and leaving in the middle of a task would be unfair to both the regular nurses and the patients. Thus an open-ended question helped to illuminate the conflicting world views these two sets of nurses held about the same emergency room experience—information that a closed-ended question, such as, "How many times do you interact with the helicopter nurses each week?" might not have elicited.

Source: Fetterman (1989, p. 54)

Be aware of these disadvantages, however:

- They frustrate people who prefer to explain and develop their answers.
- They reduce the possibility of discovering the unexpected in an interview.
- They discourage a partnership approach to interviews.
- They impede an interview from becoming a conversation.
- They discourage necessary and appropriate equivocation.

The most common closed questions seek no more than a yes or no, either–or choice, or a select-one-of-the-following type of answer. For example:

"Do you drive a car?"

Other closed questions offer choice, but within limits:

"What make of car do you drive?"

"How many miles do you estimate that you drive to work each day?"

"How often has your car needed repair in the last six months?"

"Would you describe yourself as an aggressive, moderate, or timid driver?"

Notice that although the questions elicit answers, the usefulness of the answers depends on the quality of the questioner's prior knowledge, and remains primarily limited to data collection. It's possible to explore complex motives and attitudes through a large set of closed questions (see Foddy, 1993), but closed questions do not capture personalized responses well.

Both closed and open questions are common, of course. How to use or blend them should be based on the circumstances of the interview. However, as we learn to communicate, habits develop—some influenced by our personalities, others by our environment. Without implying that openness is entirely a gender issue, Tannen (1990/2001) and other researchers have noted that men are generally more concerned with control and directness than women in their questioning behavior. Note the word *generally*; clearly many people are exceptions. People naturally emphasize one communication style over another, perhaps due to temperament or cultural influences. Knowing that, interviewers can adjust their style to the context and break away from habits or tendencies. Self-aware interviewers can adjust their style to the context and break away from habits or tendencies. Many interviews, too, will improve with a mix of interviewing approaches.

Probes

Probes follow up, extend, amplify, or clarify topics raised by primary questions. Probes belong to the family of questions in that they seek an answer or response, even though they don't always sound or look literally like questions. Some amount to silent questions; they nonverbally "ask" by a nod of the head, for example, "Would you please go on?" Three types of probes do heavy lifting in interviews: clarification, amplification, and confirmation.

Clarification probes assist understanding and resist misunderstanding. They enable interview partners to test perceptions and listening. A typical clarification probe:

"To be sure, let me restate your response: Did you mean . . . ?"

Here the probe acts as insurance against errors by reflecting, or paraphrasing, what the respondent has said. A variation on this strategy is to summarize longer, complicated answers and ask for the respondent's answers to your summary. Some clarification probes simply state, "I'm not sure I understand your answer," implicitly requesting its expansion. Despite the fear that this could suggest poor listening, most people will appreciate your efforts to understand their meaning as accurately as possible.

Amplification probes are follow-up questions that ask for an expansion of a previous response. They acknowledge that full answers rarely emerge immediately from a single primary question. A nudge or two can provide missing details or clearer context. Respondents often don't know what a questioner might be most interested in, so an amplification probe helps channel the interview. An interviewer might ask a primary question, such as:

"You were injured in an accident last year. What happened?"

After the reply, the questioner could still want to learn more. Amplification probes might include:

"I'm wondering what happened right after the accident."

"How did you feel afterward?"

"Why do you think the accident occurred?"

Silence often acts effectively as an amplification probe. It not only encourages fuller answers but also allows time for them. When a questioner is silent and does not move immediately to the next question, many people will return to their previous answer to provide an example, a reservation, a qualification, or other bits of extra information. Nonverbal cues, such as a smile, a nod, or a quizzical expression as encouragement, work well to provide amplification. Even a long "Hmmmm . . . ?" delivered with a questioning inflection, serves as an amplification probe.

Confirmative probes test the accuracy or completeness of information. At times, they serve to raise doubts or challenge answers to ensure that those answers can be trusted. Of all probes, they are most likely to apply uncomfortable but necessary pressure. Here are several examples of their intended effects:

"Are you certain that figure is correct?"

In this instance, the confirmative probe puts the respondent on notice that you're concerned about accuracy. People tend to generalize or guess when recalling dates, figures, and other types of factual data. Your probe gives your partner reason to pause and question the accuracy of a disclosure, or perhaps to retrieve documents or records that provide confirmation. At times, a probe meant to confirm a point can be shaded like a clarification probe, perhaps because you don't want to put undue pressure on your partner:

"I'm not sure of what you just said because it sounds different from your earlier comments. Are you saying you didn't get dismissed from your job?"

Journalists and others occasionally must address internal contradictions in an interview. People contradict themselves for many reasons; usually it's a memory problem or verbal slip, not intentional deception. External information that contradicts the respondent can also lead to a confirmative probe:

"Information I have from other sources differs from your account of what happened. Can you provide evidence?"

Before you can ask about a contradiction, you must listen alertly and frame the conflicting facts as at least a potential contradiction.

Confirmative probes, finally, help keep everyone in focus by seeking to establish or re-establish relevance:

"I'm not sure your answer addresses my question. Could you clarify how it relates to the subject?"

"I'm interested in getting back to what you were talking about a few minutes ago."

Questionable Questions

Certain questions should come with a warning label. Don't automatically avoid them because they're risky, but understand their possible side effects, and then handle them with care. (See Box 4.3 for an interviewer who specializes in simple, basic questions.)

Stress Questions These are questions designed to make respondents uncomfortable so the questioner can observe the effects. Of course, most interviews induce some sort of

Box 4.3

Interviewers in Action   *Brian Lamb*

Brian Lamb, host of "Booknotes," an author-interview program on the cable network C-SPAN, describes the art of asking simple questions:

"Where do you write?" "Do you use a computer?" "How did you research this?" "Why are these folks in your dedication?"

After nearly eight years and 400 author interviews, these basic questions still yield interesting, sometimes surprising answers. Forrest McDonald writes history on his rural Alabama porch—naked. Richard Ben Cramer interviewed 1,000 people for his landmark 1992 biography, *What It Takes: The Way to the White House*. Clare Brandt explored Lake Champlain and the Hudson River in small boats for her biography of Benedict Arnold. Robert Caro read through 650,000 pages from the LBJ Library for the second book in his Lyndon Johnson series. Cheryl Wudunn dedicated the book she and her husband, Nicholas Kristoff, co-authored on China to the sister she lost in the KAL airliner downing."

Source: Lamb (1997, p. xvii)

stress; is it necessary to add more? Perhaps. In certain interviews, particularly in the selection of employees who must work together in trying conditions, certain questions might reveal a problem. The emphasis is on *might*. Critics (Kanter, 1995, pp. 63, 64) contend that stress questions give interviewers unfair power and often impose an artificial situation that won't apply to the job. Stress questions vary in intensity and purpose, as these examples demonstrate:

"As a new employee of Smithton Enterprises, you discover by accident that our chief financial officer and two members of the board have invested in a company you know has produced many films of child pornography. Only you possess this information, which is potentially damaging to Smithton's reputation but unlikely to be made public. Whom, if anyone, do you tell, and why?"

"What would you do if you had to dismiss one of two equally effective employees and one of the employees was your best friend at work?"

Difficult questions like these are calculated to make you squirm. How would you answer on the spot? Some interviewers actually expect a thoughtful answer; for others, the answer is secondary to the reaction. Of course, stress questions sometimes test glibness and communication agility more than on-the-job potential. Stress questions can disclose a flaw or accomplish something positive. Be wary of them, however, as they might prompt a defensive reaction that infects the rest of the interview.

Hypothetical Questions   This form of question describes a dramatic situation and asks respondents to react as if they were participants: They usually begin with "What if . . . ?" Practical, logical respondents could bristle, "I don't deal in hypotheticals." Creative types might relish the opportunity to speculate and ponder. Yet for all, the context is crucial. Some might seem outright silly, such as this one from a personality profile interview:

"If you had to go through life as a golf club, which one would you be and why?"

If an interviewee, however, was an aspiring professional golfer, the air of silliness evaporates a bit and the response could be revealing. On the other hand, you should be aware that the quality of your interviewee's answer will widely vary according to a psychological frame over which you have no control and about which you may have virtually no information. For example, you may congratulate yourself on the cleverness of your golf question. But how clever are you, really, if the person answering knows little about golf and responds, "Putter," because it's the only club he or she knows the name for? What have you really learned?

Other hypothetical questions seek useful information and encourage respondents to think through realistic scenarios. For example, for years before the tragedy of Hurricane Katrina in 2005, reporters asked variations on this question:

"Professor, what if a Category 4 or 5 hurricane hit New Orleans head-on?"

In fact, we used this example in the first edition of this book. Such a question helps the expert place knowledge into a framework with much more human dimension. Instead of referring to meteorological descriptions of a hurricane's magnitude, the interviewee is forced to think of a phenomenon the way everyday people do, yet with added technical expertise. Obviously, Katrina taught us that such questions needed to be asked and answered persistently.

Personal Questions Personal questions ask for disclosures normally shared only among friends and family, if they are shared at all. Some interviewers' questions can venture into private zones with good reason, such as when a physician diagnoses a patient's impotence. Personal questions are appropriate when clearly justified and with the promise of confidentiality. In other instances, they raise hackles. Aside from medical conditions (illness, medications, mental health), private zones usually include sexual behavior, finances (debt, investments, salary), and family relationships (husband–wife, parent–child). In fact, most questions with no obvious relevance to the context of the interview should be construed as personal. Consider these examples:

"Are you a liberal or a conservative?"

"How would you describe your style of driving?"

"Are you a pet lover or not?"

"Are you a member of the NAACP?"

Would you consider them personal? Can you imagine circumstances that would warrant such questions? Perhaps. A veterinarian hiring an assistant might be justified in asking about pets, or a reporter writing about social justice issues in city government might think the story needs information about community leaders' affiliations, but these facts are probably irrelevant in most professional interviews.

Although some job interviewers consciously misuse their power by prying into others' private lives, people occasionally stumble innocently into private zones, such as asking a parent about a child's progress in school and opening an emotional wound. Be aware that people differ in what they consider appropriate or taboo. A sociologist interviewing exotic dancers shouldn't expect blushes or outrage over sexually explicit topics. Some people are interested in discussing their unique cultural backgrounds, whereas others might regard interviewers' inquiries about culture as emotional trespassing and become suspicious of their motives. Relevance remains the central criterion. Do the questions reflect the purpose of the interview in ways the interviewee will understand? If you're in doubt, dispense with questions that enter personal realms. A single misplaced query could erase the goodwill fostered by a dozen judicious questions.

Illegal Questions   Certain questions are forbidden by law, largely in employment contexts where people might be vulnerable to employers' power. Government regulations attempt to make the employment playing field more level by restricting employers' ability to elicit information that could be used for discrimination or prejudicial treatment. Relatively few interviewers intentionally ask illegal questions, but this is not a reason to ignore appropriate legal stipulations found in state or federal statutes, such as the Americans with Disabilities Act (ADA) or the Civil Rights Act, both of which protect against discrimination in hiring, housing, and other areas. Illegal interview questions arise most often in selection interviews.

Loaded Questions   These are questions that plant the questioner's emotional presumptions within the wording of the question. Loaded questions come in two varieties—those loaded in the sense of judgmental, potentially offensive language, and those that spring a potentially accusatory trap. In the first instance, loaded questions take these forms:

"Are you bothered by cheap foreign imports?"

"Do you think the principal is too macho?"

Including the words *cheap* and *macho* in these questions will affect respondents in a variety of ways, many of which are unpredictable. What if an interviewee wasn't particularly bothered by imported cars until your credibility momentarily convinced him or her of their "cheap" (not just inexpensive) qualities? Or what if an interviewee is bothered by import policies but doesn't consider the cars themselves to be "cheaply" made? Will this loaded question accurately probe either of these attitudes? Generally, avoid language that polarizes respondents or involves their emotions unnecessarily. Many words or phrases can be called loaded in that they carry connotations that might be offensive or judgmental to some.

The second instance is the classic loaded question that pins someone in a corner:

"When did you stop cheating at cards?"

"How did you come to be an apologist for the lunatic fringe of this country?"

If you ask questions like these, expect a defensive verbal counterpunch or an abrupt end to the interview. Those who do usually ask them for effect, not to promote understanding—as with a talk-show host seeking a tasty sound bite. That's why the word *baited* is associated with loaded questions intended to torment and incite.

In practice, few interviewers deliberately ask loaded questions. More commonly, accidental loaded questions cue us to someone's biases or insensitivity instead of their malice. Stay alert for loaded questions, and avoid asking them unless you are convinced it's the only way left to break through a logjam in the interview.

Leading Questions   These questions suggest or make much more likely a certain kind of answer. One kind of leading question encourages disclosure; another suggests answers. Questions that lead toward disclosure do so by aiding or priming an answer, and parents, counselors, and therapists find them helpful when talking to a reticent respondent or when entering into a sensitive subject:

"It sounds as if you're upset about your grade in history class."

Leading questions or statements of this kind often demonstrate active listening, and they encourage disclosure by a nonjudgmental statement of what's being heard and interpreted. They are only effective if the respondent realizes he or she has the option of denying the statement if it's not true.

Other questions lead, however, in overly manipulative ways, and they resemble loaded questions in that they rely on charged words or phrases. As a result, some experts on questions use *leading* and *loaded* interchangeably (Payne, 1951/1980). We make this distinction: Loaded questions, whether deliberate or accidental, carry an obvious indication of how you should answer if you're to meet the expectations of the interviewer. For example, if an interviewer asks "Don't you think Martha Stewart was treated unfairly by the prosecutors in her recent case?," you don't have to dig too deep to discover what you're expected to say. Leading questions rely on the power and emotional impact of language, too, but in other ways. In their suggestive form, leading questions, whether deliberate or accidental, influence answers by verbal appeals or sleight of hand. These examples illustrate further how leading questions work:

"With the rising number of DUI-related fatalities, wouldn't you say that state officials ought to crack down with random sobriety checkpoints?"

"Then, you'd agree that the company should do a better job of rewarding its employees for meritorious service?"

"Do you think the United States should allow public speeches against democracy?"

In the first example, the reference to a growing social program invites a positive response. After all, who isn't concerned about accidents associated with drunk driving? In the second example, the question all but delivers a "yes" answer. The third example comes from a classic study (Rugg, 1941) that found respondents acted in significantly different ways when the word *forbid* replaced *allow*. Faced with the question, "Do you think the United States should forbid public speeches against democracy?" 54 percent of the respondents said "yes"—that is, the government should "ban antidemocratic oratory." However, 75 percent answered "no" when asked, "Do you think the United States should allow public speeches against democracy?" In this case a much higher percentage of respondents seemed willing to let the government ban antidemocratic oratory.

Discriminating listeners may not be fooled by a leading question, but an undetected loaded question might lead to an invalid answer. In any event, questions that intentionally trick or maneuver someone into answers will undermine the legitimacy of an interview.

Threatening Questions   Threatening questions state or imply punishment or retribution if an appropriate response isn't forthcoming. Many questions could be called threatening either for their style or their content:

"Do you want to lose your job over this?"

"Do I have to call your parents to get to the bottom of your bad grades?"

Threatening questions are associated with scenes like a police interrogation, but even under adversarial conditions, a less aggressive approach generally holds greater promise for disclosure. As Yeschke (2003) observes, even investigative interviewers, such as police and military officers, have little reason to intimidate respondents: "Never ask questions in a belligerent, demeaning, or sarcastic manner. . . . Pushing interviewees into a corner where they will have to defend themselves is self-defeating. . . . Similarly, asking questions accusingly, suspiciously, or abruptly or asking 'trick questions' may arouse fear and defensiveness and will not promote cooperation. All of these tactics are counterproductive" (p. 161). Many threatening questions have power because they operate as **rhetorical questions**, ones for which the answer is so obvious that the question doesn't need to be answered at all. However, interviewees tend to close down rather than open up when confronted with them.

In a few cases, a threatening question serves as shock therapy. For example, a doctor dealing with a patient's unwillingness to treat a medical condition might threaten as a final step of intervention. If used at all, threatening questions should be asked without frustration or anger.

Blindside Questions   Some interviewers relish the power of asking questions they know to be unexpected by the interviewee. They come seemingly out of nowhere, like a sucker punch. A blindside question feels unfair and unprovoked, and thus can derail an interview and destroy an interviewer's credibility. In rare instances, however, a blindside question can offset a rehearsed answer or alibi and therefore is a tactic in used in investigative journalism, law enforcement, and courtroom interaction. A blindside question could be the first one asked, or it could come after a series of setup questions:

"Reverend Skyler, you have been a persistent critic of the mayor's marital background, including his two divorces. Am I correct?"

"And your position is that a leader loses all moral authority if he or she has been unable to keep marriages together, right?"

"Specifically, you don't like the ways that welfare mothers have been—in your words—'rewarded in the past for their sins.' True?"

"Then Reverend Skyler, as a leading advocate of family values, why have you hidden the fact that you're the father of a child born out of wedlock?"

Blindside questions are particularly dramatic in a public forum, such as a news conference. Often, those who spring surprises are more interested in the reaction than an answer. Does a question cause the interviewee to go ballistic or melt under pressure? In that sense, a blindside question functions as a stress detector.

No matter how they're used, blindside questions rarely achieve worthwhile results. Public figures are usually well prepared for surprise questions; less experienced interviewees might collapse when blindsided. But what is gained in either case?

Our list of problem question isn't exhaustive, nor is it neat and tidy. For example, some questions can exhibit multiple personalities—combining a stress question, personal question, and hypothetical question. CNN reporter Bernard Shaw asked a devastating question of Massachusetts Governor Michael Dukakis, the Democratic presidential candidate in 1988. Dukakis and Vice President George H. W. Bush met in a nationally televised debate seen by 50 million households, where Shaw, as moderator, asked Dukakis the first question: "Governor, if Kitty Dukakis were raped and murdered, would you favor an irrevocable death penalty for the killer?" Reporters in the pressroom gasped, but Dukakis answered without hesitation, "No I don't, Bernard. And I think you know that I've opposed the death penalty during all my life." Instead of answering with emotion or attacking the question, Dukakis emphasized his principles, but did so too coldly and mechanically, at least in the eyes of some critics (Simon, 1990, pp. 291–295).

The question launched a debate. Was Shaw grandstanding, or did he do his job of asking questions not to be found in candidates' briefing books—questions that reveal important facets of leadership? Should Dukakis have said, "I'd want to kill him," showing he's emotional and committed to his wife in a fundamentally human way? Or was his relatively bloodless answer justified, as a reasoned response that showed his commitment to principles? Under scrutiny, both question and answer defy easy classification. What was the "right" thing for Dukakis to have said . . . and how do you know?

Organizing Questions

Organizing questions in an interview is in some ways like a musical arrangement: It displays sequence and timing and can have elements analogous to a prelude or a crescendo. Questions can follow a detailed "score," like a symphony, or spring from disciplined improvisation, like a jazz group's jam session. Interviewers call their plan or sequence of questions a **schedule**, or, in the case of some focus group interviewers, a *question route* (Hennink & Diamond, 2000, pp. 124–126).

A structured, standardized interview, such as a survey, typically follows a set of prepared questions, asked in sequence, with no deviation. Professional interviewers often call this a **highly scheduled interview** because the question sequence is completely decided ahead of time. Most interview forms vary in organization from the informality of an **unscheduled interview** format (used, e.g., by a reporter who discovers "an interview opportunity" when a celebrity unexpectedly agrees to a conversation in the lobby of a hotel) to the middle ground of a **moderately scheduled interview**, a set of standardized "intake" questions that can set the stage for subsequent improvised and individualized questions.

Assuming you have an established, clear purpose for an interview, you'll have to decide whether the following generalized guidelines fit your needs:

• *Move from relatively simple to relatively harder questions.* A warmup period helps everyone get comfortable and mentally stretched for more demanding communication.

Saving tough questions for last minimizes the possibility that a tough question might end the interview prematurely. Don't, however, soften someone up manipulatively with easy questions only to zap them with the one explosive issue you were afraid to ask them initially. Honesty, as the cliché goes, usually is the best policy.

• *Move typically from general to specific questions—or from specific to general.* Think of the choice in terms of a funnel. At which end do you start? Imagine starting at the wide end: What interview professionals call **funnel organization** begins with general, open-ended questions, tapering down to increasingly specific questions. For example:

"What have you heard about the city's plan to build a new jail?"

"What do your friends and neighbors think of the plan?"

"What's your opinion about the proposed location?"

"Will you vote against the jail plan?"

Interviewing citizens about a proposal charged with political, economic, and social implications probably would stir a reaction from almost anyone in town. As a questioning strategy, however, the funnel approach is best suited for well-informed, articulate interviewees. The introductory question doesn't hint of an answer; it provides ample room for the interviewee to explore the issue. It's the type of question a politically active citizen would eagerly answer, even though it's general. Funnel sequence, however, might seem perfect for the interview and turn out a bust. As we've said before, asking questions requires that you remain nimble enough to adjust on the fly.

If you adopt the **inverted funnel organization**, you will progress from narrow, specific questions in the opening to broader, more general ones later (imagine turning the funnel around). For example:

"Have you read the editorial in the paper supporting the proposed new jail?"

"Have you heard Alderman Jackson speak against the jail?"

"Do you plan to vote when the proposal is on the next ballot?"

"What are your friends and neighbors saying about the jail plan?"

"Is the city's plan to build new buildings reasonable?"

The inverted funnel may coax information from someone who is not accustomed to being asked questions about government policy or politics. It's also effective as a quick assessment of a respondent's knowledge on a subject. In some cases, interviewers will provide background information to refresh memories. The respondent answers with a question: "Is that the jail that's supposed to go up near Central Elementary?" Once that's confirmed, the questioning can continue.

• *Finish a line of questioning completely before moving to another.* Inexperienced interviewers often ask a question, get an answer, then move on to the next question on the list. They fail to flesh out answers adequately. Continue asking and reasking questions, using probes as well, until you're convinced a thorough answer has emerged. This advice, however, must be qualified. Watch for an interviewee's willingness to come back to prior topics, even if the issues seem to be closed. Remember the advice from Chapter 2 about encouraging your interviewee to maintain significant control over resource factors such as content knowledge, even as you will tend to have more control over structure factors.

• *Listen and watch for a natural conclusion to your questioning.* Interview partners prepare for the heart of the interview with questions and answers. They're less apt to prepare for an ending. Commonly, interview-ending questions tie up loose ends, summarize, and check one more time for understanding and accuracy. If you've progressed through your schedule and can think of no further questions to raise, give your partner the final word by asking a **wrap-up question**, also known as a **clearinghouse question**. For example, you might ask, "Do you have anything else you'd like to discuss or tell me?" Made as a sincere offer, not a polite gesture, the question might surprise you with its results. People sometimes hold important questions and comments until they feel the interviewer is finished, or they might be reminded of additional important ideas by the overall experience. If there's an encore, let it be the interviewee's.

Wording of Questions

People don't communicate with computer-like precision. We struggle, at times, to express ourselves. Sharing a common language doesn't ensure that the words we offer to others will connect as intended. We may think they're clear and direct and discover the opposite. Misunderstandings abound, even among people with years of experience talking to one another, like spouses or old friends. Misadventures multiply when communicating with strangers, and cultural differences, often reflected in speech styles, special meanings, or different ways of evaluating context, further complicate the process.

The effectiveness of questions often depends on word choice, especially in four particularly important areas: vocabulary, connotation, ambiguity, and directness or indirectness.

Vocabulary

A well-stocked vocabulary fuels communication competence. Questioners draw from their vocabularies to construct questions, assuming that others will be familiar with the words. Unfortunately, for a variety of reasons, people miss each other's meanings. Regional differences, age, culture, education, and other social factors affect how people use and understand words. In wording your questions, try to avoid using technical, unfamiliar, or out-of-context words.

Technical or Specialized Words Complications can arise when using **jargon**, the language of particular fields, professions, or interests. For example, the term *ADHD* (attention deficit hyperactivity disorder) may be far more familiar to teachers than to lay people. If the clarity of a question depends on using jargon, try to insert a brief, informal definition when it's first said. Audience analysis is also necessary when using **euphemisms**, which are presumably inoffensive terms designed to replace unpleasant ones—as in saying *downsized* instead of *fired*. Although many euphemisms can help to take the edge off touchy questions, some listeners may find euphemistic expressions distracting; "downsized" may sound like a ludicrous substitution for the experience of losing a job to the out-of-work spot welder, if not the CEO.

Pretentious or Unfamiliar Words   Overblown, pretentious words deflect listeners' attention from the inquiry itself. Showing off your vocabulary won't impress most people—for example, saying "parsimonious" when "stingy" would be more widely understood. Questions can contain multisyllabic words (like "multisyllabic," for example), especially when a precise meaning can be achieved only by the nuance of a particular word, but simple, commonplace words generally work best. When there is doubt about use of an uncommon word, a definition can be embedded in the question. Rather than admit their unfamiliarity with words, some people pretend they know and try to discern the meaning, searching the rest of the question for clues. A job applicant, then, might successfully figure out an unfamiliar word without asking for help. (Q: "Would you say it's justified to prevaricate when someone asks you an extremely personal question?") Then again, the applicant might only come close to the meaning, guessing that *prevaricate* might mean *withhold* or *delay*. (A: "Well, yes, that happens pretty often. Though I'm open, other people don't need to know my business.") Without intending to, the applicant has admitted to lying almost as a matter of course.

A related problem arises with words that sound like ones we know, such as hearing the word *taught* when the speaker is saying *taut*. These are problems that a collaborative approach to interviews should overcome.

Out-of-Context Words   The vocabulary of teenagers, for example, differs vastly from that of most adults. Attempts to communicate in a language outside our own experience can backfire. A middle-aged white male using "dis" or "crib" in questions might not be considered cool so much as condescending or totally out of touch. Talking down to someone, by use of simplistic words and examples, can be another turnoff that results in diminished returns in an interview. A scientist would likely welcome and expect intellectually challenging questions—but so would a factory supervisor. This isn't strictly a matter of using challenging words, of course. It means asking questions that stimulate and channel constructive thinking about the subject. However, finding the appropriate vocabulary for questions involves weighing factors like these.

Connotation

Through usage and association, words and phrases acquire a reputation. The literal meaning follows the dictionary; the connotative meaning is a shadow. With some words, the connotative meaning closely follows the literal definition. The dictionary, for example, defines *timid* as "lacking courage or self-confidence." It suggests a weak, fearful, perhaps ineffectual person. Most of us wouldn't consider *timid* a complimentary word. But connotative meaning sometimes varies; in another connotative sense *timid* implies "shy" or "bashful." These, too, aren't terms of endearment, but they help illustrate the shades of gray in connotative meaning. When dealing with **denotation**, you acknowledge the literal, official definition of words; **connotation**, on the other hand, refers to the range of informal meanings a word acquires in everyday usage.

The shades of gray extend to words that, depending on circumstances, carry *either* positive or negative connotations. According to the dictionary, *shrewd* means in one sense "clever and keen" but "wily" or "tricky" in another. Applied in a corporate setting, the word implies an admirable quality. Would *shrewd*, however, positively describe the director of a charitable organization?

Precision with words should characterize all communication (see Box 4.4), but questions present a higher imperative for precision because they invite an interchange ideally leading to cooperative meaning. We ask to obtain answers, and if we want effective answers, the words we use should be chosen with care. Accounting for the impact of connotative meaning is part of that care.

Ambiguity

Ambiguous words or phrases make it hard to distinguish between two or more meanings. Sometimes people correct one another in situations of obvious ambiguity. Sometimes ambiguity serves communicators' purposes, and they use it as a strategy. At other times, we talk over and around ambiguity, with neither side recognizing a glitch that can potentially undermine effectiveness. Stanley Payne's (1951/1980) classic, *The Art of Asking Questions*, provides a rogue's gallery of ambiguous words (pp. 158–176). *You*, for one, can confuse because of its potentially ambiguous mix of singular and collective meanings.

"How many cars do you repair in a week?"

A mechanic might say, "Twenty," referring to a personal count. Another, perhaps more team-oriented mechanic might interpret *you* as applying to all the mechanics working at the shop, and respond "Oh, seventy-five to ninety." Such a misunderstanding obviously complicates the answer to a question that appears to be clear at first glance.

Abstract words present another problem of ambiguity. When you use *fair*, for example, does it mean "average," "unjust," or "unbiased"? To avoid misunderstanding, it might be necessary to either use a more explicit word or provide a definition of the word in your question.

Box 4.4

Interviewers in Action   *Seymour Sudman and Norma Bradburn*

Sudman and Bradburn, experts on strategies for questioning, offer this story about the importance of precise wording:

> Two priests, a Dominican and a Jesuit, are discussing whether it is a sin to smoke and pray at the same time. After failing to reach a conclusion, each goes off to consult his respective superior. The next week they meet again. The Dominican says, "Well, what did your superior say?" The Jesuit responds, "He said it was all right." "That's funny," the Dominican replies, "my superior said it was a sin." Jesuit: "What did you ask him?" Reply: "I asked him if it was all right to smoke while praying." "Oh," says the Jesuit, "I asked my superior if it was all right to pray while smoking."

Source: Sudman & Bradburn (1982, p. 1)

Watch out for hidden traps. The simplest of questions might be ambiguous, such as "How do you get to school?" You might answer, "Well, I take Central Avenue to Interstate 40, then exit at 33rd Street, and follow that to campus." But the seemingly plain question wasted time. The interviewer meant to ask, "What kind of transportation do you take to school?" When ambiguity isn't this obvious, the subsequent misunderstanding could derail an interview, with neither party understanding why.

Directness or Indirectness

Wording of questions also requires us to consider whether our approach will be direct or indirect. **Direct questions** usually are blunt, streamlined, and uncompromising. A doctor trying to stop someone's self-destructive behavior might say, "Do you want to die?" That's about as direct as it gets. **Indirect questions** frequently are marked by introductory phrases, related issues, or qualifiers, allowing the respondent to infer the question rather than hear it directly. Instead of a blunt question, the doctor says, "I know you love your family, so I wonder what they'd think about you ignoring this condition."

The choice of direct or indirect questions isn't always clear cut. The choice, though, should be guided by the circumstances, not by the temperament of the interviewer. If your personality is by nature more direct, it's important to consider whether the situation might call for indirect questions. If you're more comfortable with asking indirect questions, you might have to adapt in an interview with someone who prefers a direct style.

Presentation

Except for some standardized, pencil-and-paper, or self-administered survey interviews, presentational style profoundly influences how questions are perceived and answered. Delivery of a message counts. If you've driven 20 minutes to the mall to return a defective DVD player, you're not going to show much patience with a clerk who sneeringly asks, "What *seems* to be the problem?" In interviews, we are likely to be even more sensitive to tone, and when put off by what we hear, see, or sense in the questions put to us, successful communication becomes that much harder.

Four aspects of presentation play especially important roles in how the interview progresses: tone, inflection, rhythm, and pace.

Tone

Tone refers to how the manner or style of speech presumably reflects inner emotional states. Whether baritone or soprano, we're all capable of a wide range of nonverbal implications, moving, by tone of voice, from icy detachment to dripping sweetness. We aren't robots, so tone of voice, although controllable, will be dictated in part by our emotional or physical condition. People who know you well can tell, even over the telephone, if your tone isn't normal. "You don't sound like yourself," a friend might say, meaning there's something in your voice that suggests you're distracted or tired or sad. Tone might also be influenced by how we perceive our conversational partner. For example, a nurse might interview an older person as if addressing a child, or a boss might evaluate a subordinate in a condescending tone. Interviewers and interviewees should conduct what amounts to a sound check: Is my tone justified and appropriate for the interview at hand?

Tone can also be affected by other forms of nonverbal expressiveness. A question delivered without much discernible facial expression of interest or involvement sends a confusing message, at best. On the other hand, simple eye contact, a smile, or other form of reinforcement makes a big difference in people's willingness to answer. Nonverbal messages, however, can be misunderstood, a point developed more fully in Chapter 5. A nod might be construed as agreement rather than acknowledgment, for example. Moreover, if a nonverbal message seems staged, it could do more harm than good in the delivery of questions.

Inflection

Related to tone of voice, **inflection** is how we emphasize or stress certain words over others by raising the volume or pitch of our voice. Payne (1951/1980) helps us understand how inflection affects the meaning of the question. He uses a sample question, "Why do you say that?" and advises repeating the question aloud, accenting each word, one at a time (p. 204):

"*Why* do you say that?"

"Why *do* you say that?"

"Why do *you* say that?"

"Why do you *say* that?"

"Why do you say *that*?"

Do you detect a different meaning in each emphasis? Each inflection carries a shade of meaning. The first asks straightforwardly about motive; the second implies that the message could as easily have gone unsaid; the third suggests that the message might not sound right coming from this speaker; the fourth seemingly implies self-censorship would have been preferable; the last appears to signal disagreement or incredulity. Without inflection, speech is lifeless; with it, speech can become unexpectedly lively.

Rhythm

By **rhythm**, we mean a comfortable, harmonious order and progression of an interview. Interruptions, in particular, can break the rhythm of an interview, so be patient and give your partner ample time for a complete response before offering another question or comment. Questioning often takes on a give-and-take intensity, and a badly timed interruption spoils the mood and chemistry. Some people interrupt because they lack listening discipline. Others interrupt because they incorrectly sense the speaker has finished a thought. Remember that answers don't always gush out; they take time to gel.

Pace

Pace describes the timing and tempo of questions. It's related to rhythm, because bad timing and discordant tempo will affect the flow of the interview. Proper pacing, however, has more serious implications for the quality and quantity of information and insight elicited. To rush through questions or move abruptly from one question to the next can affect the outcome; people differ in their pace of answering. One person's normal rate of speech might sound as slow as molasses to someone else. Be sensitive to differences in pace and the reasons for them, such as culture or age. Interviewers should adjust their questioning to maintain a pace that is comfortable for both partners (see Box 4.5).

Getting Answers without Questions

You don't necessarily have to ask questions to get answers. In fact, at times questions can be viewed as aggressive and uncomfortable personal challenges, and provoke defensiveness or worse. Generally, questioning begins with the basics—who, what, when, where, why, how—as in the following questions:

> "Do you recycle?"
>
> "What do you recycle?"
>
> "Where and when do you recycle?"

Box 4.5

Reminders   *Asking Questions Comfortably*

- *Rehearse your interview questions and pretest them on friends or colleagues.* Read the questions aloud and then consider each: Was it clear? Fair? Could it be improved? Ask, too, about your delivery. What would a listener hear in your pacing or tone of voice?

- *Keep your questions as simple as possible.* Use concrete, everyday language whenever possible. Avoid the **suitcase question**—one crammed to overflowing with implications. Avoid, as well, **double-barreled questions**, with two or more parts to them. They leave respondents trying to decide which part to answer first, provided they can remember them distinctly. For example, are you tempted to ask, "Where did you grow up, and how did you like the kids you played with there?" If you ask two different questions instead, you'll let a respondent answer each more comfortably, and the information you'll receive will be clearer.

- *Monitor the impact of questions, being alert for verbal or nonverbal signs of misunder-* standing or hostility. Watch the respondent's eyes. They reflect boredom, confusion, anger, and many other reactions. Body movements and gestures also can be quite expressive. Ask about the question if you detect any sign that it's not being interpreted as you expected.

- *Give room and encouragement to answer.* Don't rush through your list of questions. Give yourself and your partner enough space to accomplish goals. Unless it's clearly necessary because of time constraints, don't cut short an answer. Closed questions don't allow conversation to energize the interview; relatively open primary questions are better in all but standardized, highly scheduled survey interviews. Then you can probe to flesh out the details of the interviewee's perspective.

- *Remain calm and professional as you question and listen.* You don't need to stage a totally neutral, detached demeanor. Intensity and engagement demonstrate that you're committed to the interview. But anger, frustration, or defensiveness are unlikely to advance your goals.

Trying Out Your Skills

Find a published interview in a magazine, newspaper, or book; or record a broadcast interview. Using the criteria discussed in this chapter, identify and analyze the *types* of questions, the *order* of questions, and the *effectiveness* of questions.

Such questions usually are tolerated until they cross a threshold into the realm of motivation and values. The questions may follow a logical progression from fact-finding to exploration, but clearly they are different from the preceding ones.

"You said you seldom recycle. Why not?"

The threshold has been crossed, although tentatively. Then a bolder question: "Do you believe you have an obligation to be environmentally responsible?" Judgmental inferences continue with the line of questioning. "What about future generations? Do you want them to inherit a country of landfills?"

The judgmental nature of these examples is obvious. However, even seemingly benign questions can also seem judgmental or accusatory, particularly in their cumulative effect, as they pile on, one after another. A relentless question-and-answer cycle can depersonalize communication and limit dialogue, according to Alfred Benjamin, author of *The Helping Interview* (1987). (See Box 4.6 for suggestions on how to answer questions comfortably.) Information can emerge from verbal and nonverbal statements and forms of encouragement that "ask" without the introduction of a question mark. A neutral request for information or a comment can succeed where judgmental pressure fails. "Why" questions, in particular, demand explanations, which, in turn, can compel people to incorporate excuses or justifications as part of an answer. Consider these two alternatives for eliciting a reaction:

Question: "Why did your marriage end in divorce?"

Comment/request: "I'm curious about your impressions of the divorce. Tell me about it from your perspective."

Either approach can produce an answer. Which, though, would you prefer? The neutral request puts the interviewee in control of the substance of the answer (unless it is said in a demanding tone) and tends to reduce the possibility of defensiveness.

The request approach might include using a comment to elicit a response. A comment-as-question could take a variety of forms so long as stimulating an answer is still the objective.

Comment: "You didn't make it to today's committee meeting. You must have been busy with something else."

The comment is another way of asking, "Why aren't you at the meeting?" but it downplays judgmental implications. Of course, if it's essential to obtain an overt

Box 4.6

Reminders   *Answering Questions Comfortably*

• *Prepare for the interview by anticipating the questions likely to be asked.* Remember that the prepared interviewer has thought about the questions, perhaps even to the point of mentally drafting answers. Anticipating questions obviously helps in formulating a thoughtful response instead of a spur-of-the-moment one. If the question doesn't come up, don't consider your efforts wasted. You still have acquired additional insights on your own ideas.

• *Don't rush to answer questions.* Although certain questions can be dispatched quickly, don't leap into answers you might not be comfortable with later. It's not bad form to ponder for a moment or two, perhaps saying, "Let me give that a little thought. . . ." Studies show that students tend to produce fuller, richer answers in class when they're allowed sufficient **wait time**—a significant pause of several seconds in which an inquiring teacher indicates a willingness to let students think through the implications of a point (Rowe, 1987). The same idea applies to interviewing. Because not all interviewers are used to offering wait time, you might claim it comfortably for yourself. With complex questions, simply pause

to collect your thoughts, and don't hesitate to ask for the question to be repeated if necessary. Often, the interviewer takes this as a cue to reconstruct or clarify the question.

• *Make sure you have enough information to understand and answer the question.* Notice the two parts to this reminder. First, if the language or terminology isn't familiar, it's better to ask for definitions than to answer based on a flawed understanding. Second, ask for additional information if you're not sure you know enough about the subject. A memory nudge might be all you need.

• *Discuss questions you don't feel are appropriate or relevant to the interview.* You're rarely obligated to answer all questions. Dodging a question with an evasive answer generally makes things worse. It's better to confront a problem tactfully, but directly.

• *Follow up to ensure the question was answered, or that the questioner hasn't misinterpreted your response.* Mistakes are inevitable when people communicate. Check things out before moving on to other issues or before ending the interview.

explanation of what happened and that isn't forthcoming, a direct question is probably required.

Beyond the Basics

Why People Want to Answer, Why They Don't

Questions can flatter. When someone asks us about ourselves, it's an opportunity to be heard. Yet questions sometimes cause us to demur, "Oh, you don't really want to know about my boring childhood, do you?" Do we doubt the sincerity or motives of questioners? Do we doubt our ability to provide a bright, original answer? Our reaction may depend on how we see our stake, for answering questions has consequences. Do the questions reflect a sincere interest in me? Will I feel patronized? Can I trust the person asking me questions? Do I feel exploited? Will I suffer harm or put myself in jeopardy? Will my best interests be served? Will I regret opening my mouth?

We're questioned in depth as we apply for insurance, rent a car, take out a home loan, open a checking account, fill out a patient's form, or seek financial aid for school expenses. Our habitual roles of responding explain why strangers can ask questions, even personal ones, and many of us respond without hesitation. With an interview, however, the stakes increase, and, often, so does our wariness. Interview questions put us on the spot because they demand a response, even if that response is a refusal to answer.

"Did you ever get caught shoplifting?" (Interviewer)

"I refuse to dignify that question with an answer." (Interviewee)

Questions can intrude or unsettle. They may force us into revealing part of ourselves we would rather keep private.

Here is a fundamental truth about the act of answering: *When questioned, people want to feel safe.* If they sense danger in a question, their defenses go up. Indeed, it can be perilous to provide answers. That is why empathy should accompany interviewers' questions. When questioning, try assessing each question as the other person might experience it from his or her perspective. In addition, you might use your own experience as a criterion: Would I find the question invasive? Hurtful? Insensitive? Empathy, supported by honesty of purpose on the part of the questioner, should help encourage comparable behavior by respondents. Sometimes, though, we must abandon certain questions or qualify what we ask if we want a complete, honest answer. Questioning doesn't have to be a hand-holding sensitivity session. Difficult situations may call for difficult questions. Empathy and honesty, however, can make it possible to ask tough questions and get answers. A collaborative, supportive environment encourages disclosure.

Questions aren't more important than answers, although the emphasis given them in interviewing textbooks suggests this is the case. A saying goes, "Judge people by their questions, not their answers," but clearly answers are revealing, too. Another saying advises, "There are two sides to every question." Certainly that's true when considering that a question may have different meanings for the interviewer and the interviewee. That applies to answers as well. Constant monitoring of questions and answers, often by questions about what's being said and perceived, helps keep interview participants on the same frequency.

For various reasons, people may not answer in ways that satisfy the questioner. Think of your own experience in questioning. You ask someone about her ill father ("How's your dad doing, Sarah?") and get a clipped response ("Oh, he's OK"). It seems clear that Sarah is uneasy or unwilling to say more, so you might decide to abandon the subject or ask a series of less direct questions. To you, her answer suggests another level of meaning. That happens often enough as we process answers, although perhaps not as starkly as Sarah's reticence about her father's illness.

Don't let assumptions distort your ability to discern answers. What you find evasive might not constitute an underhanded tactic; rather, it could be a justifiable attempt to protect the interviewee's privacy or emotional health. Analyze answers with an open mind, recognizing that no interviewer is omniscient. You'll make mistakes in exploring what an answer says or doesn't say, but you'll make more mistakes by neglecting to analyze and account for the meaning of the answer. If you've considered an answer carefully and still can't figure out why it seems deficient or unhelpful, evaluate the quality of your question. Answering questions constitutes an act of giving that can never be taken for granted.

Ethics of Questioning

Asking questions must include a consideration of values, biases, motivations, consequences, duties, and alternatives. Inescapable ethical implications accompany questioning. Let's start with *values* that influence our everyday communicative behavior. For example, do we respect the words and feelings of others? Raising these points involves introspective examination of our questioning orientation and motivation. Interviewing can be a heady, ego-gratifying experience. Interviewers should ask themselves questions like these: Do I ask to win? To rationalize my biases? To prove my toughness? To see others squirm or cry? Early in his career, Mike Wallace (Wallace & Gates, 1984; see also Wallace, 2005) the legendary *60 Minutes* reporter who retired in 2006, sharply questioned cartoonist Al Capp. He fixed on Capp's nervous giggle: "Why do you laugh that way, Mr. Capp? It seems compulsive, doesn't it?" Capp began to sweat and squirm, which spurred Wallace on. "Capp's distress had a mesmerizing effect on me and I persisted; I didn't let up because I felt we were getting close to the bone" (Wallace & Gates, 1984, p. 34). Wallace's reaction hints at the addictive power of questioning and underscores the advice that interviewers look deep into their motives.

Interviewers should also be concerned with the biases that prop up those motives. We all see the world in somewhat different ways. By interrogating our questions for hints of bias, we have an opportunity to compensate. Biases exist in many forms, and if we're not diligent about resisting their pull, they'll become part of our conventional way of thinking and acting. Among your biases might be a belief that females cannot manage male factory workers, that teenagers cannot be trusted to follow directions, and that people who look like you are especially well qualified to be promoted in your department. Biases also include assumptions about personality types, business procedures, and communication styles. Without an introspective attitude about your biases, you'll find it hard to be fair and, in turn, ethical, in asking questions and interpreting the answers.

As you examine your questioning orientation further, you'll confront another ethical crossroads: Whose interests are served by my questions? My own? The interviewee's? The company's? The profession's? A combination of interests? A TV reporter could say with conviction that his aggressive questions are meant to produce a fair, honest story that serves the public interest. His *motivation*, the reporter says, "is the pursuit of truth." This is a justification for questioning that most journalists would say sounds reasonable. A district manager might conduct an appraisal interview to weed out average-performing salespersons and advance the company's mission. That, too, sounds reasonable. But what about people who ask questions without regard for the *consequences* to others who have a stake in the outcome? Can you justify a purely self-serving rationale for your questions? Success in an interview can be measured in various ways. It's usually possible for everyone to succeed when an interview becomes a collaboration instead of a contest.

In Chapter 1 and elsewhere we've offered two principal ethical orientations—teleological (consequence based) and deontological (duty based). Most contemporary ethicists think that ethical decisions can involve both consequences and duties. Not every situation allows us, however, to meet all our duties, for they sometimes compete. Consequences and duties also can clash, leading to difficult decisions.

After reviewing the values, biases, and motives of questions, the next stage involves establishing our personal and professional *duties* to ask, and there can be a tug of war between the two. In some fields, among them medicine and counseling, conflicting schools of thought complicate ethical decision making. Physicians, for example, might decide a paternalistic approach to communication best serves particular patients, and therefore they withhold or disguise the purpose of the interview and their questioning. Instead of saying, "I'm interviewing you to decide whether you're a good candidate for a liver transplant," the doctor allows the patient to assume the questions are part of a standard medical history. You may say an interview of such import should keep all information strictly above board, but the doctor decides an oblique approach is both ethically and medically justified, even though she personally would prefer directness.

The general goal of questions is to seek the truth, but there must be limits to how questions are asked, even in pursuit of truth. Who could condone torture as a truth-detection method? Obviously, the ends cannot always justify the means, especially if the questioning, by intent or recklessness, hurts someone through, for example, physical pain, embarrassment, humiliation, or ridicule. Asking questions involves consequences as well. In balancing duties versus consequences, it's necessary to identify the stakeholders and consider how they might be affected by your action. The consequences of seeking the truth, for example, might result in emotional distress for the interviewee, but are larger interests at stake? The interviewer's obligation to protect an interviewee from harm may have to yield the consequence-based concept of utilitarianism—the greatest good for the greatest number.

Ethical interviewers not only weigh duties and consequences, they also factor in *alternatives* to asking questions and obtaining information. Usually, there are several possible routes to a destination. It might be safer and more effective to take a roundabout path than race down Main Street. Ethical decision making should not be done in haste. Question and justify your actions with acute ethical sensitivity to how honestly you can call for the other's participation, as well as your own responsibilities for maintaining confidentiality and avoiding deception.

Informed Consent

When police question crime suspects, they're required to issue a *Miranda* warning. The language of the warning varies by locale, but it essentially covers four points: "You have the right to remain silent. If you waive your right, anything you say may be used against you. You have the right to an attorney. If you can't afford an attorney, one will be provided without charge." The U.S. Supreme Court devised the warning as a procedural safeguard against police interrogators skilled at getting people to talk without the benefit of legal representation.

Skilled interviewers, like skilled detectives, know many shortcuts and, at times, could fool or intimidate informants to disclose more than they intend. If sensitive questions must be asked, a standard ethical guideline calls for guaranteeing **informed consent**, the Miranda warning for interviewers. Informed consent involves telling participants about the risks and benefits of answering questions. It can include a reminder that participation is voluntary and that consent can be withdrawn at any time.

Informed consent usually arises in interviews conducted by researchers. Grant guidelines and other rules governing the research, set by institutions or universities, often require a signed informed-consent form from participants as a condition for approval of a project. Informed consent, however, isn't typically required for professional interviews conducted by journalists, job recruiters, managers, or counselors, for example. In these situations, professionals frequently assume that the interviewee knows what is at stake. Ethical interviewers, however, will still fully inform their respondents about the conditions of the questioning, even when that is not required by the institutions that sponsor their work.

When is informed consent appropriate? In general, it fits any interviewing situation posing risks that may not be obvious to the interviewee. Certain interviewees warrant extra care, including children and the mentally or emotionally impaired, when there is concern about either their answering ability or vulnerability.

Informed consent almost always involves an explanation of how publicly the interview information will be shared. Thus, confidentiality becomes another serious ethical issue.

Confidentiality

Confidentiality in questioning usually covers two conditions—that the private information collected won't be made public and that the source of the information won't be identified. Of course, many interviews are conducted without a formal pledge of confidentiality, but lack of a written agreement doesn't free interviewers of a responsibility to keep confidences. With the exception of published or broadcast interviews by journalists, interviews aren't public events and, as a result, interviewees expect that what they say won't end up as office gossip or cocktail talk. People may voluntarily answer quite personal questions, but it's with a tacit understanding that the information will be used discreetly and appropriately. They don't expect interviewers to be careless about the information obtained by questioning, or to blab it to others, or to fail to ensure the security of notes or tapes.

Confidentiality—whether formally pledged or informally presumed—should not be taken lightly. It obligates interviewers to protect the content, and maybe the existence, of a conversation. You should be sure of your position guaranteeing ironclad safeguards, however. Pressure, including litigation, might force you to disclose what you've collected from a subject. Journalists have been jailed for refusing to identify anonymous sources. Ethics, however, isn't an exact science. The balance can tip in favor of disclosure over confidentiality when circumstances warrant, such as in the case of a teacher who concludes her higher ethical duty, based on weighing the consequences, is to report a child's whispered "Mommy's boyfriend hurt my brother."

Deception

Deception in questioning can come from false identification, pretense, or devious behavior. Interviewers who hide their identity do so usually because they feel deception gives them an advantage. People tend to conduct themselves in ways that seem appropriate for the situation, and that includes how to answer questions. We are different from one communication context to the next. A job applicant, for example, who is told he's going to talk to some prospective coworkers, might assume a casual demeanor, making light of some questions that he might answer more seriously if asked by a boss. In truth, several of the people he chats with are managers who want to observe the "real" person. Certainly, the interviewee suffers a disadvantage, denied the opportunity to adjust his communication style to the situation. It's difficult to justify masquerades or disguises as ethical. They're also questionable as a useful learning tactic. Above all, deception breeds distrust, and that includes its effect on those who practice deception because they assume others will deceive them.

Interviewers who resort to pretense to camouflage the actual purpose of an interview may not lie outright, but they certainly aren't being truthful. Deception about the purpose of an interview borders on entrapment, and people who engage in that tactic usually rationalize that they won't gain the interviewee's cooperation by being forthright. Once again, the deception denies the interviewee freedom of choice. Moreover, it undermines both the credibility of the interviewer and the validity of the information collected. Communication should be conducted on as equal footing as possible, but there are always exceptions.

Occasionally, something less than full disclosure may be acceptable. At times, it's in the best interest of the interviewee for researchers to withhold certain details, thus walking an ethical tightrope. At other times, it's a matter of simultaneously serving the specific interests of the interviewee without jeopardizing the important, broader interests of the interview. In a few instances, your assessment of a consequentialist greatest-good criterion might be the central factor in your decision.

Finally, deception can take the form of exploitation or betrayal, such as an interviewer who feigns empathy in asking questions or gets answers by posing as a confidant or friend. Those who pretend just act a role, and unless they are exceptionally good actors, eventually they will be exposed. It's far better to rely on ability than guile.

Toughness versus Courage

Conscientious interviewers work hard to devise the "right" questions, which often means "tough" questions. In fact, by male standards mostly, interviewers get high marks for throwing "hardball" questions and are demeaned for lobbing "softballs" or "marshmallows." Tough doesn't necessarily equate to good, although there are certainly effective, tough questions. However, concentrating on the zinger, bomb, or coup de grace elevates the negative question over those that, although less dramatic, hold greater potential for beneficial results.

Courage in questioning is another matter. Professional interviewers assume a responsibility to do their duty, even when it might be uncomfortable or painful. Avoiding that duty usually means avoiding a problem—the interviewer's or the interviewee's. Eventually, the problem must surface. For example, the supervisor who values his or her popularity avoids questioning an employee about alleged safety violations. The supervisor lacks the courage to put the safety of the workers over personal interests.

Infallible or perfect ethical criteria don't exist, but we meet our responsibilities best when we reflect as thoroughly as possible about our ethics in questioning others.

Making Your Decision

Asking

In your role as president of the campus chapter of a professional organization for accountants, you're investigating reports that the group's treasurer has been pocketing money from sales of sweatshirts instead of depositing it in a scholarship fund. You discover that an inventory of sweatshirts and receipts shows a $150 discrepancy. You cannot account for the missing funds despite repeated rechecking of the facts as you know them. Here is a situation that would challenge anyone's questioning acuity, but you conclude that questions must be asked to uncover the truth, which includes the possibility there has been no wrongdoing.

- What would you do before questioning the treasurer?

- What answers would you seek?

- How would you begin the interview?

- How would you frame and order your initial questions? Try devising a list.

Let's hope a plausible explanation emerges before you reach the ultimate question about theft of the funds. But what would you do if the answers aren't satisfactory or if they suggest the treasurer isn't telling the truth? What next? What are your ethical concerns?

Answering

Imagine yourself in the role of a woman about to graduate from college. You're making plans for finding a job in law enforcement. As a preparatory step, you schedule an interview with the campus placement director for advice. Let's assume you've encountered someone who is not known for tact, and you find yourself facing these questions:

- Why is a petite thing like you planning a career in law enforcement?

- Police agencies do thorough background checks of applicants. Have you or any of your relatives been in trouble with the law?

- What satisfaction would you get out of carrying a gun and handcuffs, and locking people up?

- Have you thought about less dangerous work?

What is your reaction to these questions? How would you respond?

Summary

You've learned from this chapter that the ability to ask questions is at the heart of effective interviewing. Questioning, though, cannot be divorced from its companion skills of listening and framing. Focusing on a purpose and a plan for questioning is an essential first step. Without clarity of purpose, shared ideally by interviewer and interviewee, the interview may drift without direction.

Questions help fuel conversation and elicit useful responses. Particularly important are those questions, called probes, that serve to bring answers to their fullest potential. The wording of questions is also important. Because misunderstandings are so common, questions should be as clear and focused as possible. Both interviewer and interviewee have responsibilities to check and recheck the condition of the interview and the quality of questions and answers.

In "Beyond the Basics" we note that the ethics of questioning involves a range of considerations, including the interviewer's communication orientation and biases. A thorough ethical audit helps reveal potential problems and conflicts. The responsibilities to gather information and safeguard the interests of the interviewee might conflict. An ethical grounding helps interviewers make justifiable decisions and avoid causing harm.

The Interview Bookshelf

On a general understanding of questions in human interaction:

Dillon, J. T. (1990). *The practice of questioning.* New York: Routledge.

Loaded with advice and insights into questioning under various conditions. Especially good sections on the notions of questioning and the alternatives to questioning. Well supported by research and theory.

On the difficulties of phrasing effective questions:

Foddy, W. (1993). *Constructing questions for interviews and questionnaires.* Cambridge, UK: Cambridge University Press.

Technical in places, but useful for its insights into how memory affects the quality of answers and what steps you can take to ensure that your questions work as intended.

Leeds, D. (1987). *Smart questions.* New York: Berkley Books.

Pitched to managers, but it's filled with good ideas about the why and wherefore of asking questions in various situations. Particularly good is a section on making questions fit certain personality types, among them the "convincers" and the "calculators."

The classic work on questioning:

Payne, S. L. (1980). *The art of asking questions.* Princeton, NJ: Princeton University Press. (Original work published 1951)

This readable classic provides a catalog of question pitfalls. Payne also suggests questions to ask about our questions, with clever, useful examples throughout.

Skillful Framing

After reading this chapter, you should be able to

- Define framing and discuss its importance relative to the other two basic skills of interviewing: speaking/questioning and listening

- Use in interviews the four basic skills of framing: metacommunicating, contextualizing, offering accounts, and reframing

- Make informed choices about when, how, and whether to use note taking, delayed note taking, and tape recording to document interviews

- Articulate your own position on a contemporary controversy about language and group identity, and use acceptance-oriented language in interviews

Famed anthropologist Clifford Geertz (2000) tells a story about his relationship with a respondent while doing field research many years ago in Java (pp. 34–37). The respondent, a clerk Geertz interviewed frequently about local customs, language, and habits, fancied himself a creative writer and asked to borrow Geertz's typewriter so he could transform his longhand prose to a more professional appearance.

The arrangement worked smoothly until one day when Geertz said he couldn't loan the typewriter, as he needed it himself that afternoon. Within minutes, the clerk sent his little brother with a note to Geertz, reporting that he'd be too busy to be interviewed the following day. Geertz, worried about the possibility of an inadvertent insult, told the brother to take a new note back to the interviewee—a note saying that Geertz could loan the typewriter that day after all, along with a profuse apology for any possible offense. Three hours later, the brother brought a new note with the clerk's reply; it said that there was no need to apologize, that the typewriter was, after all, Geertz's property, and that he wasn't affronted at all. However, the clerk reported, his literary interests had become so all-consuming that he felt he must unfortunately cancel the remaining interviews and devote the time to his writing.

The frame around a picture, if we consider this frame as a message intended to order or organize the perception of the viewer, says, "Attend to what is within and do not attend to what is outside...." Psychological frames are related to what we have called "premises." The picture frame tells the viewer that he is not to use the same sort of thinking in interpreting the picture that he might use in interpreting the wallpaper outside the frame.... The frame itself thus becomes a part of the premise system.

—Gregory Bateson,
Steps to an Ecology of Mind

Geertz tried to puzzle out how, in his words, "this molehill became such a mountain" so rapidly (p. 36), and over a simple typewriter, too. His tentative answer? The typewriter wasn't just a typewriter; it was a "complex of claims and concessions only dimly recognized" (p. 36), and it symbolized different things to the two men. For the clerk, borrowing the typewriter was an assertion that he could be taken seriously as a writer, an intellectual, and an equal. For the researcher, lending it was an assertion that he could be taken seriously as a friend and at least a temporary member of "the inner circle of [the clerk's] moral community" (p. 36). Each man had used his semifictional interpretation to convince himself that the other agreed with his own assumption. Yet despite the veneer of agreement, the two had operated from unacknowledged different interpretations of their roles. They used different *frames* in interpreting the typewriter event.

As the typewriter incident implies, many interview participants act as if their communication is entirely about speaking and listening. Yet speech is not as automatically meaningful nor listening as automatically focused as individuals might expect. What makes communication in an interview meaningful and focused enough for individuals to believe they each have been understood? The answer boils down to the different ways we frame our problems (Fontana & Frey, 2000, pp. 660–661). Framing is a term that has entered the popular vocabulary (e.g., Bai, 2005), and we can use it to describe a general approach to interpretation before we return to a more precise definition.

Speech becomes meaningful to the extent that we perceive its patterns. You can never simply "have" a conversation with someone else in the same sense that you "have" a car or "have" a cold. It can't be possessed, because conversations aren't objects but mutually coordinated action that belongs to no one. To participate in conversation means that you and your partner are always coauthoring an overall pattern of meaning into which each of the various messages will seem to fit—if you are successful. Gregory Bateson (see, e.g., 1972, 1980, 1991) believed that persons never know what is going on *in* their lives unless they can perceive the larger patterns *between* their lives that participants are always creating.

These patterns form much of the richness of talk. Communicators rarely refer to these larger patterns, even indirectly, partly because they don't think they need to and partly because they can't, as individuals, articulate the frames fully anyway. Here's an example: Martina notices that her younger brother Louis forgot about their father's birthday and has heard from a friend that he's missed quite a few classes lately at the university, too. Adopting her usual lighthearted attitude of kidding, she calls to express her concern, asking if everything is all right: "Hey, Bub. Where have you been? Dad asked about you at the birthday party. You sick, or what?" Louis, however, replies, "Why do you always have to check up on me? You're always grilling me. Let me live my own life." His response shocks Martina. What she intended as an expression of loving concern, Louis evidently interpreted as prying. How could two reasonable people frame their exchange in such opposite ways? It never occurred to Martina that Louis would take her questions as interrogation, and it never occurred to him that Martina didn't intend her inquiry as a criticism. Yet as they talked, their two different frames for the communication became more decisive than the actual words themselves.

Linguist Deborah Tannen (1986, 1990/2001) has explored dimensions of interpersonal security and insecurity that arise from different patterns of talk. For example, she observes that "if you talk to others as if you were a teacher and they were your students, they may perceive that your way of talking frames you as condescending or pedantic. If you talk to others as if you were a student seeking help and explanations, they may perceive you as insecure, incompetent, or naïve. Our reactions to what others say or do are often sparked by how we feel we are being framed" (Tannen, 1990/2001, pp. 33–34). This helps explain what Geertz's typewriter "meant" and why Louis reacted as he did to Martina despite her assurance that her question was a loving one. Such alignment of interpretive patterns explains why it's a delicate balancing act for a job applicant, for example, to come across as appropriately deferential and appropriately assertive at the same time. Does the applicant frame herself or himself as a "learner" (seeking knowledge) or a "teacher" (offering expertise)? Or is it possible to do both simultaneously? In Chapter 7, we offer suggestions for dealing with this problem head-on.

In Chapter 1 we introduced framing as the ability "to form interpretations of what we think is really going on in social situations." In addition, we discussed Agar's (1994) notion that a frame "sets a boundary around . . . details and highlights how those details are related to each other" (p. 130). Understanding the frame concept means you'll understand how people who seem to be doing the same thing together (sharing a typewriter, to Geertz, or even conducting an interview) each think they're doing something else. You frame a comment as "playful joke," whereas your friend's frame for the same words is "unfair put-down." This chapter analyzes that fundamental problem of recognizing or labeling patterns differently. In "The Basics" we (1) define the process of framing more specifically in the context of interviewing, (2) describe a set of skills and insights that can help you sharpen your understanding of framing, and (3) suggest practical approaches for a concrete problem of clarifying frames, how to take notes and record interviews. Then, in "Beyond the Basics," we return to cultural motivations more directly. We'll ask you to grapple with framing problems introduced by language habits. If naming and renaming things changes people's experience of those things, as frame theorists claim, then such matters as gender-neutral and other forms of bias-free language are extremely important. In this section you'll be challenged to think of the *political correctness* controversy in a new way. We hope to remove the controversy from a narrowly political "liberal versus conservative" context, to reframe it as a matter of clear communication.

The Basics

What Is Framing? Knowledge Interpreted in Pattern

Definitions of framing vary somewhat from researcher to researcher, although most explanations mention early works from Bateson (1972) and Goffman (1974). It might be helpful to bring the concept down to earth with another practical example from the world of interviewing.

Sonya, a personnel manager, is interviewing an applicant, Rose, who, from the first minutes of their meeting, she likes enormously. She discovers a ready rapport developing, and Sonya and Rose genuinely appear to enjoy each other's company. In a seemingly effortless way, both of them quickly shed certain more or less official aspects of their roles and engage in banter about other organizations and bosses with whom they've worked. Sonya shares a couple of minor irritations that, she realizes too late, could be thought to apply to her own company as well as to others. By the time Rose starts to answer the standard schedule of questions originally planned for all interviewees, she has gained much more inside information about the company than most interviewees can expect to learn.

Suddenly, Sonya recognizes that this session is different from the previous 12 interviews she's conducted for this position, and for the same reasons, it's likely to be different from the next ones, too. Things are going smoothly, but something is faintly troubling. It's not going to be easy to compare Rose's responses with those of the other applicants. Some questions haven't been asked at all, because Sonya thought the answers might be inferred reasonably from the bantering early in the interview. Sonya heard how some topics elicited extended stories, as if from friend to friend, and she reveled in their telling. She found herself, as well, subtly trying to sell the company by phrasing even restrictive personnel policies in their best light. A faint but real warning buzzer sounds inside Sonya, telling her that although this conversation feels right in many ways, she also feels a bit compromised. Will the tone and presumption of friendship affect her ability to make an effective recommendation on which candidate to hire? Are there aspects of her role as employment interviewer that require her to maintain some distance between her and interviewees, at least for a while?

Nervously, Sonya clears her throat, sits up straighter, and announces, "Well, let's move more directly to a series of job-related issues. We want to know how you've interceded in conflict situations in your previous leadership positions. Could you elaborate?" Sonya's language and demeanor quickly become more formal, and Rose takes the cue even without fully understanding what's happening or why. She mirrors Sonya's behavior by making her own comments sound more official: "Yes. I directed a great many projects at the National Endowment. When tempers rose, I tried to establish a buffer zone between the parties." At one level, Rose, a skillful communicator, is alert enough to see that something has changed, but at another level, inside, she's upset. What has she done wrong? Has she offended Sonya unintentionally? Why the sudden turnaround just when things have been going so smoothly? What are the new ground rules? Off balance and tentative, she stumbles through the rest of the interview, offering opinions without much confidence.

Different people could analyze what's going on here in different ways, depending on their roles. The director of the human resources department, who trained Sonya in equal employment opportunity, affirmative action, and fair hiring practices, might see an excessively friendly informal conversational tone as a breach of fairness to other applicants and applaud Sonya's change of heart. Applicant Rose might think, at least initially, that it's her good fortune to have a personality so compatible with her interviewer's. Others in the company who hope for a more friendly social climate might suggest that Sonya's conversational impulse was not wrong at all, because it discovered an excellent interpersonal fit between worker and organization. Sonya might see the whole incident as a lapse in professionalism or as a regrettable fact of an interviewer's life that she can never really be "herself." However, from the standpoint of this book, we want to understand the event simply as an example of how different frames have consequences for common action.

One particularly good way to analyze the Sonya–Rose encounter is through the actors' own definitions of the situation. Both parties sit down expecting to conform to their expectations for the social event called a "job interview." They had, in Goffman's (1974, p. 338) terms, a **clear frame**—one in which all participants operate on the basis of a similar definition. These expectations for an employment interview usually involve a relatively high degree of formality, a clear differentiation of power between interviewer and interviewee, heightened emotional tension, and reliance on a series of well-defined questions and answers. Based on Sonya's initial positive impressions and maybe Rose's successful **impression management skills** (her ability to shape her behavior to meet the demands of the situation), the distance and formality of the situation began to melt, replaced by new expectations—ones that are closer to describing informal chats between friends. The formality decreased, the mood was decidedly egalitarian and non-threatening, both felt more relaxed, and interchanges depended more on spontaneous statements than on questions and answers. The new frame, which we might call "chat," emerged—in this case, as a mutual creation formed by the talk itself as each woman let herself break out of previous assumptions. Both frames were conversations, but different types.

Yet Sonya found it necessary to shift gears abruptly, back to a formalized interview tone. Goffman (1974) calls this **breaking the frame**; that is, her talk began to violate and thus change the evidently shared assumptions. (Actually, this was the second time Sonya broke the frame in the interview, right?) Rose didn't know how to respond. How could she? In this roller-coaster ride, she understood the words, the sentences, the purpose of the meeting, and even the main nonverbal messages. Yet she still didn't get it. Despite the idea of framing being a bit abstract, it is indeed the missing piece of the puzzle for both Rose and Sonya.

Framing Skills in Action

Some aspects of dealing with frames come down to individual skills. Keep in mind, too, that if individual skills are to be effective, they must work in concert with what others are doing. With that simple qualifier, consider the following as especially important framing skills and insights that can help you become more effective in interviews.

Framing Skill 1: Metacommunicating

Metacommunication is a concept from communication research that describes the process of communicating about our communication. One form is the inevitable mix of verbal messages with nonverbal ones. In any comment you make, both how you act while saying it and how you say it (e.g., body movements or tone of voice) can be perceived as a silent commentary on how the verbal message should be interpreted. However, we want to concentrate on the second metacommunicative form—the more overt process of clarifying talk with more talk.

Most people go through life believing that communication is such a natural process that they never need to pay special attention to it, and much of the time, they are right. Most everyday exchanges are best done with little attention to analyzing them. We want to be aware of the immediate consequences of what we say and do without becoming obsessed. It's possible to overthink situations so much that you outsmart yourself.

Metacommunication, though, doesn't need to involve grand theorizing. It can exist in the moment as a brief perception check or an "active listening" assist. In this way, it averts or troubleshoots frame problems effectively. For example, as a selection interviewer, you could announce a frame shift through metacommunicating:

> "Up to this point, I've asked you about your experience working with kids at the special school district. Now, I'd like you to imagine we've already hired you for this position. Your descriptions were interesting, but let's switch gears. Here are several situations that have arisen lately around here. Give me your first impressions of how you'd respond to them, OK? It's not past experience I'm interested in, but what you'd do in new situations."

Or you could check out what you perceive as an interviewee's nonverbal discomfort:

> "You looked a lot more comfortable when we were discussing your qualifications, which are excellent. Since we starting talking about our department here, you seem . . . I don't know . . . more reserved. I'm wondering if this is beginning to sound less like an interview to you and more like a gossip session or something. If so, it's OK that you feel that way; we can take a different direction with this."

Or if you were an interviewee, you might metacommunicate to find out if an interviewer is in fact interpreting your answers from within the frame you suspect:

> (After discussing a series of hypothetical actions, triggered by interviewer questions) "Well, I've gone on quite a long time here, but it might not be my storytelling skill you're interested in. Some of my answers, I guess, were pretty personal. Was this the kind of response you had in mind?"

In metacommunicating, remember, you are explicitly bringing up what is not usually explicit in conversation. You are making the process of communicating become the content, too. If you do this all of the time, it will likely sound phony and stilted. Yet as an intervention during crucial moments of a conversation—those moments when partners are most likely to misinterpret each other—metacommunication can be a powerful skill.

Framing Skill 2: Contextualizing

Contextualizing is similar to metacommunicating (in fact, it could sound like metacommunicating at times). It involves acknowledging the full context in which a statement is made. For example, think about what makes certain words offensive in sensitive matters of cross-cultural assumptions, race, gender, class, sexual preference, or disability. Some might believe that certain words are automatically offensive, almost as if the word directly delivers the offense. In everyday life, however, that's not how we usually act.

Most people give the benefit of the doubt whenever possible. We take into account who is saying the word, her or his capacity for knowing the potentially offensive effect, and an entire range of other considerations. African Americans who object with good reason to being called "colored" or "Negro" often report that they are not offended in the same way when the speaker is an 85-year-old white man who may not be aware of contemporary dialogue about the cultural implications of language use. He may, in fact, be sincere and careful in avoiding what he considers to be the much more offensive word that his friends used in his youth.

Contextualizing does not mean you must condone the use of loaded or dismissive language, or blithely accept a variety of offending actions or misinterpretations. It only suggests that understanding context expands your range of choices for doing so. As the discussion of assertiveness in the next section suggests, you may want to reply to, or correct, the other person directly. Generally, skillful communicators give others reasonable interpretive room to move. Context matters so much in communication that the same words can be said to the same person in different situations, resulting in anger and frustration one time and amusement and entertainment the next. If this is true, the words aren't the "same," are they, when the context changes?

Another form of contextualizing is to identify and use the contextual frame most comfortable for an interview partner. You could ask an entrepreneur about the difficulties of running a small clothing store in a strip mall and get clear answers about those problems. But an interviewer skilled in contextualizing will understand that a richer explanation will emerge if the interview occurs at work, during a Friday afternoon and evening full of sales, returns, customers' complaints, and creditors' calls. On the owner's turf, you hear the answers within the interviewee's frame of reference, and your understanding will deepen.

Framing Skill 3: Offering Accounts

In many interpersonal situations that seem like miscommunication, people assume that other communicators should be able to understand them almost transparently and infallibly. The point, they think, is "already clear," or "painfully obvious." Or someone appeals to something called common sense: "I shouldn't *have* to tell you not to do that," a parent might say; "Everybody knows better than to do *that*!" These things are said (whether true or not) when people are secure in the relationship. Professional interviewing situations, though, often bring together people who have trouble saying such things to each other. Interviewers and interviewees think these things, but keep them to themselves. It might help for someone to disrupt delicately this cycle of suspected misunderstanding—not with criticism but with a more constructive approach.

One way out of a potential framing dilemma is to more or less announce the frame you're using. This clarifies the interaction for your partner and offers good evidence about whether the two of you are generally on the same wavelength or talking about two quite different things. Although the word **account** means various things in communication research, think of it here as how you make your own frame explicit when the situation is potentially fuzzy. As Heritage (1988) observes, "To make sense, the overt descriptions and explanations (or accounts) which actors provide for their actions must articulate with . . . already established implicit understandings" (p. 128). We are not all equally aware of our own frames, but we usually know whether we're speaking in a given conversation as a friend, a family member, an expert, a boss, a woman, or a man. For example, consider a defense lawyer (L) interviewing a client (C) charged with tax evasion. The lawyer assumes her client knows she is speaking in terms of legal strategy, although the two are also friends living in the same neighborhood:

L: "What caused you to withhold those other sources of income?"

C: "I didn't withhold them. I only forgot them. There are so many little piddly things—I can't keep track of them all."

L: "I don't like that explanation."

C: "What do you mean? You want me to lie? I did forget them. I can't lie about that. You'll get me into a lot of trouble!"

L (calmly): "No, I don't want you to lie. When I say, 'I don't like that explanation,' I mean that when I think about your case as a lawyer—not as your friend—I think your style of explaining things would be pretty hard to sell. That's because the prosecutor will explain everything as withholding and hiding and greed. Also, a jury won't be very sympathetic to someone who's annoyed at having a lot of different sources of income. Sounds like you're annoyed at being rich. See what I mean?"

In her last statement, the lawyer has offered an account aimed at clarifying not only the statement in question but also her overall stance or position as a communicator. She suggests that in this interview, the client shouldn't think of what is said as coming from a friendship frame but, instead, the wider professional frame of advocacy. Of course, not all occasions for offering accounts will be this obvious, so you'll have to play detective at times and ferret out when it might be best to announce your frame. Our common vernacular has an apt phrase for this: We want to know not only what someone said but also "where they're coming from." To understand persons' frame accounts is to understand where they're coming from more comprehensively.

At times, offering accounts effectively depends on other skills. Interpersonal communication teachers and trainers often distinguish among the terms *aggressiveness, acquiescence,* and *assertiveness* (see M. J. Smith, 1975, for one treatment of assertiveness). Although there are surely appropriate times and places for all three, assertiveness is the most transferable and useful response in situations of frame misinterpretation. **Aggressiveness** is the attempt to prevail in a situation (get what you want, have your say, define the outcomes as you wish) with little regard for the rights or feelings of others. It is a form of communicative selfishness. If aggressiveness is one end of a continuum of communicative respect, acquiescence is the other. **Acquiescence** is when communicators passively accept whatever comes, as though they couldn't possibly have control over the situation; thus, it amounts to letting others prevail, showing little regard for your own rights. The midpoint skill, permitting communicators the most flexibility, is **assertiveness**. Assertive communicators do not dominate situations inappropriately, nor do they automatically shrink from them. They act and express themselves when it is called for. They respect others' rights, but also respect their own. In doing so, they affirm how self and others are intertwined.

Because assertive communicators recognize this intertwining, offering an account assertively is not the same as claiming that your frame is necessarily the best or the only one possible. You simply are clarifying why the message could make more sense when understood in context. Both interviewers and interviewees will find many occasions for offering accounts. Some will require delicate tact, because interviews can become threatening, ego-involving, and emotional on other levels, too.

If you're sensitive to frame problems, you face a series of subtle dangers in choosing whether to offer accounts. If framing is signaled primarily by nonverbal **metamessages** (messages about how to interpret other messages, such as winks, clothing choices, and tone of voice), then making nonverbal context verbal by offering an account can be powerful. As many researchers (e.g., Tannen, 1986) recognize, naming a frame changes it. In a job performance appraisal interview, for example, you may want to accept your supervisor's invitation to make the occasion one for mutual feedback. You enjoy your work and particularly appreciate all the things the boss has done to help you in the past two years. You want to communicate this appreciation but don't want it to be framed as insincere schmoozing or, in the popular semicrude vernacular, "sucking up." If the two of you are both sincere in wanting to exchange honest and, let's say, appreciative feedback, then attempts to name that frame and distinguish it from other alternatives could actually be counterproductive: "I know this sounds like I'm buttering you up, and I don't want to be seen as bringing apples to the teacher, but I really think you're doing a great job managing the unit. I want you to know that." Such an account, paradoxically, could actually introduce the "schmoozing frame" inappropriately into the interview, creating ambiguity, when a simple direct compliment would suffice. In other words, most frames don't need to be named out loud when conversation is smooth. Sometimes it is downright risky to name them.

Framing Skill 4: Reframing

At times, a dominant frame can create seemingly unhealthy choices for communicators. Therapists Watzlawick, Weakland, and Fisch (1974, pp. 94–95) tell the story of a man who, out of necessity, took a job as a salesman despite being a lifelong stutterer. His speech difficulties when dealing with customers were so unsettling and embarrassing that he felt his life careening out of control. Yet he needed the job. The excruciating dilemma was real: What he *must* do was what he *couldn't* do while maintaining his self-esteem. Where could he go for a solution?

The therapists' suggestion involved **reframing**, in which someone "change[s] the conceptual and/or emotional setting or viewpoint in relation to which a situation is experienced and to place it in another frame which fits the 'facts' of the same concrete situation equally well or even better, and thereby changes its entire meaning" (Watzlawick, et al., 1974, p. 95). What the salesman experienced as an inevitable occasion of embarrassment was not the only way to frame the persuasive interviews (see Chapter 10) he had to conduct. He was asked, for example, to name some of the worst criticisms of salespeople, and he came up with such things as how ordinary people mistrust the "slick, clever ways of trying to talk people into buying something they do not want" and how customers dislike "uninterrupted sales talk[s]" that use an "offensive barrage of words." The therapists asked if he had noticed how carefully people listen to someone who stutters; and they suggested that if he could mentally compare the worst image of "slick salesman" with his particular persuasive advantage, he would never come across as slick. He would enjoy a certain level of attention and listening that many other sales professionals couldn't muster. "As he gradually began to see his problem in this totally new—and, at first blush, almost ludicrous—perspective, he was especially instructed to maintain a high level of stammering, even if in the course of his work, for reasons quite unknown to him, he should begin to feel a little more at ease and therefore less and less likely to stammer spontaneously" (pp. 94–95). By reframing, he gained a sense of mastery over his situation, instead of the reverse. Instead of framing his stuttering as an embarrassing defect, he made it a unique advantage.

Studs Terkel (1967), the radio interviewer and author of many books about the lives of ordinary Americans, had to tape his interviews, but found himself hampered by being a bit of a technological klutz. Was this a huge problem for him? No—he reframed it into an advantage. He discovered that if he mentioned at the beginning of an interview how awkward he was with tape recorders, and made jokes about how alien and mysterious they seemed, interviewees began to loosen up. In this way he demystified the experience of being tape recorded by positioning himself on the interviewee's side with respect to this potentially intrusive (although helpful) technology. Fumbling with the recorder was transformed from an embarrassing problem to an opportunity for Terkel to identify personally with the interviewee (p. xxii). His approach is another version of skillful reframing.

Freeze-Frame: Note Taking and Recording in Interviews

Throughout this book we stress the crucial role of listening in interviews (see especially Chapter 3). A discussion of framing is a good context to consider how an interviewer who listens effectively chooses to record, retain, and interpret information. Effective listening, remember, goes far beyond merely being silent and paying attention. Any listener is actively framing information, and interpreting it in alternative contexts, while ensuring that after the interview, the ideas will somehow be remembered and accessible. When it's time to make a decision, write a story, present a report, or schedule another interview, the interviewer has to rely on some method of recall. (See Boxes 5.1 and 5.2 for different experiences of recording interviews.)

The heading of this section is both illustrative and misleading. It's useful to think of methods of recording interviews as choices for how to "freeze" parts of previous communication so we can remember them better. Not all interviewers need to record their interviews, but many do so for good reasons. Journalists and celebrity interviewers listen for quotes, because these are considered the nuggets of meaning that capture the speaker's personality. In a way, we recall the quote as a vivid symbol of the person's excitement, skill, commitment, intelligence, ideology, or emotion. Psychotherapists and psychiatrists need to refer back to the exact words with which a client or patient expressed a personal problem; embedded in the language are many clues to the larger framework of a person's lived experience. To capture exact language for later reconsideration seems like freezing the frame. However, it's also a bit misleading to think

Trying Out Your Skills

Read the following interview excerpt and apply the concepts and skills of framing to help you understand how the communicators are relating to each other. The campus director of counseling services (C) is meeting a student (S) for the first time. What are likely to be the different frames involved here? Do the participants seize or miss opportunities for contextualizing and offering accounts to be understood? What are the possibilities for the student's reframing the problem here? In your opinion, should the counselor suggest a way for the student to reframe the situation? Should the counselor help the student to adapt to the realities of college life? Or should the counselor simply be a good listener?

S: Here I am, right on schedule.

C: I'm glad you came by. Our conversation on the phone the other day reminded me of some interesting things about how we make decisions here about students. I'm hoping we have the time to get into those again—if not today, then maybe next time.

S: We need to talk again? I got the impression you were just going to hear me out about this problem of professors demanding a lot of class participation and then basing your grade on it. That's not right. I know as much about Shakespeare as anyone in class, and scored higher on every exam, but because I'm shy and don't like to pop off in class, I get a B, and some people with lower scores got As!

C: Well, no, we don't need to talk again if you don't want to. But maybe you'll want to. You're really angry.

S: Damn right I am.

C: It doesn't seem fair to you that class discussion can make such a big difference in how someone evaluates your learning.

S: The way I look at it, my role is to learn, and the teacher is supposed to tell me how well I'm doing that. What difference does it make how much I talk?

C: So the talk seems extra, an add-on to the class, and the real content of the class is in the plays and the sonnets. You're mad enough to take out that insulting ad in the campus paper. What do you suppose Dr. Smith was trying to accomplish by requiring attendance and class participation?

S: That's what I don't understand.

C: I can't speak for him, but I do know that when I plan a course, I think about how students don't just want to listen to lectures all the time. They learn a lot, it seems, by testing out ideas themselves in class. I try to encourage that, too.

S: I knew you'd take his side.

C: It doesn't feel like I'm taking his side. I'm trying to understand part of what might have motivated him. Let me hear more about your side, too, OK? What makes a class "good" for you?

framing, like communication, can be frozen. It is constantly in flux and can never be fully captured or described. If, in taking notes, you write down the words "exactly," you don't preserve the exact words at all. Your notebook omits the volume, rate, and passionate inflection that were part of the speech. Even an audio recording omits as much as it captures; the words and vocal inflections are there but without the visual cues that assist a contextual interpretation. A videotape omits or distorts a whole range of cues as well, such as odor, touch, and many micromovements of facial expression; in addition, videocameras tend to focus on the behavior of interviewees, often ignoring how interviewers contribute to the mood and sense of the moment. Further, you can

Box 5.1

Interviewers/Interviewees in Action   *Lawrence Grobel and Norman Mailer*

Recording conversations . . . allows you to concentrate more on what is being said, and to respond, without having to look up from your notebook as you try to write down everything that is being said. Still, it's a good idea to jot down phrases as you listen, especially if the person you're talking with likes to jump from subject to subject. That way you can look down at your notes and refer back to something you heard but might want to delve deeper into. (p. 37)

When Norman Mailer was asked how he felt about being interviewed, he said he always sat down with a general sense of woe, because "the interviewer serves up one percent of himself in the questions and the man who answers has to give back ninety-nine percent. I feel exploited the moment I step into an interview. Of course, once in a while where is such a thing as a good interview; but even then, the tape recorder eats up half the mood. It isn't the interview I really dislike so much as the tape recorder." (p. 33)

Source: Grobel (2004)

never freeze and keep the relational or psychological frames that made the interaction uniquely immediate for participants while they were talking.

Still, many interviewers want to remember as much of what was said as possible. What are some of the practical ways of doing that? In our book on journalistic interviewing (Killenberg & Anderson, 1989), we surveyed the advantages and disadvantages of three general methods: note taking, delayed note taking, and tape recording. Except for some examples and applications, this discussion borrows heavily from that survey.

Note Taking

Taking notes is obviously helpful for an interviewer, but it also aids the interviewee. Speakers whose listeners note their words pay close attention to their own speech. They focus on a topic in especially careful ways. They can observe which parts of their message are interesting or relevant for the listener. They are encouraged to take themselves seriously. (Of course, these factors can make people nervous as well, if they are insecure about their credibility or footing.)

Because of the many advantages of note taking, effective listeners in interviews won't generally consider it to be intrusive. Consider the following advantages of an optimum level of note taking in an interview:

- It alerts interviewers, within the frame of the conversation, to how this interaction connects to previous ideas, statements, or issues.

- It can capture pithy comments from speakers relatively unobtrusively and easily.

- It is efficient—reviewing notes is more reliable than memory, and easier than reviewing an entire recorded interview.

- It can be used on-the-spot to remind the listener of probes to be used later in the interview and can be a cumulative record of impressions, not just a series of quotes from the interviewee.

Box 5.2

Interviewers/Interviewees in Action   *Jack Mendelsohn and Martin Buber*

In his book on Unitarian religious philosophy, Jack Mendelsohn recounts his interview with the renowned philosopher of dialogue, Martin Buber:

> As he began to talk, I scribbled furiously. Suddenly there was silence, and when I looked up, Buber was smiling. "Mr. Mendelsohn," he said, "either you can take notes without really listening, or you can really listen without taking notes." It was said with no trace of harshness. Firmly, I closed my notebook and "really listened." He said, "Throughout the world, there is a spiritual front on which a secret, silent struggle is being waged between the desire to be on life's side and the desire to destroy. This is the most important front of all—more than any military, political, or economic front. It is the front on which *souls are moulded*."
>
> My question was the obvious one: "What can individuals do to tip the balance?"
>
> Buber gazed out the window for a moment; then he turned to me and said: "No one can chart a day-to-day course for anyone else. Life can only be determined by each situation as it arises. We all have our chances. From the time we rise in the morning until the time we retire at night we have meetings with others. Sometimes we even meet ourselves! We see our families at breakfast. We go to work with others. We meet people in the streets. We attend gatherings with others. Always there are others. What we do with each of these meetings is what counts. The future is more determined by this than by ideologies and proclamations."

Source: Mendelsohn (1985, p. 48)

Interestingly, Buber's response to Mendelsohn's main question can also be read as a response to the interview situation, in which we must always live for the immediate meeting. Although Mendelsohn surely did not hear Buber's comment as an instruction that interviewers should never take notes, he received a forceful reminder about this interviewee, on this occasion, on this topic.

- It is a constructive task that reminds interviewers to keep the focus on the interviewee, curbing the temptation to talk too much or interrupt.
- It provides a reliable signal to interviewees about what interviewers consider important, and this can encourage further elaboration (Gorden, 1980, pp. 222–223).
- It can document an interview in case of a later dispute, legal or otherwise; a record of the conversation can also explain subsequent actions, if necessary.

Despite its advantages, note taking can create problems, too:

- It can interrupt the flow of a conversation if done awkwardly or too extensively. (See the experience of Martin Buber in Box 5.2.)
- It can deflect listeners' attention from the visual cues that influence how words should be interpreted in the interview.
- It can enmesh inexperienced interviewers in the mechanics of their task so much that they neglect to listen for basic ideas, or fail to interpret accurately the frames from which the interviewee speaks.

- It can encourage a stenographic or passive role for the interviewer, limiting the potential for fresh or surprising insights that a more active conversational approach might encourage.

- It can, if done carelessly, mix the interviewer's words and frames with the interviewee's, producing inaccurate quotations and interpretations when the notes are consulted later. Does this happen often? One study of courtrooms (see Fitzgerald, 1987) compared reporters' attributed quotes to the actual trial transcripts; researchers found that nontrivial errors occurred in at least 50 percent of cases. One newspaper misquoted 45 percent of the time, and 39 percent of these misquotes were major errors of interpretation; another paper misquoted 71 percent of the time, with 67 percent of those defined by researchers as containing significant errors.

- It can encourage listeners to jot fragmentary impressions that will not make sense later, out of context, if the notes are allowed to become stale.

Notice that many problems of note taking are simply warnings and not reasons to avoid notes. Except for some persuasion-based and broadcast interviews, virtually all interviewers work hard to polish their note-taking skills (see Box 5.3). Interviewees are wise to consider taking notes as well, despite the fact that most of the literature focuses on interviewer note taking. When you're interviewed, for instance in an employer's disciplinary interview, you might want to note especially those comments from the other person that you could easily forget because of your emotional involvement.

Delayed Note Taking

Writer Truman Capote, the subject of popular biographical films in 2005 and 2006, was reputed to have an exceptional memory, which allowed him to interview an unusually wide range of people from small-town Kansans to Hollywood celebrities simply by engaging them in spontaneous conversation (R. P. Nelson, 1979, p. 149). Then, he would cloister himself in an apartment or motel room and spend hours reconstructing how his respondents told their stories, complete with fine detail and emotional nuance. Capote claimed that without notes or audiotape, he could achieve 97 percent accuracy in these narratives. Perhaps he did. Most listeners, however, including experienced professional interviewers, couldn't come close to that mark. Contemporary life simply doesn't tune our ears or minds to listen in that way. Capote was on to something, though. To a lesser extent, his approach can be seen in the styles of many active, creative, and conversational interviewers.

These interviewers know that in sensitive situations, respondents may be reluctant to speak at all, much less speak openly to someone hanging on every word with scratching pencil or the infallible memory of a minirecorder. Overt reminders that an interviewer wants to "capture" the words can feel like a threat to fence in the interviewee, who may resist. Some interviews, therefore, call for a trade-off: The notebook is left in the car with the recorder so the interviewee will feel more comfortable. Without notes and without tapes, however, how does the interviewer keep a record of the conversation? It's difficult, but possible.

The interviewer's technique in this situation, which we call **delayed note taking**, involves (1) clearing a block of time, preferably at least 30 minutes (for a brief interview),

Box 5.3

Reminders   *The Nuts and Bolts of Note Taking for Interviewers*

- Alert your interviewees to why you're taking notes, and let them know that this is to their advantage also. For example, you might say: "Would you mind if I jot some of these things down? I want to be sure I remember all your points later."

- Smaller notebooks are generally better than legal pads or full-sized tablets, especially if you don't have a table for support.

- Write in those moments when the speaker has already clarified the main point and might simply be rephrasing or adding examples. It frustrates interviewees to get to the nub of an idea just when a listener is concentrating on writing what they said a minute or two ago.

- If you start with note taking, don't stop later in the interview without explanation. Consider what it might suggest to the interviewee if you stop writing for a long time. Does she or he assume you're less interested now? That you've gotten what you wanted already and are only biding your time until you can leave? The quality of communication will surely suffer.

- Avoid writing full sentences, except for quotes. You're writing reminders to yourself, words to jog your memory, and not an essay. Although the

teaching of formal systems of shorthand is fading from the educational scene, you should develop your own version of shorthand. For example:

   & (and)

   cd, wd, sd (could, would, should)

   w/, w/o (with, without)

   # (amount, number)

   $ (money, dollars, cost)

   pos, neg (positive, negative)

   pol (politics, politician)

- Be especially alert to figures of speech and adjectives the interviewee returns to often in the conversation. Note these. They indicate someone's values and priorities.

- Make sure you get names and titles right. Double-check the spelling of a name or the exact title of an article or report with the interviewee. In spite of an occasional interruption, this attention to accuracy will reassure almost all interviewees.

- In closing the interview, ask something like, "Before I put away my notebook, is there anything specific or especially important that you'd like to stress? I want to be sure to jot it down now."

immediately following the session; (2) ensuring that this time will be uninterrupted; and (3) reconstructing the interview on paper in as much detail as possible. For some interviewers, such a task is relatively effortless, because they've trained their minds to recall details and register their importance. For the rest of us, it's a more difficult and arduous task of systematically quizzing ourselves on what was most important in the conversation. For example, consider:

- How did the interview begin? Who initiated the talk? What was the other's mood? What were the opening comments in conducting small talk?

- What were relevant details of the physical setting? If the interview took place in a room, what were its distinguishing features? If the interviewee made any choices that affected the nonverbal setting, such as chair placement or conversational distance, note them.

• What behavioral aspects of the interaction seemed meaningful? Fidgeting or nervous tics? Steady eye gaze? Locked jaw? A ready smile? Note all that you can think of. Develop tentative statements about how these behaviors might reflect the framing process of the other persona and how you and your task might have affected these outcomes.

• Note what you considered to be the *critical incidents*, or turning points, of the interview. What were its highs and lows? The main misunderstandings? Obvious points of agreement? What surprised you and what didn't? For every main idea, ask yourself which details could help explain it. Jot them down; such clues could be important in unexpected ways later (Did she meet her husband-to-be at a traffic accident, and is this consistent with her later impulsiveness as an investor? Did he not only collect vintage motorcycles, but vintage *red* ones?)

• What was vivid, or not, about the interviewee's choice of words? Even though you weren't taking notes on the spot, some comments probably made such a firm impression that you believe you can recall them exactly. Write them down, but be wary of your ability to remember exact wording; use quotation marks in your delayed notes only for quotes that you are certain about. For example, do you have much confidence that Mendelsohn's intricate Buber quotes are exact after you read that he took no notes? (See Box 5.2.) If in doubt, write a paraphrase, such as "She talked about how frustrating it was for PR directors to feel torn between the demands of upper management and the feelings of rank-and-file employees"). Or you might write what journalists call an **essence quote**, which captures the essence of the statement and employs a particularly vivid phrase you recall the interviewee saying (e.g., "Once, she said, she got 'french fried' by her boss when she published a particularly critical letter in the company newsletter").

• How did the interview end? Was it cordial? Abrupt? Did the interviewee invite you to ask more questions later if you had them? Did you promise to get back to her to check further facts or to share a story or report you may be writing? It is imperative that you make notes reminding yourself of any such agreements.

Don't delay or compromise on following through with delayed note taking if you have no other record of the interview. It's your only chance to be systematic. With every passing minute after the interview, you'll forget or misremember more details.

Delayed note taking (especially if you're good at it, as Capote was) has the following advantages:

• It is particularly useful following atypical interview situations, such as in a car on the way to an airport or a concert, or an interview "on the move" during a factory tour.

• It requires the interviewer to process impressions as well as content, so nonverbal details of context are often recalled more completely.

• It reduces the possibility that interviewees will practice a scripted set of sound bites to deliver intact; when they see that the interviewer is not recording exact wording, they're likely to talk more conversationally, in vernacular.

• It reduces the chances of signaling special interest in a point. Although interviewing is not usually full of competitive game playing, a social worker, for example, would not want to cue a father that what he's just said contradicts what his daughter described yesterday; or an ethnographic researcher interested in a community's cultural events would prefer to participate fully in a bowling tournament rather than call attention to another bowler's juicy turn of phrase. With the right training and reminders, the researcher will remember to record the comment later.

Disadvantages are also worth noting:

- It likely sacrifices interviewers' confidence in direct quotations.
- It discourages interviewers from using **probe notes**—those notes jotted down as reminders of questions or topics to bring up later in the interview.
- Its success depends on a skill of memorization that many listeners find hard to develop (although with practice it becomes much easier).
- It eats time. Interviewers need to schedule not only the interview, and perhaps the transportation to and from it, but also an extra significant block of time to be alone while reconstructing the interview's critical issues immediately afterward.
- It entails, for some interviewing tasks, significant violations of interviewees' frames and expectations.

Dexter (1970), analyzing the problems of interviewing experts in a field, is dubious about relying too much on delayed note taking:

> Many interviewers can train themselves, apparently, to get significant parts of an interview simply by recording it afterwards from memory. However, in the type of interviewing we are here describing, this seems needlessly risky. Most [professionals] will appreciate an interviewer's need to take notes, and taking notes will give an excuse for looking back and reflecting if an interview takes an unexpected turn. (p. 86)

Thorough interviewers might combine delayed note taking with brief or sketchy notes from the conversation. This minimizes the negatives and accentuates the positives. In addition, as you will see, there are good reasons to schedule this extra note-taking time even if you tape the interview. Although your tape picks up the words, it will miss your emerging impressions and your all-important gut feelings about relevance, truthfulness, and interest. These need to be recorded, too.

Audio Recording

World-famous author Gabriel Garcia Marquez (1997) is an outspoken critic of contemporary journalism. One of the "demons" of journalism's drama, he believes, is the tape recorder (p. 32). For him, audio recording elevates mere repetition like a "digital parrot" and undermines all a journalist really needs: "the notebook, foolproof ethics, and a pair of ears" (p. 33). That will keep the interviewee talking. "Maybe," he believes, "the solution is to return to the lowly little notebook so that the journalist can edit intelligently as he listens and relegate the tape recorder to the role of witness" (p. 34). The Garcia Marquez statement, bluntly included in a 1996 speech at the International Press Association, vibrates with implications. We could disagree with him on several points (when did an entire profession ever have "foolproof" ethics? Recording technology is demonic?), but it's more important to underscore several of his underlying points.

Trying Out Your Skills

"Tape record a television or radio celebrity profile interview, perhaps conducted by Anderson Cooper of CNN, Terry Gross of National Public Radio, or Barbara Walters of ABC. Imagine yourself in the role of the interviewer who has to write an essay about this interview, but do not take notes while the tape is playing. Then, immediately following your viewing, give yourself 30 minutes of uninterrupted time to practice delayed note-taking skills:

- List all information that could be important for your article, which you hope will appear in *Rolling Stone* or *Vanity Fair*.

- Make notes about the emotional tone of the interviewee's disclosures. Was he or she excited to be interviewed? Bored? Preoccupied with nitpicking the questions?

- Make notes about topics you'd like to return to in a follow-up interview.

- Write down any striking quotations—short or long—that you remember with confidence.

Then, replay the tape and check out your memory. What do you need to work on to enhance your skill at delayed note taking? (This exercise will also enhance your ability to take notes *during* the interview.)

First, we think he's suggesting that the ultimate goal of an interviewer is not simply to capture the interview, but to apply information or insight from it to some useful purpose. In other words, the larger frame for interviewing should always be further communication, and neither party should forget this. Journalists and writers are interviewing someone to accomplish something else, such as to write an honest account of a distant military maneuver, to interpret the motivations of city council members for those who can't attend the meetings, or to give us more insight into how a president makes decisions. Too much reliance on recording puts the interview itself on a pedestal, almost as if it's a stand-alone package of meaning.

Second, Garcia Marquez implies that taping can make journalists lazy if its effect is to substitute a machine for the human effort of listening and interpreting. Understanding is a matter of framing, as we've seen, and the recorder itself never frames anything—it only reproduces talk.

Third, and especially significantly, he does not ask interviewers to avoid recording their interviews. He agrees that the machine should be used, but relegates it to the "role of witness." By doing this, interviewers can be alert listeners and still have corroboration and extra context for their interpretations later if they need it.

Contemporary technology may have progressed beyond cassettes to microchips, but the issues remain the same—and many interviewers still prefer the archival potential of taping. Therefore, we use "taping" and "recording" synonymously.

Some forms of interviewing never involve taping, such as brief survey research interviews conducted in malls or the workplace. They rely on clear-cut or forced-choice responses that the interviewer simply marks on a score sheet. Other forms inherently involve taping, and the record they produce can be invaluable. For example, cross-cultural interviewers and discourse analysts interview for the express purpose of generating transcripts of talk they will analyze later. Courtroom questioning of lawyers is preserved as an official transcript produced by court reporters who use special transcription machines. The transcriber's exact account serves the same purpose as a tape recorder. Oral historians use tapes to construct sensitive narrative portraits from a person's memories, using the interviewee's own words. However, most interviewers face a clear decision: To tape or not to tape? Consider these advantages of tape recording interviews:

• It creates an artifact of the interview that can be referred to later for clarification, support, or documentation. Although no interviewer plans on being sued, litigation is a constant threat, and professionals understand that a tape can serve as an insurance policy.

• It gives interviewers increased flexibility and versatility in noting contextual and nonverbal factors, as they don't have to listen precisely for how things are worded. That can always be picked up later. More attention can be paid to speech style, how an interviewee dismisses criticism, the development of central ideas over longer periods of time, and personal quirks and idiosyncracies.

• It flatters some interviewees, who are pleased that someone might value their words so much as to keep them. Similarly, it reassures interviewees who are concerned that a listener might miss something along the way.

• It helps interviewers operating under adverse conditions such as extreme cold or bad lighting, when it might be impractical to take thorough notes.

• It particularly assists interviewers listening for quotes. They now have proof of exact word choices. Professional writers know, along with their editors and supervisors, that quotations propel a story and pique a reader's interest.

• It provides interviewers and interviewees with a valuable educational tool. They can review tapes to hear the progress they're making as learners, and to analyze their mistakes.

Taping creates problems along with the advantages, of course. Here are some potential dilemmas faced by those who would tape conversations (see Box 5.4 for practical reminders about taping decisions):

• It intimidates some interviewees. Oriana Fallaci (1963), famous for her celebrity interviews, found that "getting them to talk in front of a machine that is recording every pause and every breath is, in 50 percent of the cases, fraught with tension (p. ix). It encourages an "Uh oh—I'm on the spot" frame for these interviews. (Do you think this factor has changed at all for celebrities in the years since 1963?)

• It can discourage candid disclosure. If someone is producing an exact record of your speech, then misstatements could easily come back to haunt you. Politicians, lawyers, arbitrators, and others who are either carefully monitored or often in the public eye are particularly sensitive to taping. They may not avoid your questions if a recorder is turned on, but you can be sure their answers will either be practiced or worded with exceptional ambiguity. One public figure we interviewed for a book on journalistic interviewing told us, "I end up talking to the tape recorder instead of the reporter."

• It isn't selective. The tape may be an hour long, with only two or three minutes of relevant material dispersed throughout in different sections. These gems can be difficult and time consuming to locate, even using digital recorders.

Box 5.4

Reminders *The Nuts and Bolts of Tape Recording for Interviewers*

• Inform your interviewees that you would like to tape, and request permission. Concealing the recorder or "wearing a wire" may be necessary sometimes for undercover cops, and certainly leads to exciting movie plots, but it is taboo for virtually all professional interviewers. The literature in communication and related fields often includes debates about exceptions based on a so-called watchdog philosophy of journalism, for example, but the majority of interviewers in organizational, governmental, academic, and personal life should not even consider deceptive taping as an option. Beyond the ethical concerns, it is illegal in 15 states to record speech without a person's consent.

• Keep the agreed-on taping as unobtrusive as possible. Use the smallest good recorder you can find, and put it a couple of feet off to the side of the conversation, where you and your partner will not fixate on it. It will probably need no further adjustment. Today's built-in microphones are quite sensitive and generally omnidirectional. They should pick up the entire interview, plus some ambient room sounds. Your best taping strategy after setup is to have no strategy; forget the machine except when you need to turn over or change the tape.

• Check to make sure the recorder works before arriving at the interview. Use new or fully charged batteries unless you're certain that an electrical outlet is handy.

• Take **tape-sensitive notes**. That is, use your notebook to write important points about where on the tape a comment or interchange will be found. For example: "Most concerned re $: t/1, s/2, 1st 5" could be your note reminding you that the interviewee was most concerned about his salary increase in a comment you'll find on tape 1, in approximately the first five minutes of side 2.

• After the interview, decide how you'll process or keep the recording. You have several options: Use **transcription** when you need or want to turn the entire interview into printed text for later analysis. This can involve laborious hours alone for you (or someone you trust), listening and typing carefully to get the wording transcribed exactly. Software that converts recorded speech into text is available, but it can be tricky to use effectively. Use **selective transcription** to listen with your goals and maybe your interview schedule in mind, transcribing only those sections of the interview (usually only from the interviewee's turns) that are directly relevant to your purposes. Use **reduced note taking** when you want to listen to the tape while reading the notes you took during the original conversation; in effect, you're using the tape to "reduce" the interviewee's words so that you can make changes or fill any gaps in your existing notes. Use **quote searching** to listen to the tape or digital record for quotes that will assist in meeting the goals you had for the interview in the first place. Finally, **archiving** means that you simply label the tape or digital record clearly (who, what was discussed, when, where, why) and keep it along with pertinent notes in a safe place.

• It can encourage laziness. Some interviewers fall victim to the "I can always find it on the tape" syndrome.

• It can be unreliable. The well-known Murphy's law says that if something can go wrong, it probably will. At the crucial moment, in hard-won interviews, batteries will fail or the cassette will jam.

Beyond the Basics

The framing concept has many implications that are readily extended and applied. Students of interviewing, for example, could look at conflict management in the interview, at deception detection, or at self-understanding. However, the conceptual umbrella of frame analysis provides an excellent opportunity for exploring one issue in particular: how the current cultural controversy about language and multiculturalism might affect interviewers and interviewees.

Political Correctness, Language, and Interviewing

Much of interpersonal style depends on nonverbal cues, but people usually interview each other to obtain information verbally. Interviews are focused language events, ideally cooperative, and designed to generate additional information or insight for one or both parties. Language is not only a medium of communicative exchange but also a reality-defining environment in which we exist; it is not only what we say to each other, but also the basis for our critical thinking and the interior dialogues that enrich our lives. With flexibility of language comes flexibility of thought, flexibility of planning, and—perhaps most important of all—flexibility in considering how different others' worlds might be. Language allows us to decenter; with it, we transcend ourselves and imagine the standpoints of others.

Interviewers who are not savvy about contemporary language trends are likely to miss important meanings. In recent years, two trends have dominated cultural assumptions about language, especially in the United States, Western Europe, and Africa. Although there are multiple perspectives on this dialogue, and although our approximations could never capture the full complexity of the arguments, it might be helpful to flesh out these two basic positions. The first trend, which has been termed *multiculturalism*, or at times, *cultural pluralism*, emphasizes that language is intimately connected with the cultural identities of all who speak and write. Society, according to the multiculturalist perspective, must listen well to be able to respect and accept the positive contributions each group, with its identity, can bring to the overall culture. Each identity brings with it a particular linguistic way of being in the world. The problems and successes of intercultural communication, therefore, are framed in terms of linguistic versatility and respect. Multiculturalists believe that language is not a neutral tool or medium for conveying thought, but that language is inevitably charged with multiple points of view and can never be completely neutral.

Multiculturalists interested in interviewing, for example, might suggest that interviewers and interviewees, especially if they represent relatively privileged social groups, keep three guidelines foremost in mind: First, they should *decenter* from their own unique perspectives while acknowledging that language is an important expression of cultural identity. Decentering doesn't mean renouncing your own identity but, rather, anticipating how you'll be understood or misunderstood by others with different linguistic habits. Second, they should *familiarize* themselves with different language styles and labels. That is, you are responsible for becoming informed about how various other cultural groups might be employing language. Third, they should *choose language with respect and sensitivity* so as not to inflame or insult other cultural groups unnecessarily.

An alternative perspective, which we might call **linguistic conservatism**, contests the assumptions of a multiculturalist philosophy. In the sense we're using the term, *conservatism* doesn't refer to conventional politics but to the goal of preserving or conserving language as a common shared experience that each person can assume all others of intelligence will employ in similar ways. Linguistic conservatives believe language is essentially a neutral medium for communication and that the goal of speakers and writers is to achieve accurate interpretations in listeners and readers. Effective communication is achieved when communication becomes, in this way, more efficient: Can you predict accurately what the other's meanings will be as a result of your word choices? Linguistic conservatives suggest that language is a system of usage guidelines legislated by educated elite speakers and writers.

Linguistic conservatives interested in interviewing would offer somewhat different advice for participants. First, they should *learn and use language as the "common coin of the realm."* That is, the best policy is to educate yourself to speak correctly, "call it as you see it," and then expect others to understand you. Second, they should *avoid linguistic compromise.* That is, the best mark of respect is to judge others by their ability to meet the same standards of language that should apply to all professionals. Third, they should *regard cultural groups' objections to some labels as oversensitivity.* For example, the differences between the terms *African American* and *Negro* are thought by some to be merely semantic and the choice shouldn't affect how sincere people relate to each other. According to this view, communicators are hindered by constantly worrying about their speech offending others, and we should all become less defensive about language.

Linguistic conservatives disdain what has come to be called **political correctness**, a belief of some critics that language use is increasingly controlled by the political and cultural agendas of minorities. By charging political correctness, linguistic conservatives and their allies assert that multiculturalists unfairly try to enforce certain ways of speaking on everyone, whether others want to use them or not. Some regard political correctness as a relatively benign way of joking with ourselves about our sensitivity to language (witness the many greeting cards and jokes about "PC," and the popularity of the term in television sitcoms and news networks). In some quarters, though, this phenomenon is not described in a lighthearted way but in the context of problems like "culture wars." In 1990, when *Newsweek* ran a cover story warning readers to "Watch What You Say," some observers thought the phenomenon might be transitory. Yet it has persisted, and more recent authors (Lakoff, 2001; Ravitch, 2003) show how the groups sometimes square off in dueling positions.

President George H. W. Bush's 1991 commencement address at the University of Michigan made serious claims:

> The notion of political correctness has ignited controversy across the land. And although the movement arises from the laudable desire to sweep away the debris of racism, sexism, and hatred, it replaces old prejudices with new ones. It declares certain topics off-limits, certain expressions off-limits, even certain gestures off-limits. What began as a

cause for civility has soured into a cause of conflict and even censorship. Disputants treat sheer force—getting their foes punished or expelled, for instance—as a substitute for the power of ideas. Throughout history, attempts to micromanage casual conversation have only incited distrust. They've invited people to look for insult in every word, gesture, action. And in their own Orwellian way, crusades that demand correct behavior crush diversity in the name of diversity. (quoted in Wilson, 1995, p. 8)

The president's speech, in fact, ignited more controversy, with a spate of television shows and newspapers editorializing about the repressions inherent in acknowledging diversity by changing our ways of speaking about it. One critic, representing a more or less multiculturalist point of view (Wilson, 1995), replied by analyzing the language of the president's charge itself. He notes that the speech denied the reality of prejudices: "which are called 'old' prejudices, as if no one believes them anymore" (p. 8). It dismisses racism: "which no longer exists except as 'debris,' since charges of prejudice are created by hypersensitive minorities who 'look for insult'" (p. 8). And it suggests that

> the danger to freedom comes not from racists (who can be dealt with using "reason") but from the "political extremists" who "roam the land, abusing the privilege of free speech, setting citizens against one another on the basis of their class or race." In this turnabout, it is not racists but leftists who abuse free speech (which has suddenly been transformed from a right into a privilege). When Bush said that "such bullying is outrageous," he referred not to those who use racial epithets to abuse other people but to the "extremists" who criticize racism. (Wilson, 1995, pp. 8–9)

Clearly, both sides engage in volatile rhetoric, and this issue tends to divide people. Each side accuses the other of political bullying. Even bringing up the controversy in a textbook could be seen as inappropriate by some. However, closing your eyes to the disagreement won't make it vanish. Your very language as an interviewer or interviewee could inadvertently make some kind of statement about endorsing cultural pluralist or linguistic conservative positions. With that in mind, and without entrenching ourselves in the anger of conservative versus liberal, right versus left, are there ways students of interviewing can acknowledge the controversy while still negotiating their way through the thicket of language decisions they must make?

Understanding the process of framing provides a key. With this concept, you can create a personal style of communication that respects a cultural pluralism that is not artificially or tyrannically politically correct. In our opinion, no one taking a position on interpersonal language can afford to dismiss the increasingly pluralist character of our cultural landscape. You may, if you choose, disagree with some arguments from the multiculturalists, but it is difficult to deny that the world itself is becoming increasingly multicultural (Childs, 2003; Dallmayr, 2002). It is no longer possible to presume there is only one "right" way of speaking.

Framing and Acceptance-Oriented Language

In this book we've tried to frame our ideas and examples in terms of gender-neutral and culturally sensitive language. We do this out of a sense of inclusiveness and fairness (you can assume we're multiculturally oriented in this way). But political correctness, narrowly defined, is not our concern. We aren't trying to conform to what someone told us we'd better do, or else. Instead, we're reaching for a more mundane ideal: We simply want to communicate clearly about a sometimes complex topic with as many readers as possible. We've tried to choose language that "lets you in" consistently without pre-judging the kind of "you" you are, and shuts no one out. We may fail more often than we'd like. Most writers are only dimly aware of their own biases, and much racism and sexism resides in unexamined nooks and crannies of everyday figures of speech. Yet our attempt to shape meaningful ideas using language that excludes no one is exactly what we suggest as the interviewer or interviewee's most reasonable path through the choices of linguistic framing.

Words always create consequences. What we call something or someone frames how we see and hear that thing or person, and the label is also noticed socially. When previous generations were using "he" and "man" virtually universally as generic words, they were inadvertently making it more difficult for women to see themselves as actors in the wider social world. If mature African American men continue to be called "boys" when white speakers typically don't refer to white Americans of the same age in the same way, who should be surprised that such references are heard as condescending and offensive?

Some might respond, "Wait a minute. Aren't we getting too sensitive here? These are only words, after all. It doesn't really matter what I call you, as long as it's not a put-down and I treat you with respect." As comforting as this sounds, it does not square well with the findings of social research. For example, in gender relations, there is evidence that "clearly indicate[s] that *man* in the sense of male so overshadows *man* in the sense of human being as to make the latter use inaccurate and misleading for purposes both of conceptualizing and communicating" (Miller & Swift, 1991, p. 28). In social science experiments, both men and women, young and old, tend to draw pictures of males when such references are used, indicating that in their minds the terms are far from truly generic. Whether or not speakers who use a supposedly generic "man" mean for it to refer equally to women, it is not evidently interpreted as such within the listener's frame. In listeners' psychology, such words appear to refer primarily to male experience.

Just as multiculturalists are rankled by the refusal to use people's preferred terms for their own group or their own experiences, linguistic conservatives are rankled by what they perceive as warped and awkward neologisms to achieve an artificial inclusiveness. Perhaps the most common object of derision is the "-person" designation in gender relations, and some people get quite upset about it. They believe women can reasonably be thought of as "chairmen," "postmen," and "freshmen" with little or no fuss. It does sound odd to say "postperson" or "freshperson," and many jokes are premised on such awkward constructions. Some changes create new problems while solving old ones. Yet when people are offended by a label, does it make sense to continue the offensiveness just because changing the label sounds unusual? All linguistic changes sound strange at first hearing. What about reframing the controversy from an I win–you lose situation to a usage that's just as clear, with neither set of emotional baggage? In interviews, we suggest you practice finding alternate terms that are just as accurate but not as awkward. For example, you might refer to neither chairmen nor chairwomen, or even chairpersons, but to "chairs" (it means the same thing); similarly, you can avoid "postman," "postwoman," and "postperson" by simply saying "mail carrier" (see Box 5.5).

Box 5.5

Reminders   *Acceptance-Oriented Language for Interviewing*

- Read widely in popular newspapers and magazines (e.g., the *Washington Post, Newsweek, Harper's*) and in academic or professional journals in your field (e.g., public relations, advertising, training, fund-raising) to get a feel for the acceptable ways of referring to people and groups. Virtually all publications now demand inclusive and gender-neutral language that recognizes diversity. If such inclusive constructions as "he or she" sound awkward to you, current style manuals list good strategies for recasting your words to achieve clarity without making reference to gender.

- Whenever you perceive a contradiction between a term that seems comfortable and one that appears to exclude or perhaps offend persons because of their gender, race, ethnic affiliation, religion, disability, age, or sexual preference, choose the inclusive term even if it sounds awkward. Remember, awkwardness is in the experience of the listener, too. If you know that a specific term risks offending even some women, some people of color, some gays and lesbians, or some older citizens, why would you want that result in even some of the cases? Even if a black woman happens not to prefer the term *African American,* it is unlikely that she'd find it offensive.

- Remind yourself that inclusive language tends to be technically more accurate. For example, if you choose to say a woman is a "chairperson" or "chairwoman," these are accurate terms (at different levels of generality). However, a generic label of "chairman" is inaccurate whenever it refers to a woman in that position.

- Perform a personal bias check. Ask yourself: Which groups do I often make fun of? Which groups do I just not understand at all? Which groups appear to have clear-cut characteristics that I dislike? In the answers to these questions lie clues to your pattern of bias and to your

frames for communicating with individuals who may be members of such groups.

- Before starting a series of important interviews, do a language check on yourself. Interview several of your friends in informal settings to get their reactions to the following questions: With what terms do I customarily refer to women? To men? To those from ethnic or racial groups other than my own? To controversial groups in political and social life? The answers may alert you to some potential linguistic minefields.

- Sensitize yourself to "red flag" messages that signal, perhaps unintentionally, either that you're insensitive to another group's experience, or that you consider large numbers of different people to lead essentially similar lives. For example, Marsha Houston and Julia Wood (1996) identify a list of phrases that might be "red flags when used by members of privileged classes and ethnic groups in conversation with members of nonprivileged classes and ethnic groups":

  "What's the black perspective on this?"

  "I've suffered discrimination too."

  "I know how you feel about racism/classism."

  "I think of you as just like me."

  "You're really exceptional."

  "Your people . . ."

  "It's remarkable how far you've come."

  "Personally, I've never discriminated against Hispanics, Asian Americans, working-class people" (and so on).

  "I've experienced sexism, so I understand racism." (p. 53)

- Consult published guidelines for more specific advice and answers to specific problems. We mention two in "The Interview Bookshelf" at the end of this chapter.

Making Your Decision

- Return to the beginning of the chapter and review the example of the Sonya–Rose employment interview. If you were Rose (interviewee), would you be tempted to metacommunicate? Offer an account? If so, how would you do so? At what point in the interview would it be most appropriate?

- Journalists and research interviewers are sometimes tempted to tape interviews when the respondent is unaware of the recording. This creates obvious frame disparities, and the tactic has generated significant controversy. Consider the following policies from the codes of ethics of daily newspapers.

From the New York Times:
"Staff members may not record private conversations without the prior consent of all parties to the conversations. In jurisdictions where recordings made secretly are legal, only the top manager of a news department may make an exception to this rule, and only after consultation with our legal department."

From the Kansas City Star:
"HIDDEN CAMERAS: The use of hidden cameras and surreptitious tape recording devices is to be avoided, except in rare cases when they are the only ways to get an important story or photo. Advance approval of a managing editor is required.

TAPING PHONE CONVERSATIONS: In most cases, inform a source before taping a telephone conversation. To make an exception—for example, if informing the source might compromise a story of compelling public importance—seek permission from your supervisor."

From the San Antonio Express-News:
"[Employees should] use their professional judgment in deciding whether to tell a source that the interview is being taped. Texas is a 'one-party' consent state, and you are allowed to tape record without the other party's consent. You may want to inform the source you are taping as a courtesy, but disclosure is not required. You should, however, inform the source if the tape will be used for broadcast on the Web, radio or television. Also, some states require both parties to consent to taping. When conducting an interstate phone interview, it is generally advisable to tell the other party if you are taping."

(Source for newspaper policies: American Society of Newspaper Editors "Codes of Ethics," 2006)

If you were a working journalist applying for jobs at these two papers, with which policy would you feel most comfortable? Suppose a managing editor from each paper interviews you, asking how you feel about the taping policy. What would you say to each editor?

- With the stipulation that no one necessarily fits any category completely, do you consider yourself primarily a multiculturalist when it comes to language frames, or a linguistic conservative? Imagine that you've been asked to conduct a series of interviews in Catholic churches throughout a major urban area (think about your nearest large city to respond to this question), for the purpose of determining parishioners' attitudes toward the local archdiocese. How do your feelings and impressions about political responses to language affect how you'll prepare?

Summary

Far from being a simple activity of speaking and listening, interviews also involve complex interpretations of people and information. The process of framing, originally discussed by social scientists Gregory Bateson and Erving Goffman, helps interviewers and interviewees get their priorities straight. Those who think they're good at asking questions and providing answers may not automatically do well at glimpsing the larger pattern in which those questions and answers could be understood.

Effective interviews involve skillful framing. This chapter suggests some abstract appreciations, but concentrates on presenting practical and concrete suggestions for improving your awareness of how people co-construct meaning. We describe four fundamental skills of framing in "The Basics": metacommunicating, contextualizing, offering accounts, and reframing. These skills are then placed in the practical context of how to record and recall what you've learned in the interview. An interviewer's choices of note taking and taping often dictate how an interviewee will choose to frame replies. In "Beyond the Basics," we introduced the contemporary controversy about political correctness, and then applied that framework to making language choices that signal your acceptance of others' perspectives.

The Interview Bookshelf

On the basic concept of framing:

Goffman, E. (1974). *Frame analysis*. New York: Harper Colophon.

The *source on the concept of framing. Although written at a fairly high level of sophistication, Goffman's work is enjoyed by a wide range of readers because he includes so many great examples.*

On an interview study of framing in everyday life:

Belenky, M. F., Clinchy, B. M., Goldberger, N. R., & Tarule, J. M. (1986). *Women's ways of knowing: The development of self, voice, and mind*. New York: Basic Books.

An eye-opening book about how women's frames, and how they communicate about them, are often different from men's. Many narratives are presented in the unique voices of thoughtful women, and the authors relate the interviewees' stories to other research in psychology, communication, and politics.

On how storytellers develop narratives in different contexts of listening:

Bauman, R. (1986). *Story, performance, and event: Contextual studies of oral narrative*. Cambridge, UK: Cambridge University Press.

Bauman studied Texas storytellers for over 15 years and found that much of their art depended on how contexts and frames could signal what was heard as truth, what was heard as playful deception, and what was heard as tall tale.

On how an interviewer could establish a new frame:

Hartshorn, N. (1996). *Catch: A discovery of America*. Denver, CO: MacMurray & Beck.

The author threw some ball gloves and baseballs into his car trunk along with a tape recorder and notebook, then hit the road to interview people "in search of a conversation." Along the way, he found the extraordinary in "ordinary" people and the accessible sides of several celebrities. His method? To ask folks to talk while they played catch with him—an unusual frame that enabled fresh kinds of communicating.

On inclusive language:

Dumond, V. (1990). *The elements of nonsexist usage: A guide to inclusive spoken and written English*. New York: Prentice Hall.

Schwartz, M., & The Task Force on Bias-Free Language of the Association of American University Presses. (1995). *Guidelines for bias-free writing*. Bloomington: University of Indiana Press.

These two books help clarify the difficult language choices that interviewers and interviewees face. Dumond includes a variety of options that avoid offending others while expressing your intentions succinctly, and a glossary of alternative nonsexist terms. Schwartz's book goes beyond gender to suggest how your language can be sensitive to differences of race, ethnicity, citizenship and nationality, religion, disabilities and medical conditions, sexual orientation, and age. Her annotated bibliography on inclusive language is also valuable.

Chapter Six

Interviews in Journalism

LEARNING GOALS

After reading this chapter, you should be able to

- **Compare and contrast traditional images and methods of interviewing with emerging concepts of the journalistic interview as a form of dialogue**

- **Recognize the differences among various types of journalistic interviews**

- **Understand the facets of interviews in journalism, from purpose to postinterview assessment**

- **Explain the different types of record keeping by reporters**

- **Discuss the ethical concerns journalists and their interviewees face**

Baseball legend Pete Rose stood in the afterglow of a 55-second ovation by fans at Game 2 of the 1999 World Series in Atlanta. For one night, he was back in baseball, given a respite from his lifetime ban for gambling on games as a manager of the Cincinnati Reds. Rose and a group of major league stars had just been recognized for their selection to the All-Century Team. Because of his ban, Rose wasn't eligible for baseball's Hall of Fame, and the fans, in part, wanted it known that they felt he deserved the honor. After the pregame ceremony, Rose faced NBC reporter Jim Gray. As Gray began his interview, Rose, still beaming, probably assumed they'd be chatting amiably about Rose's past exploits on the baseball diamond. Gray had another game plan.

Gray quickly broached the gambling controversy, asking Rose why he wouldn't just admit he bet on games in violation of the rules of Major League Baseball. Rose took offense, and said, "I'm not going to admit to something that didn't happen. It's too festive a night to worry about it" (Caesar, 1999, p. C5). Yet Gray thought he knew differently: Baseball had

Veteran newspaper reporter and editor Wendell Cochran . . . told me in an e-mail exchange that "I think interviewing is perhaps the least-appreciated and least-studied skill in journalism. There is an assumption that 'everyone' can talk and ask questions."

That's a serious ouch. In fact, it's an indictment of how we prepare for and practice our craft. If journalists aren't well-trained in the skills of interviewing, there is a much greater chance that we'll fall short in achieving ethical and excellent journalism. If we aren't proficient at asking the right questions at the right time, we'll miss on accuracy, fall short on context, and stumble on fairness. During this time of serious self-examination of journalism and journalists—not to mention the scrutiny of the public—it's essential to consider the role that interviewing skills—or the lack thereof—plays in how we measure up.

Bob Steele, Poynter Online
(http://www.poynter.org/content/content_view.asp?id=37661)

overwhelming evidence that Rose had, in fact, violated the rules by his gambling. Gray refused to change the subject to a happier frame, and pressed his question about evidence held by the commissioner. Rose's anger and resistance made the interview tense but newsworthy. Neither man backed down; it was a rare, unscripted moment of real interaction on television.

Afterward, angry fans bombarded network phone lines with objections, and players at the World Series claimed Gray clearly disrespected Rose. Some media observers said Gray ambushed Rose to make headlines for himself. But not everyone blamed Gray. Callers pointed out that Rose shouldn't have been surprised by the questions, as he'd just had a press conference at which he'd responded to many of the same issues in a more even-tempered way. His unqualified denial of wrongdoing in a live interview challenged Gray to follow up by confronting Rose—thus creating the tension. According to an Associated Press account ("Fans Upset with Gray's Interview," 1999), Murray Chass, a *New York Times* sportswriter, said, "I thought it was the best TV interview I've ever seen. It was appropriate. It was not overdone. Rose has put himself in position to be pressed like that" (p. 7). One of baseball's investigators familiar with the case said that Gray "had more guts than anyone I've ever seen," and a former baseball commissioner put the interchange in perspective as an interview when he commented: "For Pete to just stand there and look Jim Gray in the eye and deny he bet on baseball, it's obviously a challenge that any interviewer can't let go" (p. 7).

What journalists can and can't let go is a useful point to begin an inquiry into the role of interviewing in journalism. Some reporters act aggressively in interviews because they tend to frame their work as a quest for hard-won truth; theirs is a fact-finding mission in the name of the public's right to know. At times they might become so aggressive, cloaked in the First Amendment, that they unrealistically conclude that everyone owes them full and immediate answers on demand, because they're doing democracy's work. Tensions are inevitable. The public needs strong and assertive questions for public figures, and it shouldn't be surprised when interviewees maintain a wary guard, mindful of how some reporters might appear—nosy, rude, and arrogant. Not surprisingly, when neither side expects a comfortable, productive experience, the result can be a self-fulfilling prophecy.

Some news interviews may indeed be adversarial, but most go well. Given the predispositions of committed people, the challenge is often for journalists and newsmakers to work together, even in hard-news situations. In "The Basics," we discuss the traditional view of journalistic interviewing and compare it with more recent forms. We'll present an inventory of interview types that will help you understand how news is made by interviewing. In the last section of "The Basics," you'll learn about the fundamentals of news-related interviewing, insights that can be applied to a wide variety of information-gathering tasks other professionals face. "Beyond the Basics" focuses on the complex ethics of journalistic interviews, concluding with a discussion of the satisfactions of doing journalism well.

The Basics

Tradition and the News Interview

The interview has been a basic tool of journalists since the late 19th century. Media sociologist Michael Schudson (1998) has noted that although American journalists relied little on it before the Civil War, it had become so commonplace by 1880—despite attacks that it was a "barbaric contrivance"—that visitors from Europe saw it as "a distinctly American contribution to journalism" (p. 181; see also Schudson, 2003, p. 81). News, after all, is shaped by the words of legislators, judges, police chiefs, celebrities, athletes, victims, and victimizers, and Americans wanted firsthand accounts. In journalism, the adage that actions speak louder than words should be rethought; reporters and editors know that words *are* deeds. Schudson (1994) describes the remarkable influence of the news interview when he writes:

> The interview is the fundamental act of contemporary journalism. Reporters rely overwhelmingly on interviews; according to a study of Washington reporters in the 1980s, journalists depend so heavily on interviews that they use no documents at all in nearly three-quarters of the stories they write. (p. 565)

Journalists interview to satisfy the imperative of the news story: answering the who, what, when, where, why, and how of events and issues. Journalists deal in attributed facts, and interviews provide attribution. The interview also goes beyond the facts, drawing emotions, opinions, and speculation from newsmakers, often in their own words. These revelations form the essence of news.

The traditional formula of the news interview puts journalists in control. The reporter asks questions, and someone journalists call a news "source" responds. The interview appears to belong to the reporter; the interviewee is expected to provide what the journalist needs. In its bare-bones form, the news interview is economical, expedient, and valuable; it can also, given its formula, be impersonal, manipulative, and unproductive. Unfortunately, many journalists' knowledge of interviewing rests on anecdotes, folklore, and trial and error. Rarely are they aware of the solid research that could improve their skills. As the authors of *The Investigative Reporter's Handbook* claim, "Many journalists concede their shortcomings when it comes to finding documents. But few admit to shortcomings in locating and interviewing sources. Too often, they are overestimating their abilities" (Houston, Bruzzese, & Weinberg, 2002, p. 82).

Many journalists also assume interviewing comes naturally, and for some it does seem natural. However, even those with a seemingly instinctive talent are exposed to questionable advice in some newsrooms and classrooms. Here is an example from a leading introductory textbook in reporting: "When you have to ask tough questions, blame someone else." That kind of tactic isn't going to go over well with most people, who will readily recognize it as a ploy. It suggests that the reporter is playing games and not being forthright; it reinforces stereotypes in a profession that has enough trouble with its reputation already.

Writer Janet Malcolm (1990), in a controversial observation that polarized the community of journalists, helped reinforce that reputation: "Every journalist who is not too stupid or too full of himself to notice what is going on knows that what he does is morally indefensible. He is a kind of confidence man, preying on people's vanity, ignorance, or loneliness, gaining their trust and betraying them without remorse" (p. 3). Malcolm exaggerated, intentionally perhaps, in claiming that all reporters will go to unsavory extremes for a story. Critics (Anson, 1996) say that *Washington Post* reporter Bob Woodward, an icon for exposing President Nixon's role in the Watergate scandal, fits Malcolm's description. One critic, Judy Belushi, widow of comedian John Belushi, claims Woodward betrayed her in writing the book *Wired*, a devastating account of her husband's drug and alcohol abuse. "[Woodward] seemed so honest," she said. "He would say, over and over, 'John was a wonderful man. We must tell his story.'" Expecting a warm portrait, Judy Belushi helped open celebrity doors for Woodward. "I was like a Pavlovian dog," she said (p. 136). Woodward also allegedly told colleagues how he would get the girlfriend of Washington, DC Mayor Marion Barry to cooperate: "I'll play with her kid," he said. His colleagues said he did just that, and the mother, charmed, opened up to him.

Such instances might ring true to a public accustomed to stereotypes. In fairness to Woodward and all journalists, one-sided criticisms like these often come from disgruntled interviewees, including celebrities or politicians with ulterior motives. Talking to children and building rapport aren't inherently bad methods of interviewing. Journalism, however, suffers from an image of manipulation. Reporters are often driven by an overarching commitment to get to the truth, to tell the story. How far a journalist should go for a story remains a subject of sharp disagreement in the profession. A larger question, however, hasn't been as thoroughly addressed: Is there a way to get stories by collaborating with, not exploiting, interviewees?

The News Interview Revisited

Increasingly, the take-charge, pump-'em-with-questions style of interviewing is yielding to the interview-as-conversation, an approach fine-tuned by veteran writers such as Studs Terkel and the late Charles Kuralt. "I realized quite early in this adventure," Terkel (1970) said, "that interviews, conventionally conducted, were meaningless. . . . The question-and-answer technique may be of value in determining favored detergents, toothpaste, and deodorants, but not in the discovery of men and women. It was simply a case of making conversation. And listening" (p. 21). Kuralt's (1985) vivid and multifaceted portraits of ordinary people in everyday places developed in a similar way. "I have tried to go slow, stick to the back roads, take time to meet people, listen to yarns," Kuralt said, describing how he created his famous "On the Road" reports for CBS. Both journalists acknowledge their work does not involve deadline stories of crime disasters, and political intrigue—and they know that not all interviews lend themselves to informal conversational styles. But Kuralt's and Terkel's respect for people and their willingness to hear them out apply in nearly all news interviews.

Veteran editor and writer James Fallows (1996) sees interviewing as a conscientious, thorough trip of discovery, not a systematic regimen of questions and answers.

"Through the process of listening, learning, testing assumptions, and letting themselves be surprised by new evidence, reporters decide what they think is true enough to write," he wrote (p. 58). And "[you] must sometimes ask questions whose answers you think you know, so as to confirm what you have heard and to compare answers from several sources. But the main working of reporting involves asking questions whose answers you don't know, simultaneously exposing your ignorance but opening up the possibility of learning something new" (p. 143).

Fallows, Kuralt, and Terkel understand that news doesn't grow on trees, ready for plucking. Often, the stuff of news emerges from the dialogue between two people. News in this sense is a cocreation of journalists and their interviewees, and the quality of the story depends on the quality of their communication. Complete openness is an unrealistic goal. However, if trust, candor, and mutual concern are missing, the interview can hardly achieve much depth, texture, or insight.

Reporters who communicate effectively must practice empathy, which we have discussed as the ability to imagine another person's perspective on the world while recognizing that such educated guesswork can never be completely accurate. Empathy in an interview requires journalists to take seriously others' feelings, values, goals, and points of view. "If we can get out of ourselves," Murray (1988) observes, "and enter into the lives of those we interview then we may ask perceptive questions and may receive perceptive answers" (p. 2). To empathize is not necessarily to agree, nor is it an emotionless neutrality. Empathy in a news interview rests on the reporter's willingness not to be limited by his or her own experience. Genuine empathy is usually evident to interviewees and can overcome their reluctance to talk. Without empathy, interviewees might assume the worse—that the reporter is either uncaring or out for personal gain.

Public servants and other newsmakers aren't generally required to give interviews. Most people, though, readily cooperate with journalists, at least until they get burned. Those interviewed for a news story typically feel vulnerable when they allow a journalist to quote, paraphrase, or explain their views. If the journalist makes them look stupid, evasive, calculating, insensitive, careless, or rude, it is experienced as betrayal. This rarely is calculated; more likely it is caused by the reporter's inability or unwillingness to understand what is at stake for the interviewee. It's a betrayal that extends beyond the consequences for the interviewee; it betrays the fundamental responsibility that journalists profess—to get the story right.

Interviews based on empathy and a listen-to-learn attitude are more productive than the alternative model of treating an interviewee as a means to an end (see Box 6.1). Journalists depend on people for the news. They can't do their jobs without the help of others.

Types of News Interviews

Journalists specialize in information-gathering interviews, and the tasks they face are shared by all other interviewers who care about learning new and interesting insights. Even if you do not plan a career as a reporter or editor, and even if you hope never to make *Inside Edition* with your 15 minutes of fame, you'll be interviewing like a journalist whenever you are verifying information on your company's policies with the vice

---

Box 6.1

Interviewers in Action   *William Blundell*

William Blundell, author and feature writer for the *Wall Street Journal,* describes the difference between treating the interviewee as a human being as opposed to a "lemon we are trying to squeeze dry in as few minutes as possible":

> I know reporters who are chronically nagged by their failure to get good quotes. The people in their stories appear wary, blandly cautious in their statements, unwilling to show themselves. I suspect they're reacting to a quick squeeze by the reporter, who is conducting his interviews as cold, businesslike transactions when they should be conversations.

Source: Blundell (1988, p. 90)

---

president for human relations, or gathering the facts necessary for a brief article in your organization's newsletter. You're a newsperson in many ways if others in your organization treat you as an opinion leader. Virtually any leadership role can be enhanced by the attitudes of journalistic discovery.

Therefore, pay close attention to how career journalists and their sources conduct interviews. News interviews might last only a few minutes. A few may extend over a period of days. Although some are routine, all are potentially important in providing a context for news. Each type of interview serves a particular function, helping reporters verify facts, reconstruct events, gather quotable reactions, probe feelings, and clarify ambiguity.

While constructing a story, a reporter might employ a variety of methods, each with different advantages and limitations. News interviews don't necessarily fit into neat categories, of course, but here we want to introduce you to nine general types of interview choices.

Screening and Verification Interviews

A reporter's daily work could include collecting hundreds of facts and opinions, most of which never go on the air or into print. Sometimes it's a quick telephone call to confirm a fact, such as the date of a meeting or the school district's enrollment figures. A more involved inquiry might be needed to get a city official to explain arcane language in a proposed ordinance.

Reporters conduct numerous mini-interviews in the course of a day, trying to track down someone who can provide reliable information for a story, and who is willing to talk on the record. Other quick-hitting inquiries by reporters help determine whether a tip deserves consideration as a news or feature item. The fate of hundreds of potential stories rests on snap decisions by busy men and women exercising news judgment. A farmer might phone to say he's grown the largest pumpkin in Crawford County, but a few questions by the reporter who takes the call determines that another farmer set the record weight a year ago; a potential human-interest story doesn't pan out. The same reporter, with adroit questioning of a woman distraught about her mother's death from a "routine" gall bladder surgery, detects the makings of a compelling story. These are not necessarily exhaustive or carefully planned interviews, but they are important in getting to the heart of the news decision, leading perhaps to more substantive interviews later. They put a premium on spontaneous talk that opens out into significant disclosure.

Background Interviews

Some stories require reporters to take a crash course on a special topic. They are assigned to cover academic conferences, business transactions, legal hearings, scientific developments, and public policy deliberations without necessarily having expertise in the specialized subjects involved. It's imperative that they ask enough questions for basic understanding of a subject before they can translate a complex matter for the public. This is a frustrating fact of life for reporters. Few like going into a story cold, and in practice, news editors try to assign the best prepared and most knowledgeable reporter to a particular story.

The background interview exposes a common deficiency: Journalists can't be specialists on every story they cover. However, they can act as intelligent translators for experts and can help them share what they know with a general audience. The right questions put to a professor who teaches tax law can help a reporter understand and report on a subject of concern to thousands in the community, even though the expert's name never gets publicized.

News Gathering Interviews

The term *news gathering*—although widely used in journalism—is curiously misleading. News is not so much what journalists find and "gather," but more often what they help to shape through their communication skills. News is a complex phenomenon in which journalism plays a formative role. But instead of coining an entirely new term, we can simply redefine the existing one. By *news gathering*, we mean the attempt to discover facts and create opportunities for the expression of opinions, relevant to an event or issue that needs explanation.

Reporters don't get to witness a news story unfold from start to finish, except perhaps when they are on the scene by chance. More often, they must rely on the eyes, ears, and memories of others. They reconstruct what happened by learning from witnesses and those with essential information, such as emergency crews. A looming deadline may require a quick succession of basic questions: "What's your name?" "What happened?" "What did you see?" Often there isn't time to build close rapport. Everyone may be pumped with adrenaline and ready to talk immediately about the dramatic episode they lived through.

Reaction Interviews

When the governor vetoes a bill, the Supreme Court issues an opinion, or the president intervenes in a strike, reporters scurry about for "reaction" comments. Wire service reporters or national correspondents produce the big stories out of Washington, DC, or the state capitol. Reporters around the country typically localize these stories, often going to experts at nearby universities or organizations who can make a national story more immediate.

Reaction interviews frequently focus on social and political conflict. Reporters and experienced news sources understand how competing sound bites or quotes enliven a story. When reporters value merely clever or cutting comments over substantive ones, however, or when they wrongly imply that a story must be framed as an either–or battle between two factions, the public is ill served. Spokespersons are quite willing to become quotemeisters, but their comments may shed relatively little light on the underlying conflicts in question.

A special type of reaction story is difficult for all sensitive journalists—interviews with victims or survivors of tragic accidents. Despite stereotyped images to the contrary, most reporters detest prying into personal tragedies; they are not callously trying to upset people already in pain, but searching for ways to communicate an authentic context with readers and listeners in mind. It might seem heartless when a reporter shoves a microphone toward a mother whose child just died in a DUI (driving under the influence) accident: "How do you feel?" In practice, journalists seldom ask such stereotypically blunt questions, and they certainly try to avoid them at the start of an interview. Empathic reporters gently elicit information, and sometimes they must explore the feelings of grief or anger or guilt, which help dramatize the intense human cost of car accidents, drownings, drive-by shootings, drug overdoses, suicides, and other too-common heartbreaks. Box 6.2 offers a checklist for approaching reaction interviews.

In-Depth Interviews

Apart from the frantic pace of breaking news coverage, journalists occasionally enjoy the opportunity to conduct lengthy, expansive interviews that reveal people, places, and

---

Box 6.2

Reminders   *Conducting a Brief Reaction Interview*

Opening

- Introduce yourself and whom you represent.
- Explain your request clearly in terms of your story and goals. ("People are curious about the strike's effects on the town. Because you're a store owner, I'm interested in your opinion about short-term and long-term effects.")

Focused Listening

- Listen for quotes—statements that are pertinent, succinct, clear, and vivid.

- If appropriate, share previous quotes and facts with respondents to stimulate reactions.
- Verify the quotes in your notes by reading them back to the interviewee.

Closing

- Express your personal appreciation for the help.
- Invite the interviewee to contact you later with further reactions, if appropriate.

predicaments in sharp, intimate detail. In-depth interviews lead to what are called **personality profiles** of public figures. News organizations seldom pay a celebrity or politician for an interview; it's even more uncommon to allow the interviewee any form of approval over the final product. Journalists, though, sometimes accept conditions in return for a hard-to-get interview. Moreover, writers who want a fair, accurate, and complete portrayal may review their work with the subject prior to broadcast or publication, although some conditions might make such an arrangement an unacceptable threat to the interviewer's independence. What is "right" in these situations will vary. Personality stories put journalists and interviewees into an intense, often symbiotic relationship, with each party heavily invested in the outcome. Complications are bound to arise, as they did when Lawrence Grobel (2004) captured Steve Martin's sarcasm (Q: "You're forgetting that there's an art to conversation." A: "That's true. I've turned down all other requests for interviews because I want this one to have meaning" [p. 172]) and basketball coach Bobby Knight's anger. In publishing the transcript of his interview with Knight, Grobel reveals a side of Knight not commonly heard in public. You'll get a textbook version here; see Grobel's book to fill in the blanks with the coach's actual words:

> Q: Didn't the stepfather also say that he didn't think you should be fired over this [previously described] incident?
>
> [BANGS the center of the steering wheel with his fist. His rage is sudden, frightening, and unexpected.] JESUS CHRIST! THIS IS _____! I'M NOT HERE FOR A ___ ___ INQUISITION! AND IF THAT'S WHAT THIS IS THEN GET THE _____ OUT AND HITCHHIKE BACK HOME! THE _____ STEPFATHER WAS A _____ _____ _____ _____ FROM THE WORD _____ GO! HE _____ LIED AND HE LIED AND HE LIED! *JESUS CHRIST!* I MEAN THIS IS MY _____ LIFE HERE THAT WE'RE TALKING ABOUT! MY _____ *HEART* WAS RIPPED OUT BY THIS _____ _____!
>
> Q: OK . . .

In his book, Grobel interjects "Believe me, this was scary"; then, almost immediately afterward, "I'm just trying to calm him down now, he's out of control, he's still driving 70 mph, and he would like to punch my lights out. I glance at my tape recorder to make sure it's still recording" (p. 415).

Journalists also conduct in-depth interviews for *immersion reporting*. For example, reporters writing about drug abuse, poverty, AIDS, or prison life depend on interviews conducted over a period of time to tell their stories powerfully. *Washington Post* reporter Leon Dash (1996), now a journalism professor, used in-depth interviews spread over four years in "Rosa Lee's Story," the account of a 58-year-old inner-city matriarch and her family's life of crack cocaine, prostitution, crime, and poverty. His series won a Pulitzer Prize and was subsequently published as a book. The investment level for all parties to this interview type is quite high, and winning prizes doesn't ensure that everyone will be pleased with the experience. Thousands of people who read about Rosa Lee complained to the *Post* about what they considered a disturbing, depressing, invasive story. Journalism, however, contributes to our awareness of important human conditions through penetrating accounts like this. In a PBS interview months later, Rosa Lee, in tears of gratitude, told Dash, "You listened to me and you heard me."

Broadcast Interviews

Broadcast journalists interview people for the same reasons print journalists do, but they often work under very different constraints. They usually have less time to collect stories, rushing with camera crew and technicians from one event or interview to the next, with little opportunity to air more than a few seconds from the interview. When doing live interviews, of course, they have no opportunity for retakes or corrections. Broadcast reporters not only must inform; they also must perform. How they look and sound over the air can be as important as the information they provide—a fact of professional life most accept reluctantly.

Broadcast interviews serve as a centerpiece of talk shows, newscasts, and broadcast newsmagazines. Each context has its nuances and complications.

Live news provides instant coverage of breaking news, and offers a great advantage over print journalism. However, because of the inherent risks, broadcast reporters rarely snatch someone off the street and put them on the air. More often they play the odds, relying on well-informed public officials, such as a fire chief, or they prescreen interviewees to assure that they have something predictable and articulate to say. Nonetheless, when the camera rolls and people start talking—especially recounting a breathtaking event—they may blurt out reckless or profane or misinformed comments before the reporter can cut them off. Even experienced journalists swept up by a dramatic story can go overboard. The competition among broadcasting outlets to "bring you the news first" increases the pressure for frequent live interviews. Live news interviewing is not a role for excitable, rash types, either behind or in front of the microphone.

Taped/edited news is a second type of broadcast interview, designed to preserve comments that enhance stories that are being constructed: They can take the form of *actualities* for radio or **sound bites** for TV. These are intended to capture complex ideas in a few words or images. Reporters, or their producers, spend much of their days lining up people who can provide the words and visuals needed to complete a story. Such interviews rarely last longer than a half-hour, and many are far shorter. Although longer human-interest stories now appear on evening newscasts, the typical news report seldom exceeds five minutes, with many no longer than 90 seconds. Interviews conducted for local or national newscasts yield only a quote or two that will fit the time constraints, and interviewers will often cue the source to provide the kind of comment that is needed for the story. Savvy news sources prepare for this situation by compressing their knowledge and opinions into quotable nuggets. Less compelling remarks are cut as reporters and editors construct a tight audiovisual news package. With much at stake, news producers conduct considerable screening to find the right stories and the right people to tell them, even to the point of auditioning interviewees (see Box 6.3).

Newsmagazines such as *60 Minutes* established the commercial value of longer form broadcast journalism in which stories are presented with suspenseful development. Interviewing is the lifeblood of such programs, and interviewers share some of the problems and opportunities of other taped or edited news stories. Here, however, the interview becomes as much a *product* as a process. With few exceptions, *60 Minutes* and its progeny, such as *Dateline* and *20/20*, produce high ratings at far lower cost than other prime-time entertainment programs like *CSI* or *Bones*. Newsmagazine programs face

Box 6.3

Interviewers in Action   *Stephen Hess*

Washington, DC, think-tank expert Stephen Hess frequently hears from TV news outlets looking for a source:

> A producer calls to check me out, asking enough questions to know whether I am likely to say what they are after. If I do not respond appropriately, they say they will get back to me. Which means they will not. This is a big city and someone else is sure to have the magic words they are looking for.

Source: Hess (1996, p. 103)

stiff competition, and their stories must be as polished and compelling as anything coming from a network's entertainment division. Stories short on emotional electricity don't get told; interviewees lacking human-interest appeal or high drama don't get on the air; and the journalist-stars of these programs don't earn million-dollar salaries for boring interviews. Interestingly, though, broadcast news creates an illusion, intentionally at times, that stars like Diane Sawyer or Geraldo Rivera conduct every interview for a report. However, interviews sometimes are done by field producers and other staff people, off camera. The high-priced "talent," as TV's heavy hitters are sometimes called, often fly in later for the taped segments, after the groundwork is completed.

Radio journalists, with their own versions of the TV or cable newsmagazine, usually on public stations, must survive and thrive largely on how they are "heard." With no visuals to propel the broadcast and perhaps overcome a dull interview, radio journalists know listeners will not tolerate flaws in an interview. A master of radio interviews, Terry Gross (2004), host of National Public Radio's "Fresh Air," said conversations with guests "bear little resemblance to the conversations we have in daily life" (p. x). She interrupts and stops the interview to request shorter answers; she violates decorum by asking questions about religious beliefs or physical flaws of someone she has just met. Gross is not trying to embarrass her guests. Rather, she's seeking introspection and revelation. After the interview is over, her staff edits the tape, "rearranging the order of questions, if necessary, but also taking out the bluster, the dead ends, the redundancies, and the 'like's', the 'you know's', and the 'um's' that would drive even our most devoted listeners crazy if they ever heard them" (p. xxi). Print journalists often do comparable editing with interviews, and the post hoc results include, if done well, a clearer, more readable story. Never, however, should edited interviews distort the overall truth of the interviewee's words.

Talk shows provide another venue for broadcast journalism's interviews. Entertainment has become a significant component of what passes as news these days, especially in political talk shows. Few televised talk shows are completely live, but many are taped live with little opportunity for significant editing. As a result, interviews must be crisp, sharp, confrontive, interesting, and sometimes humorous. Hosts and guests are chosen for their ability to be incisive, controversial, smart, or quick with quips.

Critics say that interviews on talk shows emphasize performance art and simplistic frames far more than the sophisticated gathering and reporting of relevant information

(Jamieson & Waldman, 2003). On a larger scale, they believe that broadcast interviews too often encourage argumentation, not dialogue; that interviewers value mere quotability over substance; and that they reduce complicated issues to two-sided diatribes and a horse-race mentality (Tannen, 1998). In fairness, some print interviews deserve similar criticism, but the problems seem more serious in broadcasting.

In broadcast interviews, producers must worry about juxtaposing words and visual images, timing close-ups, and in general manipulating camera angles and background scenes so as best to tell an involving story. Interviewers must be aware of these layers of planning as well, producing a complex system in which the talk itself is only a part. Planning is a criterion that cannot be overestimated in this interview form, and most of its communication is of course rehearsed to some degree. In this somewhat artificial climate, it's natural that many interviewees are excessively self-conscious about what they're saying and the context of their talk. Talking on the record, especially when live or taped, can be harrowing. It strains communication. Yet natural, conversational interviews do occur in broadcasting, and they can be quite absorbing. Watch how Oprah Winfrey, for example, puts interviewees at ease through her skillful attention, her self-deprecating good humor, and her conversational speech style; or analyze how Ray Suarez of PBS establishes both his authority and his sensitivity in the same conversation with an interviewee. In Chapter 12 of this book, you'll read more about your role as an audience member who can analyze interviewing in media and popular culture contexts more skillfully.

If you want to hear and analyze a wide variety of actual broadcast interview examples, consider the following Web sources that offer full interviews or brief audio-video clips (only a few among many). Most use either Real Player or Windows Media Player technology:

Business Week: Clips from researchers and social scientists whose work is relevant to the business community. (http://www.businessweek.com/innovation/home/video.html)

C-SPAN: A video archive with full-length interviews, most with politicians and political figures. (http://www.c-span.org)

Daily Show: Five- to 10-minute clips of interviews with newsmakers and entertainers. (http://www.Comedycentral.com/tvshows/thedailyshowwithjonstewart)

British Broadcasting Corporation: Brief clips of interviews with filmmakers, writers, actors, broadcasters, political activists, and others. (http://bbc.co.uk/bbcfour/audiointerviews)

National Public Radio (NPR): Archive of interview shows from NPR, with precommentary that previews each interview's content. Click "Archives" in top right corner to access video interview files. (http://www.npr.org)

Telephone Interviews

The telephone both offers major advantages and necessitates major compromises in communication. Although it impressively extends the immediate reach of our messages, it sacrifices the ability to observe subtle visual cues that aid our listening. However, journalists consider telephone interviews to be undeniably efficient and indispensable. The telephone is most often a tool of print journalists, who use it from the office to substitute for much of their "legwork." Broadcast journalists need faces for their reports, so, with the exception of radio reporters, they downplay telephone interviews. The telephone has always been a good way to get to busy people, and the popularity of cell phones has enhanced this access. Voice mail and other ways of depositing and retrieving messages allow reporters to bypass a secretary and speak in direct and detailed ways about the need for an interview. A reporter's recorded message, in turn, gives a news source the opportunity to form an answer before calling back. In the interest of saving time and meeting deadlines, in fact, news sources can even leave answers on the reporter's voice mail.

The telephone offers several potential advantages (timeliness, immediacy, convenience), but it cannot be considered a direct equivalent to a face-to-face interview. In that kind of conversation, the parties can detect and assess nonverbal messages and are likely to take the exchange far more seriously. Box 6.4 offers specific advice for telephone interviewers.

Box 6.4

Reminders   *Tips on Telephone Interviews*

- Ensure that you have enough time and adequate concentration. You don't want to talk to someone who is distracted or rushed because other pressing business is on the desk or on the mind. A reporter, for example, who is trying to do several things at once while on the phone risks missing key answers; a preoccupied interviewee won't be engaged enough to notice how nuanced certain questions might be. Without a guarantee of reasonable mental focus, avoid phone interviews.

- Focus on clarifying one major question if possible, with its appropriate follow-up probes and responses. A telephone interview is not optimal for processing multilayered information, so avoid complicated schedules and convoluted answers.

- Speak slowly, distinctly, and precisely, remembering that phone talk isn't as complete and clear as face-to-face communication. Telecommunication still poses hearing difficulties in addition to the listening problems that typically accompany any interview. The hearing difficulties could be physical due to an auditory disability of a participant;

technical due to static or a bad connection; or verbal due to rapid or garbled speech.

- Avoid conducting important interviews by phone just because it's convenient. Phone interviews involve too many trade-offs. They offer a quick way to gather and exchange basic information but are inherently limiting. See if you can use the phone mainly for **preinterviews**— short interchanges that set up and coordinate longer interviews and deeper topics.

- Try to refrain from interrupting or talking over the other person's remarks. Although some kinds of interruption are common and expected in everyday talk, many of the cues that acknowledge (and repair) it are visual.

- Summarize and repeat crucial information to ensure it has been understood. Both parties benefit from reassurances that listening has been accurate. In a restricted-channel situation like telephone talk, you won't have access to many cues of attentiveness. Double-check important details, such as dates, spelling of names, and telephone numbers.

Cyberspace Interviews

Increasingly, journalists conduct interviews by e-mail and other online communication venues, such as chat rooms and blog sites. Some occur in real time, which approximates telephone interviewing but without the benefit (with most current technologies) of hearing actual voices. E-mail is also like the telephone in that messages can be left and answered at the convenience of respondents. Still, e-mail complicates interviewing. In cyberspace "talk," inflection and facial expression—by which we often signal that an "insult" should be taken as playful kidding, for example—will not be available. Symbols, known as *emoticons*, sometimes substitute for the emotional message of vocal inflection or a wink, but this system is clearly an information-thin environment. Not everyone knows (or appreciates) the specifics of e-mail conventions, and may blunder innocently into taboos such as the use of ALL CAPITAL LETTERS, for example, which is considered the equivalent to shouting. The etiquette for online talk is still evolving, and not widely shared in many instances. As a result, this communication venue poses dangers you won't confront in everyday speech.

Such interviews can be like a long-distance chess match: I make a move; you respond and wait for my next move. Although spontaneity suffers, e-mail interviews do afford more time for reflection and consideration than face-to-face or phone interviews. Sometimes, in fact, it's possible to obtain an e-mail interview with a busy person who would otherwise turn you down. *New Yorker* writer John Seabrook (1994) broke ground in electronic journalism when he based much of his portrait of Microsoft guru Bill Gates on e-mail interchanges. Seabrook thought that Gates, of all people, would be approachable through the so-called information highway. Seabrook sent a brief message identifying himself and explaining the story he was doing, ending with a question: "What do you think is unique about e-mail as a form of communication?" (p. 48). Eighteen minutes later, Gates responded. Their e-mail interview continued intermittently for a month. A productive e-mail interview can also set the stage for an eventual face-to-face meeting. Although Seabrook was successful with what we could call a spontaneous e-mail interviewing strategy, we suggest a bit more planning for the beginning interviewer in Box 6.5.

Despite the advantages of online interviews, be wary of overusing them. Cyberspace interviewing allows a lazy or computer-dependent reporter to avoid legwork—getting outside the newsroom to meet, observe, and talk with people face-to-face. When conversation occurs online, you not only miss the body language, tone of voice, visual cues, and natural dialogue of in-person interviews, but you can also risk falling victim to someone posing as a reliable source or someone they aren't, resulting in the embarrassment, when exposed, of an invented story or hoax. Even when the disclosure online is honest and truthful, it's more likely to be monitored by government agencies or corporate watchdogs. Brant Huston, executive director of Investigative Reporters and Editors, particularly worries about journalists communicating online with confidential sources. "With e-mail," he writes, "you're just laying a paper trail of what's supposed to be an anonymous source and an anonymous relationship" (Hart, 2006, p. 61).

Box 6.5

Reminders   *Conducting a Brief E-Mail Interview*

- Contact the respondent ahead of time—by phone or e-mail—to invite his or her participation and to agree on a time frame for responses and follow-up questions.

- Use the preliminary contacts for building rapport and informing the interviewee of your purpose.

- In the first content-oriented e-mail in which you pose questions, reiterate briefly the basic understandings previously reached by the two of you.

- Don't use Internet jargon or emoticons (also known as *smileys*—the symbolic representation of facial expressions portrayed by colon, semicolon, slash, apostrophe, parenthesis, and other keys), unless you're certain your partner is comfortable with such habits.

- Unless the interview is in real time (as in a chat or instant-message setting from an online service), concentrate on just a few (between three and six) open-ended questions, to which the interviewee can respond at a comfortable level of disclosure. Tell your respondent your hopes about how specific or elaborate the answers will be.

- Use probes to check out possible misunderstandings or to express unusual interest or surprise. Otherwise, assume the interviewee has told you what he or she desires to reveal.

- When replying, use your e-mail system's edit or reply features to highlight the precise statements to which you're replying. Do not reply by resending the other's entire previous message.

- Follow up with an e-mail or card, thanking your respondent.

Converged Media Interviews

Media convergence defies easy definition, in part because it is an amalgam of corporate strategy and structure, hardware and software technology, and contemporary methods of presenting and packaging the news. Media companies with converged or merged operations sometimes expect reporters to repackage stories for what the industry calls multiple "platforms," mainly print, broadcast, and online, combined under one news media roof. That means a print reporter might be asked to produce a conventional news story for the morning newspaper, repackage or "repurpose" the story for a broadcast report on the late-evening news, and finally repackage and update the story through a number of time cycles for the 24/7 online publication.

Although reporting and news interviewing share common traits and practices across platforms, in a converged-media operation, they require the special skills of journalists competent in coordinating the printed word with visual images and audiotape interviews. Although the merged media environment comprises far more than interview-based information, interviewing for information that will cross platforms alone complicates the work of reporters used to a print world. An old-school newspaper reporter—who might be young but still old-school in training and orientation—placed in a merged newsroom now may become fixated on sound, among other things. The sound issues include, of course, the technical issues, such as the quality of an audiotape. The emotional quality of taped interviews must appeal to an audience with high expectations for dramatic multimedia reporting. Factual information remains crucial, of course. Yet the interviewer must also be aware of how facts will be communicated later not just verbally but in varying visual and auditory contexts. Broadcast interview challenges related to audience appeal are now increasingly common as professionals we used to call "print journalists" are now morphing into multimedia journalists.

Fundamentals of Journalistic Interviewing

The journalistic interview takes on a unique life of its own and rarely follows a standard, predetermined pattern. Nearly all news interviews, however, include several fundamental considerations: purpose, preparation, questioning, listening, record keeping, assessment, and analyzing conditions.

Purpose

Any journalist pursuing the news wonders "What is the story here?" Usually you'd expect this to be answered early in a news assignment. Journalists, however, don't always do the expected; news emerges in strange ways. Occasionally, journalists don't find the story, or at least not the one they expected to find, until well into interviews and information gathering. Beginners risk answering "What is the story?" too quickly, thus predetermining the outcome and precluding the discovery of something truly new and especially interesting. Operating totally without a story frame, however, doesn't help either. Most reporters, based on initial information, leads, experience, and instinct, tentatively frame what the story is likely to involve. Beyond that, they learn to be flexible.

The initial conception of a story influences who must be interviewed and which goals should guide the interview. Here decisions can get tricky, especially if the story is potentially controversial, harmful, or embarrassing. Let's say the reporter's purpose is to investigate an apparent conflict of interest involving the mayor and her brother-in-law, whose company received an exclusive and lucrative contract to make repairs on city vehicles. Journalism's role as a watchdog necessitates such investigations. But what happens when the interviewer's purpose clashes with the interviewee's? Is it still realistic to envision their interview as a partnership? It probably wouldn't be a congenial partnership. Nonetheless, collaboration, to some degree, often yields better results than confrontation. The reporter can stand firm about her objective to investigate; the mayor's brother-in-law can pursue his purpose of explaining and defending his transactions with the city. Together, they can, if willing, find a common purpose of producing a story that is as truthful and fair as possible. Even with volatile stories, reporters are usually wise to share the purpose of the interview. Revealing this usually helps in obtaining an interview, and in maintaining credibility within it. Reporters often must overcome a respondent's reluctance to talk. People generally want to know what a questioner wants from them, and why. They resent being misled or kept in the dark, and a resentful interviewee is less interested in talking.

Determining journalistic purpose helps both questioner and respondent prepare for their time together. Consider how determining purpose differs according to role. As the interviewer, ask yourself the following questions:

Why do I need to know more about this topic or person?

What is the story? If you don't have much sense yet of the shape of the story, you should plan more exploratory questions.

Who will be reading or hearing my account? What will they want to know? Skilled reporters ask about what audiences want to know, not simply to follow up on their own curiosity. Therefore, sensitivity to the public's concerns is a part of the job.

Am I most interested in context, detail, or both? In deciding, don't underestimate the importance of accurate details even in nonpivotal areas. Most people are rarely if ever mentioned in print, and journalists should understand the disappointing, discouraging feeling respondents experience when they see their names misspelled, or their beloved family business misidentified, during a perhaps too-brief moment of public recognition. Remember, too, that getting a name wrong could mean an innocent person will be associated inadvertently with a misdeed.

How can I keep my mind open for new purposes that might emerge from the interview? Although each story probably begins with hunches and hypotheses, good interviews stimulate new hunches along the way, and revisions of old ones.

As the interviewee, ask yourself the following questions about purpose:

Why does the interviewer want to talk to me? What motivates the interview from his or her side? You might want to do some research if you know the interview is imminent. For example, if you're a recently elected president of the student government about to be interviewed by the editor of the campus newspaper, wouldn't it be worthwhile to review last semester's editorials and stories to determine the editor's priorities and possible hot topics?

What is my basic motivation for talking to this person? How do I want to be seen, heard, and interpreted? Are there potential pitfalls in how I talk about a topic? Ask yourself if your main purpose is to relay information or facts, or to be perceived in a certain way, or both.

Will I want or need to set any limits for the interview? Is any information out of bounds? The reminders later in this chapter concerning record keeping, assessment, and conditions will help put these questions in perspective. For now, though, consider carefully what boundaries you need or want to define, given your own purpose.

Who will be reading or hearing the journalist's account? What will these audiences want to know? How could they reward or penalize me? Do some audience analysis; your own purposes may mean this is an important opportunity to be persuasive.

Preparation

When time permits, reporters prepare for interviews by using a combination of research, reading, listening, hanging out, and reflection. To rush in with a hastily scribbled list of questions undermines an interview in several ways. First, experienced interviewees measure a reporter's credibility by the questions asked. Are they bright, provocative, thoughtful? Are they far too obvious—ones that a rookie would ask? In the eyes of many interviewees, a reporter's preparation reflects professionalism. Preparation is also a signal of respect that says to the interviewee: I care enough about you to learn who you are and not to burden you with questions I can answer online or in a newsroom library. Preparation impresses and encourages the interviewee and it bolsters the reporter's confidence.

Part of preparation also includes an awareness of whom to interview. In a world increasingly diverse in race, ethnicity, age, physical condition, socioeconomic status, and sexual orientation, journalists cannot in good conscience decide on whom to interview based on compatibility, familiarity, or similarity. Reporters who seek diversity as part of their preparation do so because they know that good journalism reflects the richness of the community. Diversity in news sources also guards against bias rooted in stereotypes, cultural ignorance, and misassumptions. A city planning official may be more comfortable to interview and will provide insight based on official policy, but a homeless veteran about to be displaced from his "home" by a condominium project backed by the city planner will have another version of the story to tell. Even an open-minded city planner will not be able to convey the veteran's experience adequately. Reporters who seek out only official sources and professionals, or interview only culturally comfortable respondents, will never grow emotionally and intellectually beyond their own socialization. Their self-inflicted narrowness ultimately penalizes the public the reporter hopes to serve.

Preparation with diversity in mind also requires that reporters anticipate the impact of differences in culture, language, and mores between themselves and the people they interview. As they encounter unfamiliar cultural contexts they must be responsible enough to consider guides, teachers, or authors who can help them prepare for the assumptions of these culturally distinctive encounters. The blind spots of individual reporters can undermine the credibility not only of stories, but of entire news organizations.

In the interest of better stories, good reporters try to give interviewees an opportunity to prepare, too. Of course, full disclosure by the reporter might give an evasive or devious news source a chance to prepare an orchestrated or calculated response, rather than one that's more spontaneous, unrehearsed, and candid. In most situations, giving an interviewee time to prepare is worth the risk. Preparation is especially helpful when seeking specialized information from an expert. Even specialists in a field cannot recall all the details of their work; sometimes, too, an interviewee who's afforded time to prepare will rethink a subject, coming up with fresh insights.

Consider the preparation choices from both sides of the interview encounter. As the interviewer, remember:

Research your partner's interests if possible. Ordinarily, you will need to understand the basics of the topic you'll be exploring with the interviewee. Although there are exceptions (e.g., broadcast interviewer Larry King claims he rarely does preliminary research on interviewees' interests because he doesn't want to stifle spontaneity), most interviewers will be more comfortable knowing possible directions the interview might take.

Anticipate vocabulary. Become familiar with the interviewee's speech habits, special jargon, or unique styles of phrasing things. You do not need to adopt all these habits yourself, talking like your conversation partner, for example, to be effective. In fact, you shouldn't try to be someone you're not. But interviewees will quickly lose interest in talking with you unless you seem at least somewhat familiar with how they express ideas, In cross-cultural settings, familiarize yourself with how the linguistic "rules" guiding the conversation itself might vary from your world to that of the other person.

Investigate the context in which someone's information might be placed. For example, before interviewing a Texaco or Wal-Mart executive about possible racial bias within her or his company, you might do an online search about other recent cases in which large corporations have been charged with discrimination, or about the particular company's recent record in affirmative action compliance.

From the perspective of the interviewee, remember:

Anticipate misunderstanding. Interviewers rarely have enough time to prepare fully for the interview; therefore, they might not have as clear or as sophisticated a purpose for the occasion as you do. Anticipate how a sincere interviewer might still misunderstand your ideas and might even frame the interview in a radically different way than you would. For example, a journalist might plan to interview you for a personality profile, but you know your company has just made a major pharmaceutical breakthrough that could make news. Wouldn't you want to talk about that, even if the reporter didn't ask?

Police your jargon. Remember that in many situations your *jargon*—the specialized language and references commonly used within your own job, hobby, or cultural position—will not be shared by the journalist or a wider audience. Plan ways to explain or frame your ideas in accessible language.

Clarify the interviewer's purpose. You have a right to inquire about the purpose of the interview. Reporters are accustomed to interviewing under different conditions and using the information they receive in varying ways. You can influence some of their interview purposes by requesting that your name not be used or that the information you supply should be used only as context for the journalist's pursuit of other information, not as news in and of itself. Journalists use several terms to describe ground rules for interviews. Please note, though, that there is no universal agreement on how to define these terms precisely. We define **not for attribution** to mean that the source of the information can be identified by a general description ("a Capitol Hill insider tells *Newsweek* that . . ."), but not by name. **On background** means that what a source says will not itself be a part of the story but will be used by the journalist to understand the subject better and possibly track down additional information. **Off the record** means the journalist will not use the information in any specific way. In the absence of universal definitions for these terms, we recommend that you establish beforehand exactly how the information you provide will be used and attributed. Without this clarification, the interviewer might incorrectly assume that anything you say is fair game.

Stay alert for interviewer strategies. Remember that although journalists aren't necessarily trying to be sneaky or deceptive, they probably know a thing or two about tactical communication. What appears to be the drift or main focus of an interview may not in fact turn out to be related to the real purpose. For example, a journalist may spend 20 minutes talking casually about the day-to-day operations of the rural school where you work, only to ask at the end of the conversation, almost as an aside, how much time the principal spends away from the school on trips and consultation visits. What you thought was an interview preparing for a light feature about the personalities of people at your school, you later discover, turns out to have been an investigation of how some administrators rip off the district. This doesn't mean journalists are basically devious or deceitful—they have a responsibility to the public as well as to individual interviewees. It only means that interviewees are well advised to be alert and consider realistically that the most obvious purposes might not be the only ones.

Questioning

As you have read in earlier chapters, interviewing is more than asking and answering questions. In fact, the question-and-answer exchange often tends to discourage natural conversation. Sometimes, however, it's the most efficient way to understand a situation. Journalists need to decide which questions to ask, as well as when and how to ask them. A few reporters make long lists, but most rely on a few primary or starter questions. They develop additional questions based on the ebb and flow of the interview. For inexperienced journalists, a question list (a *schedule* in the terminology of an earlier chapter) is a security blanket, which is OK, but adhering slavishly to such a list results in a stiff give-and-take routine. Experienced reporters work questions unobtrusively into the conversation, cued by their own curiosity.

An important part of journalists' questioning is follow-up. People seldom answer a question fully on their first attempt. They need time and help in fleshing out initial remarks. Reporters sometimes repeat a question in several forms until an answer emerges, or they might simply say, "Tell me more" or "That's interesting" while they wait for more detail. In reconstructing a news event or encouraging an anecdote, reporters ask a series of *sequence* questions, such as "What did you do when you heard the shots?" or "After the gunfire stopped, what did you do next?" The interviewee, when helped to think in terms of stages of action, provides a more detailed account.

Remember that a probe is a type of follow-up question or response that seeks clarification, elaboration, or confirmation. In a reflective probe, for example, a reporter might ask, "Let me repeat what you said to make sure I understand you." In other situations, a reporter's silence might serve as a probe that says nonverbally "Keep talking," or "Take your time in answering."

Veteran editors often tell beginning reporters to ask the questions readers or viewers would ask. People want to know how a story affects them. If it's about a pending teachers' strike, working parents will want to know, among other things, "What will I do with my kids?" That basic question might not occur to an unmarried, childless reporter.

Journalists are the public's surrogates in finding answers to questions; they are also our surrogate listeners.

In focusing on questioning, interviewers need to remember several important issues:

Prepare a schedule. You need a tentative agenda of basic questions to which you can refer easily if necessary. At the end of the interview, briefly review your schedule to ensure you haven't forgotten something crucial. Few things are as embarrassing for professional journalists as the need to recontact someone because they overlooked a question crucial to the story. Typically, journalists are taught a basic checklist that leads to full coverage of almost all stories: Who? What? Where? When? Why? How? These are the sacred *5 Ws and an H* of journalism. Although these questions needn't be asked in this order, readers, listeners, and viewers do want to know these things about events. In addition, at the end of each interview, consider *the sixth W*: What else? Get into the habit of asking something like, "Is there anything else you think you'd like me to know? Anything you think I've overlooked?" This simple, concluding probe could spare you recriminations and torment later.

Sequence your questions and topics appropriately. Plan a tentative sequence of questions adapted both to the interviewee and to your purpose. Typical journalistic patterns are **topical** (move from issue to issue), **chronological** (move from older to more recent events), **funnel** (move from general to specific), or **inverted funnel** (move from specific to general). In addition, if some areas of the interview are likely to be ticklish or tense, you might not want to lead with those and risk having the entire tone of your conversation affected by the emotional responses those questions might trigger.

Anticipate defensiveness. Remember that certain questions may provoke defensiveness. For example: "Why did you promote Ramsey after a sexual harassment complaint was filed against him?" would rarely be heard as a neutral request for a reasoned rationale. Interviewees are more likely to interpret your question as a commentary on the action. This might not always be bad (journalists are interested in how some interviewees might respond under fire, after all), but you should always be aware of the potential for defensive reaction.

Probe often. Remind yourself that all answers are not equal, nor will all respondents think of everything on the first pass. Review the uses of probes described in detail in Chapter 4. These useful follow-ups get behind or beyond the first response to explore it further. Some probes are overtly for clarification and are meant as checks on your listening.

Be aware of how your questions invite answers. Remember that different kinds of questions encourage different kinds of responsiveness and thus different qualities of answers. When seeking accurate information primarily, journalists avoid *leading questions*—those whose phrasing projects the kind of answer the questioner seems to want or expect ("You never intended to keep that plant open after acquiring it, did you?"). In other contexts, however, carefully considered leading questions can be effective in stimulating an interviewee's emotions, explanations, or argumentativeness.

Understand when questions can be counterproductive. Because the best interviews so often resemble guided conversations, they do not have to rely on a string of questions. Although questions are important, your interviewee will also respond if you characterize events in a certain inviting way. For instance, while interviewing the volleyball coach, you might say "Well, coach, your opponent, Morgan State, looks tough again this year." The coach will take your comment as a cue to talk about the upcoming game, or to speculate about final conference standings, or perhaps to complain about how Morgan State's best players are overrated. Although this can be a helpful interviewing style if it's not overdone, don't be surprised if a contrary interviewee occasionally tries to trip you up: "I'm sure it looks that way to you media types. You always give them too much ink."

When you find yourself being interviewed by a journalist, remember these points about questioning:

Verify the question. Make sure you understand questions fully before answering. It's in a journalist's nature to listen for quotes, not only for information. Editors and readers expect quotes in stories, and the more striking or unusual the better. Your problem as an interviewee is having a response wrenched out of the context of the rest of your message. Nothing can guarantee this won't happen, but asking for clarifications can often keep you out of quote trouble.

Don't take offense if a reporter doesn't seem to accept your answers at face value. A reporter's survival kit includes high doses of skepticism and a willingness to dig beneath the surface. It's usually nothing personal or suspicious that cues this kind of response.

Ask your own questions. You might ask, for example, "Who else are you interviewing on this matter?" "How is the story shaping up?" "Will this be part of a larger piece about school board policy, or is it possible that the story will be only about my actions?" Although journalists may not be at liberty to respond fully or may not know how to answer your questions, many times they'll try to clarify things for you.

Recognize the dynamics of "no comment." You need to understand that a *no comment* statement, although it may appear to be a neutral response, will still be interpreted by journalists and their audiences as meaning something (that you have something to hide? that you don't know an answer and are avoiding embarrassment? that you've been told by someone else not to talk about the subject?). Use this response sparingly, if at all.

Listening

Journalists' listening should go far beyond passive attention that simply registers comments and questions. Listening sustains and creates communication; how we listen influences how others answer our questions and what we say next. Writer Gay Talese (1995) learned to listen as a boy by hanging around his mother's dress shop, where

Trying Out Your Skills

- Writing coaches and editors often tell journalists to "ask the readers' questions," meaning they should consider what people will naturally want or need to know as they read a news story or feature. Pick a story from your local newspaper that you find lacking in important details, context, or useful information. Think of a person for whom the story's issues would be especially relevant. Then develop a set of questions you'd ask to provide this hypothetical reader the answers to questions he or she would ask. Whom would you need to interview to get the additional answers for your reader(s)?

- In another experiment, assess two of your listening skills: accuracy and note taking. Interview a friend or classmate about a vivid anecdotal experience, such as a first date or first car. Develop a brief schedule of primary questions to bring forth the anecdote, and probe to encourage the sharing of vivid details.

A five- or 10-minute interview will be sufficient. Tape your interview to produce a precise record, but also take careful notes of the interviewee's experiences. Then, without listening to the tape, reconstruct as much of the story as possible by creating a first-person account (as if in the interviewee's words) *based only on your notes*. (Note: This will be difficult, and you should not expect to do it perfectly.) Sit down with the interviewee and review the "transcript" together as a first stage of assessing your accuracy in note taking. Then compare the transcript to the tape, listening to it together, alert for lapses or errors in your note taking.

If you want to check your framing and listening skills further, use your notes to produce a brief story based on the interviewee's anecdote. Then go over the story with the interviewee, assessing both its factual and contextual accuracy.

customers would try on clothes and discuss their lives. He observed the importance of listening patiently. "I learned to listen with patience and care, and never to interrupt even when people were having great difficulty in explaining themselves, for during such halting and imprecise moments . . . people often are very revealing—What they hesitate to talk about can tell much about them" (p. 80).

Journalists who obviously don't listen can expect to get caught. A TV reporter interviewing celebrities arriving for the 1997 Academy Awards ceremony questioned Winona Ryder while looking over Ryder's shoulder to catch the eye of another Hollywood actor. After answering his question, Ryder cocked her head and said in exasperation, "Why, you're not even listening to me." The interview ended there.

As a journalistic interviewer, remember these important points about listening:

Build rapport by demonstrating your listening acuity. In other words, active listening is crucial in convincing the interviewee to trust you. Remember that active listening refers to the verbal and nonverbal behaviors by which a listener proves a message has been understood in the way the speaker hopes it would be. In a message with special relevance to journalists, psychologists Carl Rogers and Richard Farson (1957) note that "while it is most difficult to convince someone that you respect him by telling him so, you are much more likely to get this message across by really behaving that way by actually having and demonstrating respect for this person. Listening does this most effectively" (p. 11). Active listening could take several forms, but the most common is a verbal checking back—what we earlier called a clarification probe. Journalists could ask of an accident witness, "I heard you say two things a while ago. One is that you believe the truck driver cut off the pickup. Then later, you said 'maybe,' and seemed less sure about who cut off whom. Do I have that right?" Thus, at the same time you're complimenting the interviewee by paying careful attention, you're inviting a more thoughtful, and probably a more accurate, response.

Remember that listening is identified with visual cues. Listening is not just a way of registering meanings cognitively and not just a physiological process. It's also a recognizable set of observable behaviors that members of a culture will interpret in relatively predictable ways. Listening, in other words, has an appearance. In most North American cultures, listeners tend to maintain persistent, although not unvarying, eye contact. They nod and give other verbal and nonverbal encouragement for speakers to continue, they lean forward often to indicate a kind of immediacy with speakers, and they introduce no unnecessary barriers between speakers and themselves. Journalists should do a self-inventory of listening habits to isolate problem behaviors, even if they believe they remember statements accurately. Do you really need those sunglasses? Are there times when burying yourself in your notebook or scanning the horizon for other interesting people might cause someone to break off a conversation prematurely?

Let yourself be surprised by what the interviewee might say. Journalists' deadlines often encourage them to write much of the story in their heads before finishing the information-gathering process. Monitor your own habits of framing and interpreting to ensure that you're not just listening through the filters of your prejudices and earlier assumptions.

Anticipate the effects of context. Be aware of how different contexts and settings can affect listening. If you interview a doctor in the office at midday, don't be surprised if her listening is divided or diffused between your concerns and the perhaps more immediate demands of patients or her colleagues.

When responding to a journalist, remember these suggestions about listening:

Don't leave active listening to the interviewer. This skill is just as relevant for you. Openly express what you think the basic question is, from the interviewer's perspective: "You seem to want me to evaluate how easy it was to work with Paula Abdul. Is that right?" Another active listening approach is to verify the accuracy of an interviewer's interpretation by your own reflective or paraphrased response. For example, if you're a public health worker, you could say: "We've been talking for 10 minutes now about the HIV virus and I'm wondering what you think is my strongest recommendation."

Assist the interviewer's listening by providing brief informal clarifications of specialized terms or names you're using. For example, you might say, "Stuart Smith was just appointed as an 'Instructor' at the university, a less permanent academic rank that won't make him eligible for tenure."

Monitor nonverbal signals of interest or understanding from your interviewer. Watch for indications that the interviewer is confused, especially curious, or losing interest. Did he start to look at his watch or yawn? Did she quit taking notes and sigh deeply? Or did he start leaning forward expectantly, with more eye contact? You'll want to adapt your comments accordingly. It would be nice to imagine that your interviewer will be skilled, sensitive, and experienced but, frankly, this is optimistic at best. Some will be rookies, others overworked and harried because of editors' demands, and, sorry to say, still others will be arrogant know-it-alls who won't care about you. Remember that your story has to be told not just *to* them but *through* them, so help them listen by anticipating potential communication problems. Watch for signs of MEGO ("my eyes glaze over") or premature closure, and repeat significant information as needed. Slow down when introducing technical material. Summarize often. Don't let the interviewer oversimplify your points or put words in your mouth. If you think this advice is mere common sense, it's obvious that you haven't been interviewed often by busy reporters.

Record Keeping

Journalists keep a record of most interviews because it's risky not to. A clear record of notes or tapes will not only reassure editors and interviewees alike but also will help jog your memory later. Many reporters keep their notes and, less commonly, their tapes of important interviews for later reference and perhaps as context for further stories.

Sometimes, reporters delay taking notes or activating the tape recorder until they feel the interviewee is comfortable and ready to talk. Although it's difficult to keep verbatim quotes and specifics, attention to such details tells interviewees that the journalist is committed to accuracy. A careful, complete record of interviews is essential as a reporter puts together a story. It's also important if questions arise later, in the newsroom or courtroom, over the truthfulness of the story.

Record keeping involves a surprisingly complex set of choices. Reporters who focus too intently on taking notes may collect the details but not recognize the larger context and meaning of messages. Relying on a tape recorder may lead them to relax, confident that the machine is keeping track of every word. They drift mentally, and later, when replaying the tape, they realize they weren't altogether "there" for the interview and thus can't adequately put what they hear in context. Whether taking notes, using a recorder, or employing a combination of both, reporters need to balance careful note taking with concentrated mental engagement (see Box 6.6).

Assessment

Journalists must analyze and synthesize information in terms of the interview's purpose. Part of this postinterview routine involves confirming what was heard, what was learned, and what gaps might remain in the story. At times, this is as simple as going over notes, deciding what to use and what to discard. Reporters seldom use a majority of their notes in a story; they cull the immediately useful from the extraneous information. Basically, reporters prepare to write a story or put together a broadcast report by asking themselves: What do I have? What does it mean? How can I best tell this story?

Box 6.6

Reminders   *Record Keeping for Journalists*

Decide which form your record keeping for a given interview will take: direct notes, delayed notes, tape (or digital) recording, or a combination. Review Chapter 5 for an expanded discussion of the alternatives.

For most brief and straightforward journalistic interviews of less consequence, *direct notes* are not only fine but are expected by interviewees. The interviewer simply jots down important points while the respondent is talking. A small notepad is especially appropriate, but watch out for the tendency to pay more attention to the notes than to the speaker.

In some interviews, such as with an excitable or highly emotional interviewee, note taking would feel intrusive, or it could detract you from your ability to notice the nuances of nonverbal reactions. Some reporters prefer a *delayed notes* method in which they take few if any notes during the conversation but then set aside a time immediately following it to jot down as many details as they can remember. With practice in delayed note taking, even many short quotes can be recalled, although relying too much on memory is risky. Don't restrict yourself only to what was said, though. Record your estimate of how the context might have affected the interview, how the tone changed after you introduced a certain topic, when the interviewee was especially forthcoming or expansive, and definitely note whatever promises you made about calling back, when or how the story will run, whether a recheck on quotes is to be expected, and so forth. Be aware of the dangers of delayed note taking as well as its benefits.

For example, journalists may overestimate their ability to remember and introduce mistakes unintentionally; in addition, some news interviewees will get nervous if they don't see you taking notes, and your credibility will plummet.

Another increasingly common alternative is tape or digital recording. Some years ago it seemed many interviewees became squeamish and uncommunicative at the sight of a recorder, but now with the advent of tiny and unobtrusive recorders, the technology seems relatively unthreatening to most people. If you decide to tape, ensure that the interviewee understands exactly when a tape recorder is on. In a dozen states, failure to inform a source and gain permission to record a conversation constitutes a legal violation, with criminal sanctions, civil sanctions, or both. Hidden taping, although a topic of intense debate among high-profile journalists covering big stories for major networks and papers, should not be controversial at all for most journalists. Because undisclosed taping keeps interviewees from a full range of choice about their own talk, it's simply unethical in virtually all everyday journalistic occasions. A public that believes this practice is common is a public that won't trust the institution of journalism. Perhaps some stories about dangerous practices are so protected and insulated, and the people involved so despicable, that some rare deceptions could be justified. Yet this isn't journalistic "business as usual." "Beyond the Basics" in this chapter considers journalistic ethics in greater detail.

What is missing? After this round of assessment, a reporter could conclude there is more to be learned or cleared up, leading to another round of interviews.

A deeper period of assessment involves the larger picture. What's been accomplished by this interview? What's my journalistic purpose? Has it been served? How does it mesh or clash with what I perceive as the interviewee's purpose? Questions like these may lead into an ethical self-examination by the reporter or a discussion involving others in the newsroom.

Conditions

Reporters seeking interviews sometimes must submit to an interviewee's preconditions or rules. Reporters usually resist attempts to control an interview or subsequent story, but the competition for exclusive interviews, particularly with celebrities, makes it hard to take an inflexible stance. Box office stars and others in the public eye have the leverage to make all sorts of demands, including who is assigned to do the interview and what subjects are out of bounds. A reporter or editor might decide that a conditional interview is better than none at all. On the other hand, public officials and politicians tend to seek interviews rather than dodge them. However, even talkative types are likely to request at times to speak off the record, not for attribution, or on background only (see discussion earlier in this chapter). Those arrangements allow reporters to gather quotes or inside information with the typical proviso that the speaker's identity won't be revealed. In journalism, though, credibility and authenticity suffer when words and opinions are attributed to nameless sources too often. See Box 6.7 for some tips if you are the interviewee.

Beyond the Basics

Ethics

Journalism ethicists are concerned with analyzing whether certain professional behaviors and decisions are *right* to make, even if they might be efficient, persuasive, lucrative, or otherwise effective. Ethicists research and analyze everything from plagiarism to conflicts of interest to the practice of planting hidden cameras and undercover reporters posing as everyday citizens. This latter practice resulted in one of the more famous professional debates in journalism, focusing on television show *Prime Time Live's* decision to document unsanitary practices at Food Lion supermarkets by going undercover. Did the ABC journalists undertake this interview-related strategy of deceit for justifiable reasons, or bogus ones? Did the goal of publicizing unsafe public practices, and thus ending them, justify journalism's own practices, ones that some deem unsafe and dangerous as well? Is there a final ethical standard that can resolve such questions? Or is it true, as broadcast journalist Diane Sawyer said years before her involvement in the Food Lion episode, "You cannot form an exact science of ethics. . . . You can talk about it, but you can't teach it because in the end it derives out of the whole human being" ("Diane Sawyer," p. 2). We disagree with both of these positions. Admittedly, there can be no final, exact, and authoritative arbiter of all ethical controversies, but that doesn't mean that anything goes; we can still teach and learn ethics by encouraging more informed ethical choice making, and by encouraging social and cultural standards that can be internalized by individuals. In this section, we explore several key turning points commonly encountered by journalistic interviewers and interviewees.

Box 6.7

Reminders *Being Interviewed by a Journalist*

• *Speak naturally and conversationally, even when being recorded.* You needn't worry about aiming your talk directly into the microphone. Almost all recorders now have built-in omnidirectional microphones that pick up sounds throughout a room. Remember, though, that after "record" is pressed, everything you say becomes a part of the record the journalist will use to produce the story. Sometimes, for example, as broadcast reporters conclude an interview, the sound—even as equipment is being put away—may remain on. If you keep talking, the interview isn't "over."

• *Remember that you can choose to speak without being recorded.* If an interviewer doesn't ask your preference but begins to tape the conversation, you can request that the recorder be turned off.

• *You can inquire about the interviewer's record keeping.* Many reporters are willing to share at least some of the contents of their notes. Although they aren't likely to give you the notes or any kind of veto power, don't hesitate to ask about what they contain in terms of quotes, statistics, or descriptions. Both parties presumably want these things reported accurately, and you might be able to catch a mistake on the scene.

Obtaining Interviews Ethically

Some reporters have lied to get interviews. They also have used masquerades, disguises, and impersonations to gain access and get people talking. At other times, rather than using outright deception, reporters withhold their identity and strike up a conversation, hoping the news source assumes he or she isn't talking to a journalist. Another form of lying involves misrepresenting the purpose of the interview because the interviewee might cooperate for one type of story but have reservations about another.

Whenever journalists use trickery or lies to get a story, they deny the interviewee freedom of choice about talking in public. An interview obtained by dishonest means has little hope of achieving the status of partnership. A reporter's dishonesty also invites countertactics by the interviewee, with implications for the journalist's primary mission, the pursuit of truth. (You notice the irony in this description, don't you?) Is lying to obtain an interview, or any other form of deception, always unethical? That's an open question, and to answer it requires careful deliberation. Some ethicists, known as *consequentialists*, claim that the ethics of behavior must be judged by the overall good it produces, and perhaps in some cases deception could be justified. Yet surely these do not define the day-to-day responsibilities of journalists to their sources or publics. Mitch Albom, a reporter and bestselling author who writes for the *Detroit Free Press*, advises: "Never assume that you can pull the wool over anybody's eyes, just because you're a reporter and they're an average person." "I always say, 'Here's why I'm calling,'" adding that "Somebody once wrote that there's no more seductive sentence in the English language than, 'I want to hear your story,' and maybe they're right. Because often you don't have to do any more than just say that" (quoted in Scanlon, 1996, p. 56). A reasonable ethical norm should be to represent yourself as who you really are, and your purposes as what they really are.

Conducting Interviews Ethically

Several tricky issues arise in journalistic interviews. One is the use of hidden audio or video recorders, as in the Food Lion case. Reporters who secretly record interviews have different motives. Some seek candid, off-the-cuff comments, uninhibited by the presence of a recorder. Others hope to lead a news source to say something incriminating, snaring the source later with a smoking-gun tape. Are all secret or surreptitious recordings unethical? That, too, cannot be answered easily; important stories of major public interest have been told through secret recordings. The circumstances and consequences make a difference. For some reporters, when the stakes are particularly high for the public welfare and necessary information is unfairly protected by powerful interests, then secret taping might be justified. Yet as in our discussion of obtaining interviews, these are extremely rare exceptions to normal interview practice.

Skilled reporters ask incisive questions. Where do they draw a line separating the ethical from the unethical? Forceful, direct inquiries are common in journalism; loaded, leading questions meant to trap or ambush an interviewee are not. Such questions might get results, but at what cost? The notion of partnership in interviews won't survive in an adversarial, aggressive climate. Moreover, what is one's ethical responsibility regarding the subjects broached, such as asking a presidential candidate "Have you ever committed adultery?" when the journalist knows that even a rigorous denial or "no comment" nevertheless will link the candidate's name dramatically with adultery in news accounts? Ethical journalists implicitly ask several guiding questions: What is the relevant journalistic purpose of my questions? Am I exploiting interviewees to further my own interests, or those of my employers? What might be the consequences of asking about certain topics? Can I justify asking questions that have the potential to upset and hurt people?

Skilled reporters also possess a talent for getting people to speak openly, at times contrary to their best interests. This vulnerability is especially true of people unaware of how reporters operate. Should interviewers issue a warning similar to the *Miranda* warning used by police: "Don't tell me anything you wouldn't want publicized; what you say may be held against you in ways neither you nor I can anticipate"? Trust and compassion enhance communication. Manipulation and ruthless pursuit of information do not. A reporter's intentional exploitation of interviewees is hard to justify. For a brief case study of what some journalism commentators called an exploitation of a source, but that others defended as being appropriate in context, see Box 6.8.

Using Interview Outcomes Ethically

Interviews are seldom printed or broadcast in their entirety. A period of editing generally follows, with parts of the interview retained and others discarded. A degree of license must be allowed because journalists cannot be mere stenographers, taking down all that's said and conveying it to the public. The public expects them to analyze, assess, weigh, work with words and observations, and create a story. But they must not distort or misrepresent what an interview said. Beyond that, as journalists construct the story, they must not use rhetorical sleight of hand, such as quoting out of context or using words selectively in biased ways. A reporter, for example, may have good reason to use a fraction of an interview, but motives count. Did the reporter select a particular quote

---

Box 6.8

Interviewers in Action   *Connie Chung*

In a two-hour taped interview, network reporter Connie Chung induced Kathleen Gingrich, mother of then-House Speaker Newt Gingrich, to comment on her son's opinion of Hillary Clinton, at that time the First Lady. "I can't tell you what he said about Hillary," Mrs. Gingrich said at one point. "You can't?" Chung asked. "I can't," Mrs. Gingrich replied. Chung leaned toward Mrs. Gingrich and said, "Why don't you just whisper it to me, just between you and me?" Mrs. Gingrich took the bait, saying, "'She's a bitch.' That's about the only thing he ever said about her" (p. 1A). CBS aired the statement in its broadcast of the interview, opening what one account called a Pandora's box of difficult ethical issues.

Source: "Pandora's Box" (1995)

---

because it best confirmed her perceptions of the interviewee as a nitwit? Was a clarifying context for the quote omitted or distorted intentionally?

When the interview is conceived as a partnership, a reporter cannot escape the responsibility to consider the story to be a collaboration. Interviewees put themselves at the mercy of journalists, and most journalists respect the power they hold and use it honorably.

Public Dialogue

Some critics argue that traditional journalism faces a major image problem: The practice of one-way, take-it-or-leave-it, conveyer-belt news is out of touch with the needs and concerns of ordinary citizens. To these critics, journalism risks repelling its audience with a detached, aloof, elitist attitude, sending people to more user-friendly media such as online information services or call-in talk programs.

Journalism plays an important role in our shared civic experience and knowledge. It sets local and national agendas, legitimizes what it explains, and helps us connect with other people and places. In the 1990s, a movement called **public journalism,** or, to some, *civic journalism,* had many news organizations reporting stories and sponsoring activities in an attempt to become more integrally involved in their communities. Today, a central goal of public or civic journalism remains going beyond reporting the news and attempting to help people think and act more like citizens than like consumers. Newspapers have sponsored public forums on issues such as race relations, and have given people opportunities to raise questions and offer solutions to local problems. As a result, there is greater emphasis in journalism on communication, which might sound ironic. In the traditional and important journalistic role of informing, some elements of communication, particularly listening and conversation, might be deemphasized in newsrooms. However, in public journalism conceptions, the journalistic interview assumes a major role in the public dialogue because it's the fuel for much of what we call news.

Challenges and Rewards

Mike Patterson, a character in the comic strip "For Better or for Worse," discovered that reporting involves responsibilities that weren't always clear. In a series of daily strips, Mike, a journalism student, wrestles with his conscience over a feature about Mr. Bergner, a quiet, dignified custodian at Mike's university. Mike talks to Mr. Bergner one day and finds his life story fascinating. Mr. Bergner reluctantly agrees to an interview. The result is a touching story that pleases Mike, and the campus newspaper

Making Your Decision

- Sherry Johnson, an attractive, popular high school senior, disappears on her way to school. She stopped at an ATM for $50; that is the last record of her whereabouts. Sherry's on the honor roll, sings in the church choir, and plans on becoming a teacher. Her parents and the police fear she's been abducted. You're assigned to cover this developing story, reporting on the young woman, her family, and her fate.

  How far would you go in finding out about Sherry from classmates, friends, family, and church members? Would you ask about her mental health, her romances, her home life? Would you interview her parents? Her 10-year-old brother? Her former teachers? An ex-boyfriend? What would you ask those you interviewed? What would you consider out of bounds?

  What if several of Sherry's classmates told you they think she's a runaway? What if someone called you anonymously to say "Sherry ran away from home because her father has abused her." Would you investigate? If so, how deeply would you probe, and whom would you interview?

  How would you define your relationship with the worried family? Would you console them as well as question them? Or would you remain purely professional, suppressing any emotional involvement?

  As you grapple with these questions, keep in mind the divided responsibilities journalists face. This is a difficult story to report, and it presents numerous ethical issues in how to conduct interviews. You might want to conduct mock interviews with friends or classmates, asking them to play assigned roles.

- You're a reporter for a city's daily paper, engaged in your first interview with a major political official. Midway through the interview with Mayor Dooley, she evidently begins to have second thoughts about her disclosures several minutes ago about City Hall financial records. She stops in midsentence and says, "I'll keep talking with you, but only if you call me this afternoon and let me change any quotes you're going to print."

  You want to continue the interview, but wonder about the advisability and ethics of giving the interviewee this much control over your story. After all, others in City Hall also have rights in this controversy, and her changes could affect them. Consider the dynamics of the situation, and the implications of her ultimatum for future interviews. What do you say to her at this moment?

- Revisit the Pete Rose–Jim Gray interview with which we opened the chapter. Although it's easy to criticize a reporter when an interview turns sour and uncomfortable, what, if anything, would you have done differently?

accepts it for publication. Unfortunately, the custodian was under the impression that the interview was for a class project, not publication. "I don't think I want it in the paper," he says. Mike blurts back, "It's a great story!" "Yes," says Mr. Bergner, "and whose story is it, Mr. Patterson? Yours or mine?"

The question dogs Mike, but he finally decides to withdraw the story. He tells the custodian, "Maybe I'm not tough enough to be a journalist." Bergner replies, "It's not 'tough' that makes a good journalist, Mr. Patterson. It's integrity." Journalists quickly learn that they face multiple responsibilities. Overall, they have a responsibility to the truth, at least to the degree that it can be determined. This example, though, reveals additional responsibilities. Journalists are in the business to disclose information, not withhold it. Mike brought a worthy story to life; should he now kill it? He has responsibilities to his audience, too, and not only responsibilities to be accurate and fair. He must also measure the public's stake in the story. Is he duty-bound in the public interest to tell the story? Then there's Mr. Bergner. If the news amounts to a cocreation of reporters and their interview partners, then it's difficult for any reporter to say, "It's my story, not yours. I can do with it what I want."

Journalists seldom enjoy the luxury of simply "doing journalism," free from nagging concerns like these. The stakes usually are too high to pretend that getting the story defines their only responsibility. A reporter's mistakes and misunderstandings, even those that seem slight, can reverberate into the community and affect the lives of people profoundly. Journalists meet their responsibilities in different ways. Veteran reporter Richard Clurman (1990) operated from a formerly heretical view that sharing a story with its principal characters prior to broadcast or publication can only help journalists do a better job: "It can be the final step in reporting to test interpretations, facts, and conjectures with those about whom the journalist is writing." Clurman sought "new illuminations and nuances that otherwise would have escaped even careful reporting and checking" (p. 11). Journalistic interviewees get arguing rights, not editing rights, Clurman said. A news story, in this view, is the intricate interplay of journalist, interviewee, and public audience—but the journalist is the professional who bears most of the responsibility for its emergence. Considerable emotional strain accompanies the work of journalists, but most would say the pleasures outweigh the pressures. They report great satisfaction in knowing that through their efforts, people are heard, understood, and helped.

Summary

Journalists and, in turn, the public rely on interviews as a major source of news. The techniques and tasks of journalistic interviewing apply to nearly everyone responsible for gathering reliable, important information and distributing it to others. Accuracy is the primary goal of information-gathering interviews.

Journalists use interviews in various ways to fit various situations, from quick-hitting news reports to longer, textured profiles of people, but certain fundamentals apply to most interviews in journalism: purpose, preparation, questioning, listening, record keeping, and postinterview assessment. In addition, interviews can involve conditions set either by the interviewer or interviewee, such as off-the-record agreements.

Interviewees often approach journalists warily. In part, they react to stereotypes of journalists as prying, insensitive, and aggressive. In truth, most reporters approach their jobs with compassion and serious purpose. Ethics is an important concern in contemporary journalism. Although interview ethics hasn't received as much attention as other aspects of the journalist's work, certain guidelines and duties set standards of behavior. As in other fields, though, don't look for ethical absolutes. Journalists must weigh and balance their responsibilities and obligations as professionals against the consequences of their reporting. It's a job full of challenges and rewards.

The Interview Bookshelf

On the journalist's experience:

Brady, J. (1976). *The craft of interviewing.* Cincinnati, OH: Writer's Digest Books.

Wallace, M. (2005). *Between you and me: A memoir.* New York: Hyperion.

Brady's is without a doubt the best known interviewing book among journalists. He tells interesting and wise stories about resourceful journalists and the problems they solve. Wallace is perhaps the most famously aggressive interviewer of the past 50 years, and this book (with accompanying DVD) describes—and attempts to justify—his encounters with reluctant interviewees on 60 Minutes and elsewhere.

On practical problems of interpersonal communication in journalism:

Killenberg, G. M., & Anderson, R. (1989). *Before the story: Interviewing and communication skills for journalists.* New York: St. Martin's Press.

The authors frame the journalistic interview as everyday talk and the journalist as an interpersonal communicator.

On ethics in journalism:

Black, J., Steele, B., & Barney, R. (1993). *Doing ethics in journalism.* Greencastle, IN: Sigma Delta Chi Foundation and The Society of Professional Journalists.

Klaidman, S., & Beauchamp, T. L. (1987). *The virtuous journalist.* New York: Oxford University Press.

These two books manage to be both concrete and philosophically informed at the same time. They present and analyze actual cases, and challenge journalists to consider carefully the harms they might cause by sloppy communication.

On public or civic journalism:

Charity, A. (1995). *Doing public journalism.* New York: Guilford Press.

Charity reinforces our emphasis on listening and shows how a new kind of journalism has to depend on a profound respect for interviewees and audiences.

On being interviewed by journalists:

Hilton, J. (1987). *How to meet the press: A survival guide.* New York: Dodd, Mead.

Although the interview isn't really a competition, it can sometimes feel unequal to interviewees. Hilton helps anyone prepare to meet professional journalists on their own terms and with more confidence.

Chapter Seven

Interviews in Social Science and Humanistic Research

The pulse of America gets taken regularly from the Chicago, Illinois, headquarters of the National Opinion Research Center (NORC), which relies on interviews to collect much of its massive inventory of data. NORC conducts polls and surveys on major issues such as drug abuse, sexual relations, homelessness, and mental health. Its research taps into the attitudes, beliefs, and behavior of the American public, and its findings flow into a river of social science survey data used in decision-making situations ranging from marketing dog food to conducting foreign policy.

The term *social science* generally refers to attempts—such as those of NORC—to describe patterns of individual and group behavior to establish clear cause–effect relationships. Often these researchers are scholars in sociology, psychology, economics, and anthropology, but many professional fields are drawn to social science methods, including business, law, education, and medicine. Yet the social sciences don't have a monopoly on systematic research. The *humanities* include research disciplines—among them, literature, philosophy, art, and history—that attempt to discover the qualities and values that make humans particularly human. Communication researchers often stand in a fertile middle ground emphasizing both precise analysis of social behavior and

Meaning is not merely elicited by apt questioning nor simply transported through respondent replies; it is actively and communicatively assembled in the interview encounter. Respondents are not so much repositories of knowledge—treasures of information awaiting excavation—as they are constructors of knowledge in collaboration with interviewers.

—James Holstein and Jaber Gubrium,
The Active Interview

sensitive understanding of humanistic values. A wide range of social science and humanistic researchers use interviews to re-create the past, understand the present, and predict the future. Interviewing is vital work, helping to expand knowledge and offer solutions to such everyday problems as racial intolerance, teenage smoking habits, and suicide rates among the elderly. Researchers clearly play a major role in helping us understand our own lives.

Interview researcher Charles Briggs (1986) estimated some years ago that perhaps 90 percent of all studies in the social sciences used data from interviews (p. 1). Unfortunately, articles and books about interviewing tend to be the "'cookbook' type, providing recipes for better baking using interviews yet without seriously considering the nature of the interview or its inherent weaknesses" (p. 2). Despite thousands of studies, "we still know very little about the nature of the interview as a communicative event" (p. 2). Little has changed since Briggs's summary.

We are all researchers as we go about the everyday tasks of shopping, traveling, relating to coworkers, reading the paper, and voting. As everyday researchers, people sample opinions, test hypotheses, ask questions, and conduct informal interviews. However, many professional researchers elevate the collection, interpretation, and application of their inquiries to the level of science. They systematically pursue a kind of truth—at least the best available version of the truth. Others who use interviews in their work, such as journalists or social workers, may not engage in precise scientific inquiry or see themselves as researchers. They collect anecdotal evidence from interviewees, however, and weave it into literary or nonfiction forms that portray reality in a less precise but potentially more involving narrative style.

Yet even in the deadline-driven world of reporting, a level of science applies—or should apply—when news organizations administer polls and analyze data (Paulos, 1995), engaging in what some call *precision journalism* (Meyer, 2002). Some would argue that anyone pursuing knowledge should respect, and act in tune with, the spirit of scientific inquiry. Physicist Lawrence Cranberg (1989) observed that trained researchers "seek to discover hidden facts and arrive at elusive truths," and they share a "skilled determination to get at them" (p. 47). The journalist and scientist, he added, "march to the same orders and serve the common need of mankind for shared knowledge and understanding" (p. 46). Although observers define facts differently, and although facts are not like objects that can be discovered whole, Cranberg's basic sentiment applies to a wide variety of knowledge seekers.

In this chapter you will learn the fundamentals of quantitative and qualitative research interviewing. **Quantitative research** transforms experience into information by creating countable categories and units that can aid future decision making. **Qualitative research,** as the name implies, focuses less on quantities than on the qualities of data—their meaning or value. Both types of research can make scientific contributions, although science is occasionally identified more with quantitative studies. Many research projects combine quantitative and qualitative methods to help explain communication more systematically. We'll discuss more of the differences later in the chapter, but for now, we define *scientific research* as involving systematic, public, and verifiable methods for generating practical human knowledge. Scientists use a variety of methods of inquiry and measurement, and social scientists, in particular, rely on various kinds of interviews—questionnaires, telephone surveys, and in-depth conversations, for example.

After we introduce the philosophy and characteristics of scientific inquiry, we'll examine the basic form of quantitative interview research, the survey, and then move to qualitative intricacies of focus group, ethnographic, and oral history interviews. In "Beyond the Basics," we'll grapple with two ethical issues of research. First, we apply the idea of collaboration in qualitative research to the interaction of interviewers and interviewees. Second, we describe why it's important for ethical researchers to obtain the informed or implied consent of research participants.

The Basics

Philosophy of the Research Interview

How do we come to know something? This question propels **epistemology**, the study of how human knowledge develops. Kerlinger (1986) believed humans come to know things in four basic ways: tenacity, intuition, authority, and science. *Tenacity* relies on repetition and ingrained beliefs. Often it's a lesson drummed into us as children: "If you go outside with wet hair you'll catch a cold," or "Lightning doesn't strike twice in the same place." Such knowing is part of our socialization, but knowledge based on tenacity often lacks proof. It can resemble folklore more than fact. *Intuition* relies on common sense and gut feelings. A police officer, for example, employing anecdotal and impressionistic evidence, concludes violence depicted on TV instigates real-life violence. Intuition has its value, and sometimes what we know intuitively corresponds with findings of valid research. However, it can deceive us, as well, because it isn't grounded in carefully collected and analyzed empirical data from controlled, systematic observation or experimentation. When tenacity or intuition fail to answer our questions, there is the knowledge based on *authority*, such as a statement from an expert in a specialized field. In the best circumstances, an authority provides valid and sound insight. Of course, the voice of authority, while sounding sure and exact, might merely echo flawed intuition, out-of-date assumptions, or untested hypotheses.

That leaves *science*, a word most of us associate with the solid "truths" of life. The other means of knowing can be haphazard and unreliable, but Kerlinger says science offers knowledge based on proof—something to count on. Keep in mind, however, that we learn in combinations of ways. In fact, scientific investigations often spring from creative hypotheses gleaned from intuition, authority, or tenacity. Moreover, scientific knowing can be flawed, too; when framed differently by various audiences, it can, and usually does, produce conflicting conclusions. Just because a method is scientific doesn't mean that it is mistake-free. It's better at producing and clarifying some kinds of data than others. In fact, some researchers involved in "interpretive" or "naturalistic" work critique our society's near-automatic reverence for scientific method. Lincoln and Guba (1985), for example, observe that despite the successes of science, "cracks have begun to appear in science's magnificent edifice as new 'facts' are uncovered with which the old paradigm cannot deal or explain. Normal science . . . is becoming more and more difficult to sustain. Serious challenges are being mounted from the perspective of alternate paradigms that suggest new and different answers" (p. 7).

These challenges do not suggest that traditional science is irrelevant. Rather, its brands of cause–effect structure and data-based usefulness are not the only ways we can know the world. Kvale (1996) identifies epistemological positions of interviewing that aren't based on the quantitative methods of traditional science (pp. 38–50), but are more qualitative. These alternatives acknowledge that humans create meaning through their relations, that new information emerges from such communication, and that people see, interpret, and understand in different ways. Interviews that probe these nuances of meaning are, in Kvale's words, "construction sites" of knowledge (p. 42). This rough distinction might be helpful: If quantitative researchers try to *find* knowledge, qualitative ones try to discover how it is *created*.

A researcher usually chooses either quantitative or qualitative methods for a specific study, although overlap and integration of the two approaches is also possible. According to one authority (McCracken, 1988), the criterion for this choice partly reflects the scope of the study: "The quantitative researcher uses a lens that brings a narrow strip of the field of vision into very precise focus. The qualitative researcher uses a lens that permits a much less precise vision of a much broader strip" (p. 16).

Quantitative social scientists try to generate, categorize, and account for numerical data by using instruments such as questionnaires or survey interview *guides* or *schedules*. The findings reflect the mathematical precision of the research, and interpretation becomes a way of explaining or qualifying what the numbers show.

Qualitative researchers study the less tangible qualities of social experience. Their methods include fieldwork, focus groups, in-depth interviews, and participant observation. The researcher becomes an "instrument" for collecting data, using powers of communication, observation, and interpretation to conduct the research. A qualitative approach requires a personal, hands-on relationship with the data. Narratives dominate qualitative research, not numbers or charts. In political science, for example, a qualitative project might rely on in-depth interviews of voters exploring their own political beliefs, or their evaluations of the political system. It could elicit stories and interpretations that the researcher would then analyze to identify important themes. In a quantitative study, instead of face-to-face in-depth interviews or observation of political behavior, the research draws on a representative sample of voters and asks carefully constructed and administered survey questions to collect information that not only describes the voters' political beliefs and experiences but also accounts for influences of, for example, age, gender, religion, education, and income. From such data, the quantitative researcher predicts, within a range of confidence, how (for example) white males between the ages of 25 and 35 will vote on a school tax referendum. Box 7.1 outlines the basic structure of a research project.

Box 7.1

Reminders   *Stages of Research*

- *Select the problem.* You become curious about a problem that can't be explained sufficiently by existing knowledge. You tentatively decide the problem is worthy of study and consider practical and ethical implications of a possible project.

- *Review the literature.* Your **literature review**— a careful written analysis of existing research and theorizing on the proposed subject—helps narrow the study and leads to establishing a hypothesis or research question.

- *Frame a hypothesis or a research question.* A *hypothesis* is a tentative prediction about what you're likely to find in your study, based on previous research. A *research question*, especially appropriate for studies that are less associated with the traditional scientific method, asks specifically how two or more concepts are related.

- *Select a methodology.* With a hypothesis or research question, you can select a methodology appropriate for testing the hypothesis or exploring the research question. You might want to pretest the methods before data collection begins, if feasible. For example, a smaller pilot study might help you determine whether a proposed survey instrument (questionnaire) includes confusing, ambiguous, or inappropriate questions.

- *Collect data.* In most qualitative projects, you would collect information or stories through interviews, participant observation, and other personalized and often subjective methods. In a quantitative study, trained assistants could help you administer surveys or collect data in other carefully controlled and presumably objective ways.

- *Analyze data.* Qualitative research demands your personal reflection in the analysis stage, and it must be as systematic and rigorous as possible. You will develop a pattern for the analysis, such as comparing interview responses to identify emergent themes. In quantitative research, your data analysis will often involve statistical comparisons, based on coding the responses from surveys or data such as census figures.

- *Present results.* Once you've analyzed your data, your reasoning and conclusions can be shared with other researchers through professional publications or released to the public through a report or other method of dissemination. Increasingly, qualitative researchers are sharing tentative results with interviewees and other respondents whose cooperation helped produce the insights in the first place. At this stage, too, researchers will want to analyze how well the results support existing theories or point to new ones.

Survey Interviews

Researchers use quantitative and mixed quantitative and qualitative surveys for descriptive, explanatory, exploratory, and analytical purposes. In marketing, for example, surveys probe consumer behavior and attitudes, helping companies introduce new products or improve existing ones. In politics, surveys gauge public opinion on policy and campaign issues, and candidates often adjust their positions based on survey results. Academic researchers find surveys useful for a variety of projects, such as identifying attitudes of parents toward teachers' merit pay or determining the decision-making criteria of editors and other media gatekeepers.

Because researchers respect **validity** (whether a method assesses what it is supposed to assess) and **reliability** (whether it assesses the same phenomenon whenever the method is used), surveys can't be haphazardly designed or administered, unless someone doesn't want to know the truth or hopes to hide the truth. In survey research, reputations suffer when results go sour. Validity and reliability are expected, and falling short of those standards isn't acceptable.

Surveys succeed or fail to the extent that they meet three basic criteria: Do they get people to respond honestly, accurately, and completely? They ideally will encourage forthright responses, even when exploring sensitive subjects such as drug use or mental problems. The survey must avoid any ambiguity that could undermine the accuracy of its findings; if one respondent defines "well off" in terms of salary, but another defines it in terms of neighborhood safety, are they really answering the same question? Finally, the survey must gain respondent cooperation that is as thorough as possible. The design or format of a survey can either discourage or encourage participation. A survey can't accomplish its objectives if people won't participate willingly and conscientiously. Box 7.2 offers some relevant experiences from survey interviewers.

Types of Surveys

Three types of research surveys offer different advantages and limitations: self-administered questionnaires, telephone surveys, and interviewer-conducted surveys. Although each approach involves compromises, being able to compare their strengths and weaknesses allows you to select one that best meets your goals.

In **self-administered questionnaires**, respondents complete surveys received by mail or accessed by other means such as Internet Web sites. The researcher surrenders the advantage of face-to-face administration of the survey in return for efficiency—reaching a

---

Box 7.2

Interviewers in Action   *Jean Converse and Howard Schuman*

Converse and Schuman, experienced interviewers at the Survey Research Center of the University of Michigan, trained and supervised many student interviewers. Their book collected and analyzed interviewer reactions after research projects were completed. For example:

Interviewers venture out of their own small worlds. They meet people they would never otherwise meet, and they often find a degree of reflectiveness, personal candor, and genuine talk that is not even an everyday occurrence among close friends. They occasionally encounter indifference or suspicion, but they leave many an interview with the experience of a fleeting but genuine friendship.

. . . The variety of scenes and situations to which the interviewer is admitted is richer than most of us gather up in a few days or weeks within our own small worlds. The process is one of sampling not only people but moments of lives being lived.

Source: Converse & Schuman (1974, p. 1)

large number of respondents at a reasonable cost. People asked to complete such a survey might ignore it, but others might value how self-administration allows anonymity at a convenient time and place. Several companies provide mailing lists of potential respondents divided by specific demographic or lifestyle characteristics; a self-administered survey based on such a list has obvious advantages.

Self-administered surveys are a kind of interview at a distance, with prepared questions. This method forgoes such advantages as immediate feedback and interactive context. Respondents cannot clarify the meaning of the overall instructions or a particular question. Researchers can't be sure who completed the survey; it might not be the person to whom it's addressed. Another disadvantage is the return rate; it's too easy to toss a questionnaire in the trash, although reminders encourage returns. Collecting data through the mail can be agonizingly slow. Moreover, to encourage response, mail surveys must be brief—usually not more than a couple of pages. That, of course, also limits the kind and amount of data collected.

Computer-assisted self-administered interviewing (CASI) and **audio computer-assisted self-administered interviewing** (ACASI) have advantages over other more personalized interview forms in one crucial respect (Tourangeau & Smith, 1996). When personally sensitive topics such as drug use, personal hygiene, sex, or racism are involved, respondents answering questions administered by a computer (especially in the ACASI mode with an accompanying voice) are more likely to disclose acts that are potentially embarrassing. Couper and Hansen (2001) offer a comprehensive look at how computer-assisted interviewing became more sophisticated as it developed.

Telephone surveys, although not as prevalent as they once were, still can be used as an alternative to mailing questionnaires. After being contacted voice-to-voice, a respondent who might casually toss an anonymous questionnaire would be less likely to ignore a "real person" asking for assistance. As a result, response rates in telephone surveys generally run higher than those of mail surveys. Researchers also have the opportunity to establish a connection with the respondent and to provide feedback. A somewhat longer list of questions might be appropriate as well. On the other hand, in an age of pervasive marketing, many people are wary about participating in a telephone survey, as these requests can turn out to be barely disguised sales pitches even in an era of "do not call" laws. The popularity of cellular phones with unlisted numbers and call-screening technologies such as caller ID and answering machines also have decreased the desirability of telephone surveys, as has the fact that telephone interviewing is generally more costly than mail or Internet surveys. Telephone interviewers have some access to nonverbal context (e.g., inflections and pauses) but it's difficult to evaluate, and an interviewer won't know if the respondent is seriously focusing on questions instead of answering offhandedly while changing a diaper or watching a ball game on TV (see Shuy, 2001).

Interviewer-conducted surveys are the gold standard of survey interviewing for many researchers because face-to-face communication allows for more detailed and elaborate responses on a human scale, with greater opportunity for rapport, more careful listening, and higher completion rates. Although the questions come from a highly standardized schedule and there's little opportunity to adjust the questions to the needs of individual personalities, this method still encourages a more personal quality of communication and allows clarification of questions if respondents are uncertain how to respond. The advantages are bought at a fairly high price; interviewer-conducted surveys are more expensive than their alternatives, and more time-consuming, too. Despite the potential for greater rapport, the presence of an interviewer introduces new complications, such as personality conflicts, unplanned variations in how questions are worded, and different treatment for different racial and ethnic groups (see Schaeffer & Maynard, 2001, for a description of the current debate about standardization vs. flexibility in survey work). Some studies (e.g., Converse & Schuman, 1974, p. 54) have discovered **over-rapport**; that is, interviewer bias resulting from excessive closeness or cordiality. To survey a large number of people, researchers usually enlist a field staff of interviewers. Even with thorough training, these representatives will communicate somewhat differently and might fail to follow instructions for maintaining neutrality. Obviously these kinds of interviewer effects aren't found in other survey methods.

Planning and Administering Surveys

Most survey research involves five mutually supportive steps: setting a research objective; selecting a sample of respondents from the target population; constructing the survey questionnaire or instrument; administering the survey; and analyzing the data. Designing a survey project is not a simple, paint-by-numbers process. Survey researchers with large-scale projects usually possess a background in statistics, probability sampling, and the use of analytical tools. Many are highly paid for their talents; it's not a job for dilettantes. Still, the basic steps should help you get started in small-scale research projects and reinforce the importance of clear questioning. In the next few pages, we summarize common survey activities, without advocating a definitive set of instructions.

The first step, setting a *research objective*, helps researchers fine-tune the focus of the survey and determine what they really want to know. Before deciding what to ask their respondents, they ask themselves a series of questions: Will the survey collect descriptive data, such as how many people read supermarket tabloids or watch soap operas? Will the survey include questions seeking explanatory data as well, such as *why* people say they watch soap operas? Will it compare demographics, such as rate of viewership by age, race, income, and gender, to further understand *who* watches and why?

The second step, determining the sample, builds on the answers to the first set of questions about research objectives and focus. A **sample** is a group of respondents of sufficient size and type to represent fairly a larger population. Even this is a compromise. A researcher who surveys all members of a given population, such as the congregation of a church, conducts what is called a **census**. Usually, though, researchers can study only a segment of the membership and must try to generalize with some level of confidence from those results. At times the number of respondents used in survey research seems to the everyday citizen to be almost too small for drawing conclusions, but sampling procedures can be so sophisticated that results can be remarkably helpful. For example, the Gallup Organization collaborates with *USA Today* to poll on public issues. It typically interviews 1,001 individuals to gauge what 299 million Americans think about such subjects as gasoline prices, gay marriage, and the president's job performance.

The basic notion is this: If you know what you want to know, whom do you need to ask? John Allen Paulos (1995), a mathematician who studies how journalists use and misuse statistics, is concerned about the too-often blurred distinction between informal and scientific sampling:

> Too many stories (usually local) are prefaced with something like "This is not a scientific poll, but a sampling of your friends and neighbors who called our special 900 number. . . ." A more accurate prologue might be, "Here is what a few of the most fervent people in your community think about this issue." Confidence intervals for such "samplings" should be quite broad to accommodate their considerable hot air. (p. 153)

In the language of research, broad "confidence intervals" mean that you shouldn't have much confidence in the results. Paulos identifies the problems caused by shaky decisions about who to ask when you need answers. In quick-fix popular media polls, the assumption that callers represent the whole audience, and the assumption that an audience for a show represents the larger community, is rarely raised, much less tested. However, this is precisely the problem that systematic sampling tries to solve.

Survey researchers must choose between probability or nonprobability sampling. **Probability surveys** use various mathematical guidelines to ensure a representative sample of the population. The guiding principle of probability is that all members of a target population have an equal chance of being selected for the sample. Most of our previous introduction to sampling represents this type. **Nonprobability surveys** do not follow this guideline, but instead use respondents' availability or special characteristics as more important criteria than the need to generalize to a large complex population. They can be quite helpful in collecting preliminary data or in investigating a small, select, or shifting population.

Probability surveys attempt to draw a statistically representative sample of a particular population. Ideally, no member stands a greater chance of being selected for the study than any other member, a condition known as **random selection**. One researcher (see Stacks & Hocking, 1992) illustrates the process with the analogy of a jar holding 10,000 marbles—8,000 red and 2,000 blue (p. 179). You could select a sample by mixing the marbles and selecting 10, one at a time, but replacing each marble after noting its color. By chance, you could draw 10 marbles of the same color. Odds are better, though, that you'd come closer to a sampling percentage that reflects the population (several times as many reds as blues). But how close? A random sample of 100 would likely come closer to the actual 4:1 ratio, and 1,000 closer still. Probability surveys permit estimates of **sampling error**—the degree to which a given sample statistic will likely fail to correspond to the actual characteristics of the population it supposedly represents. It provides an estimate of how much the results of a sample, such as the *USA Today*/Gallup poll, may differ due to chance selection of survey participants when compared to what would have been found if the entire population had been interviewed.

Generating a genuinely random sample can be difficult, and several versions of this process have become common. Using a **simple random sample** depends on knowing and numbering the complete roster of the population. If you wanted to survey a sample of 50 professors out of a population of 500 in your city, you could assign each a number from 1 to 500. Then, locate a table of random numbers (included in many books on research methods); this table contains columns of grouped numbers arranged in a random pattern. Pick an arbitrary starting point on the table, perhaps by closing your eyes and dropping a pen point on a column. Also arbitrarily, decide whether to go up or down in columns if you don't select a number in your sample the first time. For example, your pen might land on 77,832, but the opening three-digit number, 778, is higher than any of the numbers you've assigned to the population. Because you've decided to go down the columns, say, you move to the next number down, perhaps 00789; Professor No. 7 (007) becomes the first person included in your random sample. Then select the remaining 49 numbers by moving through the table in the same way.

The **systematic random sample** resembles a simple random sample with a different selection method, one in which every "*n*th" part or unit of the population gets selected. To get a sample of 20 from a population of 100, every fifth number would be picked, starting with a number selected at random, say 9, and then moving at intervals of five (14, 19, 24, etc.). Systematic random sampling works reasonably well when the population comes from a directory or yearbook. Researchers are careful, though, when using a telephone book or other references that might not include all members of the desired population.

Earl Babbie (2007; Baxter & Babbie, 2004), author of several influential research textbooks, notes that **stratified random sampling** offers a greater degree of representativeness and a lower degree of sampling error than the other approaches. A stratified approach allows for study of subsets of a population and, therefore, enables the researcher to account for and compare variables within the population. In human groups, those variables might include ethnic identification, gender, age, education, occupation, and geography (place of residence), for example. The units of a population then are separated by common characteristics into homogeneous groups ("strata") before drawing a sample. To study voters as a population in a stratified sampling would mean looking at subsets of voters, say, by age but also, possibly, by region or religion.

Nonprobability surveys do not seek to guarantee a representative sample of the population, and thus could utilize a variety of other methods of sampling. For example, in a **convenience sample** (also called an **available sample**), respondents are chosen to participate in a research project because they can provide useful data and because they are simply available. Professors and other researchers sometimes involve college students in surveys that have nothing inherently to do with campus life; students are a group hardly known to represent larger social trends of political or economic participation, but as a group they are quite easily tapped. If the study is of group decision making, for instance, they do presumably make decisions in groups—and their ready availability and willingness (at times, at least) to participate mitigates the fact that they are unrepresentative of the entire human population in many ways. A **snowball sample** is composed of a group of respondents who then identify more respondents, who identify others, and so on. Another type uses a **quota sample** of respondents chosen to match, for example, known percentages in the larger population. Election records of a precinct might show that 40 percent of the voters are registered as Democrats, 50 percent Republicans, and 10 percent independents. You could, then, draw a sample that reflects those percentages; if known, variables of age, race, and other factors could also be included in the sample.

The third step of planning and administering surveys is question design and construction. The bare bones of a survey, whether administered on paper or orally, includes

Box 7.3

Reminders *One Common Survey Structure—Gallup's Quintamensional Sequence of Questions*

George Gallup and the American Institute of Public Opinion developed over decades a sequence of questioning that established how much information respondents might have, and how much thought they've given to a topic, before they provide significant opinions. The *quintamensional sequence*, as it's known, also increases survey validity by checking whether respondents understand the questions in roughly the same ways. William Foddy exemplifies the five-part sequence in this way:

1. A general question to establish whether respondents have the required information concerning the topic. (e.g. Have you heard of X? yes___ no___)

2. An open question to get at respondents' general perceptions or feelings about the topic. (e.g. What are your views about X?)

3. A dichotomous question to elicit perceptions or feelings about a specific aspect of the topic. (e.g. Do you favour or not favour Xi? favour___ not favour___)

4. An open question to get at reasons for responses toward the aspect of the topic specified in step 3. (e.g. Why do you favour [not favour] Xi?

5. A rating question to allow respondents to indicate the strength of their responses toward the aspect of the topic specified in step 3. (e.g. How strongly do you feel about this?; Very strongly, Fairly strongly, Not at all strongly.)

Source: Foddy (1993, p. 62)

a sequence of standardized questions preceded by an introduction and instructions. (See Box 7.3 for one particularly influential survey question sequence.) The introduction typically explains the nature and purpose of the survey; the instructions help interviewer and interviewees reduce the chances of misunderstanding or error. Introductions and instructions should be short, simple, direct, and above all, clear.

Typically, standardized questions require respondents to choose among several possible answers or ranges of response. The most common survey questionnaire employs either scales or multiple-choice selections. Often the opening questions seek demographic information—place of birth, age, occupation, residence, and so forth. For coding and comparison purposes, these questions often reflect groupings, as in this example:

What is your age?

___ 18–25

___ 26–40

___ 41–55

___ 56–70

___ Above 70

Certain scales work well with particular information-seeking objectives. For example, in measuring attitudes, a **Likert-type scale** (named after its originator, Rensis Likert) offers a statement and asks the respondent to indicate a choice from a range of agreement options:

Police should be able to conduct full car searches during routine traffic stops.

___ Strongly agree

___ Agree

___ Undecided (or neutral)

___ Disagree

___ Strongly disagree

Various forms of rating scales often include number references as codes for later calculation and analysis of the survey data:

What is your opinion of the news coverage in the *New York Times*?

Objective ___ ___ ___ ___ ___ Biased
          (5) (4) (3) (2) (1)

Semantic differential scales, similar to the preceding example, ask for a series of choices, along a continuum, between opposite descriptions. Semantic differential method probes the rater's subjective connotations—inner semantic meanings—for the item or object being rated. Varying the placement of presumably positive and negative concepts can help prevent respondents from slipping into a pattern of left-side-only or right-side-only answering, as the second line in the following example illustrates:

The president's foreign policy:

Active   ___ ___ ___ ___ ___ ___ ___ Passive

Weak   ___ ___ ___ ___ ___ ___ ___ Strong

Confident ___ ___ ___ ___ ___ ___ ___ Worried

As they explore respondents' descriptions, researchers may use a frequency scale, which provides specific data on behavioral events:

How often do you eat at a restaurant?

___ 5 or more times a week

___ 2–4 times a week

___ once a week

___ less than once a week

___ never

We've introduced elementary examples of common scale types, but other more sophisticated methods are available as well. If you must conduct complex survey research, we suggest you consult a handbook in social science survey methods or other more specialized materials (e.g., Bouma & Atkinson, 1995; Singleton & Straits, 2001), or take a survey research class. In large-scale projects, those researchers responsible for constructing the survey instrument itself may hire professional interviewers to administer the surveys, and your professional skills may involve you at that level even if you didn't design the study.

Box 7.4

Reminders *Administering Survey Interviews*

You might be asked to serve as a survey interviewer as part of your job or as a volunteer for an organization. You'll likely receive detailed instructions about the organization's expectations, but here are some general reminders:

- *Rehearse*. Go over the instrument carefully. Be familiar with the language used, consulting a supervisor or dictionary for definitions as necessary. Learn the proper pronunciation of unfamiliar words.

- *Establish a supportive climate*. Introduce yourself and the project cordially and sincerely. Dress for the occasion, as well, with clothing that fits the context. Although many interviews are reasonably formal occasions, field interviews in a factory probably shouldn't be conducted in an expensive suit.

- *Stick to the question schedule*. Don't ad lib or vary the questions, because your alterations could influence the results. Try to maintain a steady tone without inflections or pitch that could artificially lead or suggest responses.

- *Record responses accurately*. Problems of **coding** (deciding how to place responses into categories) are common even for research designs that allow little respondent choice. If questions are closed, or if respondents must choose from a list they don't appear to understand, an

interviewer must in some cases engage in what survey researchers call "training the respondent"; that is, explaining the instructions again and rereading the list. Don't interpret an interviewee's response on the spot, or give an ad hoc explanation; to do so could alter the comparability of results. Coding problems are much more challenging for open-questioning designs, because individual responses must be coded into one or more classifications of the interviewee's or interviewer's devising. If questions are open, any evidence of misunderstanding is potentially more serious, and interviewers must probe for increased clarity. In such situations, practitioners (Fowler & Mangione, 1990) suggest that you reread the question and concentrate on only three basic probes: (1) "How do you mean that?" (2) "Tell me more about that." (3) "Anything else?" (p. 41). The less intrusive the probe, the better.

- *Take your time*. Rushing might save a few minutes, but the cost can be high. You want respondents to be comfortable and confident with their answers. If they have the time to respond fully and carefully, you have the time also.

- *Reaffirm a supportive climate at the conclusion*. Close the interview with a well-phrased expression of appreciation.

The basic rules of constructing and asking questions naturally apply in survey interviews, so review our discussion in Chapter 4. Standardized social science interviewing perhaps demands even greater attention to wording questions. Foddy (1993, p. 51), after reviewing existing studies, recommends that researchers follow four basic principles in wording questions, which we paraphrase as brevity, grammatical simplicity, specificity, and concreteness. The principle of *brevity* reminds researchers to edit their questions to eliminate unnecessary words. A question that violates the principle of brevity is, "When considering the overall political and judicial scene in Washington, do you find yourself on the whole encouraged or discouraged?" Researchers achieve *grammatical simplicity* by removing "complicating phrases and clauses" and by phrasing questions in positive form. Complex grammar and negative constructions can muddy the intended question. A question that violates this principle is, "What, given the public's recent preoccupation with healthy alternatives, does not worry you about the following foods?" Researchers concerned with *specificity* choose words that have focused and clear meanings for the intended audience. A question that violates the principle of specificity for neighborhood homeowners, for example, would be, "Which educational experiences have been important for you recently?" Finally, by adopting the principle of *concreteness*, researchers provide tangible, easily understandable choices, examples, or illustrations. A question that violates the principle of concreteness is, "Would you say you go to see movies often or seldom?" Concreteness is closely related to specificity, but the emphasis in specificity is to choose words that respondents will interpret in the same way ("educational experiences" is so ambiguous that one person could call a television program on landscaping "educational," whereas another might limit the term to classroom learning). The emphasis in concreteness is not only on specificity of terms but also on providing empirical or operational definitions for respondents ("often" and "seldom" can be made empirical by substituting scales for how often the respondent goes to movies).

You might think that in social science surveys, a brief, simple, specific, and concrete schedule of questions, administered the same way to each respondent, guarantees the validity and reliability of the research. Questions are important, of course, but so is the hard-to-define cultural factor of perceived interviewer–interviewee similarity: "a guiding assumption of survey methodology is that similarity between interviewers and respondents on important social characteristics increases the validity of the information obtained in the interview. Therefore, an effort is made in surveys to match interviewers and respondents on important social characteristics such as race" (Hurtado, 1994, p. 77). Other researchers show that even interviewer matching on the basis of race is more complicated than it appears at first (Merriam, Johnson-Bailey, Lee, Ntseane, & Muhamad, 2001). Beyond the linguistic clarity of questions, survey researchers must realize that answering even "clear" questions is a social process in which people determine—rightly or wrongly—that certain answers could please or offend the social-cultural group represented by a particular interviewer, and they often adapt their responses accordingly. This adaptation could take place, of course, even with so-called "matched" interview pairs, but researchers have determined that this is a more helpful approach overall.

Trying Out Your Skills

- Reread the principles for wording questions and write out the four examples of questions that violate the principles.
- Edit or rewrite each of the questions to achieve the advantages of brevity, grammatical

simplicity, specificity, and concreteness, respectively.

- Compare your versions with those of other students.

Focus Group Interviews

What Is a Focus Group?

A **focus group** is a small group of participants recruited by researchers to discuss what draws them to certain attitudes, preferences, or products, in addition to why and how they make their social decisions. This methodology is particularly useful for determining and assessing shopping habits, product development and packaging, candidate image, and the success of persuasive campaigns. Focus groups also are valuable for organizations wanting to learn more about their employee relations, management style, and public relations. Social science researchers, too, have discovered how valuable it can be to involve research participants socially instead of questioning individuals in isolation as survey research does. In addition, social researchers often combine focus groups with other methods in an attempt to explore a phenomenon from different research directions, a technique known as **triangulation** (see Esterberg, 2002, pp. 109, 176). In recent years these directed group interviews have become perhaps the most pervasive method of qualitative research.

What Is the Communication Process of a Focus Group?

The group is facilitated by a *moderator* who asks questions, encourages interaction and comparisons of opinion, and keeps the group on-task. Researchers record salient features of the interaction for later analysis. At times, third-party sponsors or researchers are present as observers, perhaps behind one-way glass; they might in some cases communicate with the moderator to have him or her follow promising threads of conversation, ask new questions, or request clarifications. Focus groups have become so popular that variations on the methodology have proliferated, and there are now literally hundreds of different styles and models from which to choose (see Hayes & Tathum, 1989; Krueger, 1994; Morgan, 1993, 2001).

We don't have the space in this chapter to provide a comprehensive checklist for focus group studies, but you should understand that, as with other methods, focus groups must be guided by clear research questions that are consistent with the design choices. Sponsoring researchers or clients must also consider such crucial planning factors as where and when the groups will meet; how participants will be recruited and, in most cases, screened with a brief questionnaire verifying that they belong to the specific demographic group(s) probed by the study; and, perhaps most directly related to the dynamics of interviewing, how to determine the interactional role of the right kind of moderator for the group. Focus group moderators create blended roles in a sense, combining some expectations of an interviewer with the expectations of a small group facilitator or task leader. Certainly the moderator does not act straightforwardly as a survey interviewer would, sequencing a precise list of questions, each of which must be answered before moving on to the next. Nor does a moderator ask individual group members in turn to justify their decisions, attitudes, images, or product choices. Instead, using a schedule of questions similar to other interviewers (an interview *guide* or *protocol*) the moderator skillfully defines a task, then opens up areas of dialogue in which the group focuses on the designated topic (see Box 7.5).

Box 7.5

Reminders   *The* Moderator Guide *in Focus Group Research*

Prominent consultant Thomas Greenbaum recommends the following structure for a well-run schedule of activities and questions for moderators:

- *Introduction*. Here the moderator will introduce him or herself to the participants, briefly explains the purpose of the session, and alerts them to the microphones or video cameras that are recording the sessions and the one-way mirror through which observers watch the session. Finally, the participants introduce themselves.

- *A warm-up*. Here the participants are asked to discuss very general issues related to the topic. For example, if a group is being held to expose people to a new concept in dog food, the warm-up would be used to learn basic information about the participants' dogs and how they feed them, including how often and the types of dog food they purchase. The moderator guide identifies all the topics that are to be covered in this warm-up discussion.

- *A details section*. Here discussion is intended to identify important information about the product category. In the dog food example, the moderator might have the participants discuss the advantages and disadvantages of the dog [f]oods they currently buy, and what a manufacturer could do to make the optimal dog food. The moderator guide identifies in outline all the points the moderator should cover in this section of the group.

- *A key content section*. In this part of the group, input will be gained from the participants about the research topic itself. In the dog food example, the participants are exposed to several different concepts for new types of dog food. The guide identifies the areas that the moderator probes during this section in order to ensure that the discussion of the topic is thorough.

- *Summary*. The summary section gives the participants an opportunity to share any information about the topic that they may have forgotten or otherwise omitted. A common way to elicit this information is for the moderator to ask them to give "advice to the president" about the topic.

Source: Greenbaum (1993, pp. 39, 43)

Moderators must take into account the most difficult challenges facing focus group validity and negotiate among group members' own influence patterns. For example, a focus group of 8 to 10 people (common for a full group rather than a minigroup study) runs the risk of having two or three highly verbal and opinionated participants who dominate the group. Moderators must be effective enough listeners and framers to discern when other members may be intimidated or even silenced by these behaviors; gentle probing and invitational inquiries should be distributed throughout the group to give all a chance to contribute. Good moderators stimulate imaginative framing and creativity in the group. At the same time, the goal is not to have respondents react primarily to the moderator, but with each other and to the concept being probed.

The tensions introduced by this nuanced process have given critics their most potent ammunition—focus group conclusions may be based on group interaction dominated by a few highly opinionated or ideological members, or worse, by moderators. Some critics are increasingly vocal, such as social commentator Malcolm Gladwell (2005), who claims bluntly that focus groups in advertising "should be abolished" because of their inherent bias "in favor of the conservative, in favor of the known over the unknown" (p. 14). According to Gladwell, people don't necessarily have the language for the task, or the imagination to project their current likes and dislikes into the future, and are not necessarily competent judges of their own future attitudes. Gladwell seems to be arguing basically that substituting focus groups for the judgment of advertising "creatives" leads to problems, but his reasoning might also apply more broadly to the quality of data any focus group could generate. Another potential problem is more cultural in nature: The validity of the focus group depends on the assumption that participants share common assumptions and norms about group dialogue and how to participate given topics that may be personal in nature. Yet different groups respond quite differently to the task, even resisting moderators' efforts to encourage "speaking up," or suggestions to sit in a U-shaped group, as Strickland (1999, p. 195) found in her study of Indians in the Pacific Northwest of the United States (see also Barata, Gucciardi, Ahmad, & Stewart, 2006).

On the other hand, some researchers have pointed out cultural advantages of conducting more focus group research. Whereas we've seen that in one-on-one interviews the race, gender, or cultural identity of the interviewer can be a significant, if sometimes unavoidable, factor that influences how an interviewee responds, focus group methods can encourage a different dynamic of social support (Pollack, 2003). A group of mothers of disabled teenagers, for example, can find their own voices within the group in spite of the fact that the researcher is male. Kristin Esterberg (2002) notes that "by enabling women to speak with others who have had similar experiences, focus groups help empower women," and also shows how their "collective testimony" (Madriz, 1998, 2000) confirms their experiences in ways that presumably other research methods could not. By the same reasoning, focus groups may be especially powerful ways to conduct cross-cultural research as well, and this is a direction for the future (Morgan, 2001).

Oral History Interviews

One of the most exciting communication projects on the contemporary scene is Story-Corps, an organization supported since 2003 by the Corporation for Public Broadcasting. StoryCorps is establishing an archive, in cooperation with the Library of Congress, of unique stories from a wide variety of Americans. Toward that end, two buses equipped with mobile recording studios are traveling the country soliciting and documenting life experiences that might otherwise be lost to fading memories. The NPR Web site (http://www.npr.org) provides links to clear explanations for how to participate, interview, and record life story interviews. The amazing stories that emerge (listen to some online) could easily inspire ideas for your own interviews. Your grandfather started a successful business, perhaps, against all odds in a town that shunned other blacks. Your mother, amid family conflicts stretching over decades, not only held two simultaneous full-time jobs, but managed to raise four kids and support them all through college. And she wrote amazing poetry late at night at the kitchen table. StoryCorps, built on assumptions of oral history interviewing, doesn't want these emotional truths to go untold and unshared.

What Is Oral History?

Oral history is a research approach that creates a rich documentary record of an interviewee's firsthand perceptions, through the collaborative relationship of interviewer and interviewee in drawing out stories. Eva McMahan's (1989) succinct definition refers to "interview/conversations designed to record the memorable experiences of people" (p. xiv). Although this may sound at first like a simple activity that hardly deserves the label "research method," skillful oral history interviewing is a difficult and delicate application of the traditional skills of interviewers.

Some of the most involving and influential literature and history of recent decades has emerged from oral history research. Studs Terkel (1985) won the Pulitzer Prize for *The Good War*, an oral history of women and men swept into the turmoil of World War II. Terkel's impressive collection of interviewees—including a Red Cross volunteer, an atomic bomb scientist, a combat photographer, a gay Marine, and a Japanese schoolboy—reconstructed and relived the 1940s through their emotionally powerful stories. Few histories offer such a vivid overview of this wrenching world crisis.

Oral history, whether it's on Terkel's worldwide scale or on the personalized family scale described by Paul Friedman in Box 7.6, yields a rich lode of remembrances, anecdotes, and insights from people recalling their pasts. Historians traditionally have relied on documentary evidence, examining deeds, ledgers, diaries, court records, birth certificates, census data, and other tangible information sources, and de-emphasizing oral testimony from people who have lived through the events. Over time, however, historians have come to value the evidence of direct memory. Some early oral histories attempted to preserve the wisdom of "great" men and women—the wealthy, famous, or politically powerful—before they passed on. Today, oral historians also want to listen to a diversity of voices underrepresented in history books. In this way, oral history enriches and expands our sense of culture, for it enables those who might feel powerless or marginalized to add their chapters to the vibrant human narrative.

Tape and digital recorders now allow family members to construct oral histories and pass them on to future generations like portraits or heirlooms. Oral histories also nurture a growing interest in genealogy. If this possibility sounds appealing to you, realize that people do not narrate their lives simply on call. Perhaps they are willing to talk, but only under conditions in which they're convinced interviewers will listen sensitively.

Issues and Problems of Oral History Interviewing

Can human memory be trusted? Different versions of this deceptively simple question are often debated among historians and others who gather oral accounts. It certainly is an extremely meaningful question if oral testimony is the only source of detailed information about a historical event (see Sypher, Hummert, & Williams, 1994). Yet this is rarely the case. The oral historian employs the interview as an occasion for interaction, not as a test of memory. Questions are not primarily designed to elicit verifiable *facts*, but stories of a person's experience as he or she remembers it—the memories that persist, the experiences that continue to shape this unique life. Beyond unearthing facts, oral history methods produce social meaning and a context that color the documentary facts of

Trying Out Your Skills

Read the following conversational excerpt in which Audra, a college student, interviews an older neighbor who was a student activist in the 1960s. She has an assignment to do an oral history interview and wants to know more about that era. Reconsider the basic skills of journalistic interviewing (previous chapter), and decide for yourself what makes Audra's talk with Leon different from, or similar to, a journalistic interview.

AUDRA: Were the sixties a time when you felt energized?

LEON: Energized? Yeah, I guess. It was more like I never had time to stop and think about things in terms of being energized or not. Everything was charged up, not just me, at least at KU, where I went to school. You wouldn't think a vanilla place in the Midwest like that would be real politicized—and a lot of it wasn't, I guess—but it was hard for me to go anywhere and not meet dozens of people who were socially conscious.

A: "Socially conscious." What forms did that take?

L: Well, I don't know. Folks cared. It's hard to describe to students nowadays, who seem to me, at least, so concerned with slotting themselves for jobs. You had students then who would boycott classes to protest the presence of the National Guard, even though it would hurt their grades directly. Kept a lot of 'em from graduating. Graduating didn't . . . Anyway, I remember that there was this girl in my poli-sci class that was a senior, writing her honors thesis and all. She told me about this time when there was a march that she wanted to be in—felt she had to be in—and her professor had scheduled her to present the thesis to a three-person panel or something. She went in the conference room only long enough, she said, to fold the cover page into a paper airplane and float it at them, then she was out the door while it was still in the air! Man . . . I hadn't thought of her in a long time. I wonder if she ever graduated. Probably. Sometime.

A: There were troops on campus part of the time in the late sixties, right? What were you doing then?

L: I was . . . I was . . . (gulps) . . . barely hanging on. Barely. I don't want to get into it here. The atmosphere was charged, like I said, but a lot of us didn't have a clue what we were doing. I kinda crashed and burned a couple of times, lost a couple of friends. Painful . . . Maybe some other time, okay?

A: That's OK. No problem. Do you want to end our session today and pick it up tomorrow? Or do you want to just move on to another time? What did you think when the president resigned? . . .

history. Records (box scores, photos, newspaper clippings), for example, can prove that "Cool Papa" Bell played center field for the St. Louis Stars and Pittsburgh Crawfords of the old "Negro Leagues" from 1922 to 1946, compiling a .338 lifetime batting average. The records, however, fail to capture the experience of a talented athlete reflecting on why he had to play on fields of relative obscurity instead of Yankee Stadium or Fenway Park. Could an interested and committed interviewer help put flesh on the skeleton of statistics and events? How would an interviewer with this goal define the task?

First, an oral historian would emphasize the present in probing the past. Charles Briggs (1986) asserts that ignoring this "deeper issue" is a common mistake for interviewers:

> *Box 7.6*

Interviewers/Interviewees in Action

Paul Friedman • Communication professor Paul Friedman has written a manual on "life stories interviewing," a form of oral history for families. Here are some excerpts:

> Although my primary concern was to connect better with my father, I didn't want to wait for my once- or twice-a-year trips to his home to do this. I wanted to develop an approach to visiting with all persons in his generation in ways that would be meaningful and stimulating to us both, to make connecting with older persons a more regular part of my life. . . .
>
> I was . . . surprised to learn that many of the elders with whom I visited had not . . . as yet shared these accounts with their own children. At those times I often wished that I had a tape recorder available, so that our conversation could be made available to their family members, as well.
>
> Closer to home, I thought how wonderful it would be to record my own father's stories of his youth for my children. By then, however, it was too late. He had passed away, as my mother had fifteen years earlier. That opportunity was gone forever. His loss moved me, nevertheless, to launch the project that culminated in this handbook.

Source: Friedman (1983, pp. 1–3)

Ed Townley • Townley, a minister who survived a near-death experience and substance abuse, reports what it was like to be interviewed by Studs Terkel for one of his oral history projects:

> Well, the first thing is, Studs manages to make you feel like you're the only interview he's ever had. He is so committed to the matter at hand that there's no sense of this as part of a larger project. He is just genuinely interested in what you have to say. . . . You don't get the sense that he's mentally writing the book as he's talking to you. . . . You find yourself saying things you wouldn't imagine yourself saying were he less genuinely focused on the interview. He's so interested and he's so concerned about what you're saying and excited about what you're saying that it just pulls you in, gently massaging you into revealing things you might not have done otherwise.

Source: Kovach (2002)

The goal of oral history is to elicit information about past events. Researchers have noted the selectivity of memory. Yet a lack of awareness is apparent with respect to the fact that oral history interviews produce a dialogue between past and present. Interviewees interpret the meaning of both the past and the present, including the interview itself. Each query presents them with the task of searching through their memories to see which recollections bear on the question and then fitting this information into a form that will be seen as answering the question. Oral history interviews are thus related to the present as systematically as to the past. (p. 14)

Second, an oral historian would emphasize conversational teamwork. The oral history interview is a "conversational narrative" that is "jointly created by the interviewer and the interviewee" (Grele, 1994, p. 2). The interviewer knows two things: first, that the interviewee's story is paramount; second, that the interviewee's story would likely not exist in its present form were it not for the continuing attention, curiosity, and stimulating questions of an interviewer. Narratives are not just stories told, but stories heard. The opportunity for a fresh and active listener creates the essential energy for oral history.

Much of our specific advice for oral history interviewing is consistent with suggestions by James Hoopes (1979). In addition, most reminders for journalistic interviews also apply (see Chapter 6), if the more extended time frame of oral history interviews is taken into account.

Establish an Authentic Relationship   In many kinds of interpersonal encounters, such as employment interviews, it is not enough to be advised to "be yourself." You should work to be your best professional self. Hoopes believes "be yourself" is still good advice for interviewers in this highly personalized task, in which trust is essential. If the success of oral history hinges on relational meanings, give the interviewee a real person to react to.

Match Your Dress, Language, and Behavior to the Context   Are you interviewing the mayor downtown? You'll probably want to wear a suit. Are you traveling to Smithville to interview a retired factory worker at a rural cafe? Wear comfortable clothes that both reflect your personality and will not be seen as out of place at the Eat-Rite. Drop all academic jargon in interviews in favor of an informal conversational style; remember that the best interviewers familiarize themselves with the interviewee's language habits without trying to mimic them.

Seek a Location with Minimal Potential for Interruption   Although it may be tempting either to give the interviewee a choice of where to be interviewed, or to conduct the interview in a place relevant to the memories that might be evoked (e.g., a busy factory), a somewhat private environment is probably best for most interviews in the long run.

Explain Your Purpose and Procedures Clearly   Don't assume that respondents will remember what you told them last week or in an earlier phone call. Refresh their memories and redescribe your interest in their stories, perhaps while setting up and testing your audio recorder. Briefly mention why it's important to record personal narratives (it ensures you won't miss the importance of all their words, even if you're distracted momentarily by a particularly fascinating or funny story). Briefly discuss the overall reason for the study, the benefit for the interviewee in having his or her words remembered, and the purpose to which his or her stories will be put. Many interviewers will want to offer their partners a tape or compact disc recording of the interview.

Take Notes, But Not Compulsively   Even if you are recording, the notes will orient you to important insights and will ultimately save time. Judicious note taking is a reminder to you to listen carefully and a tangible demonstration to the interviewee that he or she is saying interesting things to you. Overzealous note taking subtracts you from the conversation.

Curb Your Tendency to Judge or Evaluate   Interviewers can elicit content such as racist jokes or accounts of interviewees' cruelty or violent behavior. Although you might want to argue or show your disapproval, remind yourself that this is not your role. You're not endorsing your interviewee's behavior just by listening to it. Evaluative responses create defensiveness, and your partner may simply clam up. See if you can probe and listen actively to "get inside" the other person's attitudes even further. You may find that although the interviewee uses language you don't appreciate, or has done some unsavory things, there are good-hearted touchstones of his or her humanity also. In some extreme cases, you might need to tell the interviewee that you are so uncomfortable with the language or stories that the discomfort interferes with your listening.

Word Questions as Neutrally as Possible   Although your empathy is an important addition to the interview, this does not mean that you have to load your questions with positive emotional agreement ("You were right to lash out at your father. Was he as violent after that?") or lead the interviewee toward some conclusion that might not have been reached except for your question. ("He was really a poor excuse for a parent, wasn't he?" is surely an inappropriate judgment except as a paraphrase or perception check of something the interviewee has already said.) Your primary questions or probes should help create an open space within which the other person can move, psychologically speaking.

Proceed Along Both Vertical and Horizontal Dimensions   This concept is borrowed from Paul Friedman (1983) who suggests that an excellent organizational "spine" for the interview is a chronological progression; think of this chronology as the **vertical dimension** of the interview's contents. However, at each point in this vertical, chronological progression, different things were happening in different parts of the interviewee's life. He worked in a factory and organized a new union under adverse circumstances. At the same time, he coached Little League and participated in a wide variety of civic organizations. At the same time, he experienced a disintegrating marriage and contentious family life. At the same time, he secretly donated 15 percent of his meager wages to the church for an orphan-relief program overseas. Each of these areas waiting to be explored exists in a **horizontal dimension** relative to the vertical chronology from infancy through old age. This distinction suggests a fruitful starting point for putting together a schedule of questions or topics. See if you can identify ahead of time certain landmarks that would help the interviewee place your question "vertically" and then help you follow up with "horizontal" explorations. For example, the terrorist attacks of September 11, 2001, might be such a landmark for a storyteller: "I'm curious where you and your family were living when the attacks on the World Trade Center occurred." A series of well-chosen landmarks can give your interview a stimulating and workable structure.

Review the Record for Narrative Insight   After the interview or interview series, interviewers ideally have an audio record and notes that indicate important ideas, possible kernel quotations, turning points, or other especially interesting expressions from the interviewee. Depending on your purpose, you can choose from three levels of action that might be appropriate next: (1) The *secondary notes level*: For some projects and some interviewees, it is sufficient to review the recording along with your in-process notes immediately, simply looking for overall patterns of thought and adding new notes or pages of notes written in ink of a different color and keyed to the date on which the new notes were written. Some interviewers call this "enlarging" the notes. It is particularly appropriate for preliminary or exploratory interviews or for interim analysis when several interviews must be conducted in a brief period. (2) The *notes and quotes level*: Review tape and notes by doing the first level, but transcribe significant quotes accurately and add the quotations to your notes. You may want to type your notes at this stage; in doing so, many interviewers make connections they wouldn't otherwise see. (3) The *full transcript level*: Review tape and notes as in level 1, but then transcribe (type up) the entire interview. You then might edit and shape the different stories, with the help of the interviewee, into a seamless overall narrative—producing a documentary record of the person's experience in his or her own language and voice.

Ethnographic Interviews

The oral historian attempts to enter an interviewee's personal narrative world and assist in its articulation. This is a world of subjective involvement, a world of qualitative research, and a world of relationship development that is very different from the traditional scientific goals of achieving increasingly precise knowledge of causality

Trying Out Your Skills

You could conduct a mini-oral history interview by following the guidelines in Box 7.6 and interviewing either an older member of your extended family, such as a grandfather or grandmother, or an older member of your neighborhood or community who has a particular skill or who has made a difference over the years in people's lives.

- Contact the person, describe what you'd like to learn, and ask permission to talk. *Important note:* Choose a person you are sincerely interested in knowing better, not someone you're picking just to complete the assignment. Assure the interviewee of your genuine interest, even though it might also be a course assignment.

- Agree on the ground rules of interviewing (such as the best location, or whether there are taboo topics the interviewee would like to avoid).

- If acceptable to the interviewee, a sequence of two or three shorter interviews will be more effective for your purposes than one lengthy interview.

- In addition to audio-recording and note taking, test your skill in *delayed note taking* (see Chapter 5) immediately after each interview. Analyze your own style of encouraging helpful disclosures from the interviewee.

- Don't forget a follow-up thank you to the interviewee. Many respondents will also enjoy receiving a copy of the recording or transcript.

- Write a brief paper relating what you learn about your oral history interviewing style through this experience.

and greater predictability and control over future events. Another form of qualitative interviewing, done within the ethnographic tradition, typically departs even more from traditional scientific or quantitative criteria.

What Is an Ethnographic Interview?

In one of the clearest introductions to the qualitative research methods of **ethnography**, Michael Agar (1986) defines the term and goes on to differentiate it from other forms of research:

> The social research style that emphasizes encountering alien worlds and making sense of them is called ethnography, or "folk description." Ethnographers set out to show how social action in one world makes sense from the point of view of another. Such work requires an intensive personal involvement, an abandonment of traditional scientific control, and improvisational style to meet situations not of the researcher's making, and an ability to learn from a long series of mistakes. The language of the received view of science just doesn't fit the details of the research process very well if you are doing ethnography. (p. 12)

In ethnographic studies, the researcher seeks to encounter a different culture or subculture on its own terms, by participating within it and describing its ways of experiencing reality. Although ethnographers engage in participant observation and unobtrusive methods that do not necessarily involve interviewing, one noted researcher (Fetterman, 1989) claims "the interview is the ethnographer's most important data gathering technique. Interviews explain and put into a larger context what the ethnographer sees and experiences" (p. 47). Handbooks cannot create a step-by-step formula for conducting ethnographic interviews, however, because much of the ethnographic experience must be based on spontaneous improvisation. Interview occasions often arise unexpectedly, and might not last long.

For example, Felizia, an ethnographer studying the culture of university faculty, plans to attend every open meeting of the faculty senate for an entire academic year. After the September and October meetings, the room cleared quickly. After November's meeting was adjourned, however, a brief disagreement erupted among several stragglers over the definition of "collegiality" in tenure discussions. Felizia hung around at the door as the faculty members finished up, then turned to go. Fran fell into step with her. "What did you think of all that?" Fran asked. "Well," Felizia said, "I'm just here as an observer to see how faculty make decisions, and I'm not a faculty member, but frankly, I had no idea what they were talking about." "You're right. It's unclear to me, too, and I've been teaching here for 10 years. You want to know what I think?" While walking to the parking lot, Felizia engages Fran in an "interview of opportunity." (See "Making Your Decision" at the end of this chapter for a follow-up question to this scenario.)

Although many ethnographic interviews are informal and relatively unstructured, most ethnographers also try to schedule more structured interviews with participants in an attempt to make what is strange or even incomprehensible more familiar. Fetterman (1989, p. 48) believes that the more formal interviews conducted by ethnographers tend to be "verbal approximations" of survey questionnaires with specifically worded and sequenced questions.

Issues and Problems of Ethnographic Interviewing

Ethnographic interviewers are alert to differences between a known culture and the new one being freshly experienced, and they must be open to the possibility that the differences are radical, not slight redefinitions or alterations of basic elements of the known system or culture. Ethnographers' listening becomes tuned for what Clifford Geertz (1983) calls **local knowledge**—understandings that are specifically relevant for the local and immediate context in which they are communicated. At times cultural differences can involve idiosyncrasies so striking that interviewers are thrown off stride. An excellent example from the field of communication is Drew's (2001) *Karaoke Nights: An Ethnographic Rhapsody*, in which a scholar immerses himself in karaoke performance, a personal interest that he has enjoyed without fully understanding the culture behind it. The different kinds of local knowledge at play among performers in different cities and clubs are fascinating, as are the unique communication norms that allow the performers to transcend their everyday social identities.

Even the notion of a communicative event labeled an "interview," as we've stressed, is a culturally specific idea, the characteristics of which aren't found in the same forms in all cultures. The interview plays better in cultures that are relatively individualistic in orientation. Cross-cultural interviewers may find that the whole interviewing enterprise has unfamiliar and perhaps contradictory meanings in different cultural contexts. After all, the notion of a stranger inquiring about one's business and expecting truthful and full replies seems a poor bet for universality. Sociologists (e.g., Deutscher, 1973, pp. 156–166) find that some cultures have a "courtesy bias" in response to strangers' questioning (help the stranger), whereas others normally respond with deception or a "sucker bias" (trick or "put on" the stranger) (pp. 158–159). For one interviewer's experience, see Box 7.7.

Box 7.7

Interviewers in Action   *William Foote Whyte*

In his classic study, *Street Corner Society*, sociologist William Whyte worked with a resourceful, trusted "informant" named Doc, who introduced the researcher to people in the neighborhood. When Whyte started asking sensitive questions about gambling and payoffs to police too early in his research, Doc admonished him, "Go easy on that 'who,' 'what,' 'why,' 'when,' and 'where' stuff, Bill. You ask those questions, and people will clam up on you."

Whyte said he learned a valuable lesson about interviewing:

I did not abandon questioning altogether, of course. I simply learned to judge the sensitiveness of the question and my relationship to the people so that I only asked a question in a sensitive area when I was sure that my relationship to the people involved was very solid.

Source: Whyte (1955, p. 303)

Contrary to some other research traditions in which scholars are told never to personalize their research (Chesney, 2001), in ethnography the self of the researcher is recognized as an inevitable part of the research and what is learned. This learning is accomplished not only through the normal forms of note taking and possibly recording (discussed in previous chapters), but through extensive observational **field notes**. In field notes (some authors merge the words: *fieldnotes*), the interviewer or ethnographer systematically records not only what people say but also contextual observations that help to infuse cultural communication with meaning. Although we cannot do justice to this task in just a few paragraphs, and although there are probably as many types of field notes as there are ethnographers (see Berg, 1989; Emerson, Fretz, & Shaw, 1995), three basic stages help beginners to understand the process.

In the first stage of field notes, the ethnographer records as many details about the interaction as possible, including its context. It may be necessary to take some notes at times when the researcher is not in direct interaction. The goal is to produce a descriptively rich and dense **note set**—unrefined data as complete as possible—with no regard to what the details might mean theoretically and without thinking about how they might be analyzed later. Afterward, in an inductive second stage often termed **open coding**, interpretations and labels are added to the margins of field notes to aid the researcher in analysis. "In open coding, the ethnographer should not use preestablished categories to read fieldnotes; rather he should read with an eye toward identifying events described in the notes that could themselves become the basis of categorization. . . . The ethnographer should seek to generate as many codes as possible, at least initially, without considering possible relevance either to established concepts in one's discipline or to a primary theoretical focus for analyzing and organizing this ethnography" (Emerson, et al., 1995, p. 152). Finally, after many readings and rereadings of field notes and their tentative coding, the researcher will begin to observe themes in the data. He or she is then ready for a third stage of **focused coding** (Emerson et al., pp. 160ff.), in which the researcher restudies the data with an eye toward noticing as many links between themes as possible.

At various times during their research, ethnographers write brief theoretical notes to themselves and others that they call **memos**. These simply describe the state of the researcher's understanding at that given moment. They are typically dated and kept in a notebook (looseleaf binders are most efficient) along with original proposals for the research, any relevant organizational agreements, financial records, field notes, and miscellaneous observations. By keeping and consulting a sequence of memos, the researcher checks on his or her interpretive progress as it develops.

Beyond the Basics

A persistent theme of this book has been a concern for the ethical implications of interviewing. In a variety of ways we've tried to suggest that ethical decision making helps both interviewers and interviewees to ground their communication. In "Beyond the

Basics," we explore two important issues related to the ethical involvement of interviewees in research. First, we will examine why interviewees need to be seen as full-fledged "participants," and not be treated as research "subjects." Second, we warn against a dehumanizing kind of manipulation, which can occur if researchers aren't aware of issues of consent.

Interviewees as Coparticipants

Roles are crucial in research interviews. Traditionally, the researcher, usually with relatively high prestige and institutional support, approaches individual *subjects* or *informants*, to elicit their beliefs, attitudes, values, and behaviors. When the information is obtained and analyzed, the researcher writes up "his" or "her" study, constructed with the words supplied by respondents. What's wrong with that?

Well, nothing is necessarily wrong with the data or the conclusions, but something seems at least faintly disturbing about the process. If the labels are any indication, the research enterprise tends to cast interviewees (as neutral a term as we can think of) in a one-dimensional and powerless role. Although in philosophy, "subjects" are considered to be thinking and deciding entities, being a subject also implies other less complimentary connotations. When people are subjected to a condition or treatment, they come under its influence; when people are said to be subjects of a monarchy, they are subservient to it. Calling interviewees informants, as some ethnographers do, similarly slots their role in a unidimensional and somewhat trivializing way. It implies that providing information is their only useful function when, in fact, most ethnographies emerge from interviewer–interviewee relationships that are far more richly nuanced and even emotionally based than this. An analogy in journalism is when reporters refer to "working a source," thereby objectifying a real person whose knowledge provides the basis for a story.

Students of communication know that it matters what we call things. Names and labels change perceptions. Why wouldn't we assume, knowing this, that if we apply labels that objectify and dehumanize, we might start treating subjects, informants, and sources as less-than-human objects? We can't justify manipulating *persons,* ethicists suggest, but *objects* are manipulated all the time.

Elliot Mishler (1986) devotes an entire chapter in his book on research interviewing to this "striking asymmetry of power" (p. 117) and to several ways to "empower respondents" in nonmanipulative ways. He wants "to shift attention away from investigators' 'problems,' such as technical issues of reliability and validity, to respondents' problems, specifically, their efforts to construct coherent and reasonable worlds of meaning and to make sense of their experiences" (p. 118). In other words, if an interview provides significant information for an interviewer, it provides a no less significant experience, potentially, for an interviewee. In an interview each side should have the opportunity to grow and discover something important, but, as Mishler points out, standard social science interview formats tend to alienate and dehumanize. Many contemporary interview researchers are experimenting with changes to the prevalent vocabulary emphasizing "subjects" or "informants." Thinking of interviewees as *coparticipants* or *research participants* recalibrates the power relationship. This change could create a new respect for how interviewing could potentially support and help interviewees, not just interviewers.

Consistent with this trend, most of the newer interpretive or naturalistic approaches to qualitative research advocate a **member check** (Lincoln & Guba, 1985, pp. 314–316). In this methodological move, researchers take their tentative interpretations of the data back to the interviewees, acknowledging that without their participation the study would have been impossible. Member checking increases the credibility of the study by performing the following purposes, paraphrased here from Yvonna Lincoln's and Egon Guba's work (1985, p. 314):

- It determines whether respondents intended the messages researchers heard.
- It lets respondents correct errors of fact and inaccurate interpretations.
- It stimulates recall further and encourages disclosure of extra information.
- It ultimately helps respondents understand researchers' interpretations, by inviting them to participate in evaluating results.
- It provides an occasion for summarizing data accurately.
- It provides respondents the opportunity to assess the overall adequacy of the study.

Research, Informed Consent, and Implied Consent

The history of social science research unfortunately includes occasions of deceit and deception (Korn, 1998). Some researchers misled or lied to participants while observing their behavior in unusual circumstances. In other studies, researchers never informed people that they were being manipulated systematically. Some unsuspecting people may have believed they were in stimulating conversations with potential friends, while in fact they were being interviewed by trained researchers who would use them as data sources and never see them again. At times, research participants were placed at risk, psychologically or socially, even as the researcher proceeded to publish the study and reap professional rewards. Although interviewing studies were hardly the worst culprits, contemporary research organizations have tried to ensure a more ethical research environment.

On campuses, for example, **institutional review boards** or **human studies research committees** of faculty and administrators review research proposals to reduce the possibility that research participants might be exploited, harmed, or even unduly embarrassed. Research that involves human respondents should, indeed, be screened carefully for potential dangers, and researchers must be reminded to obtain consent from interviewees and other participants. Ideally, *informed consent forms*—usually single-sheet descriptions of the study and any conceivable risks—should be read and signed by participants whenever feasible; some campuses and research organizations have printed standardized forms. **Informed consent** means that the participants acknowledge they are voluntarily cooperating with full knowledge of the kind of study in which they are involved. If respondents are to be identified in a study's public findings, permission to use names or other identifiers is absolutely required on both legal and ethical grounds.

Making Your Decision

- Review the example in this chapter of Felizia, a nonacademic ethnographic researcher studying faculty decision making. She talked to Fran, a faculty member, about her perceptions of the "collegiality" issue. Reconsider this interchange in the context of the notions of informed consent and implied consent. In your opinion, was Felizia clear enough in her statement describing her involvement? Did Fran get an accurate idea of the kind of involvement she was agreeing to by talking with Felizia?

- Hypothetical situation: An unknown benefactor has given you a grant of $10,000, which requires you to conduct an interview research study of your own choosing. Which quantitative or qualitative interviewing methodology in this chapter would you use? What made that one seem more attractive than the others? What research question or hypothesis would you investigate? Why?

- A market research company has asked you to be a moderator for a series of three focus groups discussing college students' use of cellular phones. Do an introspective self-survey of your interpersonal skills, and compare them to the demands of moderating focus groups. Do you take the job? If so, are there any necessary skills that you'd want to practice before moderating the groups? Which ones?

- A prominent social science survey researcher is giving a speech in which she justifies her methods and tells a number of humorous anecdotes. You are in the audience. You hear her say, at one point, "Social scientists have to remain neutral at all times. Although ethnographers get a lot of interesting stories, we shouldn't kid ourselves into thinking that they actually contribute to reliable new knowledge. Their subjectivity taints all of their experiences." Based on what you've read in this class and others, take a tentative position on her assertions. During the question-and-answer period, you have a chance to ask a question of her. What do you ask, and why?

In some studies, signed consent forms may be impractical or inappropriate (e.g., a large number of respondents to a mail survey questionnaire or a small number of passersby stopping for a survey at the food court of your local mall). In these instances, **implied consent** is signaled simply by the respondent's obvious willingness to participate. Even then, the interviewer or the instrument itself should describe any risks or setbacks a participant could experience. Another form of implied consent occurs in interview research. Interviewers introduce the consent issue orally with a brief description of potential risks (or their absence) and then ask if the participants understand the statement. Continuing participation signals an implied consent on the part of interviewees. Bruce Berg (1989) points out that this approach also retains the advantage of preserving anonymity and confidentiality of respondents, an important issue in many research projects (pp. 138–139).

Summary

Interviewers and their interviewees, working together to make their relationship meaningful, have produced a great deal of what we know about human behavior. Whether this knowledge comes from traditional social science philosophies that often emphasize quantitative research methods, or whether it is shaped by humanistic philosophies that employ qualitative methods, many basic principles of interviewing remain the same. As a researcher, advertise your willingness to listen, and invite the other's speech. Help the interviewee focus on what you want to know, using carefully worded questions. Create an environment in which relationships and meanings are coordinated flexibly. Check back with the interviewee's meanings to ensure you haven't misinterpreted messages. Frame messages from a variety of possible perspectives in addition to your own. Record the interchange systematically, so it might be analyzed more thoroughly.

This chapter has examined four basic types of research interviews, each of which has its own unique advantages. *Survey* interviews offer the advantage of generating a large amount of data through highly standardized questions—data that allow ready comparison across groups and conditions. *Focus groups* help researchers probe preferences and habits of a specified group of people. *Oral history* interviews supplement factual knowledge with narrative knowledge, deepening our understanding of the past. Finally, *ethnographic* interviews stress active immersion in settings where the interviewer may be in some sense a stranger; they create open possibilities for glimpsing and understanding different worldviews and cultural patterns. Finally, we offer insights and advice on an ethical approach to research, especially as it affects participants.

The Interview Bookshelf

On the role of questions in surveys:

Foddy, W (1993). *Constructing questions for interviews and questionnaires: Theory and practice in social research.* Cambridge, UK: Cambridge University Press.

Provides a thorough introduction to the linguistic and methodological issues researchers must deal with in designing questions. Very practical and also grounded in interpersonal communication research.

On classroom and home projects in oral history:

Sitton, T., Mehaffy, G. L., & Davis, O. L. (1983). *Oral history: A guide for teachers (and others).* Austin: University of Texas Press.

An explanation and discussion of oral history that moves into an interesting collection of oral history activities for teachers, students, and families. It's more than a how-to book; the authors provide an easy-to-read theoretical and practical context for conducting oral history.

On basic introductions to qualitative research interviewing:

Holstein, J. A., & Gubrium, J. E. (1995). *The active interview.* Thousand Oaks, CA: Sage.

Mishler, E. G. (1986). *Research interviewing: Context and narrative.* Cambridge, MA: Harvard University Press.

Two books that capture the excitement of interviewing. The Active Interview is shorter and tightly written, with excellent examples. Research Interviewing is possibly the best book in its field, but challenging reading if you haven't taken a communication theory course recently.

On interview studies and cultural dialogue:

Lawrence-Lightfoot, S. (2000). *Respect: An exploration.* New York: Perseus.

Smith, A. D. (2000). *Talk to me: Listening between the lines.* New York: Random House.

Two artist-scholars who use interviewing methods to encourage cultural awareness in our complex society. Lawrence-Lightfoot examines respect by interviewing six professionals who respect diversity in different ways in their everyday lives, then crafting emotionally involving essays that capture their philosophies. Smith, an actor and artist, interviews participants from all sides of such multicultural conflicts as the Los Angeles riots, and empathically makes their stories come alive by taking on all their roles on stage in her one-woman shows. Her book describes her process of interviewing and capturing the actual voices of participants.

Chapter Eight

Interviews for Employee Selection

Most people can swap stories about bizarre job interviews. Applicants tell of interviews conducted on the run, in which an interviewer was troubleshooting a factory crisis, scurrying from department to department, while the luckless interviewee hustled breathlessly behind, trying to get a word in edgewise. In other cases, interviewers have used the occasion to flaunt their power, ask for dates, brag about their own accomplishments, and spend most of the time telling each applicant how good the others have been.

Personnel managers and other job interviewers also tell nearly unbelievable tales of what some interviewees do and say. Internet sites and e-mail lists circulate several versions of stories of applicants who have shocked organizational representatives. In one instance, the applicant wore headphones and said she could listen to music and pay attention at the same time. Another asked for the interviewer's résumé to see if she was qualified to judge the candidate's credentials. In a third account, an applicant unpacked a sack of hamburgers and fries during the interview because the interview came in the middle of the day. The authenticity of these stories may be questionable, but they are believable enough to demonstrate that many people aren't aware of others' expectations and interpretations in this ticklish situation.

One of the ironies in employment practice is the emphasis that is placed on the relatively unstructured, face-to-face interview to arrive at selection decisions within organizations, despite the interview's questionable validity in predicting job success when compared to other selection techniques (i.e., biographical information, work samples, pencil-and-paper tests). Recent literature reviews have suggested that low interview validity is likely the result of both passive and active judgment errors made by interviewers as they gather, retrieve, and process applicant information.

—Robert Eder and Gerald Ferris,
The Employment Interview

Yet this isn't just any mundane ticklish situation. It is a make-it-or-break-it occasion for those with families to feed and careers to launch, seen from one perspective, or for organizations to run smoothly or serve customers with integrity and goodwill, seen from the other. The appropriate match of personality to position, and skills to jobs, can—if done well with the fullest exchange of information—create a halo of satisfaction all around. This success also extends far beyond the job location and the hiree's individual responsibilities to enhance and enrich families, neighborhoods, careers, corporate responsiveness, client satisfaction, and a variety of other outcomes.

Robert Eder and Richard Ferris (1989) found that employment interviews are notoriously weak in *predictive validity*; that is, a supposedly "good" interview is not a consistently good gauge of an employee's subsequent success in the workplace. Although their findings may seem discouraging for would-be interviewers and interviewees, Eder and Ferris suspect that interviewers lack the skills and insights to recognize what makes an interview effective or "good." In addition, recent trends indicate that both sides often prepare haphazardly for interviews. The findings of Eder, Ferris, and others should convince organizational representatives and applicants alike that interviewing should be taken seriously, prepared for carefully, practiced intensively, and followed up systematically.

Surprisingly, considering the typical frustrations and the crucial importance of successful job interviewing for both applicants and organizations, many students seem to believe that job interviewing is merely a matter of common sense. They believe they don't need to research much because the demands of interviewing are so obvious, and, in fact, "everyone already knows" what to do in an interview, how to dress, and what to say. Many want to trust blindly in the occasional apt but often misleading advice to "be natural" or "just be yourself."

In this chapter we explain why this is dangerous advice if taken too literally. First we look at what we call a rhetorical perspective, one that considers the employment interview as a focused form of interpersonal assessment based on evidence gathered, shared, and adequately analyzed by both parties. We describe the distinctive personal goals of the interview from both interviewer and interviewee standpoints, and examine also the shared goals that can emerge from the interchange. In "Beyond the Basics" you will build on your understanding of the interview as communication to consider two other detailed issues: how the legal context of employment interviewing serves as a valid constraint on what can and can't be said in the interaction; and how the principles of employment extend to other contexts of interviewing where selection is the goal.

The Basics

Beyond "Just Being Yourself": Defining the Employment Interview as Communication

Don't get us wrong. Being yourself is a fine thing. If, by "being yourself," you mean that you're comfortable with your own identity and personality, that you're reasonably confident as a communicator, and that you trust yourself to adapt to a variety of circumstances, then all of these features are certainly helpful for communicators.

However, trusting yourself to respond spontaneously is necessarily limited by the specific contexts in which you find yourself. Does it, for instance, seem to be good advice to "just be yourself " when you've agreed to be best man or maid of honor in a friend's lavish wedding ceremony? Does it seem to be good advice to be yourself when thinking about how you'll act when sitting down to take the Graduate Record Exam or LSAT? For that matter, is it a good thing simply to be yourself when you're expected to play a certain position on a soccer team or a certain role in a play? There are many ways to express your unique personality, but in none of these other contexts would it make sense to trust your personality and what you already know about yourself in lieu of specific preparation for how to merge your talents with those of others. You might also expect big problems with trusting yourself to be a good interviewee or interviewer in employment selection situations.

The **employment interview** can be defined as an encounter between a potential employee and an organizational representative or representatives for the purpose of exploring information relevant to subsequent hiring or selection decisions. Several features of the definition are especially important to emphasize in the beginning of the chapter.

First, the employment we are talking about may go beyond the normal definition of a job. Many organizations use the techniques of employment interviewing to select interns, volunteers, and other representatives; and certainly college admissions—especially for graduate school and professional programs—use comparable approaches to choose people (see Klitgaard, 1985).

Second, note that not all employment interviewing conforms to the stereotype of a lonely applicant entering an office to face a stern personnel manager sitting behind a massive desk. Some interviews are conducted in the specific work context that is relevant for the employee function, and some (especially in follow-up interviews) involve more than one organizational interviewer.

Third, we emphasize a *mutual* selection process. Because both parties need information, it's a bit misleading to say that only the employer interviews the applicant. Once the interview is framed primarily in such a limited unidirectional way, many communicative aspects of interviewing become submerged in real or imagined power relationships, and otherwise assertive interviewees turn timid and fail to get answers to their questions about the organization. Although for the sake of simplicity we often generalize applicants as "interviewees" and organizational employers as "interviewers," any effective employment interview must provide at least some opportunity for applicants to interview organizational representatives.

Finally, notice that the interview is an occasion for gathering and processing information and impressions, but this information is only useful if it leads to subsequent decision making. An employment interview is not the time to make rock-solid decisions but instead is a time to generate information and impressions that can be used later to shape fair decisions. For an employment interview to be effective for both sides, the communication has to be transactional: Each party must acknowledge how it is affected by, and how it affects, the other. From the interviewee's perspective, "Does the company want me? Did I get the job?" is only one of these decisions. Another, often just as important, is, "Do I want to work here?" Or, if an applicant is enthused about a job offer, "Should I follow up with requests for more information about benefits before making a final choice?"

In any case, this definition of the employment interview suggests it is a communication event with mutual implications, rather than just a trial in which the powerful tests the powerless. Both sides have influence, but they are different forms of influence that are enacted differently.

The main practical message of this chapter, succinctly stated, is: "Get out of yourself." Note that we are not saying, "Forget yourself " or "Don't capitalize on your own uniqueness." We are saying that interviewees and interviewers cannot stay within themselves and hope to accomplish the valid transactions that must occur in a successful interview. "Get out of yourself" suggests that you expand your focus to include the needs and goals of the other person. Interviewees cannot frame the situation selfishly, because organizations won't select employees (or graduate students, interns, or other applicants) who appear only out for themselves. Similarly, interviewers cannot frame the situation in terms of organizational demands or take-it-or-leave-it attitudes, because the best potential employees will avoid such positions, leaving such interviewers only subpar applicants to interview.

Consider this "get out of yourself" problem as it confronts both interviewee and interviewer. Employment consultant Tom Jackson, in a workshop attended by one of the authors, warned (see also Jackson, 1978) that too many job applicants frame the selection interview entirely as their own opportunity. "Why do you want this job?" the personnel manager might ask. "Because I've been out of work for so long. I need a job," replies the applicant. Think about it. This is an honest reply; the interviewee is "being himself." But, to paraphrase Jackson, "The employer doesn't give a damn if you need a job." (Actually, his words were much more colorful, but you get the idea.) Interviewers are not necessarily callous or unfeeling, but their problems transcend the interviewee's need for a job. The applicant who interviewed last hour needs a job, too, as does the next, and the next. An organization wants to hire you to add value to its own life, not necessarily to your life. Get out of yourself and see yourself in the context of the organization's goals and needs.

Of course, the same reminder applies to the interviewer, who has to consider the organization's needs in the context of the particular employee's satisfaction. In a sense, the organization that wants to hire the best possible workers with the best possible fit must, in communication terms, decenter; it must also "get outside itself," to anticipate the experience of employees. Turning Jackson's hypothetical question around, an applicant might ask, "Why would I want to work for you?" If the organizational interviewer can only respond, "Because we need someone who can sell a whole range of new customers on the need for cellular service," then the organization has not "gotten outside itself" and may lose an excellent candidate. Skillful interviewers who instead translate the organization's goals into the life goals of the applicant help create a bond that bolsters both sides. Effective communicators know themselves and the perspectives they represent, but they transcend those perspectives, too.

Employment interviewing improves when participants are primarily interested in communicating and not merely engaged in testing someone, in selecting someone, in trying out for the team, or in having an audition. Although the interview involves elements of these other tasks, don't assume they are the major frames for what is going on.

Matching applicants with organizational positions encourages a curious clash of objectives that create a rhetorical encounter—a communication situation in which each party approaches the other with relatively clear goals. We mentioned earlier that we'll take a "rhetorical" perspective on this topic. **Rhetoric**, according to Aristotle, is the study of how persons discover the available means of persuasion in their communication with others and then seek to implement persuasive strategies to influence the others. In this classical sense, rhetoric is not the same as manipulation (which involves unfair control of information or consequences), nor is it the same thing as empty public talk (the "mere rhetoric" politicians often accuse opponents of using). Ideally, rhetoric is informed, ethical communication in which participants test their ideas with their talk and writing. Yet because it often involves at least a comparison of different objectives, the rhetorical encounter can be intensely ego-involving, emotional, and, therefore, difficult. Opportunities for misinterpretation lurk everywhere.

A rhetorical approach helps you anticipate and prepare for some of the dangers inherent in the interview. Think about three specific rhetorical concerns that apply to any selection interview: *context* (the social, cultural, and physical situation in which you communicate), *persuasive proofs* (the means of persuasion with which you attempt to communicate effectively), and *ethics* (the value bases of right and wrong that help you choose how to communicate). Some researchers (Kirkwood & Ralston, 1996) imply that effective employment interviewing can reflect all three concerns—it can be adapted well to context, be persuasively oriented, and be ethical—and even that such a persuasive situation can and should be a "collaborative dialogue":

> We believe teachers are obliged to acquaint students with a vision of what employment interviewing ought to be: a collaborative dialogue that acknowledges and supports the needs of employers and applicants to make informed decisions about whom to hire or which offers to accept. If not in the university classrooms and interviewing texts, where else will students confront this possibility? Even were one to view this approach to interviewing as hopelessly idealistic (a view we do not share), it is incumbent on communication educators to raise the possibility for students. (pp. 175–176)

Context

What is the context for the employment interview? Think of *context* as a description of the background or backdrop for the content of the message participants attempt to articulate with each other; messages exist within contexts that, in turn, influence how the messages are influenced. For example, a joking remark by an interviewee about her awkward handling of a personnel conflict might be appropriate in the context of a follow-up interview in which a strong rapport has been established with the interviewer, yet the more formal context of an initial interview would make such a lighthearted approach unlikely. Surely, too, you have noticed how certain offices and placement of chairs and desks tend to formalize conversations (Is there a huge desk separating the communicators? Are the chairs eight feet apart?) or how some conversations in mid-afternoon have a slower pace than morning meetings. To imagine a different kind of context, think of interviewing a new applicant right after you've had an argument with your own boss, or think about going to a job interview when all that is really on your mind is how long you'll suffer from this tension headache. These are examples of the many different kinds of contexts that should be analyzed as you make decisions about how to communicate in an interview.

1. *Situational and social context*: What kind of situation is it? What do the communicators understand about why they are talking? If two people are talking smoothly face-to-face, how does an onlooker change the dynamics of the conversation? The goals and interpersonal rules of certain social situations might change an otherwise taboo behavior into something permissible. One university career center (Saint Louis University Career Center [SLU], 2006) asks students how they might want to—and be expected to—act differently in the following typical interview situations:

One-on-one interview (individualized attention, with one organizational representative talking with an applicant. Increasingly, these are not simple Q&A sessions, but can become **behavioral interviews**, in which an interviewee may be asked to respond to different kinds of workplace problems with accounts of previous skillful solutions to similar situations, role-play demonstrations, and the like. The approach is based upon what researchers call *behavior description theory* [Janz, 1989], which presumes interviewees' descriptions of actual past behaviors offer excellent clues to their likely performance in new jobs. Supposedly, of the four key types of interview information (credentials, experience descriptions, opinions, and behavior descriptions), "only behavior descriptions offer practical, clear data on which to base predictions of future performance" [p. 159].)

Phone interview (brief interchanges, often used to screen large numbers of candidates.)

Panel interview (several organizational representatives take turns asking questions and bringing up issues.)

Meal interview (a complex social setting often involving lunch or dinner, in which an interviewee's social and conversational skills, and the ability to concentrate informally on the questions of one or more interviewer, are paramount.)

Second interview/on-site visit (a follow-up interview, often for the purpose of further investigation and familiarization with the actual work setting; applicants will likely meet many potential coworkers in a short time and under actual organizational conditions).

2. *Temporal context*: What has happened before? How long have the participants known each other? What time of day is it? Although many people don't recognize how profoundly time affects their relationships, "time talks," as anthropologist Edward Hall (1959, pp. 128–145) put it. Think about the situational context of a meal interview and its temporal elements. For example, it's most likely to be at a certain time of day (noon),

more likely to be a second interview (with memories of the first already planted), and very likely to be of a certain predictable duration (it takes at least an hour to order, be served, converse, and conclude).

3. *Immediate nonverbal context*: How is the furniture arranged? Is the other person's speech hard to listen to because your attention is drawn so often to the odd way he or she is dressed? Does the brightly painted wall distract you? Although this type of context can't *cause* or *determine* what is said, it's safe to assume that it always will influence what is said.

4. *Psychological and physiological context*: Do you expect to succeed? To be believable and persuasive? If so, such contexts may create *self-fulfilling prophecies* that make positive outcomes more likely for competent communicators. In a self-fulfilling prophecy, what you think will happen becomes more likely to happen. Of course, negative expectations may become self-fulfilling as well. What are you worried about during the interview, and how might that distract you? If your fear of having a bad interview experience is excessive, you might be making a negative experience more likely—by distracting yourself from the very choices under your control that could make it better.

Although it seems almost self-evident to say so, job interviews take place only when there is a contextual convergence of goals: One person or organization wants to fill a position while another wants to achieve a position. Although each side is motivated, the extent to which they realize that the motivation is mutual may not be readily apparent to either party. The applicant may be too entangled in personal fears of not getting a job to realize that the employer needs to find someone; the employer may be too busy to realize fully the candidate's sincere motives. The most successful interviews are ones in which both sides converge to share information in dialogue, even if a hiring is not the result.

In spite of the fact that the physical context is usually determined by organizational interviewers and applicants or candidates usually feel less powerful and more ill at ease, researchers into the social context of employment interviews still stress the mutual influences of dialogue (Howard & Ferris, 1996, p. 112). Further, recent experience has shifted the traditional emphasis on the interviewer's perspective to a fresh interest in interviewees' perspectives (p. 125). However, the factors of context—especially how they affect interviewers' decision making—are relatively underresearched (pp. 113, 125).

Persuasive Proofs

Classical rhetorical theorists have described three basic ways communicators influence audiences: **ethos** (the persuasiveness that springs from the force of individual character), **pathos** (the persuasiveness of appealing to emotion), and **logos** (the persuasiveness of appealing to reason and logic). Why are persuasive proofs relevant in the employment interview?

In contemporary life *ethos* is usually discussed as "credibility" and, according to researchers, involves two major characteristics, expertise and trustworthiness, and a minor one, dynamism. That is, highly credible job applicants (those high on an "ethical proof" scale) are more likely to be hired when they know what they are talking about (expertise); are seen as ethical, honest, and reliable (trustworthiness); and are perceived as enthusiastic and animated (dynamism). How can applicants accomplish this? We discuss how in more detail later, but the expertise element in ethos is why interviewees want to have solid résumés that describe accomplishments well; trustworthiness is why they are sure to relate stories about positive performance appraisals of attendance, thoroughness, and honesty in past jobs; dynamism is why they want to use as many action words as possible and be wary of an excessively low-key monotonic style of speech.

Pathos is usually a less relevant and less examined factor in employment interview rhetoric, possibly because the process is presumed to be such a highly rational one. Interviewers and interviewees aren't expected to make emotionally charged decisions. Yet this fact does not mean emotions play no part in interviewing. Indeed, some evidence (Frank & Hackman, 1975) suggests that similarity between two interview partners and perceived personal attractiveness may play an important role in who is hired.

Logos, or logical proof, involves careful and systematic reasoning that demonstrates why your assertions are true: examples are appropriate, reasoning "hangs together," and the evidence used pertains directly to the claims it is used to support. An interviewer asks, "How do you know you can handle the kinds of workers and cultural tensions we have here at OneWorld Electronics?" The respondent says, "I set up a training program for similar workers three years ago at Dynamico and have studied conflict management ever since I was in college." Without saying so directly, the answer implies that these facts are not only to be taken as good evidence, but it should be assumed that they indicate an ongoing capability to accomplish the same results at OneWorld Electronics.

Ethics

What are the primarily ethical issues of the employment interview? In Chapter 1, we discussed both a *deontological* ethic, which ideally stresses principles and duties that should apply to everyone all the time—such as truth telling—and a *teleological* ethic, which ideally looks into the consequences of acts to evaluate how much good for humans can come out of those actions. Of course, life isn't lived "ideally" but in a world where important choices are rarely as clear-cut as we'd like. For example, what would you put in your résumé about managing an office when you handled the lion's share of managerial duties in your previous employment, but officially someone else held the title of "office manager"? If you put "office manager" on your résumé, are you being truthful? Some would say yes, arguing that, in truth, you managed the office. Others would argue that because you never held the title, you cannot rightfully claim it. Could such a deception ever be morally justified?

One ethical principle that applies to employment interview participants is the "test of publicity" (Bok, 1979), which asks:

> which lies, if any, would survive the appeal of justification to reasonable persons. It requires us to seek concrete and open performance of an exercise crucial to ethics: The Golden Rule, basic to so many religious and moral traditions. We must share the perspective of those affected by our choices, and ask how we would react if the lies we are

contemplating were told to us. We must, then, adopt the perspective not only of liars, but of those lied to; and not only of particular persons but of all those affected by lies—the collective perspectives of reasonable persons seen as potentially deceived. We must formulate the excuses and the moral arguments used to defend the lies and ask how they would stand up under public scrutiny of these reasonable persons. (pp. 98–99)

Boiled down to its basics, the **test of publicity** suggests that when confronted with moral choices, you can apply this criterion: Is the action I am tempted to take one that I would feel comfortable making fully public, if need be, to a wide audience of reasonable people? Not all moral dialogue has to be publicized, according to Bok. For example, you don't need to call attention defensively to your résumé item about "office manager" in each interview. However, moral decisions have to be "*capable* of being made public" (p. 97; italics added).

Over the next several sections of this chapter, we survey rhetorical goals from the standpoint of both interviewee and interviewer. We will not separate these discussions very far from each other. You'll probably find yourself in both roles in your professional career, and the rhetoric of each should help you understand the dynamics of the other.

Interviewers' Rhetoric and Goals

The interviewer's role can be distinguished by many factors, including depth and breadth of knowledge about the anticipated position; directive control over the interview setting; a perception that the interviewer is representing an organization in a legal sense; a heightened responsibility for encouraging a comfortable relationship with the interviewee; and the added decision-making responsibility of acting as a filter, narrowing the pool of interviewees the organization will be able to evaluate subsequently. The organizational responsibilities seem more politically motivating for many interviewers. The complicated nature of balancing all these tasks makes it necessary that interviewers prepare carefully in advance. Before the interview(s), interviewers should ensure that they are prepared in the following ways:

Know why you're conducting the interviews. Have a clear idea why the interviews in question are taking place, and verify with superiors their role in the selection process For example, will a given round of interviews result in a hire (**primary selection interviewing**), or will these preliminary interviews primarily serve to select a group of applicants who will be interviewed in more depth later (**two-stage screening interviewing**)? The length of the interview, its detail, the type of notes you would keep, and other decisions would hinge on the basic purpose of the interview.

Know how to describe the available position. In many cases you'll simply be given a predetermined description of the position from superiors and will be expected to shape your interviews according to its demands. If, however, you have a voice in defining the position, make the most of it. First, prepare a **needs assessment**—a systematic description of what the new hire will need to do and to know—for the position you want to fill. Be sure you have a clear, easily communicated definition of the position. It will help to develop both a **surface description version** (streamlined into one sentence) and a **depth description version** (a more specific account, perhaps with handouts, for applicants who request more information).

Know the work setting. At a concrete, everyday level, you must understand the actual work environment for a new hire; you will be a primary informant, if not the only source, for your interviewees. Visit the workplace in which the successful applicant will work, and, if necessary, briefly interview supervisors and coworkers there to get a good sense of what the job involves. Even if your superiors do not ask you to do so, develop two documents for yourself: First, write out a **profile of essential skills** that would enable someone to excel in the job setting. This profile might be used to construct a second list, a **criteria checklist**, to supplement your interview guide, and on which you could take notes during the interview.

Know the law. Familiarize yourself with all laws and regulations that affect the questions you can ask and the way you conduct the interview. In "Beyond the Basics" we provide more basic information to support and guide employment interviewers in making the difficult choices involved in questioning and responding to applicants. For now, however, you should know that a common term among those who discuss the practical and legal implications of employment interviewing is the acronym **BFOQ**. Interviewers need to focus their interviewing on **bona fide occupational qualifications**—those qualities and qualifications that are clearly and demonstrably related to how well a given job will be performed. An interviewer can't just ask anything that arises from native curiosity; some questions, if they suggest the possibility that the employer might base a decision illegally on race, gender, age, or other forms of discrimination, are unlawful.

Seek training opportunities. Don't assume that because you know the job requirements and the organization you can shortcut your preparation. Structured training in interviewing will help you reduce your interpersonal blind spots and understand your own style in more depth. There are even more practical reasons for training: Researchers have found that interviewers who have been trained systematically in the process are more alert to, and less influenced by, interviewee "self-promotion" behaviors (Howard & Ferris, 1996, p. 131).

Planning will probably be invisible to the interviewees if the interviewer does her or his rhetorical job smoothly; the interview will be experienced as conversational and natural. Competent interviewers convince applicants that it is comfortable and reasonable to disclose why they can do the job well, a result that serves both sides' interests. However, an interview differs from conversation in that most conversations don't demand as much forethought. The interviewer's primary job as a communicator is to work hard ahead of time and behind the scenes to set the stage on which spontaneous, satisfying conversation can emerge, but the interviewer cannot force that talk or guarantee it will be productive. Aside from the ultimate goals of hiring and being hired, each party mainly needs the interview to meet the goal of providing useful information. How can the interviewer structure the rhetorical encounter so that both sides achieve their informational goals? We'll look at some ways to do so in the next section.

Creative Forms of Interviewers' Questioning, Listening, and Framing

Remember that interviewing involves three fundamental processes—listening, speaking, and framing. Because employee selection interviewers typically take a directive, inquiring role, let's change the order and start with speaking and questioning this time. Speaking is an initiating process, listening is a process of active reception and conception, and framing is an overall process of helpful interpreting, understanding, and attributing meaning. The employment interviewer speaks primarily as a questioner, listens primarily as an organizational representative who attempts to address candidates' concerns, and frames information primarily as a decision maker.

Questioning from the Interviewer's Perspective

Employment interviewers are responsible for planning the basic structure of the interview. They must, therefore, be proactive when interviewees can afford to take a wait-and-see approach. The interviewer's best proactive tools are a knowledge of the typical stages of employment interviews and a clear schedule of relevant questions adapted to those stages. Because the stages really are the essential tasks accomplished by both interviewer and interviewee, each appears to demand its own particular type of questioning: Stage 1, opening and rapport building; Stage 2, interviewer inquiries; Stage 3, interviewee inquiries; and Stage 4, closing and clarifications.

Stage 1: Opening and Rapport Building Some scholars associate rapport with "coordination," "mutual attentiveness," and "positivity" (Tickle-Degnan & Rosenthal, 1990). In a condition of **rapport**, communicators create a relationship that ideally is coordinated but not manipulated, and one in which they respond attentively to each other in creating a positive tone. Rapport is *emergent* in the sense that it develops as people talk, and it cannot be forced or manipulated by techniques (Jorgenson, 1995). Rapport does not necessarily mean that participants are buddies or feel closeness. Rapport does, however, require that they become mutually and, to some extent, positively cofocused on the task at hand.

Rapport tends to emerge in situations of relatively informal but genuine small talk in a conversational style that emphasizes personal comfort and simply "being with" each other over the exchange of information. Typical rapport-building topics are weather, traffic, a particularly interesting (but noncontroversial) news event both parties have heard about, and the immediate surroundings of the interview. Family topics may be tempting, although discussions about the interviewee's family life run the risk of violating privacy and may veer into territory that is technically illegal, as we shall see in a later discussion of the legal context of interviewing. Although it seems trivial at first glance, rapport has an enormous impact on later stages of interviewing, because people use this opportunity to size up how safe it is to disclose personal details and feelings, be honest about reservations and weaknesses, and assess their own abilities. As rapport develops, you will discover appropriate ways to lay out the expectations for the interview; this kind of clarification, in the context of relaxed personal conversation, will reduce unnecessary tension in interviewees. If you are uncomfortable interviewing others, it is absolutely essential that you practice the conversational styles of rapport building.

Stage 2: Interviewer Inquiries These tend to be questions and comments about the interviewee's knowledge, skills, abilities, and appreciations. (See Box 8.1 for the questioning tendencies of one experienced interviewer.) Much of your interview of a job applicant will be guided by an *interview schedule*—a list of questions or topics with which you structure the interview. Think of your schedule as the verbal skeleton of the interview, the solid inner framework to help you ensure that the other person gets a fair chance to impress you, and that allows you to get the information you've determined you need. Having a schedule of questions does not mean that you can't raise side issues or explore interesting leads with probes (follow-up questions). It only means that you have a preplanned structure to guide you and return to when particular questioning has run its course.

Recently most employment interviewing researchers and practitioners have emphasized the need for a structured plan to enhance the odds that applicant selections will ultimately profit the organization. Wholly spontaneous interviews generally squander opportunities for information (Camp, Vielhaber, & Simonetti, 2001). A spontaneous approach also makes it difficult to compare candidates and their skills systematically when the interviews are conducted at different times or even by different interviewers.

Box 8.1

Interviewers in Action   *Nancy Austin and Mary Kay Haben*

Management consultant Nancy Austin summarizes the experience of a veteran employment interviewer, Mary Kay Haben of Kraft Foods. Note Austin's emphasis on realistic questioning that should deflect the game playing that undermines many interviews, and notice that this is a slightly different approach from the behavioral interviewing described earlier, although both rely on narrative conversation. As Austin observes:

> Old-fashioned recruiting and selection methods can't keep pace with corporations' rapidly changing needs. That's why Mary Kay Haben, executive vice president of the pizza division at Kraft Foods, spends so much time thinking about the questions she and her managers ask. "We work hard to focus our questions on the job that has to be done," she says. That means lots of open-ended inquiries to get beyond the canned responses that, let's face it, applicants are sick of giving and interviewers are sick of hearing. . . . Haben quizzes candidates in mini case studies: "I'll describe a situation and ask, 'How would you handle this?' In other words, she lays out a real, live business problem, then steps back and watches the prospect tackle it. She also relies on "multiple data points," reactions from five or six Kraft managers who individually interview the same roster of candidates, then meet later to compare notes. "In the old days," she says, "everybody followed the résumés and asked exactly the same things."

Source: Austin (1996, p. 24)

Interview schedules do not need to be elaborate (although for some positions they may be much more detailed than our examples here). Box 8.2 presents a basic format, in which an interviewer interested in hiring registered nurses for a clinical setting develops a sequence of questions to guide an interview after the basic personal data has been exchanged. The sample schedule in Box 8.2 combines behavioral interviewing questions with minicase studies to provide opportunities for candidates to describe themselves. In addition, the emphasis on more generalized questions at the beginning and on more open-ended inquiries will presumably invite candidates to adapt their explanations to the specific position being discussed (or, if they don't, that's important information, too).

Corporate consultant Arnold Kanter's (1995, pp. 85–89) advice to employment interviewers on questioning is especially relevant in the context of Chapter 4's advice

---

Box 8.2

Interviewers in Action   *A Sample Interview Schedule for a Critical Care Nurse Position*

Why are you considering/desiring Surgical Critical Care?

What are your future goals—personal/professional?

What were the circumstances concerning your leaving your last job?

Did you like your last job?

Did you encounter stressful situations?

How did you handle those situations/what did you do?

What aspects of your job (schooling) did you find most satisfying? Least satisfying?

What clinical experiences have you had?

Scenarios:

        Patient complaint: Clinical situation:

On any given shift, what is your goal with patient care?

Explain what "empowerment of patients" means to you.

Describe one of the best nursing care experiences you've ever encountered.

Describe the worst nursing care experience you've ever encountered.

What unique services do professional RNs provide that other health care workers do not?

What is your comfort level with the Nursing Process? (What is the Nursing Process?)

What adjectives do you use to describe yourself?

How would you describe your last manager?

How would you describe your previous coworkers?

Are you interviewing elsewhere? Where?

Source: Shiparski (1996, p. 32F)

about questioning styles. Here we summarize the seven basic types of questions usually asked of applicants; you will see that they aren't equally effective by any means.

Open-ended questions are effective as conversation starters and help keep the spotlight on the interviewee. (Most experts suggest interviewees should probably talk, on average, two to three times as much as interviewers.)

Closed-ended questions can be effective in eliciting specific details or keeping pressure on a respondent (if that's your goal), but they are usually not well suited to maintaining the conversational flow sought by most interviewers. They lend a staccato tone to interviews, encouraging short answers interspersed with terse questions.

Leading questions are those in which the question itself broadcasts the desired answer ("Wouldn't it be better to work in a big-city atmosphere like Atlanta?"). For most purposes, leading questions are ineffective because they don't encourage either candor or further disclosure.

Broad-brush questions like, "Tell me about your work experience last summer" (p. 87) are open and inviting, perhaps effectively so at times, but may be so imprecise that the candidate has to request clarification of terms or intent. Use these kinds of questions when you're reasonably certain that the interviewee knows your intent.

Compare-and-contrast questions have certain advantages because you can see the person's mind at work in a problem-solving mode ("Compare and contrast two types of feedback—oral and written—in their ability to encourage meaningful behavior change in workers"); be ready, though, with reasonable probes to check on what the interviewee might mean by the response.

Self-appraisal questions allow interviewees to account for why their achievements were so impressive, mitigated, or mixed. With these questions, you learn not only about their accomplishments or their opinions about them but also their theories of personal achievement or cause and affect.

Multiple questions—asking several things all wrapped up in one inquiry—usually only confuse respondents and give you vague information at best. Avoid them. Imagine being asked in a nerve-wracking situation, "Who, if any, were the most effective teachers you had at the university, what were their most interesting classroom techniques, and what did you learn about their training style as a result of interacting with them?" Huh?

Stage 3: Interviewee Inquiries These tend to be questions and comments to satisfy the interviewee's curiosity and interest concerning the description of the position and the organization. Many interviewers unintentionally hog the available time with their own questions, relegating interviewees' inquiries to an afterthought. This is one of the biggest mistakes you could make. First, the best qualified interviewees probably have been counseled, in classes, workshops, and career centers, to ask relevant, prepared questions. If denied an opportunity to inquire, competent interviewees may question the

Trying Out Your Skills

1. Review the sample interview schedule in Box 8.2.

   • Although the questions aren't overtly divided into topics and groups of issues, what is the overall organizational pattern? What are the major divisions of the organization Shiparski is recommending? Are they similar to the stages recommended in this chapter? If so, how? If not, why not? What is recommended in this chapter that doesn't appear in the schedule?

   • This schedule (an actual document, not a hypothetical suggestion) was obviously designed for a fairly long interview. Try to rewrite it to fit a 20- to 30-minute interview opportunity. Which questions could be eliminated? Which could be combined into questions that cover topics more rapidly?

2. Write a schedule of 8 to 10 questions appropriate for interviewing applicants for the latest job you've held. Try to:

   • Move from general to more specific questions.

   • Write at least two questions with behaviorally based emphases.

   • Word questions unambiguously.

   • Cover all relevant job skills.

---

overall responsiveness of your organization and decide to look elsewhere. Second, you can learn a great deal about the professional savvy, personality, and qualifications of candidates by the kinds of questions they ask. For example, if you are asked, "What are the major subsidiaries of your company?" or "Who are your major competitors in the Minneapolis market?" you can assume the interviewee hasn't spent much time researching readily available public sources of information. When newspaper editor Anders Gyllenhaal hires reporters, in fact, this question is crucial: "About the most important question to me comes toward the end when asking the candidate what questions they have. The quality and reach of their questions often tells me more than anything does. If somebody doesn't have any good questions, that usually signals problems to me" (Favre, 2001).

As a general rule, plan to set aside about a quarter of your total time for the interviewee's inquiries about such issues as working conditions, interpersonal environment, promotion potential, travel, evaluation procedures and criteria, and other matters of interest to job candidates. Some interviewees might not have this many questions. In that case, you might bring out a kind of "contingency schedule" of questions, or find a graceful way to move to the interview's closing phase.

Stage 4: Closing and Clarifications   As the name suggests, this stage serves two functions. First, many human events unfold in a narrative structure of beginnings, developments, and endings. It's as if we wish our lives to be dramatic stories that, no matter how satisfying as they play out, need a satisfying sense of closure. Think of the times when people complain about having unfinished business with someone or think they've left someone hanging in an encounter. Interviews are no different. Without a sense of closure in an interview, all participants experience at least some discomfort or uncertainty, in which they're more likely to recall the unanswered questions than the answered ones. Second, beyond the satisfactions of psychological closure lie more pragmatic concerns of ambiguity; even when there is a noticeable conclusion to the conversation, the interviewee may not know what the next step of the process is (or should be). Nor does he or she necessarily know how long it will take to be notified about the results of the organization's search process.

Interviewers can finalize the interview in a way that's satisfying for both sides:

- Summarize in general terms any very obvious strengths and potential the candidate demonstrated in the interview. But be careful to avoid appearing so enthusiastic that false hopes are raised, and keep your comments relatively unspecific. Leave conversational space for a reply in which the interviewee can also summarize impressions of your organization and the job fit.

- Describe the next step(s) in the organizational process, including relevant time frames.

- Discuss with the interviewee any follow-up information to be shared. Is either party going to send supplementary information, and, if so, when should it be expected? Is there a preferred form for such information (phone, e-mail, fax, or post)?

- Thank the interviewee, reinforcing the goodwill and rapport established in the interview.

Listening from the Interviewer's Perspective

In Chapter 3 we defined listening as "the active process through which communicators process aural (sound) stimuli, interpret them as messages, and use them to construct meanings of speech, speakers, and contexts." Listening, as this definition suggests, not only functions as the outcome of speech, but also enables speech in the first place. We don't speak meaningfully to each other unless we expect to be listened to, and if, while speaking, our listener's attention or interest wanders, we quit speaking. Speech is so thoroughly directed to an anticipated listener, in fact, that we could say that in many ways listening styles *regulate* speech styles.

If, as an interviewer, you develop the impression that a particular candidate is unenthusiastic, could it be that she's given up on your ability to listen carefully and is just going through the motions, lacking much enthusiasm? If you develop the impression that an applicant can't provide details about the computer program he claims to know intimately, it could be that your listening style has given him no evidence that you can process such detail, and he simply has chosen not to include details.

So, considering the sobering thought that interviewers may actually deter or discourage communication, how can their interviews give maximum opportunities for applicants to show what they know and what they can do? Here are some basic principles of listening for employment interviewers: wait, demonstrate, verify, clarify, record. Let's look at them one by one.

Wait Remember that interviewees are usually nervous and typically more rides on the outcome of the interview for them than for you. After you ask a question or introduce an idea, don't assume that a hesitation means your partner is having trouble answering. She or he may be balancing several effective responses but just hasn't settled down enough to form a quick answer.

In Chapter 4 we introduced a skill taught in teacher-education programs called *wait time*—meaning sufficient silence after a question to allow respondents to decide how to answer. Inexperienced teachers may ask a class, "Who were the early leaders of the civil rights movement?" and, when they get no immediate response, wrongly assume no one knows. When timed, teachers often discover they've waited barely a second or two before moving on. Moreover, many in the class may have a good response, but they need time to form answers, especially if they commit the speaker to a public position that could be judged. Interviewing is a similar challenge, and interviewers should use silence similarly—allow enough of a pause for a respondent to formulate a meaningful answer.

Demonstrate Double-check your listening style to analyze how you appear to your partner while listening. Are you attuned primarily to the conversation at hand rather than shuffling through other papers, taking phone calls, or looking at your watch? Remember from Chapter 3 that listening, when done well, is much more than a psychological process; skillful listening looks like listening on the outside, too. You can demonstrate your listening skills by practicing **attending behaviors** (nonverbal cues that reliably indicate a listener is paying attention). Nod affirmatively at points made by your partner (this kind of nodding is generally perceived not as agreement but as an indicator of interest, saying, in effect, "I'm with you, go on"). Lean forward at times to increase the immediacy between the two of you. Maintain appropriate eye contact, but more isn't necessarily better in this case. Generally, directing your gaze at your partner during especially important points helps to convince him or her that you're listening; staring constantly, however, seldom is an indicator of interest or of listening. If you fail to demonstrate your listening overtly, don't be surprised if the interviewee leaves feeling disconfirmed at best and, at worst, with an indifferent attitude toward your organization.

Verify Listen actively and, to the extent possible for you, empathetically. A basic goal of listening is to convince interviewees that they've received a full and fair hearing. One way to accomplish this is to reflect their own words back to interviewees, along with your tentative interpretations, at meaningful moments, giving your partner a chance to tell you if they've been misunderstood.

Every statement doesn't need to be reflected and verified, and if you try to do this in an information-sharing interview, the flow might be damaged irreparably. However, skillfully applied and well timed, active listening can induce further disclosures. Here's how it works:

INTERVIEWEE: When hired at my last job I became concerned that people had their own agendas and failed to work together. I thought they needed more structure.

INTERVIEWER: Things were in disarray at first.

INTERVIEWEE: Yeah. They didn't say so, but it was almost as if they brought me in to tighten up policies.

INTERVIEWER: So that's what you did?

INTERVIEWEE: It took me a year or more, but I worked to simplify things at meetings. But between our department meetings, I met with people separately and tried to clarify with them what they expected from themselves and what I expected from them.

INTERVIEWER: It sounds like you didn't want to remove all of their own agendas, or erase their feelings of autonomy, but just wanted each of them to get a better sense of the whole. Is that right?

INTERVIEWEE: Absolutely. After that first year, productivity went way up, too.

Note that the interviewer does not try to question, or pry, or even to qualify what the interviewee says. The goal is only to verify that his or her listening is more or less accurate. Even if you're wrong about the inferences you make, if you're wrong out loud, your partner can reply with a "Yes, but . . . ," or a "That's almost it. But beyond that . . . ," or "I didn't mean to suggest that." It's verification, plain and simple, but it's content verification that serves an interactional process purpose as well.

Clarify   Use your "listening spare time" (the difference between a listener's relatively rapid information processing compared to a speaker's slower speech rate) to compare and contrast what the interviewee tells you with other information you have collected. You may sense a contradiction between a story about previous employment and what the applicant put on a résumé. You may recall that early in the interview she said she always gets along with superiors but now is talking about her tension with the boss's directive style. You believe the applicant when he says that as a leader he works subtly and effectively behind the scenes, but you wonder if that claim is contradicted by the three formal complaints he filed against other employees in his previous job.

In listening to clarify, you would not interrogate, as would a prosecuting attorney. You simply use your discriminative listening skills (the skills that let you notice the differences between phenomena) to note the possible areas of misunderstanding. Effective, discriminative listeners alert to the need to clarify and willing to broach the subject openly can avert many potential misunderstandings.

Record   Review the rationale and techniques in Chapter 5 for recording information while listening. Take notes relevant to the criteria and job description you prepared beforehand. You could, for example, turn your schedule or criteria checklist into a one- or two-page form for note taking. Remember the schedule earlier in the chapter for interviewing nurses? Think of it as more than a list; it's also a criteria form, complete with blank spaces in which to record your impressions, brief quotes, and questions for follow-up. In addition to listening well within the interview to the applicant, "listen" well afterward to your own reactions to the record you've kept. If your gut feeling is that a candidate is better than your notes reflect, this is a signal for you to reconsider the record carefully. If possible, compare your notes with someone else in the organization who has interviewed this person or others for the designated position.

Interviewees might get nervous if you rarely jot down notes. They also might get nervous when you take thorough notes, thinking you're only registering flaws, problems, gaps, and gaffes. Try not to cause them unnecessary nervousness. Take enough notes to remind you later of what's crucial and to demonstrate your interest, but not so many notes that you're distracted from the conversation. A rule of thumb: If you're writing so much that the interviewee often has to pause in the conversation for you to finish, then your eye contact, as well as your listening, is probably going to suffer. This decreases the naturalness of an interview setting that is probably too artificial already.

Framing from the Interviewer's Perspective

Sociologist Erving Goffman (1974) thought that framing involves one basic question: "I assume," he wrote, "that when individuals attend to any current situation, they face the question, 'What is it that's going on here?'" Interviewers should apply Goffman's question to behaviors exhibited in selection interviews. Although framing is much more complex than his question suggests (see Chapter 5), it provides a useful starting point for sharpening our analysis here.

Interview partners never act randomly but adapt their social messages to each other, creating patterns of behavior. Those patterns, however, will not be seen or understood in the same ways by different people. At best, communicators develop similar, not identical, interpretations as they attempt to explain to themselves what is going on. Instead of just shrugging our shoulders and assuming this divergence of interpretations is inevitable, however, communication specialists, including employment interviewers, want to figure out what these differing frames mean for ongoing interaction. Let's consider a series of questions employment interviewers could ask about their own framing in relation to interviewee framing.

1. Are our frames highly congruent? What are the implications if (for instance) I define the situation as a conversation, but the applicant defines it as an audition or a test? If I start to kid the interviewee and she or he takes it as criticism? What—to apply Goffman's question—is really going on here?

It might be helpful for you to discuss your own frame assumptions in the opening of the interview. (Don't use the word *frame;* despite its usefulness in explaining the concept in a textbook, it will probably sound like jargon and give you something else to define.) You might say something like, "I know interviews often feel like nerve-wracking tests, but I really just want this to be a friendly exchange. When it's over, I want both of us to have the kinds of information we'll need to make better decisions. OK?" Don't be naïve. This won't calm everyone, but it gives the other person an opening to discuss potentially different frames or prior experiences that weren't as comfortable.

2. How do different roles make our frames even less congruent? What are the implications if I expect natural and "real" answers, but the applicant has been primed to provide "stock" answers? What is really going on here?

In most employment interviewing, you decide or influence who gets the job. That provides a power dimension to the talk that is hard to miss. These days, however, job applicants don't come without their own resources. In fact, many have received some sort of training, workshop, or mock interviewing experience in which they practiced "good" responses to common interview questions. College career counseling offices typically hand out lists of 75, 100, or even 200 frequently asked questions. Chances are you'll hear many stock answers (ones that sound right but aren't personalized) and many individually canned answers (ones that tell of personal experience but have been practiced or rehearsed so much that they sound stale). In situations like these, try *reframing* (see Chapter 5) to get the two of you out of your predesigned roles. Insert a minicase study or a hypothetical situation in which you both could imagine yourselves, perhaps, as coworkers. Reframing, although often discussed as an approach to relational and psychological health (Watzlawick et al., 1974), is also a simple way to change some conversational ground rules—potentially leveling the playing field.

3. Do my habits of attribution create problems of communication? Do our different attributions keep us from understanding each other? What is really going on here?

Attribution theory, developed by social psychologists and interpersonal communication researchers, describes how we attempt to explain other people's behaviors (see Kleinke, 1986, pp. 184–199, for a clear summary). With our great faith in cause-and-effect relationships, humans want to know the source of our actions—the reasons why people do what they do. Despite research findings that conclude social events depend on situationally embedded multiple causes and prior effects, we still strain for a clean-cut explanation, or cause, we can attribute to someone else's actions. Attributions become minitheories and, in effect, are explanation frames. For example, Molly quits her job as a copywriter for an advertising firm within two months of beginning work. Molly might not be able to pinpoint a specific reason. It just seems right to resign for a multitude of reasons: strained relations with new colleagues, dissatisfaction with the daily demands for creativity, a desire to spend more time with family at home, the possibility of a new job closer to home, and so forth. The personnel interviewer, however, won't suspect most of Molly's reasons; she likely will simply see the situation as a hire who didn't work out. Why?

Most commonly, attributions occur by assuming internal or external causation. We find explanations to support a belief that someone was motivated internally (e.g., Molly quit because she wasn't creative," or, "She's a quitter"). Or we find explanations that relate the action to external stimuli ("Sexual harassment has always been a problem in that department. They drove her out."). In either case, the explanation is probably too simplistic, but each attribution frame creates a particular kind of reality that shapes a future communication. As an interviewer, be especially careful about the **fundamental attribution error,** which is the tendency to regard others as motivated internally, say, by their "real nature," while you tend to assume that you, and others like you, are motivated by the circumstances in which you find yourself. Here's the danger: In Molly's case, it's too easy for you (as the interviewer) to believe that you wouldn't have quit, that you have what it takes, and that your own problems are attributable to unforeseeable problems out of your control, whereas Molly's problems might be explained (too easily) by character flaws or personal traits. Do you see how this could create a tendency toward unfair judgment on the part of the interviewers? The tendency to make fundamental attribution errors feeds the unfair stereotyping by narrow-minded people who think, for example, "All women are . . . ," "I knew I couldn't trust a man to do that . . . ," or "Asians have trouble with. . . ."

4. How do biases and stereotypes influence my frames? What are the implications if we each let our stereotypes govern the interaction? What is really going on here?

We described the fundamental attribution error as a tendency to regard others as motivated internally, perhaps by their "real nature," whereas you tend to assume that you, and others like you, are motivated by "circumstances." We emphasize these words here to highlight common problems in cross-cultural communication—bias and stereotyping. The fundamental attribution error is closely related to **ethnocentrism**—the sense that your own cultural group is the standard by which others must be judged (*ethno* means "people"). People often jump to the conclusion that other people's abruptness, rudeness, lateness, or decision-making style can be attributed to so-called natural characteristics of a particular culture, race, gender, sexual orientation, age group, or socioeconomic group. Ethnocentrism creates a reality of "us" (a group that does things normally and reasonably) and the alien realities of "them" (groups that demonstrate a range of irritating, wrong, irresponsible, dangerous, or unproductive behaviors).

Stereotyping, the "pictures in the head" through which we define and view others, is not always or necessarily negative. If you let your stereotypes calcify, however, your perception of a group won't let you acknowledge individual uniqueness fully. Not all people are equally prone to negative ethnocentric stereotyping, but we all probably exhibit aspects of it, which should remind you to seek out the interviewee's frame(s) for the interview and consider alternate definitions of the situation with sensitivity and empathy. (For more information on similar issues, review the discussion of framing in interviewing in Chapter 5.)

Interviewees' Rhetoric and Goals

As noted at the beginning of this chapter, many early studies of the validity of employment interviewing found that interviews didn't do much good—at least in the traditional sense of predicting who will be effective employees. What was wrong? Employers and academics alike theorized that interviewers probably hadn't taken their task seriously enough, weren't structured enough, and were too focused on opinions, claims, and what has been loosely termed *experience* (has the applicant performed a task before?). These findings have prompted a remarkable revolution in the structure and techniques of employment interviews. Box 8.3 summarizes some of the changes we've noted from a variety of authors and sources. The changes are particularly important for interviewees because they demand adjustments in your rhetorical preparation.

Overall, what should guide the interviewee's choices in preparing for the successful job interview? What are the most important rhetorical roles and goals? Answers vary, and no one has a lock on the correct ones. You should be wary about trusting anyone (including textbook authors you've never met) to prescribe answers for you. A job search is your responsibility. Many if not most career choices must be based on situational knowledge that generalizations cannot provide. Although we don't want to intrude artificially by telling you what you should do, we're not reluctant to make valid-but-general suggestions for you to consider.

Box 8.3

Reminders   *How Employment Interviews Have Changed in Recent Years:*
Implication for Interviewees

- *Interviews are much more structured.* You're less likely to get "tell me about yourself" questions that meander into a 20-minute chat. You can expect interviewers to exercise quite a bit of control over the direction of content and topics.

- *Interviews are much more focused on actual behaviors from your past.* Interviewers try to elicit your personal account of how you solved problems successfully in previous jobs and organizations through **behavior-based testing** (or *behavior-based interviewing BBI*). Interviewers are less likely to be impressed with the fact that you were a training supervisor and more likely to ask, for example, how your training program in communication skills helped to resolve interracial conflict on the assembly line. The fact that you got a performance award for excellence in 2004 may be nice, but the interviewer is more likely to be interested in how you handled actual complaints in your department.

- *Interviews are much more dependent on your abilities as a storyteller.* This is an

outgrowth of behavior-based interviewing. Interviewees are now expected not only to remember incidents, but also to frame them as interesting and relevant narratives. A much wider range of oral communication skills has become relevant.

- *Interviews might include some fairly aggressive interviewer attempts to test your problem-solving ability or creativity with "brain-teaser" or "puzzle" questions.* This minor trend toward the **brainteaser interview** is not universally seen as a good strategy (and we doubt its effectiveness), but it's gained enough popularity to make already-nervous job candidates even more fearful (Orr, 2000; Poundstone, 2003). If you are uncomfortable responding to this kind of question, you might want to review Kador's (2004) recent book, *How to Ace the Brainteaser Interview.*

- *Interviews tend to be longer.* Interviewees in past eras could expect interviewers to screen candidates, relying on résumé information

---

Considering interviewees' goals suggests new ways of thinking about defining your interviewing role. For example, most of us would assume that an applicant's overall goal is to get a job. On more careful consideration, though, would you be satisfied with *any* job? Or *equally* satisfied with a broad range of jobs? Probably not. You don't just want *a* job—you want a job that's right for you at this moment in your life, one that allows you to use your skills in satisfying ways with cooperative coworkers. Most likely, too, you want a job that advances you along a career path. A *career path* approach recognizes that each job has to be seen in the context of its unique contribution to your long-term professional life. At a given point in the flow of professional development, it may be better for you to turn down a job even if it's the only one offered you. So it's not just "a job" you're after. You won't know enough about your choices until you do your research and interviewing, but acknowledging your role as a career-planning

intensively and forming fairly rapid impressions on the basis of personality. However, employers now no longer trust rapid first impressions; they want to see how you communicate in a sustained interaction.

- *Interviews more often involve multistage* and *multi-interviewer sequences.* Consistent with the trends toward longer, more structured interviews, employers now are proactively "protecting their investments" by interviewing strong candidates more than once. They are conducting follow-up interviews and panel or series interviews, in which candidates meet a series of different people, each of whom will be looking for different things in what the candidate brings to the organization.

- *Interviews more often involve preinterview testing* or *screening.* According to one account (Neuborne, 1997), pre-employment testing, which often starts as a screening process before the interview stage, "has boomed into a more than $2 billion industry and has seeped into almost every job category, from tow-truck driver

to chief financial officer" (p. B1). Although pretest screening is controversial because of its potential for civil rights abuses and possible discrimination, employers argue such an appraisal helps match people to positions much more efficiently, with significant savings and satisfaction all around. These may be psychological tests assessing personality characteristics or straightforward skills tests designed to measure particular job-related abilities. Somewhere in the interview process of serious candidates, many employers now screen through background investigations that verify employment history, credit history, legal troubles, professional and academic credentials, licenses and degrees, and so forth. Civil libertarians rightfully worry that pretests and investigations peel another layer of individual privacy. Still, these probes are a fact of contemporary professional life, especially for managers, decision makers, and those charged with the welfare of others. You would be wise to prepare yourself accordingly, although genuinely prepared candidates always have had little to fear.

professional, not merely an applicant, can reduce the pressure you feel. Each interview is a new opportunity to learn whether the job is right for you.

Therefore, your role as an interviewee is remarkably similar to the interviewer's. Both of you are learners and both are decision makers. You're not begging and pleading. You're deciding (see Box 8.4). If you are especially good at what you do, the employer will be fortunate to hire you, and the interviewer, in fact, may have to do quite a good selling job to get you. The learning and decision-making roles of interviewees do not mean that it won't matter how persuasively you present yourself. Nor should it instill a false or strident arrogance. Simply reassure yourself that you, as well as the other person, have some decisions to make as a result of the interview process.

The job search is not easy; in fact, it can be a full-time job. Before sitting down for interviews, the ground must be prepared and cultivated with care. You're wise to see

Box 8.4

Interviewers in Action   *Bernard Milano*

Bernard Milano, partner in charge of recruiting at KPMG Peat Marwick, offers this advice for college students preparing for employment interviewing:

If you think you're going to college to land a job after graduation, maybe you should think again. Hopefully, the work you're doing now in school will serve as a down payment to the career that you ultimately want—not just a job.

. . . Career counseling, job fairs, on-campus recruitment and employment ads in newspapers, trade publications and the Internet are all good and useful things, but the selection process is about what you choose, not about what chooses you. You may use those tools as guidance, but you should be the principal actor in the decision-making process. It's not hard. It just involves viewing the whole job search procedure from a different perspective.

. . . Remember who's in charge here. It's your life, your career. Passivity is not an option. The same enthusiasm and skills you develop while positioning yourself for the job you want are the characteristics that will move you up each rung of the career ladder.

Source: Milano (1997, p. 7)

yourself as a comprehensive communicator conducting a complex campaign that demands analysis and feedback at every stage.

Preparing carefully increases your chances of getting interviews that will clear a satisfying career path. That preparation involves self-assessment, position research and assessment, persuasive cover letters and résumés, (the plural forms here are significant, as you will see), planning for nonverbal impressions, and role-playing.

Self-Assessment

None of us knows for certain what we're capable of accomplishing. We may vaguely recall what we've done, where we've been, and what we've enjoyed, but that is not enough for the specificity even of a job search, much less the daunting task of beginning to chart a career. Yet it's possible to turn those vague recollections and feelings into a sharper self-portrait if you're willing to do a little introspection (see Box 8.5).

The core question becomes "What do I know I'm good at?" and its corollary: "What evidence demonstrates my effectiveness at accomplishing these things?" Why not try interviewing as a means to learning more about yourself? Beyond asking questions of yourself, choose the person who knows you best in different components of your life: friendships, on-the-job or volunteer work efforts, academic achievement, family, organized sports, or vocational groups. Add to this select group a couple of professors or previous employers who are familiar with your work over the past few years. Tell each person you're doing an organized self-assessment, and ask them to volunteer five or more adjectives or descriptors they believe characterize your communication skills and work habits. Don't spend time arguing with them if you think they're wrong, or basking

Box 8.5

Interviewers in Action *Elsa From*

One woman's experience as job seeker illustrates the importance of honest self-assessment:

When I got back home I sat around for a few weeks still feeling sorry for myself, wondering what kind of job I could do or wanted to do. It was hard to focus on it. Jobs all seemed alike. I didn't have a clue about them.

My friend Bob . . . invited me to New York City for a week and I went. I had to get away to clear my mind. While I was there Bob set me up with a friend of his who is a career counselor, and I had a couple of great sessions with her. One of the things she had me do was go through this five-page thing she had, an exercise, I guess you call it, or process. Very interesting. I had to make lists of things about myself, what I like to do, what I didn't like, what were my skills, my interests, where did I want to live. I got to find out a lot of things about myself. Stuff I already knew, but better organized. Fascinating. I don't understand why we never did this in school. You know most of us never really look at ourselves, we just do what someone else tells us. Someone's mother tells them to be a nurse so they are, or a kid gets an erector set and his dad praises him for something he builds, and 20 years later he's a famous bridge builder.

Anyway, this woman and I went over these lists of things about me, boiled it down, and came up with a half-dozen things to look for in a job. I don't remember the list now but working with my hands was one thing, direct contact with people was another. Something about sales. Several other things.

Anyhow, I came up with a long list of jobs that fit in with things I liked to do, boiled it down with some targets and started to look.

Source: Jackson (1978, p. 25)

in glory if they're complimentary, or even asking them to come up with reasons for their impressions. Simply write down the adjectives they mention. Later, after talking with all your "informants," sit down with an "honesty partner" who knows you well enough to help you assess the other strands of feedback.

The next stage of self-assessment is to trace the adjectives back to the likely evidence each person used in forming their impressions of you. For example, the professor you served as a research assistant calls you "reliable." Focusing on this description, you re-call that in an entire academic year you never missed a meeting with her, and every time she sent you to the library to find a source citation for her research, you always came back with two or more. Through this trace-back strategy, you are not only building an inventory of skills and skill descriptions but also stockpiling stories you could relate to an employment interviewer.

Trace-back self-assessment is particularly effective because it employs **relayed feedback**. You're not saying these things about yourself (that might be perceived as boasting). In a later interview you'll simply be relaying impressions from the people who have worked closely with you. If you're like most of us, through systematic reflection you could come up with a surprisingly long list of good descriptions and evidence of your attributes. However, relayed feedback along these lines—"My final performance appraisal as an undergraduate teaching assistant said that I put in more hours assisting the COM 100 students than any other TA my faculty advisor could remember"—is much more meaningful and concrete than your own claim that you're "a hard worker."

Position Research and Assessment

When you interview for a job, don't just apply and then hope the employer will find you qualified. Take guesswork and chance out of the process by doing your homework. Several types of research are especially helpful:

• Learn about organizational structure. On virtually any four-year college campus, you will find a career center that maintains up-to-date resources: dozens of dictionaries and books that detail the organizational structure and status of many businesses, goals and activities of nonprofit organizations, representative job descriptions and listings, and so on. Check these out for every organization you target for an interview, and check for similar information available on organizational websites.

• Learn about organizational news. Do online database searches for articles in prominent publications about the organizations you're identified. Reference librarians often will help you to locate print sources relevant to your quest. Look especially for such sources as ABI/INFORM, *Trade and Industry Index, Business Wire, PR Newswire, Standard & Poor's Corporate Descriptions,* and *Standard & Poor's Register.* Pay close attention to newspapers in the city or region where you'll interview, but don't forget to check the hometown paper of the corporate headquarters as well. If the organization has a national or international profile, it's wise to check the national newspapers that are known as **papers of record** (those that try to keep track of all important national and international political, social, and economic trends). Papers of record in the United States are usually considered to be the *New York Times, Washington Post, Wall Street Journal,* and *Los Angeles Times.* Almost all of them provide online access to archives, although a fee might be charged.

• Learn about career trends. Take advantage of the Internet resources devoted to career information. Many of the most current job-search strategy books (e.g., Adams, 2001; Bermont, 2004; Kennedy, 2000; Leanne, 2003, Yate, 2006) and career counselors suggest good Web sites and approaches. Some basic examples:

Career Builder (http://www.careerbuilder.com)

Employment Guide (http://www.employmentguide.com)

Monster Board (http://www.monster.com/)

Occupational Outlook Handbook (http://www.bls.gov/oco/)

Wall Street Journal (http://www.careerjournal.com/)

To search for other online resources, go to any large university's career services Web site, or to the employment search Web site sponsored by public libraries or government agencies. For example, the Highland Park Public library online service provides many links, ranging from basic career information and organizational statistics to personal interest inventories (http://www.hplibrary.org/www/career/html).

Persuasive Cover Letters and Résumés

A **résumé** is a summary of the skills and experience that qualify you for a particular job. It is usually sent or given to an organizational representative along with a **cover letter**, a narrative description of why you believe you are a good fit for the job and can meet the organization's needs. Think of résumés and cover letters as (1) ways to qualify for interviews and (2) as preliminary responses to interview-type questions.

Résumés, like a lot of things, aren't what they used to be. Contemporary résumés are still delivered in traditional ways (postal delivery, hand carried), but increasingly, résumés are sent in electronic versions online. Not long ago the conventional wisdom for job candidates was to spend a great deal of time and energy crafting the text and design of a résumé to help it stand out. The candidate would take the typescript to a printer and order scores of résumés to send out over the next weeks and months to potential employers. These days, preparing only a single version of a résumé is not practical especially given the specialized jobs and career niches of the workplace. With word-processing programs and laser printers résumés can be—indeed, are often expected to be—tailored to each job submission. Moreover, it is usually no longer necessary or desirable, if it ever was, to produce a glitzy résumé with cute or unusual fonts, colors, or shadings. (Actually, "cute" choices were never effective, according to most experts in the field.)

Companies now use computerized résumé-tracking programs to scan electronic résumés for keywords or buzzwords, often the same terms used in the original posted job description. As a result, electronic résumés should feature a straightforward, clean style that emphasizes keyword labels or phrases to establish qualifications unambiguously. Don't be reluctant to use the jargon or special terminology of the company or industry to which you're applying. For a public relations position, for example, an electronic résumé that ties your skills to terms like "newsletter," "press release," and "image campaign" signals your qualifications with keywords that will be tracked by employers' software.

In a visual, digital world, résumés and supporting materials often come packaged in electronic portfolios that allow prospective employees a chance to review you and your credentials in an accessible, attractive format. As with traditional résumés and cover letters, avoid getting too "cute" or stylistically dramatic in your digital portfolio. Content and understated presentation work better than hyperbole and glitz.

Interviewers respond favorably to carefully prepared written materials, demonstrated skills, and clear descriptions of qualifications with examples. In a form of self-fulfilling prophecy, interviewers who read (or view) a set of strong credentials tend to use a subsequent interview to confirm that positive first impression, rather than to poke holes in it (Dipboye, 1982). In one study, researchers (Dougherty, Turban, & Callender, 1994) found that interviewers' positive first impressions "were followed by interviewers' use of confirmatory behaviors and styles, including a positive style of interviewing, selling the company, providing job information to applicants, less information-gathering from applicants, more confident and effective applicant behavior, and more rapport of applicants and interviewers." In addition, under this self-fulfilling prophecy, there was more sharing of job information with applicants and, perhaps most important, "a favorable orientation toward job offers" (p. 663). In other words, thorough presentation of materials up front pays down the road.

Think of a cover letter as a brief idealized introduction to who you are in relation to the organization's needs. The best cover letters are succinct, narratively interesting, motivating, and addressed to a specific organizational representative. Choose the content for the cover letter by asking yourself, "If someone were to meet me for a couple of minutes, what would I want to be sure to say, and how would I want to say it?" Personnel managers often skim letters rapidly and develop impressions in a matter of moments. Your cover letter, then, should emphasize short, direct sentences and paragraphs with concrete, vivid language. An effective approach is to tell a story. What, for instance, inspired you to commit to a career change, or why did recent news developments crystallize your decision to practice public relations. The cover letter additionally should lead the reader directly to a careful study of a résumé: "As you will see detailed in my résumé . . ." statements can create such a bridge. Cover letters often state a three-part goal, with major paragraphs devoted to each section: State your academic and professional relationship to the position, including why it interests you; state how your résumé reflects your qualifications for this position; and state your willingness to stay in touch (see Figure 8.1).

Résumés tend to be either chronological or functional. A **chronological résumé**—almost always a reverse chronology—charts your personal experience from job to job, from school to school, from experience to experience, from responsibility to responsibility. Within each heading, stress your skills. A **functional résumé**, alternatively, organizes your qualifications around the function you can fulfill for the new organization and the skills you bring, grouping your previous jobs and experiences underneath them. See the résumés in Figures 8.2 and 8.3 for representative hints on shaping your own résumé. Of course, you can merge or adjust the styles to fit your own personality and goals. Some additional suggestions should help you put together a clear, communicative résumé:

• A one-page résumé is often counseled in the literature, but do not shy away from a second page or more if your background and accomplishments genuinely warrant it.

• Stay away from such cute techniques as decorative fonts, wide variation in print size, excessive boldfacing, elaborate shading, and the like; let your content be the main message, even if you're submitting a digital portfolio.

• Remember the **DPFP sequence**: draft, proof, feedback, proof. (1) *Draft stage* (start by brainstorming about your skills and responsibilities by reconstructing your employment history; turn sloppy notes into a draft document). (2) *Proofreading stage* (eliminate all unnecessary words, and ensure there are no typographical mistakes, misspellings, or grammatical glitches). (3) *Feedback stage* (share proofread draft with colleagues, professors, career professionals, and friends, and systematically note their responses and suggestions; tell them your goal is credibility, which includes proof of expertness, trustworthiness, and dynamism). (4) *Second proofreading stage* (after revisions, go through your résumé again to catch errors introduced during the process).

219 South Jefferson Avenue
St. Louis, MO 63108

April 15, 2007

Ms. Francine J. Wilshore
Director of Human Resources
Storm Consulting, Inc.
1417 Ninth St. North
Kansas City, MO 64154

Dear Ms. Wilshore:

I'm responding to your advertisement for an Organizational Skills Trainer that appeared in several recent editions of the *Kansas City Star*.

As the enclosed résumé demonstrates, I've envisioned this type of position since becoming a communication major during my sophomore year. I originally declared this major after taking an exciting course in public speaking, but rapidly began to appreciate the theory and practice of leadership, persuasion, interpersonal communication, media technologies, and journalistic writing. I still enjoy the times I speak to audiences, but I have come to appreciate clear and succinct writing, as well.

With the help of committed faculty, I was able to achieve Dean's List standing throughout my junior and senior years and was elected as the first president of a recently established campus organization for communication students. My internship at Anheuser-Busch gave me a wide range of experience with everyday training activities, including computer-assisted learning and the publication of a new training manual in interviewing strategies.

My résumé will tell you much more about my qualifications. Still, I would appreciate the opportunity to discuss the position with you in person. I will be contacting your office in the near future to discuss the status of the Storm Consulting search. If there is further information I could supply, or if you would like to contact me to discuss the position further, please notify me. I appreciate your consideration.

Sincerely,

RoseAnn M. Fernandez
314-977-3196
rosean@cytrack.com

Enclosure

FIGURE 8.1 **Sample Cover Letter.**

DARYL F. YOUNG

Before May 15, 2008
Reinert Hall, Room 234
Saint Louis University
St. Louis, MO 63103
314/768-2368

After May 15, 2008
83 Chouteau Drive
Collinsville, IL 62065
618/872-5932

Career Objective

> To obtain an entry-level position in the private accounting industry utilizing education and experience in accounting.

Education

> **St. Louis University**, St. Louis, Missouri
> Bachelor of Science in Business Administration, May 2007
> Major in Accounting
> GPA: 3.65/4.0
>
> **Indiana University**, Bloomington, Indiana
> Completed 30 hours toward a Bachelor of Science degree, August 2003 to May 2004

Experience

> **Office Assistant** (August 2005 to May 2006, August 2006 to May 2007)
> Registrar's Office, St. Louis University, St. Louis, Missouri
> • Supported the assistant director with various other responsibilities, including typing, filing, and generating monthly reports.
> • Processed transcript requests

Extracurricular Activities

> Accounting Club, 2 years
> • President
> • Fundraising chair
> Pi Kappa Phi social fraternity, 4 years
> • Vice President for Alumni Affairs
> • 1995 Homecoming Program Chair
> University Choir, 2 years

Honors

> Dean's List, seven semesters
> Recipient of three academic scholarships
> Who's Who Among American College & Universities

Interests

> Enjoy golf, fishing, chess, and cooking

FIGURE 8.2 **Sample Résumé: Chronological Style.**
Adapted from: *Employment Guide 1997–1998*, p. 12, Saint Louis University Career Center (1997). Originally reprinted by permission of CASS Recruitment Media/CASS Communications, Inc. (Updated for second edition)

Jennifer R. Marconi

341 Jefferson Avenue   St. Louis Missouri   314-821-9326   jmarconi@slu.edu

Objective

To obtain a management position in public relations that will use research, writing, and program development skills.

Experience

Public Relations

- Prepared press releases and conducted press conferences.
- Organized and hosted receptions and social events.
- Spoke to various civic, business, and professional organizations.

Program Development

- Conducted research on the representation of minority students in medical colleges and developed a proposal for a major study.
- Secured funding for an $845,000 project.
- Initiated and developed a national minority student recruitment program for 20 medical colleges.

Writing

- Compiled and published educational reports.
- Produced a booklet on urban problems for general distribution.
- Published and presented conference papers.

Administration Management

- Hired and trained research assistants.
- Managed medium-sized office and supervised 30 employees.

Research

- Gathered and analyzed information on higher education.
- Utilized various statistical applications on research data.

Career-Related Employment

Assistant Manager, *ATS Research Associates*, Saint Louis University, St. Louis, MO (October 2005–Present)
Publishing Assistant, *Mosby Year-Book Publishing*, St. Louis, MO (May 2004–October 2004)

Education

Master of Arts in Journalism, *Saint Louis University*, St. Louis, MO (May 2007)
Bachelor of Arts in English, *University of Missouri St. Louis*, MO (May 2005)

Awards and Honors

Journalism Scholarship recipient, Saint Louis University, 4 semesters
Mayo Writing Prize, 2nd Place, 2005
Beta Alpha Psi (Communication Honor Society), 4 semesters

Community Involvement

Big Sisters Association, volunteer mentor, 6 years

FIGURE 8.3 **Sample Résumé: Functional Style.**
Adapted from: *Employment Guide 1997–1998*, p. 13, Saint Louis University Career Center (1997).
Originally reprinted by permission of CASS Recruitment Media/CASS Communications, Inc.

• Omit the following information from your résumé unless it is directly relevant and helpful for your desired position: physical description and health information; ethnic, religious, or cultural connections; hobbies; military experience (except for job-related experience); part-time positions; expected salary; why you left previous positions; names and addresses of your references. (An exception might be made if one or more of your references is likely to be recognized as particularly important or influential by your potential employer.)

• Omit any statement about yourself that could be interpreted as self-serving ("I am a strong motivator of people" or "I have high ethical standards"). Readers readily dismiss such rhetoric. Let your record speak for you.

• Include a job-objective statement that directly reflects or mirrors the position description. This means your résumé will be adapted in different ways to each position. Some students think this is dishonest or deceptive—how can you have so many different objectives at one time? Think of it differently by reframing the issue. Your life doesn't have one simple and overriding objective. Is it your life's objective to have a good family life, or warm friendships, or a satisfying professional life? Aren't all these objectives relevant simultaneously? The same is true of your job search. Everyone has a mix of different objectives all the time, in all arenas of life. To state one does not negate the rest. Each position you decide to apply for thus invites you to articulate a new kind of objective.

• Include keywords, such as the job category and titles of positions for which you're applying. (See the discussion at the beginning of this section for more details.)

• Stress action words along with specific evidence when describing your skills. Reduce the level of abstraction and allow readers to visualize the kinds of changes they could expect after hiring you. In other words, don't suggest that you "have" a skill called "coordination"; make the résumé vivid and active by creating lists of details describing the what, when, how many, or where of things or people you coordinated. For example, in your work as an assistant manager for a sporting goods store, you may have:

trained 20 new employees over the past three years;

resolved more than 25 customer complaints to the mutual satisfaction of customer and company;

designed weekly product displays at the store's entrance; and

communicated employee feedback to management during monthly employee staff meetings.

Planning for Nonverbal Impressions

Interviewers don't perceive job applicants by a purely rational process of evaluating credentials, skills, and reasons. As you've learned from earlier chapters and other coursework in communication, a blend of verbal and nonverbal messages influences all relationships. Each form of message, in a sense, creates the context for the other. What you

Trying Out Your Skills

• Write a rough draft of a résumé, and use it as the basis for role-playing exercises for practicing your ability to talk about yourself. Give a printed version of your résumé to three different partners—a close friend at about your same level of job experience, one of your communication teachers or graduate students, and a representative of your career center. Ask them how well your résumé characterizes you. Compare their advice, and attempt to account for any differences in what they tell you. Revise the résumé and arrange role plays with each of them. Ask yourself the following questions about this experience:

• With which role-play partner did you feel most comfortable?

• Which partner was most direct with you or gave you the most constructive feedback?

• Which partner knows most about the career objective you plan to pursue?

• Are you still uncomfortable explaining any parts of your résumé? Either revise your résumé or continue to practice your explanations of them.

claim in spoken words, for example, might be disregarded or dismissed by an interviewer if it appears to conflict with your nonverbal messages. I tell you I'm "confident," but my voice quavers and you see sweat breaking out on my forehead. Communication scholars call those contradictions between verbal and nonverbal systems **mixed messages**. You want to avoid mixed messages, but some will probably arise in any extended interpersonal situation. So rather than leaving your nonverbal presentation entirely to chance, we suggest you prepare for its crucial elements.

A common problem, researchers say, is how to dress for an interview. Clothing is a nonverbal indicator that could undermine your desired image as someone who is serious, attentive, and responsible. In other words, inappropriate choices of elements of your appearance can create mixed messages. Pat Mahony, a human resources manager, says, "I look at the way [job applicants] are dressed and figure that's the best they're going to look. If their clothes do not look good on the first day, then you know [their dress] will only be more relaxed once they come on board" (quoted in Eng, 1998, p. G20). Recent changes in on-site cultures of some companies, however, have encouraged a more relaxed style, thus creating confusion for applicants. Do you plan to "dress up" even in situations where you suspect a much more casual look is the norm? No one can answer this question definitively, but a more conservative approach is usually safer. Since the days of John Molloy's bestselling *Dress for Success*, first published in the 1970s (see Molloy, 1998), a certain kind of prescription has predominated in the literature—dark suits for men and women, solid and traditional colors, subdued hairstyles, and subdued makeup for women. We suggest that you consult one of the specialized interview-preparation books (e.g., Bixler & Nix-Rice, 2005) or professional career consultants on your campus for advice on ways to adapt appearance to expectations for a particular professional setting.

Heed, however, the warning of Richard Ilkka (1995), who says: "Attention to dress and grooming often dominate to the exclusion of other areas" of nonverbal communication given as advice to applicants. The emphasis on dress, he adds "is not surprising when selection interviewing education promotes appearance as a product to be attained, yet minimizes the study of the judgmental process" (p. 12). Ilkka is right, so you should probably also prepare for other nonverbal messages such as timing (ensuring you are punctual), posture (demonstrating attentiveness and interest), and gestures (for appropriate emphasis). Ilkka, however, notes that early impressions can be decisive in interview interactions (p. 13), and nonverbal cues of appearance and dress are crucial as interviewers form their initial impressions.

Role Playing

Putting all the elements of preparation together can be a difficult process of coordination that you can't do by yourself. You need teammates—people willing to interact with you as you try out all the things you're learning and considering. You don't want to appear phony or rehearsed. However, you've learned from other aspects of your life, such as musical performance or sports, that a discipline of practice increases your awareness of your own potential. What others can do for you is supply extra sets of eyes and ears, giving you feedback, as a teacher or coach might do. For instance, does your pause before answering a question come across as an insecure or hesitant stalling tactic or as a measured and thoughtful approach to answering fully? If the former, what would help you make the impression match the confidence you actually feel? Talk it over and experiment with ways to accentuate the positive and reduce the negative.

Creative Forms of Interviewees' Framing, Listening, and Questioning

Framing, listening, and questioning: Notice that we have again changed the order of the three basic skills to emphasize the different perspectives of the two participants. Whereas, interviewers typically approach the interview's structure first as an opportunity to question and probe the candidate's suitability for the position, then as a chance to listen to and answer the interviewee's questions, and finally as a task of assessing the overall process, the interviewee's experience is quite different. He or she enters a situation in which the frame is largely influenced by the interviewee's context, needs, and directive control. How to respond to that pre-existing interpretive frame is perhaps a more basic interviewee interactional problem than the actual responding or questioning. Then, in terms of sequence, the majority of the interview will focus on answers to the employer's questions. Finally, the opportunity for asking questions of the interviewer usually comes toward the interview's conclusion.

One other preliminary reminder: As we suggested before, it's especially effective to take a both-sides approach to understanding the interview. Although the interviewer-oriented problems and the interviewee-oriented problems usually are treated separately in textbooks and the popular media, we believe the two are intimately connected, and thus we discuss them in the same chapter. You will learn how to be interviewed only by fully recognizing the interviewer's role as well as your own; the two roles are mutually *interdependent*.

Framing from the Interviewee's Perspective

Surely the interview feels like a desperate trial at times. The successful applicants we've known, though, have defined the interview as:

- An opportunity rather than a test.
- A learning experience rather than a demonstration.
- A dialogue rather than a monologue.

If you define the interview in these more inclusive and less threatening ways, you're more likely to perceive opportunities to "get out of yourself," a concept introduced earlier in the chapter. Every comment and question, then, can be seen not only in terms of what it does or means to you, but also from the perspective of the other person. Communication theorists call this **decentering**—the ability to relate to perspectives other than your own—and it's closely associated with empathy. If you are genuinely qualified, the employer should have some good *reasons* to select you. But *reasons* and *reasoning* are different things; you have to understand that reasoning—the drawing of inferences or conclusions—can trump reasons in an interviewer's decision making.

Listening from the Interviewee's Perspective

We are potentially at our worst as listeners when we are placed in pressure-filled situations. Listening skill declines as perceived threat increases. The adrenaline flows and so does ego involvement. Therefore, communicative interviewees should pay special attention to listening skills and styles. Consider the following reminders.

• *Decenter, to understand the interviewer's context.* Perhaps the most important reminder, consistent with flexible framing, is to hear questions in the context in which the interviewer asks them. Interviewers generally don't care about how much you need a job or how the job would benefit your family or bolster your self-esteem. In fact, they probably are only indirectly impressed with what your skills have done for someone else, except inasmuch as they can translate it directly into the present selection process. They ask questions to elicit insight not into what you can do, but what you can do *for them*. Therefore, listen carefully so that you can phrase your responses with this slant:

INTERVIEWER: What qualifies you to be an editor of a major newsletter?

INTERVIEWEE: When I was at Consolidated Electric, I was the person everyone consulted about their copy, because they thought I could catch all the grammar and syntax problems. I know your newsletter, *The Coyle Call*, needs that kind of close attention from an editor. We can't afford to offend intelligent readers with sloppy publications.

Notice that the interviewee does not frame the response wholly in terms of personal qualities. To do so would miss an opportunity. Instead, the answer gives extra concrete information succinctly, relates it to the employer's need, and begins to identify with the process as a professional colleague ("we"). Even if passed over for the position, the interviewee has positioned herself in future situations as an intelligent listener who hears things from another's perspective. If you can't land the job, you can be remembered positively. Interviewers who you impress might notify someone else in the organization to see if another job fits you.

• *Verify inferences and meanings.* Do not answer a question unless you understand fully the terms of the question. Your prior research into the job, the employer, and the professional jargon should have prepared you to understand the basic terminology and duties about which you're likely to be asked. However, something unanticipated will usually come up. Instead of looking quizzically at the questioner and saying, "What's that?" apply your active listening by bringing your inferences into the open:

INTERVIEWER: Are you willing to come on board as an adjunct instructor for a year or so?

INTERVIEWEE: I think by an "adjunct" you mean someone who isn't technically going to teach full time, but who will qualify for most of the same benefits. Is that right?

You may be wrong, or you may be right, depending on the interviewer's meaning. However, you will at least avoid the trap of answering the wrong question once the interviewer provides clarification. You may also impress the interviewer with your assertiveness and thoroughness to confirm. You position yourself as a learner.

• *Look for openings that allow you to highlight or clarify your skills.* Sincere, well-intentioned people sometimes are so afraid of sounding boastful they hide behind their modesty. Communication trainers and teachers often stress *assertiveness* skills to achieve that middle ground between *aggressive personal style* (disregard for or dismissal of the rights or abilities of others) and an *acquiescent personal style* (disregard for or dismissal of one's own rights and responsibilities). In a job interview, you are expected to be assertive; you should neither dismiss your own achievements nor imply that others deserve no credit. You want to be seen as both a strong individual force in an organization and an unselfish team player. This is an admittedly delicate balance, but interviewers are taught to listen for it. For example:

INTERVIEWER: Why were you so successful as editor of the university's student paper?

INTERVIEWEE: I'm not sure, but I think it was partially because I paid so much attention the year before when I was a copy editor. I saw what the previous editor did to solidify our new readership, but I also saw firsthand the problems she had with the administration. I cut back on our emphasis on columnists, increased coverage of student organizations, and policed some writers' confrontive attitude about President Smythe. I wouldn't have been able to do this without strong support from my adviser, Dr. Jacks, and my staff. We really worked well together.

• *Regard even closed or terse questions as invitations for elaboration.* For example, what's wrong with this exchange?

INTERVIEWER: Have you ever supervised a department with more than a dozen employees?

INTERVIEWEE: Yes, of course.

INTERVIEWER: When?

INTERVIEWEE: Well, it was a few years ago.

Each answer is responsive at one level but turns the interviewer's role around to your disadvantage. Even if she or he is a poor interviewer, it's to your advantage to keep the talk from becoming an interrogation. Elaborate on what you assume to be the relevant details concerning the question's topic, and you will enhance the conversation to the benefit of both you and your interviewer.

INTERVIEWER: Have you ever supervised a department with more than a dozen employees?

INTERVIEWEE: Yes, I have. Several years ago. Martinez Manufacturing asked me to take over the public relations office on an interim basis while they searched for someone with 10 years' or more experience. At the end of that period, they hadn't found someone they liked from outside, so they asked me if I'd be interested in the job—even though I'd only worked there a year and a half.

INTERVIEWER: That's interesting. I wonder if they'd ever done that before.

In her research, Lois Einhorn (1981) found "elaboration of information" a significant factor that distinguished successful from unsuccessful interviewees: "Usually the unsuccessful applicants did not expand their answers. Fifty-eight percent of one . . . applicant's responses, for example, contained less than ten words; 29% consisted of 'um hum,' 'no,' 'okay,' or 'yeah.' By contrast, all of the successful applicants used extensive detail, treating their experiences and abilities thoroughly" (p. 223). Certainly, all elaborations won't be equally effective, and more talk isn't necessarily better talk. To talk for five minutes could quash your chances as easily as it could solidify them. Still, interviewers' questions should be taken to imply a request for detailed information, even if you're not literally asked to expand. Try for a style of focused elaboration, and look for nonverbal signals that tell you to conclude your story, such as fidgeting, glancing at a watch or clock, or removing eye contact by the interviewer.

Questioning from the Interviewee's Perspective

Toward the conclusion of your time together, most interviewers will ask you whether you have questions for them. At this point the roles shift, but they shift a bit more subtly than many interviewees realize. You might be tempted to assume that you can breathe a figurative sigh of relief now that the pressure is largely off you. You'd be wrong. The responsibilities have shifted, but one crucial factor has not changed: You are still being evaluated. Expect the kinds of questions you ask, and your style of asking them, to be noted and scrutinized with care by the organization.

In her study of interviews conducted by representatives of two firms, "Lazarus" and "Keller Crescent," Einhorn (1981) found that questioning behaviors marked the difference between successful interviewees and people the companies turned down. She writes:

> The successful applicant's communication was specific and comprehensive in questioning as well as in answering. These applicants asked the interviewers specific questions about a wide variety of subjects, and the questions tended to be focused. The following questions to the Lazarus interviewer are typical: "What brands/makers do you carry in the junior size of women's wear?" "What is the reason for your extensive point-of-purchase displays and are they means of motivating customers to start becoming innovative?" "How often do you have promotional activities?" Both successful and unsuccessful interviewees often asked questions about the companies' training programs and expansion plans, but as a group, the successful applicants asked about other matters too, such as the organization's clientele, turnover rates, and recruiting procedures. They also asked pertinent questions about the interviewers' and the companies' backgrounds and often phrased their questions in the first person. For example, instead of asking, "What are the duties and responsibilities of the job?" the successful interviewees asked, "What would be my duties and responsibilities?" By wording the question in the first person, these applicants indirectly expressed confidence in receiving offers from Lazarus and Keller Crescent. Psychologically, this phrasing also forced the interviewers to imagine the applicants in the jobs. (pp. 223–224)

With so much riding on the tone of the interview, regard your questioning period as an opportunity to solidify a relationship of mutual respect with the organizational interviewer:

• Be sure to have questions. Prepare a general list ahead of time (this is your own mini-interview schedule), and carefully note as the conversation progresses questions that have already been answered. Your prepared questions should address all areas you consider crucial in the workplace, such as how do employees interact, what means are used for evaluations, what degree of autonomy of judgment is allowed, and what value is placed on individual creativity.

• Be careful about asking picky, hyperdetailed questions, especially in a preliminary or **screening interview**. Interviewers expect more detailed questions in follow-up interviews when both sides know they are more serious about each other. (Follow-up or second interviews are sometimes specifically termed **selection interviews**, even though that word also applies to the employment interviewing process as a whole.)

• Preface your questions with expressions of interest or curiosity that put your skills in context. For example: "I've never been a part of an organization that put such a premium on monitoring the press. You must have workers who stay on top of the news by reading papers and magazines all the time. What do they look for?"

• Be sure your questions don't betray your ignorance in areas where you shouldn't be ignorant. You can't realistically be expected to know everything, and to ask questions is usually better than remaining ignorant. However, some questions have such obvious answers that your interviewer will wonder why you didn't do some of the most elementary homework: "Where is your corporate headquarters?" "I wasn't sure if your company had expanded into the radio station market yet. Has it?"

• Don't act like a persnickety shopper. We've encouraged you to frame the experience as learning and decision making, but if employers see you only in this way—as if you could get job offers so easily you merely have to choose among them—you'll sound too arrogant. Beware, in other words, of the "grocery store mentality" that characterized the unsuccessful interviewees in Einhorn's (1981) research (see also Box 8.6).

• Use questions to demonstrate your knowledge, not simply to inquire about issues and trends. For example: "In the *Phoenix Business Journal* last month, Lon Mathers speculated that online shopping had reached its peak and was on the decline. What do you think his observation means for the industry if they pan out?"

Beyond the Basics

The Legal Context of Employment Interviewing

Behind all the interactional challenges of interviewing stands another set of challenges that are often just as important. Certainly, all employment interviewing has been affected profoundly in recent decades by a legal environment of increasing governmental attention to fairness, to opportunity, to access, and to justice. Employers have a significant amount of power over their own organizational policies (which is normal and expected), and they also have power over their employees' lives (some of which might be unreasonable and illegal for a good reason).

Whether your immediate role is interviewee or interviewer, you should be aware of relevant laws governing appropriate interaction and practices in interviews. As of June 2006, the Department of Labor Web site listed relevant laws or regulations associated with "equal employment opportunity" along with associated guidelines and interpretations (http://www.dol.gov/dol/topic/discrimination/index.htm). The list covered three important areas:

• *Age discrimination*: Age Discrimination Act of 1975; Age Discrimination in Employment Act of 1967; Section 188 of the Workforce Investment Act of 1998.

• *Disability*: Section 503 of the Rehabilitation Act of 1973; Titles I and II of the Americans with Disabilities Act; the Vietnam War Veterans Readjustment Assistance Act; Section 188 of the Workforce Investment Act of 1998.

• *Ethnic/National Origin, Color, Race, Religion, Sex*: Executive Order 11246; Title VII of the Civil Rights Act of 1964; Title VI of the Civil Rights Act of 1964; Title IX of the Educational Amendments of 1972; Section 188 of the Workforce Investment Act of 1998; National Apprenticeship Act of 1937.

Box 8.6

Reminders *What Do Successful and Unsuccessful Interviewees Do Differently?*

Earlier, we cited Lois Einhorn's older (1981) but still relevant study of two employers' perceptions of college student applicants. She taped and analyzed on-campus interviews but also asked company interviewers to complete questionnaires before meeting the interviewees, based only on application materials. After the interviews, interviewers filled out other questionnaires about their impressions of interviewees. "Candidates were classified as successful if the interviewers' perception of them improved considerably and unsuccessful if the interviewers judged them more negatively after the interviews" (p. 218). You might question whether some interviewees might have been "unsuccessful" not because of their behavioral strategies but perhaps because they found these companies less desirable to work for. Still, the study discloses the inner dynamics of job interviewing as it "really" exists—in the relational realm. In this summary, we have paraphrased Einhorn's findings.

Differences in Identification with Employers

Successful interviewees emphasized or expressed

- Clearer career goals.

- Career goals consistent with the position applied for.

- Concern for careers over jobs.

- Preference for the workplace over graduate school.

- Specific interest in working for these firms.

- Reinforcement of the interviewer's ideas.

- Understanding of how the employers' job descriptions related to them.

- More context or rationale for the "negatives" in their records.

Differences in Support for Arguments

Successful interviewees used

- More evidence, especially factual and hypothetical illustrations, comparisons, and statistics.

- Less reliance on personal experience and explanations.

- More elaboration of stories of personal qualifications.

Other federal laws, for example, the Glass Ceiling Act, the Americans with Disabilities Act, and the Pregnancy Discrimination Act, also attempt to ensure basic fairness in hiring practices. In most circumstances, only legal counsel for organizations need to know all the ins and outs of these laws, as well as relevant state and local statutes on the legality of communication behaviors in the workplace. There is no need in the context of this chapter to review the laws one by one. However, general principles need to be understood by everyone involved in employment selection.

In general, the statutes address the power differences between hiring organizations—often large systems of people and practices backed by significant resources—and the individuals who apply, and are in some ways vulnerable, to them. Applicants have no reasonable way of ascertaining the accuracy of the interviewer's characterizations of the

- More comprehensive focused questioning of interviewers.

Differences in Organization

Successful interviewees used

- More active and concrete language.
- More speaking time within the interviews.
- Summary statements when interviewers moved to terminate interviews.
- Forward-looking comments to inquire about subsequent decision making.

Differences in Style

Successful interviewees used

- More active and concrete language.
- More positive descriptions of experience (fewer words of negative connotation such as "no," "awful," "difficult," or "dull").
- More technical jargon appropriate to the employers.
- More coherent sentence structure.
- Fewer grammatical errors.

Differences in Delivery

Successful interviewees spoke

- With more animation and vocal variety and forcefulness.
- With more precise articulation.
- With more natural accompanying gestures.
- With fewer nervous habits (inappropriate laughter or shaking the foot).
- With more positive nonverbal cues (smiling, nodding affirmatively).
- With better eye contact and more expressions of interest.

Differences in Images Conveyed

Successful interviewees were perceived as

- More dynamic, active, and enthusiastic.
- More professionally competent and knowledgeable.
- More assertive.

organization, promises about hiring and decision making, and description of job procedures. Prior research can help you put promises into perspective, but it will rarely uncover all you'll need to know, or, in fact, the depth of detail the organization could collect about you in just a few minutes if it wanted to invade your privacy. Legal statutes restrict an organization's ability to mislead you, lie to you, to spy on you, or treat you by different standards than it would treat another applicant. Most organizations act honorably, but it is reassuring to know that unfair, improper, and discriminatory procedures are subject to legal action.

Closely tied to power issues is the fundamental matter of fairness. Employers expect and deserve wide latitude of choice when it comes to filling their positions. After all, such concerns as company profits, organizational reputation or prestige, and even survival of an organization depend on who works there. Millions of dollars are spent retraining workers or hiring new ones to replace "bad hires"; no wonder corporations, government agencies, and nonprofits are investing money up front to improve their ability to identify competent workers. However, no organization can reasonably rationalize institutional patterns of discrimination or prejudice. People deserve access to the jobs where they can thrive, regardless of the color of their skin, their ethnicity, sexual orientation, age, gender, marital status, physical appearance, or physical disabilities. Unfortunately, we do not yet live in a society that fully values or encourages diversity. Some organizations use their inherent hiring power to practice unfair discrimination against African Americans, Latinos, and other ethnic groups; women; gay, lesbian, transgendered, and bisexual persons; applicants who are "too old" by an organization's arbitrary standard; or those physically challenged in non-job-related ways.

If you doubt that job discrimination happens often, consult recent newspaper accounts of embarrassing business scandals: The top executives of one of the largest U.S. oil companies allegedly ridiculed and told racist jokes about African Americans in boardroom meetings; major national chain restaurants counseled their personnel officers to reject black or homosexual applicants; and another major chain condoned the systematic mistreatment of minority customers. Broadcast newsmagazines have detailed how physically disabled applicants could not even obtain interviews, despite being exceptionally well qualified for the positions by all objective measures. According to one of the leading diversity consultants in contemporary management, Marilyn Loden (1996), "in a 1995 study conducted by a bipartisan congressional committee, [white men were] found to hold 95 percent of senior management positions in industry despite the fact that they represent 43 percent of the American workforce. According to the same study, despite three decades of affirmative action, glass ceilings were still firmly in place for women and people of color above middle-management levels" (p. 23). The situation for women executives has improved since then, some say dramatically so. However, according to a recent article in *U.S. Banker* (DePaula, 2003), "many executives dismiss gender as a workplace issue—even the women. Maybe they're in denial. At the highest levels in finance, equal representation of both sexes remains elusive. The numbers are particularly startling in banking, where 75 percent of the workforce is female but less than 25 percent of executives—CEOs, CFOs, COOs—are women."

Interviewing professionals and researchers refer to *bona fide occupational qualifications* (increasingly referred to as BFOQs)—those attributes reasonably considered essential to a high-quality performance within a designated job. For example, a person with no ability to vocalize could not reasonably perform as a telephone interviewer, and a company could not reasonably be criticized for denying such an applicant that position. However, research firms have other jobs for which a nonspeaking applicant would be fully qualified. Some companies might systematically hunt for "undesirables" through unfair and possibly illegal questions about such things as neighborhoods of residence and decisions about marriage or pregnancy, designed to determine—or obtain strong clues about—such things as personal plans, private family decisions, ethnic affiliations, age, social class, backgrounds, and other irrelevant issues. Without protection, applicants who rightly object to sharing such personal information could be disqualified arbitrarily.

Statutes and case law, along with Equal Employment Opportunity Commission enforcement, provide some general principles to help you recognize especially troublesome areas in interview questioning and responding. However, there is no substitute for professionals familiarizing themselves with the actual laws that define legally defensible interviewing. Be aware of these questionable areas of inquiry:

- *Race*: Requests to identify someone's race, or even produce a photograph, are unlawful.

- *Gender*: Inquiries about marital or relationship status, physical data such as height and weight, and similar questions are unlawful. Neither can interviewers inquire into child care arrangements, birth control, or pregnancy issues.

- *Religion*: Questions about styles of worshiping, affiliations with religious groups, or membership in organized religions are unlawful.

- *Disability*: Inquiries about diseases or conditions, or the experience of being disabled, are unlawful, as are probes into possible adjustments or accommodations an applicant might think he or she will need if hired. Halvorson (1997) suggests ways that classes can become more sensitive to the Americans with Disabilities Act.

- *National origin*: Asking where someone was born, or about their native language, or about the details of their U.S. citizenship are unlawful.

If it occurs to you that some of these inquiries could be relevant in the hiring process, you're right. They *could* be relevant somehow, if relevance is defined broadly enough. Yet the possibility for unscrupulous or even unwittingly prejudiced interviewers to abuse such questioning situations is high enough for agencies and courts to try to protect applicants from their potential unfairness. How can you avoid these pitfalls, then, as an interviewer? How can you respond reasonably as an interviewee if unlawful issues come up?

Several recommendations are particularly important for interviewers and organizations who value fairness (see Campion & Arvey, 1989, pp. 66–67). First, organizations should have clearly defined job descriptions from which clear performance criteria can be developed. No interview can be totally objective, but the odds of unexamined subjectivity can be reduced if the criteria are clear and fair. Second, organizations should select and train interviewers and interview teams appropriately. All-white and all-male teams, especially when inexperienced, can too easily lead to discrimination. Third, questions should not only be relevant to the job criteria, but should also be asked of *all* candidates to avoid an obvious danger of unstructured interviewing. Fourth, organizations should review the work of their interviewers, and when necessary, counter negative results of subjective discrimination with multiple- or panel-interview designs. Fifth, organizations and interviewers should keep accurate records of selection interview procedures. Sixth, the results of past interview practices should be monitored for fairness across groups. With this kind of organizational introspection, the fate of all interviewees will be in better hands.

What about the practical dilemma of being asked an unlawful question when you're the interviewee? Most authors of job-interviewing guidelines counsel you to be direct in responding, but not to answer questions with which you're uncomfortable. Be as polite as you can, but move the conversation on to what you know are your genuine employment qualifications. Later, analyze what happened. You'll probably encounter some manipulative and biased questioners, but you'll also meet some sincere interviewers who've just stumbled innocently into unlawful areas. Another strategy is to attempt to understand the interviewer's reason or motive for asking the unlawful or questionable question and then reply to that concern if possible. For example, if an interviewer appears to veer into illegal questioning about a woman's home life, it may reflect a bias that employees with strong family ties might avoid working overtime when the company faces deadlines. A possible reply might give the benefit of the doubt and focus on job-related issues: "Family is always important to me. But if the company needs me to work overtime, for example, I'll find a way to do that. I always have in the past."

Beyond the obvious legal implications, the organizational interviewer's pattern of questioning provides additional evidence you can use in deciding about where to work. When an interviewer persistently pries into your private life or your cultural beliefs ("How many children do you intend to have anyway?" or "What do you, as a black man, think about feminism and the 'glass ceiling'?"), consider the possibility that he or she may represent an organizational culture you sense as chauvinistic or racist. At times, you may simply choose to say, "I'm uncomfortable talking about that with someone I've just met. Can we move on?" Later you should assess what occurred and whether you should think twice about working in an environment that makes you feel uncomfortable.

Extensions of Selection Interview Principles

The principles of selection interviewing considered in this chapter are most commonly applied in employment interviews between two persons, in which one elicits information about the possible hiring of the other. It might be useful, however, to think in a wider frame about selection interviewing. Let's consider several areas of contemporary life that demonstrate similar laws and practices.

Service Providers

Companies, school boards, youth groups, military service groups, and many other organizations often ask service providers to make presentations before a selection group makes a decision. For example, representatives of three food-service companies appear before a university committee charged with recommending which firm should operate in the new student union. Beyond providing preliminary written materials describing their qualifications, the firms' representatives make presentations and answer questions about their services. Undoubtedly there would be opportunities, as well, for the vendors to question the committee about the plans for the student union, projections for student enrollment over the next decade, the kinds of entree selections the committee envisions, and so forth. After interviewing "applicants," the committee makes its decision in a process similar to an individual's experience when applying to a company.

Elite Selection

Although the term *elite selection* may seem odd, it refers to the situation in which a limited number of people are selected for special opportunities. If you want to attend an Ivy League university, a graduate school, a law school, or a medical school, or if you hope to be chosen for a special fellowship or prestigious award, you will go through a process of elite selection, conducted perhaps by individual preliminary interviewers, a screening committee, and a final selection board. Although the end result might not be a job, the kinds of questioning you receive and the kinds of nervousness you experience will resemble the elements of a job interview.

One of the clear differences, though, between elite selection and the job-hiring process is that in the former, most applicants are at what Robert Klitgaard (1985) calls the "right tail." That is, employment interviews usually attract a typical bell curve for applicants. (Visualize a curve in the shape of a bell, rising from the left where there are a very few totally unqualified applicants, peaking dramatically with a large number of "average" applicants, and then falling off to a very few completely qualified candidates.) The left tail is the unqualified side, and the right tail is the highly qualified side. However, in elite selection, almost all candidates represent the right tail—those who are all technically qualified for high accomplishment. When slots are few, it becomes a much more difficult and subtle task to make fine distinctions among people. Then, too, when choosing educational elites, decision makers weigh other factors that affect the learning environment for all. This is why Harvard, for example, has never chosen its student body wholly on a meritocratic basis of grades or test scores but also considers such factors as geographical roots, leadership and student activities, and cultural diversity among the highly qualified applicants. Although face-to-face interviews have never been a highly regarded means of predicting later accomplishment among such elites, the interview is an extra opportunity for applicants to impress selection bodies.

The Informational Interview

As you near the time to take job hunting seriously, we recommend setting up several informational interviews, an experience that previews an actual employment interview (Crosby, 2002). In a sense, it's a pre-employment interview or an employment reconnaissance interview. Most large organizations have personnel departments that are familiar with, and welcome, contact with students and people who are considering career shifts. With a commitment to informational interviews, organizations become better known in a community and spot exceptional candidates early in the process, sometimes long before they graduate. Occasionally, informational interviews with personnel directors result in

Trying Out Your Skills

"In your local community, pick out two prominent professional communicators who are (1) in a career field you're considering and (2) experienced interviewers.

- Structure a brief interview schedule for each that will allow you to learn both about their profession(s) and how interviewing skills play a part in their jobs.

- Schedule and conduct the interviews, at the convenience of the organizational interviewers.

For maximum learning, it's best to meet these professionals in their organizational environments. Be sure to send a follow-up note expressing your appreciation for their cooperation.

- After these informational interviews, compare their comments about effective interviewing with skills, concepts, and ideas explained in this book.

internships or other formal ongoing involvement with the organization. More often, an informal friendship or mentorship is forged, and the two people stay in touch. At the very least, setting up several informational interviews will give you insight into organizational cultures and realistic but relatively low-pressure practice in conducting yourself in an interview situation. Personnel managers who conduct these kinds of interviews often give out informational packets that help you evaluate entire job categories and industries.

Interviewing classes often feature out-of-class assignments for students to interview professional interviewers. Take any opportunity to meet interviewers in your tentative career choices. They not only could give you excellent advice about interviewing, but also advise you on working in complex organizations. In informational interviews, your goal should be to make an impression primarily as a listener—but as a listener with excellent preparation, communication skills, and potential. Do not force employment possibilities into the conversation artificially. Rather, do a good job of investigating a career or company, and use the opportunity to prepare for actual job interviews.

The Persuasive Interview: A Preview

Clearly, the employment interview involves persuasion. People's attitudes, values, and beliefs are affected by what they learn there. In addition, a body of research into the employment interview process focuses on such topics of interpersonal persuasion as impression management, compliance-gaining, exchange theory, self-monitoring, cognitive consistency research, and the like (see Dougherty et al., 1994; Stevens, 1997; Stevens & Kristof, 1995; Whetzel & McDaniel, 2000). Later, we'll devote an entire chapter to persuasive interviews as they're applied to other one-on-one interactions where attitude change is the goal—such as sales or negotiation. However, remember that all interviews have rhetorical elements in them, and all are thus persuasive to some degree.

Making Your Decision

- Refer back to the sample employment interview schedule of questions (Box 8.2), which was written to help select a registered nurse for a surgical care facility. The last item the interviewer plans to bring up is an inquiry about whether the applicant is interviewing elsewhere and, if so, where. What is your first impression of this question? If you were an applicant interviewing for the position, how would you respond?

  Still hypothetically: Assuming you're the applicant, you know you've been invited for two other interviews next week. Write out one possible realistic response to this question based on your situation.

  Now write out an alternative response that you think is appropriate, but one that takes a different approach.

  Which of your responses is more accurate? More honest? More general? More noncommittal? Does such a question seem fair? Compare and discuss your responses with others in your class. Why do you think a respected interviewer actually recommends this approach?

- Imagine a hypothetical situation in which you're asked by your boss to interview a large number of prospective employees for a cross-town delivery and messenger service. Following the reasoning that this is a high-pressure business, she asks you to make the interviews stressful and uncomfortable for interviewees. She wants you to hire only those candidates who do not buckle under the pressure.

  First, what do you suppose she means by a high-pressure interview? What would she want you to do? Be gruff, rude, and distant on purpose? Demand rapid responses? Work into your conversation a demanding tone? Insults? Take a position on the advisability of such an interview strategy. Would it, in your opinion, yield the results she expects? Why or why not? Analyze her suggestions in terms of frame analysis; that is, how would interviewees frame such an approach?

- Hypothetical: You are an African American applicant for a job in the human resources department of a major brewery. The interviewer, a white male, has made several friendly remarks about how the company has been attempting to increase the number of minority employees, "to let the rest of us know how to communicate with blacks and minorities because they, you know, don't buy our beer much." He says he thinks affirmative action is a good thing. He turns to you and asks, "Are you in favor of affirmative action yourself?"

  How do you respond? Does this question seem lawful to you? Appropriate? If so, why? If not, why not?

Summary

Contrary to the approach most textbooks use to describe employment interviewing, we weave the perspectives of interviewer and interviewee into one chapter, rather than separate what interviewers do from what interviewees do. At times we focus on one or the other, of course, but generally it is the relationship between the rhetorical roles and goals of interviewer and interviewee that interests us—and applies to you. To be effective, each person in an interview must share a knowledge of the other's concerns, what the other is trying to accomplish, and how a collaborative relationship can help the employment decisions of both parties.

According to a study (Peterson, 1997) that underscored the importance of interpersonal skills in employee selection, more than 98 percent of personnel professionals responding to a questionnaire agreed or strongly agreed that oral and nonverbal skills are significant in influencing hiring decisions. Further, deficiencies in communication skills were uncovered:

> Respondents were asked to report whether job applicants displayed adequate communication skills. Compared with their overwhelming agreement that communication skills were important, only 59.68% of respondents indicated agreement that current job applicants displayed adequate communication skills . . . Interviewers were also asked to identify the most prevalent communication inadequacies. These data identified the five most prevalent oral and nonverbal communication skill inadequacies as (a) eye contact, (b) topic relevance, (c) response organization, (d) listening skills, and (e) response clarity. (p. 289)

The topics of this chapter are at the core of your ability to improve as an interviewer or as an interviewee. We have discussed how a relational approach to interviewing can help establish an environment of collaboration. Within that environment, although rhetorical goals might differ—creating conflict of purpose at times—both sides have a similar overarching goal. Both need to have more information to make an intelligent decision; thus, both need adequate motivation and preparation to become learners. Both need to listen carefully and to frame their knowledge in a wider context.

In "Beyond the Basics" we introduced you to the relevant issues of legal context. This context, although it may not directly affect all the preparation strategies that interviewees and interviewers undertake, nevertheless influences many of the outcomes of interviewing. We suggest that legal issues generally are not cut-and-dried "do this, don't do that" stipulations that must be memorized (although organizations and individuals do need a heightened awareness of them). Instead, there are good reasons for fairness, reasonableness, and equity that we all should consider in the workplace. Finally, we have described how many of the same principles of selecting candidates and jobs can apply to other situations of selection interviewing.

The Interview Bookshelf

On the basic research that illuminates the employment interview:

Eder, R. W., & Ferris, G. R. (Eds.). (1989). *The employment interview: Theory, research, and practice.* Newbury Park, CA: Sage.

Although dated, this remains perhaps the best single-volume academic introduction to the classic studies of employee selection. The authors provide literature reviews in the areas of impression effects, interviewer decision making, context, information search strategies, applicant impression management, interpersonal dynamics, and other important areas.

On a balanced, "both sides of the table" approach:

Kanter, A. B. (1995). *The essential book of interviewing: Everything you need to know from both sides of the table.* New York: Times Books.

Kanter writes an informal, anecdotal account that is fair to both interviewers and interviewees. Although many popular books opt for easy advice and gimmicks, he attempts to explore how subtle the interview can be as a communication meeting. He does so with unusual clarity and graceful writing.

On the job search process:

Bolles, R. N. (2007). *The 2007 what color is your parachute? A practical manual for job-hunters and career-changers.* Berkeley, CA: Ten Speed Press. [updated annually]

Yate, M. (2006). *Knock 'em dead 2006: The ultimate job-seeker's handbook.* Holbrook, MA: Adams. [updated annually]

Dozens of books claim to help insecure job seekers prepare for the interview process. All give advice on what to research, how to craft a résumé, how to anticipate tough interview questions, and so forth. Most are helpful, but some seem little more than collections of quick-fix techniques. Relatively few books assist interviewees in performing realistic self-reflection about communication style and career goals, or encourage interviewees to see the interview as communication. Here are two veteran authors whose tried-and-tested books, through multiple editions, have proven especially insightful.

On the employee search process:

Camp, R., Vielhaber, M., & Simonetti, J. (2001). *Strategic interviewing: How to hire good people.* San Francisco, CA: Jossey-Bass.

This book attempts to demystify the process of deciding whether to hire applicants after meeting them for only a brief time. The authors encourage organizational interviewers to be far more systematic than many currently are.

Chapter Nine

Interviews in Organizations

(LEARNING GOALS)

After reading this chapter, you should be able to

- **Describe the role played by interviewing within contemporary complex organizations**

- **Prepare thoroughly for conducting appraisal interviews**

- **Communicate skillfully within appraisal, intervention, exit, and termination interviews, as both interviewer and interviewee**

- **Explain how conflict, trust, and supportive climates play positive roles in effective organizational interviewing**

The management of the Marriott Marquis on Times Square, flagship hotel of an international chain, thought its 400 housekeeping employees enjoyed a nearly perfect work environment of good pay, generous benefits, and satisfying work conditions. But an employee survey revealed a different story. Given a chance to speak out, employees said they wanted a level of respect and appreciation they weren't getting. "When you see us in the elevators, don't ignore us. You know our name. We're wearing it," they told managers. "And can we get some uniforms that don't look goofy?" Marriott learned an important lesson, according to motivational expert Bob Nelson (1997). Good communication makes good organizations.

Hiring competent employees through selection interviews is at the core of organizational decision making, as you learned in Chapter 8, but other kinds of interviews are also essential to the continuing success of organizations. Over time, skillful managers will interview to assess, discipline, promote, assist, reassign, or terminate employees.

Face-to-face interviewing helps organizations gather information, boost morale, solve problems, improve performance, develop talent, examine issues, explore new ideas, and interact with the public. It helps management

Communication is more than an important organization function. It reflects corporate values, maintains them, and even creates them. Communication can build or shake morale. While some see it as only one part of the organizational structure, others understand communication as the network by which the organization is held together. Organizational life is constituted by means of communication.

—Margaret Whitney,
in *Corporate Communication*

and staff collaborate in identifying, refining, and accomplishing personal and organizational goals. Ideally, it also enables organizations to listen and learn from workers, promotes a sense of shared pride and ownership, and helps employees be seen as persons, not just interchangeable cogs in a machine.

We begin the chapter by summarizing the contemporary climate of managing change, promoting teamwork, sharing information, and seeking excellence. These are hallmarks of successful and progressive organizations. We emphasize the appraisal interview in "The Basics" because of its importance for providing feedback. Interviewing skills guide the sensitive interventions and terminations managers must conduct, and many basic appraisal skills apply equally well to these other contexts of evaluation. You'll see how organizational interviewing also involves helping, information-gathering, and persuasive functions, which are covered in detail in other chapters. "Beyond the Basics" explores two interdependent special topics—conflict management and defensive/supportive climates of communication. Here you'll see how conflict and trust can coexist in organizational communication.

The Basics

Communication in Today's Organizations

Communication is the lifeblood of organizations, especially large, far-flung ones with a diverse workforce. Communication occurs inside the organization, as it defines and constitutes itself, and outside, as it extends, amplifies, and clarifies its messages for shareholders, clients, and the public at large. The means of communication include annual reports, Web sites and blogs, memoranda, press releases, publications, public forums, training videos, advertorials, and focus groups.

Face-to-face interviewing skills, however, are sometimes overlooked and underutilized. Old-school types—both workers and managers—might assume interpersonal communication training in the workplace is dispensable at best and a time-waster at worst. Evidence shows, however, that members typically want interpersonal improvement and also believe that it contributes to the bottom line. An important book, *What Workers Want* (Freeman & Rogers, 1999), reports on the results of what the authors call "the most extensive analysis of American worker attitudes toward the workplace relationships and power in more than 20 years" (p. 3). Approximately 2,500 workers were interviewed, and one sentiment in particular surfaced: Employees want more of a voice on the job. Why? The answer might surprise those who assume most employees lack motivation or commitment: They want to improve the quality of their working lives and help the company become more productive and successful. They said they wanted cooperative relations with management, and they preferred to deal with managers individually. They expect management to share power and decision making willingly. They believe management resistance is the primary reason they have not achieved their desired level of influence in the workplace (pp. 4–5). Managers, the survey found, broadly confirm the employees' conclusion about general unwillingness to share power. The workers' faith in interpersonal process is not new, and many organizations have responded by recognizing the importance of communication programs. For example, conversational approaches to organizational change are increasingly influential (see, e.g., Senge, 1990; Shotter, 1993), and they involve interviewing far beyond its information-gathering or its interrogative connotations. As Winograd and Flores suggest, "The most essential responsibilities for managers . . . can be characterized as participation in conversations for possibilities that open new backgrounds for the conversations of action" (quoted in Shotter, 1993, p. 148).

Appraisal Interviews

An organizational **appraisal interview** is conducted to share insights and information between superiors and subordinates. Generally, it serves (1) the *feedback function,* in which managers and supervisors use the interview to provide employees with evaluative information that they could use to revise their behaviors and attitudes, and to encourage feedback from the employees; and (2) the *goal-setting function,* in which superiors and subordinates collaboratively translate their current perceptions into behavioral plans.

Anecdotal evidence suggests that employees are wary of appraisal interviews because of their reputation as negative critiques of workers (Half, 1993). That is especially true in organizations with inadequate opportunities for routine communication between management and staff. Unsure of where they stand, employees enter the interview wondering, "Am I valued?" or "Am I in trouble?" If the interview goes as they fear, employees assume defensive postures: "I'm here to prove I'm a good employee. I'm ready to defend my record. I don't deserve criticism." Even when the experience isn't negative, too few appraisal interviews are seen as supportive.

A poorly conducted appraisal, even if it's positive, will not be helpful (see Box 9.1). For many employees the interview confirms what they already know and can frustrate

---

Box 9.1

Interviewers in Action   *Dorothy Leeds*

Management consultant Dorothy Leeds describes what she learned about how organizations conduct appraisal interviews:

> The performance appraisal is one of the manager's best tools for motivating people, yet it is seldom, if ever, exploited to its full potential. As typically handled, performance appraisals are virtually meaningless. When 200 managers in a large New York company were asked about their own last performance appraisal, only 10 of them said they had received a thorough give-and-take appraisal interview. Some had received no more than a token pat on the shoulder and a charge to keep up the good work. Others had been subjected to a harangue and a long list of gripes.

Source: Leeds (1987, pp. 183–184)

creativity or foster complacency. Based on preconceptions and past experience, disillusioned employees consider half-hearted appraisal interviews a waste of time: "What's the use of busting my tail when no one seems to care?" Others take a more introspective view: "Surely, there is something I can do better." At times even highly motivated employees, with positive attitudes about themselves and the organization, learn to their surprise that a new manager doesn't share their rosy assessment. In the end, many workers suffer in silence, exasperated with their relationship with the organization but afraid to say so to a superior who's blissfully unaware.

Despite being potentially uncomfortable, the appraisal interview is an important moment, and in effective organizations it can neither be avoided nor written off as a routine exercise. Besides its obvious career consequences, the appraisal interview often communicates the organization's primary, but far-from-complete, evaluation of an employee's performance and, more important, ability. When done well, an appraisal encourages dialogue and sets up the potential for future improvement.

Why Appraise?

Government and the military services developed appraisal instruments in the early 1900s to determine promotions systematically and objectively. By the 1950s, organizations and businesses had widely accepted the need for appraisals, but the methodology remained relatively unsophisticated. The Civil Rights Act of 1964 and the Equal Employment Opportunity Commission (1970) moved organizations toward clearer, more structured, and better documented procedures and guidelines by which managers could justify the legality of decisions to hire, fire, promote, or demote.

Appraisals not only can help motivate and nurture employees, stressing strengths as well as weaknesses; they also can improve relations between management and staff by bridging differences in male–female, black–white, young–old, white-collar–blue-collar, and other cross-cultural settings. Inadequate opportunities for discussion between employees and their supervisors, on the other hand, cultivate misunderstanding, resentment, low morale, and ultimately, overall dissatisfaction with the job. Appraisal interviews, conducted by competent professionals, encourage both supervisors and subordinates to be diagnostic and introspective; participants more clearly sense how they can be more communicative problem solvers and troubleshooters in their careers.

Job Satisfaction and Communication

One method of assessing job satisfaction rests on a **Quality of Work Life (QWL)** formula of eight factors (from Bruce & Blackburn, 1992):

- Fair and adequate compensation
- A safe, healthy place to work
- Opportunities to develop human capacities through meaningful work and role in new ways of doing jobs
- Growth, such as opportunities to improve skills, knowledge, and, security—a sense that job is safe
- Social integration and interaction with coworkers and management

- Fair play and recognized rights, with respect for equity and equal opportunities in a setting free of harassment
- Consideration for *total life space,* which entails the ability to balance the demand of work, home, and family
- A sense of social relevance, leading to pride in both the job and employer. (p. 15)

Notice how many QWL factors on this list depend on frank, consistent, and open communication, which even the best organizations sometimes lack. "We are always surprised at the reluctance of managers to provide regular feedback to their employees," according to organizational researchers Bruce and Blackburn (1992, p. 22). Further, "[b]y not communicating regularly with those who work for them they hamper job satisfaction and impede performance. . . . [T]hey do not give their employees the opportunity to maximize performance and satisfaction" (p. 22).

Certain themes and phrases resonate in studies of employees' attitudes about work and employers: respect, an opportunity to be heard, a stake in interesting work, appreciation for a job well done, and the chance to make a difference. QWL and other methods of determining job satisfaction rest on mutually involving interpersonal communication skills. The appraisal interview constitutes a valuable opportunity to communicate and thereby advance individual and organizational goals (see Box 9.2).

Approaches to Appraisals

The interview often is the last step of an organization's appraisal process, but its effectiveness depends on a consistent, clear, reliable, and fair emphasis on criteria and evidence. An organization that takes appraisals seriously carefully develops the objectives and methods of its appraisal system.

Four considerations influence the appraisal process: (1) the philosophy and operation principles of the organization, often expressed in a mission statement, core values, and policies; (2) the particular requirements of employment, including the individual employee's job skills and personal traits; (3) the performance expectations, or goals, set

---

Box 9.2

Reminders   *Uses of Performance Appraisals*

Appraisals are valuable in serving basic organizational functions because they:

- Critique past performance.
- Set goals for future performance.
- Determine raises, promotions, and rewards.
- Troubleshoot problems.
- Identify training, counseling, or coaching needs.

- Satisfy legal requirements to systematically assess employees, particularly if discipline is anticipated.
- Provide an opportunity for supervisors and employees to know each other better through effective communication.
- Help employees improve in terms of job satisfaction and performance.

for the employee by supervisors, colleagues, and others who depend on the employee's performance; and (4) concrete performance results, measured by standards set by the organization, ideally in consultation with employees.

Philosophy   An organization that translates its ideals into accomplishments can be expected to select and assess its employees on how well they advance these ideals. If customer service is the hallmark of the company, then appraisals are bound to assess how employees handle complaints or correct mistakes. In addition to their direct application to the job, organizational ideals, such as commitment to social responsibility, might carry over into employees' civic lives. The Ben & Jerry's ice cream business, for example, practiced "caring capitalism" that considered the impact of its business decisions on the community, and its employees were encouraged to act, in their own ways, as responsible citizens (Cohen & Greenfield, 1997).

Job Requirements   From building cars to handling insurance claims, job requirements usually spell out the skills, abilities, and traits needed for success in a particular line of work and, therefore, influence the type of appraisal that is appropriate. A job that requires outstanding writing skills might also call for someone with the temperament to accept criticism and stay cool under deadline pressure. Temperament and performance expectations aren't always compatible, however. A personable, cooperative, and loyal worker might be slow and sloppy at completing assignments; the office grinch might be a perfectionist whose work quality is unparalleled. We might usually prefer to work alongside someone with a loquacious sense of humor; but that trait, pleasant in many contexts, could undermine work that calls for serious attention and resolve.

Expectations   Appraisals sometimes go beyond performance critiques—such as pointing out a three-month decline in a sales representative's contacts—to establish more far-reaching goals. Simply satisfying a baseline norm might not be enough in organizations that stress employees' growth and development. Further, expectations can be, and usually are, highly individualized. The six-month goal set for a national sales representative, for example, might be to increase the number of units sold by 5 percent; in another department of the same organization, the production manager's goal might be to reduce defects by half. Expectations are also related to personal growth, as evidenced by, say, a willingness to take on additional responsibilities, an ability to adapt to a new operating procedure, or a willingness to undergo remedial training. Appraisals, then examine the fit of individuals within the larger organization—especially in organizations where change is continuous and creativity, advancement, and improvement are not only valued but also are integral parts of the job expectations.

Performance   The bottom line for performance usually amounts to meeting the standards of the organization in the context of its culture. Using various means, organizations measure results. Task-oriented appraisals focus on accomplishing concrete assignments—the quantity and quality of output as compared to quotas or standards or comparisons with others. Traditional ways of measuring results include recorded tallies of results or consequences, such as accident rates, absences (sick days, tardiness), sales figures, and other quantifiable measures of productivity. Although appraisals focus on individual performance, they often account for the individual's role in a *performance chain* across the organization. One worker's deliberate pace, for example, can hamper the work of others along the line, whether in an assembly plant or a claims processing office.

Organizations approach performance appraisals in many ways, but almost all assess how members adapt to the organizational mission, exhibit traits essential to the work at hand, produce quality work according to organizational expectations, and accept constructive criticism for improvement. Organizations commonly use narrative, ranking, or rating methods in their appraisal systems, and each influences the content and conduct of the interview that follows.

Narrative Methods   Among the oldest—and most subjective—appraisal methods employed by appraisal interviewers is the **narrative**, a form of written, anecdotal evaluation. A narrative approach offers many variations, but it usually is guided by some predetermined structure, such as a sequence of questions to guide appraisers. Typically, narratives are unconstrained by precise categorizing, which is why narrative appraisals sometimes take the form of **global essays**, which are narratives that respond to the supervisor's generalized, or "global," impressions of a worker's performance. A global essay would be the appraiser's response to open-ended questions such as, "Please provide an overall evaluation of this employee's performance for the period January 1, 2008–June 30, 2008."

The narrative approach tests the evaluator's compositional talents. A facile writer can produce readily a dazzling or devastating appraisal. An inexperienced writer might struggle to find words to describe an employee's strengths and weaknesses. Strong employees evaluated by weak writers may not get the appraisal they deserve. Yet this is not the only problem with a thoroughly narrative approach to appraisals. In our contemporary climate of litigation, managers are reluctant to produce a critical written report that could be used against them in court. Therefore they choose safe, nondescript language that might camouflage deeper reactions. Some writers of appraisal narratives anchor their appraisals in an overall, ambiguous label of some sort, such as describing an employee as "excellent" or "outstanding," but without providing criteria or examples to justify such generalities. Effective, focused appraisal interviews can provide the specifics to enliven and support the written narratives. Clearly, appraisals that rely on narrative methods should be based at least in part on effective interviews that elicit relevant and persuasive stories. Without such skill, supervisors will not be able to marshal the evidence to reward exemplary workers or to motivate or dismiss ineffective ones.

Narrative accounts can also include employees' **self-evaluative essays**. They, too, usually leave great leeway for literary imagination. Without clear guidance from the supervisor, perhaps in a face-to-face interview, the employee may produce what amounts to a puff piece—a portrayal based more on fancy than fact. On the other hand, self-evaluative essays can provide a useful counterpoint to a manager's view and stimulate a productive discussion to reconcile differences in their narrative descriptions. If employee narratives are the norm, and if they are taken seriously by the organization, this invitation encourages employees to see how their own stories fit within the larger narrative or culture of the organization. Not surprisingly, people who expect to be heard have more to say; thus, interviews based on such evidence can be very fruitful.

Another type of narrative account, the **critical incident report,** focuses more concretely on details and examples. It documents, through observation and note taking, specific occasions when the employee excelled or stumbled. Just as behavior-based interviewing conducted by employment interviewers will ask about specific moments in the applicant's work history and the stories that emerge from them, critical incident organizational appraisal turns on stories of organizational life. An "incident" might be an employee's exceptional speed in completing a task well, or it might be an unsolicited letter from a customer describing that same employee's attentive service "beyond the call of duty." As paper-trail documentation, the critical incident report helps organizations create a tangible record to justify performance rewards, or to justify demotion or other punitive action. However, if supervisors aren't careful, a collection of critical incidents risks a disproportionate emphasis on isolated deficiencies and inconsequential foul-ups rather than on continuing accomplishments.

Supervisors may have difficulty deciding on, and describing, the critical markers of skill, but an evaluative system that wholly depends on the evaluator's personal idiosyncrasies produces reports that are worthless to other readers. Even when critical incidents are categorized by headings such as "delegating authority" or "taking initiative," the evaluator still must decide, systematically and ahead of time, how the behavior is critical and how it contributes to the organization's mission. Although meant to be objective, the method—like other evaluative procedures—rests on some elements of subjectivity.

The **field review,** another narrative method, usually involves a manager or representative of the human resources or personnel office visiting a factory, office, or department to observe workplace activity and collect information to include in a narrative report. The field review takes two common forms. In one, the personnel representative questions the employee's immediate supervisor and elicits details to assist the evaluator in producing a narrative appraisal; in the second, the person responsible for the field review writes the report from direct observation.

Trying Out Your Skills

- Write a first draft of a one- or two-paragraph global essay appraising the work of a coworker whose situation and job you know well. (Do not attach the person's name to the appraisal, but write your essay with an actual person in mind.)

- Edit and revise your essay to insert at least one detail, illustration, or example for each evaluative statement you've made.

- Are there unstated criteria that you used to evaluate job performance? If so, try to articulate them. Is everyone in the workplace equally familiar with

these criteria? Particularly important: Ask yourself if the criteria guiding your appraisals are clear to the worker whose performance you're evaluating.

- Would the worker be surprised to read your essay? If so, why?

- If you shared it with him or her, would it provide a useful basis for a subsequent appraisal interview? See if you can create a brief interview schedule from the information in your essay. Later, compare your results in the exercise with what you'll learn about structuring the appraisal interview.

Narrative methods, even though they are variable and subjective, are especially valuable when used in conjunction with other appraisal methods and when they result from a collaboration between appraiser and appraisee.

Ranking Methods **Rankings** are quantitative assignments or estimates that compare a person or thing specifically to other persons or things on the basis of a stated criterion. As opposed to rating systems, which we describe next, a ranking pits whatever is evaluated against others by direct comparisons: "In our small department, Jan is our best writer, LaToya our second best, and Robert our weakest." Of course, Jan, LaToya, and Robert may all be awful, or wonderful, writers—thus you can see the problem with ranking systems. Direct comparisons sometimes ignore other measures of competence. Does it mean much to be the "best" writer in a department where all the employees display grammar and syntax problems? On the other hand, if you're ranked as the least effective trainer in an award-winning department, your skills may far surpass the best trainer in an ineffective group.

One common type of ranking asks an evaluator to assess someone in terms of important characteristics, such as "communication skills" or "problem solving," along a percentile continuum of other workers: top 10 percent; upper 25 percent; middle 40 percent; lower 25 percent, for example. In some ranking forms, the last item may ask the evaluator to calculate, supposedly by averaging and weighing rankings on preceding questions, an "all-purpose," "cumulative," or "overall" rank.

Ranking might require that managers create a **forced distribution** to show where individuals fit within an assessment of all employees in a department or operation. By this method, the evaluator divides a group of employees into specific performance categories, such as poor, below average, average, above average, and exceptional. In some organizations, an evaluator's rankings that fall outside a normal distribution might be met with skepticism or derision: "Can you believe McIntyre has nothing but perfect employees working for her? Who's she kidding?"

Another method, **peer ranking**, stresses colleagues' perceptions. Often the rankings are based on such collegial criteria as compatibility, teamwork, and work ethic, because coworkers may not be aware of other aspects of job performance. Peer rankings may help reveal a problem undetected by the boss, who finds her administrative assistant a model employee; peers, though, see the assistant as a menace. Personal relationships can't help but enter into the thinking of peer evaluators, even though a ranking criterion might have nothing to do with the person's physical or personality traits. Perceptions, however, do count, and the peer ranking, although rarely used as a principal method of appraisal, contributes to a broader picture.

Rankings tend to be more focused than narratives, but may not be much better at specifying criteria. For example, asking where an individual ranks on factors such as maturity or creativity doesn't provide much specific appraisal evidence. Is maturity exhibited in manner of dress, deportment, or hairstyle? ("She dresses like a teenager." "Why doesn't he act his age?") Is maturity characterized by wisdom or good judgment? Perhaps it's a mellow demeanor or a quality of age, like "mature" wine.

Nothing is wrong with striving for improvement or excellence, but a judgmental, competitive approach to ranking people can create problems. To be considered "average" usually isn't acceptable in organizations. What is average? Aren't 50 percent of people in all categories of employment—whether clerks, pilots, teachers, or electricians—below average by definition? Nonetheless, *average* suggests a condition of blandness, dullness, or even ineffectiveness. When rankings constitute the core of an organization's appraisal system, you need to avoid assuming that people are incompetent if they're merely average or even below average.

Rankings relate to, and are often combined with, rating systems, the next group of appraisal methods.

Rating Methods   Even though all evaluation is by definition subjective, some formats come closer to the goal of objective fairness. **Ratings** ask evaluators to describe and assess employees' skills in terms of a series of carefully defined categories, often with examples or specific criteria. If rankings ask evaluators to compare workers with each other, ratings ask them to compare workers with behavioral standards that are closely matched to work success.

Graphic rating scales are among the most frequently used methods of appraisal in organizations. The rating criteria reflect presumably important qualities for the job—generally a selection of traits, behaviors, and attitudes such as "resource utilization," "flexibility," "customer relations," "cooperation," or "interpersonal communication"—accompanied by one or more definitions or examples of what each category means. In nursing, for example, important health care tasks certainly receive priority, such as prompt, accurate administration of medications or careful maintenance of medical records. Less easily defined traits or behaviors, such as interpersonal warmth, could also warrant ratings, too.

Rating forms range from a single page to booklets covering hundreds of categories and questions. Rating boxes or checklists ask evaluators to distinguish the level of performance or degree of compliance, such as outstanding, satisfactory, or needs improvement, or, in another variation, exceeds, meets, or fails to meet standards. A range of ratings might be included, as well; for example, a scale for how employees follow instructions might offer these choices: always, usually, about half the time, seldom, and never.

Some rating forms, called **360-degree appraisals**, collect feedback from everyone whose own productivity and performance depend on the employee under review. For example, at a newspaper, the person responsible for supervising the printing presses works with employees in nearly every operation—news, circulation, advertising, and production. A late-breaking event, such as a World Series game, might mean starting the presses 45 minutes later than usual to ensure that a home-delivered edition contains a full account of the game. The sports editor depends on the pressroom supervisor's cooperation, and so do others who must coordinate their tasks with the printing of the newspaper.

Because a single supervisor might not be able to provide a comprehensive picture of the employee's effectiveness, the approach of a 360-degree appraisal is to "circle" the employee's contributions with impressions from coworkers who may encounter her or him from different perspectives. These comprehensive ratings work especially well when flexible interaction is important to the success of the organization, which is usually the case. A 360-degree appraisal also stresses the importance of team as well as individual performance. With input from several angles, composite ratings might reveal an inconsistent pattern of strengths and weaknesses. The employee's immediate superior sees only a piece of the operation and judges the performance "strong." At the same time, colleagues in another department find room for improvement on their ratings. It's an approach that can add balance and context to typical ratings conducted within the employee's own sphere by a single supervisor.

Many organizations encourage employees to conduct a **self-rating**. A choice might be involved: Add your own rating to your supervisor's, or be rated only by the supervisor. In another variation, both supervisor and employee independently complete the rating form, then meet to compare and discuss results. Self-rating lets employees assess their work according to defined organizational criteria, not by how they might define the job idiosyncratically. When the employee's appraisal parallels the supervisor's, there shouldn't be resentment or disagreement. If their appraisals contrast, it's not likely to be on all accounts; there will be some agreement, and disagreements can be discussed at the appraisal interview.

Although popular in organizations, rating forms have disadvantages, especially when used to the exclusion of other methods. Despite appearing to be precise in measuring traits and performance, ratings are subject to the shifting attitudes and maybe the biases of the managers who define the categories and standards. At times, evaluators find themselves trapped into assigning ratings for categories they consider irrelevant or insignificant as indicators of ability or performance. Finally, trait ratings aren't automatically designed to encourage improvement or to develop better work relations. How, for example, does one become more creative when rated low in that category? Unless accompanied by a thorough discussion of solutions, a trait rating may diagnose without proposing a treatment.

A special form of rating was developed to offset supervisors' tendencies toward leniency in assessing employees. The solution, called a **forced-choice rating**, uses four behavioral statements—two that seem favorable to the employee and two that seem unfavorable. However, the rating incorporates several wrinkles. First, one favorable statement and one unfavorable statement aren't designed to discriminate between an effective or ineffective worker. The evaluator must choose one statement that best fits the employee's performance and one that least fits it. Second, a value is assigned to each statement, but the evaluator does not know the value; the human resources office scores the forms.

In another attempt to refine ratings appraisals, industrial psychologists developed the **behaviorally anchored rating system** (BARS). The BARS approach differs from typical ratings in how the form is developed; BARS incorporates prior consultation with a large number of evaluators and, in some case, the evaluated. Developing a BARS instrument involves a thorough analysis of the job and its requirements. A guiding question to BARS development asks, "What must an employee do on this job to be considered proficient?" Based on answers to that question (or similar questions), dimensions of the job are identified; then a set of anchors—expressed in behaviors for that dimension—are described and assigned a numerical value along a continuum, ranging from high to low performance. In a sample BARS for department store sales associates, for example, one dimension of the job might be "response to customer questions," with the following set of anchors:

7—always responds with useful information in a prompt and courteous manner

6—provides useful information but lacks warmth

5—responds cheerfully but sometimes can't answer basic questions about products

4—well informed about products but occasionally responds with impatience

3—informed and respectful but doesn't go beyond the basics in answers

2—prone to disagree or argue with customers

1—frequently unable to answer questions or act courteously

Before implementation, BARS scales go through stages of pretesting and revision, again, with input from both raters and those who will be rated, to determine the validity of dimensions, anchors, and numerical values. Presumably, a BARS system, once complete, constitutes agreement among employees, supervisors, and management about evaluative criteria. Moreover, participation in creating the ratings gives people a personal stake in the system—a sense that the appraisal reflects *us* (employees and supervisors) and not just *them* (management).

The BARS philosophy is an extension of the advice for job candidates in Chapter 8: Always think of your skills and abilities in terms of behaviors and actions that translate into the organization's benefit, not, first and foremost, your own. No appraisal method is perfect. A BARS, although more participatory and precise than other approaches, takes time and money to develop; it also requires frequent modification, as job demands change in an organization.

Goals Appraisals that concentrate on a critique of performance amount to a report card. Here is how you did: A for exemplary work, B for good, C for average, D for below average, and F for unacceptable work. A different management philosophy avoids the psychological implications of grade-like procedures and emphasizes a goals orientation preferred by organizations that embrace an approach called **management by objectives** (MBO).

MBO combines a management strategy with a type of appraisal. The goals usually start with top management setting the organizational objectives. At various levels within the organization, managers determine department and unit goals and action plans to accomplish them. Eventually, the goal setting extends to individual employees, who, in collaboration with superiors, agree to goals for themselves. An MBO strategy directly depends on communication within the organization, as management and workers collaborate in forming organization, department, and individual goals. Instead of relying on inflexible standards that are presumed to be valid, MBO relies on a more local approach. Supervisors and subordinates collaborate on setting mutually agreed on objectives by which they will be evaluated later. Ideally, appraisals are based on the degree to which goals were achieved. Often an MBO program assigns priorities to different goals and weighs them by degree of difficulty. The interview is the communication laboratory in which these decisions are made (see Batten, 2003).

In summarizing the research in **goal-setting theory**, Eric Eisenberg and H. L. Goodall, Jr., (1997) suggest that intelligent and communicative managers shouldn't set the goals themselves and then hope to motivate employees to achieve them, but instead work with employees to help them set reasonable objectives that the employees then are more likely to meet. In this way, subordinates develop a sense of ownership with respect to goals that reflect their own voices. Further, Eisenberg and Goodall present this advice, consistent with goal-setting research:

1. Set clear and specific goals, which have a greater positive impact on performance than do general goals.

2. Set goals that are difficult but attainable; they will lead to higher performance than will easy goals.

3. Focus on participative rather than assigned goals.

4. Give frequent feedback about the goal-setting and work processes. (p. 245)

A related appraisal-management strategy is called a **performance plan.** William Swan (1991) endorses a continuous process of performance management, which includes appraising employees by how they follow through with and meet the performance plan. Swan includes supportive activities toward meeting goals, including **coaching** (see Box 9.3), feedback, and monitoring. The performance plan should be not only specific and challenging, but also realistic and measurable.

Goals-based appraisals usually involve a combination of self-improvement and performance objectives. These objectives may be formulated from the results of other methods of appraisal, particularly graphic scales or BARS. Based on an appraisal or another form of assessment, a plant manager, for example, agrees with a supervisor on three self-improvement goals for the coming year: complete an environmental-safety course, serve on the board of a professional organization, and publish a report in an industry periodical. (The individual goals, of course, presumably benefit the organization as well.) The plant manager and supervisor also agree on several production-performance-related goals, among them to install a computer-driven inventory system by midyear.

MBO and performance plans encourage advancement and growth in a climate of dialogue. Appraisal based exclusively on accomplishing goals poses problems when those goals aren't met satisfactorily but the organization remains successful. Does that mean the employee is a failure or that the mutual goal-setting process is off target? Goals must be realistic, considered within the framework of anticipated real conditions and institutional support. As Swan (1991) observes, an organization shouldn't demand higher achievements without clarifying appropriate incentives and support.

Whatever appraisal method is used, the interview itself should ensure that employees are heard and given a chance to act on the appraisal (see Box 9.4).

Conducting Appraisal Interviews

Remember that the appraisal interview involves both feedback and goal setting. In other words, the interviewer and interviewee ideally look both backward and forward, and

Box 9.3

Reminders   *Coaching for Performance Enhancement*

- *What is an organizational coach?* The word *coach* in sports conjures images of a charismatic authority figure who throws tantrums over bad calls, bears down on players in practice sessions, and motivates through force of will. Coaches may be good or bad, but we like to assume that they care not only about success but also about people. In organizations, coaching implies some of the same characteristics but without some of the connotations of emotional intensity. We define organizational **coaching** as a mutual activity in which one person helps another change behavior, solve problems, or develop plans, with the ultimate goal of improved performance.

- *What does a coach do?* Organizational coaching is similar to sports coaching in its emphasis on practicing fundamentals, and then progressing to higher levels of achievement. All coaching focuses on actual behavior and its consequences: "When you do this, that happens." "Why do you suppose that happens?" "Do you want it to happen?" "Why not change your approach and see what happens then?" The coach acts as a particularly committed observer who continually offers concrete and specific feedback about input–output relationships. Unlike some coaching models, however, organizational coaching isn't primarily based on ordering, lecturing, scolding, correcting, arguing, threatening, or cajoling (although in a given relationship, elements of each may develop). Although not exactly a formal interview, coaching typically relies on interview techniques, especially listening and questioning.

- *How might a coach listen and question with a worker?* The questions focus on obtaining details and descriptions of how someone works or performs, with the coach alert for flaws and potential problems in execution. The listening helps the coach decide how to provide feedback and suggestions for change. Most coaches attempt to help employees move from easy to more difficult tasks, using **microgoals** (Waldroop & Butler, 1996)—a series of systematic small steps into which a task has been divided. For example, consider microgoals in a new reporter's attempt to turn a batch of facts into a story. Writing coaches Roy Peter Clark and Don Fry (1992) believe simple questions help the coach and writer work together on improving a story:

  How do you feel about the story so far?

  What's the story about? Have you found a focus?

  What's your best quote?

  What does the reader need to know?

  Who are the most interesting people in your story?

  Questions like these help the writer find the strengths and weaknesses of the story without the coach necessarily passing judgment. A successful coaching relationship relies on rapport, trust, and praise. Impatience, negativism, and distance mark an unsuccessful experience.

- *How is coaching related to performance appraisal processes?* Coaching is related to the performance appraisal process in its interview-like interchange of questions and responses, but it should be a distinct activity. If you are a manager or supervisor, don't wait until a predetermined appraisal occasion to begin coaching; early diagnosis and attention can save you many headaches later. If you are an employee who wants to succeed, you can request a coaching relationship in many situations. Coaching is a road to development that benefits both the individual and the organization. Generally, however, it doesn't work well as a one-time or sporadic occurrence. In certain situations, especially in the early stages of learning a new job, it might be a daily routine.

Box 9.4

Interviewers in Action   *James Autry (I)*

James Autry, former president of the Meredith Magazine Group and a prominent speaker and writer on humane management, writes often about paradoxes in the business world. He captures much of what it is like to be "in charge," often evaluating others' behavior, and at the same time being a caring human being.

A young manager friend asked me to "list the paradoxes of management" sometime. I've usually avoided doing it because I don't think I know all the paradoxes of management and because I think some of them are not just restricted to management. But fools rush in, so here I go:

The leader must:

- be long-term and short-term at the same time, assuring that the quarterly earnings of the company meet the financial requirements set by the board while often sacrificing short-term earnings in order to assure the long-term growth and development of the company and its stakeholders

- be in touch and aware of what's going on without looking over people's shoulders

- inspire and often direct people in accomplishing the vision and mission and purpose of the organization while empowering people to manage themselves and make their own decisions

- accept and perform the role of spokesperson for the company, and the person in the spotlight, the person upon whom much attention is showered while letting go of ego and control and becoming a resource for the employees

- encourage and support the rights and growth and the independent thinking of individual employees without sacrificing the rights and growth and interdependence of the community of employees

- care for people and fire people, sometimes the same people

- encourage risk-taking and reward successes while preventing any mistakes that could jeopardize the survival of the enterprise

- embrace with full commitment the demands and responsibilities, as well as the rewards, of the job with all its paradoxes while embracing with full commitment the demands and responsibilities, as well as the rewards, of being a parent and spouse and friend.

Source: Autry (1994, pp. 265–266)

do so cooperatively. Done well, the appraisal interview requires sound objectives, preparation, knowledge, strategies, and attitudes.

Objectives   Planning starts with setting objectives for the meeting—what the participants hope to accomplish. The allotted time for interviews, often 30 minutes to an hour, both dictates and limits the objective. Although participants may already be friends, or may want to stretch out in a friendly rambling chat, a focused, purposeful discussion usually results. Objectives vary, but one management consultant (Skopec, 1990, p. 134) suggests six distinct topics, three of which focus on performance critique (feedback):

- Review of individual's job
- Review of standards of evaluation or appraisal
- Review and discussion of current levels of performance

The other three deal with performance planning (goal setting):

- Discussion and agreement on plans for improvement
- Deciding on support the supervisor or organization can provide
- Development of long-term prospects

That is substantial ground to cover in a brief time. Separate critique and planning interviews might work better, as long as a thorough review of feedback can also be integrated into the primary discussion of goal setting in a follow-up interview. Some experts also recommend splitting salary and promotion discussions from those involving employee development. James Goodale (1982), for example, suggests that organizations conduct performance critiques approximately three months before salary budgets are set for the coming year. Once the budget is determined, schedule another interview to explain, justify, and discuss salary and promotion decisions.

Preparation For interviewers, preparation involves a range of details, although a single guiding principle applies: Stay focused on the employee. For legal reasons, interviewers will want to conduct all performance appraisals according to a consistent set of guidelines, to ensure that some employees are not given special treatment, either intentionally or inadvertently. However, a one-size-fits-all interview is simply not realistic or productive. To be effective, interviewers must (1) develop their overall approach so that it consistently and fairly gives all employees equal opportunity; and (2) develop a personalized approach that gives each employee the sense that he or she is uniquely important. This responsibility for dual preparation is the special ethical challenge for appraisal interviewers.

Interviewers prepare by thoroughly reviewing the interviewee's performance, drawing on personal observation, employee records, and past appraisal reports. They analyze these materials for distinguishing features of the employee's personality, contributions, and potential. How, for example, does she respond to criticism? Why does he leave early so often? Are there any hidden or underdeveloped strengths? Additional homework might be necessary, such as asking discreet questions of others to fill in missing pieces or to complement inconclusive records.

Interviewees should prepare, too, by assessing the interviewer role, especially in terms of communication style, such as listening behavior, and by anticipating topics to be covered. In some cases, organizations encourage or assist employees in preparation. For example, the employee might receive appraisal information before the interview or be asked to complete a self-evaluation form or narrative as a basis for discussion. In addition, both participants should think about goals for improvement, which can be discussed at the appraisal interview or a follow-up session.

Both interviewer and interviewee also should consider scheduling details, including reasonable notice, along with date, time, and place of the interview session. Interviewers should send a detailed letter or memo about the interview well in advance; that notice should give the interviewee realistic choices for scheduling the meeting. Don't assume the date, time, and place are inconsequential considerations. For the interviewee, an interview might fall on the anniversary of a spouse's death, with disastrous emotional results. For the interviewer, it might come in the middle of a departmental crisis, to the detriment of an interviewee who could suffer the unintended negative consequence of a terse conversation. Conditions like these may warrant rescheduling.

Consider, as well, the communication implications of when during a day a meeting is scheduled. Do you interview an assembly-line worker at the end of a 12-hour shift? Should a supervisor schedule an appraisal interview right after a long, draining meeting with department heads? There may be no choice, but whenever possible, the interview should be scheduled for a time when each participant is emotionally and physically alert.

The setting can also influence the success of an interview. Certainly, appraisal interviews demand privacy and minimal interruptions. In addition, the setting should invite relaxed conversation. Many such interviews are conducted in supervisors' offices, but supervisors can reduce the power differential inherent in the setting, by choosing similar chairs, for instance. An interviewee uncomfortable in a straightback chair, confronted with the boss looming from a tall cushy chair behind her desk, may experience a conversation more as an inquisition or interrogation. The employee's discomfort doesn't serve the boss well, either, if she values a shared approach to problem solving.

A final component of preparation is training and practice. Often those entrusted with appraisal interviews learn by trial and error. A serious-minded organization prepares appraisal interviewers with videos, exercises, readings, and communication skills workshops, then follows up with critiques of the evaluator's performance, using ratings and feedback from interviewees themselves. An organization's commitment to preparation helps ensure the fullest participation by interviewer and interviewee, enabling them to communicate with comfort, clarity, purpose, and, in the end, results. Without mutual preparation, the odds of a disappointing, counterproductive outcome increase.

Attitudes An **attitude**, a predisposition to behave in certain ways, takes concrete, identifiable forms in practice. Attitudes are expressed and interpreted through words, body language, and actions. An awareness of attitudes is important for both participants in an appraisal interview, but the interviewer—usually the interviewee's boss or superior—generally sets the tone. For interviewers, the attitude of empathy should prevail, because it encourages other supportive attitudes, such as courtesy, open-mindedness, and collaboration. Empathy, of course, becomes increasingly necessary in the contemporary emphasis on culturally diverse workplaces (Kikoski, 1999).

Empathy, described in more detail in earlier chapters, is a sincere effort to identify with another person's experiences, emotions, and motivations—even as you realize you can never completely give up being yourself. Empathy is not mind-reading, although efforts to be empathic can be perceived as more or less accurate by another person.

Because appraisal interviews can be threatening and humbling for employees, with serious financial, psychological, and physical implications, empathic interviewers imagine what it's like to be evaluated. Empathic interviewees imagine the discomfort experienced by evaluators who probably don't enjoy critiquing others' behavior.

Empathy also often involves withholding judgment and setting aside assumptions. A willingness to listen and learn enhances nearly all interviews, but it's crucial in appraisal interviews. The interview isn't an occasion for personal vendettas or personalized favors. Supervisors and evaluated employees alike must resist letting feelings distort their listening and overall response to the other person ("Henderson's such a jerk"). What people do (performance) is one thing; who they are (personality or identity) is another. Effective appraisal interviewers and interviewees separate the two as much as possible, following psychologist Carl Rogers's (1961) insight that we can still extend positive regard to people whose behavior we dislike.

Approaches   An appraisal interview calls for a deft, sensitive touch because the discussion often strikes close to what most of us hold dear—our pride. Although this problem is usually discussed in terms of an unfeeling interviewer victimizing an interviewee, the emotional roles can be reversed as well. Accusations flung at interviewers also raise the level of defensiveness. An appraisal interview marked by gruff criticism or a tone of aggressive dismissal invites defensiveness. Sometimes the pressures of interviewing trigger what behavioral researchers call **flight behavior** (withdrawal-oriented choices) or **fight behavior** (confrontational choices). Several simple methods help offset defensiveness and promote thoughtful appraisal: I-messages, active listening, and questioning.

• *I-messages.* A nonjudgmental approach to discussing deficiencies or problems of performance involves use of *I-messages* that address specific behavior. To say, "You are too selfish with your coworkers" accuses the employee with finality. To say, however, "I'm noticing that you often borrow software and office materials without sharing them with coworkers so they can be more productive too," helps an employee understand your position while sounding less blaming and less judgmental. It leaves room for discussion of the interviewer's observation *and* leaves open the possibility that the interviewer may be wrong.

• *Active listening.* In an appraisal interview, active listening (see Chapter 3) is useful because it's responsive yet nonjudgmental. If an employee reacts to criticism by saying, "Why is it always *my* responsibility to be nice to the other guy?" an active listening response might be, "You believe it's unfair for me to ask you to get along better without reminding the others that they should do that, too?" Active listening mirrors essential elements of the interviewee's message as a sign of the interviewer's engagement, a way to check misunderstandings, and as an invitation for further communication.

Employees often believe that they aren't heard accurately in complex organizations. The authors of a major study of "perceived supervisor listening behavior" and its relationship to employee commitment (Lobdell, Sonoda, & Arnold, 1993) discovered that when supervisors in a large utility company are perceived as effective listeners, supervisors were evaluated as more responsive generally, increasing job satisfaction;

supervisors' effective listening was presumed to represent the entire organization positively—the organization was perceived as more open and effective; employees began to feel like they had more control over their job conditions; and employees felt more committed to the organization.

• *Questioning.* Asking good questions should be a goal of all interviews, but appraisal interviewers should expect to devote far more time to listening than questioning. Interviewers are better advised to create an interactive space in which their partners feel comfortable sharing candid evaluations. When appraisal interviewers do question, often it will be to probe, clarify, and build on the interviewer's comments. It isn't a time to gather detailed information about performance, as most of that should have been done beforehand. It is a time to confirm perceptions, seek explanations, explore solutions, and ensure feedback is understood.

For example, either participant could productively take a "what happened?" stance. In examining a critical incident, for example, the question might simply be, "What made the good (or bad) results possible?" Exploratory questions build a broad foundation supporting improved performance within the organization. Remember, though, that direct questions are often not as effective as acknowledgment of your own willingness to be surprised. Can you hear the difference in the tone of these two interviewer comments?

INTERVIEWER: Why did you cut back on production, just when we were getting a foothold in that market?

INTERVIEWEE: What makes you think I didn't have a good reason for cutting back? There's a lot you don't know about my operation.

INTERVIEWER: I noticed you cut back on production when it seemed we were getting a foothold in that market.

INTERVIEWEE: Right. I bet it surprised a few people. Let me tell you why I did that. . . .

The "what happened?" stance extends the conversation in a way that "gotcha" questions never can.

Organization   No standard script or instruction manual can guide appraisal interviews. Nonetheless, most show a progression of topics, starting with an opening that frames the interview as a positive event, with benefits for all concerned. Recall Skopec's (1990) six objectives for the appraisal; if blended a bit, they suggest an effective organizational structure for a single appraisal interview. After a rapport-building opening, a review of the job responsibilities and standards for evaluating the employee's performance can set the stage for a discussion of performance levels. Then the participants turn to the crucial task of mutual planning for future job responsibilities and how to meet them more effectively. Although different approaches are possible, we analyze the prototypical appraisal interview in five major stages that trace employee behavior in a roughly chronological manner, from previous acts and evaluations (past), through the current dialogue of the interview (present), toward an agreement about performance goals (future).

1. *Opening.* The first few moments of any interview set the tone for what follows. The organizational supervisor should take responsibility for defusing, as much as possible, the threatening character of the interview and for establishing a conversational tone of mutual respect. Both participants might experience jitters that a little informal rapport-building could dissipate:

INTERVIEWER: Tom, it's good to see you. Please have a seat. Would you like some coffee?

INTERVIEWEE: Thanks. It's colder out there than I thought when I left home. Will we ever get out of this snowy pattern?

INTERVIEWER: Probably so. Spring has to come soon, doesn't it? Do you still drive in across that dangerous bridge? . . .

Small talk needn't take more than a few minutes. In fact, too many niceties might heighten anxiety. It's best to move ahead, with the supervisor taking the lead. For example:

INTERVIEWER: Well, you know we set aside time to talk one-on-one with staff every three months. This is a good opportunity for us to see how things are going for you and discuss some things that could benefit both of us. I hope we can help each other define what we have to do for the next quarter.

INTERVIEWEE: Good. I'd like that, too. There are quite a few matters I'd like to bring up later. Some unexpected things happened in my shop, but overall, it's felt like a good year so far.

The interviewer's opening conveys an important message: This isn't just about you; it's about me, and us, too. Indeed, the person responsible for an appraisal interview should judge his or her own performance on the basis of how well the conversation flows within its stated focus.

Even when the interviewer's purpose seems self-evident, reviewing what is going to happen serves as a helpful reminder and guide. Here, the interviewer covers the main points of discussion and expectations:

INTERVIEWER: Tom, I hope we can accomplish three things in this session: review records and ratings of your performance, talk about them together, and then agree on where we go from here. I'd like to give you plenty of opportunity to discuss anything that comes up.

2. *Review.* In the second stage, participants exchange insights and perceptions to see if they are defining the position and criteria similarly. For instance:

INTERVIEWER: My notes show that last spring we agreed you would be evaluated on three primary goals—one for each of your areas of responsibility. We would look at the outcomes of your training programs—how many trainees were rated higher on communication skills. We would also look at the new database system you put in place and how satisfied office personnel were with it. Finally, we said we'd look at whether you and the PR personnel have started to get along more smoothly. Was there anything else?

INTERVIEWEE: Well, yes and no. These were the main areas, all right. But I remember being a bit more specific about the PR side of the equation, too. I think we tied that goal to the feedback/complaint incident forms. And didn't we say we would reassess my budget based on the high evaluations my people have been receiving in workshops and seminars?

3. *Evaluation and critique.* Interviewers should disclose how they apply criteria to evaluate employees' performance. Interviewees should disclose how workplace conditions, including support from relevant personnel and materials, have affected their performance. If employees seem reluctant to supply this information, interviewers may have to invite it overtly.

In most cases, interviewers won't cover every appraisal item or finding. As they prepare, they should identify and highlight major strengths and weaknesses. It's important to acknowledge achievements and contributions to the organization; unfortunately, some supervisors feel compelled to stress weaknesses, with a few rationalizing, "We pay you to do a good job. Let's spend our time talking about the areas where we need to see improvement." A sprinkling of praise followed by detractions draws the discussion too soon into the negative zone and irritates most people being evaluated. Genuine strengths can be found in virtually all employees; highlight them to reinforce effective behavior. People can't feel too secure about the areas in which they're competent. Positive feedback—that which supports existing trends—can be crucial in averting future problems.

Interviewers and interviewees should leave ample time for feedback, because the quality and substance of feedback will determine whether the interviewee finds the experience beneficial or a waste of time. People enter an appraisal interview with different objectives and expectations in mind, but few expect to listen to a supervisor's monologue. An appraisal interview, above all, should invite both sides into an exchange of feedback relevant to the interviewee's job performance. After all, it's the interviewee's career at stake. Competent, conscientious employees usually have a lot to say and relish the opportunity to react, reflect, confirm, question, discuss, and plan when it comes to matters concerning them and their jobs.

4. *Goal setting.* Participants cooperate in exploring ways to maintain the levels of effective performance or strengthen levels of substandard performance. At times, a brainstorming atmosphere will predominate at this stage, as the two attempt to solve mutual problems together. At other times, interviewers will have to emphasize unambiguously what the employee must do to improve. As this stage develops, interviewees might stress *bargaining* in their approach, in which the parties agree on future behaviors in informal but still basically contractual ways. Argyris (1960) contends that workers and organizations always maintain **psychological contracts** with each other in addition to official work agreements. These psychological contracts involve usually unstated expectations about what should be exchanged between an organization's members—for example, what employees expect to give to, and receive from, the organization; how organizations expect to support employees; and what support organizations expect in return. Because of the power differential in appraisal interviewing, the ongoing appraisal

process provides an appropriate opportunity for employees to clarify the psychological contract and perhaps to open a dialogue to establish new terms for it.

In this sense, bargaining shouldn't be thought of as a win-or-lose game in which each person tries to win resources the other will be denied, or in which a gain for one will be a defeat for the other. Rather, as experienced negotiators know, satisfying solutions often lie in the "between region" of relationships—solutions that allow each side to win at the same time but that would never be considered in a wholly competitive model of dialogue. They should adopt what Stone, Patton, and Heen (2000) call the *and stance*, a perspective that counters the either–or assumptions of much power-based talk. Instead of assuming that our positions must collide (e.g., "I want this department to get along well, but you're only selfishly looking out for yourself"), the and stance assumes that we could achieve both goals ("We could become more cooperative, and you can meet your own goals more effectively").

5. *Closing.* In the final stage, participants acknowledge or ratify the understandings they've reached together and, if appropriate, discuss who and when they will meet again. At this stage, neither interviewer nor interviewee should be unsure of whether the appraisal tone has been positive, negative, or neutral; neither party should be unsure of the next step in this process (Will there be a follow-up meeting? Allocation of additional resources to assist the employee?); neither party should be unsure about the criteria governing the next evaluation. Because appraisal interviews can involve interpersonal tension, the closing stage is an especially important time for reaffirming and supportive messages from the evaluator.

Box 9.5 provides tips for both interviewers and interviewees in appraisal sessions.

Intervention Interviews

Occasionally, supervisors have to intercede to help others do their jobs more effectively. An employee may become embroiled in an ongoing conflict with a coworker, a personal habit has begun to have negative consequences for customers, or productivity has dropped abruptly for no apparent reason. Perhaps a health problem or other personal emergency has distracted the employee from concentrating on the job, creating dangerous or disruptive consequences for all concerned. The best first step is a series of conversations designed to get information from the employees' perspectives.

An **intervention interview** can be defined as a face-to-face organizational meeting between superior and subordinate for the purpose of understanding or managing a crisis or problem more fully. At one end of the continuum, an intervention interview may be a friendly inquiry; at the other extreme, it may be an occasion for disciplining or terminating the employee.

This discussion is limited to forms of *first-level interventions,* in which supervisors diagnose and begin to address problems that are essentially interpersonal or organizational in nature. More significant actions, *second-level interventions,* are sometimes called for, and everyone in the organization should be aware of them. For example, many organizations have **employee assistance programs** (EAPs) that address serious emotional, medical, or behavioral problems. A trainer who consistently but unexpectedly cancels

Box 9.5

Reminders   *Conducting Appraisal Interviews*

Interviewers

- *Prepare adequately.* Take responsibility for giving the person evaluated a fair hearing. That requires a thorough review of the record, focusing on individualized performance, not simply on how she or he compares to coworkers. The interview isn't a time to leaf through files, trying to catch up and figure out what's going on. It's time to pay careful attention, not to do something that should have been done well before the interview.

- *Set aside assumptions.* You'll have access to a stack of evaluative materials. They represent a piece of a larger picture. The interview involves learning what goes beyond the record. Try to enter the interview with as few assumptions as possible.

- *Listen more, talk less.* Some supervisors talk more than they need to. Consider an appraisal interview from the reverse perspective—as the employee's opportunity to be heard. Guide the interview, but allow time and opportunity for the employee to determine content and direction also. At times you'll need to encourage those who find disclosure difficult. Some research into a construct called **willingness to communicate** (WTC) suggests that many otherwise exceptional workers rarely decide to volunteer their ideas and feelings openly within organizations (Richmond & Roach, 1992).

- *Reserve judgment.* At first, interviewees may react with defensiveness, anger, resentment, and other spoken or nonverbal expressions that sting interviewers. Try not to take it personally. People need to ventilate. You won't be able to listen and learn if you're caught up in your own emotions.

- *Remember, no one is perfect.* You might consider Ms. Excel to be a model employee and wish everyone in your department could be like her. They can't. She isn't perfect either. Give each employee fair, full credit for accomplishments and refrain from continual comparisons with Ms. Excel.

Interviewees

- *Prepare adequately.* Gather all documents and evidence ahead of time that can help you be introspective and realistic about your own performance. Don't try to guess what the supervisor will tell you, but familiarize yourself with the materials that may be considered in the interview.

- *Be self-critical.* Try to acknowledge areas that need improvement—do a reality check. Ask colleagues before the interview to help you see yourself more clearly. Enter the interview with an open mind and realistic perspective. It doesn't do any good to delude yourself.

- *Comment substantively, not emotionally.* When being evaluated, it's natural to be tense, and undue tension usually clouds judgment. Your goal is to avoid the appearance of defensiveness, but you do have a position you want to represent clearly and assertively. Prepare for possibly unfair adverse judgments with counterevidence—details, examples, and records. Demonstrate your point, don't just argue it.

- *Think about goals systematically.* Supervisors may appreciate what you've done, but that was yesterday. What are you going to do tomorrow and beyond? Whether it's requested or not, reflect on what you might do better and ask your supervisor for his or her opinions. When engaged in mutual goal setting, take notes (including relevant quotes) that will help you remember later what the two of you decided. Don't trust your memory when you're in an emotionally involving context.

workshops and conference trips may arouse suspicions of substance abuse. If reasonable inquiries confirm substance abuse, a second-order intervention is called for. Usually as part of a benefits package, employees can be referred to EAP-based drug and alcohol awareness training or treatment, psychological counseling, and a variety of other health-related services. Although managers need to be able to communicate responsibly about such programs and direct employees effectively to them, most supervisors are not personally qualified to act as counselors, social workers, doctors, or specialists in labor–management negotiation. Here, we discuss first-level interpersonal interventions that occur outside the cycle of regularly scheduled performance appraisal.

Performance Problems, Performance Solutions

Performance problems, which include excessive absences, errors, uncooperativeness, broken promises and deadlines, cheating, and overt conflicts, to name only a few, can signal the need for intervention. A decline in performance should be demonstrable and sustained, not a temporary slump, before intervention occurs. However, certain single instances, such as a complaint about sexual harassment or a complaint of racial discrimination, are so important that they should be addressed immediately on their own merit. Here the normal procedures of appraisal interviewing are inappropriate, and managers have to become detectives to become skilled helpers. Generally, an intervention interview—whether it is with a supposed problem person, a supposed victim, or a supposed observer or third party—accomplishes two things:

- *The intervention interview is a site of inquiry, fueled by curiosity.* The manager seeks to discover what has happened in as much detail as possible. To do this, he or she tries to avoid preframing the situation with personal expectations. (Even though Juan has a history of not getting along with customers, in *this* incident, the customer might in fact be distorting the facts unfairly by complaining about Juan.) Open questions, frequent perception checks, and behavioral demonstrations of active listening encourage interviewees to tell their own stories fully. Intervention interviews encourage the fullest possible opportunities for all concerned to give their version of what happened. They ask the journalist's questions: Who? What? When? Where? Why? How? What else? The last question—the clearinghouse "what else?"—is particularly important.

- *The intervention interview is a site of problem solving, fueled ideally by a spirit of cooperation.* A worker may feel she is unfairly branded by a manager's criticisms of how she talks and dresses and feels like a victim of a double standard. Although the interviewer might not have had anything to do with the original incident, he or she becomes a part of the woman's complex emotions about her unpleasant encounter with her manager. Merely asking questions that seem neutral can be interpreted by participants as taking sides, and merely attempting to reach a well-intentioned compromise can be perceived as a cop-out, a sellout, or a personal put-down. Consider the example in Box 9.6 for a case of how interventions could take place in volatile interpersonal circumstances. What if Joan comes to you and asks your opinion on this double standard? What if you are informed that she's filed a grievance for sexual harassment on the basis of being constantly "propositioned"? Is an intervention of any sort called for? (See

Box 9.6

Interviewees in Action   *Joan*

I worked in an office where sexual innuendo was commonplace, and I never thought anyone really took it seriously. I mean, you should hear some of the filthy jokes that we passed around. Anyway, my girlfriend Cathy used to say "Joan, you are *such* a slut" to me after I told a joke, and everyone would laugh. Then the trouble started. Men stared at my legs, my chest, looked longingly into my eyes, that sort of thing. I know I'm attractive, so I didn't pay any attention at first. But then the subtle propositions started, and that's when I got confused. Why me? Was it because I told some dirty jokes? Men do that sort of thing all the time and nobody thinks them bad or easy because of it. But it came to me that Cathy's "innocent" little statement and all that silly laughter was really just a cover for a reputation that I didn't deserve but was getting anyway. But I learned the lesson too late; during my first appraisal I was informed that my behavior was "distracting" to other workers. I knew what was meant. I only wish that I had known what was really going on before I was made a victim of it.

Source: Goodall & Phillips (1984, p. 133)

"Making Your Decision," at the end of this chapter, for other questions about Joan's experience.)

Exit Interviews

Managers often conduct **exit interviews** with employees who resign or retire from an organization voluntarily. They want to create a sense of closure for the interviewee, to request and obtain valid feedback about the organization, and to facilitate the transition for both worker and organization. Leaving a job isn't an easy step. Although it may be the employee's choice, there still may be confusion, anger, resentment, victimization, or other unresolved feelings.

The employee about to leave an organization can provide high-quality insights rarely heard from ongoing employees. When good employees quit, it is time to determine reasons and take stock of the situation (see Box 9.7). What makes other options or other companies more attractive? In a sense, managers conduct exit interviews to "debrief" people who are leaving. Let's survey the three basic functions of exit interviews and the kinds of issues and questions that characterize them.

• *Closure.* If you're the interviewer, your expressed interest and your listening style encourage the interviewee to discuss the moment as a turning point defining a time period in his or her life and in the life of the organization. Effective interviewers might, for example, ask: What successes did you achieve while you were here? What were the high points? Which were the most important projects? Which people did you most enjoy and profit from meeting and working with? Was anything important left unfinished? If so, what? How do you propose we continue the work you started here? If you're the interviewee, you'll also want to create closure for yourself. If the parting is amicable, ask

---

Box 9.7

Reminders   *Why People Quit*

- Limited opportunities for advancement
- Boredom with job
- Lack of recognition
- Unfair workplace discrimination or bias
- Unhappiness with management

- Interpersonal conflict
- Inadequate salary or benefits
- External circumstances of health, family, etc.
- Attractive opportunities elsewhere

---

about such things as how your role was perceived, what organizational advances were made with you in the position you held, and what plan the organization has in mind to fill your role.

• *Feedback.* If you're conducting an exit interview, encourage the interviewee to help you assess the organization as a communication environment. With this information, you could make positive changes that will support others. Encouraging feedback in exit interviews could take many forms: What did you see as the pluses and minuses of this organization? Do we do a good job performing our central mission? Rewarding outstanding performance? Ensuring a fair, diverse, and nondiscriminatory workplace? What kept you from doing a better job? Resources? Interpersonal rivalry? Low expectations for your performance? Unclear job descriptions?

As an interviewee, inquire about evaluative feedback that will assist you in your next position(s). What were your particular strengths? Deficiencies? On which dimension did you make your greatest progress during your stay?

• *Transition.* As an interviewer, encourage the interviewee to think about what skills, knowledge, and attitudes learned in this organization can be utilized elsewhere. What will he or she take to the next position? What new skills and practices will be more important there? Does the employee want to keep in touch with people in this organization? All such subjects will help even somewhat disgruntled employees experience you, and the organization you represent, as caring and concerned.

As an interviewee, discuss how this experience has prepared you for further skill building, and disclose what you're comfortable sharing about future plans. Solicit the reactions of your interviewer.

Termination Interviews

Being told you're out of work is one of life's most deflating and devastating messages. "You're fired," a catchphrase popularized by Donald Trump on his television show, is one particularly blunt message. These days, you're most likely to be "downsized" or laid off, but the effect is the same. Being terminated from a job doesn't always have to be a painful, shocking experience, however. It might be expected, with the employee wondering, "What took them so long?" It could even signal a positive new beginning for someone who couldn't, for whatever reason, admit the job was never a good match.

Dismissing an employee, no matter what the circumstances, should be done face-to-face, usually with the immediate supervisor taking responsibility. A dismissal interview might not be pleasant, but it's necessary for practical, ethical, and legal reasons (see Box 9.8). If there was ever an occasion in which clarity combined with supportive communication is important, this is it. In the termination interview, several interpersonal skills are necessary:

• *Rapport skills.* Difficult messages must be delivered in a context where listeners have the resources to process them fully and not be devastated by them. Managers who terminate employees are wise to discuss the circumstances that made the decision advisable or necessary, and to discuss such conditions in light of human relationships. Here is one way to start: "Marva, a number of us have had a long and productive relationship in this department, with almost no turnover. We've had good times and bad. The past six months, maybe you'll agree, haven't been pleasant—at least since our budget was cut. . . ." Remember that rapport is not a *product* that people have, but a *process* of constantly attended-to mutual interest in each other.

• *Statement skills.* As important as rapport building is, it should not detract from the clarity you need at this time. After introducing the topic, stay away from euphemisms (words or labels with which we attempt to put a more attractive spin on negative things). Stay away from soft messages that can easily be misinterpreted, such as, "Bottom Line Products has struggled recently to solidify our acceptance in variety stores, and your

---

Box 9.8

Interviewers in Action   *James Autry (II)*

No one ever believes he or she is justly fired. There must be some sort of immune system that protects us from facing the reality of our own failures.

. . . I want people I've fired to know why and to decide for themselves what might have been done. I want them to learn what to do next time. And I want them to realize that they still have a future, and they will grow enormously in embracing that future.

But I don't expect ever to convince anyone of that, and when indeed a person I've fired does learn and grow and make a better life, I don't expect to be thanked.

Nevertheless, I have the satisfaction of knowing that only one or two people did not go on to better things after I fired them. The rest of them have done well.

The nagging question, of course, is if they've done well somewhere else, why didn't they do well for me?

It's a question that can keep me awake nights.

Source: Autry (1991, p. 207)

department has had a particularly tough time. We think a change would be better for all concerned." A nervous employee might think at first, "Whew. I thought she going to fire me. I've wanted changes in this unit for years myself." Subsequent clarification can be embarrassing for both parties when an employee just doesn't "get it." A clearer, cleaner message, though still tactful, would be, "Although this is difficult, I need to tell you, Jane, that Friday has to be your last day at Bottom Line Products. I wish we could extend you until after the summer months, but the budget base just isn't there."

If the termination is tied to substandard job performance, you are doing no one a favor by disguising the fact: "We have decided to hire a marketing director who is more activist, more research oriented, and more connected with the way store managers make decisions." In addition, termination interviews need a balanced, both-sides approach. If negative factors make the termination necessary, this is also a good time to outline clearly the positive contributions made by the employee.

- *Facilitation skills.* Terminations evoke strong emotions. Through the invitational nature of your verbal and nonverbal messages, interviewees should find it possible to ventilate emotions and discuss what this action means to them. They might want to express the frustration they feel, the perceived unfairness, the anger, or perhaps the unexpected exhilaration of newfound freedom. Consider using silence productively; after you express whatever regret or other genuine feelings you are experiencing, you need not fill the air with apologies, expressions of sadness, surface compliments, or reassurances you can't back up. Most recipients of emotionally charged news simply need a little time and space to process what it means for them.

- *Clarification skills.* The next steps to be taken by the employee and the employer should be clear at the end of the interview. What should the employee do between now and Friday? How will the e-mail account be handled? Is there severance pay? Outplacement benefits? Many organizations in corporate life provide a wide range of services for outgoing employees, including job search seminars, résumé assistance, and access to phones and e-mail accounts for specified time periods. If you are the interviewer, tell interviewees about all benefits. Make sure they know what kind of help they might expect from you personally; some supervisors actively help employees look for new opportunities. Often, terminated employees are unclear about what kind of recommendation they can expect on the basis of the current employment. After all, if they're fired, how good can they be in the organization's eyes? If appropriate, clarify for the employees what kinds of helpful and positive commentary on their performance the organization could provide for future employers.

Beyond the Basics

Organizations that value dialogue, such as those influenced by MIT's dialogue project and similar programs (see Isaacs, 1993, 1997, 1999; Schoem & Hurtado, 2001; Senge, 1990; Vella, 2003), presume that a wide variety of conflicts within healthy organizations can be absorbed effectively. In fact, conflicts are essential for the organization's contin-ued vitality. As Isaacs (1997) observes, "Dialogue is a way by which better inquiry, bet-ter confrontation and clarification of thinking can come out" (p. 7). Dialogue presumes that we must take each other into account as fully as possible, that we must address ourselves to the uniquely different persons we encounter rather than to some label or stereotype, that collaboration and even conflict can produce outcomes none of us could enact separately, that genuinely open listening helps create more genuine speech, and that human life is ultimately founded on trust.

Conflict in Organizational Interviewing

Wilmot and Hocker (2005) approach conflict from a communication perspective. To them, conflict is not necessarily a negative or unproductive experience, but an "ex-pressed struggle" based on two or more people seeing how their goals are incompatible while their fates are intertwined. Several things about their approach are relevant for learning better interviewing. First, conflict is expressed somehow. People may feel resis-tance or dislike for each other, but it becomes conflict as it is reflected in their message behaviors. We are in conflict, in other words, when we act like it, and when we commu-nicate in a certain way. You could say, then, that conflict is always to a certain extent *shared*, as communication is shared, transactionally.

Second, conflict is based on perception. If interviewers and interviewees believe they are in conflict, and act as they are, they *are*. It isn't reasonable for a third party to waltz in and glibly say, "You two aren't really in conflict; you agree on many issues." Rather, they are engaging in conflict by virtue of how they are communicating. The third party may believe they *shouldn't* be in conflict, or they don't adequately recognize potential common ground, or that they are overlooking a potential for agreement. Nevertheless, the conflict is real to the participants.

Third, perceptions change, often as a result of communication. People in conflict may become less antagonistic over time, or more so. Communication does not automatically resolve conflicts, as some optimists might like to presume. Better communication could well supply the information on which a thicker, denser conflict might be built. Communi-cation, and therefore dialogue, does not solve problems nearly as efficiently as it helps to frame them, shape them, and define them. For example, an interviewer is living in a fan-tasy world if she believes that her subordinates would shape up if they would only allow themselves to understand her communication style. In fact, they may already dislike the interviewer's goals and perceived interference because they understand her style very well.

Fourth, not all conflict is bad. At times it can energize groups, organizations, and cultural groups and help them construct new possibilities for themselves. Conflict chal-lenges us to examine assumptions and reevaluate strategies. The appraisal interviewer who too readily perceives "being a team player" or "acting like a good company citi-zen" as positives to be rewarded may be undercutting the vitality of the organization. Instead, the troublemaker or gadfly, who nevertheless works hard and values the life of the group, may be a radically effective employee who deserves recognition, not suspi-cion (see Cowan, 1992).

Yet, despite the fact that some outcomes of conflict have value, interviewers and interviewees are confronted daily with unproductive forms of conflict. Consider a foreperson on the assembly line who curses new employees before they have a chance to learn their routines. Consider conflict that arises from a male vice president's persistent put-downs of women's capabilities, or the kind of cross-cultural conflict that is based on false assumptions, which a reasonably focused program of on-site job counseling, intergroup training (Schoem & Hurtado, 2001), or prior career counseling (Ponterotto, Rivera, & Sueyoshi, 2000) might help to counteract. Conflict needs to be managed if it results in polarization, ritualized competition, or dehumanization and violent inclinations toward the other side. In fact, the conflict experts suggest (Grove, 1991; Kellett & Dalton, 2001; Wilmot & Hocker, 2005), much of the time it's better to manage conflict rather than to seek to resolve it. Use it, understand it, deal with its assumptions, keep it from escalating into hate or distrust, but don't banish it (see Box 9.9).

Trust and Defensiveness

Organizational interviewers who understand conflict realize its relationship to trust. Years ago, group and organizational theorist Jack Gibb (1961) synthesized much of what researchers knew about trust into a typology of what he called defensive and supportive climates. To him, defensiveness developed (as an employee) in relatively threatening communication situations, just as the likelihood of feeling supported and understood grew in an essentially different climate. Within Gibb's typology is a wealth of advice for interviewers and managers. **Defensive climates** are those that emphasize:

- *Evaluation* (the assumption that attaching value is, and needs to be, common)
- *Control* (the assumption that people are basically untrustworthy and need to be told how to act)
- *Strategy* (the assumption that persons in social situations need to plan carefully how to persuade and dominate others)
- *Neutrality* (the assumption that leaders, for example, need to be essentially uninvolved and dispassionate to be objective)
- *Superiority* (the assumption that leaders can act as if they are better persons than the persons they "lead")
- *Certainty* (the assumption that leaders must be decisive, sure of the decisions, and unbending in implementing policies)

Gibb thought these climates of organizational life created conflict because they were built on mistrust. A supervisor who builds a managerial philosophy on them can expect a series of confrontational employee interviews, even though many employees would simply acquiesce by resigning, by leveling their productivity, or by withholding the kind of vital energy it takes to build a cooperative organization. When workers communicate defensively, in other words, they communicate unproductively.

Gibb studied other organizations that were more successful, though. Many of them had facilitated climates with completely different communication assumptions. **Supportive climates** are those in which people tend to feel secure enough to communicate honest

Box 9.9

Reminders   *Anger in the Workplace*

"Going postal" has replaced "going ballistic" as a way of describing someone whose anger crosses over into violence. The expression refers to a series of violent acts committed by employees of the U.S. Postal Service some years ago. However, anger and violence can be found in insurance offices, banks, advertising agencies, factories, and any other place people work. Sometimes, in fact, people arrive at their jobs already angry, ready for a slight nudge to send them hurtling into unproductive conflict. Although workplace anger can resemble road rage, people cannot just drive away and leave the anger in their wake. The aggression stimulated by workplace anger, in fact, can lead to physical violence, or the kind of psychological violence that damages an organization's sense of security and its ongoing operations. Intervention is often required. Communication techniques alone will not eliminate anger or lead to resolution, in part because angry people often don't think clearly or reasonably. Yet intervention interviews can help by mediating disputes and moderating tempers.

Seth Allcorn (1994) offers advice for those consumed by anger, and advice for those trying to deal with the anger of others in organizational interviews of all types. When angry (as an interviewee in an appraisal or intervention interview, for example), Allcorn suggests these steps (p. 47):

- Do not put off communicating anger for long periods.
- Think through what you want to say.
- Do not withdraw into silence.
- Avoid using strong words; do not accuse or attack.
- Be open to criticism.
- Keep focused on the problem.
- Look for a solution.

Of course, because anger distorts perceptions, following Allcorn's advice when you are angry might be difficult. It should be easier, however, for someone facing an angry person to follow these steps (p. 56):

- Do not be defensive.
- Sit back and listen.
- Sift and sort, separating facts from feelings and fantasies.
- Directly discuss the anger.
- Discover your role in the anger.
- Do not accept blame for the anger in others, even if you did provoke it.
- Remember, anger isn't bad, and it may be necessary for growth, development, and improved relations.
- Help the person focus on solutions rather than merely ventilating.

Source: Allcorn (1994)

reactions more directly; they do not feel the need to defend themselves either from attack or someone's disinterest. In his typology, Gibb created direct contrasts for purposes of illustration and diagnosis:

- Instead of *evaluation*, substitute the supportive climate of *description* (the assumption that a thorough emphasis on careful noting of behaviors and reactions is more helpful, and less threatening, than judging people constantly).

Trying Out Your Skills

- After reading the following intervention interview excerpt, list what you believe to be problems in the communication choices made by the interviewer. Be specific: What would you say and do differently?

- If you were the interviewee, would you take a more assertive stance? A less assertive stance?

- What roles do the following play in this conversation: empathy, conflict management and anger in the workplace, defensive or supportive climates, appraisal methods, problem-solving attitudes, and dialogue?

INTERVIEWER: You know, this place wasn't always this much fun. Used to be that we didn't coddle employees the way we do now. Did you realize that?

INTERVIEWEE: Since I only started last year, sir, I wasn't aware of what happened before that.

INTERVIEWER: Well, it's true. It seems to me that there's no discipline any more among workers, no self-pride in doing good work. No sense of pride in the company. It's discouraging. How many times have I had you in here to talk to you about making all your private calls during the business day? Lots. Everybody's doing this behind my back, thinking I don't know what's going on. But I do. I really do.

INTERVIEWEE: I wasn't sure what this was about. It's about taking phone calls? This is the second time you've mentioned it to me. But it's the first time you've called me into your office. I'm really sorry. When I started working here, my little girl was sick. Remember? And she or the babysitter wound up calling me several times every day. You even let me take some time off. I just kind of thought it was OK then, using the phone might still be . . . er . . . acceptable if . . .

INTERVIEWER: That's what I mean. "I just kind of thought." "I just kind of thought." Businesses don't work that way, Mardra. I'm telling you now, I want it to stop. And if it doesn't, we'll have to find someone else who can give us their full attention.

INTERVIEWEE: So I'm not supposed to call anyone at work . . . I know that.

INTERVIEWER: Right. No calls.

INTERVIEWEE: I'm sorry. I'm confused. It's not clear about taking calls. What should I do if someone calls me, like in an emergency or something? I need my job. I'm scared to lose it and don't want to. I shouldn't take any calls anymore?

INTERVIEWER: Mardra, I'm going to say this one more time. No calls. Which word isn't clear? "No" or "calls"? *No* calls.

INTERVIWEE: Even in an emergency? I've got three kids.

INTERVIEWER: Would you please get back to work?

INTERVIWEE: Yeah, will this go in my file?

INTERVIEWER: Will what go in your file?

INTERVIEWEE: Are you going to write me up in a report? Because if you do, I'd like you to note that you haven't called me in here several times about the phone calls, or whatever you thought. Maybe it was somebody else.

INTERVIEWER: Just get back to work. I'll deal with this later. . . .

- Instead of *control*, substitute the supportive climate of *problem orientation* (the assumption that a collaborative approach to problem solving and goal setting yields greater job satisfaction and better results).

- Instead of *strategy*, substitute the supportive climate of *spontaneity* (the assumption that group members appreciate leaders who can be immediately "present" in the situation, without facades or game playing).

- Instead of *neutrality*, substitute the supportive climate of *empathy* (the assumption that leaders do not have to be uninvolved in the organizational lives of group members, but can attempt to immerse themselves in the world as others experience it).

- Instead of *superiority*, substitute the supportive climate of *equality* (the assumption that, as people, leaders are no better and no worse than other group members—even though their achievements merit respect).

- Instead of *certainty*, substitute the supportive climate of *provisionalism* (the assumption that anyone's solutions are open to question and can be changed).

Gibb's supportive climate categories reinforce the kind of dialogic organizations we have described. Although he understands that such concepts as neutrality and evaluation may at times be inevitable and serve valid purposes (e.g., we cannot eliminate evaluation from an appraisal interviewing process), they do not need to be emphasized unduly in interviewing. One review of relevant research reports that criticism by appraisal interviewers "resulted in greater defensiveness, more negative attitudes toward appraisals and less improvement in subordinate performance." Yet when the criticism "was revised into goals, subordinates' performance improved" and, with more coparticipation in goal setting, defensiveness diminished (Krayer, 1987, p. 277).

When we stress in this book that interviewing can be a dialogue, we do not mean that it's a happy condition of equality, without roles or status, or that it should happen without planning. Roles are inevitable and preparation is vital. We merely suggest that a higher quality of interaction develops when the trust of supportive dialogue links communicators, even in conflict. With that quality of interaction comes better information and insight for interviewers and interviewees.

Summary

In the working world, the quality of your life is largely defined by your professional experience in organizations. Careful attention to listening, questioning, and framing practices in organizational interviewing can improve that quality of life significantly, because through interviews you begin to process the feedback you need to improve. The communication skills of listening, questioning, and framing also apply generally to organizational strategic planning, goal setting, and decision making, not just in interviewing situations.

After a brief discussion of recent trends in organizational learning, we described the mechanics and dynamics of appraisal interviewing in detail. Building on that base, we extended the same philosophy to intervention interviews, exit interviews, and termination interviews. Finally, "Beyond the Basics" took a deeper look at the communicative

Making Your Decision

- An employee you have just had to terminate comes to you and asks for advice on how to take negative feedback, thinking this will be useful in her next job. In fact, you did believe she reacted somewhat defensively over the past three or four performance appraisals. Based on your general understanding of the feedback process, and your understanding of how and why people become defensive when being evaluated, create a list of specific recommendations for how an interviewee should listen and respond to negative feedback. Be sure to include suggestions on what to do if the feedback seems undeserved, unnecessarily abusive, or otherwise off the mark.

- Your superior, the managing editor of the newspaper at which you work as a reporter, has just finished an appraisal interview with you in which she said you have no problems whatsoever. She's pleased with your initiative, your stories, and your pleasant personality around the office. The interview appears to be finished after only five or six minutes. However, you know

that you both marked off 30 minutes for the meeting, and you'd like to know more details. What questions or approaches would you use to "interview the interviewer?" Devise a rough schedule of things about which you'd like to get more detailed feedback and perhaps discover some less-than-positive reactions to your work.

- "Joan" (see Box 9.6) approaches you and asks you to talk with the men in her department about what constitutes sexual harassment. She is tired of how they treat her. You believe that all claims of sexual harassment need to be taken seriously. However, beyond that sincere concern (1) Which details of her department's situation would you want to get from Joan, so you can assess the depth of the difficulty she's experiencing? (2) Where would you find good definitions and discussions of this issue, assuming your organization has drafted no formal sexual harassment policy? (3) What do you tell her about your plans? Will you schedule interviews with each man? (4) Would you set a time frame within which you get back to her with your findings?

aspects of conflict and how conflict can be managed effectively if interviewers and interviewees recognize the influence of supportive and nondefensive conversational climates.

The Interview Bookshelf

On the organizational context surrounding interviewers and interviewees:

Eisenberg, E. M. & Goodall, H. L., Jr. (2004). *Organizational communication: Balancing creativity and constraint* (4th ed.). New York: Bedford/St. Martin's.

A comprehensive description of the contemporary complex organization, with special attention to how organizations are changing to become more dialogic and culturally sensitive.

On the demands of performance appraisals:

Bruce, W. M., & Blackburn, J. W. (1992). *Balancing job satisfaction and performance.* Westport, CT: Quorum Books.

Leeds, D. (1987). *Smart questions: A new strategy for successful managers.* New York: Berkley Books.

These two practical accounts de-emphasize theory while still placing organizational interviews in a coherent framework. Consult these books for a variety of excellent examples.

On the dilemmas of a CEO who must balance humane caring with productivity:

Autry, J. A. (1994). *Life & work: A manager's search for meaning.* New York: Morrow.

Autry is a storyteller, whether he is illustrating a point with an anecdote or a poem (he's a published poet who has been profiled by Bill Moyers on PBS). His stories show a variety of ways to be successful in organizations by emphasizing communication. "The companies," *he writes,* "that concentrate on the relationships are the ones most likely to achieve quality in everything they do" *(p. 50).*

Chapter Ten

Interviews in Persuasive Situations

(LEARNING GOALS)

After reading this chapter, you should be able to

- Enact and define persuasion as a helping relationship

- Enact the stages in a generalized process of persuasive interviewing: opening, discovering, matching, choosing, and closing

- Relate the goals of personal selling to an interpersonal ethic of communication

- Explain the fundamental skills of negotiation and interrogation/advocacy interviews

The Basics

One of the authors and his wife recently invited a representative of a large local home-improvement company into their home to get ideas and estimates for either replacing or refurbishing their kitchen cabinets. Here is their account of what happened:

> We expected a short visit, perhaps with someone taking measurements and leaving some brochures. Instead, we were interviewed thoroughly by a skillful young woman who had clearly gone through a training program that stressed the careful sequencing of topics, questions, and answers.
>
> Seated at the kitchen table with us, she talked about how much she liked "neat old houses" like ours, and how important kitchens are to the life of a family. Switching gears subtly, she asked what we knew about the company she represented. We'd heard of it through ads and because of some friends' experience using them for cabinetry work. She asked how we felt about the negative image acquired by some home-improvement companies in our area. It was an opening for her

When a professional salesperson makes a presentation, he or she will listen more than speak. In a presentation, you should listen—with the prospect speaking—at least 55 percent of the time. If you're doing more than 45 percent of the talking, it's time to pull back on the reins, talk less, and listen more. You just aren't going to persuade the prospect with your brilliant oratory. On the contrary, you persuade the prospect by getting him or her to talk. And you do that through the skillful use of questions in the sales interview. Yes, questions rather than statements. And, even though it's called a "presentation," presenting is only part of it. To be effective, a presentation is really an interview, involving a two-way dialogue between you and your prospect.

—Bob Kimball,
AMA Handbook for Successful Selling

to discuss the many decades her company had maintained its leadership and how good its reputation was with the Better Business Bureau. Presumably, we were left to conclude, a company that did shoddy work or cheated people could never stay in business in the same locale for 50 or 60 years.

Next, she took out an official-looking three-ring binder containing detailed pictures, product dimensions, and—most important of all—questions about how we use the kitchen, what we store on the shelves, how pleased we were with the present configuration of cabinets, what we had hoped to spend if we decided to do the shelves with her company, and so forth. With each answer, she paraphrased our response to ensure she understood us. At no time did she say anything that sounded like a stereotypical sales pitch, nor did she suggest we choose one product over another. She didn't even hint about whether she concurred that the existing cabinets needed replacement or remodeling.

From other pages in her notebook, she produced detailed comparisons of various plans and options, and she encouraged us to eliminate plans and options that did not meet our goals or our budget. She didn't make these decisions for us, but, rather, progressively invited us to state a series of seemingly small judgments that kept us focused on our own goals as they matched, or failed to match, the company's options. Using the criteria we supplied—budget, appearance, configuration, and minimum intrusion of workers, among others—we narrowed our choices to two or three. There was a glitch, however. The wood color we wanted wasn't listed in the package deals chosen. Would that be a problem? How big a problem? She replied frankly that she didn't know. She called her office for an answer, but it was closed for the day, so she promised to get back to us shortly, which she did. (A kept promise, no matter how tiny, is one of the best advertisements for a persuader.) Instead of losing credibility for not knowing the answer, she gained status with us by responding in what we perceived as a direct manner and by reacting with a very human expression of embarrassment for not being fully informed. Consider the frame: Instead of being a mark against her, the glitch within the context of her previously won credibility and competence led us to frame her behavior as honest and trustworthy.

We now had all the information we needed (or thought we needed) about the company, and about its cabinets and workers. She had all the information she needed about us—our budget, our goals, and our expectations. It was time to choose. Persuasion was happening, and it was set up not by manipulation, but by straightforward communication skills that emphasized clarity, listening, and caring.

This anecdote sets the stage for defining and discussing persuasion in professional and everyday life. In this chapter you'll learn about interviewing in persuasive situations. These situations include, among others, typical sales encounters, negotiations, courtroom advocacy, and law enforcement interrogation. Each of these contexts shares in common the intention of one or more parties to affect the beliefs, attitudes, values, and behaviors of other people. The intent to affect someone else is the genesis of the many definitions of persuasion throughout the centuries. **Persuasion** is usually defined, therefore, as the attempt of one communicator or group to influence the beliefs, attitudes, values, and behaviors of others. However, people often change without the conscious attempt of another person to motivate them.

The public defines persuasion too narrowly at times, identifying it almost exclusively with situations in which someone is consciously and directly trying to "sell" something, such as a bar of soap, a used car, or a senatorial candidate. Or people think they are targets for persuasion when someone speaks in the residence hall as a recruiter for student organizations, or when a minister, rabbi, or priest suggests values appropriate for moral decision making. However, in a sense, all human interaction depends on at least implicit requests that we adapt our behaviors and attitudes to each other. We gain acceptance of our points of view in close friendships just as politicians do in their congressional campaigns; we persuade in informal conversations with parents and children just as much as when we're haggling with a salesperson at the car dealer down the road. It's the goals that differ. If you define persuasion in a broader everyday sense, almost all human interactions involve persuasive goals of some kind.

Consider the following examples of persuasion, representing the other categories of interviewing treated in this book:

- In interviews for employee selection, most applicants hope to convince interviewers of their suitability and establish a personal image of competence; personnel interviewers try to maintain the credibility of the organization and persuade excellent candidates that this job is a good match for them.

- In interviews for organizational decision making, such as appraisals and interventions, employees want superiors to see their productivity within the organization; the superiors hope to convince employees to adopt mutually agreed-on strategies to increase effectiveness and teamlike cooperation.

- In interviews in journalism, interviewers hope to persuade interviewees to share information and insight about newsworthy topics; news sources often hope to influence the ultimate shape of the story or the message and information it conveys.

- In interviews in social science and humanistic research, interviewers persuade respondents that through their participation they will make valuable contributions to the researcher's study; interviewees often have a story to tell (or a set of facts to relate) that they hope will be compelling, interesting, and useful to a wider audience.

- In interviews in helping professions, effective helpers persuade clients, patients, and others that certain actions, skills, styles, or treatments will result in positive outcomes; those interview partners typically want to be seen in certain ways (e.g., as sincere, as helpless victims of circumstance, as knowledgeable partners in developing treatment, or in a variety of self-directed ways).

Therefore, *all* interviews could be thought of as persuasive interviews, if you consider persuasion's literal broad definition. Still, some interviewers consciously put persuasion front and center. Although personal selling is the most obvious form of persuasive interview, two other types of persuasive interviews are also especially prominent: negotiation and interrogation/advocacy interviews. A salesperson offers an audience goods or services but often must interview to determine the desirability or suitability for the audience. A negotiator engages in a give-and-take in which different positions could become reconciled to each other. An advocate or interrogator interviews often by probing an interviewee's well-defined point of view or version of reality to ensure its accuracy or to test its possible bias.

"The Basics" will survey principles of persuasion, noting how persuasive factors affect interviewing choices. We suggest that persuasion is ideally not a relationship of manipulation but a much more benign human relationship. Then, referring often to sales contexts as a prototypical persuasive situation, we examine how people are influenced in persuasive interviews. In "Beyond the Basics" you'll find descriptions and suggestions to help you interact in the two other common persuasive interviewing contexts—negotiation and interrogation or advocacy interviewing.

Persuasion as Helping, Not Manipulation

Some people are afraid of persuasion and want nothing to do with it. Small wonder, given the extravagant—even threatening—claims made for its power. While searching for Web sites devoted to sales and persuasion, a recent hit yielded these claims from a practitioner marketing his system of skills (capitalization, boldface, and punctuation in original):

Imagine being able to Sell, Persuade or Talk

ANYONE into ANYTHING, ANYTIME!

Further, the author suggests that "armed with [his] skills you'll find that" . . .

Your Business Profits Skyrocket.

Your Associates Beg Your Counsel.

Your Adversaries Flee.

Your Lovers Vow Eternal Loyalty.

Your Children Instantaneously Obey.

The specific Web sources don't need the advertising here, and you can find them with any search engine (just key in "persuasion" and "imagine being able"). Other Web sites touting persuasion systems similarly promise you can use their programs to learn to: "Read people instantly"; "Make people instinctively like and trust you"; "Influence anyone to give you anything, anywhere, anytime!"; "Arouse intense emotional states at will"; "Get massive cash flows surging to you"; "Astound massive audiences"; "Control how perfect strangers perceive you"; "Attract ANYTHING you choose"; and "Melt all resistance in five minutes."

All this sounds extraordinarily wonderful if you're inclined, say, to rule the world; it's less wonderful if you accidentally encounter someone with this magical power and fall under its spell. The "armed-with-skills" philosophy espouses an underlying ethic of manipulation: To be a persuader is to be an invader and controller of other people's lives. Somewhere between the extremes of shunning persuasion on one hand and abusing it on the other is the proper place of persuasion in human interaction.

Even if you consider yourself a "live and let live" person, you don't need to apologize for or feel guilty about attempting to be persuasive. People generally hope to make a difference in each other's lives, and there is nothing wrong with that. It's consistent, we believe, with the attitude that others have a right to their opinions, attitudes, beliefs, and values. Responsible persuasion does not limit other people's rights as much as it expands them. Responsible persuasion lays the groundwork for change but does not demand that change from others, nor does it seek to fence people in, limiting them to a particular point of view. The reality that there are selfish, deceitful persuaders in the world lining their own pockets by cheating others does not make unethical persuasion the norm.

Caring communicators, as James Craig describes in Box 10.1, should be responsible for telling each other what they want in their relations with others. To do less is to turn communication into more of a guessing game than it already is. This is not manipulation as much as it is clarity.

Although both interviewers and interviewees can be persuaders, most literature in the field tends to assume the persuader is the interviewer and the interviewee is the person whose attitudes or behaviors may change. In all persuasive situations, a concern for the other person should be a guiding light for all parties. The most practical ethical approach, we believe, is to consider persuasion as a helping relationship (Anderson & Ross, 2002), consistent with many of the suggestions in Chapter 11.

Box 10.1

Interviewers in Action   *James Craig*

I recently discovered that I have a long history of going around dissatisfied with contributions to joint efforts made by other members of my family, by colleagues, and by people who work for me. Either they didn't do what I wanted them to do, or they didn't do it the way I wanted it done. I generally communicated my dissatisfaction to them, either directly, or, more frequently, indirectly. I thus polluted the atmosphere of my relationships. But I now realize that I seldom got very clear with myself *in advance* as to exactly what I did want from the others. And, consequently I seldom let them know what I expected of them. That is, until I would find that they had failed to meet my previously *unvoiced* criteria.

I now know that I had been putting other people in untenable positions. I had given them great freedom to figure out what to do and how to do it. I had left them with the false impression that *whatever* they might choose to do would be o.k. with me. And then, *unless* they chose exactly what I would have chosen *if I had taken the trouble to figure it out*, I would be dissatisfied with them, and would let them know of my dissatisfaction in one way or another. . . .

Now that I'm aware of what I had been doing I take the responsibility for figuring out what I want, and for communicating it to the other people in my relationships. That doesn't mean that I dictate to them. (They wouldn't accept it if I tried to.) And we may or may not settle on a specific course of action designed to satisfy me. But we all know where we stand and what our various expectations are. People are kept out of mystery. And the atmosphere stays much clearer.

Source: Craig & Craig (1979, p. 75; italics in original)

Interaction in the Persuasive Interview

Responsible persuasion in interviewing must involve *research, audience analysis, unique discovery, matching* resources and needs, and respect for *choice*. The first two points describe preinterview factors that are extremely important but do not directly reflect the interaction of interviewer and interviewee. In developing research, the persuader inventories available resources before approaching the interview. Resources could include products, services, delivery systems, or personal experience, but the persuader must be aware of what's being offered, and should personally believe in it. In analyzing the audience, the persuader attempts to determine the valid needs, wants, and interpersonal styles that characterize how people make decisions.

The remaining three (*discovery, matching,* and *choice*) directly translate into a generalized chronology for conducting almost any persuasive interview. Although any professional interviewer could note hundreds of exceptions, the core of most interviews will be shaped by *discovering* the uniqueness of this particular relationship (using informational interviewing skills), *matching* your resources with interviewees' needs, and creating the space in which interviewees may make reasonable *choice* for themselves. When considered alongside the necessity for opening and closing the interview, they create a flexible model for persuasive interviewing.

Opening

The opening of a persuasive interview capitalizes on the willingness of participants to speak informally. As with most interview openings, it is relatively brief and stresses the task of building rapport. *Rapport building* (1) clarifies the basis for the relationship between communicators, (2) puts the communication situation on a less formal basis, and (3) ideally establishes a foundation of pleasant interaction in which, no matter how difficult the designated topic of the interaction, the interviewer and interviewee at least will like or appreciate each other. Think of rapport not as a product of a relationship but as a certain process of relationship in which the communicators are actively and civilly adapting themselves and their messages to each other.

Other than rapport building, an opening often designates the purpose for the discussion and sets the ground rules for interaction:

INTERVIEWER (financial consultant): Good afternoon, Ramona! How are things? I appreciate your calling me about that mutual fund we talked about for your dad. I've put together a few brochures and ideas here that should only take us about 15 or 20 minutes to go through. But first, how's that shortstop of yours doing? Is he leading the league in hitting and dirty caps again this summer?

This greeting gives the interaction an informal feeling and lets the interviewee know that talking about personal things won't be considered a waste of time. It both personalizes the conversation by demonstrating that Ramona's life is important enough to remember, and it signals her about how much time to expect the interview to take. Presumably the interviewer, Marion, has budgeted at least 30 minutes for the meeting.

INTERVIEWEE (coming to an appointment set up to obtain preliminary information for her father): Hey, I don't know his average, Marion, but he's sure loving his new coach. Did your boy have Jess Zamora as coach when he went through the program? Jess really works well with the kids.

INTERVIEWER: Yeah, sure I know Jess—ever since his parents lived on St. Louis Street, just down from us. His parents did business with me for years, too, before they moved to Birmingham. Maybe you didn't know that Jess and my older daughter were quite an item for a while?

INTERVIEWEE: Now that you mention it, I did hear that. Wow, things really change around here, don't they? Just a few years ago, Mom and Dad were riding herd on me, and now here I am having to run all kinds of errands for Dad. Kind of ironic.

INTERVIEWER: How's he doing since your mom's accident?

INTERVIEWEE: Well, it's hard on him, and he's not doing real well with making decisions. That's why I'm here, trying to pull some things together for him to decide. What about that mutual fund plan? Money's really on his mind these days.

INTERVIEWER: I've got it right here. Let's go over the company's reputation first, OK? . . .

The opening serves at one level to relate person with person, and persons with task at another level. It should serve as a clarifier, both emotionally and interactionally, for participants.

Discovering

Successful persuasive interviewers do not simply sell a product or a point of view to a waiting audience, despite the rich professional lore about sure-fire sales pitches. Persuasion essentially doesn't work from the outside in, as if an incoming message unlocks

Trying Out Your Skills

Think of a job you currently hold, or one that you have held in the recent past.

- Decide on one thing you'd most like to see changed about the job that could actually be changed by a superior's decision (e.g., working conditions, procedures, pay).

- How would you begin to do the informal background research necessary for requesting this change? Where would you get the information and from whom?

- Considering the idea of persuasion as a helping relationship, how would the change create advantages for people other than yourself? Specifically, if you plan to ask your supervisor or employer to make the change, how will he or she be helped?

- What would be a good time, place, and strategy for opening this persuasive discussion with your superior?

some secret place in people's decision making, and the outcome is then assured. No one else persuades you, you might say; instead, you persuade yourself by combining the reasons, materials, and ideas of another person, and then mixing these externally supplied ideas creatively with a personal awareness of your own goals and desires. External persuaders can certainly influence you at this stage, but only if they discover enough about how you frame your own situation. How can they do that? In discovering what is necessary for persuasion, interviewers *ask*, *encourage*, *listen*, and *frame*.

• Interviewers *ask questions* that provide the most helpful base of information, probably using more or less a funnel sequence. Concentrate on neutral **what-questions** (e.g., "What meals do your family members look forward to the most?" "What is the ideal percentage of attention a senator should give to foreign affairs compared with domestic?") rather than on **why-questions** (e.g., "Why do you cook so much pasta?" "Why do you give more attention to foreign policy?"). With this information, interviewers can shape and frame their suggested solutions to the problems faced by the interviewee or suggest the most helpful courses of action.

Remember that questions can backfire if an appropriate reason for them hasn't been established by the opening. If the information is seen as irrelevant, the questions will be perceived as evidence of a prying attitude or a lack of focus. People in the dominant contemporary information culture, especially that of Europe and North America, usually don't mind being asked questions about their personal affairs, but in other cultures people justifiably object to such inquiries. Privacy issues may become even more controversial as information retrieval and widespread database intrusion become more entrenched. Consider carefully whether you actually need the information before you request it.

Moreover, assume that in some cultural contexts, the request for specific information may do more harm than good unless it is handled with great tact and sensitivity. As Triandis (1994) suggests, cultures and cultural groups that value *collectivist* communication styles (in which group identification is more important than individual feelings and goals) do not usually respond positively to outsiders' probes for personal information, even though that information would be readily discussed within a family. "Collectivists," he wrote, "are especially opposed to 'washing the family's dirty laundry in public' and go to extremes to hide unfavorable information about in-group members from outsiders" (p. 230). Collectivists also tend not to disclose information easily to strangers (p. 231), although interviewers may benefit from what is called the **passant phenomenon**. In such an interaction, many people—collectivists and individualists—will disclose information if they believe the interviewer is a reliable listener and a conversation partner "in passing" (p. 232).

• Interviewers mix into the conversation strategic comments that *encourage elaborations* from the interviewee. Conversational interviewing is especially desirable in persuasive settings because the most influential messages are those perceived as nonpurposive. If a persuader, however, is seen as being self-serving, respondents will tend to become defensive if not resistant. The exclusive use of questions might suggest that the interviewee is being pumped or grilled, a feeling most of us would avert if possible. Much information comes from informal responses to interviewer observations but without some of the baggage of defensiveness. In their article "Interviewing by Comment: An Adjunct to the Direct Question," Snow, Zurcher, and Sjoberg (1981) discuss the dynamics of such an approach. They found that "questions, in contrast to comments, characteristically call forth, circumscribe, and imply answers. That is, questions 'frame' the response or talk of the interviewee" (p. 288). On the other hand, "interviewing by comment" (their phrase) "facilitates the process of discovery . . . generally associated with the creation and development of knowledge" (p. 287).

Interviewing by comment can be discerned in the following examples of nonquestions that nevertheless could elicit important information: "That real estate agent really seemed to irritate you"; "The world's getting crazy when so much of our scarce free time goes into maintaining and fixing gadgets"; "It's hard for two people to agree completely on something that costs as much money as a college degree"; "You want the contract, but you don't want it if it threatens those gains you made last year." Do you see how each of these comments invites and almost necessitates a response that could provide extra information and insight?

• Interviewers *encourage interviewees to tell stories* about their lives, their dilemmas, and their own successes in their previous experiences. If you're selling cars, for instance, it's usually a good idea to elicit and then not interrupt an enthusiastic story about how much the buyer loved a previous car manufactured by a competitor. Your first impulse might be to try to change the subject—move the speaker away from memories that might not help your cause. However, the enthusiastic willingness to tell a story is a more important positive sign than the story's content itself is a negative sign. From the story, you will discover what the interviewee enjoys about cars and what goals likely will motivate the next purchase.

• Interviewers *listen carefully* to interviewee responses to their questions and comments. Your listening must not only be accurate, but it must be demonstrated overtly, perhaps in the form of active listening. For example, in attempting to mediate between two powerful civic groups to reach an agreement about new parking regulations downtown, you might find yourself in an interchange like this:

INTERVIEWER (mediator/negotiator): John, when someone from your side talks, things are usually expressed in terms of what's going to happen down the road, in the future. Yet, at the same time, Janeece's group sounds more concerned with the short-term implications for shoppers downtown. Have I got that right? I'm wondering if I could invite more long-range observations from Janeece, or someone who'd like to speak to that, and more discussion about immediate consequences of the change from John or somebody who agrees with him.

INTERVIEWEE (Janeece): I'm sorry. I thought our position on long-term changes for downtown was obvious. [John: (muttering) "Nope. . . ."] Let me backtrack a bit. . . .

At times, listening for discovery will necessarily take another form. Part of listening is trying to figure out what is not being said and why the speaker is overlooking or avoiding those comments or observations. For example, if you were a traveling representative for a pharmaceutical company, listening for what is not said could lead you to observe, perhaps: "Doctor Fernandez, I heard you say several times you 'haven't been unhappy' with the responsiveness of the people from Rose Pharmaceuticals. But I haven't heard you say that a change is out of the question. Are there things they aren't doing, maybe, that you wish could happen?"

Is the emphasis on listening for discovery effective? When one major company had a portion of its sales personnel participate in a training program called "Selling by Listening," it discovered that one of the divisions that received training increased sales by almost 34 percent, but a comparable group that didn't receive the training increased by about 3 percent (R. Anderson, 1995, p. 169). Listening sometimes requires a persuader to suspend judgment and let the customer's views be heard. Listening expert Peter Marino (1997a) describes what happened to an interior designer while visiting the home of a potential client. The designer saw a woven tablecloth, commented on how "interesting" it was, and asked the homeowner if it was her own work. It was her grandmother's, the woman replied, done in Greece when she was a young woman. The homeowner asked, "Do you think it'll fit in with my new furniture?" Withholding her judgment, the interior designer asked for the homeowner's opinion. "I couldn't live without it," she answered, to which the designer replied: "In that case, it should remain." Later, the client revealed to the designer that she had rejected another designer who said the tablecloth had to go (see, for other relevant articles on dialogic listening in sales, Marino, 1997b, 1999a, 1999b, 1999c).

• Interviewers attempt to *frame decisions* (or issues, or ideas) in ways congruent with the interviewee's frame. Successful persuaders usually are empathizers who can consider what the world looks like to the other person(s). What, for instance, are interviewees' beliefs about how the world works? (Interviewees are unlikely to think of alternatives outside the boundaries of these beliefs.) What attitudes predispose them to evaluate options or act in certain ways? (They may not immediately understand or respect attitudes they consider inconsistent with their own.) What are the operational values that they carry with them from situation to situation? (They're unlikely to make many decisions inconsistent with long-standing values.) Then, from within the imagined alternate frame, persuasive interviewers can better understand the information and reasoning they must provide—or elicit—to clarify and assist the decision-making process for the interviewee.

Speaking and listening skills enable and support framing skills. The human relationship in persuasion, however, is being threatened as new electronic media and online database resources take the place of traditional, face-to-face persuasion. Rolph Anderson (1996) and other observers have tried to project how these changes will affect persuasion for salespersons. In the following comment by Anderson, notice how many times he places in the foreground the expected and traditional responsibilities of audience analysis, even though they are draped in new clothing:

> High-technology can never fully replace the salesperson's ability to establish trust with customers, respond to subtle cues, anticipate customer needs, provide personalized service, nurture ongoing relationships, and create profitable new business strategies in partnership with customers. However, salespeople must take on new roles and revitalize some old ones in serving customers—e.g., (1) learning more about their customers' businesses

and taking responsibility for customer profitability, (2) helping customers create long-run competitive advantages, (3) learning how to use their company resources to create added value for customers, (4) building good relationships with their own headquarters support team, (5) devoting more attention to intelligence gathering as the "eyes and ears" of their companies, (6) making use of the latest technology to increase customer contact and service while reducing costs, and (7) developing long-term, mutually profitable partnerships with customers. (p. 30)

New technologies, however, allow a persuader to discover essential facts and background about the audience. The amount of information available to communicators is staggering, in fact. We suggest you consult the many recent sources designed to guide communicators in their online research (e.g., Courtright & Perse, 1998, for a manual written especially for communication specialists and students; also see Hewson, Yule, Laurent, & Vogel, 2002; Mann & Stewart, 2000; Rubin, Rubin, et al., 2005).

Matching

Information gained in the discovery stage is useful only if you have an idea, a product, or a new perspective that an interviewee perceives as genuinely helpful, and, then, only if you convince the interviewee that your idea, product, or perspective will improve his or her current situation. Nothing sells itself by its inherent attractiveness; indeed, we "buy" based on presumed future outcomes that adopters or customers consider to be desirable or necessary.

In a complex world, though, we often are confused or intimidated by the vast array of choices we confront. Most people are knowledgeable about a number of topics, but few of us are competent to move comfortably from diagnosing engine troubles with an auto mechanic to asking a corporate lawyer sophisticated legal questions about the lawsuit filed last month by a coworker. You might know how to tell whether your computer's memory is inadequate for new software the boss wants you to run but not understand enough about operating system distinctions to ask intelligent questions of outside vendors when the department heads meet to decide on technology upgrades. We all have somewhat different bases of knowledge and competence, but we have to make decisions in many areas of relative ignorance. In the matching stage of persuasive interviewing, an interviewer shows he or she is sufficiently credible, expert, and trustworthy to assist an interviewee through an informational maze, especially when the decision maker feels overwhelmed by the task. Obviously, this is a responsibility that potentially invites misrepresentation, distortion, and selfishness. But effective persuaders understand that such tactics are ultimately counterproductive. Not only are they ethically wrong (as we discuss in more detail later), they are ineffective. When the decision maker's needs are not matched well with a product, a service, or an idea, that mismatch becomes obvious soon enough, and the persuader who urged the decision is discredited.

How do people change their minds as a result of messages they can match and align with needs and wants? A particularly revealing classic explanation is provided by social psychologist Herbert Kelman (1966). He distinguished three processes of social influence: compliance, identification, and internalization.

Compliance occurs "when an individual accepts influence from another person or from a group because he hopes to achieve a favorable reaction from the other. He may be interested in attaining certain specific rewards or in avoiding certain specific punishments that the influencing agent controls" (p. 152). For example, a person demonstrates compliance when she or he claims to agree with a comment because agreeing serves a more important need than arguing the point. Compliance also reflects a tendency of humans to seek the acceptance of others, which outweighs the intrinsic attraction of the product, the idea, or the service under discussion. "What the individual learns, essentially, is to say or do the expected thing in special situations, regardless of what . . . private beliefs may be. Opinions adopted through compliance should be expressed only when the person's behavior is observable by the influencing agent." Thus, a persuader's matching of a particular goal to systems of interviewee beliefs, attitudes, and values becomes quite dependent on the continued presence of the persuader or some similar persuasive agent. Compliance-based social influence often is transitory unless the relationship from which it springs is continually sustained. For example, some influence might be based on compliance in an ongoing superior–subordinate relationship, but when a new boss is hired, the employee wouldn't necessarily act the same way. Used car salespersons could not rely on compliance-based influence because theirs is rarely a persistent relationship with buyers.

By **identification**, Kelman means that people sometimes adopt the behaviors or preferences of other people to associate themselves with those they find desirable. Advertisers and marketers have long understood that a "me, too" or a "bandwagon" aspect motivates some consumer behavior to mimic. The fashion industry operates on this principle, and it is the reason why some people wouldn't be caught dead wearing a generic brand of jeans, even when they realize intellectually that "their" designer brand may have been assembled in the same factory, by the same workers, using the same materials, as a cheaper brand they disdain. Still, identification operates at even a deeper level, Kelman believes. We change or modify a wide range of beliefs and attitudes based on how they will be perceived by others defined as important in our lives. In a sense, identification describes our desire to see a self not only psychologically but also socially—but socially in terms of a specific other people (or groups) with whom we want to identify.

Although compliance and identification are similar in some respects (e.g., the actual content of the idea or adopted behavior is not the primary stimulus for the influence), identification differs because its influence applies in both public and private situations, whereas compliant influence is usually shown only in public or in the physical presence of influential others. Identification works as long as the person's professional or social role relative to the other is operative. For example, a car salesperson's ordinary role relative to you applies only when you're buying a car. But if she or he establishes a strong enough bond with you, later sending you Christmas cards and calling you occasionally to see how the car is working out, perhaps you'll redefine or expand the role. Instead of being merely "the person who sold you that car," she or he becomes—perhaps—"your friend who also works for a car dealership." That new role—friend—persists, and your identification with the salesperson as a friend has probably changed some of your attitudes toward, for example, the car models she or he sells. The relationship frames the product, through identification.

The deepest and most lasting process of social influence, Kelman says, is **internalization**, which develops when people discover that proposed changes genuinely fit their value systems and embrace them as a result. Although Kelman believes that internalization is often understood as rational or systematic attempts at persuasion, it doesn't necessarily operate that way. The key to internalization is that the person influenced integrates the new changes (e.g., beliefs or behaviors) into a larger pattern of values so that it makes intuitive sense.

A persuasive interviewer who seeks a lasting influence will value the process of internalization most highly, because it doesn't depend on the continued presence (Kelman calls it "surveillance") of the influencer, nor does it depend on a particular defined, continuing role definition between communicators. Internalization relies on interviewer and interviewee working mutually to match what is useful about the suggested change with what is important to the prospective adopter. These links can't be decided beforehand and told to the adopter; they must be explored together through skillful and sensitive give-and-take of interviewing. (See Box 10.2 for how two professionals describe this

---

Box 10.2

Interviewers in Action   *Maxine Dennis and Susan Fu*

Maxine Dennis

My job involves meeting with professors and discussing their textbook needs with them. Prentice-Hall publishes a huge variety of texts, so chances are we've got a book that will fit the professor's needs in either a lower- or higher-level course. My basic objective is to get a commitment from the professor that she or he will use a Prentice-Hall textbook in a particular course for the coming semester. Professors are smart people; they appreciate open, honest communication without any pushiness. And because most major textbooks are revised every three years or so, I am interested in cultivating long-term relationships with my professor-customers so that they will consider future editions of the books I sell. I listen carefully to their evaluations of the current editions of Prentice-Hall and competing texts and communicate their comments and critiques to our home office marketing and acquisitions staff people. To us, the professors' input is just as important as their choice of books, and I try to make sure that they realize this.

Source: R. Anderson (1995, p. 155)

Susan Fu

In a marketing class I took, I remember the lecture about professional selling. Like many people, I thought you had to be a smooth talker and quick on your feet to be a salesperson. But my professor stressed that the best salespeople are first and foremost excellent listeners who are sincerely interested in helping the customer fill a need or solve a problem. That sounded like something I could do well, so, after graduating in 1983 with a B.S. in Computer Science and a minor in Business, I interviewed with several firms for technical sales positions and decided to go with Hewlett-Packard as a staff sales representative. . . . On any one day, I may be on face-to-face customer calls all day, or hosting customers for a demo at our sales office, attending a trade show to generate leads, or prospecting by phone.

Source: R. Anderson (1995, p. 313)

process of exploration.) Let's try an example well suited to student decisions to attend a college or university: the interaction between a college recruitment representative and a student with her or his parents. Here are some particularly useful topics and questions for exploring a potential match:

- *Learning styles and personal preferences.* (For example: "What have been your most successful educational experiences in the past?" "Is it important to you that teachers get to know you personally?")

- *Long-term goals.* (For example: "Have you decided to focus on any particular career track, as of now?" "What do you see yourself doing in 10 or 15 years?"

- *Short-term goals.* (For example: "You played in the band in high school; is it important for you to keep up with your music, even though you're shooting for a career in international diplomacy?" "It sounds like you want to continue to play soccer. Do I have that right?")

- *Other drawbacks or advantages.* (For example: "Lexington is a surprisingly cosmopolitan city, but we've found that some students prefer a more urban environment. Have you thought about this question?" "We haven't discussed tuition, which looks pretty steep on paper. I was wondering if you'd already researched what percentage of students get significant scholarship assistance.")

Through such inquiries, the recruiter is not actively attempting to convince the student to enroll. Instead, the responses will provide information to help both parties clarify and assess what decision is right for them. The interviewer wants to suggest matches that make sense to the student and parents in meeting their goals. Indeed, the recruiter probably recognizes that it would not be in the school's best interest to lure a student who later feels misled or manipulated.

Choosing

In persuasive situations, all communicators are participants, but at the choosing stage, the primary attention turns to one person—the interviewee, for whom a change or a new decision is being suggested. Sales professionals refer to him or her as "the prospect" to emphasize the contingent nature of decision making. Despite your best persuasive efforts to represent your idea, yourself, or your product accurately, and despite a seemingly close fit between someone's desires and the changes you suggest, the final choice is not yours. Both parties typically frame a persuasive interview as leading toward the goal of choice, and in some ways, that choice will be necessarily one sided.

The best strategies for the choice stage of persuasive interviewing are the ones implemented by the sales representative we met in the story that opens our chapter (Remember? She represented a cabinet manufacturing and installation company):

- *Signal the choice.* (For example: "Well, that's about all I know. What I've tried to do is to help you clarify the decision. The ball's where it should be—in your court.")

- *Invite further questions, comments, or issues.* (For example: "If you have any other thoughts about this, or if questions come up that we didn't cover, feel free to call me any time, even at home. OK?")

- *Retreat to give the other person(s) room to decide.* In some programs encouraging dialogue among competing groups, for example, facilitators have found that they can't force dialogue to occur, but that if a space is created in which it can develop, with appropriate invitation it often will develop. Choices operate by the same principle. If you're the interviewer, you hope for a commitment that remains influential—one that's internalized, in Kelman's terms. (For example: "I'm going to leave you alone now. Take as long as you want." Or, "I'll tell you what. I've got another call to make today. Talk it over between the two of you and get back to me in a day or so. If I don't hear, should I take that as a no?)

The choice stage presents many ethical dilemmas for persuaders. Unscrupulous persuaders are tempted to use overt or covert pressure to limit others' choices, or intentionally misrepresent the choices themselves. Before participating in persuasive interviews, communicators should anticipate ethical points arising in typical influence attempts. Doing so helps ensure a realistic approach to the kinds of challenges facing both interviewer and interviewee. Almost by definition, attempts at persuasion, especially if the stakes are high, are fraught with opportunities for ethical compromises, among them that the end justifies the means.

Brown and Keller (1979; Keller & Brown, 1968) have described an especially fruitful choice-based ethic of interpersonal persuasion. Their ideas can help teach you (1) how to frame your invitations for choice making of others; (2) how to listen to influence attempts when you are the interviewee; and, in anticipation of our next stage of persuasive interviewing, (3) how to speak and listen during the all-important closing stage, whether you are interviewer or interviewee.

Approaches to interpersonal ethics frequently emphasize the content of what is said and focus on the accuracy, truthfulness, and strategic effects of words. Brown and Keller (1979, Chapter 11) take a more relational approach. Their interpersonal ethic "is more concerned with the attitude a speaker and a listener show toward each other" (p. 276). More specifically, "As communication is ethical to the extent that it accepts B's responses; it is unethical to the extent that it is hostile to B's responses, or in some way tries to subjugate B. The ethic can best be put to a test when A discovers that B rejects the message A is sending" (p. 276).

Brown and Keller's **interpersonal ethic,** based on the criterion of whether one's messages maintain or expand others' choices, has clear and demanding implications for persuaders (see Box 10.3).

Closing

Claire Kerr, a division major account manager with the NCR Corporation, describes the simplicity of what she calls her "selling style": "I find that presentations are most effective when they are clear, concise, and simple. The same rules apply to the close. Customers respect salespeople who are direct and come straight to the point. I don't use 'ulterior motive' closes, play games, or use tricks" (quoted in R. Anderson, 1995, p. 191). Her statement indicates the special meaning most sales professionals have in mind for this final stage of the persuasive interviewing process.

Box 10.3

Reminders *Implications of the Interpersonal Ethic for Persuasive Interviewers*

Brown and Keller suggest the following implications for persuaders (paraphrased here except as noted):

- "Whatever enhances the basic freedom of response . . . is more ethical; whatever either overtly or covertly attacks that energy is less ethical" (p. 279).

- Persuaders help create and maintain the full and free range of listener choices relevant to the topic at hand. Internalized attitude change happens when people realize that they've considered all reasonable options and chosen the best one (for them) on appropriate grounds.

- Persuaders know that lies, misrepresentations, distortions, and strategic omissions tend to limit the choices of listeners and are, in most cases, unethical.

- Persuaders have to be as willing *not* to make the sale, or *not* to convince the listener, as to sell or convince others. This does not mean that advocates for positions shouldn't care whether they are successful. It only means that when listeners choose otherwise, persuaders accept the result

as something that might be better for the listeners, from the listeners' frame of reference.

- Persuaders avoid assuming they can be certain about what is right or good for other people. They can be strongly committed but cannot get inside someone else's life to know what is best for them.

- Persuaders who limit the choices of others are behaving unethically toward themselves, as well. Brown and Keller write that coercive communication is not just unethical because it injures the other person, but "it is unethical for the user also, because it gradually cuts a person off from his or her own creative growth. The constant effort to exercise power over others makes one increasingly dependent on getting defeated responses from others. If the desired responses are not forthcoming, the effort to persuade must be redoubled. And this preoccupation closes the door to one's own personal development."

Source: Brown & Keller (1979, pp. 277–278)

A **close** is not just the finishing touches on the interview, or the last few things an interviewer has to say. It becomes the moment of decision itself, the psychological turf where persons commit to something. Although it's often assumed to be the time when the "prospect," the "customer," or the "decision maker" commits, it's also when the persuader commits to something—a fact missed in many discussions of selling and persuasion. Let's return to our opening anecdote and the author's account:

The representative from the home improvement company called us back with extra information about the availability of the wood we wanted, as she'd promised. She asked when we'd like to meet again with her, suggesting the final phase of her pragmatic relationship with us, the close. Then, presumably, she would have initiated a discussion of placing the order and getting the job started. By that time, however, we had changed our minds about the work, and we still live contentedly with the old cabinets. It was not the outcome she had wished for, but it was still a clarification and an unambiguous decision. Some might think she failed with us. No. She achieved for herself and her company a qualified success. She had earned our trust and goodwill to warrant a call to her firm if we needed remodeling work in the future. She also earned stories like this one, which have been told to several friends, complete with the name of the firm.

Noted leadership consultant Paul Hersey (1988), in his book *Selling: A Behavioral Science Approach,* emphasizes the importance of closing:

> Our studies indicate that the behavior of top performers is significantly different than that of average performers when closing sales. Average performers tend to become pushy and directive. But top performers recognize customer apprehension and engage in supportive behaviors instead. By enhancing the match between customer needs and product benefits, involving the customer in the decision process, and acknowledging customer objections as needs, top performers significantly increase the probability of a successful close. (p. 189)

Hersey's statement connects the closing stage to earlier responsibilities of persuaders in the stages we've labeled discovering, matching, and choosing. He justifiably emphasizes the sensitivity to listeners' cues and the ability to support the listeners' needs rather than only satisfying their own. By being creatively and ethically unselfish, then, many persuasive interviewers not only satisfy ethical criteria but also actually increase their productivity and the quality of their communication. Instead of framing what they do as meeting their own needs, successful sellers and other persuaders define themselves as "problem solvers attempting to meet other people's needs, wants, and desires" (Woodward & Denton, 1988, p. 313).

Box 10.4 presents five basic suggestions for successful closing, as described by an experienced salesman. Bob Kimball (1994) doesn't dwell on ethical concerns in this

---

Box 10.4

Reminders   *Kimball's Five Steps for Closing*

1. Ask questions and get the prospect to talk to identify needs, problems, and buying motives.

2. Confirm understanding with a reflective summary statement.

3. Present features of your product and translate those features into benefits which address the prospect's attendant buying motives.

4. Ask questions to have the customer confirm the benefits. It *may be* true if *you* say it. It *is* true if *they* say it.

5. Make a request for action.

Source: Kimball (1994, p. 171)

list and consequently could be perceived as advocating gimmicks. However, each of the suggestions builds on a valid insight on persuasion research, which, if blended with ethical sensitivity, could be as helpful for interviewee as for interviewer. Note, too, how the close recapitulates the overall process of persuasive interviewing in a microcosm.

There are lots of cute names for closing strategies. Some of these strategies are clearly ethical and mutually helpful, whereas others cut some ethical corners. For example, in what Anderson (1995, pp. 321–329) calls the **assumptive close**, the seller or interviewer assumes that the respondent has already agreed to buy the product or service, thereby making it much more difficult for a "no" response. A **standing-room-only close** implies, if not states, that the respondent must act now or forever lose the opportunity to get something he or she wants (even if this isn't true). These are examples of ethically suspect tricks of the trade that responsible communicators should not have to rely on. Other closing strategies make much better ethical sense. A persuader using a **testimonial close** simply attempts to seal a deal with a strong supportive statement about the product or service, preferably a statement from someone the respondent finds highly credible or similar to himself or herself in relevant details. A **choice close** reminds the respondent of available options and lays them out clearly so that a decision seems like a clearer, cleaner step (some unethical persuaders, of course, might artificially or unfairly limit the choices to trick listeners). A **counterbalance close** seeks to counter a respondent's valid objection with an equally valid or greater advantage that offsets the objection, and then opens discussion of decision making.

Try not to think of closing as a series of behavioral strategies that practitioners know will work for them and that they try to package for others. Sometimes they'll work for you and sometimes they won't. It's not the technique that really works (or not) but you, speaking effectively with a unique audience that responds uniquely. You're better advised to learn basic principles of persuasion and ethics, and then blend what you know with your own style within your own contexts. Staying alert to consequences and feedback will help you refine your style; maybe someday, you'll be able to recount hundreds of your own stories. However, persuasive interviewing is a process that is too dialogically based to be reduced to a list of gimmicks. Once you recognize that, however, it doesn't hurt to listen to others' stories.

We have used the sales interview encounter as a prototype, or representative example, of the problems involved in persuasive interviewing. Although only some of us become salespeople by trade, everyone attempts to sell things occasionally. We not only sell cars and old bikes, but we also persuade others every day at work to give our ideas a careful hearing. Familiarity with basic concepts of persuasive interviewing will also help you, as a respondent or interviewee, to understand the approaches of professional persuaders you'll encounter at a motivational speakers' seminar, your local furniture store, or the muffler repair shop.

The traditional sales encounter is far from the only kind of persuasive interview. In "Beyond the Basics" we survey briefly two other contexts for interviewing and point out their distinctive characteristics and skills.

Trying Out Your Skills

Assume you have just been hired by your college or university as a "student ambassador" whose responsibility is to give campus tours to prospective students and parents. Such students are expected to be guides, information providers, representatives, and persuaders. Consider carefully:

• What do you think the dean of student affairs would tell you your primary goal should be? What do you think it should be?

• Which specific skills described in this chapter would most help you accomplish this job?

• Which aspects of your personality would be your biggest assets in this job? Your biggest drawbacks?

• Every campus wants to put its best foot forward. Yet prospective students and their parents often

ask difficult questions that will test your responsiveness and Brown and Keller's *interpersonal ethic* (see earlier discussion). *Hypothetical instance:* Assuming you know that student assistants in residence halls often look the other way on alcohol violations, and that several instances of alleged date rape have been largely ignored by campus officials, how do you react to this parent's inquiry: "Martha wants to come here, but we'll be 500 miles away. How would you describe the safety of dorm life and the disciplinary system?" Write out the best response you could give. Is it persuasive? Is it fair to the parent? To the school? To Martha? Does it meet the criterion of the interpersonal ethic? If so, how? If not, why not?

Beyond the Basics

Negotiation Interviews

Management consultant Gerald Nierenberg (1987) understands the pervasiveness of negotiation in everyday life: "Nothing could be simpler in definition or broader in scope" than this process, he believes. In fact, "every desire that demands satisfaction—and every need to be met—is at least potentially an occasion for people to initiate the negotiating process. Whenever people exchange ideas with the intention of changing relationships, whenever they confer for agreement, they are negotiating" (p. 4). Parents negotiate about how to raise children. Employees negotiate pay raises. Union and management representatives negotiate collective bargaining agreements. Reporters and celebrities negotiate to determine how the results of their interviews will be presented, and in which forum.

Therefore, we define a **negotiation interview** as any situation in which parties (1) are expected to communicate intentionally and persuasively, (2) are expected to function as both interviewer and interviewee, and (3) are expected to seek agreement or consensus.

After examining each of these stipulations, we will look at negotiation in terms of interviewing's three basic processes—speaking, listening, and framing.

- *Parties are expected to communicate intentionally and persuasively.* In negotiation contexts, there are "sides," even if there is no overt conflict. One person's (or group's) goals and background are presumed to be different from another's, and this is often seen as a positive, energizing force behind negotiations. Successful negotiators value differences and seek to exploit them to discover new forms of effective relationship. In other words, negotiators are not afraid of conflict.

- *Parties are expected to be both interviewers and interviewees.* In most interview forms, the roles of interviewer and interviewee are at least relatively fixed. People generally know whose responsibility it is to initiate communication, who should take responsibility for the context, whose information is the focal point for interaction, who asks the questions, and who determines when the interaction has run its course. In negotiations, each party takes responsibility for asking questions, and each must answer them as well. In mixed-role interview situations, some logistical decisions of negotiators become complicated: Who schedules the meeting? Who speaks the most? Who requests behavior changes first? How long does the meeting last? These and other questions seldom have automatic or easy answers for negotiation sessions.

- *Parties are expected to seek agreement or consensus.* In daily life, interactions normally do not need to lead to a mutually agreed-on conclusion, but negotiation does feature this expectation. The basis for negotiating is a presumed relationship of some sort from which neither party wishes to escape. In anticipating future communication, then, one or both parties advocate a different form of relation.

Speaking

A prime goal of negotiation is to establish a *win–win outcome* in which each side can see that it has gained from the encounter. When one party wins (e.g., monetary, relational, physical, or psychological rewards) but the other clearly loses, the resulting bitterness can undercut even normal communication functions. Although not all suggestions or demands can be settled in a win–win manner, negotiators owe it to each other to explore the possibility of such thinking.

Speech in negotiation interviews, therefore, best contributes to success if it has the following characteristics:

- *Clear statements of position.* No one will continue a dialogue with you for long unless you're at least somewhat clear about what you want and why you're talking with this specific other person about it.

- *Contingent language.* Some words cut off replies from others. For example, "I know you're going to profit from exploiting these workers" is an accusation that leaves no "breathing room" for the other person. He or she can be expected to react defensively in a way that could close off future possibilities for talk. Much better (though less rhetorically flashy) would be something like, "I think the workers' predicament shouldn't lead to extra profits for the company."

- *Invitational language in questioning.* Techniques or tactics are not automatically effective in human relationships. Yet in the midst of emotional negotiations, nervous communicators often forget one of the most effective of communication "openers," which is to ask simply, "What do you think?" There are many versions of "What do you think?" questions: "How does that sound to you?" "Would your departments be able to live with that policy?" "I've talked a long time now; I want to make sure I get your point, too." Invitational language is not a language of weakness, as some people suppose, but a language of strength. Only people who feel secure in their own communication styles develop the strength to invite others to contribute significantly.

- *Assertive language.* Inviting other opinions does not mean you have to agree with them. Remember that *assertiveness* is defined as the ability to stand up for your own rights while also respecting the rights of others. If you habitually speak clearly, contingently, and invitationally, then those times when you have to state positions strongly will be particularly effective. Otherwise, an unswervingly aggressive stance will dilute others' listening just as much as a persistent acquiescence ("I'll accept anything") will.

Listening

The goal of listening in negotiation contexts is to create opportunities for others to influence you, giving yourself the information and insight needed to make sound decisions. Consider these characteristics of listening:

- *Using reflective perception checks.* Active listening skills are crucial in negotiation, and one especially helpful demonstration of them is the reflective *perception check*: "I want to make sure I heard your suggestion correctly. I think you said that instead of my current office I could count on one of those two around the corner, provided that Jane retires this year." Use as many of the other person's words as you remember, but phrase your understanding in your own words too (it's your perception, after all). Active listening doesn't parrot the other's words but simply attempts to verify your understanding of them. Effective perception checks give your negotiation partners a chance to hear their thoughts in relational context and gives them the further opportunity to correct misperceptions.

- *Holding your fire.* Complicated negotiations often turn emotional, and the potential for blaming others is high. While listening, remind yourself constantly that (1) the other person may not mean to offend you by his or her language choices; (2) you can wait to get more information before concluding that a particular phrase or strategy is meant as a put-down or an insult; (3) you can almost always respond appropriately to a negative comment later, as well; and (4) you can compartmentalize your reactions. In other words, even though the other person offends you, your overall goal may be better achieved by not making the offense an overriding issue. Listen to it to be sure, but interpret it in a broader context.

- *Corralling your biases.* We all have biases that interfere with effective, contextualized, and accurate listening. Get to know your own biases and how they might work against you. If necessary, interview friends, coworkers, and acquaintances about your listening biases before entering a significant negotiation. Negotiations aren't battles, but they often feel so much like them that it's hard to analyze your own behavior calmly within the stress of the conversation.

Framing

The goal of framing in negotiation is to understand the potential for agreement in a way that is fair both to you and to other negotiators. Although inferences are inevitable, your understanding should be based on available facts and must be realistic. Consider the following characteristics of framing:

- *Avoidance of mind reading.* Remind yourself constantly that you can know what other negotiators are saying and doing (if you train yourself to pay close enough attention), but you can't know their thoughts or motives.

- *Awareness of attribution processes.* Try to avoid what communication and social psychology researchers call the *fundamental attribution error*—assuming that others act negatively, for example, as a result of some fundamental human characteristic ("who they really are," for instance) whereas your own actions are attributable to situational factors (e.g., "anyone would have acted this way if they'd been in my situation"). It's too easy to assume that your boss fired your friend because the boss is a vindictive person, but when you fired someone, it was obviously because your employee's poor performance gave you no choice. As far as we know, people act all the time as a result of a mix of personal and contextual factors.

- *Benefit-of-the-doubt thinking.* Remind yourself that your frames for another's behavior probably won't mesh with theirs. Actively imagine what their frames *might* be. Don't leap to the conclusion that someone won't understand you, or won't believe you, or won't concede a point to you. Despite your inability (we presume) to mind read, you can creatively imagine multiple frames that might be persuasive for the other person.

Some situations demand a special form of negotiation interviewing called **mediation,** in which a third-party communicator enters especially difficult negotiations. According to one research team, "Mediation may be defined as the intervention of a neutral third party who, intervening at the request of the parties, assists the parties to find a resolution that fills their needs" (Evarts, Greenstone, Kirkpatrick, & Leviton, 1983, p. 2). The mediator's persuasive goal is to uncover the areas of potential agreement that are obscured by the conflict or mistrust separating participants. At first, neither side may be convinced that anything other than their own demands or goals would be acceptable, but effective interviewing by non-ego-involved mediators can create surprisingly fertile common ground. One of the most effective dispute-resolution experts in the field of communication was John (Sam) Keltner. See Box 10.5 for his suggestions on how mediators should try to function in their roles as persuasive interviewers.

Box 10.5

Reminders *Keltner's Functions of Mediators*

1. You do not make decisions for the parties.

2. Your job is to facilitate an agreement by the parties themselves.

3. You must be as unbiased as possible.

4. Both sides must accept your services as a third party without prejudice.

5. Your function is to persuade both parties to change positions in order to reach agreement.

6. You must keep control of communication between the parties during the mediation session(s).

7. You should help both parties find rationalizations that will justify an agreement.

8. You must know the right time to advance suggestions, bring people together, or separate them.

9. You must call the joint sessions and arrange for time, place, and facilities.

Source: Keltner (1987, p. 34)

Interrogation/Advocacy Interviews

The public now seems intensely curious about, if not obsessed by, the legal system, as demonstrated by the recent Michael Jackson trial, the disappearance of a young woman in Aruba, and other prominent, often tragic cases. The popularity of Court TV and the various *Law and Order* programs on network television also reflects our fascination with legal drama. TV has given us a close-up look at interrogation tactics of police and prosecutors. In addition, we've been exposed to the controversial methods used by our government to question "enemy combatants" imprisoned at Guantanamo, Abu Ghraib, and at alleged sites where U.S.-held prisoners had been interrogated by foreign representatives.

Officer Tom O'Connor, who has taught police how to interview suspects and witnesses since 1974 and has served as an advisor in interviewing practices for the International Association of Chiefs of Police, recounts how police interviewing has changed in recent years: "When I went to the academy, there was no 'style' of interviewing. . . . We kicked ass. I can remember hangin' 'em over the pipes and beatin' 'em with nightsticks. I can remember hangin' 'em out the window. Things have changed considerably." Now, he tells his trainees without regret, "90–98 percent of an investigation is *interviews*." He adds, "This is the area in the criminal-justice system where we are the weakest. It's the most critical aspect, and it's the area where we have the least amount of training." O'Connor, as described in a published profile, stresses "empathy . . . and establishing a rapport with the criminal and giving him, or her, a reason to confess to you. No hostile badgering, no mechanical 'Jack Webb' questioning or one-note Columbo flourishes. Just observant, thorough interviewing—with empathy. O'Connor knows the method sounds sweet. He knows a lot of cops (especially the ones who've tried once and blown it) think he's nuts. But he also knows it works" (Batz, 1999, p. 22). What works—so much for the myth that coercion is the only way to get the truth.

Most citizens will be interviewed in either a law enforcement or a courtroom context at some point in their lives. The interviewer will either be an interrogator (e.g., a police officer) or an advocate for a particular point of view (e.g., a lawyer). Although their purposes vary, interrogators and advocates are both persuasive interviewers. Respondents might be suspects, witnesses to an event, litigants in a lawsuit, members of a family under suspicion of child abuse, or just people who have talked with those who fit these categories.

An interviewer's principal purpose in an **interrogation interview** is to persuade an interviewee to disclose relevant facts fully, even when full disclosure might not be in his or her best interest. To succeed, the skillful interrogator combines the sensitive insight of counselors and social workers with the critical and analytical evaluations of a selection interviewer. Interrogators concentrate on questions, sometimes fairly aggressive or intrusive ones, to draw out what needs to be discovered. Consistent with O'Connor's practical experience, researcher J. T. Dillon (1990) advocates "human relations" qualities that help interrogators do their jobs, such as empathy, congruence, respect, and sincere concern for the other person. However, the overriding quality he emphasizes is "non-judgmental response" (p. 76). If an interviewer already seems to have made up his or her mind, what is the point of talking if you're the interviewee? Further, a variety of military and law enforcement experts (Budiansky, 2005; Yeschke, 2003) also suggest that, despite popular misconceptions, even most prisoners will be more likely to disclose information to a questioner they believe to be fair, open, and willing to be persuaded; they are less likely to cooperate after torture or rough psychological treatment. A legendary example of the effective interrogator-interviewer was World War II Marine interrogator Sherwood Moran, who followed a remarkably practical philosophy: "Know their language, know their culture, and treat the captured enemy as a human being" (Budiansky, 2005, p. 32).

Despite the obvious advantages of talking to a fair-minded, decent person, respondents to interrogations may refuse to talk or talk deceptively. They may want to hide legal or social guilt, or stay loyal to a political cause. They may withhold or conceal embarrassing facts about themselves. They may be trying to protect a loved one. Beyond obstacles like these, interrogators contend with the following problems, paraphrased here from Dillon (1990, pp. 78–79). Even sincere respondents might:

- Have faulty perception.
- Not remember the issue in question.
- Not understand what is being asked or requested.
- Believe the information requested is not relevant or important enough to mention.
- Consider the issue "too distasteful, frightening, or taboo" to discuss.
- Be affected unconsciously by bias or prejudice.

Dillon says interviewees, in fact, may "agreeably be telling you what you seem to want to know. They confirm your view without your even realizing it. Then you think you have discovered the facts about this matter. But nothing has been discovered, certainly no facts" (p. 79).

Interrogators often must dig deeper. Dillon and other experts suggest (p. 80) patience is one key. Interrogators should not rush the process by imposing artificial time limits or by failing to pause significantly after questions and answers. A second key is persistence: Interrogators may ask about a fact or issue, get one kind of answer, and then later in the interview return to the same basic inquiry by phrasing the question differently. They want to see if the response differs the second (or the third) time around. A characteristic of persistence is usually a nonaccusatory questioning tone, something consistent with a nonjudgmental attitude. Interrogations follow, as do other interview forms, a sequence, although variations are common. Questioners often start with nonthreatening topics to relax informants and let them adapt as best as they can to a threatening situation. Before direct and specific questioning begins, interviewers tend to ask what Dillon (1990, p. 85) calls a **free narrative question**—one that lets the interviewee create a free-form personal account, with no structuring from the questioner. For example, a police officer might ask, "When you were standing on the corner, a white car pulled up. Could you tell me what happened then?"

After a series of probing direct questions to ascertain the degree of truth or falsity in the free narrative, the questioner attempts to cross-check the earlier answers, asking often about seemingly unrelated details to test the consistency of an interviewee. To close the questioning, the interviewer often will ask a "what else?" question similar to the "sixth W" we advocated for journalists in an Chapter 6. "Is there anything else you'd like me to know?" a questioner might ask. Finally, experienced interrogators understand that after the tape recorder has been turned off and the notebook closed, interviewees often relax and provide useful and informative nonverbal cues, not to mention offhand comments that enhance previous answers.

In the course of a session, interrogators often must confront others' attempts to deceive. How do they do this, especially when studies consistently show how poorly most of us detect deception? A vast social science literature has developed around just this task, and we refer you to more specific sources in nonverbal communication for more precise information about the ambiguities of reliable deception detection (Burgoon & Buller, 2003). In many cases, in fact, the dividing line between truth and deceit is not as clear as most people assume. Here we paraphrase and expand on what psychologist Aldart Vrij (2000, pp. 322–324) recommends. To encounter deception in interviews, we can:

- Remain appropriately suspicious and alert to others' self-interest (automatic and complete trust is rarely justified in interview situations).

- Continue asking questions persistently if lying is suspected (many liars cannot sustain their stories over time without internal contradiction).

- Avoid revealing too much about what we understand to be accurate accounts (thus giving liars more clues about how to shape their stories).

- Ensure that we're well informed about the general topics liars are discussing (increasing the chances that deceptive statements will be obvious).
- Observe and listen carefully to nonverbal and verbal behavior as clues, always careful to note their particular contexts (there are no individual "smoking gun" behaviors, such as "gaze aversion" or "fidgeting," that are always-reliable deception cues).

Vrij and other experts caution that interviewers should not leap to conclusions too rapidly about deception and nonverbal action. He writes: "Suppose that a suspect stops fidgeting as soon as the suspect starts mentioning an alibi. You may well conclude on the basis of this behavior that something is going on. But it is impossible to say what exactly is going on. It is possible that the suspect stops fidgeting because of lying and is afraid of getting caught. But the suspect may also stop doing this when innocent, because of fear that the police will believe that fidgeting indicates lying" (p. 323).

When you are being interrogated, remind yourself that to the extent you remain calm, focused, and accurate, you will probably avoid some of the danger signs interviewers are taught to look for. Today's interrogators are less likely to play games of physical intimidation (threats, aggressive invasion of personal space), but are more likely to "Shut up and listen—let 'em talk," as police interviewing trainer Tom O'Connor says, expecting that a witness "will ramble until it jogs his memory," and "let[ting] a suspect talk herself into a corner" (Batz, 1999, p. 22).

Lawyers examining witnesses in a courtroom are concerned with similar issues of interviewing. However, lawyers operate under constraints imposed by the official presence of onlookers (a jury, a gallery of observers, sometimes even cameras broadcasting or taping trial proceedings). In addition, courtroom participants must act within a set of rules that govern their communication; for example, certain kinds of leading questions are permissible in a cross-examination of a witness that are not permitted during direct questioning. Legal systems throughout the world recognize that truth can emerge from the systematic clash of positions and proofs, with each side presented by an advocate whose responsibility is to point out the flaws in the other side's reasoning. Interviews conducted within courtrooms, then, often take the form of demonstrations of reasoning, employing a mixture of planning and spontaneity. Observers may be frustrated with the outcome of a given legal case, or with the ethical cross-pressures exerted on interviewers and interviewees who are asked to become advocates, but the overall system of legal advocacy has been proven remarkably effective at producing just results.

Advocacy interviewers, in court for example, frame their questions and comments to encourage listeners toward a certain conclusion. By the nature of the context, they are systematically and predictably biased, in other words. Yet the courtroom advocate need not become negative, as an acquaintance of the famed lawyer Rufus Choate recalled in this account:

> Commenting once on the cross-examination of a certain eminent counsellor at the Boston Bar with decided disapprobation, Choate said, "This man goes at a witness in such a way that he inevitably gets the jury all on the side of the witness. I do not," he added, "think that is a good plan." His own plan was far more wary, intelligent, and circumspect. He had a profound knowledge of human nature, of the springs of human action, of the thoughts of human hearts. To get at these and make them patent

to the jury, he would ask only a few telling questions—a very few questions, but generally, every one of them was fired point blank and hit the mark. His motto was: "Never cross-examine any more than is absolutely necessary. If you don't break your witness, he breaks you." His whole style of address to the occupants of the witness stand was soothing, kind, and reassuring. When he came down heavily to crush a witness, it was with a calm, resolute decision, but no asperity—nothing curt, nothing tart. (quoted in Wellman, 1948, pp. 209–210)

The Choate anecdote helps clarify two major differences between normal interrogation and courtroom advocacy. The interrogator seeks accurate accounts without necessarily judging them as for or against external positions, whereas an advocate elicits accounts to prove or disprove positions in a two-sided conflict; the interrogator is patient and persistent, ideally taking as much time as necessary for the interview, whereas the advocate searches for the pointedly dramatic moments in which a question or answer can best support an argument. The advocate interviewer must use responses to help frame a specific interpretation for a listening judge or jury, while recognizing, as Choate's observer reminds us, that too much hostility will stimulate listeners to react psychologically against an overly aggressive questioner.

Making Your Decision

- Some observers have argued that it is unrealistic to think salespersons and other persuasive interviewers should actively promote the freedom of choice of prospective buyers and other interviewees. Ethics demands only (the argument goes) that sales personnel not blatantly lie, but beyond that, everyone knows that their intention is to mislead. In this view, stretching the truth, making extravagant claims, intentionally distracting interviewees from registering serious objections, and withholding the negatives of one's product or service are all accepted and expected tactics. We have taken the position in this chapter that promoting freedom of choice is not only ethical but also realistic. What, in your opinion, is the best argument against our position? The best argument for it?

- Negotiation and sales interviews are not necessarily separate interviewing experiences, as you know from the last time you haggled with a used car dealer. Negotiation, however, is an uncomfortable experience for many buyers. One expert in sales research notes that a current trend in the marketplace, therefore, is an upswing in "fixed price dealers" and the increased use of "buying representatives" such as Autovantage, Autobytel, and Consumers Car Club (R. Anderson, 1996). Survey your communication skills and interests introspectively. What would you gain from avoidance of negotiation? What would you lose? To what extent would your distaste for negotiated buying (if present) be alleviated by more confidence in your skill in interpersonal interviewing?

- Many lawyers are told in law school they should never ask a witness a question to which they don't already know the answer. Yet early in this book we suggested that genuine questions are those to which you don't already know the answers and that effective interviewers should always be willing to be surprised. Are these positions contradictory? If so, how and why?

Summary

The major idea of this chapter can be stated simply: Although "interviewing" sometimes suggests a neutral pursuit of information, understanding persuasion—as a potent non-neutral force—can be crucial for interviewers and interviewees.

We begin by introducing persuasion as an interpersonal activity that occurs in various types of interviews as we constantly attempt to change others' beliefs, attitudes, and values. Even if we weren't trying to do so, such changes would happen anyway as a result of natural processes of human accommodation and adjustment. Some people, however, think that intentionally trying to change another's mind is an attempt to manipulate and serve the persuader's interests but not their own. Manipulation happens. Yet persuasion in interviewing can also be conceived as a helping relationship, a mutual process in which a persuader seeks to help the other person achieve his or her own desired goals for the mutual benefit of persuader and the one to be persuaded. This, we suggest, is clearly the rationale of ethical sales attempts, but it is the basis of other persuasive forms as well.

Using personal sales as a prototypical persuasive situation, we have developed a five-stage model for interviewers: opening, discovery, matching, choice, and closing. Communication skills are discussed in their cultural and ethical contexts, with the goal of explaining why persuasion is so complex.

In "Beyond the Basics" we look at two additional important forms of persuasive interviews that involve millions of people each year: negotiation (including mediation) and interrogation or advocacy interviews. Although these are distinct from each other, and the two of them considered together have different premises than sales interviews, the basic principles of persuasion operate in them all.

The Interview Bookshelf

On the possibilities of being fooled by persuaders:

Crossen, C. (1994). *Tainted truth: The manipulation of fact in America*. New York: Simon & Schuster.

Read this book if you think you're too sophisticated to fall for the sleazy tricks of manipulative people. Most of us even fall for shoddy reasoning that persuaders don't intend to be manipulative.

On a general appreciation of persuasion research, principles, and practices:

Simons, H. W. (2002). *Persuasion in society*. Thousand Oaks, CA: Sage.

Many excellent books on persuasion research and practice are available. This recent text foregrounds issues of framing and reframing in ways you will recognize from your study of interviewing.

On a basic approach to sales interviewing:

Anderson, R. (1995). *Essentials* of *personal selling: The new professionalism*. Englewood Cliffs, NJ: Prentice-Hall.

Rolph Anderson has provided a lively mix of stories, research, and strategies. Among the strengths of the book is its exceptional readability and its many excellent first-person accounts of interviewing.

On different forms of persuasive interviewing:

Keltner, J. W (1987). *Mediation: Toward a civilized system of dispute resolution.* Annandale, VA: Speech Communication Association.

Nierenberg, G. I. (1987). *Fundamentals of negotiating.* New York: Perennial Library.

Yeschke, C. L. (2003). *The art of investigative interviewing: A human approach to testimonial evidence.* Oxford, UK: Butterworth-Heinemann.

Wellman, F. L. (1948). *The art of cross-examination* (4th ed.). Garden City, NY: Garden City Books.

We could have included an even greater variety of suggestions here. Keltner, in the vanguard of teachers who developed academically respectable and humane interpersonal communication classes in the 1960s and 1970s, later turned his attention to consulting and dispute resolution. His book is an impressively practical account of how to help others come to agreement by using interviewing skills. Nierenberg's book is widely cited in organizational life. He helps you understand why rigid cause-and-effect thinking is not always helpful for communicators trying to reconcile different positions. Yeschke addresses the myth that interrogators have to be either threateningly nasty or deceptively syrupy to obtain useful information. Wellman's treatise on cross-examination is also a classic of sorts, but we should warn you that it's dated and veers toward racist and sexist stereotypes in many examples. His appreciation of the power of language in the legal profession, however, is otherwise impressive.

Chapter Eleven

Interviews in Helping Professions

After reading this chapter,
you should be able to

- Define essential elements of a helping philosophy

- Communicate effectively as interviewer or interviewee in diagnostic, therapeutic, and counseling interviews

- Recognize when sincere attempts to help can turn unhelpful

- Demonstrate effective empathy verbally and nonverbally

- Discuss the ethical implications of helping contexts

As a resident in psychiatry at Massachusetts General Hospital in Boston, Dr. Robert Coles (1989) came under the spell of Dr. Alfred O. Ludwig, an "affable old gent," but a "bit slow on the draw, perhaps over the hill" (p. 5). Hard of hearing, Dr. Ludwig forced Coles to speak up and speak loudly, and the older man spent far more time listening to his younger colleague than "teaching" him.

At first, Coles resisted Ludwig's unusual methods of patient care. Over time, though, Dr. Ludwig's ideas about listening and learning from patients inspired Coles to encourage patients to tell *their* stories, and Coles discovered the important role communication played in medicine. "The people who come to see us bring us their stories," said Dr. Ludwig, whose words followed Coles over three decades of practice. "They hope they tell them well enough so that we understand the truth of their lives. They hope we know how to interpret their stories correctly" (p. 7).

Despite Dr. Ludwig's sage advice, Coles found himself conflicted. "Was I to 'treat,' or was I to listen carefully, record faithfully, comprehend as fully as possible?" (p. 25). The answer seems obvious: To treat someone who wants or needs help means listening, recording, and comprehending. The interview, then, becomes a means

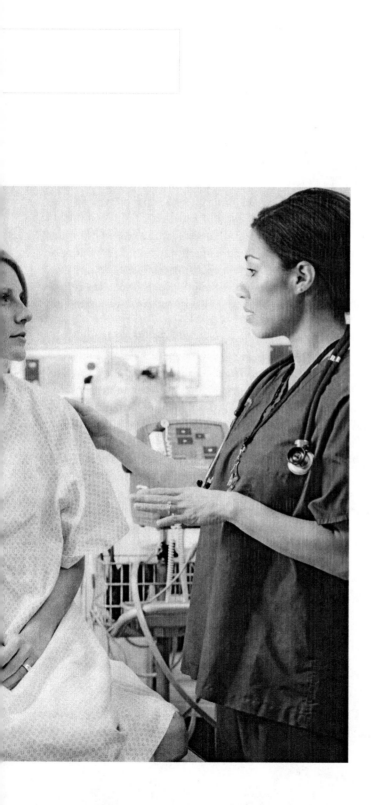

"Sacks, you're unique," the [doctor] said. "I've never heard anything like this from a patient before."

"I can't be unique," I said, with anger, and rising panic. "I must be constituted the same way as everyone else! Perhaps (my anger was getting the better of me now), perhaps you don't listen to what patients say, perhaps you're not interested in the experiences they have." "No, indeed, I can't waste time with 'experiences' like this. I'm a practical man, I have work to do."

"Experience aside, then, the leg doesn't work." "That's not my business."

"Then whose business is it? . . ."

—Oliver Sacks,
A Leg to Stand On

of helping. All interviews should to help in some way. However, when people suffer from illness, anxiety, or other conditions that they cannot deal with alone, the interview can be an essential meeting full of hope and new possibilities.

A helping interview begins with a period of discovery—a diagnostic stage that gathers information about facts and feelings, in a mutual spirit if possible. From there, the interview can develop into a form of treatment. Its therapeutic applications are broad—a professional athlete copes with Hodgkin's disease, a middle-aged executive feels mired in depression, a teenager is haunted by memories of sexual abuse.

This chapter obviously cannot fully describe medicine, psychotherapy, psychiatric social work, marriage and family counseling, or other helping professions. Professionals complete years of study, often earning a license to practice. Helping, though, is a human impulse, not just a professional task, and each of us is asked often to lend a hand, or sympathetic ear, perhaps to ease someone's disappointment or despair. We don't need a license to encourage positive communication. But don't overreach. A familiarity with skills of the helping interview will not make someone a therapist, nor does it necessarily provide reliable insight into people's inner dilemmas. Empathic listening, for example, often has therapeutic effects, but thoughtful professional helpers understand that it takes extensive knowledge and training to understand the consequences of empathy in a given situation.

"The Basics" begins by summarizing what helping means. From there, we explore ways to ask, listen, and learn as part of *diagnosis* in a wide range of helping contexts, including medical interaction between patients and health care personnel. The section on using interviews in various *therapy* settings is increasingly relevant in contemporary culture where therapeutic communication is widely discussed even in popular media. The helping role of *counseling,* which is sometimes seen as a form of therapy, focuses on everyday problems more often addressed by interpersonal communication skills rather than by extensive mental or behavioral treatment. "Beyond the Basics" explores those times when attempts to help may create unintentional limitations for people. Finally, we highlight crucial ethical aspects of helping interviews.

The interview isn't a wonder drug of conversational cure but a functional form of communication with its own limitations. Other helping methods, including medication, exercise, and diet, may build on what the interview accomplishes, but the interview does enable helpers to participate with patients, clients, or acquaintances together in determining what's wrong and what to do about it.

The Basics

Helping: Philosophy, Attitude, and Activities

In the opening quotation of this chapter, bestselling author and physician Oliver Sacks suggests that each of us has unique stories and experiences, but all of us share a desire to be understood, especially when we are in need of help. In most cultures, write Pedersen and Ivey (1993), interviewing or counseling "is the most frequently used method for supervising and/or managing people" (p. 88). Interviewing not only helps persons across many cultures to cope, but also to define the nature of self—although how it does so varies significantly from culture to culture. Not surprisingly, when people confront interpersonal crises of coping ("I think I'm always being so helpful around the dorm, but everybody just ignores me"), they usually turn to the interviewing process for help.

No single ideal approach to helping exists, and effective interview styles vary as well. Not everyone needs to show a "warm and fuzzy" style. An experienced surgeon with a curt, clinical style of communication might not be warm, but she's your first choice for a gallbladder operation. A blunt therapist might succeed in cutting through the defenses of a difficult client, where his partner's softer empathic style fails. Many models can guide helping interviews. A helper, for example, might apply different yet complementary styles of confrontation and empathy when conditions warrant.

Philosophy, Attitudes

Increasingly, helping professionals attempt to work in partnership with patients and clients. In medicine, for example, a **patient-centered philosophy** appeals to some practitioners as ultimately more helpful than disease-centered and doctor-centered philosophies (Jong & Berg, 2002; Murphy & Dillon, 2002; Okun, 2001, Sommers-Flanagan & Sommers-Flanagan, 2002; Stewart et al., 1995). Patient-centered medicine, for example, is characterized by concern for the whole person, with the doctor and medical staff exploring both the disease and the *illness experience* (R. Smith, 2002). A patient who suffered a life-changing heart attack and bypass surgery comes to his doctor upset and fearful that he can no longer participate in outdoor sports with the family. A disease-centered response might be to interpret the man's feelings as depression and prescribe medication; a doctor-centered response might be to interpret his feelings as normal and dismiss them. A patient-centered response acknowledges the man's experiences thoroughly, recognizing that unique feelings count. As Stewart and her colleagues (1995) note: "Dealing with this patient's *experience of illness* . . . may be helpful by alleviating fears, correcting misconceptions, encouraging him to discuss his discouragement, or simply by 'being there' and caring what happens to him" (p. 41). The patient-centered method encourages helpers to let people help themselves toward a solution.

The patient-centered model and similar strategies of helping were influenced by the **client-centered therapy** developed by psychotherapist Carl Rogers (1961; Thorne, 2003), a term he later expanded to the *person-centered approach.* Although he labeled concepts somewhat differently at various points in his career, his work focused on three basic processes. Rogers and others (e.g., Carkhuff, 1969; Muldary, 1983) identified three **facilitative conditions** effective helpers create with clients: respect, genuineness, and empathy.

- *Respect,* which Rogers sometimes called *positive regard* or *acceptance,* means recognizing that every human possesses inherent dignity and is worthy of being valued. In helping, it's important to accept the value of the whole person without reservations. A helper doesn't need to approve of all that the helpee does or represents. Many times the other's behavior is so dangerous, bizarre, or antisocial that it can't be encouraged or held in respect; but persons are more than the sum of their behaviors, ailments, or shortsightedness. This distinction, according to many helpers in social work, psychology, and counseling, is crucial for a helping philosophy.

- *Genuineness,* which Rogers sometimes called *congruence,* means that helping professionals try to match inner feelings and attitudes with what they say or do in the relationship. This doesn't mean that helpers blurt out everything they think or feel indiscriminately. Instead, it means that people who consistently pretend, mask their persistent feelings, or deceptively exploit others show disrespect. Phony admiration for an interview partner, for example, isn't genuinely helpful in the long run.

- *Empathy* is a form of caring that's consistent with, and supports, attitudes of respect and genuineness. Empathizers, as we've seen in earlier chapters, do their best to understand the experiences of another person—to see the world through the other's perspective—while still recognizing that it's impossible to merge completely with this other perspective or understand it fully.

People in need don't always seek out a doctor, therapist, or counselor for help. An everyday example illustrates two contrasting styles regarding the attitude of respect.

SON: I don't know how I'm going to get all these assignments in on time for my teacher. He's so demanding.

FATHER: Well, what do you expect me to do about it? You've had all term to get them done. Don't blame others for your lack of self-discipline.

SON: I'm not asking you to do anything about it. What makes you think I'd ask you, anyway? I was just talkin'. No reason.

FATHER: All right, then. Get to work.

Although the father may be technically "right," things deteriorate. Consider another approach:

SON: I don't know how I'm going to get all these assignments in on time for my teacher. He's so demanding.

FATHER: Sounds like you're really pressured and worried. More than last year, that's for sure.

SON: Yeah. I blew the whole first half of the semester. I knew this was a tough

Class, but I just went ahead and dug a deep hole for myself anyway.

FATHER: It's like you've got to do 15 weeks' work in the next 6 or 7?

SON: Uh huh. I can do it. I've just got to get to work.

Any fictionalized dialogue can be concocted to produce a predetermined result, so be wary about this one. However, Rogers's research suggested these facilitative conditions can improve everyday life. Rogers believed that people are constantly looking for ways to take responsibility for themselves, and to grow as communicators, but they're occasionally thwarted. The facilitative conditions or attitudes are his attempts to remove these blocks in a relationship, so the other person can glimpse new possibilities.

The first exchange has a tone that appeals to many people who like to think of themselves as straight talkers. It fails the practicality test however. The father doesn't empathize with his son's feelings and experience but, instead, replies with an inference (the son didn't say he was blaming the teacher) and a judgment. The son defends himself with a counteraccusation, and the problem itself is not addressed; it's unlikely he will, in fact, now "get to work." In the second exchange, the father withholds judgment, reacts simply by showing he's listening, and thereby opens a door that lets the son explore his own problem. The logic of the conversation encourages responsibility on both sides, and the son himself decides to work on the class projects. Rogers didn't claim that people always should withhold criticism of others. If help is the goal, though, listeners should demonstrate accurate understanding first. Actually, it's only after a conversation in which we feel understood well by another real person that we are really open to their feedback. This insight supports the skills of active listening and perception checking suggested by many interviewing specialists, described throughout this book.

Rogers was realistic enough to know that the act of unselfish giving sometimes might mean taking the personally difficult path of assertive intervention if that is in the interviewee's best interests. He didn't advocate passive acceptance of all behavior. We can accept *people* but still might express our problems with their *behaviors*. In fact, it's consistent with the condition of genuineness for the helping interviewer to express persistent negative feelings and perhaps even to confront directly. You might imagine, therefore, that the father in the second example will be better able to share his discomfort or irritation with the student's behavior.

Helping Activities

Many kinds of professionals help others in the ways we've described. The lines separating mental health, social service, and medical functions aren't always precise, and roles often intersect. So, rather than distinguish among helping roles by job description, we examine three common helping activities that involve interviews: diagnosis, therapy, and counseling.

- *Diagnosis*: Help-oriented interviewers need to figure out where and how help is needed and to determine tentatively the best course of action. The **diagnostic interview** is a focused inquiry into symptoms, conditions, and feelings, for the purposes of assessing the current status of a situation and determining what can be done to provide help.

- *Therapy*: In some cases, the interview becomes the heart of therapy. Certainly, therapeutic uses of the interview support other means of treatment. Therapy often unfolds over time, as interviewer and interviewee remove layers of defenses and buried feelings in a series of interviews. The **therapeutic interview** assists in systematically modifying someone's behavior, thinking, or psychological state. Obviously, diagnosis is an integral first step in an ongoing therapeutic process. We make the distinction here merely to distinguish between basic types of interviews, not to suggest that diagnosis doesn't contribute to therapeutic communication.

- *Counseling*: Counseling, too, relies heavily on effective communication but differs from therapy in scope and focus. The **counseling interview** helps people by discussing advice and strategies that could assist them in making sound decisions or working out problems in their lives. Counseling also includes related helping activities known as "coaching" or "mentoring." Therapists usually need licenses to practice because they deal, at times, with life-and-death situations; counselors are typically well trained but generally don't continue to work with someone exhibiting serious psychological or behavior problems. If they do encounter something outside their expertise, they'll refer a client to a specialist.

Helping activities aren't mutually exclusive, of course. Diagnosis might lead to follow-up counseling or therapy, and therapy might lead to follow-up counseling. Sometimes books or speakers use *therapy* and *counseling* interchangeably because they use similar methods. In some cases, all three interview activities combine to accomplish helpful results.

Diagnostic Interviews

"The diagnostic interview is the main assessment tool in mental health care" (Bogels, 1999, p. 3), and it could hardly be otherwise in the related professions of medicine and social service. Thorough diagnosis can isolate a general problem area and begin to define possible responses to it. Diagnosis is complex because people sometimes do not understand how to reveal the details of their lives, will refuse to reveal essential aspects of a problem, or will implicitly pressure the helping professional to "*do* something" about an experienced problem before the information gathering is complete (Zoppi & Epstein, 2001, p. 357). The diagnostic stage means opening issues that the interviewee may fear exploring. The person needing help might be torn by ambivalent urges to disclose or deny. "Do I want to know what's wrong? Can I face it? Do I have the strength to confront this problem?" Such concerns might require attention before an accurate and helpful diagnosis can be made. On the other hand, diagnosis might be strikingly obvious, and merely the opportunity to talk about a problem with a caring listener leads toward a resolution. Broadly defined as it is, diagnosis plays a role in nearly all helping circumstances, although some therapists and counselors, following Rogers (1961), believe that too many helpers overemphasize a precisely controlled diagnosis while underestimating the value of an accepting, empathic relationship. For example, "physicians tend to use methods of questioning that serve to allow them to keep directing the flow of the interview, rather than allowing patients to speak freely," concludes one overview of recent research (Zoppi & Epstein, 2001, pp. 357–358).

Successful diagnostic interviewers address several particularly complex problems that could undermine the helping process.

Comfort Zone

Visit a doctor's office or counselor's suite and you'll often see wall art, aquariums, comfortable furniture, soft lighting, or soothing color schemes. The comfort zone of helping sets the stage for productive talk but can never guarantee it. When people make the decision to go outside themselves to seek help with a problem, they may be anxious or embarrassed already and don't need additional threats or discomforts. A welcoming environment is a *framing* factor, in effect reassuring an interviewee that "This is a private place where I can feel secure."

Preparation

Time set aside for the interview shouldn't be used to collect basic information that could be obtained easily in other ways. In many interviews, particularly in a doctor's office, patients fill out a medical history questionnaire. Occasionally, an assistant conducts a screening interview to ensure that the problem can be addressed effectively later by another professional. Questionnaires and other means of collecting intake data probably won't lead directly to a diagnosis, but they help to rule out problems or they provide clues, such as a family history of depression or behavioral pattern of avoiding conflict.

Perceptions

People seeking help can fear they'll appear needy or even pathetic to listeners. Ask yourself how perceptions influence your assessment of others. Do you think a classmate with a model-thin figure is disgustingly self-absorbed? Do you think someone who can't stop smoking doesn't care about living or about how this action affects his or her family? Do you find yourself afraid of close contact with an AIDS patient? Do you avoid extended conversations with clients from other cultures whose language patterns are unfamiliar to you (see Ivey & Ivey, 2002)? Think of perceptions based on biases and stereotypes that lead you to judge or classify people. Who are you seeing and how are you seeing them? Then consider how those perceptions might affect you in a role as helper. Helpers who fail to offer respect and acceptance taint the diagnosis and, therefore, everything that follows.

Getting Started

If participants are meeting for the first time, introductions are crucial, including perhaps a brief exchange of names and small talk. Typically, the diagnostic interview begins without much delay.

Going to a doctor or lawyer with a vague but troubling problem usually stimulates a rapid-fire series of questions at first. One study (Branch, Levinson, & Platt, 1996) led to the estimate that the typical physician conducts over 100,000 clinical interviews in a career but never gets much beyond what they call the "Find it—Tell What to Do model" (p. 69). To "find it" (the problem), the interviewer asks and the interviewee answers. The relationship of many helping situations centers on diagnosis; because this is seen as an interview motivated by efficiency, the questioning emphasizes collecting facts rather than eliciting stories or experiences. It's also a relationship that reinforces the professional's position of authority and control.

Diagnosing is a matter of sensitive perception, so helpers must not dominate the interview. They focus on learning core background information with which they can set up their touchstone question: "How can I help?" From there, questions can and should invite the patient's involvement:

INTERVIEWER: Tell me what you want to talk about. Let me know how you feel as we go along.

Starting out can be the hardest part. Don't expect the interviewee to initiate conversation, although some will. However, don't expect reticence either. No matter how it begins, a diagnostic interview will take a while to unfold. Many medical interviewers (Branch et al., 1996) suggest starting with a broad or global question to give your partner plenty of rhetorical room to move. Robert Smith (1996) writes that the open-ended beginning question should follow "immediately after summarizing the agenda" and could sound something like, "'Given what you've told me, how are you doing (. . . how are things going)?' One links the question to the agenda to start developing the story" (p. 33). Thus, the so-called funnel sequencing of questions seems broadly applicable to diagnostic interviewing. Here's a simple, common way to start:

INTERVIEWER: How are you feeling today?

INTERVIEWEE: Oh, OK, I suppose. Maybe a little down these days.

The patient (or other helped person) who accepts this invitation is establishing an agenda that the helper is wise to note carefully. Branch and colleagues (1996) suggest that the interviewer probe to specify this agenda early in the interview and double-check to be sure the full agenda is laid out. At times, people will start with describing a single problem, only to be cut off by the assumption that it is the only thing on their minds. Doctors and other diagnosticians are wise to ask, in several different forms, the "what else?" clearinghouse question: "What else has been bothering you about this?" "Is there anything else I should know about it?" "Are there even more side effects that you haven't described yet?" These kinds of questions will frame the problem not as a single issue, waiting to be treated, but as a difficult, multifaceted experience.

In the following list, Putnam (1996, p. 78) summarizes relevant research about the medical interview with geriatric patients. The strategies suggested here also apply to other diagnostic interviewing, especially in the "getting started" stages of discovery:

- Convince the patient that you are interested in him or her, that is, that you want him or her as a customer.
- Establish the patient's agenda by eliciting his or her major concerns.
- Elicit the patient's specific requests.
- Elicit the patient's understanding of the illness.
- Look for clues of the patient's feelings and elicit them if appropriate.
- Elicit appropriate background information about the patient, that is, the social setting of the illness.
- Build and use the relationship with the patient to carry out the data-gathering and treatment functions of the interview.
- Give information after first finding out what the patient knows and then filling in the gaps.
- Finally, find out what the patient expects for treatment and negotiate a plan.

Similar advice about diagnostic interviewing comes from Lehrman's (1995) experience as a lawyer interviewing clients who have suffered domestic violence:

First, use everyday language.
Second, ask specific questions.
Third, assume nothing. (p. 39)

Trying Out Your Skills

"Become a playwright for a brief exercise. Write the dialogue for a scene in which a woman of 85, basically healthy but concerned lately about shortness of breath, brings this complaint to her doctor. You can make up details and even give the characters names, if you like. Beyond that, try to make the doctor's diagnostic interviewing style reflect the specific approaches discussed by Putnam (1996) and Rogers's (1961) general facilitative conditions of respect, genuineness, and empathy. (Note: You don't have to extend the conversation fully to the doctor's actual diagnosis; after 15 or 20 back-and-forth turns, simply close the scene with an ellipsis [. . .] to indicate that more would be said. Make sure your dialogue adequately shows the doctor's effective listening style.)

- Be prepared to share your hypothetical interview scripts with the class or with another student for feedback. Your teacher might ask you to work in groups to dramatize one or more of the scenes by acting them out.

- Be prepared to show specifically where the doctor's interviewing style demonstrates effective listening and the doctor's willingness to learn from the patient.

- Analyze how the doctor's interviewing style could be improved even further by different listening strategies.

Because she works with women who, for self-protection, might deny the events at some level, or perhaps even blame themselves, specificity is crucial after the initial rapport:

> Most clients will tell you their story twice: once to pour out their pain and a second time to answer your legal questions. As you listen, try to picture every detail in your mind. Be careful not to assume anything. For example, if your client says, "He hit me in the face," you may assume he slapped her across her cheek. But she did not say that; perhaps he punched her in the nose.
>
> Consider yourself a film director who is planning a movie of the violent incident. Every detail must be accurate. To find out exactly what took place, you might ask: Where was he? Where were you? How close to you was he? What did he do? How did he do it? How hard did he hit you? With his open hand or fist? What did it feel like? What did he say? What were his exact words? Were you afraid? Did he use a weapon? How big was the knife? Was anything in the room broken? Were there others present or within range to see or hear? What did they do? (p. 39)

Listening

Listening competence affects every interview. In contexts of helping, though, careless listening is especially damaging—there is too much at stake (see Box 11.1). Listening conscientiously and attentively comes with the territory of helping. In diagnostic interviews, though, it's especially important to listen *interpretively:* What is being said and what does it mean? Two levels of interpretive listening apply in helping interviews—content-oriented listening and feeling-oriented listening.

Box 11.1

Interviewers in Action   *Norman Cousins and Mark Cohen*

Editor and medical school professor Norman Cousins, author of *The Healing Heart,* helped young medical students learn about the human side of treating patients. Cousins drew on his experiences as a heart attack patient in describing the communication style he believes creates an "environment of healing." Here is what patients want from their physicians beyond medical competence:

They want to be looked after and not just looked over. They want to be listened to. They want to feel they are in the doctor's thoughts. In short, patients are a vast collection of emotional needs.

Source: Cousins (1983, p. 136)

Pediatrician Mark Cohen describes how he used a combination of observation and interviewing to assess a child brought to him with developmental problems:

I looked at the mother. "What do you think about him?" I asked.

Her eyes brimmed with tears. "I think he might be autistic," she said.

"What does that mean to you?" I never assume a parent's level of understanding.

"Well, I really don't know. But I know there's something different about him." Parents of children with disabilities often have tremendous insight, a quality of knowledge we doctors ignore too often. . . .

"Yes, I think you're right," I said to his mother. "there's something different about the way your son's brain works. I think that he fits into the spectrum of autism, although he doesn't fit all the characteristics of autistic children. But there are things that we can do, and that you can do, to help him grow and develop and improve."

Source: M. Cohen (2006)

Listening for content focuses on statements of fact or belief, such as a teacher's remarks about his tension headaches:

INTERVIEWEE: These headaches are killing me. Nobody seems to be able to help me. I don't feel stressed out, but I guess I am. I'm really feeling down about it all.

His words represent facts, or content, including the statement about "feeling" down. We often use the word *feel* to introduce a statement of fact or belief. The facts of the headache sufferer's comments suggest follow-up questions and another round of interpretive listening.

Listening for feelings focuses on verbal or nonverbal indicators embedded in or implied by statements, such as an angry tone of voice or excessive hand-wringing. Interpreting what these signs mean requires additional exploration, often through active listening (see Chapter 3; see also Coulehan & Block, 1992, for an application of Rogers's categories of respect, genuineness, and empathy in the medical interview context). Active listening assists helpers in responding appropriately and nonjudgmentally.

INTERVIEWER: It sounds like you're frustrated by not finding a cause or solution to your headaches.

INTERVIEWEE: Well, yes. I haven't been able to lead a normal life since they started.

INTERVIEWER: Tell me about that, would you? I wonder when they did start.

Empathic listening remains crucial in diagnosis, allowing helpers to enter the patient's world of experience, where they're most likely to be able to build a collaborative diagnosis (see Box 11.2).

Asking and Answering

Our analysis of questioning (see Chapter 4) applies to most helping interviews. In particular, effective probes bring vague or abstract statements into sharper focus, such as

---

Box 11.2

Reminders   *Empathy and Attending Skills across Cultural Differences*

Sometimes in classes we hear people say, "I know exactly what you're going through" or "All people are basically the same." Although they are almost always well intentioned, both of these conclusions are demonstrably inaccurate. No one knows exactly what my pain has been, or yours. And although people everywhere share much in common, the cultural differences are far from superficial for communicators trying to understand each other. Empathizing is tough, but cross-cultural empathy is even tougher. Consider the following research findings:

> Derald Sue and David Sue (1990) describe differences in communication styles between Native Americans, Asian-Americans, Hispanics, European-Americans, and African-Americans to demonstrate the likelihood of miscommunication across these ethnic and racial boundaries when inadequate attending skills are used. They describe Native Americans as speaking more slowly and softly, using indirect gaze when listening or speaking, interjecting less and encouraging communication less, more likely to use silence or delayed auditory response, and using

a manner of expression that is more low-keyed and indirect. Asian-Americans and Hispanics are characterized as speaking softly, avoiding eye contact when listening or speaking to high-status persons, depending on similar rules, using moderate delay in verbal response, and being low-keyed and indirect. African-Americans are characterized as speaking with affect, using prolonged direct eye contact when speaking but less when listening, interrupting or turn-taking when they can, being quicker in verbal responses, and being affective and emotional in their interpersonal responses. European-Americans are characterized as speaking loudly and rapidly in a controlling manner, using greater eye contact when listening, using head nods and nonverbal markers a lot, being quick in responding, and being objective and task-oriented. The contrasting and conflicting patterns of communication are obvious. It is easy to see how the same behavior by different ethnic groups might lead them to misinterpret that behavior.

Source: Pedersen & Ivey (1993, p. 103; see also Sue & Sue, 1990)

someone saying she's feeling "blue" or "down." Helpers working toward diagnosis, then, probe for purposes of confirmation, verification, and specificity.

One problem looms especially large in diagnostic interviews—the leading question. Some people habitually defer to the judgment and suggestions of the professional; so when a doctor says, "You don't think your anxiety is anything to worry about, do you?" the patient's own assessment (or the ability to reach one) is undercut. Leading questions seriously impair an accurate diagnosis because people in need often want to be led or can't manage to resist a professional's suggestions.

During a diagnostic interview, questioning, listening, and interpretation (framing) ideally coalesce. Careful listening and note taking facilitate effective probes; effective probes facilitate interpretation, which, in turn, should to lead to tentative diagnosis. A helping professional may want to remind the interviewee several times that questions can be directed to the helper as well. Surely no experienced diagnostic interviewer assumes that the absence of verbalized questions means that *inner* questions aren't nagging the interviewee; questions that are invited sincerely are more likely to be voiced and, therefore, answered. Asking and answering should be a two-way proposition.

Keeping a Record

Memory fails us at times, particularly when we're trying to juggle dozens of activities and responsibilities every day. Taking notes aids recall and signals that we are listening as professionals, which is why good record keeping supports many kinds of interviews.

The purpose of note taking is not only to record the other person's comments, even though this is a surprisingly common misapprehension of beginning interviewers. It also involves a listener's personal reminders to follow up or strike out in another direction, prompted by a speaker's response. However, obsessing about note taking also undercuts interpretive listening. To reduce that possibility, interviewers often take skeletal notes but flesh out details with an audio recorder or research journal immediately after the diagnostic interview. That allows them to listen intently and reconstruct what transpired before memory dims.

Resistance

Diagnosis in the face of denial or defensiveness complicates an already challenging task. Respect, genuineness, and empathy on the helper's part alone may not be enough to break through resistance. Fear of the unknown often fuels denial, but signs of defensiveness might mean the helper's attitude needs fine-tuning. It might also, though, reflect the interviewee's natural feelings of loss of control over the situation. Without cooperation, the diagnosis cannot reflect partnership. Realistically, helpers cannot always achieve cooperation no matter how hard they try.

To Withhold or Disclose?

Health care professionals often debate about how much information should be shared with patients. The debate extends, to a lesser degree, into other areas of helping. Typically, it pits those favoring full disclosure and the patient's self-determination against those favoring strategic disclosure based on what the helper considers best for the patient. Indeed, some patients don't want to know everything the doctor knows. Ethical concerns arise, requiring that helpers define and prioritize both consequences and duties. The duty to tell the truth, especially when truth in human conditions is never exact, might result in more harm than good in the helper's ethical reckoning.

We cannot tell you what to do; we can stress that rigid and automatic adherence to only one system usually isn't good practice. The helper's presumption probably should lean toward disclosure, with any exceptions made for good reasons the helper might be able to identify; phrased in terms of classical ethics, this is a largely teleological and utilitarian position.

What Happens Next?

Closing a diagnostic interview certainly demands as much care as opening one, perhaps even more. The desired result, naturally enough, is closure, leaving no serious questions and concerns unanswered. Loose ends compound problems, stress, and doubt.

The closing is also a time of reassurance from the helper. Unless the diagnosis verifies that there is nothing to worry about, the patient or client will wonder what lies ahead. Normal uncertainties include, "How is this going to change me or my life?" and "What can I expect in terms of getting better?" Although reassurance has limits, especially if the prognosis looks grim, a sense of control and hope fortifies people who are experiencing problems; there's a restorative power in knowing something is being done. The mind can do wondrous things when called on. If all the answers aren't evident by the time the interview ends, at the very least there should be follow-up encouragement: "Let's meet again and see if the diagnosis bears out." Helpers aren't omniscient, but their words can be empowering. Box 11.3 reviews key steps in diagnostic interviewing.

Therapeutic Interviews

In nearly all kinds of therapy, the interview is a primary occasion for helping. It enables therapists to uncover feelings, search for meaning, and isolate root causes. Usually the interview ventures from shallow emotional waters into the depths of feelings and experiences. Unlike a diagnostic interview that might reach the conclusion that all's well, a therapy interview means there is already a defined problem that requires attention.

People facing therapy carry heavy baggage of heightened uncertainty, anger, fear, embarrassment, or a host of concerns associated with the idea of treatment; they also carry the problems that initiated the need for therapy in the first place. Therapists might have to identify and deal with the first kind of baggage before progressing to the primary problem. Some forms of *brief therapy,* however, are specifically not focused on identifying underlying problems but instead use interviews to teach clients behavioral solutions through questioning techniques (see deShazer, 1985).

Three types of therapy-based interviews predominate in the field: behavioral, cognitive, and psychotherapeutic. The **behavioral interview** centers on breaking a cycle of behavior, such as situational panic attacks. The **cognitive interview** attempts to accomplish change by replacing negative thoughts with rational thoughts. Generally, the goal is to break habits of irrational perception and help the client construct more socially and personally realistic approaches. The **psychotherapy interview,** a broader term that

Box 11.3

Reminders   *Diagnostic Interviews*

Interviewers

- *Help the interviewee establish an agenda early in the interview.* Open-ended questions help get the process started, but specifics must be probed for the agenda setting. Then other open-ended questions can bridge to further concerns.

- *Listen for stories.* Humans use narratives to define and redefine themselves. A helper generally shouldn't discourage storytelling out of a fear that stories are diversions. Far from superfluous, narratives contain evidence and implied explanations. Let them surface, then identify their inner logic.

- *Avoid a snap diagnosis.* Initial perceptions and instant reactions act powerfully on people, including helpers. Remind yourself to guard against letting potentially inaccurate, skewed perceptions affect your ability to listen and understand.

- *Be thorough.* An accurate diagnosis takes time and concentration. Thoroughness includes keeping written records of the interview for immediate and follow-up reference. Rushing through an interview invites errors of omission and commission.

- *Don't push.* As helper, you're an authority figure to many who seek your assistance. Let them speak fully and freely, and involve them in speculating about the diagnosis. Structuring and focusing the interview isn't the same as pushing it in a particular direction.

Interviewees

- *Prepare.* You do yourself no favor by passivity; take an active role in monitoring your life. If you're voluntarily seeking diagnostic help, prepare a list of questions you want answered. Do some homework as well. An online search engine will gather a collection of references and Web sites where you can educate yourself about what you're experiencing. Remember your responsibility to your own well-being.

- *Persist in getting answers.* No matter how busy or distracted a helper might appear to you, be sure he or she understands you. Repeat important points, and persist in seeking a response to your concerns. If necessary, request that the helper listen actively by paraphrasing your concerns. You'll be able to hear where the helper has misheard or misinterpreted your words, and you can correct them.

- *Listen actively, with notes.* Check your own perceptions and meanings with the interviewer, especially if they involve technical jargon, or if you're feeling so emotional about the conversation that listening is difficult. Stated simply, this helps the helper help you.

- *Talk over what lies ahead.* Don't suffer in silence. Explore possible futures with the helper; neither of you will ever be certain what is going to happen. So let the helper's resources help to guide—but not determine—your own assessment of options.

can include cognitive approaches, focuses on investigating and confronting disabling psychological conditions, such as deep-seated depression or anxiety. Each form of therapy moves ultimately toward a goal of change.

Our advice for diagnostic interviewing can be adapted to therapeutic sessions. A comfortable, inviting setting, adequate preparation, purposeful yet delicate questioning, and careful record keeping characterize therapeutic interviews. Several other characteristics of therapy sessions, however, merit special attention. They can help even nonprofessional and informal helpers sharpen their interviewing skills.

Knowledge for Helping

Helping through therapy begins with a crucial determination on the helper's part: Who is my patient or client? A patient-history questionnaire collects certain particulars—age, occupation, marital status, medications, alcohol use, and sleep patterns. It won't reflect habits and traits; nor will a history reveal fully all the dimensions of who the person is at that moment. We are different from situation to situation, exhibiting various facets of the same self.

Role for Helping: Who Is Responsible?

Alfred Benjamin (1974) creates a pragmatic context for the issue of responsibility in helping interviews. He tells the story of a stranger who once asked him for directions but, when given them, went the other way. "You're going in the wrong direction," Benjamin shouted. The man replied, "I know. I'm not quite ready yet" (p. 1). People who ask for help may not be "quite ready" to accept it. Trying out new skills implies inner responsibility.

The therapist also remains responsible. Entering into a therapy relationship obligates the helper like an oath or contract to provide the highest possible quality of dialogue and responsiveness. Backing out isn't professionally acceptable or ethical unless continuing the relationship risks harm. Therefore, the therapist cannot shirk responsibility when a case proves especially frustrating or upsetting. Psychotherapist Harlene Anderson (1997) describes how client and therapist bring different characteristics to the interview, each with responsibilities of expertise:

> A client brings expertise in the area of content: a client is the expert on his or her life experiences and what has brought that client into the therapy relationship. When clients are narrators of their stories, they are able to experience and recognize their own voices, power, and authority. A therapist brings expertise in the area of process: a therapist is the expert in engaging and participating with a client in a dialogical process of first-person story-telling. It is as if the roles of therapist and client were reversed: The client becomes the teacher. A therapist takes more of an "I am here to learn about you from you" stance. As one young client said to her student therapist when the therapist stumbled, made mistakes, misunderstood, and did not know, "When you are as famous as Freud, you will have to tell them that I was your teacher." (p. 95)

Therapeutic interviewers, she believes, need to approach clients as expert witnesses on their own lives and as persons with whom a dialogical relationship is possible.

In addition to fidelity to the client, the therapist assumes a responsibility to maintain a professional demeanor and appropriate distance. The vulnerability and needs of the interviewee should never be exploited by the therapist, a point developed more fully in "Beyond the Basics."

Stages of Therapy Interviews

Therapists usually can't specify a sequence of questions or topics for the therapeutic interview. They therefore conduct **nonscheduled interviews**, which means that specific questions and topics cannot be preset. The creativity and spontaneity of dialogue is the overriding criterion: "The structure of the therapy conversation is spontaneous, determined by moment-to-moment exchanges that zigzag and crisscross. . . . Hence, the conversation may appear disorganized to an outside observer or one who has a preconception of what the conversation should look like" (Anderson, 1997, p. 126). However, even though individual therapists don't predetermine structure, researchers studying actual transcripts have noticed three tendencies—facilitation, transition, and action.

The first of three common stages (Carkhuff; 1969; Gazda, Childers, & Walters, 1982) of therapeutic helping, *facilitation*, starts with the therapist typically trying to establish empathic rapport and build trust. In the *transition*, or exploratory, stage the therapist examines what is causing the problem, usually proceeding from surface feelings to underlying issues. An *action* stage usually involves talking through possible solutions or strategies for change. Rarely does a single session encompass all three stages; therapy often requires multiple sessions at each stage or step.

For therapy extending over several interviews, session openings can involve reviewing what happened at the previous session and what happened for the client in the meantime. Closings often preview the goals or subjects of the next interview. In therapy, a path toward progress might mean retracing steps and incrementally reaching toward a form of progress that is mutually defined. Ending a session usually will not be a time for closure as much as for reflection and reorientation.

Sensitivity

People in need want their immediate concerns addressed. They may raise their concerns, but if a professional dismisses them as insignificant or irrelevant, clients won't usually disagree, argue, or persist. Therapeutic interviewers must resolve to listen intently to clients, especially those who meekly submit when the therapist interprets or suggests. Let's say a patient (P) sounds willing but uncomfortable about taking an antidepressant medication, and that concern generates a well-meant but curt rebuttal from the therapist (T):

P: I guess taking medication is OK, but do you think I'll experience side effects?

T: Look, every medication has side effects. Your situation requires medication. We have to get you out of this depression; the side effects are secondary.

A sensitive therapist probes signs of disquiet, through active listening:

T: It sounds as if you're worried about side effects. Let's talk about them and see what we can do to allay any fears.

A sensitive attitude isn't enough. Sensitivity refers, as well, to the skill to invite the patient or client to disclose fears, and the skill to pick up on faint signals of concern, not just booming ones. Patience, too, is part of the helper's commitment to sensitivity.

Another facet of sensitivity in therapy interviews involves providing a sense of security for the client through a method sometimes called **holding** (Tolor, 1985). In therapy, holding isn't a physical act. The therapist, through supportive talk, communicates that the client can feel safe in sharing painful or shameful details. Holding serves a figurative, verbal purpose, somewhat like a reassuring hug from a father calms an upset child.

Counseling Interviews

In a world of confusing choices and complicated problems, people need knowledgeable, helpful advisers. High school students rely on guidance counselors for advice on everything from birth control to scholarships; job seekers unsure of what work best fits their attributes seek vocational counseling; managers and supervisors in companies must help employees resolve problems and grievances through counseling skills; and people with dependencies join organizations that help them break destructive habits. Counseling can occur in prisons, offices, homes, and locker rooms. People train in specific fields of counseling, or they study counseling as part of their career preparation, as clergy or teachers do. We all do some counseling, even without a license or special training. Remember that counseling tends to have different goals than therapy, although the line dividing them can be indistinct. Whereas therapy attempts to establish a relationship in which behavior change is the focus, most counselors try to help by enabling or facilitating the client's own decision making and feelings associated with self-worth and inner control.

Counseling Principles

Authorities on counseling (Litwack, Litwack, & Ballou, 1980) suggest that counselors orient themselves by a set of guiding principles as they venture into neighborhoods and other settings to deal with families and individuals with a diverse range of problems. Here we summarize three principles that stand out from their list (pp. 25–28):

Principle No. 1: There is no single, correct way to counsel. Using a standard formula in counseling won't succeed because of the differences among people even when they go through comparable problems, such as a crumbling marriage. One couple's marital problems aren't the same as another's. Every new case doesn't require reinventing one's counseling repertoire, but each case does require an individual assessment followed by an individualized approach.

Principle No. 2: It's not the counselor's role to preach, moralize, or impose values on clients. As professional helpers, counselors see behaviors that may strike them as wrong, reckless, or unwise. Satisfaction and fulfillment, like clothing, come in assorted shades and sizes. A counselor's expectations shouldn't be imposed on others, although counseling interviews often lead to new ways of thinking. Principle No. 3 offers a partial explanation.

Principle No. 3: Individuals possess inner resources to help themselves. In other words, the counselor shouldn't assume all the responsibility for a client, even though sorely tempted to take charge. Social workers, for example, frequently find themselves drawn into the plight of a family struggling to provide for themselves. Counselors, though, must resist the temptation to let others lean on them— unless, of course, there is the possibility of imminent danger if they fail to intervene to support a client.

Setting

Counseling occurs in sun-filled offices; it also occurs on windy street corners and creaky front porches, in nursing homes and classrooms. Sometimes counselors have no control over the environment. The counselor's case assignments, for example, may require monitoring and advising clients in their homes. Even when there is a choice of settings, there are trade-offs. Counseling someone in convenient, familiar surroundings also might mean constant interruptions from phone calls or crying children. An office, although private and quiet, remains an institutional, perhaps impersonal, place. Weighing advantages against disadvantages makes sense; often the need for privacy determines where to counsel.

The "Who" of Counseling

Conditions requiring a counselor's help often sweep couples or whole families into their vortex, as with incest or spousal abuse. When an individual suffers from a consuming problem, such as an addiction, it's likely family, friends, and associates suffer as well. In counseling terms, a spouse or parent might exhibit *codependency,* a psychological condition characterized by manipulation and control by the person with the addiction. Counselors look for signs that those other than the principal subject also need their help.

Being Aware of Differences

Astute counselors learn to account for differences in culture, age, health, and social status. Those who aren't astute stumble along, failing to understand what they see and hear, which, in turn, prevents them from providing effective assistance. In the worst instances, their lack of awareness hurts rather than helps clients. Increasingly, for example, counselors encounter elderly clients, whose behavior and attitudes can perplex and irritate someone who is uninformed and insensitive about their lives (see Box 11.4). A counselor cannot take people for granted or interpret them and their problems in terms of what the counselor defines as normal. To do so is a recipe for failure.

Crisis Intervention

A crisis tests the counselor's ability under fire because an acute condition demands direct help, not tomorrow or next week, but immediately. In an everyday sense, a flat tire on a 15-year-old family car, particularly for a laid-off, single parent on food stamps, feels like a "crisis." In most counselors' worlds, however, a crisis would be a more serious threat to an individual's physical or psychological safety, one that the individual alone cannot escape or solve without outside help.

A crisis isn't necessarily defined by an event; more often it's constituted by an individual's response or perception, which challenges the counselor to judge accurately when and when not to act. When a crisis happens at work, or when work performance is affected, an organizational representative may need to appraise the situation as important enough to intervene. The employee may be referred to an *employee assistance program,* treatment opportunities offered by many employers as part of a benefits package (see Chapter 9 for more on appraisal and intervention interviewing in organizations).

Some crises are so serious and immediate that telephone intervention *hotlines* have been established at counseling centers. These allow distressed people to call and engage a responsive and trained listener (usually a volunteer) at times when they have no one else to turn to. Fish (1990), building on the work of other researchers, emphasizes an

Box 11.4

Interviewers in Action   *Maria Vesperi*

In *City of Green Benches,* a study of the elderly in St. Petersburg, Florida, anthropologist Maria Vesperi observed outreach workers interviewing candidates for adult day care. One of these candidates was Mr. Dawson, 82, a large man who walked with the aid of a cane. As the outreach worker interviewed him, Mr. Dawson remained polite but guarded. The outreach worker tried to pin him down about a date for the center's minibus to pick him up, and Mr. Dawson evaded an answer and seemingly moved into irrelevant details about his life. The worker grew impatient and abruptly ended the session with, "Well, I'm sure. We'll look forward to seeing you starting Monday morning, OK?"

Vesperi followed her account of Mr. Dawson with this cogent point:

The Messrs. Dawson of this world seem doomed to be abandoned in mid-sentence. Others invariably find them tedious, difficult to follow, boring. At worst they are labeled "Wanderers," that is, incapable of remembering the original context of a conversation. I would suggest, however, the tendency to tune out this type of monologue is a central factor in our cultural construction of old age. Perhaps if we listen a little more closely, we can understand why Mr. Dawson and the well-meaning outreach worker failed to communicate."

Source: Vesperi (1985, p. 5)

appropriate model for counselors who talk with such anonymous callers by breaking a more complex model into four sequential stages. First, the counselor must simultaneously diagnose the seriousness and urgency of the call and begin to build a relationship of mutual trust with the caller. Second, the counselor helps the caller articulate the nature of the problem—what has stimulated the call, in other words. Third, the counselor helps the caller discuss and "mobilize" (Fish, 1990, p. 158) strengths and weaknesses. Fourth, the counselor and caller attempt to reach a plan of action based on the information shared. This complex blend of therapeutic communication and counseling approaches must be formulated in *minutes*. Often, experts have found (p. 159), callers place great emphasis on receiving clear information, confidently communicated, even when there is little time to develop sustained empathy. Hotline counselors must be able to provide information, not just be sympathetic people who understand that the callers are troubled.

An interpersonal crisis doesn't necessarily erupt with sobs or violence; it can build quietly and gradually. Skilled counselors look for certain signs, including a precipitating event, vulnerability, and loss of control. The *precipitating event* poses a hazard or threat—news of a child's death or a spousal beating. *Vulnerability* accounts for emotional or physical conditions. Does the precipitating event threaten to push someone over the brink of despair? Does the individual's history suggest a strength to endure or rebound? *Loss of control* manifests itself in different ways, such as a retreat into

Trying Out Your Skills

"Many college students have participated as volunteers in hotline or peer counseling programs. They have participated in intensive workshops designed to aid them in problem recognition, empathic listening, and mutual exploration of alternatives. Some of these programs focus on substance abuse, and others focus on suicide prevention, family violence, or other serious situations.

- In your class, help to form a panel of volunteers who each will agree to speak for five minutes on the nature of their workshop training. What skills were emphasized? What is the relationship between those skills and general interviewing skills applicable to other contexts?

- After these brief presentations, the class could ask questions about specific instances and examples of therapeutic communication in these hotline or peer counseling encounters. *Note:* All stories and accounts should focus on the panel participants' experiences and impressions, not on the specific crises and problems experienced by the helpees they talked with. *Include no details that could even remotely be associated with the real identities of callers.* Confidentiality is paramount in the helping professions.

depression or a plunge into anger. When a vulnerable person cannot maintain stability or equilibrium to cope with a perceived or real threat, she or he needs rescue.

Social Work

Teachers, police officers, and ministers engage in social work, although the brunt of those duties fall to a cadre of state and local government employees working for social service agencies. Depending on particular assignments and agencies, social workers supervise child-custody cases, assist unwed teenage mothers, oversee welfare programs, and monitor boarding homes, for example.

Social workers find interviews useful for familiar purposes: information collection, evaluation, and investigation. The distinguishing feature of the social-work interview, however, is its emphasis on the relationship between clients and their place in the social system and its demands. Social workers deal with cases assigned by their agencies, which explains why they're sometimes called *case workers*. The job varies, but primarily social workers either address how individuals relate to the system or how the system relates to individuals. For example, in one case, the social worker visits parents who have been accused of child abuse by an anonymous caller to a hotline. If the accusations bear out, the social system responds on behalf of the children.

In one observer's words (Kadushin, 1972), the social-work interview generally takes place "with troubled people or people in trouble" (p. 14). There are exceptions, of course. The focus on problems, though, is an escapable aspect of social work, and the parade of problems can drain anyone's energy and emotions. A social worker's assessment of situations that an interview intervention cannot resolve can lead to life-changing recommendations, such as taking a child away from parents or closing an assisted-living center and relocating a dozen frail residents. Interviewing skills cannot solve certain problems, but certainly such skills serve social workers in making crucial yet wise decisions.

Beyond the Basics

Is Help Sometimes Hurtful?

Ram Dass and Gorman's (1985) book on service to others offers this powerful warning: "Caught up in the models of the separate self . . . we end up diminishing one another. The more you think of yourself as a 'therapist,' the more pressure there is on someone to be a 'patient.' The more you identify as a 'philanthropist,' the more compelled someone feels to be a 'supplicant.' The more you see yourself as a 'helper,' the more need for people to play the passive 'helped.' You're buying into, even juicing up, precisely what people who are suffering want to be rid of limitation, dependency, helplessness, separateness" (p. 28). Here is yet another demonstration of a skills-plus approach. "Helping" itself is not contained in a skill or a role; in fact, the skill or role may be counterproductive if you use it too zealously or too selfishly. The basis of helping is not doing something for someone else, but actively respecting the other person's own potential for accomplishment (see Box 11.5).

Not everything done in the name of helping is helpful. Help, for example, can be too directive, leaving the helped little opportunity for self-determination. It involves the therapist offering a prescription for treatment, without the full participation of the client. Earlier we suggested how a directive, dominant approach can diminish a client's self-esteem and coping skills. Most practitioners avoid dominance, but realize that assertive intervention might be necessary occasionally to accomplish helpful outcomes.

Box 11.5

Reminders   *Notes on Nursing*

Florence Nightingale, whose legendary career practically defined nursing in many people's minds, offered insight into how not to help the sick. Her words apply to a variety of caregivers, not just nurses:

No mockery in the world is so hollow as the advice showered upon the sick. It is of no use for the sick to say anything, for what the adviser wants is, not to know the truth about the state of the patient, but to turn whatever the sick may say to the support of his own argument, set forth, it must be reported, without any inquiry whatsoever into the patient's real condition.

Source: Nightingale (1969, p. 101)

In the therapy context, a professional who means to help can also cross a comparably fuzzy line from empathy to sympathy, which jeopardizes both parties' ability to remain clearheaded about what to do. For example, a client could interpret a therapist's sympathy as a sign of pity, thus deepening the problems. Empathy's keen sensitivity to the other person's experience can morph through excessive sympathy to a presumption of judging the other's feelings, as if from a superior position. It's difficult for anyone to make hard choices when guided primarily by others' feelings of sympathy. Intense emotional involvement in the client's problems also takes its toll on the therapist, perhaps to the point of compromising the treatment of other clients.

A trusting, collaborative relationship between client and therapist enhances treatment. When the relationship tilts toward dependence, however, the helping potential diminishes. Unintentionally, a therapist becomes the center of a client's existence—guru and savior rolled into one. Ultimately, answers reside in the client or the collaborative relation of "constructive dependence" (Purtilo, 1990), not in the helper—despite the temptation to adopt what Barnlund (1990) calls a "quick and dirty" fix-it-up mentality. "The key to therapeutic communication" he wrote, is "the ability to engage individuals in liberating and cathartic interaction that enhances individuals' personal insight, vigor, problem-solving resolve, and satisfaction with themselves" (p. 31).

Ethics of Helping

Helpers face competing ethical choices of duty and consequence. Earlier, we explored the ethical dimensions of truthful disclosure and strategic withholding of information. Therapists confront dilemmas, too, over their ethical responsibilities to individual and society: Is it ethical to break a pledge of confidentiality if you have evidence that a client has committed a crime or might hurt someone? Does the seriousness of the crime matter? Are there times when you need to place your own emotional interests before the client's?

The following ethical concerns arise in helping contexts. As is often the case, absolute answers are hard to find in complex webs of feelings and goals. Knowing where ethics intersects with practice can, however, lead to informed, sensitive consideration of the right thing to do.

Protecting Privacy

Helping interviews depend on a climate of trust, and trust encourages disclosure from people hoping for help. Confidentiality and privacy mark nearly all helping situations. Privacy, on one level, means care in protecting records, notes, and other documents involving the patient or client from anyone without a legitimate need to know. Confidentiality means the helper's expressed commitment not to discuss cases with outsiders, unless, again, they have a need and right to know.

Fiduciary Responsibilities

Helpers often assume an obligation to help those who cannot help themselves. That's particularly true with clients in vulnerable positions because of physical or mental impediments. *Fiduciary* refers to holding something in trust; applied to helping contexts, fiduciary responsibilities resemble a guardianship, like a family member assigned or chosen to look after a child's welfare. Fiduciary responsibilities have limits. At a minimum, however, a helper must monitor the condition of those who can't help themselves and, if warranted, serve as an advocate to ensure their well-being.

Clear and Present Danger

Counselors deal with people with violent tempers and reckless tendencies. Despite the professional standard of respecting and protecting privacy, there may come a time when an interviewer must put the interests of others, or the safety of the client, ahead of wishes expressed by the client. The point isn't usually reached until the helper believes a clear and present danger exists to either the client or someone the client might hurt. What is "clear" and what is "present" will depend on circumstances and indicators that the helper must weigh, but if warning bells ring, the ethical helper cannot ignore them.

Safety Precautions

Safety precautions relate directly to the dictum guiding many health professionals: Do no harm. Helpers cannot ethically engage in unnecessarily risky experiments or endanger clients by methods of treatment. Using humans as guinea pigs was denounced long ago, but the practice perhaps continues in subtle ways if clients are not kept informed of the potential range of consequences in the relationship. In the interest of helping someone else who needs help, clients sometimes agree to try unconventional or experimental treatment, but in those instances, the helper should secure informed consent beforehand. A helper who embarks on a questionable course of treatment or therapy without the client's knowledge might say, "The ends justify the means." That can be an exercise in ethical rationalization.

Making Your Decision

Imagine someone saying to you, "I need help." It happens frequently enough in our lives, although the request isn't always so direct. Here's a situation that could call any of us:

> Over coffee in the university commons, a friend confides in you about her growing discomfort over a professor's behavior toward her. Although your friend doesn't act overtly concerned on the surface, you sense something more serious is bothering her. The fact that she initiated the conversation suggests to you she wants and needs your input.

What kind of listening and responding would be appropriate? Do you encourage her to get into particulars about the professor? How deeply do you delve? What do you do if she reveals apparent instances of sexual harassment but attempts to pledge you to confidentiality? How do you advise her, if at all? Where do your primary responsibilities lie?

Work through this scenario, incorporating what you know about helping interviews.

Beyond avoiding clearly unsafe practices, the helper's responsibility extends to every facet of care. Helpers must ask continuously: Is there any danger in what I'm doing, or not doing, in my relationship with the client? The ethics of helping demands diligent attention to safety considerations.

In most of the preceding situations, legal implications also arise. Unethical conduct can result in litigation against helpers. Carelessness or moral shortcuts, even when the helper is otherwise sincere, invite malpractice suits. Conscientious care remains the hallmark of the helping professional.

Summary

Helping others places great demands on professional therapists, doctors, teachers, supervisors, managers, and all those whose jobs and responsibilities include caregiving and counseling. The fragile condition of people who need outside help for their problems requires a deft and delicate touch in nearly all aspects of helping.

The interview serves helpers by facilitating communication, building rapport and trust, exploring problems, and collaborating in finding solutions. The techniques and principles generally associated with effective interviewing apply to helping interviews as well. Special circumstances, however, require heightened concentration and sensitivity by helpers as they listen and interpret what transpires in interviews and other communicative encounters.

Diagnosis begins many helping interventions, followed, when needed, by treatment, various forms of therapy, or counseling. Therapy involves people's intense emotions and psyches over time, and the helper's responsibilities increase with the severity and depth of problems. Counseling helps people deal with more everyday—but still serious—problems of family life and individual coping. Dealing with the problems of others can be stressful to helpers; they also run the risk of getting too involved in their clients' lives.

Ethical and legal issues further complicate the helper's work. In short, helpers face major challenges, but the rewards make the effort and complications worthwhile.

The Interview Bookshelf

On the philosophy and practice of the helping interview:

Benjamin, A. (1974). *The helping interview* (2nd ed.). New York: Houghton Mifflin.

Full of metaphors, personal experiences, and story-quality examples, the author lays out a philosophy of helping along with practical advice.

On therapy and counseling:

Rogers, C. R. (1961). *On becoming a person.* Boston: Houghton Mifflin.

Thorne, B. (2003). *Carl Rogers* (2nd ed.). London: Sage.

Anderson, H. (1997). *Conversation, language, and possibilities: A postmodern approach to therapy.* New York: Basic Books.

Bohart, A. C., & Greenberg, L. S. (Eds.). (1997). *Empathy reconsidered: New directions in psychotherapy.* Washington, DC: American Psychological Association.

Carl Rogers's "technique," according to some people, was "reflecting feelings" through active listening. However, Rogers himself disavowed the whole notion of relating to others by techniques; he simply wanted to let others know they could be understood, no matter how unusual their experiences might seem. Harlene Anderson respects clients in what Rogers would call "person centered" ways, and this is clear from her sensitive descriptions of therapeutic conversations. Her writing has many examples and insights about language and empathy, topics explored in depth in the APA-sponsored anthology.

On medical interviewing:

Coulehan, J. L., & Block, M. R. (1992). *The medical interview: A primer for students of the art* (2nd ed.). Philadelphia: Davis.

Smith, R. C. (1996). *The patient's story: Integrated patient–doctor interviewing.* Boston: Little, Brown.

Both books are practical introductions to interviewing that avoid overgeneralization and prescription. Highly recommended.

Chapter Twelve

Understanding and Analyzing Interviews in Popular Media Culture

LEARNING GOALS

After reading this chapter, you should be able to

- Understand the extent to which popular culture relies on information obtained through interviews

- Describe how broadcast interviews differ from other forms of professional interviewing, because of overhearing audiences, dramatic requirements, the need for illustration, pervasive streamlining, and transitory content

- Conduct a basic broadcast-type interview as interviewer or interviewee

- Analyze broadcast interviews by observing how interviewers and interviewees enact identity codes, situational codes, verbal codes, and nonverbal codes

- Adapt broadcast interviewing styles and skills to other interview situations

If you doubt the impact of popular media culture in your life, consider the following commonplace ways we satisfy our craving to know what's going on outside our personal spheres.

• Do you follow the careers of professional basketball players LeBron James or Diana Taurasi? Singers Shakira or Kanye West? Film stars Denzel Washington or Salma Hayek? If you do, what you've learned about your favorite celebrity has been provided by a raft of zealous interviewers. Have you looked up advice recently about, say, how to break into network news? In all likelihood, that advice—from interviewers Anderson Cooper, Matt Lauer, or Soledad O'Brien, for example—was obtained through interviews. Interviews help us learn about intriguing people and subjects that interest us.

• Your book collection might include an autobiography of a celebrated musician. Perhaps you don't realize that many "autobiographies" of famous people are not produced by the star writing down memories but by a writer who has interviewed the celebrity and shaped the recollections into a coherent and (they hope) engrossing narrative. Interviews are also crucial for writers of fiction. Listen to them talk about their research (on an interview talk show, for instance), and you'll hear how often they had to interview public defenders or judges

Broadcast news should aim to stimulate its audiences to take up its information and insert it into the culture of their everyday lives. It should aim to be talked about, which means it must discard its role of privileged information giver, with its clear distinction between the one who knows (the author) and those who do not (the audience), for that gives it the place and the tone of the author-god and discourages popular productivity. Rather, it should aim to involve its viewers in making sense of the world around them, it should encourage them to be participants in the process, not recipients of its products: it should . . . aim to make them readers rather than decipherers. Instead of promoting a final truth, then, it should promote discussion . . . or disagreement.

—John Fiske,
Reading the Popular

or medical examiners before adding the nuances of detail to that courtroom thriller you admire. Interviews support our literature by giving it a structure of vivid facts and realistic details.

• You might enjoy listening to or watching talk shows on radio or television; if so, you should realize that most shows Oprah Winfrey presents (or Montel Williams, Ellen DeGeneres, Howard Stern, Regis Philbin and Kelly Ripa, Maury Povich, Rush Limbaugh, and others) are little more than occasions for one-on-one or group-on-one interviews in front of an audience. Some shows are morally uplifting (e.g., Oprah interviewing Elie Wiesel or Maya Angelou), and others can be dispiriting (e.g., someone learning via a Maury Povich interview that a spouse is having an affair). Others, such as infomercial testimonials solicited by celebrity hosts, relate the wonders of the latest fashion or consumer craze. Interviews entertain us, shock us, and provide revealing glimpses into the human condition.

• Do you respect the local member of Congress or school board president, or do you consider them self-serving and overly political? Without information gleaned through public and quasi-public interviews, you likely would have scant evidence to support your attitudes. Imagine a political campaign without popular media interviews on television and radio. You'd have to attend each speech, and follow each candidate around, to gather your own idiosyncratic information. You have neither the time nor the inclination to do that, even if you had the money or curiosity. Interviews serve our decision-making process.

• You've heard much about the relatively new world of *blogging* (That is, "Web logging," or posting a running log of personal experience and opinion on the Internet), and how it creates new avenues for interviewing skill. If you participate, you know the range of content and agendas advanced daily on sites operated by businesses, politicians, organizations, celebrities, and ordinary people. The Internet's bloated blogosphere contains plenty of juvenile, exploitive, and, at times, dangerous communication. Despite its flaws and failings, blogging has opened a vast world of vital, useful information about subjects that until the last decade or so had been the exclusive province of those who owned the traditional, commercial means of mass communication. The Internet, of course, paved the way for a wide open, virtual marketplace of ideas, but the blogging phenomenon dramatically has exposed the desire of people to converse beyond the confines of family and friends. Blogs differ in purpose and format, but those most linked to interviewing encourage the asking and answering of questions. The average person can more readily interview and engage people in public life, from the school superintendent of Pinellas County, Florida, to the owner of the NBA's Dallas Mavericks, Mark Cuban. What's more, one question, followed by an answer, can ignite follow-up questions and answers. In the blogosphere, information and understanding proliferate in ways impossible when the Oprahs and David Lettermans of the world control with whom, when, and to what extent the rest of us can engage in the dialogue. Interviews through blogging can grant us unprecedented opportunities to participate in local, regional, and global conversations.

• A calamity strikes the Gulf Coast, such as Hurricane Katrina. Within minutes, network and local reporters are talking with people who thought just last week that their lives were ordinary. Now, breathless questioners with microphones transform them into heroes, fools, victims, and storytellers. The president flies to New Orleans to visit the horrible scenes, and the public observes him talking to survivors, asking about their resources and provisions, eliciting stories of their courage. Here is yet another kind of interview. After *Air Force One* takes off, a press secretary briefs reporters and the assembled citizens on the president's impressions and then invites questions in a group interview. We'd like to be symbolically assured, whether in Waukegan or Waikiki, not only that residents of the Gulf Coast are going to be well cared for, but so will we all if such a disaster strikes in our community. When government response to tragedy fails miserably, as it did in New Orleans and other regions hit by Katrina, we're doubly shocked by the eyewitness accounts. Normally interviews are occasions of social order, and we use them to reassure ourselves that at least some events can be orderly and predictable, somehow knowable and therefore manageable.

These are only a few of the ways our popular culture exists in and through interview styles that help create and sustain a mediated reality. Although some critics bemoan this technological condition, it makes little sense to ignore it. Instead, this chapter looks at the assumptions behind interviews in popular media culture to see what they reveal about culture generally. Here, we are less concerned with the behavioral skills you can develop as an interviewer or an interviewee and more concerned with the analytical skills you can develop to understand how interviews function in popular culture. Studying interviewing is closely linked with other skills in a communication curriculum, such as those taught in media literacy, persuasion, public relations campaign, or rhetorical criticism courses.

"The Basics" will examine media assumptions about how interviews should be conducted; we'll try to take you behind the scenes and encourage you to think about interviews in a new way. For purposes of clarity and focus, we've decided to concentrate on broadcast interviews rather than discuss all popular culture media forms. These broadcast forms include interviews that are live and taped, in front of a studio audience and without a studio audience, in one-on-one or panel settings, on radio or television. In "Beyond the Basics" we ask you to become a critic in accomplishing two tasks. You'll discover new ways to listen to and observe broadcast interviews more systematically and develop strategies for importing or adapting broadcast styles for your own improvement as interviewer and interviewee in other interview situations.

The Basics

Learning and Interviewing

Most interviews in everyday professional life are motivated by interviewers who have a clear and immediate learning goal: To gain information or insight someone else possesses. For example, social science researchers, oral historians, journalists, medical personnel, and salespersons all do their jobs by developing a solid understanding of the other person's perceptions, even if they have to start from a base of little or no knowledge.

Media interviews, however, especially in the broadcast media, typically make very different demands on participants; interviewers already may know the other person's basic message (or they think they do), and they attempt to elicit an interesting or dramatic articulation of it for a proposed audience. Ken Metzler (1997) suggests a number of other differences between broadcast interviewers and their cohorts in other professions. Broadcast interviewers "tend to dive for what glitters" in "short, provocative, usually superficial interviews." They emphasize the dramatic and "colorful" response, often in a scene or location that itself is designed to suggest a message to an audience. They "[cut] quickly to the essence of a situation," with a "firm and narrow sense of purpose" that often can be achieved in four to six minutes. They encourage respondents to adopt a "performance attitude," because opportunities to impress an audience are fleeting (pp. 145–146). Such characteristics leave little room for the same kind of learning attitude stressed earlier in this book. Broadcast interviewers must be flexible enough and prepared enough to know before the interview what the content is likely to be, yet at the same time be skilled enough as a listener to follow unexpected threads of meaning that arise (see Box 12.1). Interviews in popular media culture are indeed a different animal, but ignoring their demands can be a big mistake for communicators who justifiably seek a wider audience for their ideas and goals.

Interviewers in any situation can learn important insights about technique from skilled broadcast communicators. However, broadcast interviewers have some goals that are distinctive from, if not contradictory to, those of other interviewers. The nature of the goals and the assumptions that guide broadcast interviewers must be considered

---

Box 12.1

Interviewers in Action   *Susan Stamberg*

Noted radio host Susan Stamberg—renowned for her public affairs interviews—offers advice on the relationship between planning and spontaneity in broadcasts:

I think it's good to go in with a sense of what it is you want to happen in the course of the conversation. . . . What points do you want to get made? What information do you want to elicit? Then you have to be ready to abandon that at any moment if something comes up that you hadn't thought about before, but that strikes you as far more interesting.

The biggest mistake is coming in with a list of 10 questions and then not paying any attention to the answers that are being given. . . . The guest may get off on a tangent, but it can be much more interesting than anything you've got on paper.

Source: Biagi (1992, p. 116)

when applied to other situations. Beware, especially, of simply trying to import media interviewing styles into your other interviewing tasks in businesses, schools, or in such specialized communication tasks as fund-raising, training, public relations, personnel management, or sales. A given strategy or technique might appear to work for Oprah, but few of us play in her league, with her budget, or with her rules.

Media Assumptions about Interviews

Five assumptions, or tendencies, drive media interviews. They are interrelated, and careful observers will notice exceptions to all of them, but they help us see the media in ways that tend to be overlooked in the everyday bustle of tuning in to our favorite television and radio programs (and, more recently, our favorite Web sites).

Interviews Must Be Framed for an Overhearing Audience

Larry King (1989) is an unusual interviewer. The CNN talk-show host, who also has been a dominant force in radio talk over the years, says he never wants to read the books of authors before he interviews them. To read the book, he thinks (p. 136), is to reduce the element of surprise he wants to feel when the author starts explaining plots, characters, and ideas. He tries to enter the situation as the "typical" audience member who, in all likelihood, is unfamiliar with the book but might want to read it. He tries to ask the audience's questions, in other words. Most interviewers want to give the appearance of insiders probing with the author into deep issues, but King evidently is unafraid to appear ignorant on occasion about those issues.

Although his methods are uncommon, King's approach exemplifies one of the most basic assumptions of media interviewing—the always-present audience. His interview style is informed not by his own curiosity alone, and perhaps at times not by his own curiosity at all, but by *an inferred curiosity of others* that he wants to represent. This condition in some ways frees him to ask different questions from different perspectives than he otherwise would if the interview were a private one-on-one affair. Just as newspaper reporters are often substitute listeners for the rest of us as they write about news events, media interviewers are surrogate inquirers for the public when they have access to celebrities, stars, athletes, and politicians.

However, King and other media interviewers also are constrained by the presence of the unseen audience. He has to speak at least partly with our vocabulary and language habits rather than his own, and he must be ready at a moment's notice to rephrase subtly an interviewee's lofty rhetoric into everyday vernacular. Although he might be weary personally of a prosecuting attorney's account of a president's legal trouble, King knows he'll have to ask anyway.

The presence of the audience might mean at times that interviewers adopt pretenses of not knowing. "When did you write your first book?" for instance, would be an odd and possibly insulting question to ask if you were interviewing a well-known writer such as Stephen King for the college literary magazine. You would be expected to know such basic facts before you arrive for the interview; you should have done your homework on his career. Yet if he hears the same question during a radio interview downtown, she is unlikely to think anything unusual has been asked. Rather than assuming the interviewer to be lazy or ignorant, he'll assume the question is designed to help the overhearing audience put his work in context.

Sociologist Erving Goffman (1981) refers to the audience in broadcast situations as a **ratified participant,** even though it's one that will not assume a speaking role. He means that the audience is taken into account as if it were participating but without ever actually being able to participate. In cases like "'on the spot' interviewing," he writes, "the announcer may turn from . . . fellow participants at the microphone and acquaint the audience with background matters. He may even go so far as to let the audience know what has already transpired between the talkers just prior to the broadcast. . . . In these ways the audience can appear to be brought into the conversation as it unfolds, knowing enough to follow the talk, in principle no less knowledgeable than the platform listeners themselves as to what is about to be said" (pp. 234–235). The "ratified participant"—audience that might participate only tangentially—is nevertheless in charge throughout the interview, in a sense: Heritage and Greatbatch (1991) conclude that "the footing of news interview talk as oriented towards the overhearing audience is managed at all points over the course of the talk and not merely at those points where an overt reference to the audience . . . takes place" (p. 109). Both interviewer and interviewee implicitly understand throughout the interview that they are ultimately making their remarks to and for the audience—even when they aren't mentioning the audience (see also Heritage, 1985; Livingstone & Lunt, 1994).

Interviews Must Be Engaging

Because broadcast interviews in popular culture are framed with large unseen audiences in mind, what those audiences expect becomes paramount. It's not as though the listeners have made a large commitment of time and energy to attend an event, as they would by purchasing a ticket to a show, driving to a theater, parking, and sitting down for an hour or more of performance. The interview can vanish from the tube or the radio in a flash if a listener gets bored. Physical presence presumes a continuing attention to talk that electronic presence does not.

Interviewers and interviewees in media contexts know that audiences must be caught, enticed, given emotional and dramatic reasons to continue a psychological commitment to listening (see Box 12.2 for a vivid example). They must frame the event almost from the start as relevant. The best way to ensure this kind of commitment, interview participants know, is to lead with dramatic, surprising, shocking, or at least highly involving aspects of a narrative. Then participants work to intersperse other such interesting moments throughout the course of the interview. This requirement, of course, usually makes for a very different interview structure than so-called ordinary interviewing.

An example of one form of media interviewing that particularly exploits drama is the daytime talk show on television. According to Shattuc (1997) in her analysis of one talk show, such programs

> stage a highly standardized drama of the disenfranchised. The *Donahue* program sets
> up veiled class, education, and gender distinctions as the image, primarily of women,

Box 12.2

Interviewers in Action   *David Frost*

British interviewer David Frost negotiated to interview ex-President Richard Nixon in 1976 about the Watergate issues and other aspects of his presidency:

> "Ah," said Nixon as I entered his office. "The Grand Inquisitor." "No, no," I said, "just your friendly neighborhood confidant."
>
> In fact, of course, I knew I would probably have to play both those roles, and several more besides. But then that's one of the things that interviewing is all about. We discussed makeup and how his office could be effectively lit.
>
> "It's the way you look that I'm really worried about," Nixon said almost playfully. Then he added, "After all, you've got a whole career ahead of you." (pp. 70–71)
>
> We would, with Nixon and myself as the alchemists, be using our own raw material to provide a better quality of source material for journalists, historians, and political scientists to ponder. Some questions which we knew would produce news stories might never be asked. Others, unless of overriding importance, might be edited out. News per se was not our first priority. Insight into the man and his administration was. . . .
>
> I would remain ever alert, of course, for targets of opportunity, for moments of potential openness, such as would occur months later when Nixon himself introduced the topic of his alleged foreign bank accounts and his rumored love affair with a European countess. But that was different. That was seizing the moment. In our general preparation, the thrust of every line *of* questioning had to grow out of that which we already knew. A proper foundation for each line of questioning was critical. (p. 41)

Source: Frost (1978)

the working class, and ethnic people exploited by powerful male lawyers. The power polarities are usually not so clearly portrayed as in this program . . ., but talk shows always build a sense of a victim (someone who has been cheated, emotionally hurt, physically beaten, or otherwise mistreated) and a perpetrator (boss, parent, husband, lover) into the conflict. (p. 80)

Shattuc amplifies her point:

> Talk radio offers a set of traits similar to those of the TV talk show in that the format combines call-in shows on social issues, interview shows, and psychological advice shows that provide the range of topics found on the latter. Talk radio also stages controversy to create dramatic appeal. Additionally, talk radio is wholly dependent on audience participation by means of listener call-ins. (p. 7)

Although we certainly find many differences among the different forms of broadcast talk shows, all of them introduce drama and controversy through the mechanism of a host or expert who *interviews*—that is, who interprets a topic and explores it through questions phrased for a guest, a panel, a studio audience, a call-in audience, or in some cases, all of these.

The audience must be served, no matter what the program's format. Terry Gross hosts "Fresh Air," the Peabody Award–winning weekday magazine of contemporary arts and issues. It is one of public radio's most popular programs; each week nearly 4.5 million people tune in to the prerecorded show's intimate conversations with authors, artists, and authorities in current events. Gross (2004) acknowledges that her audience, despite its loyalty, can begin to literally tune out when the talk for which she and her guests are noted fails to engage or entertain. So she has few qualms about asking guests to retape a muddled response; shutting them up when she senses the yawn gauge rising dangerously high; or liberally editing transcripts to remove dead spots or rearrange taped comments for better cohesiveness. So what sounds like a warm, spontaneous, eloquent conversation is, to a degree, a broadcast illusion. Most of the time, Gross sits alone in a studio and her guests "visit" by phone. After the taped interview concludes, Gross and her production crew fine polish and reassemble the "conversation" for its maximum appeal to the audience.

Interviews Must Involve a Degree of Collusion

Face-to-face interviewing, as we have seen, usually involves the interviewer communicating with an interviewee, each with separate goals of learning or discovering something new. Media interviewers know that if the interview is defined in this way, genuine learning can become a recipe for risky, boring, and possibly dangerous broadcasts (for one host's experience, see Box 12.3). Why is this true?

Media interviews feature a peculiar kind of unspoken collusion—or even teamwork—between interviewer and interviewee. This form of teamwork is not when the two people get together beforehand and decide on a script or set up answers artificially. Instead,

---

Box 12.3

Interviewers in Action   *Jim Loughman*

Loughman, a longtime host on the prominent Chicago talk radio station WGN, discusses his best and worst guests:

- The best guests: "Basically I wanted interesting people with strongly held views. All the better if they were newsmakers. . . . The best guests I interviewed were not necessarily ultra-high-profile. It gets back to what I mentioned a moment ago about strongly held views. The other side of the coin is the willingness, even eagerness, to express and defend those views; to mix it up with friends and foes alike; to be stimulating and provocative."

- The worst guests: "They were the ones who acted like all they had to do was show up; people who rested on their press clippings, or put on airs, or spoke condescendingly to the audience. Politicians come to mind. Lots of them."

Source: Hilton (1987, p. 76)

on an informal basis and often without deciding overtly on how it will happen, the two adapt their behaviors mutually to a commonly understood purpose and set of roles. Heritage and Greatbatch (1991) found that on broadcast news shows, interviewees naturally allocate certain rights to interviewers, such as opening and closing shows, deciding when topics will shift, and making conversational interruptions. On the other hand, interviewers, Claflin (1979) notes, typically will not press interviewees on how their talk conflicts with that of other public figures or even how it conflicts with their own prior statements. Despite the absence of formal planning, in other words, interviewers and interviewees appear to collaborate in saving face and carrying off the event without a hitch. Interviewers will ask questions in such a way that interviewees will be able to meet at least some of their objectives and vice versa. Because interviewers are often at least public figures who are potentially "known quantities" before the conversation takes place, interviewees understand what kind of communication to expect, even if they do not know the exact questions that will arise. Because interviewees are usually chosen because of their notoriety or celebrity or newsworthiness, they also are at least somewhat predictable communicators to interviewers.

To use prominent examples, on successive days CBS's Katie Couric and CNN's Anderson Cooper interview the CEO for a pharmaceutical company under public scrutiny for a government-ordered recall of its popular pain-reducing drug. Because the drug executive and his public relations handlers have access to a backlog of similar interviews conducted by the two interviewers, they can plan for the encounter. The executive understands that Couric's style is more folksy and informal, with "fastball" questions often framed by a cushion of seemingly pleasant conversation. Cooper's style is known to be more tenacious, as he often launches a series of probes bluntly phrased to illuminate flaws in reasoning. What kinds of "teamwork" can the executive expect if an interviewer presents such threats? How does this qualify as teamwork? The answer is that the media interview is usually a transaction in which an interviewer, producer, program, or network negotiate a trade with an interviewee. The network gets a dramatic event to fill time, make news, and interest an audience. The interviewee gets access to the program's audience and therefore obtains exposure for his or her ideas, explanations, or self-defense. Of course, double crosses and ambush interviews occasionally occur. Yet in most radio and television interviews—even with accused child abusers and traitors—audiences will hear interviewers creating a relatively open and congenial space for interviewees to frame their actions.

Public officials of the highest rank often get the most preferential treatment. When Dan Rather in 2003 scored an exclusive interview in Baghdad with Saddam Hussein, less than a month before President George W. Bush ordered the invasion of Iraq, a media critic said the dictator's effusive and frequent use of the words "peace" and "humanity" seemed "to lull Rather in hopeful complacency: Mustn't upset the dictator" (Franklin, 2003, p. 28). Rather got his big interview, but did he play slow-pitch softball with Hussein to keep the interview going, avoiding tough questions that might have prematurely ended his exclusive access? The interview so pleased Hussein that he decided to broadcast it on Iraqi television shortly after it aired in the United States. Rather's approach is supported by research findings from Heritage and Greatbatch (1991), that such interviewers are constrained to be "neutralistic" in much of the conversation. They're not expected to argue or nitpick answers the respondent provides. Interviewees, by the same token, do not normally complain that interviewers' questions put them on the spot too much or are too unfair. The rules often are mutually understood and roles mutually agreed on. Remember, there are always exceptions to the norm, but by and large, the current conventions of interviewing encourage politicians and advocates of all stripes to advertise their positions in the media without having to defend them against authentic and heartfelt disagreement.

New York Times media critic John J. O'Connor offers another reason broadcast interviews usually fail to cross the neutrality threshold:

> Most (television) panel formats are carefully designed to protect the interests of the guest. When questions are rotated among a group of journalists, the results are virtually guaranteed to be superficial. A questioner getting close to the core of one subject will find that his time is up. Another questioner takes over and, more often than not, begins to pursue an entirely different subject. The reason for this standard routine is purely practical. Without some built-in safeguards, prominent politicians, the kind most courted for television, would simply refuse to appear on panel shows. (quoted in Claflin, 1979, p. 12)

O'Connor's observation dates to the late 1970s, but his complaint will probably be confirmed to a disturbing degree if you watch Sunday morning's network political interview programs or the president's next press conference.

Broadcast interviewers not only face rules and conditions that call for self-imposed restraint, they also increasingly face interviewees coached by communication experts whose advice includes how to dodge tough questions and answer easy ones; pitch platitudes and remain unflinchingly polite; and spread the party line through catchy, prepared, self-serving themes (Lieberman, 2004). Coached to control interviews, public officials rarely say or do anything that could inflict damage on themselves, their bosses, and the institutions they serve.

Claflin (1979) wants to increase dialogue in the public sphere because most news interviewers are too docile; they allow respondents to make unsupportable if not ludicrous claims and get away with this tactic. Instead of allocating the responsibilities of interviewing to media representatives who don't sufficiently press public figures on the implications of their positions, Claflin offers a "radical proposal" for dialogic free speech in public discourse: Why not have advocates on different sides of controversial issues interview each other in public? The public would learn much from such interchanges, not the least of which is who can phrase a clear and fair question, who listens well to opposing positions, and who respects the other side enough to frame it as a serious possibility. None of these types of information is generally a part of the puzzle that voters, for example, piece together at election time.

Although popular media culture has not fully adopted Claflin's suggestion of expert spokespersons interviewing other experts in public, we have perhaps moved somewhat further in that direction since his book appeared. News and public events talk shows now feature a more rigorous interaction among different representatives, as on PBS's *McLaughlin Group*. Unfortunately, participants almost always talk over each other's words, competing for airtime with loud and rapid speech. Claflin's innovative suggestion for media reform in which disagreements are explored through clearly framed interviewing roles has not been tried seriously. If it were to be tried, it might create a new version of public dialogue in which genuine learning could take place among interview participants, not just the representation of positions they wish to illustrate or illuminate.

Interviews Must Be Streamlined

Media interviewers often experience a series of time-management problems that set their context apart from other interview situations. One analyst (A. Cohen, 1987) describes how:

> time constraints pose a special problem in television interviewing. Getting to a story and setting up the interview is logistically more complex in television than in any other medium. More equipment is needed to record the interview and to transmit it, both in live or in prerecorded formats. Also, television scheduling is very precise, more so than in any other mass medium (mainly in the United States). As a result, the timing of the interview, live or recorded, and the editing process must all be done with careful consideration of the program context in which the interview will be telecast. Despite what appears to be a tendency for shrinking news-holes in newspapers, it is likely that newspaper editors are still more flexible in deciding to allocate more space to a particular story if they deem this necessary. In the television industry, however, given the more severe constraints, comparable decisions are more complex and, therefore, less likely to be made. (p. 27)

A factor influencing the relative brevity of media interviews is that a wide variety of technicians and planners must be on the job to support the occasion. Another is that time equals space in the broadcast industry, and few shows can afford to allocate sufficient space to long-form interviews with individual respondents (although exceptions such as Charlie Rose, Barbara Walters, and Brian Lamb come to mind). Longer interviews, therefore, are either discouraged or are edited to highlight their juiciest, most newsworthy, most conflictual, or most embarrassing moments.

Savvy interviewees realize that if they can say something memorable in a brief interview, it probably will be shortened even more if it is rereported. The media tend to quote and requote **sound bites**, those short slogan-like statements that supposedly capture longer and more complex modes of thought in a few words. In 1968, network newscasts ran uninterrupted quotes from presidential candidates that averaged 42.3 seconds; by 1988 that figure had dropped to 9.8 seconds (Davis, 1993, pp. 58–59). Although we haven't found a more recent statistic, such a trend can't continue much further, although it probably has become even more entrenched. Media consultants like Jack Hilton (1987) train political and corporate interviewees to speak in sound bites in the first place:

> Extemporaneous speech combines . . . composition and presentation . . . simultaneously. Because that's fraught with peril for a speaker much of my work as a consultant is aimed (yes, manipulatively, but not sinisterly) at separating the two.
>   This kind of forethought and preparation was demonstrated . . . in the second TV debate in 1984 between President Reagan and Walter Mondale. After the President's frankly doddering performance in the first debate two weeks previously, senility became

an issue in the campaign, and the Reagan brain trust anticipated a question from someone on the panel of reporters about the President's age.

On stage in Kansas City, they were accommodated in spades before 80,000,000 television viewers by Henry Trewhitt of the *Baltimore Sun*. And Mr. Reagan ad-libbed his reply just as he had written it on a legal pad several days before, flawlessly and verbatim: "I will not make age an issue in this campaign," he said. "I'm not going to exploit for political purposes my opponent's youth and inexperience."

Twenty-three words, or about eight seconds at my rate of speech (not including the audience's explosive response). I'll wager $50 that you saw it on the late-evening newscasts of October 21st, unless you were visiting the Australian outback. An additional $25 says that you'll see it replayed on television every four years until the tape wears out. (p. 39)

Interviews Must Produce Transitory Content

Perhaps because of the brevity of media interviews, their content is usually short-lived and ephemeral. Although the occurrence of an interview—the fact that it was arranged—is undoubtedly important, what is said usually has a short shelf life. Think about what kinds of talk qualify for newsworthiness or requoting: the juicy comment, the accusation, the characterization so intense or unusual that it shocks audiences, an expressed conflict with another public figure, a statement so embarrassing or difficult to explain that listeners' attention becomes drawn to it. Although all of these comments will raise eyebrows, they rarely have an impact over a sustained period, and they rarely come to characterize someone's career.

We expect other speech occasions and genres to produce memorable quotations, but expectations for the broadcast interview appear to be lower. From a speech, for example, we gather presumably significant statements about a person's future, or plan for a campaign, or the potential for larger cultural change. Interviews are important but usually not as a source for these types of statements. Another speech genre, testimony, also creates serious content to which we expect public figures to adhere closely.

The typical broadcast interview, however, is considered by audiences to be a creative mix of information, entertainment, public relations, propaganda, and advertising. It is quickly forgotten or dismissed. If you doubt this, track the talk-show appearances (e.g., on *Meet the Press, Face the Nation,* or *Paula Zahn Now*) of a prominent and controversial spokesperson for a point of view, such as cultural critics William Bennett or Tavis Smiley, or lawyers doing daily analysis of extended cases such as the Michael Jackson trial in California. Surely most analysts do not attempt to lie or deceive in their commentaries, but neither do they go out of their way to explain or reconcile inconsistencies between what they said last night and what they asserted last week, last month, or last year. They assume—rightly—that because of how the public listens to media interviews, their observations are valuable for the moment in which they're uttered but become disposable almost immediately. Unless they are formalized as part of a speech or testimony of some sort, the statements enter what Booth (1988, p. 184) calls the "meaning chopper" of the news, never to be heard of again in their appropriate context.

Some observers (e.g., Postman, 1988) have suggested that this lack of concern for historical context is a function of the broadcast medium itself, which supposedly trivializes genuine knowledge. Television, and to a lesser extent, radio, encourages us to think primarily in terms of a brief and generally ahistorical perspective. You don't have to agree fully with critics like Neil Postman to acknowledge that electronic media have helped to change some human perceptual habits. Electronic media, especially television, have made it possible to reach vast audiences with crucial information and interesting entertainment possibilities. It is senseless to lash out at a medium of our own devising. It is not senseless, however, to note that it might have some specific effects on a particular communication context, such as interviewing.

Bill McKibben (1993) watched an entire day of television taped (with the help of friends) from more than 90 channels on the Fairfax, Virginia, cable system. McKibben wrote a book describing the important and trivial messages he saw and their relationship to his life. One of the things he noticed most was how much television deals with itself and other transitory messages, and how much it glorifies its own historically brief time period of the past few decades. "Which is fine—but nothing," according to McKibben, "that comes *before* television is covered in any detail at all" (p. 64). There are exceptions, such as Ken Burns's PBS series on the Civil War, baseball, and the Lewis and Clark expedition, but in general, "The brightness surrounding the last forty years [now, of course, more than fifty years] blinds us to all that preceded it—and forty years is a very short time, even to an individual" (pp. 64–65). He adds:

> Bob Hope, for instance, came on the J. C. Penney shopping channel to hawk his new book. We know Bob Hope from years of specials, from footage of him entertaining the troops. But he is an old man, too. He's talking about World War II, and tells a joke about how FDR trained his dog Fala on the *Chicago Tribune*. The interviewer brays—convulses—but it's hard to believe he has any idea about Colonel McCormick's feud with Roosevelt; Bob might as well tell Saint Thomas Aquinas jokes. The past fills our minds, but only the past of the last four decades. As a result, those four decades seem utterly normative to us, the only conceivable pattern for human life. (p. 65)

The plight of the hapless interviewer in McKibben's example capsulizes the status of media interviews in our culture, in which the fact that the interview took place overshadows the content of what is actually said. Although McKibben strongly suspects the interviewer doesn't get the joke (which depends on remembering a historical relationship between two men now long dead), that is not the important thing. The important thing is that Bob Hope—a comedian whose career spanned generations—is *on*. The important thing is that he has told a joke on the air, and a distant audience expects laughter. No one needs to understand, much less remember, the joke, but the interviewer wants to avoid the immediate impression that a respected comedian told a joke that got no response. So he plays out a charade, representing "our" appreciation of Bob Hope. If McKibben had not been chronicling his experience for a book, no doubt he would have forgotten where and when he saw Bob Hope, what he said, and why he appeared. Most media interviews are produced, in other words, with the assumption that they'll be transitory.

In a general sense, media interviews serve three masters: information, entertainment, and recognition. They must be informative and entertaining while they ensure that certain spokespersons and their issues become recognizable. Ideally, the interview threads these three functions together, as interviewer and interviewee cooperate to produce informative

Box 12.4

Reminders   *Practical Tips for Media Interviews*

For the Interviewer

- *Remember the audience*: Ask their questions, and translate answers so they will understand the issues; prepare carefully, even though you want to let yourself be surprised by some disclosures. Make sure you have all the facts straight (e.g., titles and qualifications of interviewees).

- *Help the interviewee to dramatize*: Unearth conflicts, contradictions, disagreements, choice points, problems of analysis, and threats to audience members; if appropriate, encourage two or more interviewees with strong opinions to "interview" each other and state the others' interpretations fairly. Most experienced interviewers believe it's fair to brief interviewees on the projected topics (to allow them to prepare, too), but they do not disclose specific questions.

- *Streamline the interaction*: Ask brief, well-focused questions; redirect the discussion if the interviewee gets off track or too long-winded; cover ground, but do it economically. Remind interviewees ahead of time that short, punchy examples help audiences relate to them but that extended narratives usually fall flat. Don't be timid about interrupting long-winded talkers.

- *Help the interviewee to emphasize a point or case*: Although you might disagree, defer your disagreement until you're sure the point has been stated clearly.

- *Summarize the interview's major points and contributions*: If it's important to do so, create a historical context for the interviewee's ideas, to counteract the tendency for audiences to forget the content of broadcast interviews.

For the Interviewee

- *Remember that you're both talking to, and talking through, the interviewer*: By engaging in an illuminating conversation with him or her, you're reaching many more people in an unseen audience.

- *Answer the questions, but also use them to bridge to other points you want to make*: Your reason for appearing may be different from their reason for choosing you to interview, and a good bridge is a transition to new conversational territory. Sometimes you'll have to create your own openings. For example (after an answer): "You know, a similar question arose when Marge Kennedy was mayor, and nobody paid attention. She and I believe . . ."

- *Dramatize and streamline your ideas with direct examples*: Audiences won't follow lengthy chains of reasoning, and they tend to get lost in a thicket of statistics. Although it might offend your sense of subtlety, try to boil down ideas to striking comparisons: "Harvard's endowment *increase* for last year alone was more than four times the *total* endowment of our university." Relate the unfamiliar to the familiar in brief stories, and the audience is more likely to remember your idea because of this reframing.

- *Show, don't smother, your personality*: Audiences recall impressions much more clearly than content. Often a person who makes a mistake or is nervous comes across as more believable and likable than the slick operator who has everything figured out and states a case with glibness. We're not suggesting that you "be yourself" as much as we're encouraging you to be conversational and avoid trying to be someone else.

and memorable entertainment (or entertaining and informative memories, or impressive and entertaining information). Box 12.4 reviews how participants in media interviews can acknowledge and include the audience.

Beyond the Basics

In this section we suggest ways to build on the foundation of your understanding of interviewing in popular media by exploring your interests in the context of radio and television interviews. So far, the focus has been on differences between forms of interviews and other interviewing tasks and functions, but it's also important to acknowledge the similarities. Interviewing is so pervasive in popular culture, with so many positive and negative models available, that we shouldn't overlook this interesting learning opportunity.

Observing Broadcast Interviews Systematically

In a survey of professional studies of television news interviews, Akiba Cohen (1987, pp. 49–63) organizes the literature under these headings:

- General preparation and control
- Identity codes
- Situational codes
- Verbal codes
- Nonverbal codes

These five categories provide an effective checklist to observe and analyze broadcast interviews systematically. Let's look at each of them in turn, exploring their potential for understanding the process and structure of interviewing.

General Preparation and Control

The **literature** (what professionals and scholars call the body of knowledge in a particular field of study) focuses on the role of interviewer and abounds with advice about how to prepare for and maintain control of the interaction. Interviewers are advised to familiarize themselves with relevant topics of the interview, of course, and also with backgrounds of the people they'll interview. Cohen appears surprised at how often in the literature the interviewer is assumed to be in the position of controlling the action, almost like a general in a battle.

When observing media interviews, try to answer these questions about preparation and control:

- How does an interviewer signal—consciously or unconsciously—the level and quality of preparation he or she has done?

Trying Out Your Skills

For this activity, you will need two partners, a video camera and monitor, and—if your video camera records to tape—a VCR.

- Assume that a series of interviews from 10 to 15 minutes long will be broadcast on a local cable channel, on a show titled *The American College Student Today: Direction and Drift*. Thus, it is important for interviewers to be professional in demeanor and interviewees (as themselves) to be personable and full of opinions.

- Record a round of interviews (A interviews B with C as observer/critic; B interviews C with A as observer/critic; C interviews A with B as observer/critic). Each interviewer must take the

broadcast nature of the occasion into account in conducting the interview, but beyond that you can focus on any aspect of college life that you think illustrates the show's theme. Be creative in asking questions and equally creative and thoughtful when answering them. See if you can approximate broadcast quality appearance and interestingness.

- Afterward, discuss the activity from the standpoint of your roles as observer/critics. How did interview participants talk differently compared to other interview assignments during the semester? How did you act or move differently? What accounts for the differences?

- What is the interviewer trying to accomplish by discussing this preparation? (Alternatively: What does the interviewer inadvertently suggest about the interview if he or she betrays a lack of preparation?)
- What are the control mechanisms of the interview?
- Who states the purpose and topic of the interview?
- Who introduces topic changes?
- Who interrupts whom?
- Who summarizes?

Identity Codes

Our use of *code* here shouldn't imply direct linguistic subterfuge, as in wartime codes or ciphers that keep the other side from understanding your messages. Rather, a **code** in communication scholarship is an organized and interlinked set of conditions that characterize a situation. To study this type of code is akin to getting inside the logic of a situation to understand more completely how it works. When you analyze codes, you are not trying to be ultrasensitive to single instances, nor are you seeking to assign blame to persons. You are looking for patterns of behavior that may be so woven into the fabric of interviews that they are hard to see at first glance.

Cohen (1987) analyzes interview identity (who someone is, in terms of their perceived characteristics) in three ways: demographics, social roles, and relationship to the story. **Demographics** refers to gender, age, ethnic group, and similar characteristics.

Trying Out Your Skills

Videotape or digitally record a sample interview from a network morning news and entertainment show such as *Good Morning America* or *Today*.

- Watch the recording at least three times, making notes each time about when and how the two participants appeared to be in "collusion" (see discussion in text). What specific behavioral or linguistic evidence suggested the collusion? Do

you think the interviewer or the show's producer talked so much about the interview in advance that the interview was, in effect, rehearsed?

- Write an essay on conversational teamwork, using the evidence you gathered from the tape. (You might also want to review the research literature on this phenomenon of speakers working to help each other look good in front of others.)

Social roles are the positions interviewers and interviewees are assumed to hold, along with the behaviors associated with them. Roles in society range from specific elected jobs, such as senator, to family roles, such as parent. Different roles provide potentially different levels of credibility for speakers. **Relationship to the story** is Cohen's term suggesting that some people are more closely tied to certain topics by virtue of their interests, skills, or background experiences.

When observing media interviews, try to answer these questions about identity codes:

- Why was *this* interviewer selected to conduct this interview? Who else could have been chosen? What might this choice say about the relationship between the sponsoring organization (e.g., TV station) and the story? Between the organization and the interviewee? Who decided to match a particular interview assignment with a particular interviewer?

- How might the interviewer be tied to the topic or interviewee through demographics, social roles, or relationship to the story? Are there possible patterns of special insight, expertise, or bias? Are some identity code decisions made with audience appeal in mind? (For example, is the ex-athlete sportscaster more likely to interview Tiger Woods or Martina Navratilova when they come to town, even if their appearance is for a news event like a charity ball? Is the station's African American reporter dispatched automatically to black neighborhoods to cover a teachers' strike?)

- What criteria might have determined that *this* interviewee would be chosen to answer questions? Have some individuals become identified as "experts" primarily because they've made themselves available often to answer questions? Consider professional qualifications: Why are journalists experts on governmental affairs, and why are they interviewed more often than political scientists by other journalists? Consider race, gender, and class issues: Note, for example, the number of times the same white males turn up to comment as "experts" on prestigious interview shows like *Face the Nation*. Consider what you know about interviewers: Is it possible that some interviewees are selected because they are easy to find, because their ideologies are highly predictable, or because they are friends of the interviewer or producer?

- How is the interviewee's identity framed and represented by the interviewer? Race, gender, and class issues are relevant here also. Can you identify differences between how women and men, homosexuals and heterosexuals, blacks and whites, or rich and poor are addressed by interviewers (e.g., by first names or honorific titles)? Women and marginalized minority groups notice these things more readily than dominant cultural groups. For example, a host interviewing a panel of experts may refer consistently to "Professor Hartley" (a white male academic), but call a woman professor "Janeece." Or you might notice that an interviewer might ask local white politicians about policy or budget issues, but ask black officials only about neighborhood crime or social conflicts, thus "slotting" certain officials into particular areas of expertise that can further distance minorities from power centers.

Situational Codes

Researchers of nonverbal communication understand that where an interview takes place can profoundly affect participants. On-location interviews are sometimes quite brief not because the interviewer planned them that way but, for example, because it's cold or wet, and there are no chairs. Less obvious, perhaps, is the effect on an audience. The situation and how it is handled tells the audience how to "take" the interview—whether they should interpret its statements as definitive, tentative, emotional, objective, reasoned, or spontaneous. NBC correspondent Arthur Kent and CNN correspondent Peter Arnett became famous during the first Gulf War through their interview reports in Israel or Baghdad, conducted with missiles passing overhead and explosions going off nearby. Many "embedded journalists" have discussed their similar experiences in the recent Iraq war (Borjesson, 2005). Although participants rarely refer directly to their surroundings in more normal circumstances, some sort of context is always available for audiences to interpret. Situational codes are particularly pronounced on television, of course, but they also become surprisingly influential in radio interviews: NPR producers, for example, often have their field producers on location record interviews with indigenous background sounds such as crickets or crackling fire, to suggest the experience of "being there."

When observing media interviews, try to answer these questions about situational codes:

- What is in the background, visual or aural, of the interview conversation? Presuming that participants had some choice of time and place, what made this situation attractive?

- What clues within the interview might indicate whether the site was chosen by interviewer, interviewee, both, or neither?

- How does the situation reinforce the content of the interview? How does the situation detract from it? Do the participants appear to be aware of these influences?

- Do contextual design factors symbolize or represent the status of interviewer or interviewee, perhaps affecting your estimate of other codes? For example, if an interview is held in an executive's office, does he or she sit behind a massive mahogany desk, symbolizing power, prestige, and distance? What does this suggest about the meaning of the interaction and about what topics are more, or less, likely to come up?

- Is the interview conducted live or recorded for later broadcast? At one extreme, live interviews suggest immediacy, involvement, and a high level of implied importance of an event for an audience, such as covering a hostage crisis after a bank robbery. At the other extreme, live interviews might simply be a choice of convenience, such as an anchorperson on the midday news interviewing a cookbook author on a publicity tour.

- How has a taped interview been edited, if at all? Look for shifts in background, clothing, camera angle, and facial expressions, to name only a few cues. Most editing is benign and necessary to fit complex messages into tight broadcast schedules. It's not unheard of in the broadcast world, however, for a less prestigious employee to conduct a personality profile interview, only to have the respondent's words later interlaced with edited-in reaction shots of a star interviewer. Such practices validly raise ethical concerns. If the interviewer or producer is willing to shortcut the process in this way, what else might have been shortchanged?

- Are situational codes mixed with identity codes in predictable ways? Does a station only interview African American adolescent males, for example, in gyms? Teenage girls only when they are cheerleading or sitting in honors classes? Retired people only in nursing homes? What's the message here? What do such examples tell you about media perspectives on these groups?

Verbal Codes

Specialized rules appear to guide interviewers and interviewees in their talk. Although broadcast interviews are commonly conversational, they are often only distantly related to everyday conversations as you might have them around the cafeteria table or at a ball game.

When observing media interviews, try to answer these questions about verbal codes:

- What rules guide the phrasing of questions? When are they broken and by whom? What happens after the violation? Generally, given the brevity of this type of interview, questions will be short and direct. When, if ever, does an interviewer ask a lengthy question—say, 100 or more words—and achieve a helpful and positive response? Further, how are questions "formulated" (set up, introduced, signaled)?

- What does the interviewer disclose about himself or herself? Why, and to what purpose, is the disclosure included? What effect does interviewer self-disclosure have on the interviewee?

- How are the especially meaningful questions or answers "marked"? That is, when and why do interviewers say things like, "Now we're getting to the crux of the matter," or interviewees say things like, "If there is one thing I want you to understand about me, it is. . . ." In your opinion, what motivates communicators to mark their speech in this way?

- Are there discernible verbal turning points, or critical incidents, after which the tone of the talk changes significantly? These might be breaches of etiquette, real or imagined insults, or misunderstandings of words or stories.

- Whose vocabulary predominates? Does the interviewee adapt to the linguistic habits of the interviewer, or vice versa, or do you perceive evidence of mutual adaptation? What might such observations tell you about the relationship that develops between them?

Nonverbal Codes

A. Cohen (1987, pp. 59ff.) highlights three nonverbal areas that have clear relevance for interviewing—*space*, *artifacts*, and *filmic procedures*. By **space**, he means that the way people choose distances for communication and how they sit or stand relative to each other send their own set of messages in interviewing. **Artifacts** are objects we display intentionally or unintentionally that might contribute to interpersonal meaning. **Filmic procedures** are conventions that tell us how to interpret other messages. Filmic issues are examples of the importance of framing in interviewing, because through them an audience understands important aspects of a communicator's intent. Cohen's interest in televised interviews leads him to stress visual cues rather than the nonverbal **paralinguistic** vocal cues (inflection, pitch, rate, volume) that are discernible in radio interviews as well as on television.

Researchers of nonverbal communication warn that it is futile to try to decide what a behavioral message "means," as though it carries a single certifiable meaning. Instead, nonverbal messages are perceived within patterns of other nonverbal and verbal messages. Within a given context, a message might be seen or heard as consistent or inconsistent, but it never means only one thing. Thus, as with the rest of communication, analysis has to be contingent; it is based on a great deal of guesswork.

When observing media interviews, try to answer these questions about nonverbal codes:

- How do participants manipulate the space between them? How much space is maintained, and do you notice differences between interviewers? Between an interviewer and his or her different interviewees? Between an interviewee and his or her different interviewers? What motivations might lie behind these differences? Does the spatial arrangement shift when a topic, or emotional tone, changes? If so, how? Are there times when a participant literally retreats or advances spatially?

- How do participants use posture or other spatial messages to indicate interest or willingness to change topics? For example, turning away might be seen as consistent with a desire to change the subject, whereas a respondent who leans into a question at least appears to be anxious to answer it. Normal conversation is usually conducted at a slight angle between conversants—not straight on or (obviously) not turned away. Deviations from this usually unstated expectation might be an interesting signal for analysts to consider.

- How do participants use eye contact, or the absence of it, to indicate closeness, truthfulness, confirmation, or willingness to answer?

- Do participants use props to signal their intentions, affiliations, or allegiances? If so, how? And if so, does the interview partner call attention to it? On March 11, 1998, NBC's *Today* anchor Matt Lauer interviewed Casey Martin, a professional golfer whose lawsuit stimulated the sport's governing association to change its rule forbidding players to use motorized carts in sanctioned tournaments. Martin, whose painful and chronic leg condition would keep him from competing otherwise, was discussing how pleased he was to be able to continue on the tournament circuit. Late in the interview, Lauer said he couldn't help noticing the "swoosh" (the Nike logo) on a couple of articles of clothing Martin wore. He asked a difficult, but fair, question invited by Martin's display of these artifacts: Did this controversy, however unpleasant, open some economic doors for Martin that would not have been possible considering only his skill at golf?

- How are the participants portrayed in the two filmic codes that A. Cohen (1987) emphasizes: "the angle of the shooting of the interview" and "the closeness of the shot" (p. 60)? Most broadcast interviews longer than a sound bite feature one or more **establishing shots**—visuals in which both participants are shown interacting together, within an identifiable context, sometimes with a **voice-over** (explanatory commentary added to the tape later). This tells viewers both what is taking place and where. In the interviews you choose to analyze, what is *established* in the establishing shot?

  Moreover, what seems to be the rationale by which producers vary the three major kinds of shots of interviewees and interviewers? A **medium shot** depicts what conversation partners know as a "social distance," including most of the body and some of the background context in which the person speaks. The **head and shoulders close-up** conforms more to "personal" distance, bringing the viewing audience to within the equivalent of touching distance of the speaker. The **tight shot** (extreme close-up) brings the viewer to a hyperintimate distance uncharacteristic of ordinary conversation. Assume that each time you see a certain shot, it's a result of someone's choice. Some changes in shots are undoubtedly to increase variety and interest audiences. For other camera changes, rhetorical purposes might dictate the shift. What might the producer be trying to "say" by zooming in on forehead perspiration, a wink to someone off camera, a smirk, or an eyelid twitch?

Trying Out Your Skills

Obtain a video recording of an interview from *60 Minutes*, perhaps the most famous investigative reporting television show ever. List all the nonverbal code elements you believe were intentionally structured by the producer or interviewer. What is the probable effect, in your opinion, on the audience?

Adapting Broadcast Interview Styles for Your Own Interviewing Goals

Clearly, communication choices appropriate and necessary for broadcast interviewers do not necessarily translate well to other interview tasks. You would have a hard time adapting Ellen DeGeneres's loose and friendly talk-show banter to a survey or oral history interview or to a serious attempt to address an employee's problem behaviors in an intervention interview. Tim Russert's or Jon Stewart's approach to exposing inconsistencies in the rhetoric of public officials and Barbara Walters's warm personality profiles of celebrities are effective within their own contexts, but they provide largely disastrous models for employment interviewers to emulate.

At the same time, let's recognize that these famous interviewers have become successful for reasons that make sense. Many aspects of popular broadcast interviewers' communication can be incorporated effectively into general interviewing styles if we are careful in making the connections. Read the following descriptions as tendencies; they are behavioral styles that tend to be appealing in the broadcast context and could have a wider application, too. To make that application, interviewers must be both knowledgeable about the process and introspective about themselves.

Effective broadcast interviewers must be extraordinarily flexible communicators. Look for ways to adapt each of their strengths to whatever interviewing task you're asked to perform. Interviews differ significantly, but all depend to some degree on these general skill areas. Broadcast interviewers can teach all of us something about being conversationalists, sensitive time managers, comprehensive listeners, contextualizers, and culturally sensitive communicators.

Conversationalists

Broadcast interviewers tend to be appropriately informal and spontaneous, or they find another line of work. This does not mean that they like to "wing it" in interviews, although some undoubtedly must work without a safety net at times. Being a conversationalist means that interviewers look for openings to put others at ease with everyday language, informal gestures, and perhaps well-placed humor. Conversations tend to be "locally managed" interactions, according to communication researchers, which means in everyday terms that the talk is experienced as having an immediate importance for the communicators. Despite the advantages of preparation, no one can script a genuine conversation. Effective interviewers are as fully "with" interviewees as possible.

Sensitive Time Managers

Broadcasters develop excellent time-management skills. They often work live, so they accept the responsibility for regulating the interchange to produce a seamless occasion. Even when interviews are taped for later broadcast, they work to ensure relevant topics are covered within a target time frame, so that intrusive and perhaps expensive editing isn't necessary. Although other interview occasions might not be as time sensitive as broadcast interviews, many participants unfortunately forget, or become oblivious to, the expressed time constraints of an interview partner. Many interviewers, therefore, could profit from observing how broadcasters make transitions from topic to topic ("You know, that's an unexpected side of you that we don't often see. I'm curious whether your parents encouraged you to take that direction. What was your early life like?"). Similarly, interviewers in other professions could study how broadcasters close interviews with respect and appreciation for their partner's contribution ("Thanks so much for talking with me today. I learned not only about your commitment to the industry but also about your concern for the culture as a whole. You've put things in a fresh perspective.").

Comprehensive Listeners

Interviewers in popular media tune themselves as listeners to nuances of wording and nonverbal context. Through experience, they learn to tell when someone is getting uncomfortable or tired, or when they've just disclosed something unintentionally. Working in tight time constraints fine-tunes their diagnostic abilities in communication, and they develop fairly accurate assessments of others' internal frames of reference. This comes from an immersion in a special kind of interviewing that most of us don't experience, however; interviews aren't everyday occasions for most other professional interviewers, who can be at least as nervous or ill at ease as their interviewees. Nervousness impedes their listening skill, because listening involves a kind of relaxed concentration on a variety of cues, both verbal and nonverbal. Pay attention to how broadcast interviewers pick up on small cues and use them to check out possible meanings ("A while ago you said you were 'happy' with your career. Just now, though, you started to say 'happy' but changed it to 'happier.' It's like you're moving in the right direction, but might not be there yet. Am I sensing an ambiguity here?").

Contextualizers

Successful broadcast interviewers learn to place interaction in a wider context. They understand that the interview is only a small slice of someone's life and an atypical one at that. Its importance may come as much from what isn't said as from what is said. Interviews are often important, in other words, in their relationship to the rest of someone's life and not in and of themselves. The contextualizing perspective is particularly useful for journalistic and employment interviewers who encounter others every day in situations that are much more uncomfortable for the interviewee than for the interviewer. Is Tamika Jones a nervous person because she acts nervous around a reporter? Is Robert Hawkley a forgetful or unreliable person because he neglects to mention his experience as a supervisor at Walgreen's, even though it's listed in his résumé?

Culturally Sensitive Communicators

Because broadcasters are constantly thinking of potential audience responses to what they say and do, interviewers must develop culturally flexible communication styles. This does not mean that they have learned to mimic different groups' cultural speech practices and can do so on demand. Nor are we referring to the ability to do accents or dress in trendy ways. These usually are perceived as affectations. Rather, many broadcasters analyze audiences well and can anticipate the most troublesome or offensive zones in communication. This ability relates to the use of sensitive language discussed in Chapter 5. The principle is relatively simple: Discover what labels or styles potentially offend people, and then avoid these messages whenever possible.

Making Your Decision

• Imagine you are a producer for *Meet the Press* or *Face the Nation*. The head of the news division has suggested that the show include more video clips of politicians' speeches, entrances, photo ops, and the like, and fewer "talking heads" sitting around a table arguing. Do you agree that this is a good move? It will surely cut down on the opportunities for extended interviews of political figures and for roundtables—the interview-like discussions among political analysts. What is your position? What arguments would you put in a memo to support your position?

• Several scenes in the film *Broadcast News* illustrate the ethical dilemmas associated with how to broadcast videotaped interviews. In controversial situations, how much of the interview could be considered fair context if the segment presents a negative criticism of the interviewee? Is it ethical to intercut reactions from the interviewer that were taped outside the actual interview? View the film and keep a log of each "decision point" that involves an ethical choice about interviewing. For each ask yourself: (1) Why did the character(s) make a particular choice? (2) What would I have done, given similar situations, responsibilities, and pressures?

• Famed broadcaster interviewer Larry King (1989) once wrote: "I try to follow a few other rules for interviewing. For openers, I ask short questions. The longer you take, the less the audience is learning. Good questions start with the words *Why* or *How*. Bad questions start with the words *Did* and *When*. With *Why* or *How* questions, I can get some elaboration from the guest. With the others, I'm inviting one-word answers, which everyone hates" (p. 135). In your opinion, is King right about "Did" and "When" questions? Imagine yourself in King's position, interviewing celebrities and politicians. Pick a celebrity you'd like to meet, and prepare several "Did" and several "When" inquiries. What would the interviewee likely answer? Are there occasions in which "Did" and "When" questions are helpful?

• A number of comedy TV shows, including the "fake news" of *The Daily Show* on Comedy Central, have started airing "real" interviews edited for humorous effect. Some public officials, including governors and mayors, have agreed to be interviewed in this way, although they surely must suspect they will be mocked later. Why do you believe they agree to do this? What do they get out of the experience?

Summary

This chapter is unlike previous chapters that introduced you to basic skills of interviewing or to the application of those skills to a particular professional context. It is possible that you will enter a profession in which one or more of these well-defined applications is necessary for performing your job. You need to know not only the how-to aspects of interviewing in professional life but the "why to" aspects and at least some of the research and theory that support the skills.

This chapter and the next attempt to expand the skills application context to a wider social context. Professions and careers are affected by an increasingly global popular media culture. All informed citizens hear hundreds of interviews on television or radio each week and are often influenced deeply by their style and content. It's tempting at times to think that we can learn something about interviewing from these unique personalities, who are public celebrities in their own right. Students bring to class examples of Oprah

Winfrey's interviewing style, or Carson Daly's, or Leslie Stahl's, and they are understandably intrigued. Can we learn from them? Of course we can, with reservations.

In this chapter we've attempted to place this culture-wide obsession with interviewing into professional perspective. The differences between broadcast interviewing (where most influential popular culture interviews occur) and other interviewing occasions are enormous. At the same time, certain prominent skills of broadcast interviewers are clearly transferable. After reading this chapter, you should have a more balanced view of our interview-immersed media culture.

The Interview Bookshelf

On how television has become its own reality:

McKibben, B. (1993). *The age of missing information*. New York: Plume.

McKibben wondered what it would be like to watch all available programming that was aired on a single day in the nation's (then) largest cable system—all the sitcom repeats, all the infomercials, all the local interviews, all the cooking shows. His book contrasts what he learned from the screen with what he learned from a day alone in the Adirondacks.

On planning broadcast interviews:

Biagi, S. (1992). *Interviews that work: A practical guide for journalists* (2nd ed.). Belmont, CA: Wadsworth.

Biagi's excellent discussion of broadcast interviewing points out similarities and, more important, differences between broadcasters' jobs and other journalists' goals.

On the inside track of broadcast interviewing:

Gross, T. (2004). *All I did was ask: Conversations with writers, actors, musicians, and artists.* New York: Hyperion.

Joyce, E. (1988). *Prime times, bad times.* New York: Anchor.

Hilton, J. (1987). *How to meet the press: A survival guide.* New York: Dodd, Mead.

Gross, one of the most famous of the "conversational" broadcast interviewers, shows how planning and editing are essential in the performance interview. Joyce, a former president of CBS News, takes us behind the scenes of network news, often including fascinating, if gossipy, portraits of well-known interviewers. Hilton fancies himself on the other side. A former broadcaster and political commentator for ABC, he now trains public figures to "get their message across" even when talking to ignorant, hostile, or incompetent interviewers. Joyce's and Hilton's analyses probably will make you wince and worry about ethics at times, but they, with Gross, at least help us know what to trust—and fear—in an interview-driven culture.

On critiques of television culture:

Livingstone, S., & Lunt, P. (1994). *Talk on television: Audience participation and public debate.* London: Routledge.

Mander, J. (1978). *Four arguments for the elimination of television.* New York: Quill.

Postman, N. (1985). *Amusing ourselves to death: Public discourse in the age of show business.* New York: Penguin.

Mander and Postman offer polemics—extended arguments advancing a position. Be careful when reading them, but read them. Ad executive Mander's book is often simplistic, and many communication scholars frankly hate its tone. Still, it's been quite influential in the wider cultural discussion of media. Postman is much more scholarly and subtle in supporting his warnings. Livingstone and Lunt have a position, too, but it is more hopeful about the future of public dialogue.

Wrapping It All Up: Professional Interviewing

There are many new things under the sun. However, in their classic early interviewing text published more than 50 years ago, Kahn and Cannell (1957) highlight important issues that are still crucial. They stress how a supposedly straightforward communication act is in reality a complex system of interwoven psychological and sociological processes. Interviewing isn't what one person does to another but a process that develops when two interdependent communicators collaborate to create information and insight. Simplistic research methods and prescriptive training just won't work if an interview is to fulfill its promise.

The Centrality of Interviewing

As an effective interviewer and interviewee, you have found the front door for entering the social conversation about organizational decision making and public policy.

In an era when so many compete to make your decisions for you, interviewing skills and values allow you

If we are to understand the process of interaction between interviewer and respondent, we cannot concern ourselves only with the mechanics of the interviewing process, nor can we be satisfied to study the interview as a series of discrete stimulus–response episodes. We must be concerned instead with the goals, attitudes, beliefs, and motives of the principals in the interview.

. . . Influence between the interviewer and the respondent is by no means a one-way process. The relation is reciprocal, with the psychological fields of both the interviewer and respondent constantly in process of modification because of cues each receives from the other. Most students of interviewing recognize that the motivation of the respondent depends to a considerable extent upon interviewer characteristics and behavior. It is less frequently recognized, however, that the interviewer's behavior depends in part on the respondent.

—Robert L. Kahn and Charles F. Cannell,
The Dynamics of Interviewing

to find answers for yourself. They let you go to the source, to test solutions, to check information, and to personalize your particular professional quest. Interviewing lets your learning be firsthand and personalized, rather than a batch of warmed-over ideas received from others. It lets you take charge of more of your own learning in many of the most crucial arenas of professional life.

Rather than prescribe answers or make your decisions more automatic, we've tried to suggest a two-sided approach to problems of obtaining more information and insight. First, learning about interviewing in this book will help to clear the muddy waters of interpersonal hesitation, apprehension, and fear. Many of us are justifiably afraid of encountering others face-to-face or through other forms of direct and immediate contact. Interviewing involves learning the fundamental skills of interpersonal communication. Second, studying interviewing will muddy some waters that might have previously seemed clear. This is a good thing. That is, without overcomplicating things, we've tried to show how this topic, which some presume is straightforward and nonproblematic, is actually more complex than it is often assumed to be. Throughout this book, therefore, we've encouraged interview participants to see themselves not only as speakers and listeners enacting skills, but also as thinkers. Effective interviewers and interviewees prepare carefully, diagnose and troubleshoot possible problems, assess their experiences, project the probabilities for future success, and adjust accordingly. They need a familiarity with the broader psychological, social, and cultural contexts of interpersonal relationships. They frame their experiences in ways that are not always observable in the simple behaviors people demonstrate for each other.

Some kinds of learning tend to close people down, whereas others can open people up. Think about a professor who teaches poetry writing by having you memorize and copy Shakespeare's sonnets. Surely your time wouldn't be completely wasted, because Shakespeare is worth studying and you can learn much about rhyme and meter by modeling and emulating his work. However, the outcome of this learning isn't likely to help you glimpse the wider range of functions poetry can serve, nor will it necessarily help you develop your own creativity as a poet. Something enlightening has happened, but you've also been closed down, in one sense, by someone else's experience being imposed on you. Experiencing other poems, other poetries—including your own first attempts in your own voice—would develop your own artistic abilities. Keep an interest in Shakespeare, or rhymed poetry, but not as your sole focus. Skills help, but you go beyond them to other appreciations and applications to open yourself up to a new area like poetry.

Interviewing is a bit like learning poetry in this sense. We encourage you to develop a wide range of appreciations and curiosities to go along with your basic communication skills. Trust the advice of experienced practitioners, but don't swallow it whole and indiscriminately. We've included many boxes in which practitioners discuss real-life dilemmas they face, and you'll notice they don't all agree on what to do about these problems. We've included many boxes asking you to make your own decisions in hypothetical and real cases. An education in interviewing involves not only learning how to speak and listen, but also how to think.

Skills-Plus Interviewing

We have framed this book as a *skills-plus approach* for a good reason. It's important to know what to do, which is the focus of a skill-building approach. But it's equally important to know why it works and to be flexible in atypical situations. Don't shirk either the "What?" or the "Why?" questions in studying interviewing. Without a broad base of behavioral and cognitive skills, you won't be able to perform competently in everyday interview situations. You won't have the raw materials to build with. On the other hand, if you *only* stress such skill building, you miss much of the context in which those skills exist. You'll be able to deal with the so-called normal situations but will be shocked or immobilized when creativity is necessary.

We divided each chapter into (1) basic issues, and (2) ideas that build on or extend them—"The Basics" and "Beyond the Basics." Experts might disagree about some of these choices and believe we've relegated some truly basic information to the ends of chapters. In no sense are the "Beyond the Basics" sections impractical, marginal, or dispensable. Rather, they describe issues that, in our opinion, might be addressed best with the rest of the chapter's content firmly in mind. We thought it would aid your reading to defer some topics until a baseline understanding of terms and concepts was built. In some cases instructors will assign entire chapters, whereas other instructors might assign only "The Basics," leaving the later topics for other courses or your personal reading.

The major themes of a complex subject are difficult to summarize. However, a final chapter is a good place to attempt to boil things down. When you think back over all of what you've read, what basic ideas seem most relevant across contexts? Regardless of what specific interview contexts or roles in which you might find yourself, we believe all interviewers and interviewees should keep the following basic principles in the front of their minds.

Remember That Interviewing Is Focused Conversation

Chapter 1 defined an interview as an interpersonal or public communication situation in which one or more persons seeks information and insight from another or others. Although interviewing is occasionally described as a one-sided activity of extracting information, the best interviews tend toward conversational talk in important ways. The term itself discloses a clue to the potential of interviewing: Interviews can become "inter-views." By interviewing, we learn what we have in common with others, what they have to share with us, and vice versa. "Inter-view": Views can become shared between (inter-) communicators, just as in conversations.

However, interviewing is different from having everyday spontaneous conversations; if it were no more difficult than that, taking classes in it would not be necessary. Instead, an interview is a *focused* conversation. Interviewers and interviewees build on the skills of normal talk, whether they are discussing a potential job, a new treatment for cancer patients, a product preference in a brief mall survey, or a politician's campaign promise.

Let Curiosity Guide You

People presumably want to interview because they want to learn something new, and they consent to be interviewed because they have something to say. Both of these insights rely on a faith in our human capacity for speech to improve our relationships. When we need to know about something, we usually seek out someone to ask; when asked, we tend to respond. This reciprocal relationship, so often at the heart of friendships and families, is also at the core of career success for communication professionals. Having good questions and being willing to respond appropriately are in many ways the hallmarks of professional success in any career.

Nurture Dialogic Skills and Appreciations

Dialogic skills and appreciations ideally motivate interview communicators. This means that each respects the uniqueness of the other person, and each attempts to create occasions in which both go beyond what they already know to achieve new insight. It means that the best interviews are prepared for carefully but not prefabricated or scripted. It means that the participants value their differences as much as their similarities. It means that each side tries to imagine the reality of the other, communicating empathically even when intimate communication is not involved. It means that each communicator speaks ethically and authentically to preserve the range of choices of the other. The three dialogic skills emphasized in this book are listening, questioning, and framing.

Listening Sets the Stage

Listening is the baseline skill that lets an interview develop between two or more people. Concepts of listening and speech cannot be separated easily in everyday life, even for analytical purposes. However, one insight does clearly suggest the importance of listening. Without the expectation of being heard and, at a deeper level, listened to, we don't even begin to consider the possibility of asking questions. Speakers who are self-absorbed don't progress very far in any human endeavor. Instead, the more common experience for speakers is to imagine their partner's style and capacity of listening and then fit speech to that estimate.

Listening, as we've stressed it in this book, is an active process of understanding and checking meanings with others. It is not merely a passive reception of others' messages. You listen actively by paying attention, to be sure, but also by reflections, paraphrases, and perception checks that let others know when they've been misunderstood. With effective listening, questioning and framing become meaningful.

Questioning Fuels Listening

As we intend the term, questioning implies both the act of asking questions and the attitude of checking reality. Genuine questioning in an interview demonstrates how you want to learn, when you have a desire to learn, and why you're willing to inquire.

A friend of ours intersperses his conversations, about topics large and small, with a simple verbal habit—every so often he'll ask, "What do *you* think?" Then he waits to hear what you'll say. It's surprising how many good ideas he hears and how people feel good about being asked. Of course, not all questions operate that way; some questions can be taunts, or manipulations, or sarcastic comments, or attempts to embarrass others: "What makes you think *that*?" "I got an A, just like last week. What did you get?" "You don't really agree with Senator Hudson's vote on schools, do you?"

Questioning, as we've stressed, is an open invitation that convinces others that you're going to listen carefully to how they respond. But beware of too much, or too little, reliance on questions. Without them, interviews don't seem like interviews, but with only questions, interviews seem like interrogations and cross-examinations.

Framing Creates Perspective

People don't just accumulate information, as if facts were packages of meaning that they need to gather. Interviewers sometimes overgeneralize by referring to "information gathering" as though the information was sitting only slightly under the surface of life, "out there" somewhere waiting to be found by an industrious truth seeker. In fact, as evidence cited throughout our book verifies, communicators never collect information neutrally in that sense; they are forever interpreting, infusing perceptions with feelings, investing them with connotations of good or bad, perceiving their importance in light of this or that goal.

Framing, as we've discussed it in this book, probes how interviewers and interviewees interpret information in their own contexts and put it to their own uses. The question becomes: How can we recognize and gain access to others' frames? Interviewers experience this problem, for example, when they decide how to establish rapport and open up conversations—where is this other person coming from? Interviewers experience this also when they try to figure out, often with fragmentary clues, what the questioner really wants to know.

Continue to Learn

When concluding a class, many students pack up their notes, sell their textbooks to the campus bookstore or an online vendor, buy new texts, and start thinking about a vacation or next semester. This might be one class where you should keep your notes and books handy and ideas in the front of your mind. In addition to their obvious relevance for professional careers, interviewing skills and appreciations are extraordinarily helpful for completing assignments in other college classes.

You're fishing for a good term paper topic in your Persuasion class; interviewing a political science, law school, or media ethics professor could lead you to some interesting controversies in government–media relations—prior restraint of publications, definitions of hate speech, or political implications of pornography definitions, for example. Or you're having trouble in your Philosophy of Communication class and need to ask your teacher specifics about how Wittgenstein relates to conflict management. Or you are studying for your first exam in Communication Research and realize you need a refresher in qualitative interviewing skills. Or your Public Affairs Reporting class requires you to spend a day at the county courthouse and write at least two stories; is it possible you'd want to talk to lawyers or to police officers? Or the Women's Studies Program is being reviewed by the campus administration, and you'd like to survey recent graduates to discover their impressions of the faculty and curriculum. To keep your learning about interviewing fresh, we suggest you do the following:

- Keep an informal interviewing log in which you note especially good examples of effectiveness in interviewers and interviewees. Who are the best interviewers in popular media? What are their strengths? How can you build those strengths into your own interpersonal style? Who are the least effective interviewers in popular media? What are their weaknesses? How can you avoid those weaknesses in your own style?

- Read more about famous interviewers, such as Barbara Walters, Ray Suarez, Charles Kuralt, Studs Terkel, or Terry Gross.

- Volunteer for any interviewing tasks that come up in your student activities group, civic or neighborhood club, or political action group.

- Interview several interviewers to see if their experiences match ideas and advice you've read in this book and other textbooks or articles. One particularly practical suggestion is to conduct informational interviews with several successful professionals in the career area you're considering. Ask them not only for opinions but also for stories—anecdotes that illustrate the centrality of effective interviewing in their jobs. Find out from them firsthand whether interviewing skills are practical in the world of work.

- Write at least two forms of your résumé, and update them regularly whether you're applying for jobs or not. This personal habit will remind you to be systematically introspective about your qualifications and your communication skills. Work with the career center on your campus to stay current with new expectations employers might have about résumé format and content, including online innovations.

- Schedule role-play employment interviews with career center personnel and with several professors in your department who understand the career for which you're preparing yourself. Make sure they feel comfortable giving you both positive (reinforcing) and negative feedback and that they have enough time to coach you fully on options for adapting your behavior.

Summary

Studying interviewing can be based on conversational dialogue. Although this approach might sound nonthreatening, it does put your ego on the line. Interviews are collaborative, but their participants encounter each other as unique individuals, too.

We wrote this book for students in performance courses that combine practice in professional tasks with insights about interpersonal communication. It has asked you to monitor your communication competence in front of other people and to practice better ways to listen, speak, and frame information to learn. In doing so, you integrate skills with attitudes, theory, and research in the best tradition of the communication disciplines.

account A statement offered to make your frame clear and explicit in response to a possible misunderstanding with a communication partner. *See* **frame (framing)**.

acknowledgment cluster In confirmation theory, a group of statements or behaviors that indicate a willingness to follow or remain engaged with someone's words, expressed through verbal or nonverbal signs.

acquiescence When communicators passively accept whatever happens or is said, acting as though they have no right to exert control in the situation.

active listening A style of responding in which the listener is willing to test his or her interpretation aloud, with the intention of enhancing and refining communication. Active listening often is expressed by a communicator saying, for example, "I'm hearing that your main idea is . . . ," followed by a paraphrase of the speaker's meaning.

affective/behavioral inference response A listener's verbalized attempt to note and interpret a speaker's behavioral or nonverbal messages.

aggressiveness When communicators attempt to prevail or control communication with little or no regard for the feelings or rights of other participants.

amplification probe Follow-up questions or comments that ask for an expansion of a response to a primary question.

appraisal interview An organizational interview designed to allow a superior to assess and communicate with a subordinate through mutual feedback and goal setting.

appreciative listening Listening to enjoy the creative or aesthetic features of a message.

archiving Labeling a tape or other recording clearly, with a date, place, and subject, and keeping it, along with written notes or other interview material, in a safe place.

artifacts Objects people display intentionally or unintentionally that are meaningful in a relationship. An executive's desk, for example, is an artifact that may symbolize status, and the photographs displayed on that desk may suggest commitment to family life.

assertiveness A midpoint between **acquiescence** and **aggressiveness** in communication, when speakers act or express themselves in ways that protect their own rights while respecting the rights of others.

assumptive close When a seller in a persuasive encounter concludes the interview by assuming the respondent has made a commitment to buy, complicating the process if there is a "no" response.

attending behaviors Nonverbal cues that indicate a listener is paying attention.

attitude A person's predisposition to behave in certain ways.

attribution theory A description of how people attempt to explain, or attribute, behaviors to either internal or external causes.

audio computer-assisted self-administered interview (ACASI) A form of survey research interview in which the interviewee, working at his or her own pace, privately responds to questions from a computer program that includes an interviewer's voice. *See* **computer-assisted self-administered interview (CASI)**.

behavior-based testing In selection settings, an interview in which the interviewee is asked either to describe handling a crisis situation or to demonstrate a skill—an approach based on the presumption that past behavior often predicts future performance. Known also as *behavior-based interviewing (BBI)*. In therapy settings, a behavioral interview centers on breaking a cycle of behavior.

behaviorally anchored rating system (BARS) A form of appraisal rating that assesses workers' performance according to standards based on a thorough analysis of job requirements.

369

blindside questions   Questions the interviewer knows the interviewee will not expect; used to surprise and either test reactions or obtain an unrehearsed answer.

bona fide occupational qualifications (BFOQ)   A legal term used to describe the qualities and qualifications demonstrably related to effective performance on a given job.

brainteaser interview   An employment interview that tests on applicant's problem-solving ability with so-called "puzzle" questions.

breaking the frame   When one of the two or more communication partners violates shared assumptions regulating their interaction.

census   A group of survey respondents that includes all members of a given population.

choice close   A method of closing a persuasive interview by laying out options to help the prospective buyer reach a decision.

chronological organization   An interview style in which questions move from past toward recent or current events or details.

chronological résumé   A résumé that summarizes an applicant's qualifications, experiences, and other attributes from most to least recent. *See* **functional résumé.**

clarification   Similar to **paraphrasing**—a skill of critical listening that helps communication partners ensure that each understands the other.

clarification probe   A type of follow-up question or comment that assists understanding by enabling communication partners to test perceptions and listening acuity.

clear frame   A description of a situation in which participants clearly share very similar definitions and expectations for what they are doing together.

clearing   The psychological and physiological process of eliminating distractions that could interfere with the ability to listen.

clearinghouse questions   See **wrap-up questions.**

client-centered therapy   To Rogers, a term for a therapeutic relationship focusing on nonjudgmental listening and therapy rather than on a therapist's behavioral or analytical techniques.

close   A term for the final stage of persuasive interviewing when a commitment or binding decision occurs.

closed questions   Sometimes called closed-ended questions, they seek specific information and limit the range of a respondent's answers. *See* **open-ended questions.**

coaching   A mutual activity of one person helping another improve performance by changing behavior, solving a problem, or developing a plan.

code   In the context of communication studies, an organized and interlinked set of conditions that characterize a situation; the internal logic of a context that may sometimes be difficult to see.

coding   A system researchers use to place responses or collected data into categories.

cognitive interview   A therapeutic approach that focuses on helping a client replace negative with rational thoughts.

communication   The complex process of developing shared meaning through messages, both verbal and nonverbal, between persons in a relationship.

communication competence   Knowledge, skills, and motivation to behave appropriately in communication relationships.

communication noise   See **noise.**

communication rule   An implicit social agreement that helps people decide what behavior is obligated, preferred, or prohibited in certain social contexts.

compliance   The process of accepting the influence of another person in the hope of achieving a favorable reaction from that person.

comprehensive listening   Listening to comprehend a speaker's meaning or intention.

computer-assisted self-administered interviewing (CASI)   A form of survey research interviewing in which the interviewee, working at his or own pace, privately responds to questions from a computer program. *See* **audio computer-assisted self-administered interviewing (ACASI).**

concentration   The ability to filter out the effects of distractions when listening.

confirmative probe A follow-up question or comment that attempts to challenge the reliability of answers.

confirmation theory Suggests that communication quality often depends on the acknowledgment and recognition people receive from others.

connotation The range of informal meanings words acquire in everyday usage.

content inference response A way of telling a speaker that you have both heard and attempted to understand what has been said.

contextualizing Acknowledging for yourself, and perhaps for your communication partner, the full context in which the communication is occurring.

convenience (available) sample In research interviewing, a sample group of respondents selected on the basis of availability or convenience rather than representativeness.

conversational maxims Four factors—quantity, quality, relevance, and manner—that help conversants determine when and how they need to be flexible.

cooperative principle The presumption that each speaker should contribute appropriately to the purposes and directions of a conversation.

counseling interview An interview context in which professionals help clients discuss strategies that might assist them in making sound decisions or working out problems.

counterbalance close A persuasive interviewing strategy that sellers use to encourage acceptance of an idea or product by matching a respondent's reservations with an offsetting benefit.

cover letter A narrative description to introduce yourself and explain why you're qualified and a good fit for a job.

credibility In communication, a listener's estimate of a speaker's expertise, and, to a lesser extent, dynamism. *See* **ethos.**

criteria checklist A list of qualifications and other employment considerations that help selection interviewers supplement a list of essential skills. *See* **profile of essential skills.**

critical incident report A narrative assessment that focuses on concrete examples of a worker's ability to carry out job responsibilities.

critical listening Listening that focuses on judging the worth and quality of messages.

decentering The ability to see things from perspectives other than your own; closely related to **empathy.**

defensive climate An interpersonal context, often stimulated by unnecessary judgment or criticism, that encourages communicators to react as if they are protecting themselves from attack.

delayed note taking A style of recording interview information that relies on memory to collect details and later recall an interview; used when on-the-spot note taking isn't possible or advisable.

demographics Characteristics such as gender, race, or age used by researchers to define or identify segments of a population.

denotation The literal meaning of words as defined, for example, in dictionaries.

deontology An ethical orientation that stresses strict adherence to rules or duties in one's behavior and decision making.

depth description version A detailed position description for job applicants.

diagnostic interview A focused inquiry into the possible causes of a physical or psychological problem; takes into account symptoms, conditions, and feelings for the purpose of assessment and possible treatment.

dialogue Moments of communication that depend on mutually interactive, reciprocal relationship, not technique or strategy. In dialogue, communicators become partners in producing insights and understanding of each other and the topics they explore.

direct questions Questions that are blunt, to the point, and specific.

discriminative listening Listening to determine types and subtleties of differences in messages.

disqualifying response In **confirmation theory,** when a communicator dismisses, trivializes, or disparages the words and ideas of others.

double-barreled questions Questions with two or more parts to them, making them difficult to answer.

DPFP sequence An abbreviation for the *draft, proof, feedback,* and *proof* method for creating, refining, and checking a résumé.

egoism A branch of ethics that emphasizes an individual making the decisions most likely to produce the greatest good for that individual.

emotional sensitivity The ability to infer from a speaker's words and behaviors the emotional state of mind behind messages.

empathy Sensing someone else's world accurately, as they sense it, without leaving your own. In part, both an attitude and an ability to detect and appreciate another person's feelings, emotions, and concerns.

employee assistance programs Programs sponsored by, or contracted by, large corporations in which employees can find help for serious emotional, medical, or behavioral problems. These options are often recommended during intervention or appraisal interviews for employees whose work may be suffering temporarily.

employment interview An encounter between an applicant and an organizational representative for the purpose of mutually exploring information and subjects relevant to hiring or selection decisions.

endorsement cluster In confirmation theory, a group of statements or behaviors that accept and treat a speaker's messages as important or OK.

epistemology The study of how human knowledge and insight develop.

essence quote Description that paraphrases a respondent's basic meaning and includes a particularly vivid quoted phrase.

establishing shots Visuals used in television or video to help audiences see how participants are oriented physically to each other within a context.

ethnocentrism The attitude suggesting that all cultural groups should be judged by the standards of the perceiver's own culture.

ethnography A form of research in which an interviewer or participant observer attempts to experience as directly as possible a different culture's expectations, values, beliefs, and behavioral patterns.

ethos In classical rhetoric, one of three ways communicators persuade others (*see* **logos** and **pathos**). Ethos is a persuasiveness that comes from force of character; often known in contemporary communication studies as **credibility**.

euphemisms Presumably inoffensive words used as replacements for words that are considered unpleasant or offensive.

exit interview An interview by an organizational representative with an employee who resigns or retires; conducted for purposes of closure or feedback, and assistance with the transition to new jobs or tasks.

facilitative conditions To Rogers, the qualities of respect, genuineness, and empathy found in effective relationships between helpers and clients.

field notes An ethnographer's detailed, written record of cultural communication, including contextual observations, that can make unfamiliar cultural patterns more meaningful.

field review A narrative assessment conducted by a manager or supervisor who observes a worker's performance on the job and uses those observations for a written report.

fight behavior A confrontive reaction to criticism.

filmic procedures Broadcast decisions involving how to film or videotape interaction, such as televised interviews; these decisions key audiences to how they should frame or interpret that interaction.

flight behavior Withdrawal and passivity in the face of criticism.

focus group An approach to research in which respondents are recruited by a researcher to discuss in groups what draws them to certain attitudes, preferences, or products. Moderators in such studies are, in effect, group interviewers.

focused coding Stage of fieldnote coding in which the researcher restudies the data and tentative themes, looking especially for links between themes.

forced-choice rating A special type of rating system designed to channel raters' responses into a limited number of categories.

forced distribution A ranking approach that requires managers to show where individual workers fit within categories in relation to an assessment of all employees of a particular department or operation.

frame (framing) The complex inner process of interpreting and evaluating patterns of messages according to the contexts in which they occur.

free narrative question An inquiry that allows a respondent to create a personal account with no structuring from the interviewer.

full mental focus A skill of **comprehensive listening** that capitalizes on the "spare time" created by the difference between the rate of speech and the rate of thought.

functional résumé A résumé that organizes an applicant's qualifications around the functions of a particular job, such a "office management" or "writing skills." *See* **chronological résumé.**

fundamental attribution error The tendency for an interviewer or other communicator to regard others as motivated by internal forces while assuming his or her own motivation is determined by the circumstances at hand.

funnel organization A method of interviewing that begins with general, open-ended questions and moves to increasingly specific and narrow ones.

global essay A form of narrative assessment by which a supervisor writes generalized, or "global" impressions of a worker's performance.

goal-setting theory A concept based on the belief that managers and workers should jointly identify and seek attainment of a set of performance objectives.

graphic rating scales Common method of organizational appraisal in which criteria (traits, behaviors, and attitudes) are accompanied by definitions and examples of what each category means.

head and shoulders close-up A camera perspective that brings the audience within the equivalent of touching distance of the speaker.

hearing The psychological or biological process by which sounds are perceived by the human ear and auditory apparatus. Compare with **listening.**

high-flex communicator Someone who understands, appreciates, and adapts to the context and the process of **communication rules.**

highly scheduled interview A structured interview planned in advance that follows a detailed and prescribed organization.

holding A therapeutic method that employs supportive talk to make a client feel safe in sharing painful or embarrassing details.

horizontal dimension In oral history, areas or branches of an interviewee's life to explore relative to the **vertical dimension** of chronology.

human studies research committee *See* **institutional review board.**

hypothetical question A form of question that creates a dramatic or narrative situation and asks respondents to react as if they were participants.

identification In the process of social influence, how people sometimes adopt the behaviors or preferences of others they admire or model.

I-message A nonjudgmental way of responding to a speaker's statements without raising defensiveness. An I-message indicates only that a speaker believes or feels something, without implying that someone else necessarily is responsible for causing that state.

immediacy theory Explains how face-to-face communication that is verbally and nonverbally close and direct increases communicators' satisfaction. Nonverbal immediacy can be increased, for example, by more eye contact or by reducing interactional distance; verbal immediacy can be increased by substituting personalized phrases such as, "I am pleased with your department's work this quarter, Jeanne," for "The marketing department is improving this quarter."

impervious response When one communicator, such as an interviewer, acknowledges the presence of another but fails to act as if the other person could make a significant difference in the relationship.

implied consent A research interviewee's unstated but obvious willingness to participate in a study. *See* **informed consent.**

impression management skills The ability to adjust talk and nonverbal messages successfully to meet the demands of a communication situation and to present an appropriate image to others.

indifferent response Words or actions by which someone suggests he or she doesn't care about a speaker or the speaker's words.

indirect questions Questions, often marked by introductory phrases or qualifiers, that allow the respondent to infer intentions and meanings rather than be confronted directly.

inflection How speakers emphasize certain words over others by varying vocal volume or pitch.

information gathering interview An interaction that focuses on learning something specific from another person or group.

informed consent In an interview or other research setting, the oral or written assurance that participants understand the risks and benefits of answering questions.

institutional review board A body charged with reviewing research proposals and sometimes monitoring research that involves potential risk to participants. Known by other names, such as *human studies research committee.*

internalization The process of social influence by which people conclude a proposed change fits within their values systems and adopt it for that reason.

interpersonal ethic An ethical approach that weighs the implications of one's messages for their impact on the communication rights of others. In general, an interpersonal ethic is guided by the maintenance or expansion of choices available to communicators.

interrogation interview An interview designed to persuade an interviewee to disclose all relevant facts fully even when disclosure may not be in the individual's best interest.

intervention interview A face-to-face interview between a superior and a subordinate in an organization for the purpose of dealing with a crisis or problem attributable to the subordinate's behavior.

interview An interpersonal or public communication event in which one or more persons seek information and insight from another or others.

interviewer-conducted survey Highly standardized survey completed face-to-face with the researcher.

interviewing by comment A means of using comments or statements to elicit important information.

inverted funnel organization A method of interviewing that progresses from narrow, specific questions and widens to broader, general ones.

jargon The "inside language" of particular fields, professions, or interests that is often unfamiliar to outsiders.

leading questions Questions that suggest by their form the kind of answer desired by the questioner.

Likert-type scale An instrument to measure attitude; it asks respondents to consider an issue or statement, then indicate where they stand on a scale of approval or agreement.

linguistic conservatism The attitude that society should preserve or "conserve" language as a commonly shared experience; this perspective assumes that words should be applied and understood by similar ways by communicators, whatever their cultural backgrounds. *See also* **multiculturalism, political correctness.**

listening The holistic activity of processing aural stimuli, interpreting them as messages, and using them to construct meanings of speech, speakers, and contexts.

literature The current body of knowledge in any field of study.

literature review A careful written analysis of existing research and data on a proposed topic to be studied.

loaded questions Questions that plant a questioner's emotional presumption within the wording, often using judgmental or accusatory language.

local knowledge In ethnography, understandings specifically relevant for the local and immediate context in which they are communicated.

logos In classical rhetoric, one of three ways communicators influence audiences (*see* **ethos** and **pathos**). Logos refers to persuasiveness that comes from appeals to logic.

management by objectives (MBO) A management philosophy that values attainment of organizational goals.

meal interview A complex interview setting often scheduled for lunch or dinner, in which an applicant's ability to converse and interact with one or more interviewers is tested by the need to divide attention among several different tasks.

mediation An interaction that involves a neutral third-party interviewer to help settle difficult negotiations.

medium shot A camera perspective that approximates what is considered the proper social distance for interpersonal communication.

member check A qualitative researcher's method of asking interviewees from researched groups to review tentative interpretations and conclusions to guide against errors.

memos Brief theoretical notes a researcher writes to self, to describe his or her current state of understanding.

metacommunication The process by which communication partners address the state of their communication through either implicit, silent commentary or explicit verbal analysis.

metamessages Messages (often tone of voice or visual clues, like a wink) used to tell others how to interpret other messages.

microgoals A series of small steps systematically leading to the attainment of a major goal.

mirror response Reflecting or repeating a speaker's statement to help verify and note that the speaker has been heard accurately.

mixed messages Perceived contradictions between verbal and nonverbal messages sent by a communicator.

moderately scheduled interview An interview that mixes standard, preestablished questions with improvised and individualized ones.

multiculturalism A term with various meanings, it particularly suggests an emphasis on how language and mannerisms can communicate powerful messages about or affecting cultural identities. Multiculturalists, therefore, tend to conceive of language as an arena to affect cultural change. *See* **linguistic conservatism, political correctness**.

narrative The human tendency to tell and appreciate dramatic stories. Also, an appraisal method based on an anecdotal evaluation, written either after, or as the basis for, an appraisal interview.

needs assessment A systematic description of what a job calls for in terms of a new employee's skills and knowledge; an aid in interviewing.

negotiation interview Any situation in which competing parties function as both interviewer and interviewee in exchanges expected to result in agreement or consensus.

noise Any psychological or physiological interference with a listener's attempt to tend to messages.

nonjudgmental response A listening approach that avoids attacking or otherwise judging a speaker's words or actions.

nonprobability survey In interview research, a sample population selected without the use of mathematical guidelines of probability.

nonscheduled interview An interview determined by moment-to-moment exchanges rather than questions or topics set in advance; nonscheduled interviews are common in many therapy sessions and on-the-scene journalistic settings.

not for attribution An understanding in a journalistic interview; when an individual, usually a public figure, agrees to an interview on the expressed condition that he or she will not be identified in a reporter's story as the source of the information. *See* **off the record, on background**.

note set The raw, dense collection of interview data that the researcher later refines by analysis.

off the record An understanding in a journalistic interview; when someone supplies a journalist with information with the stipulation that it is not to be published. *See* **not for attribution, on background**.

on background An understanding in a journalistic interview; when someone agrees to provide a journalist with off-the-record information with the agreement that it will not be published or broadcast, or attributed to the source. It can however, be used by the journalist to discover further relevant information about a story. *See* **not for attribution, off the record.**

open coding Interpretations and labels added in the margins of field notes to aid the qualitative interviewer in later analysis.

open questions Questions that invite respondents to choose their own direction, depth, and context for answers. *See* **closed questions.**

oral history A rich documentary record produced from an interviewee's firsthand perceptions or memories.

over-rapport Interviewer bias resulting from excessive closeness or cordiality.

pace The timing and tempo of an interview.

panel interview A form of selection interview in which several organizational representatives take turns asking questions and seeking information from an applicant.

papers of record Periodicals, such as the *New York Times*, considered authoritative sources on political, social, and economic information.

paralinguistic cues Nonverbal vocal variations, such as pitch and volume, that influence how a speaker's message will be interpreted.

paraphrasing The repetition of a speaker's ideas or statements in a listener's own words to verify accurate listening.

passant phenomenon A condition in which people will disclose highly personal information to a stranger they do not expect to meet again.

pathos In classical rhetoric, one of three ways communicators persuade others (*see* **ethos** and **logos**). Pathos is persuasiveness that comes from appeals to emotion.

patient-centered philosophy An approach to helping interviews in medicine; characterized by concern for the whole person, with medical personnel exploring the illness experience from the patient's perspective.

peer rankings A method of appraisal that evaluates an employee or group member on the basis of colleagues' assessments of his or her work relative to the performance of other colleagues.

performance plan An outcome of organizational interviews that help employees set realistic goals for attaining measurable improvement.

personality profile A journalistic article or report on an individual based on in-depth reporting.

persuasion The communication process in which beliefs, attitudes, values, or behaviors are influenced by others' messages.

political correctness A term describing a belief that society is increasingly controlled by political agendas of various cultural groups, particularly efforts to enforce rules about acceptable language and behavior.

preinterview A short interchange that sets up or coordinates longer interviews.

preparatory questions In an interview, communication that helps show hospitality, establish rapport, or screen information in a nonthreatening way.

primary questions Interview questions the purpose of which is to open areas of inquiry and discover basic information. *See* **probes.**

primary selection interviewing A single round of interviewing intended to identify and select a particular employee for a particular position.

probability survey Interview research using a sample population drawn by mathematical guidelines to represent a larger population accurately.

probe notes An interviewer's written reminders to help recall questions or topics he or she wants to address later in the interview.

probes Questions or inquiries that confirm or amplify information elicited by **primary. questions** or by previous probes. Also called probe questions.

profile of essential skills A document that lists the main qualities and qualifications necessary to excel in a given job. *See* **criteria checklist.**

psychological contract Unstated expectations about appropriate behaviors or attitudes by members within an organization.

psychotherapy interview Treatment that focuses on investigating and confronting enabling psychological conditions, such as deep-seated depression; typically, psychotherapy is conducted in face-to-face interview settings.

public journalism A movement that stresses greater involvement by news organizations in community life and resolution of community problems.

punctuation The mental act by which people attribute causes and effects, stops and starts, and other indicators of meaning to what they see and hear.

qualitative research An inquiry, often using interviewing methods, that concentrates on less tangible qualities of experience that characterize social action. *See* **quantitative research.**

Quality of Work Life formula (QWL) A method of assessing job satisfaction according to a set of criteria.

quantitative research An inquiry to generate, categorize, and analyze statistical data by use of instruments such as questionnaires and surveys. *See* **qualitative research.**

quota sample A group of respondents selected to match, for example, known percentages of subsets found in a larger population.

quote searching Listening to a taped account of an interview until you hear the quotes that best meet your goals.

random selection A mathematical method of ensuring that every member of a population has an equal chance of being selected for a **sample.**

rankings Quantitative assignments or estimates that compare a person or thing to other persons or things based on a stated measure. In ranking procedures, each member must be designated as first, second, or third, and so on, in a given group. *See* **ratings.**

rapport Positive, natural, and mutually attentive talk and behavior that encourage further talk by creating an environment of comfort and cooperation.

ratified participant A concept that accounts for the silent, but fully recognized as important, participation of the audience in broadcasts.

ratings Evaluations that assess persons or things on the basis of a series of carefully defined performance criteria. Ratings differ from **rankings** in that they reflect individual performance quality, whereas rankings reflect performance quality in direct comparison of other persons or things.

recognition cluster In **confirmation theory,** a group of statements or behaviors that indicate direct engagement with, and focused attention on, a speaker.

recognition skills In **discriminative listening,** attentiveness to verbal, vocal, and behavior cues of meaning.

reduced note taking Reading the written notes of an interview while listening to the taped conversation, comparing the two, and filling in the gaps in the notes.

reframing Consciously developing a new context in which to interpret phenomena; often involves recasting a potentially negative or unhelpful frame to one that is positive and helpful.

regulation skills In **discriminative listening,** being sensitive to acting on cues that signal turn taking and other behaviors that govern conversation.

relationship to the story An aspect of analyzing identity codes in media interviews, referring to a participant's ties to certain topics.

relayed feedback A skill that allows job applicants or other interviewees to pass along positive assessments others have made of them without appearing boastful.

reliability Whether a research measures the same phenomenon whenever it is used. *See* **validity.**

résumé A succinct summary of the education, work experience, and skills that qualify a person for a job. *See* **chronological résumé, functional résumé.**

rhetoric The study of intentional communication, often involving how people implement strategies to influence others.

rhetorical questions Questions for which the answer is so obvious that they don't need to be answered at all.

rhythm A comfortable, harmonious order and progression of an interview.

sample A group of respondents for an interview or study that represents a larger population.

sampling error The degrees to which a given sample statistic will likely fail to correspond to the actual characteristics of a population.

schedule An interviewer's planned organization of questions or topics.

screening interview Preliminary interviews designed to determine whether a job applicant meets requirements and warrants a fuller second interview or follow-up interview.

second interview/on-site visit A follow-up interview, often for the purposes of exposing an interviewee to the work setting and meeting potential coworkers under actual organizational conditions.

selection interview An interaction designed to determine whom to hire for a job or select for an honor or award; the term is sometimes used to describe the employment interview process as a whole.

selective transcription Transcribing sections of a taped interview most relevant to the interviewer's purposes.

self-administered questionnaire Instrument completed at respondents' own initiative often after mail or Internet distribution.

self-evaluative essay A type of narrative assessment based on a worker's personal portrayal of his or her performance.

self-fulfilling prophecy A phenomenon in which prior perceptual habits and expectations at least partially determine what people find in new situations, thereby "fulfilling" their own expectations.

self-rating An employee's appraisal of personal performance, based on criteria or standards on a rating form provided by the organization.

semantic differential scale A measurement instrument that asks respondents to consider a concept along a continuum, ranging from one quality to its opposite: hot–cold, active–inactive, and so forth.

simple random sample A sample based on assigning each member of a population a number and then choosing a sample from a table of random numbers.

skill The ability to adapt behaviorally to meet the demands of different contexts.

skills-plus approach Communication that emphasizes skills in the context of the values and motivations of the people using them.

snowball sample A sample developed as a group of respondents identifies more respondents, who identify others, and so on.

social roles The positions assumed by interviewers and interviewees along with behaviors associated with those positions.

sound bites Short, slogan-like statements that supposedly capture longer, more complex ideas in a few quotable words; often used in media coverage.

space In nonverbal communication, how persons use distance to define relationships and meanings.

standing-room-only close A tactic used by sellers to imply or state that a respondent must act now or forever lose the opportunity to buy something framed as desirable or wanted.

stereotyping Using mental pictures or expectations to predict and explain others.

stratified random sample A sample that takes into account and studies various subsets, such as age and occupation, of a random sample.

stress questions Questions expressly designed to make respondents uncomfortable so the interviewer can observe reactions.

suitcase questions Questions crammed to overflowing with implications or details.

supportive climate An interpersonal atmosphere or context that encourages communicators to seek ways of supporting each other. *See* **defensive climate**.

supportive questions Questions or probes that help direct and advance interviews by bolstering, setting up, or following up primary questions.

surface description version A concise statement prepared by an organization for applicants, describing a job position.

surplus of seeing To Bakhtin, the idea that each person in a communication relationship sees, hears, and thus contributes perspectives that the other partner cannot.

systematic random sample A method of selecting a sample based on every nth part or unit of a population.

tape-sensitive notes Notebook entries an interviewer uses to remember important points or statements and specify where they can be found on the tape.

teleology An ethical orientation that emphasizes the importance of outcomes and consequences in actions and decisions.

telephone survey Brief, highly scheduled, and focused interview conducted over the telephone.

test of publicity An ethical principle based on asking whether a communicator would feel comfortable in publicizing an action to a wide audience of reasonable people.

testimonial close A seller or persuader's strategy to close a deal by introducing a statement from someone a potential buyer finds credible.

testing A skill of critical listening that involves a constant willingness to detect and assess communication problems and discuss them openly.

therapeutic interview Designed to assist in systematic modification of interviewee's behavior, thinking, or psychological state.

therapeutic listening Listening to help others accomplish their goals through supportive styles and behaviors.

360-degree appraisal An appraisal method based on collecting feedback from everyone whose productivity and performance depend on the employee under review.

tight shot In television or film, an extreme close-up of a speaker; displays for the audience a perspective uncharacteristic of ordinary conversational distance.

tone An aspect of self presentation that refers to vocal inflection and how it presumably reflects inner emotional states.

transcription Converting the entire taped record of an interview into a printed account that can be more easily analyzed than extensive replaying of the tape.

triangulation Use of multiple methods to research a single phenomenon.

two-stage screening interviewing Employment interviewing strategy in which a preliminary screening stage selects applicants for additional in-depth interviews.

unscheduled interview An informal interview opportunity in which the interviewer does not prepare a set of specific questions.

utilitarianism An ethical approach that stresses concern for consequences of acts, particularly favoring those acts that produce the greatest good for the greatest number.

validation Acknowledgment through words or actions that there has been a sincere, cooperative exchange of views.

validity Whether a research method measures what it purports to measure. *See* **reliability.**

vertical dimension In oral history interviewing, the chronological progression of an interviewee's recollections.

voice-over Explanatory commentary added later to video recording.

wait time A significant pause of several seconds used to elicit fuller, richer answers by giving a respondent time to think through the implications of a point.

what-questions Neutral, information-seeking inquiries used in interviews to help frame suggested solutions or courses of action.

why-questions Inquiries that focus on explanations and justifications rather than information useful in working out solutions or courses of action.

willingness to communicate (WTC) This concept concludes that many otherwise exceptional employees will rarely volunteer their ideas or feelings openly within organizations.

wrap-up questions Known also as *clearinghouse questions*, these give the respondent a final word or opportunity to supply information the questioner has not covered.

you-messages Judgmental responses that tend to cause a defensive reaction, such as, "You made me mad."

References

Adams, B. (2001). *The everything job interview book: Answer the toughest job interview questions with confidence.* Cincinnati, OH: Adams Media.

Agar, M. H. (1986). *Speaking of ethnography.* Newbury Park, CA: Sage.

Agar, M. (1994). *Language shock: Understanding the culture of conversation.* New York: Morrow.

Allcorn, S. (1994). *Anger in the workplace.* Westport, CT: Quorum.

Anderson, H. (1997). *Conversation, language, and possibilities: A postmodern approach to therapy.* New York: Basic Books.

Anderson, R. (1995). *Essentials of personal selling: The new professionalism.* Englewood Cliffs, NJ: Prentice-Hall.

Anderson, R. E. (1996). Personal selling and sales management in the new millennium. *Journal of Personal Selling & Sales Management, XVI*(4), 17–32.

Anderson, R., Baxter, L. A., & Cissna, K. N. (Eds.). (2004). *Dialogue: Theorizing difference in communication studies.* Thousand Oaks, CA: Sage.

Anderson, R., & Ross, V. (2002). *Questions of communication: A practical introduction to theory* (3rd ed.). New York: Bedford/St. Martin's.

Anson, S. A. (1996, June/July). Off the record. *George,* pp. 110–114, 134–140.

Argyris, C. (1960). *Understanding organizational behavior.* Homewood, IL: Dorsey.

Austin, N. K. (1996, March). The new job interview: Beyond the trick question. *Working Woman,* pp. 23–24.

Autry, J. A. (1991). *Love and profit: The art of caring leadership.* New York: Avon.

Autry, J. A. (1994). *Life and work: A manager's search for meaning.* New York: Morrow.

Babbie, E. (2007). *The practice of social research* (11th ed.). Belmont, CA: Wadsworth.

Bai, M. (2005, July 17). The framing wars. *New York Times Magazine,* pp. 36–45, 68–71.

Bakhtin, M. M. (1986). *Speech genres & other late essays* (V. W. McGee, Trans.; C. Emerson & M. Holquist, Eds.). Austin: University of Texas Press.

Barata, P. C., Gucciardi, E., Ahmad, F., & Stewart, D. (2006). Cross-cultural perspectives on research participation and informed consent. *Social Science & Medicine, 62,* 479–490.

Barnlund, D. C. (1990). Therapeutic communication. In G. Gumpert & S. L. Fish (Eds.), *Talking to strangers* (pp. 10–28). Norwood, NJ: Ablex.

Bateson, G. (1972). *Steps to an ecology of mind.* New York: Ballantine.

Bateson, G. (1980). *Mind and nature: A necessary unity.* New York: Bantam.

Bateson, G. (1991). *Sacred unity: Further steps to an ecology of mind* (R. E. Donaldson, Ed.). New York: HarperCollins.

Batten, J. D. (2003). *Beyond management by objectives: A management classic.* Eugene, OR: WIPF and Stock.

Batz, J. (1999, December 9–15). Good cop, good cop. *Riverfront Times,* 22–26.

Bauman, R. (1986). *Story, performance, and event: Contextual studies of oral narrative.* Cambridge, UK: Cambridge University Press.

Baxter, L., & Babbie, E. (2004). *The basics of communication research.* Belmont, CA: Wadsworth.

Belenky, M. F., Clinchy, B. M., Goldberger, N. R., & Tarrule, J. M. (1986). *Women's ways of knowing: The development of self, voice, and mind.* New York: Basic Books.

Benjamin, A. (1974). *The helping interview* (2nd ed.). Boston: Houghton Mifflin.

Berendt, J. E. (1992). *The third car: On listening to the world* (T. Nevill, Trans.). New York: Henry Holt Owl Books.

Berg, B. L. (1989). *Qualitative research methods for the social sciences*. Boston: Allyn & Bacon.

Bermont, T. (2004). *Ten insider secrets to a winning job search: Everything you need to know to get the job you want in 24 hours or less*. Franklin Lakes, NJ: Career Press.

Biagi, S. (1992). *Interviews that work: A practical guide for journalists* (2nd ed.). Belmont, CA: Wadsworth.

Bird, S. E. (1987). Anthropological methods relevant for journalists. *Journalism Educator, 41*, 5–10, 33.

Bixler, S., & Nix-Rice, N. (2005). *The new professional image: Dress your best for every business situation* (2nd ed.). Avon, MA: Adams Media.

Black, J., Steele, B., & Barney, R. (1993). *Doing ethics in journalism: A handbook with case studies*. Greencastle, IN: The Sigma Delta Chi Foundation and The Society of Professional Journalists.

Blundell, W. E. (1988). *The art and craft of feature writing*. New York: Plume/Penguin.

Bogels, S. M. (1999). Diagnostic interviewing in mental health care: Methods, training, and assessment. In A. Memon & R. Bull (Eds.), *Handbook of the psychology of interviewing* (pp. 3–20). Chichester, UK: Wiley.

Bohart, A. C., & Greenberg, L. S. (Eds.). (1997). *Empathy reconsidered: New directions in psychotherapy*. Washington, DC: American Psychological Association.

Bok, S. (1979). *Lying: Moral choice in public and private life*. New York: Vintage.

Bolles, R. N. (2007). *The 2007 what color is your parachute? A practical manual for job-hunters and career-changers*. Berkeley, CA: Ten Speed Press.

Bommelje, R., Houston, J. M., & Smither, R. (2003). Personality characteristics of effective listeners: A five factor perspective. *International Journal of Listening, 17*, 32–46.

Booth, W. C. (1988). *The vocation of a teacher: Rhetorical occasions 1967–1988*. Chicago: University of Chicago Press.

Borjesson, K. (Ed.). (2005). *Feet to the fire: The media after 9/11: Top journalists speak out*. Amherst, NY: Prometheus.

Bouma, G. D., & Atkinson, G. B. J. (1995). *A handbook of social science research: A comprehensive and practical guide for students* (2nd ed.). Oxford, UK: Oxford University Press.

Brady, J. (1976). *The craft of interviewing*. Cincinnati, OH: Writer's Digest Books.

Branch, W. T., Levinson, W., & Platt, F. W. (1996, July 15). Diagnostic interviewing: Make the most of your time. *Patient Care, 68–70, 75, 79–83*.

Brian, D. (1973). *Murderers and other friendly people*. New York: McGraw-Hill.

Briggs, C. L. (1986). *Learning how to ask: A sociolinguistic appraisal of the role of the interview in social science research*. Cambridge, UK: Cambridge University Press.

Brown, C. T., & Keller, P. W. (1979). *Monologue to dialogue: An exploration of interpersonal communication* (2nd ed.). Englewood Cliffs, NJ: Prentice-Hall.

Bruce, W. M., & Blackburn, J. W. (1992). *Balancing job satisfaction and performance*. Westport, CT: Quorum.

Buber, M. (1965). *Between man and man* (R. G. Smith, Trans.). New York: Macmillan.

Buchanan, E. (2004). *The corpse had a familiar face*. New York: Pocket Books. (Original work published 1987.)

Budiansky, S. (2005, June). Truth extraction. *The Atlantic Monthly, 32–35*.

Burgoon, J. K., & Buller, D. B. (2003). Interpersonal deception theory. In J. Seiter & R. Gass (Eds.), *Perspectives on persuasion, social influence, and compliance gaining* (pp. 239–264). Boston: Allyn & Bacon.

Burleson, B. R., & MacGeorge, E. L. (2002). Supportive communication. In M. L. Knapp & J. A. Daly (Eds.), *Handbook of interpersonal communication* (3rd ed., pp. 374–422). Thousand Oaks, CA: Sage.

Caesar, D. (1999, October 26). NBC's Gray has no regrets about his interview of Rose. *St. Louis Post-Dispatch*, p. C5.

Camp, R., Vielhaber, M., & Simonetti, J. (2001). *Strategic interviewing: How to hire good people*. San Francisco, CA: Jossey-Bass.

Campion, J. E., & Arvey, R. D. (1989). Unfair discrimination in the employment interview. In R. W. Eder & G. R. Ferris (Eds.), *The employment interview: Theory, research, and practice* (pp. 61–73). Newbury Park, CA: Sage.

Carkhuff, R. R. (1969). *Helping and human relations: A primer for lay and professional helpers* (Vols. I and 2). New York: Holt, Rinehart & Winston.

Charity, A. (1995). *Doing public journalism.* New York: Guilford.

Chesney, M. (2001). Dilemmas of self in the method. *Qualitative Health Research, 11,* 127–135.

Childs, J. B. (2003). *Transcommunality: From the politics of conversion to the ethics of respect.* Philadelphia: Temple University Press.

Cissna, K. N., & Anderson, R. (1994). Communication and the ground of dialogue. In R. Anderson, K. N. Cissna, & R. C. Arnett (Eds.), *The reach of dialogue: Confirmation, voice, and community* (pp. 9–30). Cresskill, NJ: Hampton.

Cissna, K. N., & Keating, S. (1979). Speech communication antecedents of perceived confirmation. *Western Journal of Speech Communication, 43,* 48–60.

Cissna, K. N., & Sieberg, E. (1981). Patterns of interactional confirmation and disconfirmation. In C. Wilder-Mott & J. Weakland (Eds.), *Rigor and imagination* (pp. 230–239). New York: Praeger.

Claflin, S. T., Jr. (1979). *A radical proposal for full use of free speech.* New York: Philosophical Library.

Clark, R. P., & Fry, D. (1992). *Coaching writers.* New York: St. Martin's Press.

Clurman, R. M. (1990). *Beyond malice.* New York: New American Library.

"Codes of ethics." (2006). *American Society of Newspaper Editors* (online). Retrieved February 19, 2008, from http://www.asne.org/index.cfn?id=387

Cohen, A. (1987). *The television news interview.* Newbury Park, CA: Sage.

Cohen, B. R., & Greenfield, J. (1997). *Ben & Jerry's double-dip.* New York: Simon & Schuster.

Cohen, M. (2006, April). The boy who stopped talking. *Discover* (online). Retrieved August 6, 2006, from http://www.discover.com/issues/apr-06/departments/vital-signs/

Coles, R. (1989). *The call of stories.* Boston: Houghton Mifflin.

Converse, J. M., & Schuman, H. (1974). *Conversations at random: Survey research as interviewers see it.* New York: Wiley.

Coulehan, J. L., & Block, M. R. (1992). *The medical interview: A primer for students of the art* (2nd ed.). Philadelphia: F. A. Davis.

Couper, M. P., & Hansen, S. E. (2001). Computer-assisted interviewing. In J. F. Gubrium & J. A. Holstein (Eds.), *Handbook of interview research: Context and method* (pp. 557–576). Thousand Oaks, CA: Sage.

Courtright, J. A., & Perse, E. M. (1998). *Communicating online: A guide to the Internet.* Mountain View, CA: Mayfield.

Cousins, N. (1983). *The healing heart.* New York: Norton.

Cowan, J. (1992). *Small decencies: Reflections and meditations on being human at work.* New York: Harper Business.

Craig, J. H., & Craig, M. (1979). *Synergic power: Beyond domination, beyond permissiveness* (2nd ed.). Berkeley, CA: Proactive Press.

Cranberg, L. (1989). Plea for recognition of scientific character of journalism. *Journalism Educator, 43,* 46–47.

Crosby, O. (2002). Informational interviewing: Get the inside scoop on careers. *Occupational Outlook Quarterly, 46,* 32–37.

Crossen, C. (1994). *Tainted truth: The manipulation of fact in America.* New York: Simon & Schuster.

Dallmayr, F. (2002). *Dialogue among civilizations: Some exemplary voices.* New York: Palgrave Macmillan.

Daly, J. A., & McCroskey, J. C. (Eds.). (1984). *Avoiding communication: Shyness, reticence, and communication apprehension.* Beverly Hills, CA: Sage.

Dash, L. (1996). *Rosa Lee: A mother and her family in urban America.* New York: Basic Books.

Davis, D. (1993). *The five myths of television power.* New York: Simon & Schuster.

DePaula, M. (2003, January). How long will women have to wait? *U.S. Banker* (online). Retrieved July 2, 2006, from http://www.us-banker.com/article.html?id=200404153wtwtumj

deShazer, S. (1985). *Keys to solution in brief therapy*. New York: Norton.

Deutscher, I. (1973). *What we say / what we do: Sentiments and acts*. Glenview, IL: Scott, Foresman.

Dexter, L. A. (1970). *Elite and specialized interviewing*. Evanston, IL: Northwestern University Press.

Diane Sawyer: Conscientious voice of "60 Minutes." (1988, May). *In Touch*, pp. 1–2.

Dillon, J. T. (1990). *The practice of questioning*. London: Routledge.

Dipboye, R. L. (1982). Self-fulfilling prophecies in the selection-recruitment interview. *Academy of Management Review, 7*, 579–586.

Dougherty, T. W., Turban, D. B., & Callender, J. C. (1994). Confirming first impressions in the employment interview: A field study of interview behavior. *Journal of Applied Psychology, 79*, 659–665.

Drew, R. (2001). *Karaoke nights: An ethnographic rhapsody*. Lanham, MD: AltaMira Press.

D'Souza, D. (1992). *Illiberal education: The politics of race and sex on campus*. New York: Vintage.

Dumond, V. (1990). *The elements of nonsexist usage*. New York: Prentice-Hall.

Dunbar, C., Rodriguez, D., & Parker, L. (2001). Race, subjectivity, and the interview process. In J. A. Gubrium & J. A. Holstein (Eds.), *Handbook of interview research* (pp. 279–298). Thousand Oaks, CA: Sage.

Eder, R. W., & Ferris, G. R. (1989). Preface. In R. W. Eder & G. R. Ferris (Eds.), *The employment interview: Theory, research, and practice* (pp. 11–14). Newbury Park, CA: Sage.

Einhorn, L. J. (1981). An inner view of the job interview: An investigation of successful communicative behaviors. *Communication Education, 30*, 217–228.

Eisenberg, E. M., & Goodall, H. L., Jr. (1997). *Organizational communication: Balancing creativity and constraint* (2nd ed.). New York: St. Martin's Press.

Eisenberg, E. M., & Goodall, H. L., Jr. (2004). *Organizational communication: Balancing creativity and constraint* (4th ed.). New York: Bedford/St. Martin's.

Emerson, R. M., Fretz, R. L., & Shaw, L. L. (1995). *Writing ethnographic fieldnotes*. Chicago: University of Chicago Press.

Eng, S. (1998, January 18). Company culture sets dress for job interviews. *St. Louis Post-Dispatch*, p. G20.

Esterberg, K. G. (2002). *Qualitative methods in social research*. New York: McGraw-Hill.

Evarts, W. R., Greenstone, J. L., Kirkpatrick, G. J., & Leviton, S. C. (1983). *Winning through accommodation: The mediator's handbook*. Dubuque, IA: Kendall-Hunt.

Fallaci, O. (1963). *The egotists: Sixteen surprising interviews*. Chicago: Henry Regnery.

Fallows, J. (1996). *Breaking the news: How the media undermine American democracy*. New York: Pantheon.

Fans upset with Gray's interview (Associated Press). (1999, October 26). *Edwardsville Intelligencer*, p. 7.

Farson, R. (1996). *Management of the absurd: Paradoxes in leadership*. New York: Touchstone.

Favre, G. E. (2001). The art of the job interview: Eighteen editors reveal what they're looking for and how they find it. *Poynter Online*. Retrieved February 19, 2006, from http://www.poynter.org/content/content_view.asp?id=5081

Fetterman, D. M. (1989). *Ethnography: Step by step*. Newbury Park, CA: Sage.

Fish, S. L. (1990). Therapeutic uses of the telephone: Crisis intervention vs. traditional therapy. In G. Gumpert & S. L. Fish (Eds.), *Talking to strangers: Mediated therapeutic communication* (pp. 154–169). Norwood, NJ: Ablex.

Fiske, J. (1989). *Reading the popular*. Boston: Unwin Hyman.

Fitzgerald, M. (1987, June 6). Don't (mis)quote me on that!. *Editor & Publisher*, 114.

Fiumara, G. C. (1990). *The other side of language: A philosophy of listening* (C. Lambert, Trans.). London: Routledge.

Foddy, W. (1993). *Constructing questions for interviews and questionnaires: Theory and practice in social research.* Cambridge, UK: Cambridge University Press.

Fontana, A., & Frey, J. H. (2005). The interview: From neutral stance to political involvement. In N. K. Denzin & Y. S. Lincoln (Eds.), *The Sage handbook of qualitative research* (3rd ed., pp. 645–672). Thousand Oaks, CA: Sage.

Fowler, E. J., & Mangione, T. W. (1990). *Standardized survey interviewing: Minimizing interviewer-related error.* Newbury Park, CA: Sage.

Frank, L. L., & Hackman, J. R. (1975). Effect of interview–interviewee similarity in on interviewer objectivity in college admission interviews. *Journal of Applied Psychology, 60,* 356–360.

Frankfurt, H. (2005). *On bullshit.* Princeton, NJ: Princeton University Press.

Franklin, N. (2003, March 10). Must-see Saddam. *The New Yorker, 79*(3), 28–30.

Freeman, R. B., & Rogers, J. (1999). *What workers want.* Ithaca, NY: Cornell University Press.

Friedman, P. G. (1983). *The life stories interview: Creating a portrait on tape.* Lawrence: University of Kansas, Department of Communication Studies.

Frost, D. (1978). *"I gave them a sword": Behind the scenes of the Nixon interviews.* New York: William Morrow.

Gadamer, H.-G. (1982). *Truth and method* (G. Barden & J. Cumming, Trans.). New York: Crossroad.

Garcia Marquez, G. (1997, July). The roving recorder. *Harper's Magazine,* 32–34.

Gazda, G. M., Childers, W. C., & Walters, R. P. (1982). *Interpersonal communication: A handbook for health professionals.* Rockville, MD: Aspen.

Geertz, C. (1983). *Local knowledge: Further essays in interpretive anthropology.* New York: Basic Books.

Geertz, C. (2000). *Available light: Anthropological reflections on philosophical topics.* Princeton, NJ: Princeton University Press.

Gibb, J. R. (1961). Defensive communication. *Journal of Communication, 11*(3), 141–148.

Gladwell, M. (2005, August 8). Focus groups should be abolished. *Advertising Age, 76,* 14.

Goffman, E. (1974). *Frame analysis: An essay on the organization of experience.* Cambridge, MA: Harvard University Press.

Goffman, E. (1981). *Forms of talk.* Philadelphia: University of Pennsylvania Press.

Goodale, J. G. (1982). *The fine art of interviewing.* Englewood Cliffs, NJ: Prentice-Hall.

Goodale, J. G. (1989). Effective employment interviewing. In R. W. Eder & G. R. Ferris (Eds.), *The employment interview: Theory, research, and practice* (pp. 307–323). Newbury Park, CA: Sage.

Gorden, R. L. (1980). *Interviewing: Strategy, techniques, and tactics.* Homewood, IL: Dorsey Press.

Gordon, T. (1975). *P.E.T: The tested new way to raise responsible children.* New York: New American Library.

Greenbaum, T. L. (1993). *The handbook for focus group research* (Rev. ed.). New York: Lexington.

Grele, R. J. (1994). History and the languages of history in the oral history interview: Who answers whose questions and why? In E. M. McMahan & K. L. Rogers (Eds.), *Interactive oral history interviewing* (pp. 1–18). Hillsdale, NJ: Erlbaum.

Grice, H. P. (1975). Logic and conversation. In P. Cole & J. Morgan (Eds.), *Syntax and semantics: Vol. 3. Speech acts* (pp. 41–58). New York: Academic Press.

Grobel, L. (2004). *The art of the interview: Lessons from a master of the craft.* New York: Three Rivers Press.

Gross, T. (2004). *All I did was ask: Conversations with writers, actors, musicians, and artists.* New York: Hyperion.

Grove, T. G. (1991). *Dyadic interaction: Choice and change in conversations and relationships.* Dubuque, IA: Brown.

Grudin, R. (1996). *On dialogue: An essay in free thought*. Boston: Houghton Mifflin.

Gubrium, J. F., & Holstein, J. A. (Eds.). (2001). *Handbook of interview research: Context and method*. Thousand Oaks, CA: Sage.

Half, R. (1993). *Finding, hiring, and keeping the best employees*. New York: Wiley.

Hall, E. T. (1959). *The silent language*. New York: Fawcett.

Hall, E. T. (1966). *The hidden dimension*. Garden City, NY: Anchor.

Halvorson, S. (1997). Interviewing: Role playing to understand the Americans with Disabilities Act. *The Speech Communication Teacher, 11*, 1–3.

Hart, K. (2006, December–January). Inbox journalism: The e-mail interview. *American Journalism Review* (online). Retrieved August 2, 2006, from http://www.ajr.org/Article.asp?id=4005.

Hartshorn, N. (1996). *Catch: A discovery of America*. Denver, CO: MacMurray & Beck.

Hayes, T. J., & Tathum, C. B. (1989). *Focus group interviews: A reader* (2nd ed.). Chicago: American Marketing Association.

Heidegger, M. (1982). *On the way to language* (P. D. Hertz, Trans.). New York: Perennial Library.

Hennink, M., & Diamond, I. (2000). Using focus groups in social research. In M. Memon & R. Bull (Eds.), *Handbook of the psychology of interviewing* (pp. 113–144). Chichester, UK: Wiley.

Heritage, J. (1985). Analyzing news interviews: Aspects of the production of talk for an overhearing audience. In T. A. van Dijk (Ed.), *Discourse and dialogue: Handbook of discourse analysis: Vol. 3* (pp. 95–117), London: Academic.

Heritage, J. (1988). Explanations as accounts: A conversation analytic perspective. In C. Antaki (Ed.), *Analysing everyday explanation: A casebook of methods* (pp. 127–144). London: Sage.

Heritage, J., & Greatbatch, D. (1991). On the institutional character of institutional talk: The case of news interviews. In D. Boden &

D. H. Zimmerman (Eds.), *Talk and social structure: Studies in ethnomethodology and conversation analysis* (pp. 93–137). Berkeley: University of California Press.

Hersey, P. (1988). *Selling: A behavioral science approach*. Englewood Cliffs, NJ: Prentice-Hall.

Hess, S. (1996). *News & newsmaking*. Washington, D.C.: Brookings Institute.

Hewson, C., Yule, P., Laurent, D., & Vogel, C. (2002). *Internet research methods: A practical guide for the social and behavioral sciences*. Thousand Oaks, CA: Sage.

Hilton, J. (1987). *How to meet the press: A survival guide*. New York: Dodd, Mead.

Holstein, J. A., & Gubrium J. E. (1995). *The active interview*. Thousand Oaks, CA: Sage.

Hoopes, J. (1979). *Oral history: An introduction for students*. Chapel Hill: University of North Carolina Press.

Houston, B., Bruzzese, L., & Weinberg, S. (2002). *The investigative reporter's handbook: A guide to documents, databases, and techniques* (4th ed.). Boston: Bedford/St. Martin's.

Houston, M., & Wood, J. T. (1996). Difficult dialogues, expanded horizons: Communicating across race and class. In J. T. Wood (Ed.), *Gendered relationships* (pp. 39–56). Mountain View, CA: Mayfield.

Howard, J. L., & Ferris, G. R. (1996). The employment interview context: Social and situational influences on interviewer decisions. *Journal of Applied Psychology, 26*, 112–136.

Hurtado, A. (1994). Does similarity breed respect? Interviewer evaluations of Mexican-descent respondents in a bilingual survey. *Public Opinion Quarterly, 58*, 77–95.

Ihde, D. (1976). *Listening and voice: A phenomenology of sound*. Athens: Ohio University Press.

Ihde, D. (1983). *Sense and significance*. Atlantic Highlands, NJ: Humanities Press.

Ilkka, R. J. (1995). Applicant appearance and decision making: Revitalizing employment interview education. *Business Communication Quarterly, 3*, 11–18.

Isaacs, W. (1993). Taking flight: Dialogue, collaborative thinking, and organizational learning. *Organizational Dynamics, 22*, 24–39.

Isaacs, W. (1997, August). Restoration of common sense: An interview with William Isaacs. *Executive Excellence*, p. 7.

Isaacs, W. (1999). *Dialogue and the art of thinking together*. New York: Currency.

Ivey, A. E., & Ivey, M. B. (2002). *Intentional interviewing and counseling: Facilitating client development in a multicultural society* (5th ed.). Belmont, CA: Wadsworth.

Jackson, T. (1978). *Guerilla tactics in the job market*. New York: Bantam.

Jamieson, K. H., & Waldman, P. (2003). *The press effect: Politicians, journalists, and the stories that shape the political world*. New York: Oxford University Press.

Janz, T. (1989). The patterned behavior description interview: The best prophet of the future is the past. In R. W. Eder & G. R. Ferris (Eds.), *The employment interview: Theory, research, and practice* (pp. 158–168). Newbury Park, CA: Sage.

Johannesen, R. (2002). *Ethics of human communication* (5th ed.). Prospect Heights, IL: Waveland.

Jong, P., & Berg, I. (2002). *Interviewing for solutions* (2nd ed.). Belmont, CA: Brooks-Cole.

Jorgenson, J. (1995). Re-relationalizing rapport in interpersonal settings. In W. Leeds-Hurwitz (Ed.), *Social approaches to communication* (pp. 155–170). New York: Guilford.

Joyce, E. (1988). *Prime times, bad times*. New York: Anchor.

Kador, J. (2004). *How to ace the brainteaser interview*. New York: McGraw-Hill.

Kadushin, A. (1972). *The social work interview*. New York: Columbia University Press.

Kahn, R. L., & Cannell, C. F. (1957). *The dynamics of interviewing: Theory, technique, and cases*. New York: Wiley.

Kanter, A. B. (1995). *The essential book of interviewing: Everything you need to know from both sides of the table*. New York: Times Books.

Keller, P. W., & Brown, C. T. (1968). An interpersonal ethic for communication. *Journal of Communication, 18*, 73–81.

Kellett, P. M., & Dalton, D. G. (2001). *Managing conflict in a negotiated world: A narrative approach to achieving productive dialogue and change*. Thousand Oaks, CA: Sage.

Kelman, H. C. (1966). Three processes of social influence. In M. Jahoda & N. Warren (Eds.), *Attitudes* (pp. 151–162). Baltimore: Penguin.

Keltner, J. W. (1987). *Mediation: Toward a civilized system of dispute resolution*. Annandale, VA: Speech Communication Association.

Kennedy, J. L. (2000). *Job interviews for dummies* (2nd ed.). New York: Hungry Minds.

Kerlinger, F. N. (1986). *Foundations of behavioral research*. New York: Holt, Rinehart & Winston.

Kikoski, J. F. (1999). Effective communication in the performance appraisal interview: Face-to-face communication for public managers in the culturally diverse workplace. *Public Personnel Management, 28*, 301–322.

Killenberg, G. M., & Anderson, R. (1989). *Before the story: Interviewing and communication skills for journalists*. New York: St. Martin's Press.

Kimball, B. (1994). *The AMA handbook for successful selling*. Chicago: American Marketing Association/NTC Business Books.

King, L., with Occhiogrosso, P. (1989). *Tell it to the king*. New York: Jove.

Kirkwood, W. G., & Ralston, S. M. (1996). Ethics and employment interviewing. *Communication Education, 45*, 167–179.

Klaidman, S., & Beauchamp, T. L. (1987). *The virtuous journalist*. New York: Oxford University Press.

Kleinke, C. L. (1986). *Meeting & understanding people*. New York: Freeman.

Klitgaard, R. (1985). *Choosing elites: Selecting the "best and the brightest" at top universities and elsewhere*. New York: Basic Books.

Koile, E. (1977). *Listening as a way of becoming*. Waco, TX: Regency.

Korn, J. (1998). *Illusions of reality: A history in social psychology*. Albany: State University of New York Press.

Kovach, R. (2002). Studs Terkel on the art of interviewing. *Writer, 115*(5), 26–31.

Krayer, K. J. (1987). Simulation methods for teaching the performance appraisal interview. *Communication Education, 36*, 276–283.

Krueger, R. A. (1994). *Focus groups: A practical guide for applied research*. Thousand Oaks, CA: Sage.

Kuralt, C. (1985). *On the road with Charles Kuralt. New York*: Putnam's.

Kvale, S. (1996). *Inter-views: An introduction to qualitative research interviewing*. Thousand Oaks, CA: Sage.

Lakoff, R. (2001). *The language wars*. Berkeley: University of California Press.

Lamb, B. (1997). *Booknotes: America's finest authors on reading, writing and the power of ideas*. New York: Times Books.

Lawrence-Lightfoot, S. (2000). *Respect: An exploration*. New York: Perseus.

Leanne, S. (2003). *How to interview like a top MBA*. New York: McGraw-Hill.

Leeds, D. (1987). *Smart questions: A new strategy for successful managers*. New York: Berkley Books.

Lehrman, F. L. (1995, February). Strategies for interviewing domestic violence clients. *Trial,* 38–43.

Lieberman, T. (2004, January–February) Answer the &%$#* question! *Columbia Journalism Review,* 40–44.

Lincoln, Y. S., & Guba, E. G. (1985). *Naturalistic inquiry*. Beverly Hills, CA: Sage.

Litwack, L., Litwack, J., & Ballou, M. (1980). *Health counseling*. New York: Appleton-Century-Crofts.

Livingstone, S., & Lunt, P. (1994). *Talk on television: Audience participation and public debate*. London: Routledge.

Lobdell, C. L., Sonoda, K. T., & Arnold, W. E. (1993). The influence of perceived supervisor listening behavior on employee commitment. *Journal of the International Listening Association, 7*, 92–110.

Loden, M. (1996). *Implementing diversity*. Chicago: Irwin.

MacHovec, F. J. (1989). *Interview and interrogation*. Springfield, IL: Thomas.

Madriz, E. (1998). Using focus groups with lower socioeconomic status Latina women. *Qualitative Inquiry, 4*, 114–129.

Madriz, E. (2000). Focus groups in feminist research. In N. K. Denzin & Y. S. Lincoln (Eds.), *Handbook of qualitative research* (2nd ed., pp. 835–850). Thousand Oaks, CA: Sage.

Malcolm, J. (1990). *The journalist and the murderer*. New York: Knopf.

Mander, J. (1978). *Four arguments for the elimination of television*. New York: Quill.

Mann, C., & Stewart, F. (2000). *Internet communication and qualitative research: A handbook for researching online*. Thousand Oaks, CA: Sage.

Marino, P. (1997a, October 1). Listening, the often ignored skill. *Furniture World Online Magazine*. Retrieved March 12, 2006, from http://www.furninfo.com/absolutenm/ templates/Article_Retailing.asp?articleid=13 99&zoneid=4

Marino, P. (1997b, November 1). Relationship selling. *Furniture World Online Magazine.* Retrieved March 12, 2006, from http://www. furninfo.com/absolutenm/templates/Article_ Retailing.asp?articleid=1395&zoneid=4

Marino, P. (1999a, June 1). Listening to your customers: Part 1. *Furniture World Online Magazine*. Retrieved March 12, 2006, from http://www.furninfo.com/absolutenm/ templates/Article_Retailing.asp?articleid=10 89&zoneid=4

Marino, P. (1999b, August 1). Listening to your customers: Part 2. *Furniture World Online Magazine*. Retrieved March 12, 2006, from http://www.furninfo.com/absolutenm/ templates/Article_Retailing.asp?articleid=10 85&zoneid=4

Marino, P. (1999c, October 1). Listening to your customers: Part 3. *Furniture World Online Magazine*. Retrieved March 12, 2006, from http://www.furninfo.com/absolutenm/ templates/Article_Retailing.asp?articleid=10 73&zoneid=4

McCracken, G. (1988). *The long interview*. Newbury Park, CA: Sage.

McKibben, B. (1993). *The age of missing information*. New York: Plume.

McMahan, E. M. (1989). *Elite oral history discourse—A study of cooperation and coherence.* Tuscaloosa: University of Alabama Press.

Medley, H. A. (1992). *Sweaty palms: The neglected art of being interviewed.* Berkeley, CA: Ten Speed Press.

Mehrabian, A. (1981). *Silent messages: Implicit communication of emotions and attitudes* (2nd ed.). Belmont, CA: Wadsworth.

Mendelsohn, J. (1985). *Being liberal in an illiberal age: Why I am a Unitarian Universalist.* Boston: Beacon Press.

Menuhin, Y. (1992). Foreword. In J.-E. Berendt, *The third ear: On listening to the world* (p. 7). New York: Henry Holt Owl Books.

Merriam, S. B., Johnson-Bailey, J., Lee, M.-Y., Ntseane, G., & Muhamad, M. (2001). Power and positionality: Negotiating insider/outsider status within and across cultures. *International Journal of Lifelong Education, 20,* 405–416.

Metts, S., & Planalp, S. (2002). Emotional communication. In M. L. Knapp & J. A. Daly (Eds.), *Handbook of interpersonal communication* (3rd ed., pp. 339–373). Thousand Oaks, CA: Sage.

Metzler, K. (1997). *Creative interviewing: The writer's guide to gathering information by asking questions* (3rd ed.). Boston: Allyn & Bacon.

Meyer, P. (2002). *Precision journalism* (4th ed.). Lanham, MD: Rowman & Littlefield.

Milano, B. J. (1997, September 5). Preparation proves productive. *The University News,* p. 7.

Miller, C., & Swift, K. (1991). *Words & women: New language in new times* (Updated ed.). New York: HarperCollins.

Mishler, E. G. (1986). *Research interviewing: Context and narrative.* Cambridge, MA: Harvard University Press.

Molloy, J. T. (1998). *John T. Molloy's new dress for success.* New York: Warner Books.

Morgan, D. L. (1993). *Successful focus groups: Advancing the state of the art.* Newbury Park, CA: Sage.

Morgan, D. L. (2001). Focus group interviewing. In J. F. Gubrium & J. A. Holstein (Eds.), *Handbook of interview research: Context & method* (pp. 141–159). Thousand Oaks, CA: Sage.

Muldary, T. W. (1983). *Interpersonal relations for health professionals.* New York: Macmillan.

Murphy, B., & Dillon, C. (2002). *Interviewing in action: Relationship, process, and change* (2nd ed.). Belmont, CA: Wadsworth.

Murray, D. (1988, January). Writing on writing. No. 3, *Boston Globe,* pp. 1, 2.

Nelson, B. (1997). *1001 ways to energize employees.* New York: Workman.

Nelson, R. P. (1979). *Articles and features.* Boston: Houghton Mifflin.

Neuborne, E. (1997, July 9). Employers score new hires *USA Today,* pp. 1B, 2B.

Nierenberg, G. I. (1987). *Fundamentals of negotiating.* New York: Perennial Library.

Nightingale, E. (1969). *Notes on nursing.* New York: Dover.

Okun, B. (2001). *Effective helping: Interviewing and counseling techniques* (6th ed.). Belmont, CA: Wadsworth.

Orr, T. B. (2000). Interview horror stories. *Career World, 29,* 15–17.

Pandora's box of an interview. (1995, January 5). *St. Petersburg Times,* pp. 1A, 12A.

Paulos, J. A. (1995). *A mathematician reads the newspaper.* New York: Basic Books.

Payne, S. L. (1980). *The art of asking questions.* Princeton, NJ: Princeton University Press. (Original work published 1951)

Pearce, W. B., & Cronen, V. (1980). *Communication, action, and meaning.* New York: Praeger.

Pedersen, P. B., & Ivey, A. (1993). *Culture-centered counseling and interviewing skills: A practical guide.* Westport, CT: Praeger.

Peterson, M. S. (1997). Personnel interviewers' perceptions of the importance and adequacy of applicants' communication skills. *Communication Education, 46,* 287–291.

Phillips, G. M. (1981). *Help for shy people.* Englewood Cliffs, NJ: Prentice-Hall.

Phillips, G. M. (1984). Reticence: A perspective on social withdrawal. In J. A. Daly & J. C. McCroskey (Eds.), *Avoiding communication: Shyness, reticence, and communica-*

tion apprehension (pp. 51–66). Beverly Hills, CA: Sage.

Phillips, G. M. (1991). *Communication incompetencies: A theory of training oral performance behavior.* Carbondale: Southern Illinois University Press.

Pollack, S. (2003). Focus-group methodology in research with incarcerated women: Race, power, and collective experience. *Affilia, 18,* 461–472.

Ponterotto, J. G., Rivera, L., & Sueyoshi, L. A. (2000). The career-in-culture interview: A semi-structured protocol for the cross-cultural intake interview. *The Career Development Quarterly, 49,* 85–94.

Postman, N. (1985). *Amusing ourselves to death: Public discourse in the age of show business.* New York: Penguin.

Postman, N. (1988). *Conscientious objections: Stirring up trouble about language, technology, and education.* New York: Knopf.

Poundstone, W. (2003). Beware the interview inquisition. *Harvard Business Review, 81*(5), 18–19.

Prewett-Livingston, A. J., & Field, H. S. (2000). The employment interview and race: A review. In A. Memon & R. Bull (Eds.), *Handbook of the psychology of interviewing* (pp. 239–252). Chichester, UK: Wiley.

Purdy, M., & Borisoff, D. (Eds.). (1997). *Listening in everyday life: A personal and professional approach* (2nd ed.). Lanham, MD: University Press of America.

Purtilo, R. (1990). *Health professional and patient interaction.* Philadelphia: Saunders.

Putnam, S. M. (1996). Nature of the medical encounter. *Research on Aging, 18,* 70–83.

Ram Dass, R. & Gorman, P. (1985). *How can I help?: Stories and reflections on service.* New York: Knopf.

Ravitch, D. (2003). *The language police: How pressure groups restrict what students learn.* New York: Knopf.

Richmond, V. P., & Roach, K. D. (1992). Willingness to communicate and employee success in U. S. organizations. *Journal of Applied Communication Research, 20,* 95–115.

Roach, C. A., & Wyatt, N. J. (1988). *Successful listening.* New York: Harper & Row.

Rogers, C. R. (1959). A theory of therapy, personality, and interpersonal relationships, as developed in the client-centered framework. In S. Koch (Ed.), *Psychology: A study of a science: Vol. III. Formulations of the person and the social context* (pp. 184–256). New York: McGraw-Hill.

Rogers, C. R. (1961). *On becoming a person.* Boston: Houghton Mifflin.

Rogers, C. R., & Farson, R. E. (1957). *Active listening.* Chicago: University of Chicago Industrial Relations Center.

Rowe, M. B. (1987, Spring). Wait time: Slowing down may be a way of speeding up. *American Educator,* 38–40.

Rubin, H. J., & Rubin, I. S. (2005). *Qualitative interviewing: The art of hearing data.* Thousand Oaks, CA: Sage.

Rubin, R. B. (1990). Communication competence. In G. M. Phillips & J. T. Wood (Eds.), *Speech communication: Essays to commemorate the 75th anniversary of the Speech Communication Association* (pp. 94–129). Carbondale: Southern Illinois University Press.

Rubin, R. B., Rubin, A. M., & Piele, L. J. (2005). *Communication research: Strategies and sources* (6th ed.). Belmont, CA: Wadsworth.

Rugg, D. (1941). Experiments in wording questions: II. *Public Opinion Quarterly, 5,* 91–92.

Ryen, A. (2001). Cross-cultural interviewing. In J. F. Gubrium & J. A. Holstein (Eds.), *Handbook of interview research: Context and method* (pp. 335–354). Thousand Oaks, CA: Sage.

Sacks, O. (1984). *A leg to stand on.* New York: Summit Books.

Saint Louis University Career Center. (1997). *Employment guide: 1997–1998.* St. Louis, MO: Author.

Saint Louis University Career Services. (2006). *Interviewing: Putting your best YOU forward.* St. Louis, MO: Academic Resources Center, Saint Louis University.

Sampson, E. E. (1993). *Celebrating the other: A dialogic account of human nature.* Boulder, CO: Westview.

Scanlon, C. (Ed.). (1996). *The best newspaper writing of 1996*. Chicago: Bonus Books.

Schaeffer, N. C., & Maynard, D. W. (2001). Standardization and interaction in the survey interview. In J. F. Gubrium & J. A. Holstein (Eds.), *Handbook of interview research: Context & method* (pp. 577–602). Thousand Oaks, CA: Sage.

Schoem, D., & Hurtado, S. (Eds.). (2001). *Intergroup dialogue: Deliberative democracy in school, college, community, and workplace*. Ann Arbor: University of Michigan Press.

Schudson, M. (1994). Question authority: A history of the news interview in American journalism, 1860s–1930s. *Media, Culture, & Society, 16*, 565–587.

Schudson, M. (1998). *The good citizen: A history of American civic life*. New York: Free Press.

Schudson, M. (2003). *The sociology of news*. New York: Norton.

Schumacher, M. (1990). *Creative conversations: The writer's complete guide to conducting interviews*. Cincinnati, OH: Writer's Digest Books.

Schwartz, M., & the Task Force on Bias-Free Language of the Association of American University Presses (1995). *Guidelines for bias-free writing*. Bloomington: Indiana University Press.

Seabrook, J. (1994, January 10). E-mail from Bill. *New Yorker*, pp. 48–52, 54–61.

Senge, P. (1990). *The fifth discipline: The art and practice of the learning organization*. New York: Doubleday.

Shah, S. (2004). The researcher/interviewer in intercultural context: A social intruder. *British Educational Research Journal, 30*, 549–575.

Shattuc, J. M. (1997). *The talking cure: TV, talk shows, and women*. New York: Routledge.

Shimanoff, S. (1980). *Communication rules: Theory and research*. Beverly Hills, CA: Sage.

Shiparski, L. (1996). Successful interview strategies. *Nursing Management, 27*, 32F, 32H.

Shotter, J. (1993). *Conversational realities: Constructing life through language*. London: Sage.

Shuy, R. W. (2001). In-person versus telephone interviewing. In J. F. Gubrium & J. A. Holstein (Eds.), *Handbook of interview research: Context & method* (pp. 537–556). Thousand Oaks, CA: Sage.

Simon, R. (1990). *Road show*. New York: Farrar, Straus, Giroux.

Simons, H. W. (2002). *Persuasion in society*. Thousand Oaks, CA: Sage.

Singleton, R. A., & Straits, B. C. (2001). Survey interviewing. In J. F. Gubrium & J. A. Holstein (Eds.), *Handbook of interview research: Context and method* (pp. 59–82). Thousand Oaks, CA: Sage.

Sitton, T., Mehaffy, G. L., & Davis, O. L. (1983). *Oral history: A guide for teachers (and others)*. Austin: University of Texas Press.

Skopec, E. W. (1990). *Communicate for success*. Reading, MA: Addison-Wesley.

Slim, H., & Thompson, P. (1995). *Listening for a change: Oral testimony and community development*. Philadelphia: New Society.

Smith, A. D. (2000). *Talk to me: Listening between the lines*. New York: Random House.

Smith, M. J. (1975). *When I say no I feel guilty*. New York: Bantam.

Smith, M. J. (1984). Contingency rules theory, context, and compliance-behaviors. *Human Communication Research, 10*, 489–512.

Smith, R. C. (1996). *The patient's story: Integrated patient–doctor interviewing*. Boston: Little, Brown.

Smith, R. (2002). *Patient-centered interviewing: An evidence-based method* (2nd ed.). Philadelphia: Lippincott, Williams, & Wilkins.

Snow, D. A., Zurcher, L. A., & Sjoberg, G. (1981). Interviewing by comment: An adjunct to the direct question. *Qualitative Sociology, 5*, 285–311.

Snyder, M., Tanke, E. D., & Berscheid, E. (1977). Social perception and interpersonal behavior: On the self-fulfilling nature of social stereotypes. *Journal of Personality and Social Psychology, 35*, 656–666.

Sommers-Flanagan, J., & Sommers-Flanagan, R. (2002). *Clinical interviewing* (3rd ed.). Indianapolis, IN: Wiley.

Stacks, D. W., & Hocking, J. E. (1992). *Essentials of communication research*. New York: HarperCollins.

Steele, B. (2003, June 16). Interviewing: The ignored skill. *Poynter Online*. Retrieved July 2006, from http://www.poynter.org/content/content_view.asp?id=37661.

Stevens, C. K. (1997). Effects on preinterview beliefs on applicants' reactions to campus interviews. *Academy of Management Journal, 40*, 947–966.

Stevens, C. K., & Kristof, A. L. (1995). Making the right impression: A field study of impression management during job interviews. *Journal of Applied Psychology, 80*, 587–606.

Stewart, M., Brown, J. B., Weston, W. W., McWhinney, I. R., McWilliam, C. L., & Freeman, T. R. (1995). *Patient-centered medicine: Transforming the clinical method*. Thousand Oaks, CA: Sage.

Stiel, L. K., Barker, L. L., & Watson, K. W. (1983). *Effective listening: Key to your success*. Reading, MA: Addison-Wesley.

Stone, D., Patton, B., & Heen, S. (2000). *Difficult conversations: How to discuss what matters most*. New York: Penguin.

Strickland, C. J. (1999). Conducting focus groups cross-culturally: Experiences with Pacific Northwest Indian people. *Public Health Nursing, 16*, 190–197.

Sudman, S., & Bradburn, N. (1982). *Asking questions*. San Francisco CA: Jossey-Bass.

Sue, D. W., & Sue, D. (1990). *Counseling the culturally different. Theory and practice*. New York: Wiley.

Swan, W., with Margulies, P. (1991). *How to do a superior performance appraisal*. New York: Wiley.

Sypher, H. E., Hummert, M. L., & Williams, S. L. (1994). Social psychological aspects of the oral history interview. In E. M. McMahan & K. L. Rogers (Eds.), *Interactive oral history interviewing* (pp. 47–62). Hillsdale, NJ: Erlbaum.

Talese, G. (1995, December). The art of hanging out. *Writer's Digest*, pp. 61–64, 80.

Tannen, D. (1986). *That's not what I meant! How conversational style makes or breaks relationships*. New York: Ballantine.

Tannen, D. (2001). *You just don't understand: Women and men in conversation*. New York: Quill. (Original work published 1990).

Tannen, D. (1998). *The argument culture: Moving from debate to dialogue*. New York: Random House.

Terkel, S. (1970). *Division street: America*. New York: Avon Discus Books.

Terkel, S. (1985). *The good war: An oral history of World War Two*. New York: Ballantine.

Thompson, T., & Parrott, R. (2002). Interpersonal communication and health care. In M. L. Knapp & J. A. Daly (Eds.), *Handbook of interpersonal communication* (3rd ed. pp. 680–725). Thousand Oaks, CA: Sage.

Thorne, B. (2003). *Carl Rogers* (2nd ed.). London: Sage.

Tickle-Degnan, L., & Rosenthal, R. (1990). The nature of rapport and its nonverbal coordinates. *Psychological Inquiry, 1*, 285–293.

Tolor, A. (1985). *Effective interviewing*. Springfield, IL: Charles C. Thomas.

Tourangeau, R., & Smith, T. W. (1996). Asking sensitive questions: The impact of data collection mode, question format, and question context. *Public Opinion Quarterly, 60*, 275–304.

Triandis, H. C. (1994). *Culture and social behavior*. New York: McGraw-Hill.

Truss, L. (2004). *Eats, shoots, and leaves: The zero tolerance approach to punctuation*. New York: Gotham.

Ullmann, J., & Colbert, J. (Eds.). (1991). *The reporter's handbook: An investigator's guide to documents and techniques*. New York: St. Martin's Press.

Vella, J., and Associates. (2003). *Dialogue at work: A case book*. San Francisco, CA: Jossey-Bass.

Vesperi, M. D. (1985). *City of green benches*. Ithaca, NY: Cornell University Press.

Vrij, A. (2000). Interviewing to detect deception. In A. Memon & R. Bull (Eds.), *Handbook of the psychology of interviewing* (pp. 317–326). Chichester, UK: Wiley.

Waldroop, J., & Butler, T. (1996, November–December). The executive as coach. *Harvard Business Review*, pp. 111–117.

Wallace, M. (2005). *Between you and me: A memoir.* New York: Hyperion.

Wallace, M., &. Gates, G. P. (1984). *Close encounters.* New York: Morrow.

Watzlawick, P., Beavin, J. H., & Jackson, D. D. (1967). *Pragmatics of human communication: A study of interactional patterns, pathologies, and paradoxes.* New York: Norton.

Watzlawick, P., Weakland, J., & Fisch, R. (1974). *Change: Principles of problem formation and problem resolution.* New York: Norton.

Wellman, F. L. (1948). *The art of cross-examination* (4th ed.). Garden City, NY: Garden City Books.

Wheatley, M. (2002). *Turning to one another: Simple conversations to restore hope to the future.* San Francisco, CA: Berrett-Koehler.

Whetzel, D. L., & McDaniel, M. A. (2000). The employment interview. In A. Memon & R. Bull (Eds.), *Handbook of the psychology of interviewing* (pp. 213–226). Chichester, UK: Wiley.

Whitney, M. A. (1994). Analyzing corporate communications policy using ethnographic methods. In M. B. Goodman (Ed.), *Corporate communication* (pp. 185–197). Albany: State University of New York Press.

Whyte, W. E. (1955). *Street corner society* (2nd ed.). Chicago: University of Chicago Press.

Wilmot, W. W., & Hocker, J. L. (2005). *Interpersonal conflict* (7th ed.). New York: McGraw-Hill.

Wilson, J. K. (1995). *The myth of political correctness: The conservative attack on higher education.* Durham, NC: Duke University Press.

Wingert, P., & Brant, M. (2005, August 15). Reading your baby's mind. *Newsweek,* 32–39.

Wolvin, A., & Coakley, C. G. (1996). *Listening* (5th ed.). Dubuque, IA: Brown & Benchmark.

Woodward, G. C., & Denton, R. E., Jr. (1988). *Persuasion and influence in American life.* Prospect Heights, IL: Waveland Press.

Yate, M. (2006). *Knock 'em dead: The ultimate job seeker's handbook.* Holbrook, MA: Adams.

Yeschke, C. L. (2003). *The art of investigative interviewing* (2nd ed.). Amsterdam: Butterworth Heinemann.

Zimbardo, P. G. (1977). *Shyness: What it is, what to do about it.* New York: Jove/HBJ.

Zoppi, K. A., & Epstein, R. M. (2001). Interviewing in medical settings. In J. F. Gubrium & J. A. Holstein (Eds.), *Handbook of interview research* (pp. 355–384). Thousand Oaks, CA: Sage.

Index

CPSIA information can be obtained at www.ICGtesting.com
Printed in the USA
BVOW02s0541021214

377216BV00003B/8/P